Insert this Pocket Part in the back of the Restatement of the Law Third, Unfair Competition (1995)

CASE CITATIONS TO THE RESTATEMENT OF THE LAW

Cumulative Annual Pocket Part For Use In 2024

Reporting Cases From July 1987

Through June 2023 That Cite

Restatement of the Law of Torts §§ 708–761 and

All Cases Through June 2023 That Cite

Restatement of the Law Third, Unfair Competition §§ 1 to End

This Pocket Part contains all citations to the Restatement of the Law Third, Unfair Competition, as well as citations, for the period from July 1987 through June 2023, to §§ 708–761 of the original Restatement of Torts. For earlier citations to §§ 708–761, see the following two Volumes titled "Torts 2d Appendix §§ 708–840E:

"Reporting Cases through December 1977

"Reporting Cases through June 1987."

For subsequent citations, see also the *Interim Case Citations to the Restatements and the Principles of the Law* pamphlets designated for use with the 2024 Pocket Parts and Supplements.

The American Law Institute
4025 Chestnut Street
Philadelphia, PA 19104

ST. PAUL, MN
AMERICAN LAW INSTITUTE PUBLISHERS
2024

32

Mat #43312916

YOUR COMPLETE **UNFAIR COMPETITION** LIBRARY SHOULD CONTAIN:

One Volume

§§ 1–End (1995) with Pocket Part for use in 2024

The American Law Institute

COUNCIL[†]

[†] As of January 23, 2024

COUNCIL

---

* *Director Emeritus*

COUNCIL

COUNCIL EMERITI

COUNCIL

INTRODUCTION

This Cumulative Annual Pocket Part contains all citations, through June 2023, to the Restatement of the Law Third, Unfair Competition (1995). It also contains citations, for the period from July 1987 through June 2023, to §§ 708–761 of the original Restatement of Torts. These sections, dealing with unfair competition, were omitted from the Restatement of the Law Second, Torts 2d. Citations to the original Restatement of Torts appear first, followed by citations to the Restatement of the Law Third, Unfair Competition. Earlier citations to §§ 708–761 of the original Restatement of Torts will be found in the two Torts 2d Appendix Volumes covering §§ 708–840E through 1977 and through June 1987.

This Pocket Part includes court citations to Introductions, Introductory Notes, black letter, Comments (including Illustrations), and Reporter's (or Reporters') Notes of the Restatements and Principles of the Law. Reporter's Notes discuss the legal and other sources relied upon by the Reporter in formulating the black letter and Comments, and enable the reader better to evaluate those formulations; they also provide avenues for additional research. Reporter's Notes are regarded as the work of the Reporter and do not represent the position of The American Law Institute, but courts may nevertheless find them useful.

Grateful acknowledgment is made to Thomson Reuters for furnishing the Institute with citations of decisions noted herein.

The American Law Institute

Philadelphia, PA
March 2024

INTRODUCTION

This Cumulative Annual Pocket Part contains all citations through June [illegible], to the Restatement of the Law Third, Unfair Competition (1995). It also contains citations for the period from July 1987 through June [illegible] to §§ [illegible] of the original Restatement of Torts. These sections, dealing with unfair competition, were omitted from the Restatement of the Law Second, Torts 2d. Citations to the original Restatement of Torts appear first, followed by citations to the Restatement of the Law Third, Unfair Competition. Earlier citations to §§ [illegible] of the original Restatement of Torts will be found in the Torts 2d Appendix Volumes covering §§ [illegible] through 1977, and through June 1987.

This Pocket Part includes court citations to Introductions, Introductory Notes, blackletter, Comments (including Illustrations), and Reporter's (or Reporters') Notes of the Restatement and Principles of the Law. Reporter's Notes discuss the legal and other sources relied upon by the Reporter in formulating the blackletter and Comments and enable the reader better to evaluate these formulations. They also provide a guide for additional research. Reporter's Notes are regarded as the work of the Reporter and do not represent the position of The American Law Institute, but courts may nevertheless find them useful.

Grateful acknowledgment is made to Thomson Reuters for furnishing the Institute with citations of decisions noted herein.

The American Law Institute

Philadelphia, PA
[illegible]

TABLE OF ABBREVIATIONS USED IN THIS VOLUME

Ch.—Chapter
cit.—cited
cl.—clause
com.—comment
conc. op.—concurring opinion
disc.—discussion
diss. op.—dissenting opinion
dist.—distinguished
erron.—erroneously
fol.—followed
ftn.—footnote
illus.—illustration
Intro.—Introductory
Prop.—Proposed
quot.—quoted
Rptr's—Reporter's
rev.—revised
sec.—section
Stat.—Statutory
subsec.—subsection
sup.—support
Supp.—Supplement
T.D.—Tentative Draft

CASE CITATIONS TO THE RESTATEMENT OF THE LAW CUMULATIVE ANNUAL POCKET PART FOR USE IN 2024

TORTS

Note: The Restatement of the Law of Unfair Competition, published in 1995, supersedes and replaces Chapters 34, 35, and 36 (§§ 708–761) of the original Restatement of Torts. The subject matter of these chapters was omitted from the Restatement Second of Torts on the ground that it was no longer a subcategory of Torts but a distinctive area of the law calling for separate treatment. Citations to §§ 708–761 of the original Restatement of Torts, addressing interference with business relations, are reproduced here for the reader's convenience. For citations to these sections of the original Restatement of Torts prior to July 1987, please consult the Torts 2d Appendix Volume covering §§ 708–840E through 1977 and the Appendix Volume covering §§ 708–840E from 1978 through June 1987.

DIVISION NINE. INTERFERENCE WITH BUSINESS RELATIONS

PART 1. BY TRADE PRACTICES

Generally

C.A.5, 2007. Part 1 cit. generally in ftn. (general cite). Assignee of rights to computer program brought trade-secret-misappropriation claim against developers of competing program that was based in large part on assignee's program. On remand, the district court granted summary judgment for defendants. Affirming, this court, inter alia, upheld the magistrate judge's definition of "use" with respect to the third element of trade-secret misappropriation. The court reasoned, in part, that, under Texas law, which followed the Restatement Third of Unfair Competition, defendants "used" plaintiff's program by continuing to rely on it, either directly or on those portions incorporated into the competing program, to accelerate the development and marketability of the competing program. General Universal Systems, Inc. v. HAL, Inc., 500 F.3d 444, 451.

CHAPTER 34. THE PRIVILEGE TO ENGAGE IN BUSINESS

D.N.M.2010. Cit. in sup. §§ 708-710, constituting all of Ch. 34. Buyer of endodontic equipment sued sellers for breach of contract and unfair trade practices; sellers brought various counterclaims sounding in contract and tort. Granting in part and denying in part buyer's motion for summary judgment on sellers' counterclaims,

Cit.—cited; com.—comment; fol.—followed; sup.—support.
A complete list of abbreviations precedes page 1.

this court held, in determining that New Mexico law applied, that sellers' counterclaims of unfair competition, violation of the New Mexico Unfair Practices Act, and unlawful misappropriation fell into the category of torts. The court noted that the causes of action in the Restatement Third of Unfair Competition appeared to have grown out of the Restatement of Torts, implying that they should be categorized as torts. Guidance Endodontics, LLC v. Dentsply Intern., Inc., 708 F.Supp.2d 1209, 1225.

§ 708. Engaging in Business in Good Faith

Conn.1987. Quot. but dist. After the state board of examiners in podiatry issued a declaratory ruling that the treatment of ankle problems was within the scope of podiatry practice in Connecticut, an orthopedic specialist appealed, claiming that the ruling was arbitrary, erroneous, and in excess of the board's statutory authority. The lower court dismissed the appeal on the ground that the plaintiff was not aggrieved under state law and that therefore the court lacked jurisdiction over the subject matter. Citing error, this court set aside the judgment and remanded, concluding that, because the plaintiff had effectively alleged that his anticipated loss of revenues upon the ruling of the board would result from competition that was unfair or illegal, the plaintiff had standing to appeal the ruling. State Med. Soc. v. Board of Exam. in Podiatry, 203 Conn. 295, 524 A.2d 636, 640, appeal after remand 208 Conn. 709, 546 A.2d 830 (1988).

§ 710. Engaging in Business in Violation of Legislative Enactment

C.A.1, 2021. Quot. in case quot. in sup. Taxicab corporations sued transportation-network company, alleging, inter alia, that defendant engaged in unfair competition against plaintiffs, because it operated its ride-sharing business in violation of state and local taxicab regulations. The district court entered judgment for defendant. This court affirmed, holding that the fact that defendant's conduct violated taxicab regulations did not mean defendant engaged in unfair competition against plaintiffs. The court explained that plaintiffs failed to show, as required under Restatement of Torts § 710, that the relevant taxicab regulations were enacted to protect them from unauthorized competition, and observed that language suggesting that the regulations were designed to prevent unreasonable competition was deleted by the legislature before the regulations were enacted. Anoush Cab, Inc. v. Uber Technologies, Inc., 8 F.4th 1, 23.

CHAPTER 35. CONFUSION OF SOURCE (PASSING OFF, INFRINGEMENT OF TRADE-MARK OR TRADE NAME AND IMITATION OF APPEARANCE OF GOODS)

D.Ariz.2010. Cit. in disc. §§ 711-743, constituting most of Chapter 35. Insured sued insurer, seeking to establish that insurer had a duty to defend insured in an underlying patent-infringement action filed against it by a competitor. Granting summary judgment for insurer, this court held, among other things, that a "knowledge of falsity" exclusion in the policy applied and relieved insurer of any potential duty to defend. The court pointed out that competitor made specific allegations of fraud, because it asserted violations of the Delaware Deceptive Trade Practices Act, violations of the Lanham Act, and common-law unfair competition, all of which required a plaintiff to prove some type of deception or falsity on the part of the defendant, and insured had not shown that those claims had any alternative negligence theory that could be covered under the policy. Ventana Medical Systems, Inc. v. St. Paul Fire & Marine Ins. Co., 709 F.Supp.2d 744, 760.

N.D.Cal.2009. Cit. in case quot. in disc. §§ 711-743, constituting most of Ch. 35. Insured under a commercial-liability policy sued insurer, alleging that insurer breached its duty to defend insured against defamation cross-claims asserted against it by a third party in underlying state-court litigation. Granting insured's motion for partial summary judgment, this court held, inter alia, that insurer owed a duty to defend, because the policy's intellectual-property exclusion did not apply to the alleged defamation in the cross-complaint. The court noted that, while the exclusion included "unfair competition," it used that

For earlier citations, see the Appendices, Supplements, or Pocket Parts, if any, that correspond to the subject matter under examination.

term in the context of "passing off" and analogous acts by which a person exploited a competitor's reputation in the market, and there was no relationship between the injury caused by insured's alleged defamatory statements and insured's conduct with respect to intellectual property rights. Align Technology, Inc. v. Federal Ins. Co., 673 F.Supp.2d 957, 970.

S.D.Cal.2012. Cit. in disc. §§ 711-743, constituting most of Ch. 35. City and its public financing authority sued applicant who sought to register certain trademarks that were similar to plaintiffs' marks "Crossings at Carlsbad" and "TCAC," asserting, inter alia, a claim for common-law unfair competition. This court entered judgment for plaintiffs, holding that, by registering infringing domain names, incorporating California corporations with infringing names, and purchasing yellow pages directory listings using the name "The Crossings at Carlsbad Golf Course," defendant appropriated, at little or no cost, trademarks developed, registered, and used by plaintiffs, and thus his conduct constituted fraud under California's unfair competition law; defendant's actions suggested a false designation of origin, were likely to cause confusion, and were likely to deceive as to the affiliation of defendant with city and its golf course. City of Carlsbad v. Shah, 850 F.Supp.2d 1087, 1110.

Cal.1992. Cit. in disc. §§ 711-743, constituting most of Ch. 35. Bank, after settling a consumer class action, asserted that the claims against it alleging violations of the state's unfair business practices act were covered by its comprehensive general insurance policy. Insurer sought a declaratory judgment that the policy did not provide coverage. The trial court granted the insurer's motion for summary adjudication; the court of appeal found coverage and vacated the trial court's order. Reversing, this court held that, while the policy covered damages for "unfair competition" that occurred in the course of the bank's "advertising activities," the policy referred to the common law tort of unfair competition and not to conduct prohibited under the unfair business practices act. Bank of the West v. Superior Court, 2 Cal.4th 1254, 10 Cal.Rptr.2d 538, 544, 833 P.2d 545, 551.

Cal.App.1999. Cit. in disc. §§ 711-743, constituting most of Ch. 35. Insurer sought declaration that it was not obligated to defend and indemnify insured against competitor's business-tort claims. The trial court entered judgment on a jury verdict for insured. Reversing, this court held, in part, that "passing off" claims based entirely on advertising conduct infringing competitor's trade dress or trademark were expressly excluded under the policy provision barring coverage for claims for unfair competition arising from trademark infringement. Industrial Indem. Co. v. Apple Computer, 79 Cal.App.4th 817, 95 Cal.Rptr.2d 528, 535.

Introductory Note

U.S.2014. Intro. Note cit. in disc. After supplier of toner cartridges brought a copyright-infringement action against manufacturer of components used by supplier's competitors to refurbish and resell used cartridges, manufacturer counterclaimed, alleging that supplier engaged in false or misleading advertising in violation of the Lanham Act, and that its misrepresentations that manufacturer's business was illegal had caused manufacturer lost sales and damage to its business reputation. The district court dismissed manufacturer's Lanham Act claim, holding that manufacturer lacked "prudential standing" to bring that claim; the court of appeals reversed. Affirming, this court held that manufacturer had standing to bring a false-advertising claim under the Lanham Act against supplier. The court concluded that manufacturer came within the class of plaintiffs to whom Congress gave authorization to sue for false advertising under the Lanham Act, because it adequately pleaded that, pursuant to the zone-of-interests test, it suffered an injury to a commercial interest in sales or business reputation, and that the injury was proximately caused by supplier's misrepresentations. Lexmark Intern., Inc. v. Static Control Components, Inc., 134 S.Ct. 1377, 1390.

C.A.Fed.2022. Intro. Note quot. in sup. Owner of trademarks brought a claim under the Lanham Act to cancel trademark registrations of competitor, alleging that defendant registered and used marks that were nearly identical to marks that plaintiff used in India. The U.S. Trademark Trial and Appeal Board canceled defendant's marks. This court reversed, holding that plaintiff failed to establish a statutory cause of action, because plaintiff failed to demonstrate that defendant's use of the

Cit.—cited; com.—comment; fol.—followed; sup.—support.
A complete list of abbreviations precedes page 1.

marks in the United States diverted sales and reputation away from plaintiff. Citing the Introductory Note to Chapter 35 of the Restatement of Torts, the court explained that it was baseless to assume that the fact that the marks were well known in India meant they were well known among Indian Americans in the United States, thus diverting sales away from plaintiff, and plaintiff submitted no further evidence beyond single instances of U.S. consumer awareness that plaintiff's marks were used in India. Meenaxi Enterprise, Inc. v. Coca-Cola Company, 38 F.4th 1067.

S.D.Fla.2021. Intro Note cit. in sup. In multidistrict litigation, automotive-part recyclers that purchased vehicles equipped with airbags containing the propellant ammonium nitrate filed a class action against manufacturers of the vehicles, alleging that manufacturers knew or should have known that the propellant posed an unreasonable risk of serious foreseeable harm or death. This court granted manufacturers' motion to dismiss recyclers' claims for false advertising under the Lanham Act, holding that recyclers lacked statutory standing because they were not competitors of manufacturers of the vehicles or airbags. The court cited the Restatement of Torts in reasoning that unfair competition had historically been understood as injuries to business reputation and to present and future sales and, even though recyclers' business model was to eventually re-sell used cards and car parts, their relationship to manufacturers was one of disappointed consumer to hoodwinking supplier, rather than competitors. In re Takata Airbag Products Liability Litigation, 524 F.Supp.3d 1266, 1286, 1287.

D.N.J.2000. Intro. Note quot. generally in case quot. in disc. Unsuccessful trademark applicant sued stock brokerage for unfair competition and trademark infringement. Entering partial summary judgment for defendant, the court held that material factual issues existed as to whether defendant had engaged in unfair competition by misappropriating plaintiff's confidential and proprietary information through fraud and breach of a fiduciary relationship, since the evidence tended to show that plaintiff had spent substantial time and money to formulate an idea for novel financial products, that he had submitted a proposal marked "proprietary and confidential" to defendant and had sent additional information at defendant's request, and that defendant then began marketing products similar to plaintiff's samples. Duffy v. Charles Schwab & Co., Inc., 97 F.Supp.2d 592, 600.

§ 711. General Principle

D.Conn.1987. Cit. in disc. An Arizona company manufactured and marketed products under trademarks substantially similar to trademarks owned by a Connecticut company. The Arizona company advertised its products, with the infringing trademarks, in numerous national publications that reached Connecticut, and contracted with an Illinois distributor to have its catalogs and products distributed in a geographic area that included Connecticut. The Connecticut company sued the Arizona company for trademark infringement in the federal district court in Connecticut. This court denied the defendant's motion to dismiss for lack of personal jurisdiction, holding, inter alia, that jurisdiction was proper under the tortious act subsection of Connecticut's long-arm statute because tortious conduct in a trademark infringement action takes place where the passing off occurs, and the passing off required only the distribution of catalogs offering goods under the infringing trademark. Whelen Engineering v. Tomar Electronics, 672 F.Supp. 659, 662.

E.D.Pa.1991. Quot. and cit. in sup. A manufacturer of a roofing system sued a competitor for unfair competition, inter alia, alleging that the defendant used the plaintiff's trademark and trade dress in the manufacture and marketing of its product and passed them off as its own. The court granted the plaintiff's motion for a preliminary injunction, finding that the plaintiff was subject to irreparable harm and was likely to succeed on the merits of the case. The court stated that the plaintiff's evidence that the defendant intentionally copied the plaintiff's unique nonfunctional trade dress and thus used a confusingly similar trade dress in marketing its product constituted proof of unfair competition under New Jersey law. Merchant & Evans v. Roosevelt Bldg. Products, 774 F.Supp. 1467, 1480, 1483.

For earlier citations, see the Appendices, Supplements, or Pocket Parts, if any, that correspond to the subject matter under examination.

TOPIC 1. FRAUDULENT MARKETING

§ 712. General Principle

D.N.M.2010. Cit. in sup. Buyer of endodontic equipment sued sellers for breach of contract and unfair trade practices; sellers brought various counterclaims sounding in contract and tort. Granting in part and denying in part buyer's motion for summary judgment on sellers' counterclaims, this court held, in determining that New Mexico law applied, that sellers' counterclaims of unfair competition, violation of the New Mexico Unfair Practices Act, and unlawful misappropriation fell into the category of torts. The court noted that the causes of action in the Restatement Third of Unfair Competition appeared to have grown out of the Restatement of Torts, implying that they should be categorized as torts. Guidance Endodontics, LLC v. Dentsply Intern., Inc., 708 F.Supp.2d 1209, 1225.

Mass.App.2009. Coms. (b) and (c) cit. in disc. After proprietor sold the assets of his roofing and siding business to his son-in-law, proprietor's son and son's incorporated roofing and siding business brought suit for trade-name infringement, inter alia, against proprietor's son-in-law and son-in-law's corporation. The trial court entered judgment for plaintiffs. Affirming, this court held that plaintiffs showed that their use of the trade name "Castricone Roofing and Siding" had acquired a secondary meaning. The court reasoned that, at the time of trial, plaintiffs had used the name for almost 30 years; the parties' trade names, products, and markets were very similar, if not exactly the same; and the trial court's findings that defendants' use of the name had caused substantial confusion between the two businesses and had resulted in lost profits for plaintiffs' business were supported by the evidence and were not clearly erroneous. Castricone v. Mical, 74 Mass.App.Ct. 591, 594, 909 N.E.2d 29, 34.

§ 713. Inducing Fraudulent Marketing

D.Md.1996. Quot. and cit. generally in disc., cit. in case quot. in disc. In action brought under the Lanham Act, charity sued publisher for contributory trademark infringement in connection with the use of charity's name and mark in a book designed to instruct readers on ways to make money from "business opportunity" frauds and scams. Publisher moved to dismiss on the ground that charity could not sustain a claim for contributory infringement absent proof of direct infringement. Denying the motion, the court held, in part, that dismissal was inappropriate because it could not say, as a matter of law, that charity would be unable to present evidence of direct infringement. N.F.B. v. Loompanics Enterprises, 936 F.Supp. 1232, 1245.

TOPIC 2. INFRINGEMENT OF TRADE-MARK AND TRADE NAME

§ 716. Definition of Trade Name

Or.App.1995. Com. (b) quot. in case quot. in disc. Hardware company brought an action for trade-name infringement and trade-name dilution against home center using a similar business name. Affirming the trial court's dismissal of the complaint, this court held that, because plaintiff failed to prove that the name Ernst, when used as part of the name of plaintiff's business, had acquired a secondary meaning, plaintiff did not have a protectible interest in that name. Ernst Hardware Co. v. Ernst Home Center, 134 Or.App. 560, 565, 895 P.2d 1363, 1366.

§ 717. General Statement of Conditions of Infringement

D.Conn.1987. Cit. in disc. An Arizona company manufactured and marketed products under trademarks substantially similar to trademarks owned by a Connecticut company. The Arizona company advertised its products, with the infringing trademarks, in numerous national publications that reached Connecticut, and contracted with an Illinois distributor to have its catalogs and products distributed in a geographic area that included Connecticut. The Connecticut company sued the Arizona company for trademark infringement in the federal district court in Connecticut. This court denied the defendant's motion to dismiss for lack of personal jurisdiction, holding, inter alia, that jurisdiction was proper under the tortious act subsection of Connecticut's long-arm statute because tortious conduct in a trademark-infringement

Cit.—cited; com.—comment; fol.—followed; sup.—support.
A complete list of abbreviations precedes page 1.

action takes place where the passing off occurs, and the passing off required only the distribution of catalogs offering goods under the infringing trademark. Whelen Engineering v. Tomar Electronics, 672 F.Supp. 659, 662.

Mass.App.2009. Com. (b) cit. in disc. After proprietor sold the assets of his roofing and siding business to his son-in-law, proprietor's son and son's incorporated roofing and siding business brought suit for tradename infringement, inter alia, against proprietor's son-in-law and son-in-law's corporation. The trial court entered judgment for plaintiffs. Affirming, this court held that plaintiffs showed that their use of the trade name "Castricone Roofing and Siding" had acquired a secondary meaning. The court reasoned that, at the time of trial, plaintiffs had used the name for almost 30 years; the parties' trade names, products, and markets were very similar, if not exactly the same; and the trial court's findings that defendants' use of the name had caused substantial confusion between the two businesses and had resulted in lost profits for plaintiffs' business were supported by the evidence and were not clearly erroneous. Castricone v. Mical, 74 Mass.App. Ct. 591, 594, 909 N.E.2d 29, 34.

§ 718. Affixation

Mo.App.1993. Com. (b) cit. in sup. and in ftn. Gearbox manufacturer sued competitor and former employees working for competitor to enjoin them from revealing its trade secrets and using its trademark without authorization and requested other relief. The trial court granted plaintiff injunctive relief. Affirming in part, reversing in part, and remanding with directions, this court held, inter alia, that, since any use competitor made of the accused mark before selling or distributing any gearboxes was not sufficient to create protectable trademark rights, plaintiff engaged in protected use of its mark before competitor engaged in such use of it, considering additionally competitor's knowledge of plaintiff's logo, indicating that its subsequent decision to use the accused mark was made in bad faith. Superior Gearbox Co. v. Edwards, 869 S.W.2d 239, 252.

§ 719. Adoption and Use

C.A.3, 1994. Com. (a) quot. in sup. Manufacturer of plastic garden planters shaped like Grecian urns brought a trade-dress-infringement action against competitor and moved for a preliminary injunction. Affirming the district court's denial of plaintiff's motion, this court held that, since plaintiff was unable to show that its product's configuration was either inherently distinctive or had acquired a secondary meaning, plaintiff failed to demonstrate a likelihood of success on the merits. The court rejected the application of traditional trade dress doctrine to a claim that product configuration had been infringed. Duraco Products v. Joy Plastic Enterprises, Ltd., 40 F.3d 1431, 1450.

§ 720. Geographical Names

C.A.Fed.2015. Com. (c) cit. in sup., com. (d) quot. in case quot. in sup. Housewares manufacturer headquartered in Newbridge, Ireland sought protection of the mark NEWBRIDGE HOME in the United States. The Trademark Examiner refused to register the mark as being primarily geographically descriptive when applied to manufacturer's goods; the Trademark Trial and Appeal Board affirmed. Reversing and remanding, this court held that the evidence as a whole suggested that Newbridge, Ireland—a town of less than 20,000 people—was not generally known, thus, to the relevant public, the mark was not *primarily* geographically descriptive of the goods. The court cited Restatement of Torts § 720 in noting that the rationale for allowing registration of marks that relevant consumers did not view as primarily geographic was that the consumer would consider such marks arbitrary. In re The Newbridge Cutlery Co., 776 F.3d 854, 860.

§ 721. Generic and Descriptive Designations

S.D.N.Y.1987. Com. (a) quot. in case quot. in disc. A corporation sued to enjoin another corporation and others from using a certain mark on its goods or in its corporate name, for the cancellation of the defendants' trademark registration, and for an accounting. The court denied the plaintiff's motion for a preliminary injunction. The court noted that the distinction between a generic term and a descriptive term was one of degree. A descriptive term conveyed information on the characteristics and qualities of an article and would receive protection only when it had become distinctive of the applicant's goods in commerce, provided it had a secondary meaning. A generic term provided information on the nature or class of an article and was not

For earlier citations, see the Appendices, Supplements, or Pocket Parts, if any, that correspond to the subject matter under examination.

eligible for trademark protection. The court examined certain accepted definitions of the word gear and concluded that it was generic with respect to clothing. Gear, Inc. v. L.A. Gear California, Inc., 670 F.Supp. 508, 514.

E.D.Pa.1988. Com. (a) cit. in disc. An apple juice producer sold its product in a bottle with a label that showed several apples and a drop of juice. When a competitor started selling apple juice in a carton with a similar label, the producer sued the competitor for trademark infringement. The court found for the defendant, holding that the plaintiff's unregistered label was not entitled to protection because it was merely descriptive rather than distinctive. The court stated that a descriptive trademark was one that permitted the consumer to determine attributes of the product without having significantly to use his or her imagination. The court noted that many companies that sold apple juice employed labels depicting apples; the greater the number of similar trademarks in use, the less likely that the trademark would be afforded legal protection. Ginger Group, Ltd. v. Beatrice Companies, Inc., 678 F.Supp. 555, 559.

§ 728. Confusing Similarity

C.A.8, 1998. Com. (a) quot. in case quot. in sup. Manufacturer of children's toys sued competitor for Lanham Act violations. The district court entered judgment for defendant. Affirming, this court held, in part, that even though some of plaintiff's products were inherently distinctive and nonfunctional, they were not entitled to trade-dress protection because consumers were not likely to be confused as to the source of the goods. Children's Factory, Inc. v. Benee's Toys, Inc., 160 F.3d 489, 496.

Wyo.1992. Quot. in case quot. in disc. Oil company sued petroleum company with a substantially similar name for trade-name infringement and unfair competition. The trial court granted defendant's motion for summary judgment. Reversing and remanding, this court held that the 25-year-long use by plaintiff of its trade name, as well as its establishment of a dominant place in the market, warranting protection of its reputation, created an issue of fact as to whether plaintiff had developed a secondary meaning in its trade name. The court also stated that the trial court erred in restricting its analysis to confusion among customers, because this devalued other policy considerations that resulted in trade-name protection, such as consumer protection, property rights, economic efficiency, and universal concepts of justice. Powder River Oil v. Powder River Petroleum, 830 P.2d 403, 412.

§ 729. Factors in Confusing Similarity

C.A.2, 1996. Com. (b) quot. in case quot. in disc. Maker of SPAM luncheon meat brought trademark-infringement action against filmmaker whose latest movie featured a puppet named "Spa'am," seeking to enjoin filmmaker from using Spa'am in connection with movie-related promotional merchandise. Plaintiff feared that consumers would confuse the puppet with "SPAM-man," plaintiff's own promotional character. After a bench trial the district court entered judgment for filmmaker and denied plaintiff's request for a permanent injunction. Affirming, this court held that plaintiff failed to establish the elements of trademark infringement, since, among other things, the marks Spa'am and SPAM were highly dissimilar, a finding that was helped by the fact that the two marks would always appear in dramatically different settings and project completely different visual displays. Hormel Foods Corp. v. Jim Henson Productions, Inc., 73 F.3d 497, 503.

C.A.2, 1995. Com. (b) quot. in sup. Manufacturer of a hand-operated staple gun bearing the registered trademark "T-50" brought a trademark-infringement action against a competing manufacturer of pneumatic staplers, based on competitor's use of the mark "T50" as part of the model number on its staplers. Connecticut federal district court held that defendant infringed on plaintiff's valid trademark. This court reversed, holding that where the allegedly infringing use concerned inclusion of the symbol T50 in a six-digit model number used to identify a product different from the plaintiff's in price and in function, the court could not conclude that plaintiff had established that an appreciable number of prudent purchasers were likely to be misled or confused. While the "T" and "50" both appear in defendant's designation and plaintiff's mark, the total effect of defendant's multi-digit model numbers was decidedly different from plaintiff's "Model T-50." Arrow Fastener Co., Inc. v. Stanley Works, 59 F.3d 384, 395.

Cit.—cited; com.—comment; fol.—followed; sup.—support.
A complete list of abbreviations precedes page 1.

C.A.2, 1993. Cit. in case quot. in sup. Owner of trademark "Sportstick" for lip balm brought a trademark-infringement action against owner of trademark "Right Guard Sport Stick" for deodorant. Affirming the district court's entry of judgment for defendant, this court held that plaintiff failed to prove its allegation of a likelihood of "reverse confusion," i.e., that potential customers would assume that defendant was the source of plaintiff's mark and thus believe that plaintiff was the infringer, and therefore could not establish its claim of trademark infringement. W.W.W. Pharmaceutical Co., Inc. v. Gillette Co., 984 F.2d 567, 572.

C.A.2, 1991. Cit. in case quot. in disc. A publisher of a book and audiotapes on the development of charisma that used the trade name "New Choices Press" sought to enjoin a magazine publisher from using the name "New Choices for the Best Years" for its magazine on retirement living. The district court granted the defendant's motion for summary judgment. Affirming, this court held that the plaintiff failed to raise a genuine issue of fact as to the likelihood of confusion. The court concluded that the plaintiff's trade name was weak because it was not widely known. Lang v. Retirement Living Pub. Co., Inc., 949 F.2d 576, 580.

C.A.5, 2008. Com. (f) quot. in case quot. in sup. and cit. in ftn. Four universities sued apparel company and its principal, alleging that defendants infringed their trademarks in violation of the Lanham Act and state law by selling t-shirts with universities' color schemes and other identifying indicia. The district court granted summary judgment for plaintiffs. Affirming, this court held, inter alia, that the colors, content, and context of the offending t-shirts were likely to cause confusion as to their source, sponsorship, or affiliation. The court pointed to the strong similarity between defendant's t-shirts and plaintiffs' licensed products, as well as defendant's admitted intent to copy, as strong evidence of a likelihood of confusion. Board of Supervisors for Louisiana State University Agricultural and Mechanical College v. Smack Apparel Co., 550 F.3d 465, 482.

C.A.5, 1998. Com. (b) quot. in case quot. in disc. Assignee and registrant of all trademarks, copyrights, and publicity rights belonging to Elvis Presley estate sued owner of bar operating as "The Velvet Elvis" for, inter alia, trademark infringement and unfair competition. The district court entered judgment for defendant. Reversing and remanding, this court held that the district court erred in isolating its consideration of defendant's advertising practices from its consideration of whether the name "The Velvet Elvis" infringed plaintiff's trade and service marks and therefore created a likelihood of confusion; that the strength of plaintiff's mark, the similarity of the parties' marks, and the similarity of products and services weighed in favor of finding a likelihood of confusion; that defendant's actions suggested an intent to confuse customers as to the source of its mark; and that the evidence supported a finding that defendant's advertising practices caused actual confusion among customers. Elvis Presley Enterprises, Inc. v. Capece, 141 F.3d 188, 197.

C.A.6, 1991. Com. (g) cit. in headnote and quot. in sup. Two companies utilized service marks containing the same initials. One company sued the other company seeking injunctive relief and cancellation of the other's federally registered mark. The district court granted summary judgment in favor of the plaintiff, holding in part that the plaintiff's mark was sufficiently strong and well established. Reversing and remanding, this court held, inter alia, that genuine issues of material fact were raised with respect to whether a likelihood of confusion existed in the marketplace due to the parties' use of their respective marks. The court stated that extensive third-party uses of a trademark might have the effect of substantially weakening the strength of a mark, and that evidence of such numerous third-party registration of marks consisting of the plaintiff's initials should have been considered. Homeowners Group v. Home Marketing Specialists, 931 F.2d 1100, 1101, 1108.

C.A.6, 1988. Com. (f) quot. in case quot. but dist. A holder of a trademark and a car wash company sued an independent car wash owner for, inter alia, trademark infringement for operating car washes under the same name as the registered trademark held by the plaintiffs. The trial court found for the defendant on the ground that there was no real "likelihood of confusion" between the two businesses. Reversing and remanding, this court held that there was substantial likelihood of confusion between the two names, and that a lack of evidence

For earlier citations, see the Appendices, Supplements, or Pocket Parts, if any, that correspond to the subject matter under examination.

showing that the defendant intended to profit from using the plaintiffs' name did not preclude the finding of infringement. Wynn Oil Co. v. Thomas, 839 F.2d 1183, 1189.

C.A.8, 1987. Cit. in case cit. in sup. In a suit for trademark infringement, a seller of high-fashion cosmetics moved to enjoin the marketer of an imitation fragrance from using certain packaging and display materials in the distribution and sale of its products. The trial court determined that the plaintiff would probably be successful in demonstrating a likelihood of confusion and granted in part the plaintiff's motion for a preliminary injunction. Affirming in part, reversing in part, and vacating without prejudice, this court held that the trial court abused its discretion in issuing the preliminary injunction because it erroneously concluded on the basis of insufficient evidence that the plaintiff demonstrated probable success on the merits. Noting that a multitude of factors to determine likelihood of confusion have been articulated by the courts, the court stated that the trial court's in-chambers visual inspection by itself, in the absence of reference to any other supporting evidence that could give rise to an inference of likely consumer confusion, was too narrow a context on which to base a conclusion of probable success on the merits. Calvin Klein Cosmetics Corp. v. Lenox Laboratories, 815 F.2d 500, 504.

C.A.8, 1987. Cit. in disc., coms. (b) and (g) cit. in sup. A cereal manufacturer sought a preliminary injunction to prevent another cereal manufacturer from using a name for a new cereal that was similar to the name of a cereal already existing and manufactured by the plaintiff. The trial court denied the injunction. Affirming, this court held that the plaintiff failed to demonstrate that it would suffer irreparable harm absent a preliminary injunction. The court reasoned that the plaintiff manufacturer presented insufficient evidence that the defendant's mark would create a likelihood of consumer confusion, deception, or mistake. General Mills, Inc. v. Kellogg Co., 824 F.2d 622, 626, 627.

C.A.9, 1999. Com. (f) quot. in case quot. in disc. Entertainment industry information provider using "MovieBuff" as trademark sought to enjoin video-rental chain from using "moviebuff.com" as its web site domain name. The district court entered judgment for defendant. Reversing and remanding, this court held that plaintiff established itself as the senior user of the mark, and that, given the similarity of the marks, the relatedness of product offerings, and the overlap in marketing and advertising channels, likelihood of consumer confusion existed. That defendant did not intend to confuse consumers was irrelevant under the circumstances. Brookfield Communications v. West Coast, 174 F.3d 1036, 1059.

C.A.9, 1993. Com. (f) quot. in sup. Phone company sued communications company for infringement of its service mark. District court enjoined defendant from using the service mark "telesis," holding that defendant's use of the mark constituted federal and state service-mark infringement, federal false designation of origin, and state of California trademark infringement and unfair competition. Affirming, this court held that district court's finding of likelihood of confusion was not clearly erroneous. The court stated that, although plaintiff offered no evidence disproving defendant's contention that buyers of its services would exercise considerable care in determining their origin, district court's ultimate factual finding was supported by its finding on character and strength of plaintiff's mark; by its finding on similarity of the services offered and the markets addressed; and by its findings on plaintiff's priority in use of the mark and defendant's attempt to get the benefit of goodwill and reputation acquired by plaintiff. Pacific Telesis v. International Telesis, 994 F.2d 1364, 1369.

C.A.10, 1999. Cit. in sup. Seller of camouflage-patterned outdoor clothing under "King of the Mountain" trademark brought trademark-infringement action against promoter of "Jeep KING OF THE MOUNTAIN DOWNHILL SERIES" ski races. Affirming the district court's grant of summary judgment for defendant, this court held, in part, that no likelihood of confusion existed as to sponsorship of ski races. King of the Mountain Sports, Inc. v. Chrysler Corp., 185 F.3d 1084, 1089.

C.A.10, 1996. Com. (b) quot. in part in sup. Bank sued competitor for trademark infringement, seeking to prevent competitor's use of the phrases First Bank, First Bank Kansas, and First Bank System on the ground that those terms were confusingly similar to bank's own FirstBank logo. The district court granted competitor's motion for summary judgment, concluding

Cit.—cited; com.—comment; fol.—followed; sup.—support.
A complete list of abbreviations precedes page 1.

that competitor's 1971 federal registration of the term First Bank System and an accompanying design provided constructive notice to others that they could not adopt a confusingly similar mark, and that "First-Bank" was confusingly similar. Reversing and remanding, this court held that, when all the relevant factors were considered and the marks at issue were compared to each other in their entirety, they were not confusingly similar. First Savings Bank, F.S.B. v. First Bank System, 101 F.3d 645, 653.

C.A.10, 1994. Com. (g) quot. in case quot. in sup. One corporation sued another for violation of federal trademark laws and for unfair competition under state common law as a result of defendant's use of the word "Universal" to describe its combination telephone and retail credit card. This court affirmed the district court's granting of summary judgment for defendant, noting that the term was used by a significant number of entities and was thus a relatively weak mark, and that the district court had concluded that the record was void of any evidence that defendant chose the term "Universal" with the intent of copying plaintiff's mark or confusing the public as to the sponsorship or affiliation of its card. Universal Money Centers v. AT & T, 22 F.3d 1527, 1533, cert. denied 513 U.S. 1052, 115 S.Ct. 655, 130 L.Ed.2d 558.

C.A.10, 1990. Cit. in disc. A telephone company, operating under some form of the name "General Telephone" since 1935, registered those words as a service mark for the provision of telephone services in 1982. It then sued for infringement the owner of a mobile telephone and paging services business who had been using the same name in an area of Utah since 1974. The district court held that the businessman was entitled to concurrent registration of the mark for his geographical area, and to its exclusive use in that region, finding that his use of the mark was not likely to cause confusion in the marketplace and that he had established the common-law defense of good faith adoption in a remote area. This court affirmed, holding, inter alia, that the district court had applied the proper legal standard for likelihood of confusion in its finding that the businessman's use of the mark was not likely to cause confusion in the marketplace regarding the source, origin, or sponsorship of his services. GTE Corp. v. Williams, 904 F.2d 536, 539, certiorari denied 498 U.S. 998, 111 S.Ct. 557, 112 L.Ed.2d 564 (1990).

C.A.10, 1987. Quot. in case quot. in disc., com. (f) cit. in disc. A blue-jeans manufacturer sued the manufacturers of jeans for larger women, alleging trademark infringement. The trial court found for the defendants. Affirming, this court held that the trademarks used by the plaintiff and the defendants were not confusingly similar, reasoning that the striking dissimilarities in the designs used in the two marks greatly outweighed any similarities; that the defendants did not intend to confuse the public, but rather intended to parody the plaintiff when they adopted their trademark; and that the plaintiff's mark was not tarnished because the public would not associate the defendants' jeans with the plaintiff or, if it did, it would only make the association because of the parody and not because of the belief that the plaintiff manufactured the defendants' jeans. Jordache Enterprises, Inc. v. Hogg Wyld, Ltd., 828 F.2d 1482, 1484, 1485.

C.A.Fed.1993. Quot. in case quot. in disc., cit. in sup. A shoe retailer sued for a declaration that its shoes did not infringe a manufacturer's trademarks, trade dress, or design patents; the manufacturer counterclaimed for infringement, unfair competition, and other claims. Vacating the district court's denial of the manufacturer's motion for a preliminary injunction and remanding for reconsideration of the motion, this court held, inter alia, that the district court focused on marketplace confusion but should have also considered the extent of possible post-sale confusion, as the marks and trade dress of the retailer's shoes were remarkably similar to the manufacturer's. Payless Shoesource, Inc. v. Reebok Intern. Ltd., 998 F.2d 985, 988, 989.

N.D.Cal.2009. Com. (f) quot. in case quot. in sup. Companies that owned 12 trade names and one trademark all incorporating the word "Rearden" brought trademark-infringement and other claims against another company after it changed its name to "Rearden Commerce." Granting summary judgment for defendant, this court held, inter alia, that no reasonable jury could find that defendant's use of "Rearden" created a strong likelihood of confusion in the minds of the relevant consuming public. The court rejected plaintiffs' argument that defendant acted in bad faith, noting that the record was devoid of evidence suggesting any intent to deceive; defendant allegedly selected the name due

For earlier citations, see the Appendices, Supplements, or Pocket Parts, if any, that correspond to the subject matter under examination.

to its founder's fondness for a fictional character named "Hank Rearden" and apparently thought plaintiffs had abandoned the marks when it changed its name. Rearden LLC v. Rearden Commerce, Inc., 597 F.Supp.2d 1006, 1025.

D.Colo.2001. Cit. in disc. Tire-store owner brought suit against manufacturer of tie-down straps and cargo-control products for infringement of its "Bigfoot" trademark. Granting plaintiff's motion for a preliminary injunction, the court held, inter alia, that plaintiff showed a likelihood of success on the merits based on evidence that defendant's use of the mark was likely to cause confusion in the marketplace concerning the source or quality of the products. Big O Tires, Inc. v. Bigfoot 4X4, Inc., 167 F.Supp.2d 1216, 1222.

D.Colo.1990. Quot. in case cit. in disc. A corporation that developed and marketed an electrosurgical coagulation device sought a preliminary injunction against a competitor for alleged violations of its trademark rights and unfair competition. The court denied the motion for a preliminary injunction, holding that the plaintiff was not likely to succeed on the merits since the terms in dispute were generic rather than suggestive or descriptive. In light of the degree of dissimilarity between the competing terms and the defendant's apparent lack of malintent in adopting the designation, the court found that the competitor's use of its mark was not likely to cause marketplace confusion. Birtcher Electro Med. Systems v. Beacon Laboratories, 738 F.Supp. 417, 426.

D.Colo.1990. Cit. and quot. in case cit. in disc., com. (f) cit. in case quot. in disc., com. (g) quot. in disc. A laser manufacturer that promoted products sold under the "Coherent" name and trademark sued a developer of coherent laser radar systems for trademark infringement. The court entered judgment for the defendant on the ground that the plaintiff failed to demonstrate the likelihood of confusion among its customers due to the similarity in the parties' names. The court said that the plaintiff's customers were sophisticated and exercised great care in their purchase of its products and services, and therefore the likelihood that the defendant's name would cause confusion among them was small. Coherent, Inc. v. Coherent Technologies, Inc., 736 F.Supp. 1055, 1064, 1066, judgment affirmed 935 F.2d 1122 (10th Cir.1991).

M.D.Fla.1991. Com. (f) cit. in sup. Publisher of Yellow Pages, which was given exclusive rights to publish the classified directory, sued publisher of tourist's guide, claiming, inter alia, unfair competition and trademark infringement after defendant inserted a similar directory next to the Yellow Pages in phone books distributed to tourist sites and businesses. The court granted a preliminary injunction enjoining defendant from using a slogan similar to the Yellow Pages' slogan and from inserting the guide into phone books. It held that a jury could find a confusing similarity between the directories and, therefore, find for plaintiff based solely on defendant's demonstrated intent to derive benefits from plaintiff's well-established reputation. BellSouth Adv. & Pub. v. Real Color Pages, 792 F.Supp. 775, 783.

S.D.Fla.1986. Quot. in disc. A clothing dealer made and sold inferior-quality clothing under a trade name and trademark substantially similar to that of a renowned manufacturer of quality clothing. The trademark owner sued for damages and injunctive relief. This court entered judgment for the plaintiff on all claims, holding that the defendant was liable for infringement because there was a likelihood of confusing the public between the products of the plaintiff and those of the defendant through the defendant's deliberate use of substantially similar trademarks and trade names. Polo Fashions, Inc. v. Rabanne, 661 F.Supp. 89, 94.

D.Kan.2008. Com. (g) quot. in case cit. in ftn. University and university athletic corporation sued t-shirt seller and manufacturer, alleging violations of state and federal trademark laws through the unauthorized and unlicensed sale of university apparel. This court, inter alia, denied plaintiffs' motion in limine to exclude evidence concerning third-party use of plaintiffs' marks, finding that evidence of such use was relevant to the issues of the marks' strength and fame. The court noted that, in general, the greater the number of identical or more or less similar marks already in use on different kinds of goods, the less was the likelihood of confusion between any two specific uses of a weak mark. University of Kansas v. Sinks, 565 F.Supp.2d 1216, 1231.

D.Kan.2006. Adopted in case quot. in sup. Sauna dealer sued competitors that allegedly used its trademark in a domain

Cit.—cited; com.—comment; fol.—followed; sup.—support.
A complete list of abbreviations precedes page 1.

name and an e-mail address to communicate injurious falsehoods about its products to third parties, asserting, among other claims, false description under the Lanham Act. After jury exonerated one defendant and found remaining defendant liable for $1 in actual damages on the false-description claim, the district court overruled remaining defendant's pending motion for judgment as a matter of law. The court held, inter alia, that plaintiff produced strong evidence of a likelihood of confusion, showing that defendant used plaintiff's trademark with malicious intent to harm plaintiff, and that both parties marketed their products through similar means. Sunlight Saunas, Inc. v. Sundance Sauna, Inc., 442 F.Supp.2d 1160, 1169.

D.Kan.2006. Adopted in case quot. in sup. Sauna dealer sued competitors that allegedly used its trademark in a domain name and an e-mail address to communicate injurious falsehoods about its products to third parties, asserting, among other claims, false description under the Lanham Act. This court denied in part defendants' motion for summary judgment, holding that a question of fact remained as to whether defendants intended to infringe on plaintiff's mark and consumers were likely to be confused regarding the sponsorship of the website and e-mail account; although defendants did not use the site or account to sell goods or services, a reasonable jury could conclude, in regard to one relevant factor in the inquiry, that defendants' intent was to enhance their competitive positions at plaintiff's expense, not to educate consumers. Sunlight Saunas, Inc. v. Sundance Sauna, Inc., 427 F.Supp.2d 1032, 1062.

D.Kan.1997. Quot. in case cit. in disc. A Missouri corporation sued an Oklahoma corporation for trade-dress infringement, commercial misrepresentation, and unfair competition, alleging that the defendant corporation and its president infringed the trade dress of two of plaintiff's chemical injection pumps in violation of the Lanham Act. This court entered judgment for defendants, holding, inter alia, that plaintiff failed to establish that there was a likelihood of confusion by purchasers at the point of sale of plaintiff's and defendant's pumps. Several witnesses testified that consumers in the chemical injection pump market usually understood that different manufacturers made products with similar designs. The manner of marketing the pumps also suggested that there was little likelihood that direct purchasers were confused as to the origin of the pumps. Finally, defendant's intent in manufacturing the pumps suggested that there was little likelihood of confusion. Western Chemical Pumps, Inc. v. Superior Mfg., 989 F.Supp. 1112, 1124.

D.Kan.1995. Cit. in case cit. in sup. Manufacturer of plastic dinnerware sued manufacturer of cookware for trademark infringement, inter alia, seeking a preliminary injunction against defendant's use of the term "Casual Elegance" with its new product line. Denying plaintiff's motion for a preliminary injunction, the court held that plaintiff failed to show that there was a substantial likelihood that it would succeed on the merits and thus it did not establish its right to preliminary injunctive relief. The court stated that differences in the appearance of the two marks significantly outweighed any similarities. Packerware Corp. v. Corning Consumer Products Co., 895 F.Supp. 1438, 1448.

D.Kan.1992. Quot. in case quot. in sup. Shoe company sought declaratory judgment against competitor that it had not infringed on defendant's patents or trademarks. Defendant counterclaimed and moved for a preliminary injunction. The court denied defendant's motion for preliminary injunction, noting insufficient evidence that consumers would be likely to confuse plaintiff's and defendant's shoes. It explained that the two manufacturers put their own names on the shoes, the two types of shoes were never sold in the same retail outlets, and that consumers made the conscious choice to patronize plaintiff's store to find nonname-brand, inexpensive shoes. The court denied as moot plaintiff's motion for leave to file a supplemental memorandum. Payless Shoesource, Inc. v. Reebok Intern. Ltd., 804 F.Supp. 206, 210, vacated by 998 F.2d 985 (C.A.Fed.1993).

D.Kan.1992. Quot. in case quot. in sup. Regional manufacturer and distributor of petroleum products sued a national oil company for infringement of plaintiff's registered trademark (DYNA-PLEX 21C), alleging that after it had marketed a certain line of diesel engine lubricants for 20 years, defendant introduced a similar line of products with a name (AMOCO 21C) likely to cause confusion among the parties' customers. The court denied plaintiff's motion for summary judgment on the ground that genuine issues of material fact existed as to the likelihood of confusion. Universal Motor Oils Co., Inc. v. Amoco Oil Co., 809 F.Supp. 816, 820.

D.Kan.1989. Quot. in disc. A motion picture producer that placed commercials at the beginning of its videocassettes sued a corporation that recorded advertisements without the plaintiff's authorization and consent on videocassettes containing the plaintiff's motion pictures and bearing the plaintiff's trademark on theories of trademark and copyright infringement, inter alia. The court denied the plaintiff's motion for a preliminary injunction, holding that there was no evidence that the public perceived the videocassette purchased or rented from a video retailer to be a unit package containing only the plaintiff's products and added that the plaintiff came forth with no evidence of actual confusion. Paramount Pictures v. Video Broadcasting Systems, 724 F.Supp. 808, 815.

D.Kan.1987. Cit. in disc. A manufacturer and distributor of retail barbecue products sued a competing barbecue-sauce manufacturer, contending that the defendant's use of "Kingsford, Inc.," on its product infringed on the plaintiff's registered trademark "Kingsford." The court denied the plaintiff's motion for a preliminary injunction, holding that, although the plaintiff might eventually win judgment because of the likelihood of confusion in the marketplace caused by the defendant's use of the trademark, the plaintiff failed to show irreparable injury and a favorable balance of hardships, since a preliminary judgment would impose severe financial hardship on the defendants. Kingsford Products Co. v. Kingsfords, Inc., 674 F.Supp. 1428, 1430.

E.D.Ky.2014. Com. (f) quot. in case quot. in sup. Owners of a barbeque restaurant and registered trademarks for the restaurant brought claim for, among other things, trademark infringement against former business partner who, after parting ways with plaintiffs, continued to cater and provide food services while using the same trademarks to advertise his business. This court granted plaintiffs' motion for partial summary judgment, holding that defendant's use of identical trademarks was likely to cause confusion among customers, because the parties both sold barbecue, had nearly identical menu items, and competed directly against each other. The court cited Restatement of Torts § 729 in noting that, when it could be shown that a defendant's intention in using a trademark was to benefit from the reputation of that trademark, then that fact alone was potentially sufficient to justify the inference that there was confusing similarity. EAT BBQ LLC v. Walters, 47 F.Supp.3d 521, 532.

M.D.La.1985. Com. (f) quot. in case cit. in disc. A grocery-store chain sued an insurance company of the same name for trademark infringement. Finding for the defendant, the court stated that, if the name was adopted with the intent to derive benefit from the reputation of the plaintiff, the intent alone might be sufficient to justify the inference that there was confusing similarity. The court held, however, that in this case no evidence was presented of the defendant's intent to pass its product off as the plaintiff's product in such unrelated fields as insurance and groceries. Safeway Stores, Inc. v. Safeway Ins. Co., 657 F.Supp. 1307, 1316, affirmed 791 F.2d 929 (5th Cir.1986).

E.D.Mich.2003. Com. (g) quot. in case quot. in disc. Michigan ticket broker that did business as "BIG TIME WORLDWIDE" brought trademark-infringement action against Missouri ticket seller that used federally registered mark "BIG TIME TICKETS." Denying plaintiff's motion for a preliminary injunction, the court held that plaintiff failed to show a strong likelihood of success on the merits; because plaintiff's mark lacked distinctiveness and, thereby, lacked strength, the likelihood of confusion between the two marks was low. Big Time Worldwide Concert & Sport Club at Town Center, LLC v. Marriott Intern., Inc., 236 F.Supp.2d 791, 799.

D.N.J.1989. Com. (g) quot. in case cit. in disc. (Erron. cit. as com. 8.) An insecticide manufacturer sought a preliminary injunction to restrain a competitor from using the designation MAX or any other designation that allegedly infringed on the plaintiff's MAXFORCE trademark for pesticides. The court denied the plaintiff's motion, holding that the plaintiff had failed to establish a likelihood of consumer confusion between the products and marks in question. The court stated that the word "Max" was a weak element of the plaintiff's trademark, pointing out that it was simply a descriptive term and that it had commonly been used for similar products. American Cyanamid Co. v. S.C. Johnson & Son, Inc., 729 F.Supp. 1018, 1025.

Cit.—cited; com.—comment; fol.—followed; sup.—support.
A complete list of abbreviations precedes page 1.

E.D.N.Y.2018. Com. (f) quot. in case quot. in sup. Owner of various trademarks containing the word "BOLD" brought a lawsuit against competitors, alleging that defendants sold competing bathroom-fixture products using a text logo with the word "BOLD" that infringed on plaintiff's trademarks. This court adopted the recommendation of a magistrate judge and granted in part plaintiff's motion for default judgment on other grounds, holding, inter alia, that defendants' continued use of plaintiff's marks did not support an inference that they did so with the intent to confuse. The court quoted Restatement Third of Unfair Competition § 22, Comment *c*, and Restatement of Torts § 729, Comment *f*, in observing that defendants' continued use of the marks did not conclusively prove defendants' intent to create confusion, but provided evidence suggesting that defendants knew their infringing use could create confusion under the current market conditions. Kohler Co. v. Bold International FZCO, 422 F.Supp.3d 681, 728.

N.D.N.Y.2002. Com. (b) quot. in case quot. in disc. Stethoscope manufacturer that owned "Tycos" trademark sued competitor for trademark infringement and dilution. Granting in part and denying in part plaintiff's motion for preliminary injunction, the court held that plaintiff failed to prove a likelihood of confusion with respect to those products in conjunction with which defendant currently used the "Tyco" or "Tyco/Healthcare" trademarks, but barred expansion of those marks' use to other medical instruments during the pendency of this action. The court said that, based on their total effect, the parties' marks were somewhat, but not strongly, similar. Welch Allyn Inc. v. Tyco Intern. Services AG, 200 F.Supp.2d 130, 139.

N.D.N.Y.1997. Com. (f) quot. in case quot. in disc. A designer and manufacturer of child carriers sued a competitor for trade-dress infringement and unfair competition, alleging that the competitor had copied plaintiff's product, causing cheaper, inferior, and confusingly similar child carriers to be manufactured abroad. This court granted defendant summary judgment, holding, inter alia, that plaintiff failed to state a viable claim for trade-dress infringement. The court determined that plaintiff failed as a matter of law to overcome the presumption that its dress was weak. However, although there was serious doubt as to whether bad faith existed in this case, the court was required to resolve such doubt in plaintiff's favor; therefore, this factor, while not conclusive, weighed in support of a likelihood of confusion. While the record supported the conclusion that defendant intentionally copied the design of plaintiff's carrier, the presence of a prominent label bearing the parties' trademarks on the product and the lack of similarity between the parties' respective trademarks argued against any finding of a bad-faith intent to confuse. Tough Traveler, Ltd. v. Outbound Products, 989 F.Supp. 203, 214, affirmed 165 F.3d 15 (2d Cir.1998), cert. denied 527 U.S. 1036, 119 S.Ct. 2394, 144 L.Ed.2d 795 (1999).

S.D.N.Y.1993. Cit. in case quot. in disc. The owners of a major league baseball team and a corporation that performed licensing and marketing functions for major league baseball sued the owners of restaurants, alleging unauthorized use of a trademark in unfair competition under New York law. Defendants counterclaimed for cancellation of the trademark registrations. This court dismissed the claims and denied the counterclaims, holding that plaintiffs had failed to establish actual or likely confusion, and thus failed to establish trademark infringement or unfair competition, and plaintiffs had abandoned use of the mark when the team moved to another city and ceased using the former city's name, which was part of the trademark. Major League Baseball Properties, Inc. v. Sed Non Olet Denarius, Ltd., 817 F.Supp. 1103, 1118.

S.D.Ohio, 1996. Com. (g) quot. in disc. "Daddy's Junky Music Stores," a company that operated retail stores in the Northeast, sued "Big Daddy's Family Music Center," an Ohio sole proprietorship engaged in retail sales of musical instruments, alleging trademark infringement, among other claims. This court granted defendant summary judgment, holding, inter alia, that defendant's use of its name did not constitute trademark infringement and unfair competition because no likelihood of consumer confusion existed. The court stated that plaintiff's "Daddy's" marks were not strong, since the word "Daddy's" was abundant in American nomenclature and there were a significant number of registrations using the word "Daddy's." On the other hand, plaintiff's mark "Daddy's Junky Music Stores" was

For earlier citations, see the Appendices, Supplements, or Pocket Parts, if any, that correspond to the subject matter under examination.

entitled to a finding of moderate strength. Daddy's Junky Music Stores v. Big Daddy's Fam. Mus., 913 F.Supp. 1065, 1072, reversed 109 F.3d 275 (6th Cir.1997).

E.D.Pa.2009. Subsec. (a) cit. in sup. Seller of toy marbles that contained laser-etched three-dimensional figures under the name "Warbles" brought trademark-infringement and other claims against competitor that sold a trading-card game using marbles under the name "Warballs." Denying plaintiff's motion for a preliminary injunction, this court held, inter alia, that plaintiff failed to demonstrate a likelihood of success on the merits based on the likelihood of confusion. Analyzing the degree of similarity of the two marks under the "sound, sight, and meaning trilogy" and in their market context, the court concluded that, while the sounds of the trademarks were nearly identical, the difference in the trade dresses of the trademarked goods were substantial. Noasha LLC v. Nordic Group of Companies, Ltd., 630 F.Supp.2d 544, 553.

E.D.Pa.1988. Com. (g) cit. in sup. An apple juice producer sold its product in a bottle with a label that showed several apples and a drop of juice. When a competitor started selling apple juice in a carton with a similar label, the producer sued the competitor for trademark infringement. The court found for the defendant, holding that the plaintiff's unregistered label was not entitled to protection because it was merely descriptive rather than distinctive. The court stated that a descriptive trademark was one that permitted the consumer to determine attributes of the product without having significantly to use his or her imagination. The court noted that many companies that sold apple juice employed labels depicting apples; the greater the number of similar trademarks in use, the less likely that the trademark would be afforded legal protection. Ginger Group, Ltd. v. Beatrice Companies, Inc., 678 F.Supp. 555, 559.

N.D.Tex.2009. Com. (f) quot. in case quot. in sup. Professional football team, along with football league's marketing arm, sued owner of a federally registered trademark, which dated to 1990, alleging that defendant's trademark infringed their common-law rights in the trademark "America's Team," which plaintiffs had used since 1979, and their state trademark registration, which dated to 1992. Granting summary judgment for plaintiffs, this court held, inter alia, that there was a likelihood of confusion between defendant's and plaintiffs' marks. The court noted that if a plaintiff could show that a defendant adopted a mark with the intent of deriving benefit from a plaintiff's reputation, that fact alone could justify the inference that there was confusing similarity, and pointed to defendant's prior attempts to sell its federal registration to plaintiffs just six months after obtaining it. Dallas Cowboys Football Club, Ltd. v. America's Team Properties, Inc., 616 F.Supp.2d 622, 640.

N.D.Tex.1991. Cit. in ftn. The owner of a trademark for platen printing presses brought an action for trademark infringement and unfair competition against a company that rebuilt and resold the plaintiff's used presses. The court dismissed the action, holding that the plaintiff had not shown any likelihood that consumers would be confused as to the source of the rebuilt presses. The court also held that the plaintiff could not regulate the rebuilding and resale of its presses unless it could prove trademark infringement or unfair competition. Brandtjen & Kluge, Inc. v. Prudhomme, 765 F.Supp. 1551, 1566.

S.D.Tex.2009. Coms. (b) and (f) quot. in case quot. in sup. Real estate broker sued competitor, alleging that defendant's real-estate yard signs and other advertising materials had a design and color arrangement confusingly similar to plaintiff's trademarks. Granting summary judgment for plaintiff on its trademark-infringement and unfair-competition claims, this court held, inter alia, that, despite some differences, the signs were similar enough in their most significant features to cause confusion in the market for real-estate-brokerage services; a real-estate yard sign was intended to catch the attention of people driving past, and, to a consumer driving by, the red, white, and blue tri-bar design common to the parties' signs, not the differences in smaller, less-significant design elements, stood out. The court further held that, while the record did not permit the conclusion that, as a matter of law, defendants acted with the intent to deceive, an intent to deceive was not required for a finding of infringement. RE/MAX Intern., Inc. v. Trendsetter Realty, LLC, 655 F.Supp.2d 679, 701, 702.

S.D.Tex.1999. Com. (g) quot. in case quot. in disc. Manufacturer/distributor of

Cit.—cited; com.—comment; fol.—followed; sup.—support.
A complete list of abbreviations precedes page 1.

weight-training equipment brought trademark infringement action against health club, alleging that the name of defendant's facility was confusingly similar to plaintiff's marks. Granting plaintiff's request for injunctive relief, the court held that plaintiff's mark was arbitrary and sufficiently strong in the fitness industry that defendant's use of a similar mark was likely to cause consumer confusion, as was the visual similarity of the marks and the similarity of the parties' products and services; that irreparable injury was likely to result absent of injunctive relief; and that protecting plaintiff's mark by use of an injunction served the public interest. Quantum Fitness Corp. v. Quantum LifeStyle Centers, 83 F.Supp.2d 810, 820.

S.D.Tex.1997. Com. (f) cit. in case quot. in ftn. Valve manufacturer brought trademark infringement and unfair competition action against companies that reconditioned and resold plaintiff's valves without indicating that the items were not new from the factory. Plaintiff moved for partial summary judgment. Denying the motion, the court held, in part, that material factual issues existed as to, among other things, the identities and expectations of the parties' potential customers, the similarity of the parties' advertising efforts, defendants' intent, and the extent of actual confusion generated by defendants' actions. Neles-Jamesbury, Inc. v. Valve Dynamics, Inc., 974 F.Supp. 964, 973.

S.D.Tex.1996. Com. (f) quot. in case quot. in disc. Tennessee holder of trademarks, copyrights, and publicity rights belonging to the estate of Elvis Presley sued owner of "The Velvet Elvis," a Texas bar, for, inter alia, trademark infringement and violation of the right of publicity. Following a two-day bench trial, the court held, in part, that defendant's use of the service mark "The Velvet Elvis" did not constitute trademark infringement because, among other things, defendant adopted the mark for the purpose of parodying a faddish and tasteless era, not with the intent of deriving benefit from plaintiff, and because no actual confusion had resulted from defendant's actions; however, the advertisements used in connection with the bar were likely to cause confusion. As for plaintiff's "right of publicity" claim, the court determined that Texas law applied because Texas had a more significant relationship to the dispute than Tennessee, and that plaintiff's right of publicity was violated inasmuch as defendant had appropriated Presley's name and likeness without consent. Elvis Presley Enterprises, Inc. v. Capece, 950 F.Supp. 783, 795, judgment reversed 141 F.3d 188 (5th Cir.1998).

E.D.Va.2006. Cit. in sup. User of trade name "Worsham Sprinkler Company" brought infringement action to permanently enjoin competitor and its majority shareholder from using the trade name "Wes Worsham Fire Protection, LLC." Entering judgment for defendants, this court held, inter alia, that plaintiff failed to carry its burden of establishing a likelihood of confusion. The court stated that while the similarity of the competing trade names might create, in theory, the impression that the parties were related, that possibility was mitigated because of the notoriety of majority shareholder's name, "Wes Worsham," in the industry, the disclaimer printed on competitor's public documents, and the sophisticated and tight-knit nature of the fire protection/construction industry in the Virginia area. Worsham Sprinkler Co., Inc. v. Wes Worsham Fire Protection, LLC, 419 F.Supp.2d 861, 877.

Alaska, 2001. Cit. in ftn. Theater owner sued operator of trolley tour service named "Fourth Avenue Theater Trolley Tours" for infringement of its trade name "Fourth Avenue Theatre." The trial court entered judgment on a jury verdict for plaintiff. Affirming in part, this court held, inter alia, that defendants infringed plaintiff's trade name. The court said that "Fourth Avenue Theatre" had acquired a secondary meaning prior to its use by defendants, and that the jury's finding of a likelihood of confusion was supported by the evidence. Alderman v. Iditarod Properties, Inc., 32 P.3d 373, 391.

Miss.App.2021. Com. (f) quot. in case quot. in sup. Owner of the service mark "Midtown Wine & Spirits" filed an action for infringement against competitor that operated under the name "Midtown Market Wine & Spirits." After a bench trial, the trial court found that, although plaintiff had the right to use the service mark at issue, defendant did not infringe on the mark. This court affirmed, holding that there was no evidence that defendant adopted plaintiff's mark with any intent to confuse, mislead, or deceive the public, such that an inference of confusing similarity was justified under Restatement of Torts § 729. The court pointed out that defendant

For earlier citations, see the Appendices, Supplements, or Pocket Parts, if any, that correspond to the subject matter under examination.

had not attempted to pass off its products or services as those of plaintiff, that defendant's principal testified that he was unaware of plaintiff's business, and that defendant's search of the Secretary of State's website failed to identify plaintiff's mark because plaintiff had not registered the mark as a fictitious name. T.M.T., LLC v. Midtown Market Wine & Spirits, LLC, 310 So.3d 1217, 1226.

N.D.1997. Cit. in disc. An audio and visual production services company (KAT Video) brought suit seeking to enjoin a radio station from using the name "Kat" and a tiger logo, in violation of North Dakota's tradename and trademark laws. Trial court granted the radio station summary judgment. This court reversed and remanded, holding that fact issues existed as to similarity of the marks, proximity of the products, evidence of actual confusion, and degree of care used by an ordinary purchaser. The court applied the six-step analysis of likelihood of confusion as adopted by the Eighth Circuit. KAT Video v. KKCT-FM Radio, 560 N.W.2d 203, 208.

Wyo.1992. Cit. in case quot. in disc. Oil company sued petroleum company with a substantially similar name for trade-name infringement and unfair competition. The trial court granted defendant's motion for summary judgment. Reversing and remanding, this court held that the 25-year-long use by plaintiff of its trade name, as well as its establishment of a dominant place in the market, warranting protection of its reputation, created an issue of fact as to whether plaintiff had developed a secondary meaning in its trade name. The court also stated that the trial court erred in restricting its analysis to confusion among customers, because this devalued other policy considerations that resulted in trade-name protection, such as consumer protection, property rights, economic efficiency, and universal concepts of justice. Powder River Oil v. Powder River Petroleum, 830 P.2d 403, 413.

§ 730. Limitation of Protection with Reference to Kind of Goods, Services or Business

C.A.2, 1993. Cit. in case quot. in sup. Owner of trademark "Sportstick" for lip balm brought a trademark-infringement action against owner of trademark "Right Guard Sport Stick" for deodorant. Affirming the district court's entry of judgment for defendant, this court held that plaintiff failed to prove its allegation of a likelihood of "reverse confusion," i.e., that potential customers would assume that defendant was the source of plaintiff's mark and thus believe that plaintiff was the infringer, and therefore could not establish its claim of trademark infringement. W.W.W. Pharmaceutical Co., Inc. v. Gillette Co., 984 F.2d 567, 572.

C.A.2, 1991. Cit. in case quot. in disc. A publisher of a book and audiotapes on the development of charisma that used the trade name "New Choices Press" sought to enjoin a magazine publisher from using the name "New Choices for the Best Years" for its magazine on retirement living. The district court granted the defendant's motion for summary judgment. Affirming, this court held that the plaintiff failed to raise a genuine issue of fact as to the likelihood of confusion. The court concluded that the plaintiff's trade name was weak because it was not widely known. Lang v. Retirement Living Pub. Co., Inc., 949 F.2d 576, 580.

S.D.N.Y.1993. Cit. in case quot. in disc. The owners of a major league baseball team and a corporation that performed licensing and marketing functions for major league baseball sued the owners of restaurants, alleging unauthorized use of a trademark in unfair competition under New York law. Defendants counterclaimed for cancellation of the trademark registrations. This court dismissed the claims and denied the counterclaims, holding that plaintiffs had failed to establish actual or likely confusion, and thus failed to establish trademark infringement or unfair competition, and plaintiffs had abandoned use of the mark when the team moved to another city and ceased using the former city's name, which was part of the trademark. Major League Baseball Properties, Inc. v. Sed Non Olet Denarius, Ltd., 817 F.Supp. 1103, 1118.

M.D.Tenn.1994. Com. (b) quot. in sup. and cit. in headnote. A company that repackaged and marketed imported surgical instruments to physicians and a hospital sued a competitor, alleging infringement of its trade dress. This court, granting partial summary judgment for the defendants, concluded that plaintiff's trade dress was ineligible for protection under the Lanham Act. The court held, inter alia, that expansion of its product line by the alleged infringer was not indicative of infringement, as the likelihood of customer confu-

Cit.—cited; com.—comment; fol.—followed; sup.—support.
A complete list of abbreviations precedes page 1.

sion was not indicative of infringement, even though the parties competed in the same market. The court stated that notwithstanding the relatedness of the products, some similarities of the marks, and the similarities of the marketing channels used, those factors were outweighed by the weakness of plaintiff's mark, the high degree of purchaser care and sophistication, and the presence of the logos of both parties on the respective element of their trade dress. Specialty Surgical Instrumentation v. Phillips, 844 F.Supp. 1211, 1214, 1220.

Mass.App.2009. Com. (a) cit. in disc. After proprietor sold the assets of his roofing and siding business to his son-in-law, proprietor's son and son's incorporated roofing and siding business brought suit for tradename infringement, inter alia, against proprietor's son-in-law and son-in-law's corporation. The trial court entered judgment for plaintiffs. Affirming, this court held that plaintiffs showed that their use of the trade name "Castricone Roofing and Siding" had acquired a secondary meaning. The court reasoned that, at the time of trial, plaintiffs had used the name for almost 30 years; the parties' trade names, products, and markets were very similar, if not exactly the same; and the trial court's findings that defendants' use of the name had caused substantial confusion between the two businesses and had resulted in lost profits for plaintiffs' business were supported by the evidence and were not clearly erroneous. Castricone v. Mical, 74 Mass.App. Ct. 591, 594, 909 N.E.2d 29, 34.

§ 731. Factors in Limitation of Protection with Reference to Kind of Goods, Services or Business

C.A.1, 2008. Com. (e) quot. in case quot. in disc. Company that offered sightseeing tours via land and water, using amphibious vehicles commonly referred to as "ducks," sued competitor for trademark infringement, inter alia. The district court granted plaintiff preliminary-injunctive relief, enjoining defendant from using the phrase "duck tours" in its trade name. Reversing and remanding, this court held, inter alia, that the district court committed clear error by finding the term "duck tours" to be nongeneric and therefore capable of trademark protection. The court concluded that an analysis of the evidence did not establish a likelihood of confusion between the parties' marks, and thus plaintiff failed to prove a likelihood of success on the merits of its trademark-infringement claim. Boston Duck Tours, LP v. Super Duck Tours, LLC, 531 F.3d 1, 13.

C.A.2, 1993. Cit. in case quot. in sup. Owner of trademark "Sportstick" for lip balm brought a trademark-infringement action against owner of trademark "Right Guard Sport Stick" for deodorant. Affirming the district court's entry of judgment for defendant, this court held that plaintiff failed to prove its allegation of a likelihood of "reverse confusion," i.e., that potential customers would assume that defendant was the source of plaintiff's mark and thus believe that plaintiff was the infringer, and therefore could not establish its claim of trademark infringement. W.W.W. Pharmaceutical Co., Inc. v. Gillette Co., 984 F.2d 567, 572.

C.A.2, 1991. Cit. in case quot. in disc. A publisher of a book and audiotapes on the development of charisma that used the trade name "New Choices Press" sought to enjoin a magazine publisher from using the name "New Choices for the Best Years" for its magazine on retirement living. The district court granted the defendant's motion for summary judgment. Affirming, this court held that the plaintiff failed to raise a genuine issue of fact as to the likelihood of confusion. The court concluded that the plaintiff's trade name was weak because it was not widely known. Lang v. Retirement Living Pub. Co., Inc., 949 F.2d 576, 580.

C.A.6, 2012. Com. (c) quot. in sup. Manufacturer of paper-towel dispensers and disposable paper products brought a trademark-infringement action against distributor of janitorial supplies in connection with distributor's sale of off-brand paper towels for use in manufacturer's dispensers. The district court granted summary judgment for defendant. Affirming, this court held, among other things, that plaintiff's expansion of its product lines did not significantly increase the likelihood of confusion; the focus was on the expansion of the defendant's business that could lead to confusion, not the plaintiff's, and, in any event, plaintiff's market penetration, no matter how aggressive and successful, would not result in direct competition between the parties; while defendant distributed paper and janitorial supplies, it did not manufacture commercial paper systems. Georgia-Pacific Consumer

For earlier citations, see the Appendices, Supplements, or Pocket Parts, if any, that correspond to the subject matter under examination.

Products LP v. Four-U-Packaging, Inc., 701 F.3d 1093, 1101.

C.A.6, 1997. Subsec. (b) and com. (c) cit. in case quot. in disc. An operator of a chain of retail musical instrument stores doing business as "Daddy's Junky Music Stores" brought an action for trademark infringement against an Ohio competitor named "Big Daddy's Family Music Center." The district court granted summary judgment for defendant, finding that there was no likelihood of confusion between the parties' marks. Reversing and remanding, this court held, in part, that an issue of fact regarding whether plaintiff would expand its product line in central Ohio precluded summary judgment on the issue of the likelihood of confusion. Daddy's Junky Music v. Big Daddy's Family Music, 109 F.3d 275, 287.

C.A.6, 1991. Subsec. (b) and com. (c) cit. in sup. Two companies utilized service marks containing the same initials. One company sued the other company seeking injunctive relief and cancellation of the other's federally registered mark. The district court granted summary judgment in favor of the plaintiff, determining in part that a likelihood of geographic expansion by the defendant did exist. Reversing and remanding, this court held, inter alia, that genuine issues of material fact were raised with respect to whether a likelihood of confusion existed in the marketplace due to the parties' use of their respective marks. The court stated that a trademark owner is afforded greater protection against services which directly compete with his own, and that a strong possibility that either party will expand his business to compete with the other or be marketed to the same consumers will weigh in favor of finding that the present use of the mark is infringing. Homeowners Group v. Home Marketing Specialists, 931 F.2d 1100, 1112.

C.A.9, 1997. Subsec. (b) cit. in case quot. in sup. Television actors whose likenesses were made into animatronic robotic figures that were placed in bars sued creator of figures for, inter alia, unfair competition, alleging that, by using an imitation of their physical characteristics, defendant misrepresented plaintiffs' association with and endorsement of defendant's bar concept. The district court granted defendant's motion for summary judgment and, on remand, again entered summary judgment for defendant, having found no similarities between plaintiffs and the figures. Reversing and remanding, this court held, in part, that a jury could find that defendant's conduct had created a likelihood of confusion as to whether plaintiffs were endorsing its product, since, among other things, plaintiffs' mark was strong, there was evidence of actual confusion, and there was a real possibility that further confusion would result from future attempts to expand product lines. Wendt v. Host Intern., Inc., 125 F.3d 806, 814.

C.D.Cal.2006. Subsec. (b) and com. (c) cit. in case quot. in sup. Manufacturer of musical instruments sued competitors, seeking, inter alia, a declaratory judgment that the body shape of its guitars did not infringe on competitors' trade dress. This court granted plaintiff's motion for summary judgment as to the trade-dress claim, holding, among other things, that plaintiff's and defendants' product lines were substantially similar and that there was no evidence showing that any party intended to expand its line of guitars. The court noted that a strong possibility that a party would expand its business to compete with another would weigh in favor of finding that the present use was infringing, since when goods were closely related, any expansion was likely to result in direct competition. Switchmusic.com, Inc. v. U.S. Music Corp., 416 F.Supp.2d 812, 825.

C.D.Cal.2003. Subsec. (b) and com. (c) cit. in case quot. in sup. Celebrity tennis player sued publisher of adult-entertainment magazine under Lanham Act, alleging, in part, that publication of partially nude photographs of another woman falsely identified as plaintiff constituted false endorsement. Granting summary judgment for defendant, the court held that plaintiff's claim failed because plaintiff did not show that defendant intentionally designed magazine edition in a way that was likely to confuse the average reader into believing that plaintiff endorsed or approved the magazine. The court said that plaintiff was not entitled to protection as a trademark owner who might expand her business to compete with defendant, since she had stated that she had no intention of entering the adult-entertainment market. Kournikova v. General Media Communications, Inc., 278 F.Supp.2d 1111, 1127.

N.D.Cal.2012. Subsec. (b) and com. (c) cit. in case quot. in sup. Boutique winemak-

Cit.—cited; com.—comment; fol.—followed; sup.—support.
A complete list of abbreviations precedes page 1.

ers and sellers brought a trademark-infringement action against winemaking subsidiary of an international beverage conglomerate, alleging that the mark for defendant's "Stark Raving" wine was confusingly similar to plaintiffs' "Stark Wine" and "Stark Thirst" marks. Plaintiffs moved for a preliminary injunction to stop the advertisement, promotion, distribution, and sale of defendant's wine. This court granted plaintiffs' motion as to their existing market in one county in California, but otherwise denied it, holding, inter alia, that plaintiffs did not show generally a likelihood of success on the merits on their trademark-infringement claims outside of that county. The court reasoned, in part, that the factor of "the likelihood of expansion into other markets" weighed against a finding of confusion except as to that county; while defendant was fully capable of accessing plaintiff's established market in that single county, the possibility remained speculative as to whether plaintiff could expand into defendant's current nationwide market position. Stark v. Diageo Chateau & Estate Wines Co., 907 F.Supp.2d 1042, 1064.

S.D.Fla.1986. Cit. in disc. A clothing dealer made and sold inferior quality clothing under a trade name and trademark similar to that of a renowned manufacturer of quality clothing. The trademark owner sued for damages and injunctive relief. This court entered judgment for the plaintiff on all claims, holding that the defendant was liable for infringement because there was a likelihood of confusing the public between the products of the plaintiff and those of the defendant through the defendant's deliberate use of substantially similar trademarks and trade names. Polo Fashions, Inc. v. Rabanne, 661 F.Supp. 89, 94.

E.D.Ky.2014. Subsec. (b) and com. (c) cit. in case quot. in sup. Owners of a barbeque restaurant and registered trademarks for the restaurant brought claim for, among other things, trademark infringement against former business partner who, after parting ways with plaintiffs, continued to cater and provide food services while using the same trademarks to advertise his business. This court granted plaintiffs' motion for partial summary judgment, holding that defendant's use of identical trademarks was likely to cause confusion among customers, because the parties both sold barbecue, had nearly identical menu items, and competed directly against each other. The court reasoned, in part, that, although plaintiffs provided no evidence of plans for future expansion, defendant was already competing with plaintiff for the same consumers and using the same channels of commerce as plaintiffs, which supported the finding of a likelihood of confusion under Restatement of Torts § 731. EAT BBQ LLC v. Walters, 47 F.Supp.3d 521, 532.

W.D.Ky.2021. Subsec. (b) and com. (c) cit. in case cit. in sup. Bourbon distiller sued competitor, alleging that defendant infringed upon plaintiff's trademark by using the family history and name of the ancestor of defendant's founders, because plaintiff acquired the brand and goodwill of ancestor and ancestor's bourbon-brewing techniques. This court granted in part plaintiff's motion for preliminary injunction, holding that plaintiff demonstrated a strong likelihood of success on the merits of its underlying trademark-infringement claim against defendant. Citing Restatement of Torts § 731, the court explained that the facts weighed in favor of finding that defendant's trademark had a strong likelihood of infringing upon plaintiff's, because defendant expressly stated its intent to expand its geographic and market presence, and plaintiff's brand would similarly expand due to increases in the bourbon market. Heaven Hill Distilleries, Inc. v. Log Still Distilling, LLC, 575 F.Supp.3d 785, 839.

W.D.Ky.2020. Subsec. (b) and com. (c) cit. in case quot. in sup. Owner of a federally registered trademark for nationwide cleaning, restoration, and remediation services filed an infringement action against competitor that operated in Kentucky, alleging that it used plaintiff's trademark in its domain name, website, and online advertisements without authorization. This court granted in part plaintiff's motion for summary judgment, holding that no reasonable jury could find that there was no likelihood of confusion. The court cited Restatement of Torts § 731 in noting, however, that the "likelihood of expansion" factor was neutral, because, while the parties overlapped in their internet marketing and offered similar services, neither party offered any evidence regarding whether defendant was likely to expand its business further to overlap with plaintiff's services. ServPro Intellectual Property, Inc. v. Blanton, 451 F.Supp.3d 710, 727.

For earlier citations, see the Appendices, Supplements, or Pocket Parts, if any, that correspond to the subject matter under examination.

W.D.Mich.2004. Subsec. (b) and com. (c) quot. in case quot. in disc. Manufacturer of industrial presses and components sued competitor for trademark infringement and unfair competition, inter alia, alleging that defendant used plaintiff's trade secrets and confidential information to manufacture a machine and parts identical to plaintiff's clutch and parts, and used plaintiff's "Torc-Pac 40" mark without identifying plaintiff as manufacturer or license holder. This court denied in part defendant's motion for summary judgment, holding, inter alia, that factor of product-line expansion suggested likelihood of confusion from defendant's use of plaintiff's mark. Even though sale of new Torc-Pac units was in decline, there would still be demand for replacement parts in the future. Bliss Clearing Niagara, Inc. v. Midwest Brake Bond Co., 339 F.Supp.2d 944, 968.

S.D.N.Y.1993. Cit. in case quot. in disc. The owners of a major league baseball team and a corporation that performed licensing and marketing functions for major league baseball sued the owners of restaurants, alleging unauthorized use of a trademark in unfair competition under New York law. Defendants counterclaimed for cancellation of the trademark registrations. This court dismissed the claims and denied the counterclaims, holding that plaintiffs had failed to establish actual or likely confusion, and thus failed to establish trademark infringement or unfair competition, and plaintiffs had abandoned use of the mark when the team moved to another city and ceased using the former city's name, which was part of the trademark. Major League Baseball Properties, Inc. v. Sed Non Olet Denarius, Ltd., 817 F.Supp. 1103, 1118.

S.D.N.Y.1988. Subsec. (f) and com. (e) cit. in sup. An automobile manufacturer announced its intention to market a new line of automobiles under a brand name ("LEXUS") that was similar to the name of an established computer-assisted legal-research service ("LEXIS"). The corporation, which provided the research services and owned the LEXIS mark, filed an action seeking injunctive relief against the manufacturer alleging, inter alia, dilution of its trade name pursuant to New York's antidilution statute. This court held that the LEXIS mark was a strong and distinctive trademark which was likely to be diluted by the defendant's LEXUS mark. It stated that the LEXIS mark distinguished the LEXIS service from other products and was uniquely associated with the source of that product. The court rejected a view taken by other courts that only the most famous trademarks could be diluted, noting that distinctiveness was essentially a synonym for strength. As a remedy, the court permanently enjoined the manufacturer from using the LEXUS name unless it elected alternative relief described in the court's opinion. Mead Data Cent., Inc. v. Toyota Motor Sales, U.S.A., 702 F.Supp. 1031, 1042, reversed 875 F.2d 1026 (2d Cir.1989).

S.D.Ohio, 2010. Subsec. (b) and com. (c) cit. in case quot. in sup. State university sued publishers of website promoting university's athletics, alleging that defendants' website, as well as electronic and print publications, contained infringing uses of plaintiff's trademarks, including school colors and symbols. Granting plaintiff's motion for a temporary restraining order and preliminary injunction, this court held that plaintiff had demonstrated a strong likelihood that it would succeed on the merits of its claims of trademark infringement and unfair competition. The court cited evidence that defendants were poised to expand the market and distribution channels for their products, and reasoned that such expansion would undoubtedly enlarge the breadth of the competition between the parties and illustrated the likelihood that confusion among customers would be compounded over time to plaintiff's detriment. Ohio State University v. Thomas, 738 F.Supp.2d 743, 755.

S.D.Ohio, 2002. Subsec. (b) and com. (c) cit. in case quot. in disc. Clothing store that sold girls' fashions sued retailer of off-price merchandise for trademark infringement, trademark counterfeiting, and unfair competition, alleging that defendant was offering for sale 31 styles of its garments that were unauthorized or counterfeit. This court granted in part plaintiff's motion for preliminary injunction, holding that plaintiff had substantial likelihood of success on claim of trademark infringement based upon unauthorized production. It noted that there was no evidence that either party would expand its product line to compete with each other in same market. Plaintiff did not engage in sell-offs, nor did defendant exclusively target teenage girls; thus, absence of expansion by either party of product lines did not increase or reduce chances for consumer confusion. Too, Inc. v.

Cit.—cited; com.—comment; fol.—followed; sup.—support.
A complete list of abbreviations precedes page 1.

TJX Companies, Inc., 229 F.Supp.2d 825, 836.

S.D.Ohio, 1996. Subsec. (b) cit. in case cit. in disc. "Daddy's Junky Music Stores," a company that operated retail stores in the Northeast, sued "Big Daddy's Family Music Center," an Ohio sole proprietorship engaged in retail sales of musical instruments, alleging trademark infringement, among other claims. This court granted defendant summary judgment, holding, inter alia, that defendant's use of its name did not constitute trademark infringement and unfair competition because no likelihood of consumer confusion existed. The court stated that plaintiff's speculative plans to enter the central Ohio musical instrument market were not entitled to significant weight in determining whether there was any likelihood of confusion. Daddy's Junky Music Stores v. Big Daddy's Fam. Mus., 913 F.Supp. 1065, 1076, reversed 109 F.3d 275 (6th Cir.1997).

M.D.Tenn.1994. Subsec. (b) and com. (c) cit. in case quot. in sup. and cit. in headnote. A company that repackaged and marketed imported surgical instruments to physicians and a hospital sued a competitor, alleging infringement of its trade dress. This court, granting partial summary judgment for the defendants, concluded that plaintiff's trade dress was ineligible for protection under the Lanham Act. The court held, inter alia, that expansion of its product line by the alleged infringer was not indicative of infringement, as the likelihood of customer confusion was not indicative of infringement, even though the parties competed in the same market. The court stated that notwithstanding the relatedness of the products, some similarities of the marks, and the similarities of the marketing channels used, those factors were outweighed by the weakness of plaintiff's mark, the high degree of purchaser care and sophistication, and the presence of the logos of both parties on the respective element of their trade dress. Specialty Surgical Instrumentation v. Phillips, 844 F.Supp. 1211, 1214, 1220.

Alaska, 2001. Cit. in ftn. Theater owner sued operator of trolley tour service named "Fourth Avenue Theater Trolley Tours" for infringement of its trade name "Fourth Avenue Theatre." The trial court entered judgment on a jury verdict for plaintiff. Affirming in part, this court held, inter alia, that defendants infringed plaintiff's trade name. The court said that "Fourth Avenue Theatre" had acquired a secondary meaning prior to its use by defendants, and that the jury's finding of a likelihood of confusion was supported by the evidence. Alderman v. Iditarod Properties, Inc., 32 P.3d 373, 391.

Fla.1993. Cit. in disc. The First Southern Bank sued to enjoin another bank from using the name "Great Southern Bank," alleging infringement and dilution of its trademark name and unfair competition. Trial court granted plaintiff injunctive relief and certified the question whether the plaintiff bank's name was descriptive or generic so as not to be entitled to protection in the absence of proof that it had acquired a secondary meaning. This court remanded, holding that the plaintiff bank's name contained laudatory, generic, and merely geographically descriptive elements so as not to be entitled to protection under either common or statutory law, but determination was necessary whether a secondary meaning in the name had developed in order to decide the dilution claim. The court noted its approval of the factors set forth in this Restatement section as being appropriate to determining both registrability and infringement. Great Southern v. First Southern, 625 So.2d 463, 469.

§ 732. Extent of Protection with Reference to Territorial Markets

C.A.10, 1990. Com. (a) cit. in disc. A telephone company, operating under some form of the name "General Telephone" since 1935, registered those words as a service mark for the provision of telephone services in 1982. It then sued for infringement the owner of a mobile telephone and paging services business who had been using the same name in an area of Utah since 1974. The district court held that the businessman was entitled to concurrent registration of the mark for his geographical area, and to its exclusive use in that region, finding that his use of the mark was not likely to cause confusion in the marketplace and that he had established the common-law defense of good faith adoption in a remote area. This court affirmed, holding, inter alia, that the finding that the businessman had adopted the mark in good faith despite his actual knowledge of the telephone company's use was not clearly erroneous, since mere knowledge would not defeat a finding of good faith unless it was coupled with an intent to benefit from the telephone company's reputation or good will. GTE Corp. v. Williams, 904 F.2d 536, 541, certiorari denied 498 U.S. 998, 111 S.Ct. 557, 112 L.Ed.2d 564 (1990).

§ 738. Inducing or Aiding One's Purchasers to Infringe on Resale

D.Md.1996. Quot. and cit. generally in disc, cit. in case quot. in disc. In action brought under the Lanham Act, charity sued publisher for contributory trademark infringement in connection with the use of charity's name and mark in a book designed to instruct readers on ways to make money from "business opportunity" frauds and scams. Publisher moved to dismiss on the ground that charity could not sustain a claim for contributory infringement absent proof of direct infringement. Denying the motion, the court held, in part, that dismissal was inappropriate because it could not say, as a matter of law, that charity would be unable to present evidence of direct infringement. N.F.B. v. Loompanics Enterprises, 936 F.Supp. 1232, 1245.

TOPIC 3. IMITATION OF APPEARANCE

§ 741. Elements of Unprivileged Imitation

C.A.3, 1994. Com. (j) cit. in case cit. in disc. Manufacturer of plastic garden planters shaped like Grecian urns brought a trade-dress-infringement action against competitor and moved for a preliminary injunction. Affirming the district court's denial of plaintiff's motion, this court held that, since plaintiff was unable to show that its product's configuration was either inherently distinctive or had acquired a secondary meaning, plaintiff failed to demonstrate a likelihood of success on the merits. The court rejected the application of traditional trade-dress doctrine to a claim that product configuration had been infringed. Duraco Products v. Joy Plastic Enterprises, Ltd., 40 F.3d 1431, 1444.

C.A.8, 2000. Subsec. (b)(ii) cit. in disc. Sponsor of home shows sued competitor for, inter alia, violations of the Lanham Act, alleging that defendant was sponsoring shows with names deceptively similar to those used by plaintiff. The district court entered judgment for plaintiff. Affirming, this court held that the names at issue constituted descriptive marks that had acquired secondary meaning. Home Builders Ass'n v. L & L Exhibition Management, 226 F.3d 944, 950.

D.Kan.1995. Cit. in headnote, quot. in sup. Manufacturer of plastic dinnerware brought, in part, a state-law claim of unfair competition against manufacturer of cookware, seeking a preliminary injunction against defendant's use of the term "Casual Elegance" with its new product line. Denying plaintiff's motion for a preliminary injunction, the court held that plaintiff did not establish its right to preliminary injunctive relief, since it failed to show a substantial likelihood of prevailing on its unfair competition claim under the standard requiring a showing of unprivileged imitation by defendant of the physical appearance of plaintiff's goods. Packerware Corp. v. Corning Consumer Products Co., 895 F.Supp. 1438, 1440, 1452.

§ 742. Functional and Non-Functional Features

C.A.2, 2012. Sec. and com. (a) quot. in ftn. Designer of women's high-heeled shoes with high-gloss red lacquer outsoles that contrasted sharply with the color of the rest of the shoes brought a trademark-infringement action against competitor that marketed and sold a monochrome red shoe with a red sole. The district court denied plaintiff's request for a preliminary injunction. Reversing in part and remanding, this court held that the trademark was valid and enforceable as modified to limit the registration to a red lacquered outsole that contrasted with the color of the adjoining upper. The court explained that the district court could not adopt a per se rule of aesthetic functionality for color marks in the fashion industry that would effectively deny trademark protection to any deployment of a single color in an item of apparel; rather, a highly fact-specific analysis was required to determine whether recognition of trademark rights in the use of the color would significantly hinder competition by putting competitors at a significant non-reputation-related disadvantage. Christian Louboutin S.A. v. Yves Saint Laurent America Holdings, Inc., 696 F.3d 206, 220.

C.A.6, 2003. Com. (a) cit. generally in

Cit.—cited; com.—comment; fol.—followed; sup.—support.
A complete list of abbreviations precedes page 1.

disc. Scrapbook-album manufacturer sued competitor for trade-dress infringement. Affirming the district court's grant of summary judgment for defendant, this court held, inter alia, that plaintiff's album-design features, including a dual strap-hinge, concealed binding, padded album covers, and reinforced pages, were functional, and thus were not entitled to trade-dress protection. The court said that the concept of aesthetic functionality did not apply to plaintiff's album design. Antioch co. v. Western Trimming Corp., 347 F.3d 150, 155.

C.A.8, 1994. Com. (a) cit. in diss. op. Packager of potpourri fragrances sued competitor in state court for infringement of trade dress. The case was removed to federal district court after amendment of the complaint to allege infringement of registered federal trademarks. Reversing and vacating the district court's finding of infringement, this court held that packaging in pillow-shaped double cellophane bags, closed at the top by gathering the excess cellophane and closing it with a colored cord tied in a square knot bow with an oval label, did not identify the manufacturer's product and did not have a secondary meaning. The trade dress, said the court, was merely functional. The dissent argued that defendant had engaged in a studied and extensive imitation of plaintiff's trade dress. Aromatique, Inc. v. Gold Seal, Inc., 28 F.3d 863, 886.

C.A.9, 2006. Com. (a) cit. and quot. in disc. and quot. in sup. Maker of key chains and license-plate covers that bore exact replicas of two automobile manufacturers' trademarks sued the manufacturers for a declaratory judgment that its activities did not constitute trademark infringement, trademark counterfeiting, or trademark dilution. The district court granted partial summary judgment for plaintiff. Reversing and remanding, this court held, inter alia, that because plaintiff failed to show that defendants' logos and marks were aesthetic functional elements of plaintiff's products, the marks were entitled to trademark protection. The court rejected plaintiff's argument that the trademarks were functional features of plaintiff's products on the basis that they constituted the actual benefit that the consumer wished to purchase, stating that plaintiff's approach distorted basic principles of trademark law and the doctrine of functionality in particular. Au-Tomotive Gold, Inc. v. Volkswagen of America, Inc., 457 F.3d 1062, 1068, 1074, cert. denied 549 U.S. 1282, 127 S.Ct. 1839, 167 L.Ed.2d 323 (2007).

C.D.Cal.2011. Com. (a) cit. in case quot. in sup. (general cite). As part of a consolidated action, doll manufacturer sued competitor, alleging, among other things, that competitor's sale of doll products in a type of heart-shaped packaging that was already used by manufacturer constituted trade-dress infringement. This court granted summary judgment for competitor on manufacturer's claim of trade-dress infringement, holding, among other things, that manufacturer's heart-shaped packaging was aesthetically functional; heart-shaped packaging was aesthetically pleasing to children and thus enhanced the value of a product independent of its source-identifying function. Mattel, Inc. v. MGA Entertainment, Inc., 782 F.Supp.2d 911, 1007.

N.D.Cal.2019. Com. (a) quot. in case quot. in sup. (general cite). Owner of registered federal trademarks in the pun "LETTUCE TURNIP THE BEET" brought an action for trademark infringement against competitor that sold products featuring the same phrase or similar phrases. This court granted summary judgment for defendant, holding that plaintiff was not entitled to preempt defendant's use of the pun, because there was no evidence of source confusion; the accused products merely displayed the pun as a graphic-design element without any indication that they were produced or licensed by plaintiff, and the evidence showed that consumers were not seeking to purchase defendant's products based on plaintiff's reputation, but rather, because they displayed the pun. The court cited the Restatement of Torts, which described the doctrine of aesthetic functionality, in explaining that decorative or ornamental features were not subject to trademark protection. LTTB, LLC v. Redbubble, Inc., 385 F.Supp.3d 916, 920.

D.Del.1990. Com. (a) quot. in case cit. in disc. A manufacturer of dental products sued a competitor for trademark, trade dress, and patent infringement. The dispute centered on dental restorative material inserted by the plaintiff and the defendant into single-dose ampules. This court denied the defendant's motion for summary judgment, holding that genuine issues of material fact existed concerning whether the plaintiff's ampule was entitled to trademark or trade dress protection, which was dependent on whether the ampule was functional. Dentsply Intern., Inc. v. Kerr Mfg. Co., 732 F.Supp. 482, 486.

D.Mass.2021. Com. (a) quot. in case quot. in sup. Seller of a device used to clean continuous positive airway pressure machines filed a claim for trade-dress infringement against competitor that sold replacement filters for seller's device. This court granted in part seller's motion for a preliminary injunction, holding that seller had a reasonable likelihood of prevailing on competitor's challenge to the validity of its marks based on non-functionality, because the marks comprised both functional and non-functional features. The court cited Restatement of Torts § 742 in noting that the evidence of other design options for competitor's filter did not, by itself, compel competitor to use an alternative design if the design seller chose was essential to the use or purpose of the device or affected the cost or quality of the device, but it did constitute evidence that there were some arbitrary elements to seller's filter that competitor decided to copy where functionality had not otherwise been established. SoClean, Inc. v. Sunset Healthcare Solutions, Inc., 554 F.Supp.3d 284, 301.

D.N.J.1989. Cit. in case quot. in sup. The manufacturer of a well-known mouthwash sued the retailer of a similar mouthwash for using the same trade dress as the manufacturer and sought a preliminary injunction against the retailer's sale of its mouthwash. This court held that the plaintiff had not adequately demonstrated that it faced irreparable harm or was likely to succeed on the merits of the action, and a weighing of equities and the public interest revealed that a preliminary injunction was not called for. The court noted that, although the shape of the product's bottle might be protected if it were nonfunctional, the shape of the mouthwash bottle in this case was possibly functional, and the court therefore was not persuaded that the plaintiff had sufficiently shown that it was likely to prevail on the merits. Warner Lambert Co. v. McCrory's Corp., 718 F.Supp. 389, 397.

TOPIC 4. REMEDIES

§ 747. Profits

C.A.11, 2019. Com. (b) quot. in sup. Owner of trademarks that it licensed to a cosmetics producer for use in the sale of cosmetics brought an action under the Lanham Act against competitor of producer, seeking an injunction to prevent future infringement, an accounting, disgorgement of profits, and declaratory relief, along with fees and costs. The district court denied plaintiff's request for a jury trial, noting that plaintiff had disclaimed any request for actual damages and was seeking only equitable remedies, and, after a bench trial, ruled that there was no likelihood of confusion and that defendant made out a fair-use defense to infringement. Affirming, this court held, among other things, that plaintiff was not entitled to a jury trial on its claim for an accounting and disgorgement of profits. The court cited Restatement Third of Unfair Competition § 37 and Restatement of Torts § 747 in explaining that the remedies sought by plaintiff in the form of an accounting and disgorgement of profits were historically equitable, rather than legal, in nature. Hard Candy, LLC v. Anastasia Beverly Hills, Inc., 921 F.3d 1343, 1356, 1357.

N.D.Ill.2015. Com. (b) quot. in ftn. Seller of power tools brought patent-infringement and trademark-infringement claims against competitor. This court denied defendant's motion to strike plaintiff's jury demand with respect to its trademark-related claims for defendant's profits, in which defendant argued that plaintiff's request for profits was a demand for equitable relief that was not subject to jury determination, holding that plaintiff claimed profits as a proxy for damages. The court cited the first Restatement of Torts § 747 in explaining that, in the context of trademark-infringement cases, courts historically allowed parties to pursue an award of profits as a proxy for damages because of the evidentiary barriers to proving damages. Black & Decker Corporation v. Positec USA Inc., 118 F.Supp.3d 1056, 1062.

E.D.Va.1988. Com. (g) cit. in sup. A corporation that had contracted with a restaurateur for the exclusive use of the corporation's service mark in a designated area contracted with a hotel owner in the

Cit.—cited; com.—comment; fol.—followed; sup.—support.
A complete list of abbreviations precedes page 1.

same area for the use of the corporation's mark. The corporation sought a declaration of its right to grant the hotel owner the use of the service mark. The court issued an injunction to prevent the corporation from allowing anyone other than the restaurateur to use the service mark in the designated area, because the corporation was breaching its contractual duty of forbearance by allowing others to use the mark. The court stated that an injunction was appropriate, as the restaurateur's damages were impossible to determine because the hotel was not actually diverting business from the restaurant. Shoney's, Inc. v. Schoenbaum, 686 F.Supp. 554, 568, affirmed 894 F.2d 92 (4th Cir.1990).

CHAPTER 36. MISCELLANEOUS TRADE PRACTICES

Generally

N.D.Cal.1999. Cit. generally but not fol. Owner of patent for security device sued competitor for, in part, misappropriation of trade secrets. Granting defendant's motion for summary judgment, the court held, inter alia, that plaintiff's trade-secret misappropriation claim was same as claim alleged in prior lawsuit, even though regarding earlier product, and was released by prior settlement between parties. Security People, Inc. v. Medeco Security Locks, 59 F.Supp.2d 1040, 1043, affirmed 243 F.3d 555 (Fed.Cir.2000).

§ 757. Liability for Disclosure or Use of Another's Trade Secret—General Principle

C.A.1, 2002. Cit. generally in case cit. in disc., com. (d) quot. in disc. Tobacco companies sued state of Massachusetts, alleging that state's Disclosure Act, which allowed disclosure of companies' ingredient lists whenever such disclosure could reduce risks to public health, created an unconstitutional taking and violated companies' due process rights. District court granted plaintiffs summary judgment. Affirming, this court held, inter alia, that Massachusetts law protected plaintiffs' ingredient lists as trade secrets, and that plaintiffs had a property interest in their trade secrets that was implicated by the Disclosure Act, which violated the takings clause. Philip Morris, Inc. v. Reilly, 312 F.3d 24, 31, 32.

C.A.1, 2001. Cit. generally in ftn. After cookware corporation brought claims for trade-dress infringement, unfair competition, and patent infringement against marketer of kitchen products, marketer sued insurer for breach of duty to defend and indemnify marketer under policy coverage for advertising injury. New Hampshire federal district court entered judgment for marketer. This court reversed and remanded, holding that the policy term "advertising" referred to conventional advertising, separate from the product itself, and that marketer failed to establish causal connection between claim for misappropriation of tea-kettle design and "advertising injury" coverage clause in policy. Ekco Group, Inc. v. Travelers Indem. Co. of Illinois, 273 F.3d 409, 412.

C.A.2, 1999. Com. (b) quot. in case quot. in sup. and in diss. op. Employer sued former employee and the employee's subsequent employer for misappropriation of trade secrets, alleging that defendants solicited plaintiff's client contacts contained in a list misappropriated from plaintiff. District court entered an order preliminarily enjoining defendants from soliciting the client contacts, holding that the list was a protectable trade secret. This court affirmed, holding that plaintiff demonstrated a likelihood of success on the merits of its claim. The court stated that New York law imposed a duty not to use trade secrets in competition with a former employer, and the employment agreement reinforced this duty, requiring that the former employee keep all trade secrets and client lists strictly confidential. Dissent argued that when, as here, there is any ambiguity about what constitutes a trade secret, the court should not affirm an injunction order that forbids its use. North Atlantic Instruments, Inc. v. Haber, 188 F.3d 38, 44, 50.

C.A.2, 1997. Cit. in headnote, cit. in sup., com. (b) cit. in disc. and quot. in case quot. in sup. Computer software company sued designer of medical and scientific communications programs for, inter alia, misappropriation of trade secrets and copyright infringement in connection with defendant's reproduction and misuse of codes contained in plaintiff's programs. The district court entered judgment in part for plaintiff, but rejected the claims insofar as

For earlier citations, see the Appendices, Supplements, or Pocket Parts, if any, that correspond to the subject matter under examination.

they related to programs defendant created after the commencement of the litigation. Affirming in part, vacating in part, and remanding, this court held, among other things, that, with respect to the post-litigation programs, the manner in which plaintiff combined various design elements in its software constituted a protectible trade secret, the novelty of which plaintiff was not required to establish, and that further factfinding was necessary to determine whether the manner of combination was copyrightable. Softel v. Dragon Med. & Scientific Communications, 118 F.3d 955, 957, 968, cert. denied 523 U.S. 1020, 118 S.Ct. 1300, 140 L.Ed.2d 466 (1998).

C.A.2, 1993. Cit. in disc., cit. in case cit. in disc., cit. generally in case cit. in ftn. com. (b) quot. in disc. and in ftn. Hotel chain's principal officer approached another hotel chain's CEO to describe concept about a small-size, upscale hotel room he designed to capture low-budget market segment of hotel industry. The two companies discussed joint venture, but they both developed separate small-size, upscale hotel chains on their own. Company that had idea first sued other hotel chain for misappropriation of trade secret. Federal district court entered judgment on jury verdict for plaintiff. Vacating and remanding with instructions to dismiss, this court held that, even assuming that an idea embodied in product or concept can constitute trade secret in premarketing stage, district court erred as matter of law in allowing this action for misappropriation of "Microtel" concept to proceed to trial under trade secret theory once plaintiff had affirmatively abandoned novelty claim. The court suggested that a new product idea cannot constitute a trade secret; however, it declined to reach that conclusion, since it confined its holding to determination that a non-novel idea was not a trade secret. Hudson Hotels Corp. v. Choice Hotels Intern., 995 F.2d 1173, 1176, 1177.

C.A.2, 1992. Cit. in sup., subsec. (c) cit. and quot. in sup., com. (1) quot. in disc. Owner of copyrighted computer program sued computer software corporation for misappropriation of trade secrets under state law, inter alia. The district court held that plaintiff's claim had been preempted by the federal Copyright Act. Vacating in part and remanding, this court held that plaintiff stated a nonpreempted trade-secret claim against defendant on the theory that defendant had used plaintiff's trade secrets while on constructive or actual notice of the fact that plaintiff's former employee had breached his duty to plaintiff of confidentiality by stealing plaintiff's trade secrets and incorporating them into defendant's computer programs. Computer Associates Intern., Inc. v. Altai, Inc., 982 F.2d 693, 718.

C.A.2, 1991. Com. (b) cit. in disc. A tour and travel business sued a former employee for misappropriating trade secrets, seeking damages and an injunction against any use by the employee of the confidential information. Without evaluating the merits, the district court summarily dismissed on jurisdictional grounds. The defendant argued that the district court did not dismiss on jurisdictional grounds and that summary judgment on the merits was proper. This court vacated and remanded for further proceedings, holding that the dismissal on jurisdictional grounds was improper. The court noted that even if the defendant were right in his contention that the court dismissed the plaintiff's trade secrets claims on the merits rather than for lack of jurisdiction, the dismissal could not stand. The plaintiff had produced evidence that it took reasonable measures to protect the secrecy of its customer list and that the information could not be obtained from other sources; therefore, a genuine issue of material fact remained as to whether the list constituted a trade secret. A.F.A. Tours, Inc. v. Whitchurch, 937 F.2d 82, 89.

C.A.2, 1990. Cit. in disc., com. (b) cit. and quot. in sup. and quot. in case quot. in sup. A computer software company developed generic programs that could be easily customized to meet a client's specific needs. Former employees of the company were hired by a competitor, which soon created substantially similar programs. The software company sued its competitor and former employees, claiming that its combination of generic programs deserved protection as a trade secret. The district court found that the defendants had misappropriated trade secrets and used them to develop the competitor's programs, and granted injunctions against the defendants. This court affirmed, upholding the district court's finding that the overall structure of the company's program was a protectable trade secret. The court concluded that the manner in which the company's programs interacted was not generally known outside

Cit.—cited; com.—comment; fol.—followed; sup.—support.
A complete list of abbreviations precedes page 1.

the company, nor had it been disclosed by the company's promotional material. The court also noted that the company had taken measures to protect the secrecy of its program architecture, had invested heavily in research and development, and cited expert testimony that the product's overall structure could not be readily duplicated without the secret information obtained by the company through years of research. Integrated Cash Mgmt. Serv. v. Digital Transactions, 920 F.2d 171, 173, 174.

C.A.3, 2020. Cit. in sup. Hydraulic-systems designer brought a lawsuit against former employee, competing company created by former employee, competitor, and employees of competitor, alleging, inter alia, that former employee provided plaintiff's proprietary information to competitor and company in order to wrongfully undermine plaintiff's bid to provide hydraulic systems to spaceflight authority, and that defendants misappropriated plaintiff's trade secrets regarding hydraulic-engineering drawings that plaintiff created under a work-for-hire agreement with spaceflight authority. The district court entered judgment for plaintiff. This court affirmed, holding that, as a matter of law, defendants' conduct constituted misappropriation of trade secrets under Restatement of Torts § 757. The court explained that plaintiff's trade secrets were not undermined by the fact that plaintiff provided the information to a public entity subject to state open-records law, without a formal confidentiality or nondisclosure agreement, because, inter alia, spaceflight authority honored plaintiff's proprietary designation and did not disclose such information except as needed to operate a space-launch program. Advanced Fluid Systems, Inc. v. Huber, 958 F.3d 168, 179.

C.A.3, 2019. Cit. in sup. (general cite), cit. in case cit. in sup., cit. in cases cit. and quot. in sup. (general cite); com. (c) quot. in sup. Manufacturer brought a lawsuit against owner of competitor, alleging that defendant misappropriated plaintiff's trade secrets when it acquired, through its wholly owned subsidiary, a third-party company to whom plaintiff had disclosed the trade secrets more than twenty years prior, and used them to manufacture competing products. The district court granted defendant's motion for summary judgment. This court reversed in part and remanded, holding, inter alia, that the district court erred by finding that the statute of limitations barred plaintiff's claims. The court explained that, under Restatement of Torts § 757, Comment *c*, defendant's ongoing usage of the misappropriated trade secrets created a cause of action separate from the disclosure. Heraeus Medical GmbH v. Esschem, Inc., 927 F.3d 727, 736, 739.

C.A.3, 2006. Com. (b) quot. in case cit. and quot. in sup. Corporation that handled sales and distribution for family seed-corn partnership sued partnership for, in part, misappropriation of trade secrets in connection with the brand names of certain hybrid strains of corn seed. The district court granted summary judgment for plaintiff. Reversing and remanding, this court held, among other things, that it could not conclude that the brand names attached to the hybrids were trade secrets as a matter of law. The court pointed out that the facts suggested that corporation did not consider the names of its hybrids to be trade secrets, and that, while it was unclear which of the disputed brand names were variety names, the Federal Seed Act required different sellers to use the same variety name for the same hybrid of corn seed. Doeblers' Pennsylvania Hybrids, Inc. v. Doebler, 442 F.3d 812, 829.

C.A.3, 2004. Com. (b) quot. in case quot. in disc. (Erron. cit. as Restatement Second of Torts.) Two Arab nationals appealed their convictions for mail fraud and conspiracy, arising out of allegations that nationals paid impostors to take requisite standardized English-language exam on their behalf so as to ensure that they kept their student visas. Affirming the convictions, this court held, inter alia, that federal government adequately alleged that defendants knowingly and willfully engaged in a scheme to defraud the testing service of a traditionally recognized property interest, namely, its tangible score reports and other confidential business information. Here, testing service was deprived of its recognized property interest in the right to decide how to use its language exam when it unknowingly granted unauthorized persons access to the test. U.S. v. Hedaithy, 392 F.3d 580, 594, cert. denied 544 U.S. 978, 125 S.Ct. 1882, 161 L.Ed.2d 731 (2005).

C.A.3, 2003. Cit. in sup., cit. and quot. in ftn. Inventor sued manufacturer for trade-secret misappropriation. The district court entered judgment on a jury verdict for defendant. Affirming, this court held, inter alia, that, under Pennsylvania law, independent development was not an affirmative defense; raising independent development simply shifted the burden of production to defendant, with the burden of persuasion remaining with plaintiff. Thus, the district court's jury charge placing on plaintiff the ultimate burden of disproving independent development was correct. Moore v. Kulicke & Soffa Industries, Inc., 318 F.3d 561, 566, 569.

C.A.3, 2000. Quot. in disc., cit. in ftn., subsec. (c) cit. in case cit. in disc. British corporation sued Taiwanese corporation and Pennsylvania corporation with its principal place in business in New Jersey, alleging that defendants misappropriated trade secrets. Applying New Jersey law, New Jersey federal district court entered preliminary injunction for plaintiff. This court reversed, holding that Taiwanese law governed, because Taiwan had the greater interest in whether plaintiff had a protectible interest in information licensed to a Taiwanese licensee and whether defendant Taiwanese corporation acted unlawfully in acquiring it. New Jersey's interest in protecting trade secret holders who exported their intellectual property to Taiwan was greatly outweighed by Taiwan's interest in setting standards for the protection of intellectual property in Taiwan. BP Chemicals Ltd. v. Formosa Chemical & Fibre Corp., 229 F.3d 254, 264, 265.

C.A.3, 1989. Com. (b) quot. in disc. and cit. in cases quot. in disc. After the plaintiff's wife died of severe burns sustained as the result of an exploding cigarette lighter and the plaintiff suffered injuries, he brought this suit for products liability, inter alia, on behalf of his wife's estate and in his own right against the manufacturer of the lighter. The defendant moved for a protective order in response to the plaintiff's interrogatories, arguing that the information sought was a trade secret. The district court denied the motion, finding that the information was not a trade secret because it did not give the defendant a competitive advantage. This court reversed the denial of the defendant's motion for a protective order with regard to confidential design, safety, and quality test information and affirmed the denial of the protective order with regard to information concerning other accidents or complaints. The court held that the district court's requirement that the defendant prove that its design information gave a competitive advantage in order to show the existence of a trade secret was an erroneous application of Pennsylvania law. Smith v. BIC Corp., 869 F.2d 194, 199, 200.

C.A.3, 1988. Com. (b) cit. in sup. A lighter manufacturer, the defendant in an earlier personal-injury action, sought to prevent an intervening newspaper publisher from gaining access to certain trial exhibits because they were confidential corporate documents, the disclosure of which was prohibited by a protective order. The manufacturer also sought a contempt order against the original plaintiff's attorney, contending that he retained confidential documents in violation of the protective order. The district court granted the newspaper access to the contested documents and refused to hold the original plaintiff's attorney in contempt. Affirming in part and reversing in part, this court held, inter alia, that the district court's finding that the manufacturer's documents did not contain trade secrets was not clearly erroneous. The court explained that nontrade-secret information, which was what the manufacturer contended the documents in question contained, was not entitled to the same level of protection from disclosure as trade-secret information. Littlejohn v. BIC Corp., 851 F.2d 673, 685, on remand 697 F.Supp. 192 (E.D.Pa.1988).

C.A.3, 1987. Com. (b) cit. in case cit. in disc. The FDA rejected a manufacturer's application to produce a generic animal drug because it failed to submit original safety and effectiveness data. When the manufacturer asked the trial court to direct the FDA to rely on the data previously submitted by the manufacturer of the predecessor brand name drug, the court granted the FDA's motion for summary judgment. Affirming, this court held that the new data was required by statute. The court noted that, prior to the passage of the applicable statute, data submitted by an original manufacturer was held by the U.S. Supreme Court to constitute a property interest of that manufacturer under state law. Tri-Bio Laboratories, Inc. v. United States, 836 F.2d 135, 140.

C.A.4, 2018. Com. (b) cit. and quot. in sup., cit. in case cit. in sup., quot. in ftn. Company that analyzed airline ticket fares brought an action against former employee who, among other things, accessed his company account after resigning and down-

Cit.—cited; com.—comment; fol.—followed; sup.—support.
A complete list of abbreviations precedes page 1.

loaded two flowcharts displaying ticket-price rules derived from the Airline Tariff Publishing Company, alleging, inter alia, misappropriation of trade secrets. After a bench trial, the district court entered judgment for defendant. This court vacated and remanded, holding that the district court erred in finding that the flowcharts were not trade secrets under Maryland law. The court noted that, prior to enactment of the applicable Maryland law, Maryland had applied the factor-based definition of "trade secret" set forth in Restatement of Torts § 757, Comment *b*, and reasoned, citing Comment *b*, that, here, the flowcharts were valuable because the evidence showed that plaintiff intended to keep the flowcharts confidential and that, even though the information on the flowcharts was publicly available, it was not readily ascertainable. AirFacts, Inc. v. de Amezaga, 909 F.3d 84, 95-97.

C.A.4, 1994. Com. (b) quot. in sup. Computer products marketer sued employee, among others, for copyright infringement of a computer program and misappropriation of trade secrets in the program, inter alia. The trial court entered judgment for plaintiff on the trade-secrets misappropriation claim, and this court vacated in part and remanded, holding that a finding on remand by the district court that copyright in the program vested in defendant would mean that, from the moment of the program's inception, defendant had owned the exclusive right to license uses of the original and any derivative works; thus, absent a written agreement regarding plaintiff's use of the program, any use license held by plaintiff would be implied and nonexclusive and could not support the reasonable expectation or right of secrecy necessary for plaintiff's trade-secrets misappropriation claim under Virginia law. Avtec Systems, Inc. v. Peiffer, 21 F.3d 568, 575.

C.A.4, 1993. Com. (a) quot. in part in sup., com. (b) quot. in part in sup. and in ftn., com. (c) cit. in disc. The owner of computer software sued its licensee and the licensee's contractor for, among other claims, misappropriation of trade secrets, alleging that the licensee improperly disclosed and the contractor improperly acquired and used plaintiff's computer program. The jury found for plaintiff and awarded compensatory and punitive damages. Affirming in part, this court held, inter alia, that plaintiff failed to prove that the engineering formulae and methods of calculation and structure and organization of the software program's modules were trade secrets under the Maryland Uniform Trade Secrets Act, as plaintiff had refused to explain at trial how the program was structured or organized, but that the program's source and object codes constituted trade secrets, since an individual could use them to offer the same services as plaintiff and thus plaintiff could derive independent economic value from secrecy of the codes. Trandes Corp. v. Guy F. Atkinson Co., 996 F.2d 655, 660, 661, 663, 665, cert. denied 510 U.S. 965, 114 S.Ct. 443, 126 L.Ed.2d 377 (1993).

C.A.5, 2016. Quot. in case quot. in sup.; subsec. (c) cit. in sup. Developer of software under a government subcontract filed an action in state court against competitor hired by the government to replace plaintiff's software, alleging, among other things, trade-secret misappropriation in violation of Texas law. After defendant removed the action, the district court entered judgment on a jury verdict for plaintiff. Affirming, this court held that plaintiff's claim was not preempted by federal copyright law, because plaintiff was required to establish an additional element in support of its misappropriation claim, namely, that the protected information was taken via improper means or by breach of a confidential relationship. The court explained that Texas followed the approach set forth in Restatement of Torts § 757, which required additional wrongful conduct beyond mere reproduction. GlobeRanger Corporation v. Software AG United States of America, Incorporated, 836 F.3d 477, 488, 492.

C.A.5, 2013. Com. (b) quot. in case quot. in sup. Developer of complex-services software for oil companies sued consulting firm, alleging that defendant misappropriated its trade secrets. The district court entered judgment on a jury verdict for plaintiff. Affirming, this court held that reasonable jurors could have found that defendant misappropriated plaintiff's trade secrets under Texas law. The court concluded that sufficient evidence existed to support the jury's finding that plaintiff's technology contained trade secrets, pointing out that plaintiff was the only company offering complex-services software from 2000 to 2005 (the years prior to defendant's alleged misappropriation), that it guarded the secrecy of its technology by placing its software behind a firewall and sharing it subject to confidentiality agreements, and that its technology had value. Wellogix, Inc. v. Accenture, L.L.P., 716 F.3d 867, 875.

C.A.5, 2010. Cit. in case cit. in sup., com. (b) cit. and quot. in case cit. in sup. (general cite). Owner of copyrighted software sued former customer, after a group of defendant's employees obtained a copy of plaintiff's software from an unknown source and used it without authorization. The district court entered judgment on a jury verdict in favor of plaintiff. This court reversed as to plaintiff's claims for misappropriation of trade secrets and unfair competition and rendered a take-nothing judgment for plaintiff, holding that, while plaintiff demonstrated defendant's total revenue, it failed to deduct unrelated revenue and costs to demonstrate defendant's profits related to the infringement. The court rejected plaintiff's argument that its exhibit showing total revenue satisfied its burden of proof with regard to defendant's "sales" and that defendant subsequently had the burden of demonstrating which portions of its revenue were not attributable to the state-law claims, concluding that the Texas Supreme Court would not adopt the burden-shifting procedures of Restatement Second of Torts § 45, Comment *f*. MGE UPS Systems, Inc. v. GE Consumer and Indus., Inc., 622 F.3d 361, 370.

C.A.5, 2009. Quot. in case quot. in sup., com. (b) quot. in sup. Company that specialized in cleaning a type of low grade coal known as lignite sued mining company in connection with a failed partnership to clean lignite at two mines. The district court granted defendant's motion for a take-nothing judgment on plaintiff's claim for misappropriation of trade secrets. Affirming, this court held, inter alia, that plaintiff's recommendation that defendant focus on high-quality "ROM lignite" rather than waste lignite was not a trade secret under Texas law, because it did not involve a previously unknown process or method for cleaning lignite, was not a process or device for continuous use that offered defendant an advantage over its competitors, and was tailored to defendant's initial cleaning project, rather than to the mining industry generally. CQ, Inc. v. TXU Min. Co., L.P., 565 F.3d 268, 274.

C.A.5, 2007. Com. (b) quot. in sup. (general cite). Producer of golf clubs sued competitor for, in part, misappropriation of trade secrets. The district court granted defendant's motion to limit the evidence to two of defendant's clubs that plaintiff initially identified in discovery as the only clubs relevant to its trade-secrets claims. Affirming as to that portion of the decision, this court held, inter alia, that plaintiff was prohibited from offering evidence of defendant's use of allegedly non-trade secret "confidential information," including "design sketches," as to any clubs that plaintiff could have, but did not, include in its trade-secrets claims; while "confidential business information" could in some cases be distinct from "trade secrets," plaintiff's design sketches clearly fell into the category of trade secrets. Triple Tee Golf, Inc. v. Nike, Inc., 485 F.3d 253, 267.

C.A.5, 2004. Cit. generally in ftn., com. (j) cit. in ftn. Developer and licensor of tracking software for shipping industry sued licensee who, without authorization, created similar tracking system that incorporated elements of licensor's software. The district court granted summary judgment for defendant on plaintiff's copyright-infringement claims, and subsequently dismissed plaintiff's conversion, misappropriation, and trade-secret claims. Reversing only as to the trade-secret claim, this court held, inter alia, that a genuine issue of material fact existed as to whether plaintiff had formed a partnership with defendant that imposed a duty on each party to not breach their confidential relationship by misusing the trade secret of the other partner. General Universal Systems, Inc. v. Lee, 379 F.3d 131, 151, on remand 2005 WL 1828565 (S.D.Tex.2005).

C.A.5, 1999. Com. (f) cit. in ftn. Manufacturer of telephone switching equipment sued competitor for copyright infringement, trade-secret misappropriation, and unfair competition. Affirming the district court's entry of judgment awarding plaintiff damages on its trade-secret misappropriation claim, this court held, inter alia, that defendant obtained plaintiff's trade secrets through improper means by unlawfully acquiring a copy of plaintiff's operating-system software from plaintiff's customer and then using the knowledge it gained from the purloined software to interpret the trade secrets contained in plaintiff's firmware. Alcatel USA, Inc. v. DGI Technologies, Inc., 166 F.3d 772, 785.

C.A.5, 1996. Cit. in ftn. in sup. A manufacturer of above-ground storage tanks sued a fiberglass-products manufacturer

Cit.—cited; com.—comment; fol.—followed; sup.—support.
A complete list of abbreviations precedes page 1.

under Texas law for theft of trade secrets regarding the manufacture of its tanks. After the jury returned a verdict awarding plaintiff $2 million in compensatory damages and $3 million in exemplary damages, the district court granted defendant's motion for judgment n.o.v., holding, in part, that plaintiff's evidence of damages was too speculative to support the compensatory damages award. Reversing and remanding, this court held, inter alia, that a plaintiff's costs of development were one possible, and allowable, component in the calculation of damages and that uncontroverted evidence existed that plaintiff's demand during licensing negotiations with defendant for an up-front payment of $2 million was reasonably based on its cost of research and development. The court noted that, although its holding was based on a decision under the Georgia law of trade secrets, Georgia, like Texas, based its law of trade secrets on the Restatement of Torts § 757. Texas Tanks, Inc. v. Owens-Corning Fiberglas Corp., 99 F.3d 734, 739.

C.A.5, 1994. Com. (c) quot. in disc. Roach spray manufacturer sued potential purchaser of its assets for misappropriation of trade secrets, inter alia, after negotiations between the parties broke down. The trial court granted judgment as a matter of law for defendant on plaintiff's trade secrets claim, inter alia. Affirming in part and reversing and rendering in part, this court held that plaintiff's claim for misappropriation of trade secrets failed for the reason that there was insufficient evidence as a matter of law that defendant improperly disclosed or used any of plaintiff's confidential or proprietary information as a result of which defendant gained some sort of unfair trade advantage. Omnitech Intern., Inc. v. Clorox Co., 11 F.3d 1316, 1325, cert. denied 513 U.S. 815, 115 S.Ct. 71, 130 L.Ed.2d 26 (1994).

C.A.5, 1994. Subsec. (b) quot. in case cit. but dist., com. (b) cit. in headnote and quot. in disc., com. (j) cit. in case cit. but dist. Business owner sued prospective buyers of his business for misappropriation of trade secrets under the guise of purchasing the business. The district court entered judgment on a jury verdict awarding plaintiff damages. Affirming, this court held, inter alia, that, although plaintiff never explicitly requested that the secret of his manufacturing process be held in confidence, plaintiff took steps to protect his trade secret by not disclosing the process to anyone until sales negotiations with defendants commenced; thus, his disclosure was made within a confidential relationship that placed defendants under a duty to keep the secret. The court stated that the jury was justified in finding that defendants knew or should have known that the information was a trade secret and that the disclosure was made in confidence. Phillips v. Frey, 20 F.3d 623, 624, 628, 631, 632.

C.A.5, 1991. Cit. in case cit. in sup. A Mexican restaurant chain sued an imitator chain for trade-dress infringement under the Lanham Act and misappropriation of trade secrets under Texas law. The district court entered judgment on the jury's verdict in favor of the original chain and denied the imitator's motion for judgment n.o.v. Affirming, this court held, inter alia, that the original chain's disclosure of architectural plans to contractors who considered them to be confidential and to the municipality in order to obtain a building permit did not extinguish the restaurant chain owner's proprietary interest in preserving the secrecy of these plans. The court stated that architectural plans and kitchen equipment layouts and designs were trade secrets because they were used by the restaurant chain to give them an advantage over their competitors. Taco Cabana Intern., Inc. v. Two Pesos, Inc., 932 F.2d 1113, 1123.

C.A.5, 1987. Quot. in disc., subsec. (b) quot. in disc., com. (j) cit. in ftn. An inventor sued a tool manufacturer for misappropriation of a trade secret, alleging that he had submitted a suggestion for a tool in confidence, and that the manufacturer misappropriated it and was liable for damages. The trial court found for the plaintiff. Reversing, this court held that there was no confidential relationship between the plaintiff and the defendant; therefore the defendant was free to use the trade secret and it violated no obligation to the plaintiff by manufacturing the tool. The court reasoned that the defendant was not liable because the plaintiff never requested that his disclosure be held in confidence, he disclosed the invention on his own initiative, and he never indicated that he wanted any pecuniary recompense for his suggestion. Smith v. Snap-On Tools Corp., 833 F.2d 578, 579, 580.

C.A.7, 2003. Cit. in sup., cit. generally in sup. Toy-design company sued toy manufacturer and its representatives for misappro-

For earlier citations, see the Appendices, Supplements, or Pocket Parts, if any, that correspond to the subject matter under examination.

priation of a trade secret in a realistic toy railroad track under Illinois Trade Secrets Act. Jury awarded plaintiff a royalty for a license, but district court granted judgment as a matter of law for defendants, holding that plaintiff did not have a protectable trade secret. This court reversed, reinstated jury verdict, and remanded for trial on damages, holding that plaintiff presented sufficient evidence for jury reasonably to conclude that factors of Restatement of Torts § 757 weighed in plaintiff's favor. The court construed six-part Restatement test as instructive guidelines, and not requisite elements, for ascertaining whether trade secret existed under Act. Learning Curve Toys, Inc. v. PlayWood Toys, Inc., 342 F.3d 714, 722, 723.

C.A.7, 1993. Cit. in case cit. in disc., cit. generally in sup. Employer sued former employees to enforce an agreement not to compete after employees left to work for a competitor. The district court granted plaintiff's request for a preliminary injunction. Reversing the decision below, vacating the injunction, and remanding, this court held, inter alia, that since paragraph three of the employment agreement was not a noncompetition clause, but a prohibition against releasing confidential customer information that the court determined did not qualify as a trade secret, the lack of any time limitation on the restriction on release of the customer information was unreasonable and therefore paragraph three was void and unenforceable. Nalco Chemical Co. v. Hydro Technologies, Inc., 984 F.2d 801, 804.

C.A.7, 1991. Cit. generally in ftn. A defendant who was convicted of mail fraud sought postconviction relief after learning that a codefendant's conviction had been vacated by a subsequent United States Supreme Court ruling. The district court vacated his mail fraud conviction on the ground that the objective of the underlying scheme did not constitute a property interest under the new Supreme Court ruling. Reversing, this court held that the conviction was valid because the defendant's scheme to obtain a village's cable television franchise contract by means of false and fraudulent representations had in fact deprived the village of a valid property interest. Borre v. U.S., 940 F.2d 215, 219.

C.A.7, 1991. Cit. in disc. A manufacturer of newspaper printing presses sued a competitor and the competitor's president for misappropriation of trade secrets and RICO violations. The district court entered summary judgment for the defendants. Reversing and remanding, this court held that factual issues existed as to whether the plaintiff took reasonable precautions to keep its piece part drawings secret and whether the defendants obtained the drawings by improper means. Rockwell Graphic Systems, Inc. v. DEV Industries, Inc., 925 F.2d 174, 178.

C.A.7, 1990. Com. (b) cit. in case quot. in disc. The developer and manufacturer of a boat speedometer sued a competitor alleging several counts including breach of contract and misappropriation of trade secrets. The district court granted summary judgment for the defendant on several counts and granted directed verdicts for the defendant on other counts, including a count of unfair competition for which the jury had awarded the plaintiff compensatory damages. Affirming, this court held, inter alia, that the district court properly granted summary judgment for the defendant on the misappropriation of trade secrets count. The court stated that the plaintiff took no measures to guard the secrecy of his information either from other boat speedometer manufacturers or from the competitor's employees. Further, the plaintiff's "idea" could not be considered novel when articles were previously published in fishing publications about the use of the competitor's speedometers for trolling. Wilson v. Electro Marine Systems, Inc., 915 F.2d 1110, 1115.

C.A.8, 2011. Com. (b) quot. in case quot. in sup. Manufacturer of helicopter engines sued third-party overhaul shop, alleging that defendant had violated the Lanham Act by misappropriating trade secrets from an informational letter that plaintiff issued exclusively to its authorized maintenance centers. The district court granted summary judgment for plaintiff, finding that, while prior versions of the letter were publicly available, the most recent revision of the letter was a protected trade secret. Affirming, this court rejected defendant's argument that only a trivial amount of information in the most recent revision was not readily ascertainable from prior revisions, holding that the existence of a trade secret was determined by the value of the secret, not the merit of its technical improvements. The court noted that, because trade-secret laws provided more

Cit.—cited; com.—comment; fol.—followed; sup.—support.
A complete list of abbreviations precedes page 1.

limited protection than patent laws, they did not require the kind of novelty and invention that was a requisite of patentability. AvidAir Helicopter Supply, Inc. v. Rolls-Royce Corp., 663 F.3d 966, 973.

C.A.8, 1994. Subsecs. (a) and (e) cit. in sup., com. (a) quot. in disc., com. (b) cit. in disc. Breeder of corn seed sued competitor for trade-secret misappropriation. Affirming the district court's entry of judgment for plaintiff, this court held that the district court's finding of misappropriation was not clearly erroneous in light of substantial circumstantial evidence giving rise to an inference of defendant's acquisition of the genetic makeup of plaintiff's seed corn by improper means and defendant's inability to meet its burden of showing lawful acquisition; moreover, the district court's damages award to plaintiff of lost profits was reasonably based on evidence of defendant's actual sales figures, plaintiff's profitability history, and a reasonable estimate of plaintiff's lost market share. Pioneer Hi-Bred Intern. v. Holden Foundation Seeds, 35 F.3d 1226, 1235, 1238, 1239, 1244.

C.A.8, 1992. Com. (b) quot. in case quot. in sup. California employee of microbiological equipment manufacturer signed an employment agreement that included a one-year noncompete covenant. Later, employee resigned his position and accepted employment with a Missouri competitor. Former employer sued employee in federal district court, seeking to enjoin employee from misappropriating trade secrets and to enforce the noncompete provision. District court refused to enforce the noncompete provision but enjoined the employee for one year from using or disclosing certain confidential information. The court determined that employer had met its burden of proving that at least some of the information in question constituted trade secrets which deserved protection. Affirming, this court held, inter alia, that the district court did not abuse its discretion by crafting an injunction that protected employer from harm, while imposing no greater restraint than necessary on employee. Baxter Intern., Inc. v. Morris, 976 F.2d 1189, 1193.

C.A.8, 1989. Com. (b) cit. generally in disc. and quot. in case quot. in disc. A railroad sued a public power district to prevent disclosure of its contract with another public power district to transport coal. The district court held that the contract was a trade secret and thus not subject to disclosure. Affirming, this court stated that the railroad had developed at considerable effort and expense a formula for the escalation of the base contract rate for coal transportation, which was designed to give the railroad a competitive advantage in attracting utility customers and was in continuous use in its operations, and that it had gone to great lengths to prevent disclosure of the information, negotiating the contract to include a strict confidentiality requirement and vigorously prosecuting this action to prevent disclosure. Burlington Northern v. Omaha Public Power Dist., 888 F.2d 1228, 1231, 1232.

C.A.10, 2022. Com. (b) quot. in case quot. in sup. Owner of brand of homemade bread products sued baker, son of baker, and competitor, alleging, inter alia, that defendants misappropriated plaintiff's trade secrets by using plaintiff's compilation of specific ingredients and production techniques to create competing homemade bread products. The district court entered judgment on a jury verdict for plaintiff. This court reversed in part and remanded, holding that plaintiff's compilation was not a protectable trade secret, because it was generally ascertainable and readily known to those in the baking industry. Citing Restatement of Torts § 757, the court explained that plaintiff's use of potato flour and dry yeast was printed on its products' nutrition labels, the amount of those ingredients could be ascertained by defendants with simple trial and error, and the proofing and baking techniques used by plaintiff was common among bakers. Bimbo Bakeries USA, Inc. v. Sycamore, 39 F.4th 1250, 1261.

C.A.10, 2022. Com. (b) quot. in sup. Assignee of bakery sued, among others, competitor, alleging that defendant misappropriated plaintiff's trade secrets by working with plaintiff's former partner in order to develop homemade bread products that were substantially similar to plaintiff's. The district court entered judgment for plaintiff. This court reversed in part and remanded, holding that plaintiff's compilation of recipes and processes used to make its homemade bread products was not a trade secret. Quoting Restatement of Torts § 757, Comment *b*, the court explained that the compilation constituted information that was well known outside plaintiff's business, because it was readily ascertainable by those in the baking industry. Bimbo Bakeries USA, Inc. v. Sycamore, 29 F.4th 630, 641.

C.A.10, 2011. Cit. in disc. (general cite). Developer of audio teleconferencing equipment sued former employees and their new employer, alleging misappropriation of trade secrets pursuant to the Utah Uniform Trade Secrets Act. The trial court issued a permanent injunction against defendants, and entered judgment on a jury verdict for plaintiff. In affirming, this court rejected defendants' argument that, had the district court correctly applied Massachusetts law, it would have been required to conclude that plaintiff's sound-enhancement algorithm did not constitute a valid trade secret because plaintiff had, prior to the alleged misappropriation, ceased using the algorithm and declared that it had no value; defendants had abandoned their position that Massachusetts law applied to the misappropriation claim, subsequently arguing that Utah law applied. ClearOne Communications, Inc. v. Bowers, 643 F.3d 735, 769.

C.A.10, 2009. Cit. in case quot. in sup. (general cite). Employer sued competitor and former employees who resigned to work for competitor, alleging, among other things, that defendants misappropriated plaintiff's confidential pricing information, in particular, a price quote that plaintiff generated for its longtime customer, which ultimately placed its order with competitor. After a bench trial, the district court found in favor of plaintiff on several of its claims. This court reversed as to plaintiff's claim for misappropriation of trade secrets, holding that the price quote did not qualify as a trade secret because plaintiff disclosed that quote and other pricing information to its customers without reservation. The court noted that the quote was known outside of plaintiff, that plaintiff took no measures to prevent customer from disseminating the information, and that competitor could properly acquire the information simply by requesting it from customer. Southwest Stainless, LP v. Sappington, 582 F.3d 1176, 1189.

C.A.10, 2006. Com. (b) cit. generally in sup. Manufacturers of indoor tanning lotions and their exclusive distributor sued family and its businesses that resold the lotions over the Internet without authorization. The district court, inter alia, granted plaintiffs' motion for sanctions against defendants based on defendants' refusal to disclose their list of suppliers on trade-secret grounds. Affirming, this court held that the district court did not abuse its discretion in determining that the trade-secrets privilege did not apply. The court concluded that defendants failed to meet their burden of proof in establishing a trade secret under Oklahoma law, because the list contained information that was widely known outside of defendants' business, presumably widely known by employees and others involved in the business, and easily acquired or duplicated by others. Australian Gold, Inc. v. Hatfield, 436 F.3d 1228, 1245.

C.A.10, 1994. Com. (b) cit. and quot. in case quot. in sup. Lumber wholesaler sued its competitor and a former employee, alleging theft of trade secrets and other claims. Reversing the district court's grant of summary judgment for competitor and remanding, this court held that a fact issue existed as to whether plaintiff's computerized price quoting system was a trade secret, as the evidence was that there was integration obtained by the software, it was a total package for immediate use, and it was the only system in the industry that could provide immediate pricing. Rivendell Forest Products, Ltd. v. Georgia-Pacific Corp., 28 F.3d 1042, 1043, 1044.

C.A.10, 1993. Com. (a) cit. in disc. Owner of copyright on software sued competitor, seeking a permanent injunction against defendant's use of an allegedly infringing program. The district court granted in part plaintiff's motion for the injunction. Affirming in part, this court held, inter alia, that because plaintiff's claim for trade-secret misappropriation under Colorado trade-secret law required proof of a breach of trust or confidence, proof that was not required under the Copyright Act, plaintiff's state law claims were not preempted by federal law. Gates Rubber Co. v. Bando Chemical Industries, Ltd., 9 F.3d 823, 848.

C.A.10, 1993. Com. (b) quot. in case quot. in ftn. The developers of an auto mall sued the city of proposed location, alleging deprivation of property interest without due process in trade secrets regarding the proposed mall and other civil rights claims. Affirming the district court's grant of summary judgment for the city, this court held, inter alia, that, under Utah law, the developers had failed to demonstrate ownership of any trade secrets as a basis for claiming a property interest in the concept of the

Cit.—cited; com.—comment; fol.—followed; sup.—support.
A complete list of abbreviations precedes page 1.

auto mall, as they had disclosed information regarding the mall to entities other than the city, and they knew that they would have to disclose certain information to the city in the process of developing the mall and that this information would become public. Jensen v. Redevelopment Agency of Sandy City, 998 F.2d 1550, 1557.

C.A.10, 1990. Com. (b) quot. but not fol. and cit. generally but not fol. in case quot. in sup. A woman sued a chemical manufacturer in state court for injuries allegedly caused by an injection of liquid silicone produced by the manufacturer. The Food and Drug Administration (FDA) rejected the woman's request for documents submitted regarding the liquid silicone under the Freedom of Information Act (FOIA). The woman sued the FDA to compel disclosure of the documents. The district court granted summary judgment for the FDA, holding that the requested documents contained confidential information that was exempt from FOIA disclosure requirements. This court reversed and remanded for further examination of the documents and findings as to the justifications for the exemptions. The court ruled that a narrow definition of "trade secrets" should be applied, which required a direct relationship between the trade secret and the productive process, and noted that a broader definition of the phrase would render superfluous other exempted categories enumerated within the FOIA. Anderson v. Department of Health & Human Services, 907 F.2d 936, 943, 944.

C.A.11, 2001. Com. (b) cit. in case quot. in ftn. After college student died in car accident, his parents sued tire manufacturer for negligent design and manufacture. The parties settled, and confidential discovery documents were ordered to remain sealed. Members of the press then sought to intervene to unseal manufacturer's documents, and district court ordered documents unsealed. This court vacated and remanded with instructions for district court to determine whether good cause existed for maintaining documents under seal. The court stated that, should district court determine that documents contained trade secrets, it was to balance manufacturer's interest in keeping information confidential against press's contention that disclosure served public's interest in health and safety. Chicago Tribune Co. v. Bridgestone/Firestone, Inc., 263 F.3d 1304, 1314.

C.A.D.C.2004. Com. (b) quot. in conc. and diss. op. Aircraft-maintenance contractor sued Air Force, challenging as arbitrary and capricious Air Force's decision to release to plaintiff's competitor pricing information contained in contract Air Force awarded to plaintiff for maintenance of two aircraft. District court upheld Air Force's decision. This court affirmed in part and reversed in part, holding that Air Force could release "over and above work" prices but could not release option-year prices. Concurring and dissenting opinion argued that, since plaintiff did not prove that Air Force disclosures were likely to cause substantial harm to plaintiff's competitive position, it concurred with majority's decision that "over and above work" prices could be disclosed, but it dissented from majority's determination that vendor-pricing and option-year line items could not. It raised issue of whether prices paid by government should be trade secrets. McDonnell Douglas Corp. v. U.S. Dept. of the Air Force, 375 F.3d 1182, 1204.

C.A.D.C.1987. Com. (b) quot. in disc. The FDA denied a hair-care products manufacturer's application for trade-secret status for a secret ingredient. After the trial court invalidated the FDA's procedures on due-process grounds, the FDA revised its procedure for handling trade-secret applications. The plaintiff reapplied and was again denied trade secret status by the FDA. The trial court affirmed a magistrate's ruling rejecting the plaintiff's claims. Reversing and remanding, this court held that the denial was arbitrary and capricious. The court reasoned that any formula that was used in one's business and gave its manufacturer an opportunity to obtain an advantage over competitors who did not know of it or use it qualified as a trade secret. Zotos Intern., Inc. v. Young, 830 F.2d 350, 352.

C.A.Fed.2018. Cit. and quot. in case cit. and quot. in sup.; subsec. (b) cit. in disc., quot. in case quot. in sup.; com. (j) quot. in case quot. in sup. Developer and seller of ambient-light sensors that had confidentially shared information with competitor during negotiations regarding a potential merger filed, inter alia, a claim for misappropriation of trade secrets against competitor, alleging that competitor released new sensors with the technical design plaintiff had disclosed. The district court entered judgment in part on a jury verdict for plaintiff, finding that the jury awards

For earlier citations, see the Appendices, Supplements, or Pocket Parts, if any, that correspond to the subject matter under examination.

on the breach-of-contract and tortious-interference claims were duplicative. This court affirmed liability for trade-secret misappropriation but on a more limited basis than plaintiff presented to the jury. Relying on Restatement of Torts § 757, the court determined that plaintiff failed to show that defendant had acquired plaintiff's packaging roadmap and cost-breakdown information by misappropriation, because defendant was already using low-cost plastic rather than glass packaging prior to plaintiff's disclosure of its confidential information and defendant could not misappropriate information it already had. Texas Advanced Optoelectronic Solutions, Inc. v. Renesas Electronics America, Inc., 888 F.3d 1322, 1330, 1331, 1333.

C.A.Fed.2013. Com. (b) quot. in sup., cit. in case cit. in sup., quot. in ftn. Manufacturer of smartphones and tablets brought a patent-infringement action, inter alia, against competitor. The district court, relying on an opposition filed by a nonparty media organization, denied in part the parties' pretrial motions to seal certain documents containing, among other things, confidential financial information, even though those motions were unopposed by the parties; after the parties filed a joint stipulation in which they agreed to rely on less detailed financial information at trial, and a jury found in favor of plaintiff, the district court denied defendant's post-trial motion to seal the material plaintiff had designated as confidential, but stayed the order pending appeal. Reversing and remanding, this court held that the district court abused its discretion in ordering the detailed financial information unsealed, because the parties had a significant interest in preventing the release of that information. The court reasoned, in part, that it was likely that the information at issue would meet the Restatement's relatively broad definition of "trade secret," because the parties could suffer competitive harm if the information was made public. Apple Inc. v. Samsung Electronics Co., Ltd., 727 F.3d 1214, 1222, 1225.

C.A.Fed.2013. Cit. in disc. Military shipbuilder brought an action for misappropriation of trade secrets against the United States under the Federal Tort Claims Act (FTCA), alleging that defendant wrongfully disclosed plaintiff's proprietary technical drawings for a special-operations craft to its rival for use in designing and constructing a nearly identical craft. After the district court entered judgment for plaintiff, the Fifth Circuit Court of Appeals vacated and remanded for transfer to the Court of Federal Claims on the basis that plaintiff's claim was rooted in breach of contract. This court affirmed the district court's transfer of the case, holding that, while plaintiff's stated claim was a tort-based claim for liability based on the Virginia law of trade-secret misappropriation and, on its face, was within the district court's jurisdiction under the FTCA, the Fifth Circuit did not clearly err in holding that plaintiff's claim depended on an adjudication of the government's contract obligation not to disclose plaintiff's designs and thus was presumptively limited by the Tucker Act to the Court of Federal Claims. U.S. Marine, Inc. v. U.S., 722 F.3d 1360, 1365.

C.A.Fed.2011. Com. (b) cit. in disc. In an action by domestic manufacturer of cast steel railway wheels, the International Trade Commission found that importation of foreign competitor's wheels violated the Tariff Act, because they were made using trade secrets that competitor had misappropriated from manufacturer's foreign licensee. Affirming, this court noted that, in analyzing the alleged misappropriation, the commission applied general principles of trade-secret law, including the six factors defining a trade secret set forth in the comments to Restatement First of Torts § 757. TianRui Group Co. Ltd. v. International Trade Com'n, 661 F.3d 1322, 1325.

C.A.Fed.1991. Com. (b) cit. and quot. in disc. and cit. generally in case cit. in disc. A federal prison inmate sued a government corporation, alleging that the corporation had violated his Fifth Amendment right by taking his invention without paying him just compensation. The United States Claims Court granted the defendant summary judgment, holding that the plaintiff did not possess a protectable property right in the invention because he did not keep the invention secret. This court reversed and remanded, holding, inter alia, that the plaintiff's invention was a protectable trade secret under Texas law, even though the plaintiff demonstrated the invention to the defendant, who was both his employer and a potential customer. The court found that the demonstration was not a release of the plaintiff's secret information to a

Cit.—cited; com.—comment; fol.—followed; sup.—support.
A complete list of abbreviations precedes page 1.

competitor. Lariscey v. U.S., 949 F.2d 1137, 1141-1142, vacated 962 F.2d 1047 (1992).

C.A.Fed.1989. Com. (b) quot. in case cit. in disc. The holder of a patent on a motorcycle rear-wheel suspension system sued a motorcycle manufacturer for misappropriation of trade secrets, inter alia, after unsuccessful licensing negotiations. The district court entered judgment on a jury verdict that 9 of the plaintiff's 11 asserted trade secrets were not trade secrets and granted the defendant's motion for a new trial on the validity of the two asserted trade secrets that the jury had upheld. This court reversed the trial court's order for a new trial and reinstated the jury verdict, inter alia, holding that the district court's erroneous instruction that, because the defendant might have developed or could have developed on its own the information it received from the plaintiff, that information could not be protected as a trade secret imposed a higher standard for trade secret status than was contained in California law and placed a prejudicially heavy burden on the plaintiff. Richardson v. Suzuki Motor Co., Ltd., 868 F.2d 1226, 1243, certiorari denied 493 U.S. 853, 110 S.Ct. 154, 107 L.Ed.2d 112 (1989).

Ct.Int'l Trade, 1987. Cit. in ftn. An importer sought judicial review of an antidumping duty order and made a motion seeking the disclosure of nonpublic confidential information, including trade secrets, in the administrative record to its in-house counsel. This court denied the motion, holding that disclosure to the in-house counsel would create an unacceptable risk of inadvertent disclosure, since the in-house counsel was not sufficiently isolated from the commercial activities of the plaintiff, and denial of access would not prejudice the plaintiff because the outside counsel retained by the plaintiff had already been allowed access. A. Hirsh, Inc. v. U.S., 657 F.Supp. 1297, 1301.

Ct.Fed.Cl.2012. Sec. and com. (a) quot. in sup.; cit. in ftn. and cit. in case cit. in ftn. (general cite). Developer of proprietary technology for the remote detection of microwire sued the United States, alleging, among other things, that the National Nuclear Security Administration breached express and "implied in fact" contracts to maintain plaintiff's trade secrets in confidence. Denying defendant's motion to dismiss plaintiff's claim for misappropriation of trade secrets, this court held that it had subject-matter jurisdiction over that claim, because, while the court generally had no jurisdiction over tort claims, here the claim arose from an alleged breach of contract. Demodulation, Inc. v. U.S., 103 Fed.Cl. 794, 812, 813.

Ct.Fed.Cl.2010. Cit. in case quot. in sup. Vendor that had, at federal agency's request, generated a budgetary proposal containing cost information for mobile medical trailers sued United States, alleging, among other things, that agency improperly disclosed to other potential bidders plaintiff's proprietary information contained in the proposal, including the design layout and integrated equipment list for its mobile surgery unit. Dismissing the action, this court held, among other things, that plaintiff's design layout and equipment list were publicly available and therefore did not constitute proprietary or trade-secret information. The court pointed out that plaintiff had displayed a fully equipped model unit at trade shows, which revealed plaintiff's design layout, and that an educated observer could recreate plaintiff's equipment list by viewing the model unit. Mobile Medical Intern. Corp. v. U.S., 95 Fed.Cl. 706, 734.

Ct.Fed.Cl.2003. Cit. in ftn. Patent owner sued United States for infringing his patent by producing fighter planes that used his process for making a silicon fiber sheet product. Court of Federal Claims initially granted defendant partial summary judgment, holding that because fibers were manufactured in foreign country, plaintiff's suit was barred by 28 U.S.C. § 1498(c) because it was based on a claim arising in a foreign country. After staying defendant's motion pending additional briefing, the court denied defendant's motion, holding that plaintiff could assert a claim outside of § 1498 for a taking of its patent rights under Fifth Amendment. The court cited a prior Supreme Court case holding that intellectual property interest deserved Fifth Amendment protection and finding a Tucker Act remedy even though disclosure of trade secret was a tort. Zoltek Corp. v. U.S., 58 Fed.Cl. 688, 705.

N.D.Ala.1987. Quot. in case quot. in sup., com. (b) quot. in case quot. in sup. A paper products salesman who had acquired knowledge of the needs of his employer's major customers, military installations contractors, resigned his position and immediately began employment with his for-

For earlier citations, see the Appendices, Supplements, or Pocket Parts, if any, that correspond to the subject matter under examination.

mer employer's competitor, where he solicited sales from the former employer's customers. The former employer sued the salesman to enforce the one-year written covenant not to compete he had signed. This court granted the plaintiff a preliminary injunction on the ground that the restrictive covenant was enforceable because the plaintiff had a legitimate interest in restraining the defendant from appropriating the plaintiff's valuable, confidential trade and customer information. Affiliated Paper Companies, Inc. v. Hughes, 667 F.Supp. 1436, 1446.

D.Ariz.2015. Cit. in case quot. in disc. Financial advisor and his insurance agency brought claims for, among other things, unfair competition against competitor and former agency employees who left to work for competitor, alleging that defendants committed computer fraud, trespass, conversion, and other illegal acts in an effort to gain an unfair competitive advantage over plaintiff. This court granted, with leave to amend, defendants' motion to dismiss plaintiffs' claim for unfair competition, holding that Arizona did not appear to recognize a common-law claim for unfair competition as alleged in plaintiffs' complaint. The court noted that, while the first Restatement of Torts §§ 757 and 759 enumerated several theories of liability for unfair competition, including disclosure or use of another's trade secret and improper acquisition of information to advance a rival business interest, the Arizona Supreme Court had held that the universal test for unfair competition was whether the public was likely to be confused. Joshua David Mellberg LLC v. Will, 96 F.Supp.3d 953, 961.

D.Ariz.2010. Com. (b) quot. in sup. and adopted in case cit. in sup. Patent holder sued competitor for infringement of its patent for the design of a motorized mini bike. This court granted defendant's motion to seal an exhibit—the license agreement between the parties—in its answer and complaint, holding that defendant made a sufficiently particularized showing of good cause to seal the document; the license agreement fell within the definition of a trade secret, because it contained information, such as the royalty rate charged to licensees and other terms and conditions of the license, that would have economic value to defendant's competitors, and that was not generally known by others or readily ascertainable by proper means. MMI, Inc. v. Baja, Inc., 743 F.Supp.2d 1101, 1106.

E.D.Ark.1994. Com. (b) quot. in part in case quot. in sup. (Erron. cit. as Restatement (Second) 1979.) Farm-supply business sued former manager, former employees, and new employer for misappropriation of trade secrets, among other claims, after manager left plaintiff, bringing with him his former co-workers to start business financed by new employer, and plaintiff's customers followed. The court entered judgment in defendants' favor on this claim, holding, inter alia, that state trade secrets act was plaintiff's exclusive remedy and that all information plaintiff contended was entitled to act's protection, including names of plaintiff's customers, was readily ascertainable. Vigoro Indus. v. Cleveland Chemical of Arkansas, 866 F.Supp. 1150, 1163.

N.D.Cal.2018. Com. (b) quot. in case quot. in sup. Consumers sued manufacturers of a soft drink, alleging that defendants defrauded California consumers by, among other things, marketing the drink as "Made from Real Ginger," when it was made with a ginger derivative known as ginger oleoresin, rather than with ginger root. This court granted in part defendants' administrative motion to seal certain documents, holding that there were compelling reasons sufficient to outweigh the public interest in disclosure to seal portions of the documents that discussed trade secrets or other confidential information. The court noted that the Ninth Circuit had adopted the definition of trade secrets set forth in Restatement of Torts § 757, and that, under the Federal Rules of Civil Procedure, courts had broad discretion to permit sealing of court documents for the protection of a trade secret or other confidential research, development, or commercial information. Fitzhenry-Russell v. Keurig Dr. Pepper Inc., 345 F.Supp.3d 1111, 1120.

N.D.Cal.1995. Com. (b) cit. in case quot. in disc. Nonprofit religious corporation sought preliminary injunction to prevent former Church of Scientology member from disseminating over the Internet copyrighted "course" materials for which corporation claimed an exclusive license. Corporation alleged that member's actions constituted copyright infringement and misappropriation of trade secrets. The court issued an injunction prohibiting member from posting copyrighted materi-

Cit.—cited; com.—comment; fol.—followed; sup.—support.
A complete list of abbreviations precedes page 1.

als, but held that corporation failed to show a likelihood of success on the merits of its trade-secret claim where, among other things, it did not define with particularity those aspects of the course materials it considered secret, and the materials at issue had already appeared on the Internet prior to member's posting. The court noted that as long as a religious organization took reasonable steps to protect the confidentiality of materials that gave it a competitive economic edge over others who did not possess them, the materials could not be denied trade-secret protection solely because of their religious nature. Religious Technology Center v. Netcom On-Line Com., 923 F.Supp. 1231, 1234, 1235, 1250-1253.

N.D.Cal.1993. Cit. in disc. and in ftn., cit. generally in disc., com. (a) quot. in sup. Texas company sued former employees in 1985, alleging that they had disclosed their trade secrets to California competitor. That suit was dismissed in 1986. In 1990, company sued same defendants on same theories. This court granted defendants summary judgment, holding that statute of limitations barred prosecution against these defendants of any claims arising out of or dependent on any alleged misappropriation of any of alleged trade secrets or confidential information reached by plaintiff's claims. Citing its prior ruling that California law applied to this case, the court rejected plaintiff's assertion that Texas law should determine whether to treat trade-secret claims as continuing wrongs. It noted its belief that Texas courts, which apply this Restatement section instead of Uniform Trade Secrets Act, also would reject "continuing wrong" theory because Restatement clearly rejects notion that interest protected by trade secret law is some species of "property." Intermedics v. Ventritex, Inc., 822 F.Supp. 634, 643, 644, 653.

S.D.Cal.1993. Com. (b) cit. in disc. (Erron. cit. as com. 6.) Religious organizations sued seller of course for copyright infringement and misappropriation of trade secrets. The court held that plaintiffs were entitled to judgment as a matter of law, since the undisputed evidence showed that defendant copied or directed her students to copy plaintiffs' copyrighted materials, which were the product of an author's creative thought processes, as part of a course that she offered for sale. The court granted plaintiffs' request for a permanent injunction and noted that the undisputed evidence showed that defendant's copying was not limited and spontaneous, but was extensive and methodical, and consisted of copying from the same author, time after time. Bridge Publications, Inc. v. Vien, 827 F.Supp. 629, 633.

S.D.Cal.1986. Com. (b) quot. and cit. in sup. A chemical company sought a preliminary injunction to prevent a competitor, which had hired two of the company's former employees, from producing, using, selling, or directly or indirectly licensing a foam product produced by the company's patented processes. The court issued the injunction pending trial, holding that the plaintiff had shown that it would suffer irreparable harm if the competitor was allowed to continue producing the foam product. The court said that the foam-producing processes were trade secrets that the competitor could have obtained only through the violation of the plaintiff's former employees' employment/confidentiality contracts. Imi-Tech Corp. v. Gagliani, 691 F.Supp. 214, 230, 231.

D.Colo.1993. Com. (b) quot. in case quot. in sup. Lumber wholesaler sued its competitor and a former employee, alleging theft of trade secrets and other claims after employee was hired away by competitor. Granting defendants' motion for summary judgment, this court held that plaintiff's mere conclusory allegation that it held a secret method of combining concepts and ideas for computerization of the lumber business, without more, did not establish issues of fact sufficient to defeat the summary judgment motion. Plaintiff offered no facts to suggest either that it had a protectible methodology for implementing the combination of concepts and ideas; that competitor appropriated any protected implementing methodology, rather than the unprotectable elements or functions common to both programs; or that competitor's resulting program was similar to plaintiff's in protected particulars. Former employee merely took to competitor his knowledge that certain databases and business techniques lend themselves to speedy customer service. Rivendell Forest Products v. Georgia-Pacific, 824 F.Supp. 961, 967, reversed 28 F.3d 1042 (10th Cir.1994).

D.Conn.2014. Quot. in ftn. Company that designed, manufactured, and supplied products for the military and aerospace

For earlier citations, see the Appendices, Supplements, or Pocket Parts, if any, that correspond to the subject matter under examination.

markets sued former employee, asserting claims for unfair competition and misappropriation of company's confidential information and trade secrets. Granting summary judgment for defendant, this court held, inter alia, that plaintiff's causes of action for unfair competition and misappropriation of trade secrets failed because the undisputed facts showed that defendant, even if he possessed any trade secrets (as defined in Restatement of Torts § 757), was not using, or unfairly competing with, that information; additionally, plaintiff failed to prove that it incurred damages. Amphenol Corp. v. Paul, 993 F.Supp.2d 100, 112.

D.Conn.1997. Com. (b) cit. in headnote, adopted in case cit. in ftn., and cit. and quot. in sup. (Erron. cit. as Restatement (Fourth) of Torts.) An employer sought a preliminary injunction against a former employee to prevent him from violating the noncompetition provision of his employment agreement and the provisions of a confidentiality agreement by commencing employment with employer's principal competitor. The court granted plaintiff's motion for a preliminary injunction, finding it likely that defendant would disclose plaintiff's trade secrets and other confidential information either intentionally or inadvertently in his position with plaintiff's competitor. Weseley Software Development Corp. v. Burdette, 977 F.Supp. 137, 138, 145.

D.Conn.1994. Subsec. (c) cit. in disc. Holder of a patent on electrical substrate material for printed circuit boards sued a competitor for infringement, and competitor counterclaimed. Plaintiff then instituted a second suit for misappropriation of trade secrets and other claims. Granting competitor's motion for summary judgment and denying plaintiff's motion for summary judgment as to issues presented in the second action, the court held, inter alia, that, as competitor had only disseminated alleged trade-secret information internally and not to any third party and as competitor had not used the information in any other way, competitor could not be held liable on a misappropriation basis. Rogers Corp. v. Arlon, Inc., 855 F.Supp. 560, 571.

D.Conn.1988. Com. (b) cit. in disc. (Erron. cit. as Restatement (Fourth).) An insurer sued its former agent, seeking a preliminary injunction to prevent the agent from misappropriating the insurer's trade secrets. This court held that the insurer was not entitled to a preliminary injunction requiring its former agent to return customer files in his possession and to stop misappropriating the insurer's trade secrets because there was no showing that the files and the information warranted protection where the employer had taken no special measures to limit access to the information and where it was arguable that the agent had a superior proprietary interest in the files. Nationwide Mut. Ins. Co. v. Stenger, 695 F.Supp. 688, 691.

D.Del.2015. Com. (b) quot. in case quot. in sup. Buyer of all of corporation's stock under a stock-purchase agreement sued sellers and others, alleging, among other things, that defendants misappropriated trade secrets contained in corporation's documents in order to form a competing business. After a bench trial, this court found in favor of defendants on plaintiff's claim for misappropriation of trade secrets, holding that plaintiff failed to show that the claimed documents were or contained trade secrets under New York law. The court noted that the definition of a trade secret set forth in Restatement of Torts § 757 had been cited with approval by New York courts, and that plaintiff did not present any evidence to show that the documents were trade secrets pursuant to the factors set forth in § 757. Enzo Life Sciences, Inc. v. Adipogen Corporation, 82 F.Supp.3d 568, 601.

D.Del.Bkrtcy.Ct.2018. Com. (b) quot. in case quot. in disc. Chapter 11 debtor filed an adversary complaint against former chief operations officer (COO) and her new employer, alleging that defendants used plaintiff's trade secrets and misappropriated information to steal plaintiff's customers and employees as part of a premeditated course of action that included having COO leave her employment with plaintiff to join new employer. This court granted in part and denied in part defendants' motion for summary judgment. The court noted that Missouri, the state with the most significant relationship to the claim, looked to Restatement of Torts § 757, Comment *b*, in defining "trade secret," and the court examined Missouri case law in reasoning that plaintiff's customer list did not constitute a "trade secret" under Missouri law, but that there were sufficient facts to support that the non-customer list materials could rise to level of "trade secrets." In re Patriot National Inc., 592 B.R. 560, 574.

Cit.—cited; com.—comment; fol.—followed; sup.—support.
A complete list of abbreviations precedes page 1.

D.Del.Bkrtcy.Ct.2002. Cit. but dist., com. (b) adopted in case cit. in disc. Debtor, which was in the business of providing rehabilitation and nursing services and personnel to healthcare facilities, sued to enjoin its former officers from using or disclosing any of debtor's confidential information or trade secrets. Granting in part debtor's motion for a preliminary injunction, this court held, inter alia, that debtor's business plan to provide temporary nursing staff to nursing homes nationwide was entitled to protection as a trade secret, since the business plan was a compilation of diverse information, like pricing, marketing, and customer information, contained information that was not in the public domain, and was kept confidential by debtor. In re Integrated Health Services, Inc., 281 B.R. 231, 237.

D.D.C.2019. Com. (b) quot. in case quot. in sup. Investment-research firm that purchased former employer's assets sued former employee who left firm soon after the acquisition to form a competing company, alleging that defendant breached his fiduciary duty by misusing plaintiff's proprietary information, including business cards that defendant obtained during his employment with former employer and plaintiff. This court denied in part defendant's motion for summary judgment, holding that, because defendant used the business cards to compete with plaintiff, questions of fact remained as to the ownership and status of the cards, and whether the cards were the equivalent of confidential customer lists that plaintiff acquired when it purchased former employer. The court noted that a question of fact also remained as to whether the cards were trade secrets under the factors set forth in Restatement of Torts § 757. Hedgeye Risk Management, LLC v. Heldman, 412 F.Supp.3d 15, 29.

D.D.C.Bkrtcy.Ct.1988. Cit. in disc., quot. in case quot. in disc., com. (b) quot. in disc. A Chapter 11 debtor brought an adversary proceeding to establish its proprietary interest in computer program enhancements it had developed through the use of private funds and to enjoin the government from misappropriating the enhancements in an alleged violation of the parties' licensing agreement. The court held, inter alia, that whether the developer's privately financed enhancements to a computer program that was itself in the public domain qualified as trade secrets and were protected from subsequent misappropriation was a question for the finder of fact. The court noted that software code constituted intellectual property that may be protected under trade-secret laws. The court defined a trade secret as any formula, pattern device or compilation of information that is used in one's business and that gives one an opportunity to obtain an advantage over competitors who do not know or use it. In re Inslaw, Inc., 83 B.R. 89, 158, 159, vacated 132 B.R. 808 (D.D.C. 1991).

M.D.Fla.1999. Subsec. (b) cit. generally in disc. Corporation that built boat ramps and that submitted a copy of a boat-ramp design to county for proposed use in two parks sued the county for an injunction and damages, alleging copyright and unfair competition and violation of the Uniform Trade Secrets Act after county used the design. This court granted defendant's motion for judgment on the pleadings as to the count under the Trade Secret Act, holding, inter alia, that, because the design was copyrighted, plaintiff lost all claims to a misappropriation of a trade secret. Tedder Boat Ramp Systems, Inc. v. Hillsborough County, Florida, 54 F.Supp.2d 1300, 1302.

M.D.Fla.1995. Com. (g) quot. in disc. Anheuser-Busch, a beer producer, sued A-B Distributors, its former beer distributor, for, among other claims, violation of the Lanham Act. This court denied plaintiff's motion for an injunction to stop defendant's post-termination use of plaintiff's trademarks, holding, inter alia, that defendant's use of "A-B" in its corporate name did not infringe on plaintiff's "A B" trademark, because there was no likelihood of confusion in the marketplace between the two marks. The court cited the lack of similarity between the marks "A B" and "A-B Distributors," as well as the lack of similarity of products, services, purchasers, or retail outlets, now that defendant was no longer in the beer distribution business. Furthermore, defendant presented evidence of extensive use of "A B" in businesses in the Jacksonville area alone. Anheuser-Busch, Inc. v. A-B Distributors, Inc., 910 F.Supp. 587, 593.

S.D.Fla.2006. Cit. in ftn. After competitor of pharmaceutical company hired private investigative agency to conduct a campaign of corporate espionage against company, company sued competitor and agency for misappropriation of trade secrets and other claims, seeking lost-profit damages. This court vacated a jury verdict awarding plaintiff nominal damages and, inter alia, granted judgment as a matter of law for agency, holding, in part, that plaintiff could not recover under Florida's codification of the Uniform Trade Secrets Act because it failed to present any evidence of damages. The court noted that proof of damages was also required in states where misappropriation of trade secrets was a common-law tort based on Restatement First of Torts § 757. Alphamed Pharmaceuticals Corp. v. Arriva Pharmaceuticals, Inc., 432 F.Supp.2d 1319, 1338.

S.D.Fla.1990. Quot. in disc., com. (b) quot. and cit. in disc. The plaintiff, a Florida corporation, offered a Massachusetts company the services of its resource system in issuing a secured credit card whereby the guaranteed cash surrender value of life insurance policies would be employed to secure credit-card debt. After the Massachusetts company engaged third parties to promote the system and denied the plaintiff's proprietary interest therein, the plaintiff sued the company, alleging, inter alia, unfair competition and fraud. This court denied the defendant's motion for summary judgment, holding that genuine issues of material fact existed as to whether the plaintiff had a trade secret in the resource system. The court indicated that the plaintiff's allegation that its creation of a method of securing credit-card debt constituted a trade secret was sufficient to establish a triable issue of fact on the issue. Default Proof Credit Card System v. State St. Bank, 753 F.Supp. 1566, 1571, 1573.

N.D.Ill.1998. Com. (b) quot. in disc. A manufacturer of telecommunications hardware brought suit seeking a declaratory judgment absolving it from any severance liability to a former president of one of the manufacturer's divisions. The former president counterclaimed for breach of contract, equitable estoppel, fraud, and bad-faith termination. This court denied the manufacturer's motion for a protective order for its proprietary business information, holding that the manufacturer failed to make the necessary showings for entry of a protective order. Although the manufacturer regarded nearly everything concerning its business as confidential and employed extensive security measures to protect the security of its office, the court found this evidence to constitute self-serving statements and could not determine whether the manufacturer's assertions were legitimate. Andrew Corp. v. Rossi, 180 F.R.D. 338, 341.

N.D.Ill.1990. Cit. generally in sup., com. (b) quot. in disc. and quot. in case quot. in disc. A printing-equipment business sued several competing businesses for violations of trade-secret laws, inter alia, alleging that the defendants had acquired and used secret drawings that contained the information necessary to duplicate machine parts. Granting the defendants' motion for summary judgment, the court held that, since the plaintiff failed to take reasonable security precautions to protect its drawings from disclosure to potential competitors who would use them to the plaintiff's disadvantage, the plaintiff could not establish that the drawings in the defendants' possession were secret. Rockwell Graphic System v. DEV Industries, 730 F.Supp. 171, 177, 178, judgment reversed 925 F.2d 174 (7th Cir.1991).

N.D.Ill.1988. Com. (b) quot. in case quot. in disc. A metal finishing company that did work for an airplane parts supplier on a chemical milling facility provided information to the supplier on its bid for a defense project subcontract. The finishing company brought this action for injunctive relief against the supplier, alleging that the supplier had wrongfully divulged the plaintiff's confidential, proprietary information and trade secrets to a competitor. This court denied the plaintiff's motion for a temporary restraining order barring the defendant from divulging certain information obtained during the course of the two projects, finding that it did not stand a reasonable chance of prevailing on the merits of any of its claims. Regarding the claim for misappropriation of confidential, proprietary information and trade secrets, this court held that the information in question did not rise to the level of a trade secret in light of uncontroverted evidence that the plaintiff did not treat the information confidentially, but rather freely divulged it to many of its employees as well as to individuals outside its business. Ecologix, Inc. v. Fansteel, Inc., 676 F.Supp. 1374, 1382.

N.D.Ind.1997. Com. (b) cit. in disc. A former employer sued its former employee and the employee's current employer for breach of a noncompetition agreement and moved for injunctive relief, arguing that it would suffer irreparable harm in the absence of a preliminary injunction because the disclosure of its trade secrets and other confidential information would prove damaging in the competitive market. Granting in part plaintiff's motion for a preliminary injunction to enforce the terms of the noncompetition agreement, the court held, inter alia, that the noncompetition agreement was enforceable to the extent reasonably necessary to protect plaintiff's confidential information. The court said that plaintiff failed to present sufficient evidence that defendants were utilizing or disclosing plaintiff's trade secrets. Ram Products Co., Inc. v. Chauncey, 967 F.Supp. 1071, 1087.

S.D.Ind.2001. Com. (b) quot. in case cit. in disc. Medical-device manufacturer sued competitor for patent infringement. Denying the parties' cross motions for protective orders covering trade secrets and other commercially sensitive information, the court held, inter alia, that plaintiff's proposed order failed to include any requirement that the competitive value of the information must have arisen from the information's secrecy, or that the designating party must have exerted reasonable efforts to maintain that secrecy. Cook Inc. v. Boston Scientific Corp., 206 F.R.D. 244, 248.

S.D.Ind.2001. Com. (b) quot. in ftn. Tobacco company sued state, alleging that statute enacted by general assembly violated equal protection, due process, compact, and commerce clauses of United States Constitution. Plaintiff moved for protective order to shield certain information from discovery by third parties. Finding plaintiff's proposed protective order overbroad, this court denied plaintiff's motion, but entered its own protective order, holding that plaintiff's sales and manufacturing information constituted protectible trade secrets. Star Scientific, Inc. v. Carter, 204 F.R.D. 410, 414.

S.D.Ind.1998. Com. (j) cit. in disc. Manufacturer/seller of oxygen regulators sued competitor for misappropriation of trade secrets. Denying plaintiff's request for injunctive relief, the court held, in part, that plaintiff did not show a likelihood of succeeding on the merits of its claim, as the information sought to be protected was readily ascertainable through reverse engineering of plaintiff's products, which had been on the market for some time; plaintiff failed to take reasonable steps to protect the confidentiality of the allegedly protected information; and defendant, to whom plaintiff once voluntarily disclosed the information at issue, never consented to keep it confidential. Flotec, Inc. v. Southern Research, Inc., 16 F.Supp.2d 992, 1006.

N.D.Iowa, 2006. Com. (b) cit. in case cit. in disc. After former employee quit to work for competitor, manufacturer of ice cream sandwich wafers sued employee and competitor for, in part, misappropriation of trade secrets. This court granted in part plaintiff's motion for a preliminary injunction against defendants, holding, inter alia, at least provisionally, that plaintiff's recipes and manufacturing processes, with respect to ice cream sandwich wafers, constituted "trade secrets" within the meaning of Iowa's Uniform Trade Secrets Act. The court pointed out, in regard to the requirement of "derived economic value," that the entirety of plaintiff's manufacturing process gave it a unique and unrivaled competitive advantage in the marketplace as evidenced by its almost 95% market share, and that defendant's CEO and president had conceded that the formulas used in the process were valuable. Interbake Foods, L.L.C. v. Tomasiello, 461 F.Supp.2d 943, 963.

N.D.Iowa, 1998. Com. (b) quot. in case cit. in disc. Insurance agent and his agency sued insurers for breach of contract, intentional interference with plaintiffs' contracts with manufacturer association groups, fraudulent misrepresentation, and misappropriation of trade secrets after termination of cooperative effort to market recreational vehicle insurance. The jury entered a verdict for plaintiffs. This court denied in part defendants' motion for judgment as a matter of law or for a new trial. The court held, inter alia, that a reasonable jury could have found that defendants misappropriated marketing information and other business information constituting trade secrets that had independent economic value, and that plaintiffs kept the information secret to an extent that was reasonable under the circumstances. S & W Agency, Inc. v. Foremost Insurance Company, 51 F.Supp.2d 959, 977.

N.D.Iowa, 1996. Com. (b) cit. in case cit. in disc. Bagel manufacturer sought preliminary injunction to prevent former employee from disclosing trade secrets concerning manufacturer's recipes, production,

For earlier citations, see the Appendices, Supplements, or Pocket Parts, if any, that correspond to the subject matter under examination.

and packaging for its "fresh, never-frozen" line of bagels. Manufacturer alleged, among other things, that former employee misappropriated the trade secrets in violation of the nondisclosure/noncompete agreement that all employees were required to sign. Issuing the injunction, the court held that the information at issue constituted a trade secret because its economic value derived from the fact that it was not readily ascertainable by competitors and because manufacturer made reasonable efforts to maintain its confidentiality; that manufacturer would likely suffer irreparable harm if the injunction did not issue; the balance of harms tilted in favor of issuance; and that the public interest was served by protecting trade secrets. Uncle B's Bakery, Inc. v. O'Rourke, 920 F.Supp. 1405, 1426.

S.D.Iowa, 2008. Com. (b) quot. in case quot. in disc. Advertising company sued television broadcasters for trade-secret misappropriation, among other claims, after defendants discontinued use of plaintiff's services, yet allegedly continued using plaintiff's advertising methods. Granting defendants' motion for summary judgment, this court found that plaintiff's assertion that its trade secrets were not the items provided to prospective clients—the prices, brochures, or market determinations themselves—but rather the methods, i.e., the "how" and the "why" used to determine those prices, markets, layouts, and language to create an effective campaign, was simply too ephemeral to qualify for trade-secret protection. Sun Media Systems, Inc. v. KDSM, LLC, 564 F.Supp.2d 946, 972.

D.Kan.2001. Cit. in disc., cit. in case cit. in disc. Aircraft navigational instrument provider sued competitor for Lanham Act violations and unfair competition, among other claims, alleging that defendant improperly obtained plaintiff's trade secrets, altered documents to misrepresent the Federal Aviation Administration's position on plaintiff's products, and provided the altered documents to plaintiff's customers. This court overruled defendant's motion to dismiss plaintiff's unfair-competition claim, predicting that the Kansas Supreme Court would apply the general principles outlined in the Restatement (Third) of Unfair Competition and allow an unfair-competition claim based on misuse of trade secrets and other confidential business information. Airport Systems Intern., Inc. v. Airsys ATM, Inc., 144 F.Supp.2d 1268, 1270.

D.Kan.2001. Cit. in ftn. Buyers of Mexican restaurant sued sellers' daughter, who had opened a similar restaurant across the alley from their restaurant, alleging, in part, that defendant misappropriated plaintiffs' trade secrets by hiring away two of plaintiffs' cooks. Granting in part defendant's motion for summary judgment, this court held, inter alia, that plaintiffs could not obtain through a tort theory of trade-secret misappropriation what they could not have obtained through a preemployment covenant not to compete, which the Kansas courts would have struck down as unreasonable because too general, with no limitation as to time or geographic area, and which in effect would have prevented the cooks from working in the Mexican-restaurant industry. Vasquez v. Ybarra, 150 F.Supp.2d 1157, 1173.

D.Kan.2000. Cit. in ftn. Wholesale and retail sellers of fireworks sued former employee and his competing business for, in part, misappropriation of trade secrets, seeking to enjoin defendants from using plaintiffs' customer lists. Granting plaintiffs' motion for a preliminary injunction, the court held, inter alia, that plaintiffs showed a substantial likelihood of success on the merits with respect to their trade-secrets claim, since it was undisputed that plaintiffs expended a great deal of time, effort, and expense in developing the lists, the evidence showed that the lists gave plaintiffs a competitive advantage in the fireworks industry, and former employee was aware that it was plaintiffs' policy to keep the lists secret. Fireworks Spectacular v. Premier Pyrotechnics, 86 F.Supp.2d 1102, 1106.

E.D.La.1987. Com. (b) cit. in disc. An inventor sued a motorcycle manufacturer for misappropriation of trade secrets and unjust enrichment after the manufacturer used the inventor's idea to correct a defect in the motorcycle's air-intake system. This court granted the defendant's motion for involuntary dismissal, holding that the plaintiff did not establish that the device was a trade secret. The court noted that the plaintiff took no precautions to preserve the secrecy of the device, to reserve any economic or other benefit from the device, or to prevent its use by others. Nevertheless, the court found that the plaintiff was entitled to sanctions against the defendant because the defendant had acted both negligently and in bad faith in needlessly increasing the costs of litigation and in failing to cooperate in pretrial discovery. Sheets v. Yamaha Motors Corp., U.S.A., 657 F.Supp. 319, 327, affirmed in part, remanded in part 849 F.2d 179 (5th Cir.1988).

D.Me.2004. Com. (e) cit. in sup. Developer of automated trading program sued custom software company and its owner for misappropriating its trade secret and violating the parties' nondisclosure agreement. After the jury returned a verdict against defendant owner, plaintiff moved for injunctive relief, seeking, in part, to permanently enjoin defendant from all programming of any automated trading systems. Granting in part plaintiff's motion, the court held, inter alia, that plaintiff was entitled to an injunction prohibiting defendant from using plaintiff's computer program or its concepts; however, an injunction barring defendant from all programming of automated trading systems was broader than the terms of the nondisclosure agreement and was not warranted. Pearl Investments, LLC v. Standard I/O, Inc., 297 F.Supp.2d 335, 337.

D.Me.2004. Com. (b) cit. in disc. and cit. generally in disc. Trade association for pharmaceutical-benefits-management companies sued state attorney general, seeking preliminary injunction against enforcement of new statute that regulated the benefits-management industry. Association alleged that enforcement was preempted by Employee Retirement Income Security Act, would constitute an unlawful taking of trade secrets, and violated the commerce clause. Granting the injunction, this court found, inter alia, that the statute required companies to disclose trade secrets, specifically, certain confidential information that derived independent economic value from not being readily available to the public, such as the companies' contract terms with drug suppliers and pharmacies. Pharmaceutical Care Management Ass'n v. Rowe, 307 F.Supp.2d 164, 177, 178.

D.Md.2020. Com. (b) cit. in case cit. in sup. Developer of senior-living community sued former employees, alleging that defendants misappropriated plaintiff's trade secrets and engaged in unfair competition when they downloaded plaintiff's confidential heat maps, pricing sheets, and underwritings during their employment and used them to create a competing business. This court granted plaintiff's motion for preliminary injunction, holding that plaintiff established the likelihood of success on the merits of its claims, because it provided sufficient evidence that the misappropriated information constituted trade secrets. The court examined the factors set forth in Restatement of Torts § 757, Comment *b*, in determining that the underwritings constituted trade secrets, and observed that the information was not disseminated outside of plaintiff's business, only a select number of plaintiff's employees had access to them, and their disclosure to outsiders would result in plaintiff's proprietary formulas and data being used by competitors to improve their own underwriting tools and better predict financial success. Brightview Group, LP v. Teeters, 441 F.Supp.3d 115, 129.

D.Md.2013. Com. (b) quot. in case quot. in sup. Contractor sued former employees who had engaged in a competing business venture after being terminated by plaintiff, alleging, among other things, that defendants misappropriated plaintiff's "pricing structure, pricing knowledge and research, and established customer relationships" in violation of the Maryland Uniform Trade Secrets Act. Granting in part defendants' motion to dismiss, this court held that the complaint lacked sufficient factual allegations and clarity to present a plausible claim that the information relied upon was protectable as a trade secret under the Act. The court reasoned that it was unclear what the term "established customer relationships" meant and how such relationships were plausibly construed as a trade secret; moreover, the complaint did not allege facts upon which a reasonable inference could be drawn that the claimed trade secrets held independent economic value because such information was not generally known to or readily ascertainable by others in the relevant business. Structural Preservation Systems, LLC v. Andrews, 931 F.Supp.2d 667, 679.

D.Md.2007. Com. (b) cit. in case cit. in sup. (general cite). Franchisor of lawn-care services brought various claims against former franchisees for allegedly using franchisor's confidential information and trade secrets in the operation of a competing business. Granting plaintiff's motion for a preliminary injunction, this court held, inter alia, that plaintiff's customer lists were trade secrets. The court pointed out that the information on the lists was not widely known by individuals other than plaintiff's employees and franchisees, that the franchise agreements specifically provided for return of the lists on termination of the agreements, that the lists were potentially valuable to competitors such as former franchisees, and that plaintiff developed the lists over time. NaturaLawn of America, Inc. v. West Group, LLC, 484 F.Supp.2d 392, 399.

D.Md.2004. Cit. generally in disc. Military-style private school sued school's former principal and Internet-based university, alleging, in part, that former principal violated the Maryland Uniform Trade Secrets Act by using proprietary information to complete doctoral program offered by university. Denying in part university's motion to dismiss, the court held, inter alia, that a genuine issue of material fact existed as to whether university misappropriated plaintiff's trade secrets. Role Models America, Inc. v. Jones, 305 F.Supp.2d 564, 568.

D.Md.2001. Com. (b) cit. in case quot. in disc. Seller of petroleum-refining technology sued buyer and buyer's parent for, in part, misappropriation of trade secrets in connection with their transfer of the technology to a sister corporation. Granting in part defendants' motion for summary judgment, the court held, inter alia, that plaintiff's misappropriation claim failed because plaintiff produced no evidence that the technology qualified as a trade secret under the Maryland Uniform Trade Secrets Act, that it took any reasonable steps to ensure the secrecy of the technology, or that the transfer was improper. Contracts Materials Processing, Inc. v. Kataleuna GmbH Catalysts, 164 F.Supp.2d 520, 533.

D.Md.2001. Com. (a) cit. in case quot. in disc. Real-estate listing service sued operator of web-site on which brokers could post listings of commercial real estate available for lease, alleging copyright infringement of over 300 of its photographs and asserting state-law claims for, in part, unfair competition, unjust enrichment, and tortious interference with business relations. Granting in part defendant's motion to dismiss, the court held, inter alia, that plaintiff's state-law claims were preempted by the Copyright Act because they required no additional elements of proof beyond those necessary to recover for copyright infringement. The court said that the Copyright Act did not preempt trade-secret misappropriation claims, for example, because such claims required proof of improper means, which was an additional element of proof. Costar Group Inc. v. Loopnet, Inc., 164 F.Supp.2d 688, 713, judgment affirmed 373 F.3d 544 (4th Cir.2004).

D.Md.2000. Cit. generally in disc. Parent of chemical distributor sued manufacturer of product for, inter alia, misappropriation of trade secrets, alleging that defendant disclosed a list of distributor's customers to one of distributor's competitors. Entering summary judgment for defendant on this count, the court held, in part, that the information revealed was easily obtainable, and therefore could not be said to amount to a trade secret. Home Paramount Pest v. FMC Corp./Agr. Products, 107 F.Supp.2d 684, 692.

D.Md.1987. Quot. in disc. A woman who contracted pelvic inflammatory disease from her use of an IUD sued the manufacturer of the IUD on theories of negligence, strict liability, and fraudulent misrepresentation. The manufacturer refused to produce without a protective order transcripts of depositions from similar litigation and clinical studies, claiming that the documents were trade secrets. The court denied the manufacturer's motion for a protective order and ordered production of the requested documents, holding that the manufacturer had failed to establish that they were trade secrets. The court stated that the manufacturer merely claimed the documents' confidential nature and did not explain why they were confidential. The court, however, entered an interim protective order pending the manufacturer's appeal so that discovery could proceed. Deford v. Schmid Products Co., 120 F.R.D. 648, 653.

D.Md.Bkrtcy.Ct.2010. Com. (b) quot. in ftn. Biomedical equipment company brought adversary proceeding against Chapter 7 debtor, alleging that debtor, while employed by company as its regional manager, wrongfully diverted business to plaintiff's competitor and violated his duties under the parties' employment agreements by using confidential information, including trade secrets, other than in the service of employer. This court entered a nondischargeable judgment in favor of plaintiff in the amount of debtor's salary for the years that he had diverted plaintiff's business, holding, among other things, that while it would hold debtor liable for his misuse of plaintiff's proprietary informa-

Cit.—cited; com.—comment; fol.—followed; sup.—support.
A complete list of abbreviations precedes page 1.

tion, such information did not amount to trade secrets. In re Janssens, 449 B.R. 42, 71.

D.Mass.2017. Com. (b) cit. in case quot. in sup. Software developer sued former employee and his new company, alleging that defendants misappropriated plaintiff's trade secrets related to certain software. This court denied defendants' motion for summary judgment, holding that a reasonable jury could find that defendants misappropriated trade secrets from plaintiff and either used or attempted to use the secrets in its competing software product. The court noted that Massachusetts law and Restatement of Torts § 757 defined a trade secret as any formula, pattern, device, or compilation of information that was used in a party's business and that gave the party an opportunity to obtain an advantage over competitors who did not know or use it. Iconics, Inc. v. Massaro, 266 F.Supp.3d 449, 452.

D.Mass.2017. Com. (b) quot. in disc. (erron. cit. as Restatement Second § 727). Seller of custom quilts and pillows made from customers' t-shirts sued, among others, video production and advertising company that it hired to make videos for its website, alleging that defendants stole plaintiff's trade secrets, including its e-commerce marketing strategies. Granting summary judgment for defendants, this court held that, while marketing strategies could potentially attain trade-secret status under Restatement of Torts § 757, plaintiff failed to show that it took affirmative steps to preserve the secrecy of the information from defendants, that defendants actually used or disclosed plaintiff's trade secrets, or that plaintiff suffered damages as a result of defendants' use of its trade secrets in the form of loss in sales or a drop in revenue or market share. Repat, Inc. v. Indie-Whip, LLC, 281 F.Supp.3d 221, 227.

D.Mass.2014. Com. (b) quot. in case quot. in sup. Pharmaceutical company brought an action for, inter alia, false advertising under the Lanham Act against competitor; defendant counterclaimed for misappropriation of trade secrets, alleging that plaintiff misappropriated an undisclosed number of pages of defendant's training materials and the trade secrets contained therein. Granting in part plaintiff's motion to dismiss defendant's counterclaim, this court held that defendant failed to state a claim for misappropriation of trade secrets, because, while the materials at issue contained some information about defendant's marketing strategy, that information was not protected by Massachusetts law. The court relied on caselaw quoting Restatement of Torts § 757, Comment *b*, which provided that matters of public knowledge or general knowledge in an industry were not trade secrets, in determining that the training materials that defendant admitted as evidence contained publicly available information about defendant's pharmaceutical products, not trade secrets. Ferring Pharmaceuticals Inc. v. Braintree Laboratories, Inc., 38 F.Supp.3d 169, 175.

D.Mass.2012. Com. (b) quot. in case quot. in sup. Coin collector who claimed to have invented a new method to grade the "eye appeal" of coins sued coin-grading service and service's competitor, alleging that defendants misappropriated his trade-secret grading system after he approached them to promote his system. Granting in part and denying in part defendants' motion to dismiss plaintiff's misappropriation claim, this court held, inter alia, that plaintiff did not take reasonable steps to maintain the secrecy of his grading system, but rather, published articles about the system that were available to the public, and, while plaintiff allegedly did not disclose the entirety of his system to defendants, he did not describe with sufficient particularity which portion remained a trade secret at the time it was disclosed. Blake v. Professional Coin Grading Service, 898 F.Supp.2d 365, 393.

D.Mass.2011. Com. (b) quot. in case quot. in sup. Company sued competitor for, inter alia, theft of trade secrets, alleging that company's former employee gave competitor information about company's customers, which competitor used to further its business. This court granted plaintiff's motion for a preliminary injunction to prevent dissemination of any allegedly proprietary information. The court reasoned, in part, that plaintiff would likely establish that its customer list was a trade secret, despite defendant's assertion that, because customers' contact information was available on plaintiff's website, the information in the list was a matter of public knowledge. The court pointed out that the list, which included specific contractual, financial, and service request information pertaining to 3500 customers, was acquired at considerable cost, and not known in its entirety

For earlier citations, see the Appendices, Supplements, or Pocket Parts, if any, that correspond to the subject matter under examination.

outside of plaintiff, and defendant's claim that it could have obtained this information through individual phone calls to each customer was highly doubtful. Optos, Inc. v. Topcon Medical Systems, Inc., 777 F.Supp.2d 217, 238, 239.

D.Mass.2007. Com. (b) cit. in ftn. (general cite). Software developer sued competitor for, in part, trade-secret violation, alleging that competitor wrongfully stole and incorporated developer's software into its own product. Allowing in part defendant's motion to dismiss, this court held, inter alia, that plaintiff's trade-secret-violation claim failed because plaintiff did not allege that the relevant trade secret was in continuous use, as required by Massachusetts law. The court noted that the continuous-use requirement was adopted from the first Restatement of Torts, and that, whatever its wisdom, it was part of Massachusetts law, and this court was powerless to remove it. Portfolioscope, Inc. v. I-Flex Solutions Ltd., 473 F.Supp.2d 252, 255.

D.Mass.2004. Quot. in case quot. in sup. (Erron. cit. as Rest. Second of Torts § 727.) Software company sued former customer, alleging that defendant misappropriated design of plaintiff's software package in violation of trade-secret law. This court allowed in part plaintiff's motion for preliminary injunction, holding that there was substantial likelihood that plaintiff could prove existence of trade secret. The court said that it was easy to discern nature of the trade secret, the product's design gave plaintiff a distinct competitive advantage not possessed by competitors, and while defendant was developing similar technology, it did not possess mature design that plaintiff offered. TouchPoint Solutions, Inc. v. Eastman Kodak Co., 345 F.Supp.2d 23, 27-28.

D.Mass.2001. Cit. in disc., cit. in case quot. in disc.; com. (b) cit. in sup., quot. in disc., and quot. in case quot. in disc.; com. (j) quot. in disc. (cit. as com. on clause b). Medical-pump manufacturer brought suit for, in part, misappropriation of trade secrets against former employee who developed a competing line of medical pumps. Denying defendant's motion for summary judgment, the court held, inter alia, that genuine issues of material fact existed as to whether the source code for plaintiff's pump was a trade secret, and whether defendant used the source code in breach of the confidence reposed in him. Harvard Apparatus, Inc. v. Cowen, 130 F.Supp.2d 161, 174-177.

D.Mass.2000. Com. (b) cit. and quot. in sup. Tobacco companies sought to enjoin state from enforcing the Disclosure Act, under which plaintiffs would be compelled to list the additional ingredients in their cigarettes and smokeless tobacco products, arguing, among other things, that the effect of enforcement would be a taking of their private property without just compensation. Entering summary judgment for plaintiffs, the court held, in part, that compliance with the Act would force plaintiffs to disclose trade secrets of real economic value, thereby depriving them of a significant property interest and amounting to an unconstitutional taking. Phillip Morris Inc. v. Reilly, 113 F.Supp.2d 129, 135, 136, judgment reversed 267 F.3d 45 (1st Cir.2001), judgment affirmed 312 F.3d 24 (1st Cir.2002).

D.Mass.1999. Cit. generally in ftn., com. (b) quot. in case cit. in disc. Manufacturer of X-ray equipment used to detect contraband sued competitor, among others, for misappropriation of trade secrets, inter alia, seeking to enjoin defendant from performing a government contract allegedly secured as a result of defendant's tortious conduct. Denying the motion for injunctive relief, the court held, in part, that plaintiff had failed to establish that the backscatter technology it sought to protect constituted a trade secret. American Science and Engineering, Inc. v. Kelly, 69 F.Supp.2d 227, 238, 239.

D.Mass.1999. Com. (b) quot. in case quot. in disc. An inventor sued two corporations for trademark infringement and trade-secret misappropriation, among other claims, alleging that defendants expropriated plaintiff's idea for a dual-protection product to screen children and adults from harmful ultraviolet sunlight and insects. This court granted in part and denied in part defendants' motion to dismiss, holding, inter alia, that even though plaintiff adequately alleged that he took reasonable steps to preserve the product's confidentiality in the negotiations with defendants, these precautions could not restore the product's secret status. Swartz v. Schering-Plough Corporation, 53 F.Supp.2d 95, 100.

D.Mass.1997. Cit. in ftn. Manufacturer of system that used a specialized hose for removing sludge deposits in nuclear boilers

Cit.—cited; com.—comment; fol.—followed; sup.—support.
A complete list of abbreviations precedes page 1.

sued competitor for, inter alia, misappropriation of trade secrets. Competitor moved for summary judgment. Denying the motion, the court held, in part, that material factual issues existed as to whether the components of manufacturer's hose type and design were either in the public domain or were obvious extensions of known technology. Foster-Miller, Inc. v. Babcock & Wilcox Canada, 975 F.Supp. 30, 35.

D.Mass.1997. Com. (b) cit. in case quot. in sup. Football coach who developed foam ball for use in training exercises sued sporting goods manufacturer for, inter alia, misappropriation of trade secrets after the parties' attempts to establish a joint business venture failed and defendant proceeded to market the device on its own. Defendant moved for summary judgment. Granting the motion in part and denying it in part, the court held that recovery under a theory of misappropriation of trade secrets was precluded where there was no confidential relationship between the parties, and where the information sought to be protected was in the public domain and thus could not be considered a trade secret; however, material factual issues existed as to whether defendant was unjustly enriched as a result of having allegedly feigned interest in plaintiff's proposal in order to induce plaintiff to provide it with free marketing advice. Moore v. Marty Gilman, Inc., 965 F.Supp. 203, 217.

D.Mass.1995. Cit. in headnotes, quot. and cit. in sup., com. (b) cit. in disc. and sup. In action for misappropriation of trade secrets, manufacturer of computed tomography (CT) scanners sought to enjoin competitor from using in its CT scanner servicing business materials improperly acquired or stolen from manufacturer. Issuing the injunction, the court held that manufacturer's diagnostic software, service handbooks and manuals, and training materials constituted proprietary information entitled to trade secret protection; that materials to which competitor's principal had access as a trainee of manufacturer did not lose their protection; that competitor's unauthorized use of software and related documents received from former employee of manufacturer in violation of his noncompete agreement amounted to misappropriation; and that competitor's use of confidential service manuals kept on site with manufacturer's customers constituted conversion. Picker Intern. Corp. v. Imaging Equipment Services, Inc., 931 F.Supp. 18, 18-21, 23, 35, 38, 40, 42, 43, affirmed 94 F.3d 640 (1st Cir.1996).

D.Mass.1993. Com. (b) quot. in part in cases quot. in sup. A computer manufacturer sued its competitor, alleging misappropriation of trade secrets and other claims. This court, disposing of post-trial motions after awarding damages to plaintiff manufacturer, held, inter alia, that sufficient evidence supported the jury's conclusion that a diagnostic software program used to service and maintain certain computers was a trade secret under Massachusetts law. Several witnesses, including two defense witnesses, testified that the software contained trade secrets, and the evidence, said the court, showed that the software was unique, effective, and conferred a competitive advantage to the plaintiff manufacturer in the computer service business. Furthermore, plaintiff sufficiently proved that defendant knowingly misappropriated the program, since there was credible evidence from which the jury could infer that defendant obtained the program by taking property known to belong to another or by knowingly participating in the breach of an express or implied confidentiality agreement by, for example, a former employee or customer of plaintiff. Data General Corp. v. Grumman Systems Support Corp., 825 F.Supp. 340, 359, 360, remanded in part 36 F.3d 1147 (1st Cir.1994).

D.Mass.1992. Quot. in sup. A computer repair services provider sued competitor for copyright infringement, pursuant to federal copyright laws, after defendant allegedly used and copied software developed by plaintiff for use in diagnosing computer problems. Plaintiff also alleged several state law claims, including conversion and misappropriation of trade secrets. Denying defendant's motion for partial summary judgment on the statutory and common law counts for trade-secret misappropriation, this court held, inter alia, that the evidence was sufficiently ambiguous to preclude summary judgment, and that, since the claim was premised in part on the alleged wrongful acquisition or retention of trade secrets, the claim was not preempted by federal copyright law. The court noted that plaintiff argued its trade secrets were wrongfully retained by former employees and customers in violation of their duties of confidentiality to plaintiff, that defendant knew software's contents were trade secrets, and that defendant knowingly benefited from the wrongful conduct by acquiring, possessing, and using the software. Data General v. Grumman Systems Support Corp., 795 F.Supp. 501, 507, motion denied 803 F.Supp. 487 (D.Mass.1992).

E.D.Mich.2012. Com. (a) cit. in ftn., com. (b) quot. in case cit. in sup. Provider of software for companies in the security-alarm industry sued competitor, alleging, inter alia, that defendant violated the Michigan Uniform Trade Secrets Act by accessing plaintiff's servers and stealing its software. Granting summary judgment for defendant, this court held that plaintiff's trade-secret-misappropriation claim failed because plaintiff established none of the three elements required to prove its claim. The court concluded that the information at issue was not a trade secret, in that the pertinent data file was not kept secret from plaintiff's customers, and, moreover, the relevant information in that file belonged to a former customer of plaintiff; the information was not copied or otherwise acquired by defendant; and there was no evidence that plaintiff made any unauthorized use of plaintiff's trade secrets. Dice Corp. v. Bold Technologies, 913 F.Supp.2d 389, 406.

E.D.Mich.2012. Com. (b) quot. in case quot. in sup. Manufacturers of polysilicon products, including trichlorosilane, brought an action for misappropriation of trade secrets against competitor, alleging that defendant misappropriated plaintiffs' trade secrets regarding "first generation" fluid bed reactor technology and used the secrets in multi-million dollar contracts with foreign firms. This court denied defendant's motion to compel plaintiff to disclose its trade secrets regarding subsequent generations of the technology, holding that defendant did not carry its burden of establishing that the information sought was necessary. The court explained that a later generation of a technology did not necessarily render a prior generation obsolete and unprotectable for lack of economic value, because the value of information contained in a trade secret associated with a prior generation depended on how much someone was willing to pay for it; in addition, trade-secret law did not require a plaintiff to show that technology was "optimal" in order for it to be protected, but merely that it was valuable to the plaintiff and its competitors. Dow Corning Corp. v. Jie Xiao, 283 F.R.D. 353, 357, 358.

E.D.Mich.2006. Com. (b) quot. in ftn. Securities-investment brokerage firm sued former employee who, after resigning, solicited firm's clients whom he had serviced, alleging, in part, that its customer lists were a trade secret. Denying plaintiff's motion for a preliminary injunction, this court held, inter alia, that plaintiff was not likely to succeed on the merits of its claim for misappropriation of trade secrets. The court stated that the customer lists were not entitled to trade-secret protection; although plaintiff claimed to protect the secrecy of this information by keeping it in a password-protected database and requiring employees to maintain its confidentiality, the goal of secrecy was defeated by plaintiff's practice of allowing its brokers to maintain posting pages that contained the same information, yet were the broker's property that broker was free to take with him when he departed from the firm. Raymond James & Associates, Inc. v. Leonard & Co., 411 F.Supp.2d 689, 695.

E.D.Mich.2001. Com. (b) quot. in case quot. in disc. Developer of computer software for building-construction industry sued former employee and his current employer for, in part, misappropriation of trade secrets, after employee resigned and removed certain information from his workplace computer, including a database of customer leads. Granting in part defendants' motion for summary judgment, the court held, inter alia, that although a question of fact existed as to whether the database of customer leads contained trade-secret information, plaintiff's claim failed because there was no evidence that defendants actually used any of plaintiff's trade secrets. Electronic Planroom, Inc. v. McGraw-Hill Companies, Inc., 135 F.Supp.2d 805, 819.

E.D.Mich.2000. Com. (b) quot. in case quot. in disc. Developer of metal-flake formulas for quick-drying nail polish sued cosmetics company, among others, for, in part, breach of their confidentiality agreement. Granting summary judgment for defendant, this court held, inter alia, that plaintiff's use of "public domain" information in its formulas and its widespread dissemination of its formulas defeated its claims of confidentiality under the parties' agreement. Rainbow Nails Enterprises v. Maybelline, Inc., 93 F.Supp.2d 808, 827.

E.D.Mich.1999. Com. (b) quot. in case cit. in sup., quot. in ftn., and cit. generally in disc. Software user moved for reconsideration of district court's denial of its motion for summary judgment on software owner's claim of trade-secret misappropriation. Denying the motion for reconsideration, this court held, inter alia, that owner's submission of unredacted copies of its user manuals to the United States Copyright Office did not constitute a publication that undermined its claim of secrecy as a matter of law; therefore, neither an error of law nor any palpable defect existed that would warrant reconsideration of the court's order. Compuware Corp. v. Serena Software Intern., Inc., 77 F.Supp.2d 816, 820-822.

E.D.Mich.1999. Com. (b) quot. in case quot. in disc. Manufacturer of mineral-insulated cable sued competitor and individual defendants who were plaintiff's former employees, alleging misappropriation of trade secrets. Granting defendants' motion for summary judgment, this court held that plaintiff failed to establish that the information that would inevitably be disclosed was peculiar to plaintiff's own business, and not generally known in the industry. Hoskins Manufacturing Co. v. PMC Corp., 47 F.Supp.2d 852, 857.

E.D.Mich.1998. Com. (b) cit. in ftn. Patentees of gravity-flow sand-reclamation system sued competitors for patent infringement. Plaintiffs also contended that defendants, with whom contract negotiations had fallen through, engaged in unfair competition by utilizing various proprietary materials and information furnished by plaintiffs during the negotiations period. Entering summary judgment for defendants, the court held, in part, that federal patent infringement laws were inapplicable where the accused activities took place outside the United States. Furthermore, the unfair competition claim, which was more correctly termed an action for misappropriation of trade secrets, failed, since plaintiffs were unable to show that defendants actually used plaintiffs' alleged proprietary information. Rothschild v. Ford Motor Co., 2 F.Supp.2d 941, 950.

W.D.Mich.2008. Cit. in case quot. in disc. (erron. cit. as Restatement 2d). Railcar-maintenance company sued its former employee, alleging that defendant provided a competitor with plaintiff's confidential and proprietary information—including its internal bid and pricing information—for use in undercutting plaintiff in its bid on a maintenance contract. Granting in part and denying in part defendant's motion for summary judgment, this court held that, while a genuine issue existed as to whether defendant sent confidential internal bid and pricing information to competitor, such information constituted a trade secret under the circumstances, and thus the Michigan Uniform Trade Secrets Act (MUTSA) applied and preempted plaintiff's claim for breach of the common-law duty of confidentiality as to that particular disclosure; MUTSA did not, however, preempt plaintiff's claim for breach of defendant's contractual duty of confidentiality. Appalachian Railcar Services, Inc. v. Boatright Enterprises, Inc., 602 F.Supp.2d 829, 852.

E.D.Mo.2021. Com. (a) quot. in case quot. in sup. Entities that owned deceased political figure's intellectual property and publicity rights sued decedent's daughter and others, alleging that defendants infringed and misappropriated decedent's information by copying it from plaintiffs' database without permission and using it to promote their own activities. This court denied in part defendants' motion to dismiss, holding that plaintiffs' allegations were sufficient to state a claim for misappropriation of a trade secret. The court cited Restatement of Torts § 757 in explaining that neither the lack of confidentiality agreements for employees with access to the database nor the fact that decedent's son—who wrote the source code and application software that allowed plaintiffs to manage the database, but was not an employee of plaintiffs—had access to the database showed as a matter of law that plaintiffs failed to take reasonable steps to keep the contents of the database secret. Phyllis Schlafly Revocable Trust v. Cori, 512 F.Supp.3d 916, 932.

E.D.Mo.2004. Com. (a) quot. in case quot. in disc. Computer-software developer sued licensee and third party after licensee allowed third party to copy and download software that plaintiff designed specifically for licensee's exclusive use. Denying in part defendants' motions to dismiss, the court held that plaintiff's claim for misappropriation of trade secrets was not preempted by the Federal Copyright Act, in order for plaintiff to succeed on the merits, he would have to prove under state law that the software was a trade secret misappropriated by the third party from licensee, and

For earlier citations, see the Appendices, Supplements, or Pocket Parts, if any, that correspond to the subject matter under examination.

that the licensee had a duty to maintain the secret and limit its use. Because such elements were qualitatively different than the unauthorized copying necessary to establish federal copyright infringement, the claim was remanded to state court for lack of subject-matter jurisdiction. Huckshold v. HSSL, L.L.C., 344 F.Supp.2d 1203, 1209.

E.D.Mo.2001. Subsec. (a) cit. in disc. British corporation sued Chinese company, alleging that defendant wrongfully acquired plaintiff's trade secrets and incorporated them into an acid plant in China. This court granted defendant's motion to dismiss, holding, inter alia, that defendant was immune from suit under the Foreign Sovereign Immunities Act (FSIA). Where defendant acquired plaintiff's technology from a Chinese or Taiwanese source and merely disclosed plaintiff's trade secrets to American vendors, the suit was not based upon "an act performed in the United States in connection with a commercial activity of a foreign state elsewhere," as defined in the FSIA. BP Chemicals Ltd. v. Jiangsu Sopo Corp., Ltd., 144 F.Supp.2d 1140, 1145, judgment reversed 285 F.3d 677 (8th Cir.2002).

W.D.Mo.1992. Subsec. (b) cit. in disc. and quot. in case cit. in disc. A rifle owner who was injured when the rifle accidentally discharged sued the rifle's manufacturer for product defect, negligence, and other tort claims. Granting in part plaintiff's motion to compel production of documents related to defendant's development of a new rifle, this court held that, although defendant had demonstrated that the documents in question were entitled to protection as trade secrets, plaintiff had established that the documents were relevant and necessary to his claims, so that disclosure, with certain exceptions, was appropriate under the safeguard of a protective order. The court noted that since many of the documents pertained to the new rifle, which remained in the development stage, the court, giving a broad interpretation to defendant's privilege claim, found that the trade-secret privilege applied to those documents and to other documents included in the files. Hartman v. Remington Arms Co., Inc., 143 F.R.D. 673, 675.

D.Neb.2010. Adopted in case cit. in sup. Software licensee that was incorporated in Delaware and headquartered in Nebraska sued Texas licensor for breach of contract; defendant counterclaimed. This court granted summary judgment for plaintiff on defendant's counterclaim for misappropriation of trade secrets under the Nebraska Trade Secrets Act, but allowed the counterclaim to proceed under Texas law, holding that the contract's Texas choice-of-law provision encompassed the counterclaim because the counterclaim was closely related to the contractual relationship between the parties. The court noted that Texas law recognized misappropriation of trade secrets as a valid cause of action and cited a Texas Supreme Court case adopting the definition of a trade secret set forth in the first Restatement of Torts. Peter Kiewit Sons', Inc. v. ATSER, LP, 684 F.Supp.2d 1126, 1136.

D.Neb.2004. Com. (b) cit. in case quot. in disc. Family of woman struck and killed by truck driver in a motor-vehicle accident brought products liability suit against truck manufacturer. Plaintiffs sought, in part, to compel defendant's responses to plaintiff's request for production of documents. Granting plaintiff's motion in part, the court held, inter alia, that defendant's trade-secret defense for withholding discovery failed because defendant did not meet its burden of proving that any of the documents submitted in camera constituted a trade secret such that, if released, a competitive business advantage would be lost. Carlson v. Freightliner LLC, 226 F.R.D. 343, 364.

D.Neb.1988. Com. (b) cit. and quot. in sup. A railroad carrier developed a confidential rate-setting formula used in the pricing of coal transportation for utilities. The railroad sought declaratory and injunctive relief against a public utility to prevent the disclosure of their contract containing the formula to another public utility. This court denied the other utility's motion for summary judgment on a cross-claim against the utility contracting with the railroad carrier, stating that the Nebraska Public Records Act exempted trade secrets from disclosure requirements. The court reasoned that the confidential formula was a competitive device, not generally known in the industry, and that the formula was so vigorously protected that it qualified as a trade secret. Burlington Northern R. Co. v. Omaha Public Power Dist., 703 F.Supp. 826, 831, affirmed 888 F.2d 1228 (8th Cir.1989).

D.Nev.1993. Cit. in ftn. in sup. Developer of a skinless fried-chicken product sued restaurant franchisor for trade-secret

Cit.—cited; com.—comment; fol.—followed; sup.—support.
A complete list of abbreviations precedes page 1.

misappropriation. Granting defendant's motion for summary judgment, the court held that the procedure that defendant allegedly misappropriated did not constitute a protectible trade secret under the Uniform Trade Secrets Act, since the general process of skinning, cutting, marinating, dipping, breading, and frying chicken to produce a skinless fried-chicken product was obvious and not new or a secret and it was generally known to and readily ascertainable by others who could obtain independent economic value from its use. Hutchison v. KFC Corp., 883 F.Supp. 517, 521.

D.N.J.2013. Com. (b) quot. in case quot. in disc. (erron. cit. as Restatement (Second)). Disbursing agent for Chapter 11 debtor/former business brought an adversary proceeding against, among others, debtor's corporate affiliate, which was substantially owned by the same shareholders as debtor, alleging misappropriation of trade secrets and other claims. Granting defendants' motion to dismiss the misappropriation claim, this court held that plaintiff failed to identify or define what trade secrets or proprietary information belonging to debtor defendants allegedly misappropriated. While plaintiff claimed that defendants misappropriated debtor's assets through fraudulent transfers of equipment and certain improper payments made by debtor on behalf of defendants, plaintiff failed to allege that these "assets" constituted trade secrets or proprietary information. Jurista v. Amerinox Processing, Inc., 492 B.R. 707, 771.

D.N.J.2009. Com. (b) quot. in sup. (erron. cit. as § 787, cmt. a). Debt-collection agency sued former employee and former client, alleging that employee falsely informed client, among other things, that agency's employees were stealing confidential client information from agency, and that client conveyed the false allegations and certain confidential documents provided by employee to two of agency's other clients. Granting summary judgment for client, this court held, inter alia, that agency failed to show in support of its claim for breach of contract that employee's letter to client, which reiterated her allegations against agency in writing, included confidential business information protected by agency's contract with client. The court pointed out that the allegations were not the sort of confidential business practices protected by the common-law tort for disclosure of business secrets. Professional Recovery Services, Inc. v. General Elec. Capital Corp., 642 F.Supp.2d 391, 409.

D.N.J.2004. Cit. generally in disc. and in case cit. in disc. After pharmaceutical company sued prospective manufacturers of a generic drug for patent infringement, a company that provided research and analysis to investors on patent-related issues intervened in the case, seeking access to documents submitted in connection with parties' summary-judgment motions. Magistrate denied company's application to modify blanket protective order and unseal numerous documents filed pursuant to that order. This court affirmed magistrate's ruling, holding that magistrate's conclusion that the summary-judgment papers consisted largely of protectable trade secrets was soundly supported. Thus, the court concluded that company was entitled to access summary-judgment papers redacted of trade secret and proprietary information, but must bear costs of redaction process. In re Gabapentin Patent Litigation, 312 F.Supp.2d 653, 667.

D.N.J.2000. Com. (b) quot. in case quot. in disc. Provider of "report card" for summarizing mutual fund performance sued securities brokerage firm, alleging trademark infringement, misappropriation of ideas, unfair competition, and breach of implied-in-fact contract. Following dismissal of claims relating to trademark, firm moved for dismissal of remaining claims. Granting the motion in part, this court held, inter alia, that plaintiff's "report card" idea was not sufficiently novel to warrant protection as a confidentially submitted idea. Duffy v. Charles Schwab & Co., Inc., 123 F.Supp.2d 802, 813.

D.N.J.1997. Cit. generally in ftn., com. (b) cit. and quot. in disc., com. (d) quot. in disc., coms. cit. generally in headnotes (erron. cit. as Restatement (Second) of Torts). A German drug manufacturer brought suit against several competitors, alleging that defendants misappropriated its trade secrets involved in the manufacture of a laboratory version of erythropoietin. Denying defendants' motion for summary judgment, the court held, inter alia, that genuine issues of material fact existed as to whether plaintiff's purported trade secrets were, in fact, secret; whether plaintiff took reasonable precautions to protect the secrecy of its alleged trade secrets; and whether one defendant used plaintiff's alleged trade secrets to plaintiff's detriment. The court refused to find that the defendant's use of plaintiff's purported trade secrets for evidentiary purposes during prior commercial litigation was privileged. Merckle GmbH v. Johnson & Johnson, 961 F.Supp. 721, 722, 730-732.

D.N.J.1992. Com. (b) quot. in part in disc. A corporation that manufactured and sold pollution control chemicals and related equipment sued its former agent in the Philippines, alleging various claims, including unfair competition from misappropriation of trade secrets, and seeking preliminary injunctive relief. Plaintiff had entered into direct dealings with a major Philippine government customer after its agency agreement with defendant expired, but defendant had attempted to reposition itself as middleman in transactions between plaintiff and the customer and then represented itself to the customer as being able to provide competing chemicals and equipment at reduced prices. This court, determining that plaintiff was not entitled to injunctive relief, held, inter alia, that plaintiff had not demonstrated a likelihood of success on its unfair-competition claim, even if defendant had obtained confidential information, including access to prices and discounts offered to the customer, as plaintiff had failed to establish, among other things, that defendant had gained unfair competitive advantage from its relationship with plaintiff. Apollo Technologies Corp. v. Centrosphere Indus. Corp., 805 F.Supp. 1157, 1197, 1198, 1200, 1201.

D.N.J.1991. Cit. in disc., cit. generally in disc., com. (b) quot. in case quot. in disc. Food manufacturer that had been working on new nutritional frozen-food product line sued for preliminary injunction for misappropriation of trade secrets, inter alia, after one of its product development technologists resigned and accepted a position with a competitor, which subsequently patented a similar food product. Employee had an agreement with manufacturer not to divulge trade secrets and business ideas to competitors after termination of employment. This court granted plaintiff's application for preliminary injunction, holding, in part, that plaintiff had proved likelihood of prevailing on the merits on its claim that its process for making a nonfried frozen chicken product was a trade secret and that defendant misappropriated it. Plaintiff's process was not known by others in the industry, plaintiff took measures to guard trade secret, and plaintiff spent significant amount of effort in testing formula and procedure. Campbell Soup Co. v. Conagra, Inc., 801 F.Supp. 1298, 1304, 1305, vacated by 977 F.2d 86 (3d Cir.1992).

E.D.N.Y.2013. Com. (b) quot. in case quot. in sup. Former chapter of association dedicated to fighting Alzheimer's disease brought unfair competition and other claims against association, alleging that, after the parties disaffiliated, defendant sent out direct mass mailings in an attempt to solicit donations for itself using plaintiff's return address and the name and forged signature of plaintiff's executive director/CEO. Granting defendant's motion to dismiss that claim, this court held that, although a cause of action based on unfair competition could be predicated upon the alleged bad faith misappropriation of a commercial advantage belonging to another by exploitation of proprietary information or trade secrets, the use of publicly available information like plaintiff's officer's name and address did not qualify as a trade secret. Alzheimer's Disease Resource Center, Inc. v. Alzheimer's Disease and Related Disorders Ass'n, Inc., 981 F.Supp.2d 153, 162.

E.D.N.Y.2012. Com. (b) quot. in case quot. in sup. Provider of merchandising services sued grocery cooperative that hired it to develop checkout display units for its members to place at or near cash registers, alleging, among other things, that defendant breached the confidentiality and nondisclosure provisions of the parties' agreements by misappropriating its confidential information and trade secrets to create a competing checkout display program. Denying defendant's motion to dismiss, this court held that the complaint was sufficiently specific to support plaintiff's claim that the allegedly misappropriated information was "confidential" or a "trade secret." The court noted that trade secrets included information used in running the business, like the formulas or processes used in manufacturing, and that plaintiff identified the alleged confidential information as "checkout counter programs and its business model, plan-o-grams and designs, methods and procedures," including creating and designing the specific program for defendant. Dorset Industries, Inc. v. Unified Grocers, Inc., 893 F.Supp.2d 395, 411.

E.D.N.Y.2012. Com. (b) quot. in sup. Receiver for company, who was appointed by this court in an underlying action, sued company's officers, among others, for misappropriation of trade secrets, inter alia, alleging that, in an attempt to sabotage company, officers transferred company's trade secrets to another corporation. Denying defendants' motion to dismiss, this court held that plaintiff sufficiently pled that the items allegedly transferred to corporation—namely, certain customer lists, as well as the rates charged to and correspondence with those customers—were trade secrets. The court noted that, while a customer list, on its face, was not a trade secret, a customer list developed by a business through substantial effort and kept in confidence could be treated as a trade secret provided that the information it contained was not otherwise readily ascertainable. Friedman v. Wahrsager, 848 F.Supp.2d 278, 301, 302.

E.D.N.Y.2009. Com. (b) quot. in case quot. in ftn. in sup. Customers sued tax-service company, company's agent, and company's franchisee, alleging deceptive pricing practices in the sale of tax-return-preparation services; franchisee counterclaimed, alleging that plaintiffs misappropriated confidential information by inducing defendants' employees during pretrial discovery to bring them unredacted third-party customer bills and computer screen shots itemizing how much third-party customers paid for services. This court granted plaintiffs' motion to dismiss franchisee's counterclaim, holding, inter alia, that even if a misappropriation action was cognizable, the counterclaim failed on its face because franchisee did not allege that the third-party information constituted a trade secret; it alleged only that the information was confidential, and this allegation, by itself, failed to satisfy the pleading requirement, since confidentiality was only part of the trade-secret analysis. Watts v. Jackson Hewitt Tax Service Inc., 675 F.Supp.2d 274, 279-280.

E.D.N.Y.2007. Com. (b) quot. in case quot. in sup. Manufacturer of retail wall systems brought, in part, claim for misappropriation of trade secrets against its former director of engineering and the company that director left to form. This court found defendants liable on the claim and awarded damages. The court held, inter alia, that the information misappropriated, including drawings, schematics, photographs of previous installations, and a range of customer and other business data constituted trade secrets. The court pointed out that the information was not known outside of plaintiff's business and was not openly available within the business; plaintiff had numerous safety measures in place to protect it; the information gave defendant company a great advantage, saving it years of development time; and director wrongfully took and retained the information. Paz Systems, Inc. v. Dakota Group Corp., 514 F.Supp.2d 402, 407.

E.D.N.Y.2006. Com. (b) quot. in case quot. in sup. Former employer sued former salesperson and his subsequent employer, seeking to enjoin them, in part, from soliciting business from clients known to them as a result of data obtained by salesperson during his employment with seller. Denying plaintiff's request for a preliminary injunction, this court held, inter alia, that plaintiff failed to establish a likelihood of success on the merits in demonstrating that certain of its customer lists were entitled to trade-secret protection. The court noted that the lists were developed largely through the efforts of salesperson both before and during his employment with plaintiff, in a market that was not specialized but had many, easily identifiable, potential customers. Iron Mountain Information Management, Inc. v. Taddeo, 455 F.Supp.2d 124, 138.

E.D.N.Y.2002. Com. (b) quot. in case quot. in disc. Former employer sued, among others, former employee and his spouse for breach of the employment agreement's restrictive covenant, after employee's spouse formed a competing company. Granting in part plaintiff's motion for a preliminary injunction, the court held, inter alia, that the restrictive covenant should be enforced to prevent disclosure of plaintiff's trade secrets in the form of customer lists, pricing, and volume information. Unisource Worldwide, Inc. v. Valenti, 196 F.Supp.2d 269, 278.

E.D.N.Y.2000. Com. (b) quot. in case quot. in sup. Holder of patents for sound-masking equipment and licensed manufacturer of the equipment brought suit for, in part, misappropriation of trade secrets against distributor that had promoted and sold plaintiffs' products as its own. Denying defendant's motion to dismiss, the court held, inter alia, that plaintiffs' allegation that defendant had obtained through deception specifications and drawings of plaintiffs' products from plaintiff manufacturer, which had provided them in confidence in the good-faith expectation that they would be used solely to promote plaintiffs' interests, was sufficient to state a cause of action under state law for trade-secret misappropriation. 777388 Ontario Ltd. v. Lencore Acoustics Corp., 105 F.Supp.2d 56, 65.

E.D.N.Y.2000. Com. (b) quot. in case quot. in disc. Distributor of industrial filters sued manufacturer for, inter alia, misuse of proprietary information and unfair competition in connection with defendant's termination of plaintiff's exclusive distribution agreement and subsequent acquisition of customer lists compiled by plaintiff. Granting in part and denying in part defendant's motion for summary judgment, the court held, among other things, that the customer lists constituted a trade secret, that defendant used those lists after terminating plaintiff, and that a reasonable jury could find that the parties shared a confidential relationship that gave rise to a duty of fidelity on defendant's part. Abernathy-Thomas Engineering Co. v. Pall Corp., 103 F.Supp.2d 582, 600.

E.D.N.Y.1998. Com. (b) quot. in sup. and quot. in case quot. in sup. A seller of medical supplies sued three former employees for breach of fiduciary and misappropriation of confidences and secrets, among other claims. Defendants argued that plaintiff's customer list was not a "secret" because it was readily ascertainable from sources outside the plaintiff's business. This court granted in part and denied in part defendants' motion to dismiss, holding, inter alia, that plaintiff sufficiently alleged a cause of action for misappropriation of trade secrets. Plaintiff alleged that defendants stole its customer list as well as other confidential company files, and this information allegedly was gathered at considerable expense and effort over a 23-year period. Universal Marine Medical Supply, Inc. v. Lovecchio, 8 F.Supp.2d 214, 222.

E.D.N.Y.1997. Cit. generally in cases cit. in sup., com. (b) quot. in sup., com. (c) quot. in case quot. in sup. A software licensor sued a licensee for, in part, misappropriation of trade secrets in connection with licensee's modifications of computer software provided by licensor. Granting in part defendant's motion for summary judgment, the court held, inter alia, that, as a matter of law, plaintiff could not prove that defendant misappropriated plaintiff's trade secrets, since plaintiff failed to allege that defendant disclosed the trade secrets to any third party or that defendant had used the trade secrets or would use them in competition with plaintiff. Applied Information Management, Inc. v. Icart, 976 F.Supp. 149, 156.

E.D.N.Y.1997. Cit. in disc. An airline magazine distributor sued a competitor and the competitor's employees for violations of the Sherman Act, Clayton Act, Lanham Act, and state law claims. Plaintiff alleged that defendant infringed upon plaintiff's name and logo and that the individual employees had violated noncompetition and nondisclosure covenants through the use of trade secrets and other proprietary information. This court granted plaintiff's motion for a preliminary injunction, holding, inter alia, that plaintiff's proposals, customer contracts, binding equipment, and the binding process were protected trade secrets. The court stated that the only way defendants could gain access to the cumulative proposal information, which was developed and protected by plaintiff through considerable time, expense, and effort, was through their employment with plaintiff. However, plaintiff's customer lists and its computer system were not entitled to trade secret protection. Inflight Newspapers, Inc. v. Magazines In-Flight, 990 F.Supp. 119, 126.

E.D.N.Y.1995. Com. (b) quot. in case quot. in disc. Corporations that were in the business of importing and distributing at wholesale seasonal or general merchandise to major American retailers sued former sales representatives after they went to work for a competitor. The magistrate recommended that plaintiffs' motion for a preliminary injunction enjoining the employment of the individual defendants be denied, holding, inter alia, that plaintiffs were not likely to succeed on the merits in demonstrating that the identity of their customers or information concerning customer preferences and ordering patterns qualified as a trade secret. There was no evidence that plaintiffs expended substantial time, effort, or money to develop their list of customers or that they made efforts to guard the secrecy of information concerning their customers. This court accepted the magistrate's recommendation and denied plaintiffs' motion for a preliminary injunction. Ivy Mar Co., Inc. v. C.R. Seasons Ltd., 907 F.Supp. 547, 556.

E.D.N.Y.1993. Cit. in disc. The owner of a copyrighted computer program sued a competitor, alleging infringement and trade-secret misappropriation. Circuit court vacated district court's ruling that the Federal Copyright Act had preempted the Texas law trade secret claim. On remand, this court dismissed plaintiff's action, holding that the discovery rule did not apply to toll the limitations period applicable to the trade-secret misappropriation claim. The court stated that it would be presumptuous to assume that the Texas Supreme Court would extend the discovery rule to all misappropriation claims, as well as inappropriate for a New York Federal district court to expand Texas law in this manner. Computer Associates Intern., Inc. v. Altai, Inc., 832 F.Supp. 50, 52, affirmed 61 F.3d 6 (2d Cir.1995).

E.D.N.Y.1992. Com. (b) quot. in case quot. in disc. The manufacturer of a computer software program sued a former employee for misappropriation of trade secrets combined and contained in the plaintiff's program and allegedly used to create and develop the defendant's own software program. The court granted the plaintiff's motion for a preliminary injunction pending the outcome of the action, holding that the plaintiff had established both irreparable harm and a likelihood of success on the merits. The court found that the plaintiff had established by clear and convincing evidence that his product contained protectable trade secrets. Computer Associates Intern., Inc. v. Bryan, 784 F.Supp. 982, 987.

E.D.N.Y.1992. Cit. generally in case quot. in disc., com. (b) quot. in disc. Holder of a patent on the radiation processing of polytetrafluoroethylene for use in printing ink powders sued a former employee and his current employer for damages for, inter alia, misappropriation and disclosure of confidential and trade secret information. Entering judgment for plaintiff, the court held that because plaintiff took reasonable precautions to guard its trade secret and because the issuance of a British patent on the process did not disclose the improved procedure under plaintiff's newer patent, defendant employee's disclosure of the disputed information and use of the procedure during his tenure with his current employer entitled plaintiff to damages. Shamrock Technologies v. Medical Sterilization, 808 F.Supp. 932, 936, 938.

E.D.N.Y.1991. Cit. in disc. The owner of a copyright protecting a computer software program and its components sued a competing computer software company, alleging that the competitor had infringed the copyright and misappropriated trade secrets by incorporating elements of the operating system compatibility component of its copyrighted program. This court entered judgment for the plaintiff, holding, inter alia, that § 301 of the federal copyright act preempted the owner's misappropriation-of-trade-secrets claim because the copyright owner had pleaded and proven facts establishing that the same act, incorporating portions of its copyrighted program into the competitor's program, constituted both copyright infringement and misappropriation of trade secrets. In noting the differences between copyright and trade secret law, the court stated that trade secret law may be enforced only against defendants having a special relationship to the plaintiff, while copyright law may be enforced against the world; however, merely because the elements of a trade secret and a copyrightable work were different did not avoid preemption. Computer Associates Intern., Inc. v. Altai, Inc., 775 F.Supp. 544, 564, affirmed in part, vacated in part 982 F.2d 693 (2d Cir.1992).

E.D.N.Y.1991. Cit. generally in disc., quot. in case quot. in disc. A seller of computer hardware and software sued a former employee, seeking to enjoin trademark, trade name, and copyright infringements. The court granted in part the plaintiff's request for a preliminary injunction, holding that the defendant, whether an employee of or a joint venturer with the plaintiff, had breached his fiduciary duty to the plaintiff by disclosing the plaintiff's trade secrets. Panther Systems II v. Panther Computer Systems, 783 F.Supp. 53, 64.

E.D.N.Y.Bkrtcy.Ct.2015. Com. (b) quot. in case quot. in sup. Chapter 7 trustee for the estate of debtor brought an adversary proceeding for misappropriation of trade secrets against debtor's wife and corporation nominally controlled by wife, alleging that debtor, as a part of a fraudulent scheme, transferred trade secrets owned by his closely-held company to corporation. This court denied in part defendants' motion to dismiss, holding that there were genuine issues of material fact. Citing Re-

For earlier citations, see the Appendices, Supplements, or Pocket Parts, if any, that correspond to the subject matter under examination.

statement of Torts § 757, Comment *b*, for the factors used in determining whether a trade secret existed, the court explained that whether the information that debtor allegedly transferred to corporation was available to the public, and thus did not constitute trade secrets, was a question of fact for the jury to decide. In re Collins, 540 B.R. 54, 63-64.

E.D.N.Y.Bkrtcy.Ct.1995. Subsec. (b) cit. in disc. Chapter 11 pharmaceutical company sought preliminary injunction to prevent former employee from working for its competitor and disclosing certain alleged trade secrets. Debtor contended that employee was bound by the terms of noncompetition and confidentiality agreements distributed to her when she accepted her position with debtor. Denying the motion, the court held that employee's refusal to sign the noncompetition agreement rendered it unenforceable and that the remedy for a breach of the valid confidentiality agreement would be money damages, not injunctive relief. The court explained that, while debtor's client and physician lists constituted trade secrets in that their compilation resulted from many years' expenditure of time and money and could only be discovered by competitors through extraordinary efforts, there was no evidence that employee had disclosed or intended to disclose their contents to her new employer, debtor's rival. In re American Preferred Prescription, Inc., 186 B.R. 350, 356.

N.D.N.Y.2018. Cit. in sup.; com. (b) quot. in case quot. in sup. In an action by manufacturer of drug testing kits against competitor, plaintiff filed a motion to amend or supplement the complaint to add claims for, among other things, misappropriation of trade secrets against its former employee, who left plaintiff to work for defendant. This court granted plaintiff's motion in part, holding that plaintiff stated a claim for misappropriation of trade secrets by pleading facts that plausibly alleged the existence of trade secrets under New York law and Restatement of Torts § 757, and that it made an effort through a confidentiality agreement to keep the trade secrets confidential. The court pointed to plaintiff's allegations that employee had access to proprietary and confidential information regarding plaintiff's contracts, pricing, product costs, internal sales strategies, legal and regulatory procedures, and competitive positions within plaintiff's industry during his employment with plaintiff. American Bio Medica Corporation v. Bailey, 341 F.Supp.3d 142, 157, 158.

N.D.N.Y.2011. Com. (b) cit. in cases quot. in sup. Financial-services company sued competitor and two former employees who resigned to work for competitor, alleging, among other things, that employees misappropriated confidential information and trade secrets. Granting plaintiff's request for preliminary injunctive relief, this court held, inter alia, that it would apply New York law to plaintiff's tort claims. The court cited New York decisions relying on Restatement of Torts § 757 in support of its conclusion that no actual conflict existed between New York and California law on plaintiff's claim for misappropriation of trade secrets. Ayco Co., L.P. v. Frisch, 795 F.Supp.2d 193, 203, 204.

N.D.N.Y.2005. Cit. in case quot. in disc. Commercial rock-salt producer sought post-judgment relief from the trial court's entry of a jury verdict holding it liable for misappropriating trade-secret information divulged by patentee of commercial deicing agent at a meeting between the parties, alleging, inter alia, that patentee's claim for misappropriation of trade secrets was actually a breach-of-contract claim that could not independently form a basis for tort liability. This court ruled that the jury's verdict finding liability on both theories could stand, holding that the two interrelated claims were sufficiently distinct as to allow them to coexist, since the parties' confidentiality agreement precluded unauthorized disclosure of the information exchanged, whereas the tort of misappropriation guarded against producer's use of the information to patentee's detriment. Cargill, Inc. v. Sears Petroleum & Transport Corp., 388 F.Supp.2d 37, 64, appeal dismissed 163 Fed.Appx. 894 (Fed.Cir. 2006).

N.D.N.Y.2003. Com. (b) quot. in case quot. in sup. Manufacturer of products used in papermaking process sued former employee and his new employer for unfair competition, trademark infringement, and misappropriation of trade secrets, inter alia. Denying in part plaintiff's motion for a preliminary injunction, district court held that plaintiff failed to establish that its customer databases and design specifications were entitled to trade-secret protection at this stage of proceedings, since customer addresses and contact informa-

Cit.—cited; com.—comment; fol.—followed; sup.—support.
A complete list of abbreviations precedes page 1.

tion were ascertainable from other sources, and since there was no evidence that defendants used improper means when they used reverse engineering to discover plaintiff's design specifications. Kadant, Inc. v. Seeley Machine, Inc., 244 F.Supp.2d 19, 35.

N.D.N.Y.2003. Cit. in sup., cit. generally in sup., com. (b) quot. in sup. and quot. in case quot. in sup. Manufacturer of veterinary penicillin products sued competitor for misappropriation of a trade secret. Granting plaintiff's motion for a preliminary injunction, the court held, inter alia, that plaintiff established a claim under New York law for trade-secret misappropriation because it showed that its method of manufacturing veterinary penicillin constituted a trade secret, and that defendant improperly obtained the trade secret from plaintiff's former employee. Norbrook Laboratories Ltd. v. G.C. Hanford Mfg. Co., 297 F.Supp.2d 463, 482-484, 488.

N.D.N.Y.1999. Cit. in disc., com. (b) cit. and quot. in cases quot. in disc. American distributor of snow-removal equipment sued Canadian competitor for, inter alia, misappropriation of trade secrets. Defendant had purchased the assets of plaintiff's Canadian sibling corporation, which had recently consolidated with plaintiff, and began marketing similar equipment in the United States, allegedly by copying wrongfully obtained designs created by plaintiff. Entering partial summary judgment for defendant, the court held that any secrecy existing in plaintiff's designs was easily acquired by competitors, and was therefore lost when the end product was placed upon the market; thus, information contained in plaintiff's engineering and production drawings and fixtures did not constitute a protectable trade secret. Frink America, Inc. v. Champion Road Machinery Ltd., 48 F.Supp.2d 198, 206-207.

N.D.N.Y.1999. Com. (b) cit. in headnote, quot. in case quot. in disc., quot. in case cit. in ftn., and cit. generally in disc. The seller and developer of a high-protein energy bar sued the manufacturer of the bar, seeking to enjoin defendant from misappropriating plaintiff's trade secret. This court denied plaintiff's motion for a preliminary injunction, holding, inter alia, that plaintiff had not shown a likelihood of success on the merits on its trade-secret claim. The use of beef-based gelatin was common in the industry, as was the use of hydrolyzed gelatin in combination with glycerine. Worldwide Sport Nutritional Supplements, Inc. v. Five Star Brands, LLC, 80 F.Supp.2d 25, 30, 32.

N.D.N.Y.1998. Com. (b) quot. in case quot. in disc. A carpet seller sued a competitor and its vice president for misappropriation of trade secrets, among other claims, alleging that defendants used proprietary information to steal plaintiff's subcontractors, employees, and customers. Plaintiff argued that in hiring two of plaintiff's key employees, defendants acquired access to trade secrets involving costs, products, and prices, and the identity, source, and price of plaintiff's floor covering products. This court granted in part and denied in part plaintiff's motion for a preliminary injunction, holding that plaintiff had not met its burden of demonstrating that its costs, prices, budgeting, and general business information were entitled to trade-secret protection. However, the court determined that plaintiff had demonstrated that it was likely to succeed on its claim that its product specifications were entitled to trade-secret protection. Carpetmaster of Latham v. Dupont Flooring Systems, 12 F.Supp.2d 257, 261.

N.D.N.Y.1998. Com. (b) quot. in case quot. in disc. (erron. cit. as Torts (2d)). Manufacturer sued competitor for violating the Sherman Act, alleging that defendant initiated a baseless state court lawsuit against it that was solely intended to prevent competition and ensure its monopoly. Defendant sought to obtain plaintiff's customer list and information about plaintiff's manufacturing process. This court held, inter alia, that plaintiff's manufacturing process was a trade secret, because the way in which plaintiff's bearings were made make them unique in the market and this information could not easily be duplicated or acquired by others. Defendant's customer lists were trade secrets, because the names of potential purchasers of this specialized product were not readily ascertainable outside of the business itself. DDS, Inc. v. Lucas Aerospace Power Transmission Corp., 182 F.R.D. 1, 5.

N.D.N.Y.1996. Com. (b) cit. generally in headnote and cit. in case quot. in sup. Purported designer of a folding window crank brought an action for trade-secret misappropriation, inter alia, against window-crank manufacturer. Granting in part defendant's motion to dismiss, or in the alternative for summary judgment, the

For earlier citations, see the Appendices, Supplements, or Pocket Parts, if any, that correspond to the subject matter under examination.

court held that the design at issue was not within the scope of trade-secret protection, since the design, when put in production, yielded a product of the business, a device that upon marketing and sale was open to public inspection of all of its features and thus not secret; under New York law, for a process or device to be a trade secret, it must be something used to run a business, rather than a product of the business. Blank v. Pollack, 916 F.Supp. 165, 167, 174.

S.D.N.Y.2022. Com. (b) cit. in sup. and in ftn. (general cite). International executive-recruitment firm sued two former partners of the firm, alleging that defendants were liable under the Defend Trade Secrets Act and the common law for taking plaintiff's proprietary information and using it to unfairly compete with plaintiff. This court denied in part defendants' motion to dismiss, holding that plaintiff stated a claim for misappropriation of trade secrets under the Act. The court reasoned, in part, that plaintiff sufficiently alleged the existence of trade secrets under the six-factor test set forth in the Restatement of Torts, in the form of candidate- and client-specific information that was developed through its own diligence and expenditure of resources and was not known or easily obtainable outside of plaintiff's business. Catalyst Advisors, L.P. v. Catalyst Advisors Investors Global Inc., 602 F.Supp.3d 663, 672, 674, 675.

S.D.N.Y.2021. Com. (b) quot. in ftn.; com. (f) quot. in cases quot. in sup. Manufacturer of consumer products filed claims for misappropriation of trade secrets against retailer that sold goods on a television station and online, retailer's subsidiary, and subsidiary's founder in connection with certain projects that the parties began developing together but that defendants eventually hired another entity to produce instead of plaintiff. This court granted in part defendants' motion to dismiss, holding that plaintiff forfeited any trade-secret protection under Restatement of Torts § 757, because it disclosed the alleged trade secrets to several factories and third persons without taking any measures to ensure that the factories or third persons would not disclose that information to others. Town & Country Linen Corp. v. Ingenious Designs LLC, 556 F.Supp.3d 222, 255, 258, 262, 265.

S.D.N.Y.2017. Cit. in sup.; com. (b) cit. and quot. in cases quot. in sup. Licensor of software for the ticket-broker industry sued former licensees, alleging that licensees improperly used their access to licensor's software to acquire the knowledge and information they needed to build a competing product. This court denied licensor's motion for a preliminary injunction on its claims for trade-secret misappropriation, holding, among other things, that the information that licensees allegedly misappropriated from licensor did not qualify as a trade secret, because licensor failed to show that it undertook reasonable measures to protect the secrecy of that information, as required for information to be trade secret under New York law and Restatement of Torts § 757. The court pointed to evidence that licensor regularly disclosed its alleged trade secrets to each of its licensees without notifying them of the information's confidential nature or binding them to confidentiality agreements. Broker Genius, Inc. v. Zalta, 280 F.Supp.3d 495, 513, 514, 517, 519.

S.D.N.Y.2014. Cit. in case quot. in sup., com. (b) quot. in case quot. in sup., com. (f) quot. in sup. Digital-printing company sued competitor, alleging, among other things, that defendant misappropriated plaintiff's five-element trade-secret method for producing recyclable banners over the course of three laboratory trials conducted by plaintiff and a nonparty. Granting summary judgment for defendant, this court held that plaintiff failed to identify all but one element of its trade secret with sufficient particularity, and that, even if plaintiff had adequately identified a viable trade secret, its claim would fail because defendant did not discover that trade secret through improper means and did not misappropriate it. The court pointed out that defendant was invited to participate in the laboratory trials, and reasoned that, simply accepting an invitation to participate in a potential customer's laboratory trials did not constitute improper means that fell below the generally accepted standards of commercial morality under Restatement of Torts § 757. Big Vision Private Ltd. v. E.I. DuPont De Nemours & Co., 1 F.Supp.3d 224, 257, 268, 273.

S.D.N.Y.2014. Com. (b) quot. in case quot. in sup. Environmental organization brought suit under the Freedom of Information Act, requesting appraisal records of coal-mining leases previously awarded by the Bureau of Land Management (BLM) to private mining companies, in order to

Cit.—cited; com.—comment; fol.—followed; sup.—support.
A complete list of abbreviations precedes page 1.

determine whether BLM complied with federal law requiring it to sell federal coal for no less than its fair market value. Granting in part the government's motion for summary judgment, this court held that, in rare cases, including the case here, the government's legitimate commercial interests could require the protection of information even after a contract was awarded. The court noted that BLM's methodology for determining fair market value of government property was a close, indeed compelling, analogue of a commercial "trade secret" as defined by the factors set out in Restatement of Torts § 757, Comment *b*. Natural Resources Defense Council, Inc. v. Dept. of Interior, 36 F.Supp.3d 384, 412.

S.D.N.Y.2013. Adopted in cases cit. in sup., cit. in sup.; com. (f) quot. in sup. Provider of litigation funding and support to parties in divorce proceedings brought a claim for misappropriation of trade secrets against, among others, competitor's co-founder, alleging that defendant induced plaintiff's client to breach her confidentiality agreement with plaintiff by providing him with copies of her agreements with plaintiff. This court denied defendant's motion to dismiss the misappropriation claim, holding that plaintiff's complaint plausibly alleged that defendant obtained the agreements through improper means under New York law, which looked to the Restatement of Torts § 757 in defining the elements of that cause of action. The court that pointed to plaintiff's allegations that such agreements were confidential in the litigation-funding industry, that defendant was aware that such agreements were confidential, and that defendant nevertheless sought out information that he knew to be confidential. Balance Point Divorce Funding, LLC v. Scrantom, 978 F.Supp.2d 341, 353, 354.

S.D.N.Y.2013. Com. (b) cit. and quot. in cases cit. and quot. in sup. Former employee brought a declaratory-judgment action against former employer/pharmaceutical company, challenging, among other things, the validity of the nondisclosure provisions of the parties' restrictive-covenant agreement. Denying in part employee's motion for summary judgment, this court held that genuine issues of material fact existed as to whether employer's information concerning patients, referral sources, and treatment constituted a trade secret, so as to justify the nondisclosure provisions. Applying the factors of Restatement of Torts § 757, Comment *b*, which New York courts used in determining whether information was worthy of trade-secret protection, the court pointed to evidence that the compilation of employer's information was largely specific to its business, only certain employees had access to the information, and employer secured the information on a password-protected database. Poller v. BioScrip, Inc., 974 F.Supp.2d 204, 215, 219.

S.D.N.Y.2013. Adopted in case quot. in sup. and cit. in ftn., com. (b) quot. in case quot. in sup. and cit. in ftn. Market-research companies sued assignee of a patent related to a method for correlating ads that consumers viewed with their purchasing behavior, seeking a declaration that they had not infringed that patent; assignee counterclaimed, alleging, inter alia, misappropriation of trade secrets. Granting summary judgment for companies on assignee's counterclaim, this court held that there was no evidence that companies used assignee's protected trade secrets, for purposes of proving trade-secret misappropriation under New York law. The court noted that the New York Court of Appeals had adopted the definition of a trade secret provided by Restatement of Torts § 757 as any formula, pattern, device, or compilation of information that was used in one's business, and that gave him an opportunity to obtain an advantage over competitors who did not know or use it. TNS Media Research, LLC v. TRA Global, Inc., 984 F.Supp.2d 205, 237, 238.

S.D.N.Y.2013. Com. (b) quot. in case quot. in sup. and cit. in ftn. Market-research company sought a declaration that it had not infringed a patent for a method of correlating ads that consumers viewed with their purchasing behavior; assignee of the patent counterclaimed, alleging, among other things, misappropriation of trade secrets. This court granted plaintiff's motion to dismiss defendant's counterclaim, holding that defendant failed to identify its alleged trade secrets with specificity prior to the close of discovery. The court noted that, in any event, the documents that defendant eventually identified in support of its claim failed to evidence protectable trade secrets under the definition set forth in Restatement First of Torts § 757, which had been adopted by the Court of Appeals of New York. TNS Media Research, LLC v.

TRA Global, Inc., 977 F.Supp.2d 281, 312, 313.

S.D.N.Y.2011. Com. (b) cit. in case cit. in sup. Employer sued former employee and business competitor for which former employee had begun working, alleging that former employee misappropriated plaintiff's trade secrets. This court ruled that fact issues precluding summary judgment existed as to whether the information that former employee forwarded from his e-mail account with plaintiff to his personal e-mail address—consisting of lists of plaintiff's clients and revenue associated with those clients, and documents concerning clients' coverage and insurance policies—was protectable as a trade secret; the record showed that plaintiff treated the information confidentially, its employees were required to sign confidentiality agreements, and it would take a significant effort to compile the information at issue. USI Ins. Services LLC v. Miner, 801 F.Supp.2d 175, 195.

S.D.N.Y.2009. Com. (b) quot. in sup. and cit. and quot. in cases cit. and quot. in sup. In a consolidated securities class action litigation involving a collapsed Italian conglomerate, lead plaintiffs moved to unseal certain discovery materials that certain defendants designated as confidential pursuant to a protective order. Granting plaintiffs' motion, this court held, inter alia, that defendants failed to show that the disclosure of any of the particular documents at issue would reveal business information that was sufficiently valuable and secret that it could cause competitive harm to them. The court noted that, although a business's information did not have to be a "true" trade secret in order to warrant protection from disclosure under federal discovery rules, trade-secret law was instructive in gauging whether information constituted sensitive business information that courts should shield from public scrutiny. In re Parmalat Securities Litigation, 258 F.R.D. 236, 245.

S.D.N.Y.2009. Com. (b) quot. in case quot. in disc. Former employee of United States subsidiary of a Japan-based global-trading corporation brought claims for, inter alia, race and national-origin discrimination under Title VII against employer and supervisors. Granting partial summary judgment for employer on its counterclaim for misappropriation of trade secrets, this court found plaintiff culpable of trade-secret misappropriation based on his disclosure to third parties of information about employer's strategic weaknesses that could give a competitor an advantage over employer. The court rejected plaintiff's argument that employer failed to make a showing of pecuniary damages stemming from the trade-secret disclosure; there was no requirement to demonstrate pecuniary damages to prevail on a trade-secrets misappropriation claim, since injunctive relief could also be a proper remedy in the trade-secrets context. Schanfield v. Sojitz Corp. of America, 663 F.Supp.2d 305, 349.

S.D.N.Y.2008. Cit. in sup. Holder of an expired patent for a railway brake unit sued company to which it licensed manufacturing information for the product, alleging that defendant wrongfully continued to use its trade secrets to manufacture the product after the parties' license agreement was terminated. Granting in part plaintiff's motion for preliminary injunctive relief, this court held, inter alia, that the information contained in plaintiff's manufacturing drawings constituted a trade secret under New York law. The court concluded, among other things, that the information was not widely known outside of the business, since there was no evidence to suggest that those few companies that sold certain component parts of the product in direct competition with plaintiff produced the parts by drawing on plaintiff's confidential knowledge or information, and the fact that some others knew of a trade secret independently did not deprive it of its trade-secret status. Faiveley Transport Malmo AB v. Wabtec Corp., 572 F.Supp.2d 400, 404.

S.D.N.Y.2008. Com. (b) quot. in sup. and adopted in case cit. in sup. Holder of a patent for an over-the-counter dental protection device sued, among others, competitor that began selling an allegedly infringing device and two former employees of plaintiff's predecessor-in-interest who allegedly divulged plaintiff's confidential and proprietary information and material to competitor. Denying in part defendants' motions to dismiss, this court held, inter alia, that plaintiff sufficiently alleged a claim for trade-secret misappropriation. The court cited plaintiff's allegations that employees had access to critical information about the design and manufacturing process for the device, which information enabled competitor to cut out the research and development phase of creating a com-

Cit.—cited; com.—comment; fol.—followed; sup.—support.
A complete list of abbreviations precedes page 1.

peting device on an expedited basis in order to take advantage of a limited window of opportunity with a large retailer. Medtech Products Inc. v. Ranir, LLC, 596 F.Supp.2d 778, 804.

S.D.N.Y.2008. Com. (b) quot. in case quot. in sup. Investors in corporation's common stock, on behalf of a prospective class, sued corporation and others, alleging, among other things, that corporation made materially false and misleading statements that caused corporation's stock to trade at an artificially inflated price. Granting corporation's motion to dismiss, this court held, inter alia, that defendant's use of the term "proprietary technology" was not false and misleading merely because defendant did not have any patents or pending patents for the technology. The court reasoned that the legal definition of proprietary technology was broader than simply holding a patent, and could encompass defendant's confidential manufacturing process, since legal protections extended not just to patents, but also to trade secrets. Tabor v. Bodisen Biotech, Inc., 579 F.Supp.2d 438, 452.

S.D.N.Y.2007. Com. (b) quot. in sup. and quot. in case quot. in sup. Employer sued former employee after employee resigned and began working for employer's direct competitor. This court granted employer's request for a preliminary injunction to prevent employee from working for competitor or disclosing confidential or proprietary information related to employer's software application project. The court held, inter alia, that because it was more likely than not that employee was knowledgeable about the overall design of the application, and employer kept the application secret and spent more than five years and $750,000 to develop it, employee was in possession of a trade secret; while employee contended that he was not involved at the technical or source-code level, he was one of only six employees with password access to the application and was responsible for supervising its development and implementation. Payment Alliance Intern., Inc. v. Ferreira, 530 F.Supp.2d 477, 481.

S.D.N.Y.2006. Com. (b) cit. in case quot. in sup. Former employee sued former employer, a market-research and consulting firm, for unpaid commissions, and employer counterclaimed, alleging that employee had operated a competing consulting firm while employed by employer. This court, inter alia, denied summary judgment for employee on employer's claim for misappropriation of trade secrets. The court held that, while elements of employer's methodology were common tools in the industry, a fact issue existed as to whether the aggregation of those tools was novel and not generally known in the trade so as to constitute a trade secret, and that it was also unclear whether employer's business practices, including its dealings with clients, employees, and consultants, were trade secrets under the six-factor Restatement test. Derven v. PH Consulting, Inc., 427 F.Supp.2d 360, 371, 372.

S.D.N.Y.2006. Com. (b) quot. in sup. Skin-and hair-product manufacturer sued former employee after he accepted employment with a competitor, in alleged violation of the parties' noncompete agreement. Granting employer's motion for a preliminary injunction, this court held, inter alia, that plaintiff demonstrated that the measure of damage caused by the misappropriation of its trade secrets was unquantifiable and that, therefore, it would suffer irreparable injury absent the injunction; employee possessed trade secrets through his knowledge of plaintiff's confidential products under development and its innovations scheduled for the future, information that would be advantageous in the hands of plaintiff's competition. Estee Lauder Companies Inc. v. Batra, 430 F.Supp.2d 158, 175.

S.D.N.Y.2005. Cit. in disc., com. (b) quot. in sup. and quot. in case quot. in disc. Secured lender sued borrower for breach of contract, after borrower refused to pay expenses of securitization. Granting lender's motion to dismiss borrower's counterclaim for misappropriation of trade secrets, this court held, inter alia, that information allegedly disclosed by lender did not constitute protected trade secrets; financial information could not be regarded as processes or devices for continuous use in operation of borrower's business. Instead, the financial information here simply constituted independent and ephemeral facts, insufficient to be classified as trade-secret information. Bear, Stearns Funding, Inc. v. Interface Group-Nevada, Inc., 361 F.Supp.2d 283, 304, 305.

S.D.N.Y.2005. Cit. in ftn., com. (b) quot. in sup. Chewing-gum manufacturer that licensed the right to sell, manufacture, and distribute its products, along with the technology needed to produce them, to Argentine corporation sued corporation, alleging breach of contract, fraudulent inducement, and trade-secret misappropriation. The court denied in part defendant's motion for partial summary judgment, holding, inter alia, that punitive damages might be available on plaintiff's claim for misappropriation of trade secrets. The court concluded that this claim was an independent tort that was not grounded solely in the contractual relationship between the parties, and therefore was not subject to the applicable common law test for determining the appropriateness of punitive damages for breach of contract, which required a public wrong. Topps Co., Inc. v. Cadbury Stani S.A.I.C., 380 F.Supp.2d 250, 266, 267.

S.D.N.Y.2004. Com. (b) quot. in ftn. Jewelry transportation facilitator sued national shipping company for, in part, state-law misappropriation of trade secrets, after defendant canceled exclusive contract and directly solicited plaintiff's clients. Dismissing the claim, the court held, inter alia, that the customer information that plaintiff provided to defendant for shipping purposes did not constitute a trade secret subject to protection, because the Airline Deregulation Act preempted the manner in which carriers received their shipping information. A.I.B. Express, Inc. v. FedEx Corp., 358 F.Supp.2d 239, 252.

S.D.N.Y.2004. Com. (b) quot. in case quot. in disc. Stent manufacturer brought action against distributor with whom it had an extensive contractual relationship, alleging breach of contract, misappropriation of trade secrets, and various statutory and common-law violations. Distributor counterclaimed for breach of contract, improper termination of agreement, and breach of covenant of good faith and fair dealing. On cross-motions for summary judgment, the court dismissed plaintiff's claim of misappropriation, and held, inter alia, that while protectible trade secrets must contain a formula, pattern, device, or compilation of information not known to competitors, here, the design embodied in one of plaintiff's stents was not protectible because the stent was either held out to the public for sale or was intended to be marketed in the future. Medinol Ltd. v. Boston Scientific Corp., 346 F.Supp.2d 575, 607.

S.D.N.Y.2002. Com. (b) quot. in case quot. in sup. Owner of perfume trademarks sued former "turnaround" managers, hired under retainer agreements, for infringement, trade-secret misappropriation, and other torts. Denying in part defendants' motion to dismiss, this court held, inter alia, that owner stated claim for trade-secret disclosure where genuine issue of fact existed as to whether disclosure took place after defendants were hired. Houbigant, Inc. v. Development Specialists, Inc., 229 F.Supp.2d 208, 221.

S.D.N.Y.2002. Com. (b) quot. in sup. and quot. in case quot. in disc. Computer-software developer sued competitor for, in part, misappropriation of trade secrets. Granting in part defendant's motion for judgment as a matter of law, the court held, inter alia, that plaintiff's software architecture was not a trade secret, because the architecture was easily ascertainable by the public and could be duplicated once the product was marketed. LinkCo, Inc. v. Fujitsu Ltd., 230 F.Supp.2d 492, 498.

S.D.N.Y.2002. Com. (b) quot. in case quot. in disc. Optical-coating firm sued a former employee and the optical-coating business he started, seeking injunctive relief and damages for misappropriation of trade secrets and unfair competition. After a bench trial, this court concluded, inter alia, that defendants violated plaintiff's trade secrets by unlawfully soliciting one of plaintiff's most lucrative customers and creating a rotation device that was nearly identical to the unique device originally crafted by plaintiff. The court determined that existence of the customer as plaintiff's customer constituted a trade secret. It also found that plaintiff's unique, almost completely hand-crafted and superior planetary device was a trade secret, because it provided plaintiff with a competitive advantage over other optical coaters in the industry. Thin Film Lab, Inc. v. Comito, 218 F.Supp.2d 513, 520.

S.D.N.Y.2001. Com. (b) quot. in ftn. Former employee sued business consulting firm, claiming termination without cause, thereby triggering stock-repurchase requirement. Firm counterclaimed to enforce noncompete agreement. Granting relief to both parties, the district court held that notice sent to employee eight months after termination was insufficient, and noncompete agreement would be enforced to the extent the court found reasonable. The court said that noncompete covenants were enforceable under Massachusetts law

Cit.—cited; com.—comment; fol.—followed; sup.—support.
A complete list of abbreviations precedes page 1.

even where no trade secrets were involved. Markovits v. Venture Info Capital, Inc., 129 F.Supp.2d 647, 657.

S.D.N.Y.2001. Com. (b) quot. in case quot. in sup. Original distributor of beauty-care products sued manufacturer, new distributor, and former employees now working for manufacturer, alleging, inter alia, misappropriation of trade secrets, and seeking preliminary injunction prohibiting defendants' use of marks pending litigation. This court issued the injunction but held, inter alia, that plaintiff failed to show that former employees were misappropriating trade secrets. Tactica Intern., Inc. v. Atlantic Horizon Intern., Inc., 154 F.Supp.2d 586, 606.

S.D.N.Y.1999. Com. (b) quot. in disc. Creator of vaginal lubricant sued health and beauty aid conglomerate for, inter alia, misappropriation of trade secrets, alleging that defendant rejected her proposal for a joint venture and, instead, used confidential information to produce a similar item. Entering summary judgment for defendant, the court held, in part, that plaintiff's concept was not a protectable trade secret, since, among other things, it was familiar to those in the industry, had already entered the public domain, and was not novel. Brandwynne v. Combe Intern., Ltd., 74 F.Supp.2d 364, 376.

S.D.N.Y.1999. Cit. generally in disc., com. (b) quot. in cases cit. in disc. Provider of on-line products and services sought to enjoin former vice president from accepting a position with its competitor, to whom plaintiff argued defendant would disclose trade secrets. Entering judgment for defendant, the court held, in part, that the contractual noncompete provision that plaintiff sought to enforce was overbroad, and that, in any event, plaintiff had failed to show that its strategic-content planning, licensing agreements and acquisitions, and advertising and technical knowledge constituted protectable trade secrets. Earth-Web, Inc. v. Schlack, 71 F.Supp.2d 299, 314, 315.

S.D.N.Y.1998. Cit. in disc., com. (b) quot. in case quot. in disc. Cable-television-programming producer sued cable-television programmer and system operators for copyright and trade-secret violations, among other claims. This court granted in part and denied in part defendants' motions to seal portions of the record, holding, inter alia, that, with the exception of the fee that programmer paid plaintiff for a pilot show, the information that defendants sought to seal was confidential. Given the extent of the confidentiality and the importance of the information to defendants, the information that defendants sought to seal comprised trade secrets. Encyclopedia Brown Productions v. Home Box Office, 26 F.Supp.2d 606, 613.

S.D.N.Y.1997. Cit. in headnotes, com. (b) cit. in case quot. in disc. A broker for the sale of computers sued companies that developed and distributed computer hardware and software, alleging tort and contract claims. Plaintiff, which was in the business of providing intelligence about the business landscape in China, moved to add a claim for misappropriation of trade secrets. The court denied the motion, holding, inter alia, that plaintiff's information was not protectable and that defendants did not violate a confidential relationship. Four Star Capital Corporation v. Nynex Corporation, AGS Computers, Inc., 183 F.R.D. 91, 108.

S.D.N.Y.1996. Com. (b) quot. in ftn. Creator of computer program for theater-ticket sales sued program's alleged licensee and others for, inter alia, misappropriation of trade secrets, alleging that defendants not only displayed, publicized, and distributed its copyrighted program but did so in violation of an agreement to keep the trade secrets contained in the program confidential. Denying in part defendants' motion to dismiss, the court held that, because plaintiff's claim for trade-secret misappropriation required the "extra element" of proof of a breach of confidence, it was not preempted by federal law. Ez-Tixz, Inc. v. Hit-Tix, Inc., 919 F.Supp. 728, 737.

S.D.N.Y.1993. Cit. in disc. Several calling card holders sued a telephone company for fraudulently inducing them to obtain card under presumption that it would be free of service costs. The court granted in part defendant's motion to dismiss and granted defendant's motion to seal trial exhibits from public view. The court held that, while defendant's allegedly deceptive advertising strategies were not "trade secrets" in the traditional sense, their potential to do commercial harm prior to trial and the fact that the information was generally a part of defendant's effort to gain competitive advantage were dispositive to the court's decision to seal the exhibits in

For earlier citations, see the Appendices, Supplements, or Pocket Parts, if any, that correspond to the subject matter under examination.

question. Gelb v. American Tel. & Tel. Co., 813 F.Supp. 1022, 1034.

S.D.N.Y.1993. Cit. in disc., com. (b) cit. in disc. and quot. in case cit. in disc. Insurance brokerage firm sought a preliminary injunction barring a former employee and his new employer from using plaintiff's customer lists and conducting any other acts of unfair competition in connection with them, inter alia. Denying plaintiff's motion for a preliminary injunction, the court held that plaintiff made no showing adequate to support a preliminary injunction that it had met the criteria for trade secrecy or similar protection. Licata & Co. Inc. v. Goldberg, 812 F.Supp. 403, 409, 410.

S.D.N.Y.1993. Com. (b) quot. in case cit. in disc. Former fraud investigator for a private employer sued employer for breach of contract and violations of state whistleblower act, alleging that employer prevented him from pursuing various reports of financial wrongdoing in ways he thought were appropriate and then fired him for continuing to raise those issues. This court denied employer's motion to dismiss, subject to renewal of the motion after 45 days, during which plaintiff could supplement complaint by submitting certain information outlined in the opinion. In addressing plaintiff's allegation that he was forced to enter into a commitment to withhold from proper authorities information with respect to employer's illegal activities, the court stated that plaintiff could supplement complaint by furnishing concrete, specific details concerning any reports concerning ongoing wrongdoing that he attempted to make. It noted that disclosures of wrongdoing did not constitute revelations of trade secrets that could be prohibited by agreements binding on former employees. McGrane v. Reader's Digest Ass'n, Inc., 822 F.Supp. 1044, 1052.

S.D.N.Y.1992. Com. (b) quot. in case cit. in sup. Employee sued former employer; employer counterclaimed to enjoin plaintiff from using employer's customer lists pursuant to a confidentiality covenant in the employment contract. The trial court denied employer relief, holding that customer lists did not constitute protectable trade secrets. It found that the employee could easily obtain the lists by purchasing them, that most of employer's clients were obtained by randomly calling names on the list, and that employees were never told that the lists were confidential. It also noted that employer and employee executed a release barring any claims against the employee. Hancock v. Essential Resources, Inc., 792 F.Supp. 924, 926.

S.D.N.Y.1992. Com. (b) quot. in sup. and quot. in case cit. in sup. Inventor of an electronic photographic retouching and imaging system sought to enjoin the system's former marketer, among others, from marketing, selling, or promoting a similar system, which allegedly was developed by defendant's contractor as a result of defendant's misappropriation of plaintiff's trade secrets. Granting defendant's motion to dismiss, the court held, inter alia, that plaintiff failed to surmount his threshold burden of establishing that there was in fact a trade secret or in defining what the trade secret was for which protection was sought. The court said that plaintiff appeared merely to have followed the suggestions of the imaging/retouching software's manufacturer as to how to obtain the best results with the software's usage. Julie Research Laboratories v. Select Photographic, 810 F.Supp. 513, 517, 520, affirmed in part, vacated in part 998 F.2d 65 (2d Cir.1993).

S.D.N.Y.1989. Cit. generally in disc., quot. in part in sup. A construction technology firm sued competitors for common law misappropriation of technology. This court dismissed the claim without prejudice, stating that the plaintiff failed to show a required element of its claim, that the defendants knew or had notice that the information they received was confidential. The court explained that, although one defendant arranged to imitate a design and improperly received information for its completion, the plaintiff did not allege that the defendant had notice that the information was confidential. Absent such an allegation, the court said that it would not presume that the defendants possessed the requisite knowledge. Construction Technology v. Lockformer Co., Inc., 704 F.Supp. 1212, 1225, 1226.

S.D.N.Y.1989. Com. (b) quot. in case quot. in disc. A developer of financial software sued a competitor, inter alia, alleging that certain proprietary information of value to the plaintiff was misappropriated by the plaintiff's former employees who went to work for the defendant. The court found that the source code and combination of modules of some of the plaintiff's generic programs constituted trade secrets entitled to protection from misappropriation. The court, therefore, enjoined the defendant for a period of six months from utilizing as parts of its systems any versions of the programs created in whole or in part by the plaintiff's former employees. Integrated Cash Mgmt. Serv. v. Digital Transactions, 732 F.Supp. 370, 375, judgment affirmed 920 F.2d 171 (2d Cir. 1990).

S.D.N.Y.1988. Com. (b) cit. in disc. A marketing and research firm sued a defunct corporate competitor for copyright infringement, violation of the Lanham Act, and unfair competition and trade-secret practices, alleging, inter alia, that the defendants had unlawfully appropriated the plaintiff's customer list. This court held in part that the plaintiff had failed to take steps necessary to maintain its customer lists as trade secrets where the plaintiff had no formal policy in existence regarding the customer lists, no special access code was needed to access the lists on the computer, copies of the customer lists were discarded in hallways and were handled by general building personnel, and there was a complete lack of confidential treatment of the lists. Business Trends Analysts v. Freedonia Group, Inc., 700 F.Supp. 1213, 1236.

S.D.N.Y.1988. Com. (b) quot. in disc. A financial-information service sought a preliminary injunction to prevent a software company from manufacturing, selling, or distributing to the service's customers a software package that copied and analyzed the data provided by the service. The plaintiff alleged that the use of the package constituted a misappropriation of trade secrets, a violation of copyright and telecommunications laws, and interference with contractual relations. The court granted the plaintiff's motion for a preliminary injunction, holding that the plaintiff had shown its probable success on the merits and demonstrated that it would suffer irreparable harm without an injunction. Telerate Systems, Inc. v. Caro, 689 F.Supp. 221, 231.

S.D.N.Y.1988. Quot. in case quot. in sup. The father of a boy who was injured while driving an all-terrain vehicle (ATV) sued the Japanese manufacturer of the ATV and its American subsidiary on a theory of products liability. In response to the plaintiff's discovery requests, the subsidiary moved for a protective order to limit the dissemination of its communications with the Consumer Products Safety Commission, alleging that many of the communications involved trade secrets. The court denied the subsidiary's motion, holding that the defendant had failed to show the confidential nature of the documents or that its competitive position would be damaged by disclosure. Turick by Turick v. Yamaha Motor Corp., USA, 121 F.R.D. 32, 35.

S.D.N.Y.Bkrtcy.Ct.2007. Com. (b) quot. in case quot. in sup. Chapter 11 debtor brought adversary proceeding against its former employee and a competing company formed by employee, alleging, among other things, that defendants misappropriated its customer lists, which constituted trade secrets because they included confidential customer information, were compiled using software that was unique to debtor's business, and were protected by a three-tier security structure that only certain employees had access to based on their role in the company. This court entered judgment in favor of defendants, holding, inter alia, that, while plaintiff's customer lists were protected trade secrets, plaintiff failed to prove by a preponderance of the evidence that the lists were misappropriated by defendants. In re Cross Media Marketing Corp., 367 B.R. 435, 457.

S.D.N.Y.Bkrtcy.Ct.1991. Com. (b) cit. in case quot. in sup. A Chapter 11 debtor sued its former sales people to enjoin them from unfairly competing with the debtor and soliciting business from customers who formerly dealt with the debtor. The debtor offered into evidence that the sales people took with them confidential information maintained by the debtor, such as customer lists, credit terms, and price schedules. The sales people maintained that the customer lists, credit terms, and price schedules were retained by memory and then drafted into vacation lists compiling that information. The court dismissed the complaint against the sales people and denied the requested injunctive relief, finding that the vacation lists did not contain confidential information. It reasoned that the information contained in the vacation lists was easily acquired from other sources, the debtor's customers' names, addresses, and contact people were known outside of the business, and there was no evidence that the debtor made any effort to guard against the release of the information contained in

For earlier citations, see the Appendices, Supplements, or Pocket Parts, if any, that correspond to the subject matter under examination.

the vacation lists. In re Golden Distributors, Ltd., 134 B.R. 750, 757.

W.D.N.Y.2021. Com. (b) quot. in case quot. in sup. After general contractor that was hired to build dormitory buildings on a college campus brought a claim for breach of subcontract against subcontractor, subcontractor counterclaimed for misappropriation of trade secrets, alleging that general contractor's employee sent photographs of subcontractor's trade secrets to another company working on the project. This court granted summary judgment for general contractor on subcontractor's counterclaim for misappropriation of trade secrets. The court reasoned that, even if the information constituted a trade secret under Restatement of Torts § 757, it was undisputed that subcontractor failed to maintain the secrecy of its alleged trade secrets, because it permitted general contractor's employee to access the information with no restriction on his subsequent dissemination of the information. Pike Company, Inc. v. Universal Concrete Products, Inc., 524 F.Supp.3d 164, 181.

W.D.N.Y.2001. Com. (b) cit. in disc. Insurance agent whose agency with particular insurance company was terminated brought breach-of-contract action against company to recover deferred compensation; company counterclaimed, alleging that agent breached the agency agreement by, in part, misappropriating trade secrets, including customer lists and other proprietary information. Denying the parties' cross-motions for summary judgment, the court held, inter alia, that genuine issues of material fact existed as to the exact nature of the materials allegedly taken by agent, particularly how much effort was involved in obtaining the information, and how difficult it would be to obtain that information from other sources. Cray v. Nationwide Mutual Ins. Co., 136 F.Supp.2d 171, 176.

W.D.N.Y.2000. Quot. in case quot. in disc. Manufacturer of automated self-checkout system for use in retail establishments sued to enjoin one of its former salesmen from disclosing confidential information or trade secrets to a competitor. Denying plaintiff's motion for a preliminary injunction, the court held, inter alia, that injunctive relief was not necessary because defendant former salesman was already bound not to disclose confidential information by dint of his employment contract with plaintiff and the legal requirements resulting from that employment. The court said that defendant could be held accountable in provable damages if he violated his contractual obligations. PSC, Inc. v. Reiss, 111 F.Supp.2d 252, 254.

W.D.N.Y.1999. Com. (b) quot. in case quot. in disc. Seller sued buyer's new supplier, among others, for, inter alia, misappropriation of trade secrets, alleging that defendant unfairly used proprietary information belonging to plaintiff in its quest to become buyer's exclusive provider of regulators. Denying defendant's motion for summary judgment, the court held, in part, that material factual issues existed as to whether certain information, processes, and inventions claimed by plaintiff constituted trade secrets. BBS Power Mod, Inc. v. Prestolite Elec., Inc., 71 F.Supp.2d 194, 202.

W.D.N.Y.1995. Cit. in headnotes, cit. in sup., com. (b) quot. in sup. and quot. in case quot. in disc., com. (a) quot. in ftn. (erron. quot. as com. (b)). Licensor and licensee of single-screw compressor technology brought misappropriation-of-trade-secrets action against sublicensee's former employee, seeking to enjoin him from using and/or disclosing the technology. Defendant moved for summary judgment maintaining, inter alia, that he had developed the technology before his former employer became a sublicensee and received any confidential information from plaintiffs. Denying the motion and issuing a permanent injunction, the court held that knowledge of the single-screw compressor technology constituted a trade secret, which defendant had misappropriated. In support of its finding, the court noted, among other things, that knowledge of the disputed technology was not widespread, licensor had taken substantial steps to protect its secrecy, and the information was of great value to him, as he had spent more than 20 years and large sums of money developing it. Monovis, Inc. v. Aquino, 905 F.Supp. 1205, 1205, 1223-1224, 1224.

E.D.N.C.1996. Cit. in headnote (erron. cit. as Torts (2d)), com. (b) quot. in ftn. in sup. Pharmaceutical company sued competitor for, inter alia, misappropriation of trade secrets, alleging, among other things, that competitor discovered the mysteries of ranitidine hydrochloride crystallization only because its expert witness was able to analyze data in confidential documents made available by company during discovery in the parties' first lawsuit. Following a bench trial, the court entered judgment for competitor, holding that information did not become a trade secret merely because the document containing it was stamped "confidential," and that, in any event, the allegedly secret information here was readily discoverable by chemists. Glaxo Inc. v. Novopharm Ltd., 931 F.Supp. 1280, 1302, affirmed 110 F.3d 1562 (C.A.Fed.1997).

E.D.N.C.1992. Com. (b) quot. in disc. A travel agent who developed an idea to help finance vacations sued a travel agency and its president for misappropriation of trade secrets. The travel agent had disclosed his idea to several banks and travel agencies as well as to this agency in conjunction with his application for a managerial position with them. The court granted defendants' motion for summary judgment, determining that even if the concept could be found both unknown and not easily ascertainable, the travel agent's repeated disclosure of the details of the plan without any attempt to ensure the information's confidentiality, voided any claim to trade-secret protection. Bank Travel Bank v. McCoy, 802 F.Supp. 1358, 1360.

W.D.N.C.1989. Com. (b) cit. in case cit. in disc. An employee sued his employer for misappropriation of a trade secret, inter alia, alleging that his invention constituted a trade secret when his employer disclosed and began use of it in connection with its business. The court denied the defendant's motion for summary judgment, rejecting the argument that the court could not grant state law protection to an invention that was patented under federal law. The court stated that it had jurisdiction over a claim of unfair competition when it was joined with a substantial and related claim under the patent laws and that a trade secret may be, but need not be, a device or process that was patentable. Additionally, the court noted that the plaintiff's invention fit the definition of a trade secret, since it was a device used in one's business that gave him an opportunity to obtain a competitive advantage. Moore v. American Barmag Corp., 710 F.Supp. 1050, 1060, affirmed 902 F.2d 44 (Fed.Cir.1990).

N.D.Ohio Bkrtcy.Ct.2009. Com. (b) cit. and quot. in sup. After creditor was instructed by the bankruptcy court to file with the court an agreement it had entered into with another company for the provision of administrative loan default services with respect to Chapter 7 debtors' note, it moved for a protective order, seeking to prevent the disclosure of certain allegedly proprietary information in the agreement. Denying the motion, this court held that creditor did not meet its burden of proving that the agreement or any part of it, including the identity of the other company's corporate officers and the kinds of insurance that the company carried, was either a trade secret or confidential information, and certain schedules that included pricing information were similar to a publicly filed document in a prior case. In re Waring, 406 B.R. 763, 768.

S.D.Ohio, 1997. Cit. generally in disc., com. (b) cit. in disc. (Erron. cit. as Restatement (Fourth) of Torts.) Pharmaceutical company moved to enjoin physician, one of its former clinical investigators, from distributing information that he had obtained from company while conducting clinical trials on its acne medication, arguing that the material constituted trade-secret information under Ohio's Uniform Trade Secrets Act. Plaintiff also maintained that defendant owed it a common law duty not to disclose the information. Denying the motion, the court held that, while the documents at issue were of some economic value, the information contained therein was readily ascertainable from medical literature, and, moreover, plaintiff did not make reasonable efforts to keep the information secret. As for the remaining claim, the court explained that Ohio did not recognize a common law duty not to disclose trade secrets. Hoffmann-La Roche Inc. v. Yoder, 950 F.Supp. 1348, 1357, 1358, 1364.

S.D.Ohio Bkrtcy.Ct.1993. Cit. in sup., com. (b) quot. in sup. Occupational health care provider sought to enjoin its former employee and a competitor from using proprietary information the employee acquired during his business relationship with the provider. This court, granting a preliminary injunction, held, inter alia, that "green sheets," financial data, and fee or rate schedules used in the provider's business were trade secrets, as the information in them was not generally known outside the provider's business and the provider took steps to protect access to the documents. In re Urgent Medical Care, Inc., 153 B.R. 784, 788.

E.D.Pa.2021. Cit. in sup. University researcher brought a claim for trade-secret misappropriation under the Defend Trade

For earlier citations, see the Appendices, Supplements, or Pocket Parts, if any, that correspond to the subject matter under examination.

Secrets Act against, among others, university, alleging that defendant misappropriated plaintiff's pig-based model for studying heart failure and used it to file patent applications. This court denied in part defendant's motion to dismiss, holding that plaintiff satisfactorily alleged that a trade secret existed, because plaintiff alleged that he took reasonable measures to protect trade secrets regarding his pig-based model. The court explained that, under Restatement of Torts § 757, plaintiff was not required to take every possible measure to shroud the model in absolute secrecy, and that he complied with industry recommendations in securing the trade secrets, he used passwords and locks to protect the laboratory containing the secrets, and the trade secrets were obtained by improper methods when a colleague made false representations to plaintiff's student in order to gain access to the model. Houser v. Feldman, 569 F.Supp.3d 216, 230.

E.D.Pa.2018. Com. (b) cit. in case cit. in sup.; com. (j) cit. in sup. Employer sued former employee, competitor, and competitor's CEO, who was also employee's romantic partner, alleging that employee passed employer's trade secrets to CEO and competitor in breach of her fiduciary duty to employer. This court denied in part employee's motion to dismiss, holding that employer sufficiently stated a claim for conversion against employee by alleging that employee knowingly provided employer's trade secrets to CEO and competitor, who used the trade secrets to compete with employer to its detriment. The court pointed out that trade secrets were treated as convertible property under Pennsylvania law and Restatement of Torts § 757. Teva Pharmaceuticals USA, Inc. v. Sandhu, 291 F.Supp.3d 659, 680.

E.D.Pa.2013. Com. (b) cit. in ftn., illus. 3-4 cit. in sup. Apparel manufacturer brought an action for willful misappropriation of trade secrets under the Pennsylvania Uniform Trade Secrets Act (PUTSA) against distributor of its products. Denying defendant's motion to dismiss this claim, this court held that plaintiff's allegations that its method and formula for manufacturing a nonflaking coating on its apparel was a trade secret, that defendant misappropriated the information, and that defendant "used" the trade secret were sufficient to state a claim for trade-secret misappropriation under PUTSA. The court noted that PUTSA was a relatively young statutory creature, and Pennsylvania courts continued to look to pre-PUTSA case law interpreting Restatement of Torts § 757, Comment *b*, for guidance on determining whether information constituted a trade secret. Alpha Pro Tech, Inc. v. VWR Intern. LLC, 984 F.Supp.2d 425, 435, 442.

E.D.Pa.2012. Quot. in sup. Alleged inventor/developer of a sandpaper-based trigger for heat packs sued, among others, individual who founded a competitor of plaintiff, alleging trade-secret misappropriation, inter alia. Granting in part defendant's motion for summary judgment, this court held that this claim failed, because plaintiff failed to show that defendant learned of plaintiff's confidential information while standing in a position of trust and confidence, or that he used plaintiff's intellectual property adversely; no evidence supported plaintiff's allegation that defendant spoke to plaintiff to set up a confidential disclosure agreement regarding the trigger. Nova Design Technologies, Ltd. v. Walters, 875 F.Supp.2d 458, 468.

E.D.Pa.2009. Com. (b) cit. in case cit. in disc. Former employee sued former employer and employer's parent company, alleging, among other things, that defendants improperly and illegally assigned the agreement to another subsidiary of parent company; defendants counterclaimed for, among other things, misappropriation of trade secrets and/or confidential or proprietary information. Denying without prejudice the parties' cross-motions for summary judgment on defendants' counterclaims, this court held, inter alia, that it could not rule on whether the counterclaims were preempted by the Pennsylvania Uniform Trade Secrets Act (PUTSA), because neither party had properly briefed whether the information at issue qualified as a trade secret under the PUTSA and the applicable Restatement factors. Youtie v. Macy's Retail Holding, Inc., 626 F.Supp.2d 511, 522.

E.D.Pa.2008. Com. (b) cit. and quot. in sup., quot. in ftn., and cit. and quot. in cases quot. in sup. Former employees sued securities-trading employer for a declaration of the invalidity of covenants not to compete that were part of their employment contracts; employer counterclaimed for, inter alia, misappropriation of trade secrets. This court entered judgment for former employees on employer's misappropriation counterclaim, finding that em-

Cit.—cited; com.—comment; fol.—followed; sup.—support.
A complete list of abbreviations precedes page 1.

ployer failed to meet its burden of proving under Pennsylvania law the existence of a protected trade secret in its proprietary trading formula. The court concluded that the concept, formula, and spreadsheet were too widely known and too easily ascertainable to be protected as trade secrets, pointing out that one of employer's traders had derived both the concept and the formula by watching competing traders who were beating him on trades and observing how they traded. Fishkin v. Susquehanna Partners, G.P., 563 F.Supp.2d 547, 582-584.

E.D.Pa.2006. Cit. in case cit. in sup., com. (b) quot. in sup. Employer sought enforcement of a 12-month noncompetition agreement against a former senior executive who resigned to accept a position with employer's most significant competitor in the region. Granting plaintiff's motion for preliminary injunction, this court held, inter alia, that because plaintiff established that defendant had information entitled to trade-secret protection and he intended to work for a direct competitor, employer demonstrated irreparable harm. The court concluded that trade-secret protection applied because defendant had inside information about highly confidential marketing plans pertaining to plaintiff's services, which, if disclosed to competitor, would allow competitor to gain an unfair competitive advantage. Verizon Communications Inc. v. Pizzirani, 462 F.Supp.2d 648, 658.

E.D.Pa.2004. Com. (b) quot. in case cit. in sup. (Erron. cit. as § 474.) National association of hearing health care professionals sued manufacturer of hearing devices with which it had contracted to sell products to its members at discounted prices, alleging that manufacturer, which had bypassed association and made direct sales to its members, had converted association's member list and breached contract and covenant of good faith and fair dealing. Granting summary judgment for manufacturer on all counts, this court held, inter alia, that the conversion claim failed because association could not prove that its member list, which was posted on the association's website, was a trade secret that gave association a competitive advantage in the marketplace. American Hearing Aid Associates, Inc. v. GN ReSound North America, 309 F.Supp.2d 694, 705.

E.D.Pa.1998. Quot. in ftn. Insurance company sued former agent for, inter alia, tortious interference with contractual relations, misappropriation of trade secrets, and unfair competition. Granting in part and denying in part defendant's motion for summary judgment and denying that of plaintiff, the court held that the evidence was sufficient to allow a finding that defendant's actions in writing policies for plaintiff's former clients and in failing to return all of his client files and cards to plaintiff in a timely manner constituted tortious interference with contractual relations, and that material factual issues existed as to whether the client files, cards, and other items contained trade-secret information; however, there was no support for the allegation that defendant engaged in unfair competition. Prudential Ins. Co. of America v. Stella, 994 F.Supp. 318, 323.

E.D.Pa.1997. Cit. in headnotes, com. (b) quot. in sup. and quot. in case cit. in disc. Operator of high-end costume-jewelry retail stores located throughout the United States and Canada sought injunctive relief to prevent its former in-house attorney from accepting employment with operator's competitor, with whom operator frequently competed for selling space as well as for customers. Granting in part operator's motion for a preliminary injunction, the court held that attorney's knowledge of facts and numbers acquired during lease negotiations on behalf of operator constituted trade secrets entitled to protection, as did attorney's knowledge of operator's individual store profitability, and that attorney was therefore enjoined from representing competitor in lease negotiations upon which he worked for operator, from disclosing information relating to operator's retail leases, and from disclosing information relating to the profitability of operator's stores. Hyman Companies, Inc. v. Brozost, 964 F.Supp. 168, 169, 174.

E.D.Pa.1997. Cit. in disc. Pennsylvania corporation brought RICO action against British medical schools and their agents, alleging that defendants misappropriated plaintiff's proprietary interest in medical scanner equipment and technology. Defendants moved to dismiss, arguing, among other things, that the court lacked personal jurisdiction over them. Denying the motion, the court held, in part, that in personam jurisdiction was proper under the "tort-out/harm-in" provision of the Pennsylvania Long Arm Statute, since defendants' alleged misappropriation of plaintiff's trade secrets in England caused harm to plaintiff

For earlier citations, see the Appendices, Supplements, or Pocket Parts, if any, that correspond to the subject matter under examination.

in Pennsylvania, and that defendants had sufficient minimum contacts with Pennsylvania such that exercising jurisdiction over them would not offend traditional notions of fair play and substantial justice. Supra Medical Corp. v. McGonigle, 955 F.Supp. 374, 381.

E.D.Pa.1995. Cit. in headnote, quot. in disc. Creditor sued guarantors for breach of credit agreement when loan recipient defaulted. Guarantors contended, inter alia, that a novation occurred whereby the original credit agreement was superseded by two new contracts. They also filed a counterclaim charging, inter alia, that creditor tortiously interfered with the contract with loan recipient and misappropriated certain trade secrets. Granting in part and denying in part creditor's motion for summary judgment, the court held that there was no novation, only an executory accord, the terms of which guarantors had breached. The court interpreted the claim of tortious interference with contract as accusing creditor with attempting to prevent guarantors, rather than loan recipient, from performing. Considering the relevant factors, chief among them the nature of the alleged conduct, the court concluded that creditor had not acted sufficiently egregiously to support this claim. However, factual questions existed as to whether guarantors' plan to provide financing for affordable housing was a protectable trade secret that creditor had misappropriated. GE Capital Mortg. Serv. v. Pinnacle Mortg. Inv., 897 F.Supp. 854, 858, 871.

E.D.Pa.1993. Com. (b) quot. in sup. (Erron. cit. as Torts 2d and as § 797.) A corporation that marketed self-funded workers' compensation programs sued its current and former employees and a competitor formed by them for, among other claims, trade secret infringement and tortious interference with contract. This court, concluding that no trade-secret violations took place but that defendants interfered with plaintiff's contractual relations, awarded plaintiff compensatory and punitive damages and held, inter alia, under Pennsylvania law, that plaintiff's customer list was not a "trade secret" entitled to protection, as all of the customers were required to register as nonprofit organizations with the state and their names were a matter of public knowledge. A proposal book freely distributed to potential clients was also not a "trade secret," as plaintiff took no steps to keep its contents secret. National Risk Management, Inc. v. Bramwell, 819 F.Supp. 417, 430.

E.D.Pa.1992. Com. (b) quot. in sup. and quot. in case quot. in disc. Licensor of technology related to aluminum-zinc steel coating sought preliminary injunction against former employees, alleging misappropriation of trade secrets, intentional interference with contractual relations, and diversion of corporate opportunities, inter alia. The court granted the preliminary injunction, holding that, while licensor could not claim trade-secret protection in the manufacturing process of the coating or the names of its customers, since this information was public, licensor could claim protection in its own manuals, license agreements, business plans, projections, and strategies that resulted from its own precise configuration and assemblage of this information. It also held that while licensor could not prevent employees from soliciting past, present, and potential licensees' business, employees' attempts to induce existing licensees to breach confidentiality clause with licensor constituted interference with licensor's contractual relations and diversion of its corporate opportunities. BIEC Intern., Inc. v. Global Steel Services, Ltd., 791 F.Supp. 489, 539.

E.D.Pa.1988. Com. (b) quot. in disc. The administrator of a decedent's estate sued a manufacturer for injuries the decedent received from the explosion of a disposable butane lighter. The magistrate denied the defendant's motion for an order allowing them to withhold from discovery, certain design information that allegedly constituted trade secrets. This court affirmed, stating that, because the information the defendant sought to protect was already in the public domain and did not provide the defendant with any competitive advantage, the defendant had not met its burden of showing the existence of a trade secret or other good cause for the court to issue a protective order. Smith v. BIC Corp., 121 F.R.D. 235, 239.

M.D.Pa.2018. Cit. in case quot. in disc. Manufacturing company brought an action for misappropriation of trade secrets against former sales manager who had worked remotely from his home in Pennsylvania, seeking a preliminary injunction to restrain defendant from disclosing trade secrets and working for plaintiff's competitors in violation of a confidentiality agree-

Cit.—cited; com.—comment; fol.—followed; sup.—support.
A complete list of abbreviations precedes page 1.

ment he had executed with plaintiff. This court granted in part and denied in part plaintiff's motion for a preliminary injunction, holding that, under Pennsylvania law, while plaintiff demonstrated entitlement to injunctive relief enjoining defendant from disclosing certain trade secrets, plaintiff was not entitled to relief enjoining defendant from working for a direct competitor, given the significant harm that defendant would suffer if barred from working for any period of time. The court determined that no true conflict of law existed between the trade-secret analysis laws of Illinois, the state chosen by the parties to govern the confidentiality agreement, and Pennsylvania, because both forums derived definitions of "trade secret" and "misappropriation" from Restatement of Torts § 757. Cerro Fabricated Products LLC v. Solanick, 300 F.Supp.3d 632, 648.

M.D.Pa.2001. Cit. and quot. in ftn., cit. in sup., com. (b) quot. in ftn. and cit. in sup. State prescription-drug-plan contractor brought claims for trade-secret misappropriation, breach of contract, and tortious interference against former employee and competitor. On plaintiff's motion for preliminary injunction, this court held, inter alia, that plaintiff would likely be able to establish damages based on misappropriation of trade secrets, as well as other claims, but the court denied plaintiff's motion for preliminary injunction, stating that plaintiff would not suffer irreparable injury in absence of injunctive relief. First Health Group Corp. v. National Prescription Adm'rs, Inc., 155 F.Supp.2d 194, 217, 218, 227.

M.D.Pa.1995. Cit. in headnotes, com. (b) quot. in case quot. in disc. Manufacturer and servicer of precision balances and other instruments sought preliminary injunction to prevent former employee from using its specialized customer list in his competing business. Employee, who returned all files, customer lists, data bases, and microfiche films belonging to manufacturer when he resigned, located potential customers by looking in telephone, hospital, and university directories and cold-calling them, as well as by contacting customers for whom he recalled providing service while with manufacturer. Denying the injunction, the court held, inter alia, that manufacturer failed to establish a likelihood of success on the merits since its customer list was easily obtainable from directories and other publicly available sources and, therefore, did not constitute a protectable trade secret. Mettler-Toledo, Inc. v. Acker, 908 F.Supp. 240, 240, 241, 246.

W.D.Pa.2014. Cit. in case quot. in sup., com. (b) cit. in case cit. in sup. Insured manufacturer of respiratory-protection products sued insurer, alleging that insurer failed to indemnify it against hundreds of underlying products-liability actions, some of which were still pending. This court denied insured's motion to file certain documents under seal, holding that documents discussing insured's defense, valuation, or settlement of the underlying actions were not trade secrets under Restatement of Torts § 757. The court pointed out that a document did not contain a trade secret merely because a party deemed it to be confidential, and, while insured sought to protect its settlement strategy from public disclosure in order to protect its own financial well-being in connection with pending and future cases, the information it sought to seal was not the type of trade secret or proprietary commercial information that traditionally received protection from public disclosure to avoid harm to competitive market activity. Mine Safety Appliances Co. v. North River Ins. Co., 73 F.Supp.3d 544, 560.

W.D.Pa.1988. Cit. in sup., com. (b) cit. and quot. in disc. A former employee of a hospital management consulting firm formed his own business and began marketing computer software programs that he had developed while working for the consulting firm. The consulting firm sued the former employee for, inter alia, misappropriating trade secrets to which he had access and of which he had knowledge. This court granted the plaintiff's request for a preliminary injunction against the defendant, concluding that the plaintiff had sustained its burden of demonstrating a substantial likelihood of success on the merits of its trade-secret claim. The court held that based on a consideration of all relevant factors, the plaintiff had established that its methodologies of developing computer software programs constituted trade secrets. Healthcare Affiliated Services, Inc. v. Lippany, 701 F.Supp. 1142, 1154.

E.D.Tex.2019. Com. (b) cit. in case cit. in sup. (general cite). Business and subsidiaries brought a lawsuit against former employees and competitors, alleging that defendants misused plaintiffs' trade secrets

For earlier citations, see the Appendices, Supplements, or Pocket Parts, if any, that correspond to the subject matter under examination.

regarding products for spraying limestone, which defendants obtained during inquiries into an investment agreement with plaintiffs. This court adopted the recommendations of a magistrate judge and granted in part and denied in part defendants' motion for summary judgment, holding, inter alia, that plaintiffs failed to provide evidence that the allegedly misappropriated information, except for certain formulas, were trade secrets. The court explained that plaintiffs' non-formula information did not constitute trade secrets as defined by Restatement of Torts § 757, Comment *b*, because such information did not exist or was publically available. StoneCoat of Texas, LLC v. ProCal Stone Design, LLC, 426 F.Supp.3d 311, 321.

E.D.Tex.2012. Com. (b) cit. in sup. Software developer sued competitor, asserting, inter alia, a claim for infringement of its patent for technology that permitted automobile shoppers to use the Internet to compare vehicles available for purchase; competitor counterclaimed for misappropriation of trade secrets. After the jury found that developer misappropriated competitor's trade secrets, and awarded competitor damages, this court denied developer's motion for judgment as a matter of law. The court concluded that there was sufficient evidence at trial to support the jury's verdict that developer used competitor's alleged trade secrets in an unauthorized manner to secure a commercial benefit. The court rejected developer's argument that competitor failed to prove that its algorithm qualified as a trade secret under Texas law, pointing to evidence that, despite certain differences in the combination and ordering of steps in the parties' algorithms, developer's algorithm embodied the essence of competitor's algorithm. Versata Software, Inc. v. Internet Brands, Inc., 902 F.Supp.2d 841, 852.

E.D.Tex.2002. Com. (b) cit. in case quot. in sup. Putative holder of copyright in various computer programs sued alleged infringer. Granting defendant's motion for partial summary judgment, the court held, inter alia, that the programs' author was not an employee of plaintiff at the time the copyrighted programs were created; as a result, the programs were not works made for hire, and the copyrights were held by their author, not by plaintiff. The court also held that author's sole ownership of the copyrights precluded plaintiff's pendent claim for misappropriation of the trade secrets that consisted of those programs, since plaintiff could not establish the required element of secrecy necessary for it to maintain a misappropriation claim. Alcatel USA, Inc. v. Cisco Systems, Inc., 239 F.Supp.2d 645, 660.

N.D.Tex.2014. Subsec. (c) and com. (*l*) quot. in case quot. in sup. Developer of radio-frequency-identification technology that was installed for the U.S. Navy as part of a subcontract sued competitor, alleging that defendant improperly gained access to plaintiff's technology while working on a subsequent project for the Navy, and then used that access to reverse-engineer its own similar technology. This court denied defendant's motion for summary judgment on plaintiff's claim for misappropriation of trade secrets, holding, among other things, that genuine factual issues existed as to whether defendant had notice of the impropriety of its trade-secret acquisition, because plaintiff submitted sufficient evidence for a reasonable juror to conclude that defendant was on inquiry notice of the facts that the Navy's project contained plaintiff's trade secrets and that the Navy did not have the undisputed right to disclose those trade secrets. The court explained that, under Restatement of Torts § 757, plaintiff did not have to show that defendant actually knew its acquisition of plaintiff's trade secrets was improper; it was enough if defendant should have known of the impropriety of its acquisition. GlobeRanger Corp. v. Software AG, 27 F.Supp.3d 723, 750.

N.D.Tex.1990. Quot. in cases cit. in disc., com. (b) quot. in case cit. in disc. A manufacturer of medical diagnostic equipment sought a preliminary injunction to enjoin a former employee from further disclosing the plaintiff's confidential, proprietary, and trade secret information and using that information to do business with the plaintiff's former customers and to otherwise compete with the plaintiff in servicing the plaintiff's equipment. Because the court found that the defendant was in possession of over 7,000 pages of the plaintiff's confidential training manuals and that he had provided technical information regarding the servicing of the plaintiff's magnetic resonance imaging system to his current employer, it held that there was substantial likelihood that the plaintiff would prevail on its claim for misappropriation of trade secrets and it

Cit.—cited; com.—comment; fol.—followed; sup.—support.
A complete list of abbreviations precedes page 1.

granted the plaintiff's motion for injunctive relief. Picker Intern., Inc. v. Blanton, 756 F.Supp. 971, 979.

S.D.Tex.2015. Quot. in sup.; com. (b) quot. in sup. and cit. in cases cit. in sup.; com. (b) quot. in sup. (erron. cit. as Restatement Third)). Supplier of materials to the oil-and-gas industry filed a claim for misappropriation of trade secrets against competitor and former employee who left plaintiff to work for competitor in connection with allegations that employee stole confidential information from plaintiff and provided it to competitor. This court denied summary judgment for defendants, holding that questions of fact remained as to whether plaintiff's list of customer contacts and their personal email accounts was protectable as a trade secret under Texas law, noting that some Texas courts had held that even if customer information was readily available in the industry, liability would be upheld if the defendant gained the information in usable form while working for the plaintiff. The court noted that, under Texas law and the first Restatement of Torts § 757, a trade secret included information that was neither generally known by others in the same business nor readily ascertainable by an independent investigation. A.M. Castle & Co. v. Byrne, 123 F.Supp.3d 909, 915, 916.

S.D.Tex.2015. Com. (b) quot. in sup. (erron. cite as Restatement Third of Torts). Former employer brought a claim for misappropriation of trade secrets, inter alia, against former employee and his new employer, alleging that former employee misappropriated confidential customer lists, vendor lists, sales data, and other information from former employer and subsequently provided the information to new employer. Plaintiff moved to compel defendants to submit to a court-supervised forensic inspection of defendants' computers and other electronic equipment. The magistrate judge denied plaintiff's motion. Affirming, this court held that plaintiff was not entitled to the inspection of defendants' computers and other electronic equipment, because plaintiff failed to identify any specific confidential information of which defendants were in wrongful possession. In making its decision, the court referred to Restatement of Torts § 757, Comment *b*, as setting forth the criteria for determining whether something was a trade secret under Texas law. A.M. Castle & Co. v. Byrne, 123 F.Supp.3d 895, 901, 902.

S.D.Tex.2015. Com. (b) quot. in case quot. in sup. Designer of a smartphone application brought a claim for trade-secret misappropriation, inter alia, against former business partner, alleging that defendant sold the application to unnamed parties without authorization. Granting summary judgment for defendant on that claim, this court held that plaintiff failed to identify any trade secrets in a pitch deck for the application that plaintiff emailed to defendant. The court explained that, although the pitch deck included seven screenshots and a paragraph of text about the application's functionality, those were all readily ascertainable from the application itself, which was available to the public for free at the time of the alleged misappropriation. The court noted that Texas courts applied the six-factor test set forth in Restatement of Torts § 757 in determining whether a trade secret existed. Beardmore v. Jacobsen, 131 F.Supp.3d 656, 671.

S.D.Tex.2015. Cit. in sup. Ohio insurer brought an action in Ohio federal court for, among other things, breach of contract and misappropriation of trade secrets against former employee, after employee resigned to work for Texas wholesale insurance broker. Following transfer of the action, this court denied the parties' cross-motions for summary judgment, holding that genuine disputes of material fact remained as to whether employee breached the noncompete and nondisclosure provisions in the parties' contract as a matter of Ohio law. The court rejected defendants' argument that the contract's Ohio choice-of-law clause was unenforceable because the application of Ohio law would be in violation of a fundamental Texas public policy. While Ohio's definition of trade secrets was slightly different from Texas's definition, which followed the first Restatement of Torts § 757, Ohio had adopted the Restatement's six-factor test to determine whether a trade secret existed, and the definitions of trade secret in Ohio and Texas were not substantially different such that applying Ohio law would be repugnant to Texas public policy. McGowan & Co., Inc. v. Bogan, 93 F.Supp.3d 624, 637.

S.D.Tex.2014. Com. (b) quot. in cases quot. in sup. Former employer sued competitor and former employee who left employer to work for competitor, alleging, among other things, that defendants misap-

For earlier citations, see the Appendices, Supplements, or Pocket Parts, if any, that correspond to the subject matter under examination.

propriated plaintiff's trade secrets. This court granted in part defendants' motion for summary judgment, holding that plaintiff failed to state a claim against defendants for misappropriation of trade secrets. While defendants conceded that a reasonable jury could find that plaintiff's product costs, pricing information, and sales data were "trade secrets" under the definition set forth in Restatement of Torts § 757, there was no evidence that defendants used that information, and, while plaintiff also claimed that defendants took its customer lists, target-customer lists, cost-reduction case studies, proposal documents, financial information, and customer-treatment information, the court had previously ruled that plaintiff's evidence related to defendants' alleged misappropriation of that information was inadmissible; thus, plaintiff could not establish that the trade secrets were acquired through a breach of a confidential relationship or discovered by improper means. GE Betz Inc. v. Moffitt-Johnson, 301 F.Supp.3d 668, 689.

S.D.Tex.2013. Quot. in case quot. in sup., com. (b) quot. in sup. and cit. in case cit. in sup., com. (f) quot. in sup. Manufacturer of butterfly valves used in the transportation industry brought a trade-secret-misappropriation claim, inter alia, against competitor, among others, alleging that defendant unlawfully obtained plaintiff's trade secrets when it hired plaintiff's former employee to develop a competing line of valves. Denying defendant's motion for partial summary judgment, this court held that genuine issues of material fact existed as to whether plaintiff's drawings and dimensions rose to the level of trade secrets, whether plaintiff took reasonable steps to protect them, whether the information had been publicly disclosed, whether plaintiff's former employee wrongfully used the trade secrets, and whether plaintiff was damaged. Ultraflo Corp. v. Pelican Tank Parts, Inc., 926 F.Supp.2d 935, 948, 959, 961.

S.D.Tex.2011. Adopted in case cit. in sup., com. (b) cit. in case cit. in sup. Software developer sued, among others, consulting firm, alleging, among other things, misappropriation of trade secrets and theft of trade secrets in violation of Texas statutory and common law. After a jury returned a verdict in favor of developer, this court denied firm's renewed motion for judgment as a matter of law, holding, among other things, that developer presented sufficient evidence to allow a jury to conclude that trade secrets existed. The court pointed to developer's evidence that the source code for its software was maintained behind a firewall to ensure its secrecy, and that, though the functions of developer's software were known to the industry, other software companies did not have identical functions in their software. Wellogix, Inc. v. Accenture, LLP, 823 F.Supp.2d 555, 562.

S.D.Tex.Bkrtcy.Ct.2014. Cit. in case cit. in sup. Claimant/manufacturer filed a proof of claim in Chapter 11 debtor's bankruptcy proceeding, alleging, inter alia, that debtor and its employees civilly conspired to misappropriate claimant's trade secrets. Debtor moved to estimate the claim, and filed an objection to the claim. This court found, among other things, that claimant failed to legally justify its request for multiple damages for its trade-secret misappropriation claim, but was entitled to recover debtor's net profits earned using some of claimant's drawings. Noting that Texas based its law of trade secrets on Restatement of Torts § 757, the court stated that, in an action for trade-secret misappropriation, a plaintiff could recover actual damages based on either the value of what had been lost by the plaintiff or the value of what had been gained by the defendant. In re Mud King Products, Inc., 514 B.R. 496, 522.

W.D.Tex.2013. Com. (b) quot. in case quot. in sup. Nonprofit organization that developed and administered examinations for individuals seeking certification in medical radiologic technology sued provider of test-preparation services for the examinations, alleging, inter alia, that defendant misappropriated plaintiff's trade secrets by improperly soliciting, obtaining, and distributing questions appearing on plaintiff's examinations. Denying defendant's motion for summary judgment, this court held, among other things, that plaintiff's examination questions constituted trade secrets. The court pointed out that the questions were not published or otherwise made known to the public, that only certain employees of plaintiff were able to access the questions, that the questions were kept in a secure area and were only revealed to test-takers after they signed a nondisclosure agreement, that the questions were valuable because they enabled plaintiff to provide states with licensing exami-

Cit.—cited; com.—comment; fol.—followed; sup.—support.
A complete list of abbreviations precedes page 1.

nations, that plaintiff had committed a significant amount of resources to developing the questions, and that it would be very difficult for a competitor to acquire the specific questions developed by plaintiff. American Registry of Radiologic Technologists v. Bennett, 939 F.Supp.2d 695, 711.

W.D.Tex.Bkrtcy.Ct.2012. Cit. in disc. and in sup., cit. in ftn., quot. in case quot. in sup., com. (b) adopted in case cit. in ftn. and quot. in cases quot. in sup. Chapter 11 debtor/oil and gas production company brought an adversary proceeding for, inter alia, misappropriation of trade secrets against potential prepetition buyer of its assets, alleging that defendant impermissibly used plaintiff's confidential information and trade secrets to acquire oil and gas leases in a hydrocarbon-rich area of south Texas. This court entered judgment for debtor on this claim, holding that: debtor's subsurface, production, and operations data qualified as trade secrets under the six-factor test of Restatement of Torts § 757, Comment *b*; defendant obtained those trade secrets through improper means—requesting and receiving debtor's secrets from debtor's employees and a contractor retained by debtor; and defendant used debtor's trade secrets in a way that was competitively disadvantageous to debtor and benefited defendant. In re TXCO Resources, Inc., 475 B.R. 781, 803-807, 811, 813, 815, 818, 822.

W.D.Tex.Bkrtcy.Ct.2010. Com. (b) quot. in case quot. in sup. Mining company brought adversary proceeding against mineral lessee/debtor, asserting breach-of-contract, fraud, and other claims; debtor brought, inter alia, a counterclaim for misappropriation of trade secrets arising from the actions of debtor's one-time business associate in breaking into debtor's office and pilfering various documents. Denying this counterclaim, this court held that debtor failed to prove that plaintiff misappropriated trade secrets, since the pilfered documents were merely an assortment of documents that were unrelated to one another, aside from the fact that they all pertained generally to debtor's business activities, and did not amount to "trade secrets" under Texas law. In re ACM-Tex., Inc., 430 B.R. 371, 430.

D.Utah, 2012. Com. (b) quot. in case quot. in sup. (general cite). University sued pharmaceutical company for misappropriation of trade secrets. Denying defendant's motion for summary judgment, this court held that disputed issues of material fact existed as to whether university researcher's vision to find a certain type of drug, accompanied by the tools developed to accomplish that goal, could be a compilation trade secret, and, if so, whether defendant misappropriated that trade secret. The court rejected defendant's argument that no disputed facts existed as to whether the purported trade secret lacked specificity and uniqueness, concluding that a vision was protectable if, based on the defendant's knowledge and experience, the information was not known or ascertainable, and, here, plaintiff claimed that, at the time it was sharing information with defendant, no other research group had access to the unique combination of researcher's clones, antibodies, research data, expert advice, and project. Brigham Young University v. Pfizer, Inc., 861 F.Supp.2d 1320, 1326.

D.Utah, 1991. Cit. in case cit. in disc., com. (b) quot. in cases cit. in disc. The plaintiffs in a products-liability case moved to remove the confidentiality designation from various documents in the defendant's possession covered by a protective order. The court granted the plaintiffs' motion, holding that the defendant had failed to show good cause for the continued confidentiality of the documents. The court said that the defendant had not shown that release of the documents would jeopardize its trade secrets. Grundberg v. Upjohn Co., 137 F.R.D. 372, 393, 394.

E.D.Va.2004. Com. (b) quot. in case quot. in sup. Provider aeronautical engineering services sued competitor for, among other things, misappropriation of trade secrets in connection with information contained in competitor's proposal for government contract. Granting in part and denying in part defendant's motion to dismiss, this court held,inter alia, that provider sufficiently stated claim for misappropriation of trade secrets where it alleged that it made efforts to preserve secrecy of test materials, former employee provided materials to competitor, and competitor used materials in proposal for government contract; however, provider's patents were publicly disclosed and did not provide basis for claim for trade-secret misappropriation. Tao of Systems Integration, Inc. v. Analytical Services & Materials, Inc., 299 F.Supp.2d 565, 574.

E.D.Va.1995. Com. (a) quot. in case quot.

For earlier citations, see the Appendices, Supplements, or Pocket Parts, if any, that correspond to the subject matter under examination.

in sup. Religious group sued newspaper for, inter alia, copyright infringement and misappropriation of trade secrets after newspaper published portions of an affidavit filed by a dissatisfied former group member. Newspaper moved for summary judgment. Granting the motion, the court held that newspaper's publication came within the fair-use exception to the law of copyright infringement and that the document at issue did not constitute a trade secret, as it was part of an unsealed court file for 28 months and had been posted on the Internet, where it was potentially available to millions of Internet users worldwide. Furthermore, even if the document could be considered a trade secret, there was no liability where newspaper did not acquire it improperly. Religious Technology Center v. Lerma, 908 F.Supp. 1362, 1369.

E.D.Va.1995. Cit. in headnote, com. (c) cit. in sup. Food manufacturer sued its sauce packager for misappropriation of trade secrets and tortious interference with existing and prospective contractual relations after packager developed an imitative barbecue sauce and began selling it to manufacturer's longstanding customer. The court denied packager's motion for summary judgment, holding that material factual issues existed as to its misconduct. It also rejected the argument that manufacturer could receive a double recovery if both claims went forward, since one could not steal trade secrets without interfering with a rightful owner's business relations. The court explained that the two causes of action were independent, it being well settled that the harm in misappropriation was the wrongful acquisition of the trade secret, regardless of the wrongdoer's method of obtaining it or his decision to use it competitively. Smithfield Ham and Products Co. v. Portion Pac, 905 F.Supp. 346, 347, 350.

E.D.Va.1992. Com. (b) cit. in case quot. in disc. A marketer of computer products sued its former employee and a satellite products developer, alleging infringement of its copyright on a computer software program and other claims, including misappropriation of trade secrets; defendants counterclaimed on various bases. This court, while denying plaintiff's claim for copyright infringement, held, inter alia, that plaintiff's use of an earlier version of the program as a demonstration and marketing device qualified as a trade secret, and defendants misappropriated plaintiff's trade secret by marketing an enhanced version of the program as a stand-alone product. Avtec Systems, Inc. v. Peiffer, 805 F.Supp. 1312, 1320, affirmed in part, vacated in part 21 F.3d 568 (4th Cir.1994).

E.D.Va.1989. Cit. in case cit. in disc. A facsimile-machine manufacturer, which sold its machines only to the government, claimed that its various machine signals, called protocol variations, deserved trade-secret and copyright protection and sued a competitor, alleging trade-secret misappropriation, conversion, and copyright infringement, after the defendant used a government-owned machine that was manufactured by the plaintiff to achieve interoperability between the two parties' machines through reverse engineering. The court granted the defendant summary judgment, stating that the plaintiff, by selling its machine without reserving proprietary rights, disclosed its protocol variations; moreover, since the government owned all the rights to the machine, the defendant's acquisition of the machine and reverse engineering of the protocol variations were proper. The court concluded that the plaintiff's failure to protect this information when it sold the machine to the government rendered the information ineligible for trade-secret protection. Secure Services Tech. v. Time and Space Processing, 722 F.Supp. 1354, 1361.

S.D.W.Va.2018. Adopted in case cit. in sup.; com. (b) quot. in sup. Provider of software and related support services to county clerks' offices sued competitor and former employee who left plaintiff to work for competitor, alleging, among other things, that defendants misappropriated plaintiff's trade secrets, including the source code for its software programs. This court granted in part defendants' motion for summary judgment, holding that the source code for plaintiff's software did not qualify as a trade secret under the West Virginia Uniform Trade Secrets Act or Restatement of Torts § 757, because it was readily ascertainable by proper means by other persons who could obtain economic value from its disclosure or use. The court pointed to evidence that plaintiff placed the source code on county servers without encrypting or password-protecting it, labeling it as confidential, or mandating any requirements that it be kept confidential. CSS, Inc. v. Herrington, 306 F.Supp.3d 857, 876, 877.

Cit.—cited; com.—comment; fol.—followed; sup.—support.
A complete list of abbreviations precedes page 1.

S.D.W.Va.2013. Com. (b) quot. in sup. Environmental groups filed a citizens' complaint against energy companies, alleging that defendants' coal mining operations contaminated streams in violation of federal laws. After defendants inadvertently produced internal survey reports that documented water-contamination levels, without first marking them confidential or otherwise limiting their use, and plaintiffs refused to return the reports, defendants filed motions for a protective order and to seal the reports. This court, relying on the factors set forth in the original Restatement of Torts for determining whether information rose to the level of a trade secret, denied the motions, holding that the reports did not constitute confidential commercial research information entitled to a protective order. The court reasoned, in part, that defendants had not demonstrated that keeping the reports private provided it with an independent commercial advantage that would morph into a substantial competitive harm if the reports were disclosed. Ohio Valley Environmental Coalition v. Elk Run Coal Co., Inc., 291 F.R.D. 114, 119.

S.D.W.Va.2008. Cit. in case quot. in sup. Buyer of PVC pipe sued seller for damages, alleging that the couplings joining lengths of the pipe together failed. This court granted buyer's motion to allow public release of documents that seller marked as confidential pursuant to a protective order, which documents suggested that the presence of di-octyl phthalate caused the couplings to fail in pipes carrying water for human consumption. The court held, inter alia, that the documents did not contain "confidential commercial information" similar to a trade secret with independent economic value, noting that seller failed to show what efforts it took to keep the information contained in the documents a secret, and that the documents were not marked as confidential or privileged prior to being disclosed to buyer. Massey Coal Services, Inc. v. Victaulic Co. of America, 249 F.R.D. 477, 482.

E.D.Wis.2010. Com. (j) quot. in sup. Auto parts supplier that sought to purchase competitor's assets sued competitor and two of its employees for misappropriation of trade secrets, alleging that defendants disclosed to a nonparty highly sensitive and valuable internal documents that plaintiff had provided to defendants during purchase negotiations. Denying defendant's motion to dismiss, this court held, among other things, that plaintiff sufficiently alleged that defendants were under a duty to maintain the secrecy of the information at issue; a duty to maintain secrecy could arise in the context of a business acquisition, such that one party had the duty not to disclose a trade secret provided to it for a limited purpose in the course of negotiations. Radiator Exp. Warehouse, Inc. v. Shie, 708 F.Supp.2d 762, 768.

E.D.Wis.1993. Cit. generally in sup., com. (b) quot. in part in sup. A chemical company sued a competitor and former employees, asserting violation of the Wisconsin Uniform Trade Secrets Act and other claims after the employees began working for the competitor. This court, entering various orders including a denial of plaintiff's motion for a preliminary injunction, held, inter alia, that it was unlikely the plaintiff would be able to establish that product bulletins given out upon request, "confidential" product profiles containing virtually the same information, personal service reports left with customers after service calls, daily logs of customers contacted by company salesmen, and customer lists containing volume and dollar values of chemicals purchased were trade secrets or that they were misappropriated. In any event, said the court, statutory damages would provide an adequate remedy at law. Nalco Chemical Co. v. Hydro Technologies, Inc., 149 F.R.D. 686, 691-692.

E.D.Wis.1993. Com. (b) cit. in sup. An employer sued its former employees and their current employer, alleging breach of their employment agreements and misappropriation of trade secrets. Granting in part defendants' motion to compel discovery, this court held, inter alia, that sales information and other materials the employer had collected on competitors' prices and products was relevant to the trade-secret claim, so as to be discoverable. Nalco Chemical Co. v. Hydro Technologies, Inc., 148 F.R.D. 608, 616.

Ala.1996. Com. (b) quot. in case quot. in sup. Sole proprietor of a paintless-dent-removal (PDR) business sued former employee for breach of the employment agreement, which contained both a noncompete and a nondisclosure clause. The jury determined that defendant breached the noncompete clause, but also concluded that PDR did not constitute a trade secret. The

For earlier citations, see the Appendices, Supplements, or Pocket Parts, if any, that correspond to the subject matter under examination.

trial court entered judgment for plaintiff and permanently enjoined defendant from engaging in the business of PDR for two years, but refused to enforce the nondisclosure clause. Affirming, this court held, in part, that the PDR system was not a trade secret because, among other things, it was commonly known and readily ascertainable to those in the automobile body industry. Buckley v. Seymour, 679 So.2d 220, 223.

Ala.1992. Cit. in quot. but dist. The federal district court certified questions to this court to determine whether plaintiff, a defendant in a pending action, violated state legislation or common law in disclosing trade secret that she did not know was misappropriated by a third party at the time she obtained it. This court held that plaintiff violated state law when she disclosed the trade secret because she knew before disclosure that it was misappropriated. It explained that the legislature intended for the statute to impose liability for knowledge of misappropriation at the time of disclosure regardless of the fact that plaintiff did not know the secret was misappropriated at the time she obtained it. IMED Corp. v. Systems Engineering Assoc., 602 So.2d 344, 348.

Ala.1988. Quot. in case quot. in disc., com. (b) cit. generally and quot. in part in case quot. in disc. A manufacturer of enamel-coated pipe sought a permanent injunction against a former employee for violating a trade secret. The trial court granted the injunction. Affirming, this court held that several factors were to be considered in determining whether the plaintiff's manufacturing process constituted a trade secret and whether a trade-secret violation by the defendant had been established. The court noted that there was proof that the defendant misused knowledge of the plaintiff's production process since he was aware of his former employer's efforts to keep the process secret. State law had adopted the "comparative injury doctrine" for determining whether an injunction was warranted. Saunders v. Florence Enameling Co., Inc., 540 So.2d 651, 653, 654.

Ala.App.1987. Cit. generally in case cit. in disc., com. (b) quot. in disc. A restaurant owner sued a distillery, one of its sales representatives, and its parent corporation, alleging, inter alia, that the defendants misappropriated his recipe for a beverage. The trial court entered judgment on a jury verdict in favor of the plaintiff for nominal damages of one dollar. Reversing and remanding, this court held that the defendants were not entitled to a directed verdict, since the plaintiff presented some evidence that his recipe was a trade secret. Mason v. Jack Daniel Distillery, 518 So.2d 130, 132, 133.

Alaska, 2012. Com. (b) quot. in ftn. Village, along with manufacturer of a component for power-generation facilities, sued quasi-independent state agency, alleging, among other things, that agency erroneously awarded certain contracts for power generation in remote Alaskan villages to manufacturer's competitor and that agency's employees improperly disclosed manufacturer's trade secrets to competitor. The trial court granted agency's motion for summary judgment. While affirming, this court held that plaintiffs raised a fact issue as to the existence of a trade secret with regard to manufacturer's method of programming or wiring a certain type of controller. The court cited manufacturer's evidence regarding the value of its information to its business and to its competitors, the amount of effort and money expended in developing the information, how difficult it would be for others to properly acquire or duplicate the same information and methods, and manufacturer's efforts to keep its information secret. Powercorp Alaska, LLC v. Alaska Energy Authority, 290 P.3d 1173, 1187.

Alaska, 1991. Com. (b) quot. in ftn. Oil drillers sued state oil and gas conservation commission, among others, for a declaration that statutory disclosure provisions were unconstitutional and sought to enjoin defendant from disclosing oil well data. Reversing the trial court's decision for plaintiffs and vacating the injunction granted to plaintiffs, this court held that although plaintiffs' oil well data constituted trade secrets and were protected as property under both the federal and state constitutions, disclosure of the data to the state's department of natural resources for internal departmental purposes following an initial confidentiality period as provided by state statute did not constitute an unconstitutional taking. State DNR v. Arctic Slope Reg. Corp., 834 P.2d 134, 138.

Ariz.2014. Cit. in disc. Public-relations company brought unfair-competition and other claims against its former president and her competing company, alleging that defendants learned confidential and trade-secret information about plaintiff and intended to steal and exploit that information and plaintiff's customers to gain a competitive advantage. The trial court granted defendants' motion to dismiss, finding that the Arizona Uniform Trade Secrets Act (AUTSA) preempted plaintiff's common-law tort claims arising from the alleged misuse of confidential information even as to information not asserted to rise to the level of a trade secret. The court of appeals reversed in part. Agreeing with the result reached by the court of appeals, this court reversed the trial court's dismissal of plaintiff's unfair-competition claim and remanded that claim to that court, holding that the AUTSA did not displace common-law claims based on alleged misappropriation of confidential information that was not a trade secret. In making its decision, the court noted that it did not decide whether Arizona recognized a common-law claim for unfair competition under Restatement of Torts §§ 757 and 759. Orca Communications Unlimited, LLC v. Noder, 236 Ariz. 180, 184, 337 P.3d 545, 549.

Ariz.App.1999. Com. (b) cit. in ftn. Automobile leasing company filed a motion for a permanent injunction against former senior-level manager, alleging that defendant misappropriated trade secrets. Reversing the trial court's denial of the motion and remanding, this court held, inter alia, that plaintiff's internal financial information and its customer-service worksheet were trade secrets entitled to protection according to the nondisclosure provision in the employment agreement. Enterprise Leasing Co. of Phoenix v. Ehmke, 197 Ariz. 144, 3 P.3d 1064, 1069.

Ariz.App.1987. Subsec. (b) quot. in sup., com. (b) quot. in disc. An insurance agency sued a former employee for unfair competition, breach of contract, and intentional interference with contract, alleging that the defendant unlawfully retained information on the plaintiff's policyholders after resigning and used it to sell the policies of other insurance companies. The trial court enjoined the defendant from soliciting business from the plaintiff's policyholders, stating that the defendant wrongfully used the unlawfully retained information. Affirming, this court held that the trial court's wrongful-use finding was sufficient to establish liability for use of a trade secret, since part of the retained information was available nowhere else except through contact with an individual policyholder and the information was useful for soliciting new business. Prudential Ins. Co. of America v. Pochiro, 153 Ariz. 368, 736 P.2d 1180, 1183.

Ark.2002. Com. (b) cit. in disc. Poultry producer sued competitor, seeking an injunction against disclosure of its trade secrets and damages for their misappropriation. After the jury returned a verdict for plaintiff, the trial court granted defendant's motion for judgment n.o.v. Affirming, this court held, inter alia, that plaintiff's nutrient profile for poultry feed did not qualify as a trade secret because plaintiff failed to take any precautionary measures to protect it. Tyson Foods, Inc. v. ConAgra, Inc., 349 Ark. 469, 79 S.W.3d 326, 332.

Ark.2002. Com. (b) adopted in case cit. in sup. Financing company brought suit against wholesale warehouse club for misappropriation of a trade secret. The trial court entered judgment on a jury verdict awarding plaintiff damages. Reversing and dismissing, this court held that plaintiff's concept of wholesaling by buying goods in bulk at a favorable price and selling them at a markup to preordained customers was not a trade secret, since the basic economic components of the concept were generally known in the business world, and the combination of the components into the concept was not unique but rather was readily ascertainable. Wal-Mart Stores, Inc. v. P.O. Market, Inc., 347 Ark. 651, 66 S.W.3d 620, 630.

Cal.2003. Com. (f) quot. in ftn. to conc. op. Trade association for motion-picture industry brought suit for injunctive relief against web-site operator's republication of source code for software designed to circumvent the encryption of movies stored on DVDs, alleging that defendant misappropriated trade secrets. The trial court issued a preliminary injunction. The court of appeal reversed. Reversing and remanding, this court held that the preliminary injunction did not violate defendant's free-speech rights under either the state or federal constitution. A concurring opinion argued that plaintiff did not establish a likelihood of prevailing on its trade-secret claim, noting that it was doubtful that the alleged trade secret, which was obtained through reverse engineering, was acquired by improper means. DVD Copy Control Associa-

For earlier citations, see the Appendices, Supplements, or Pocket Parts, if any, that correspond to the subject matter under examination.

tion, Inc. v. Bunner, 31 Cal.4th 864, 901, 4 Cal.Rptr.3d 69, 101, 75 P.3d 1, 28, on remand 116 Cal.App.4th 241, 10 Cal.Rptr.3d 185 (2004).

Cal.App.2014. Cit. in ftn. (general cite). Company that invented a process for creating self-authenticating documents through the use of barcodes sued manufacturer of multifunction printers, alleging trade-secret misappropriation. After a bench trial, the trial court entered judgment for plaintiff. Affirming, this court held that the trial court's finding that defendant misappropriated plaintiff's trade secrets was amply supported by the evidence in the record and the relevant legal authorities; defendant's secret filing of patent applications disclosing plaintiff's ideas and its subsequent acquisition of patents covering those ideas were classic violations of trade-secret law. The court noted that, prior to the 1984 enactment of the Uniform Trade Secrets Act (UTSA), California had followed the similar, though not identical, Restatement of Torts definition of a trade secret. Altavion, Inc. v. Konica Minolta Systems Laboratory Inc., 226 Cal.App.4th 26, 41, 171 Cal.Rptr.3d 714, 726.

Cal.App.1990. Cit. in disc., cit. and quot. in ftn., subsec. (b) and com. (j) cit. in ftn., com. (b) quot. in ftn. An insurance company acquired rights to a software system of a collateral insurance tracking service and hired the director of the service as a consultant. Several years later, the consultant started his own company in competition with his former employer. The insurance company sued the consultant for unfair competition, alleging that the defendant had copied its software, had induced its employees to work for him, and had solicited its clients. The trial court ruled for the plaintiff. Affirming, this court rejected the defendant's argument that the plaintiff's cause of action was preempted by federal copyright law. The court held the complaint was not preempted because, in addition to elements of copyright infringement, it included elements of breach of fiduciary duty, breach of confidential relationship, and unauthorized disclosure of trade secrets. Balboa Ins. Co. v. Trans Global Equities, 218 Cal.App.3d 1327, 267 Cal.Rptr. 787, 796-801, certiorari denied 498 U.S. 940, 111 S.Ct. 347, 112 L.Ed.2d 311 (1990).

Cal.App.1989. Com. (f) cit. and quot. in disc. A Japanese manufacturer secretly arranged for its distributor to purchase ultrasonic imaging equipment from the plaintiff manufacturer, allegedly for comparison to its own imaging equipment. The plaintiff, on discovering that this Japanese competitor had received the equipment, demanded its return, but the competitor refused. The plaintiff filed suit, claiming that the competitor had misappropriated its trade secrets. The trial court subsequently issued a broad preliminary injunction prohibiting the competitor's use of information it had garnered from its study of the plaintiff's product. This court reversed, ruling, inter alia, that the product had been publicly disclosed, since hundreds of the product had already been sold on the open market, and therefore the information acquired through the competitor's examination could not be considered a trade secret. The court also concluded that the competitor's unethical concealment of its identity in obtaining the publicly available product did not create liability under trade-secret law. It stated that unless what is sold contains a trade secret in the first place, concealment of one's identity as a competitor does not violate trade-secret law. Acuson Corp. v. Aloka Co., Ltd., 209 Cal.App.3d 425, 257 Cal.Rptr. 368, 381.

Colo.App.2016. Com. (b) quot. in sup. Owner of the rights to the design of a component for a tool used in oil-and gas-drilling operations sued designer of the component and designer's new employer after he created a similar component for the new employer, alleging misappropriation of trade secrets and conversion. The trial court entered judgment on a jury verdict for plaintiff. Reversing in part and remanding, this court held that the record lacked sufficient evidence to support a conclusion that plaintiff's design was secret, because plaintiff did not establish that its design, in whole or in part, was substantially different from designs that were publicly available at the time of its creation. The court pointed out that, under Restatement of Torts § 757, the subject matter of a trade secret had to be secret, and matters of public knowledge or of general knowledge in an industry could not be appropriated by an individual as his or her secret. Hawg Tools, LLC v. Newsco International Energy Services, Inc., 411 P.3d 1126, 1134, 1135.

Colo.App.2001. Com. (b) quot. in case quot. in disc. Plumbing subcontractor for home developer sued independent contrac-

Cit.—cited; com.—comment; fol.—followed; sup.—support.
A complete list of abbreviations precedes page 1.

tor who had done plumbing work for subcontractor, alleging trade-secret misappropriation and unfair competition based upon defendant's use of subcontractor's confidential contract-pricing and bid information. Trial court entered judgment on jury verdict for subcontractor. This court affirmed the judgment and reversed the order denying subcontractor injunctive relief, holding, inter alia, that there was substantial evidence to support subcontractor's trade-secrets claim. The trade secret claimed by subcontractor was the bid itself, rather than the methods of calculating bid or bid's elements. The court declined to adopt a per se rule that a bid on a contract could not be a trade secret as a matter of law. Ovation Plumbing, Inc. v. Furton, 33 P.3d 1221, 1224.

Colo.App.1988. Com. (b) quot. in sup. An employment agency sued a former account executive for violating his employment contract's covenants not to compete, after the executive started his own agency and made several placements involving either his former employer's candidates or clients. The trial court held that the defendant had misappropriated trade secrets and violated the covenants not to compete by using his former employer's information on candidates. Affirming in part, reversing in part, and remanding, this court held that the employer's list of candidates was a trade secret. Management Recruiters of Boulder v. Miller, 762 P.2d 763, 765.

Colo.App.1988. Quot. in sup., com. (b) cit. in disc. A manufacturer of mining equipment lent a new product to a potential customer, presumably for the customer to test the product's efficiency. The customer removed the label indicating that patent applications were pending and gave the product to another person to duplicate. Upon discovery of these facts, the manufacturer sued the men involved for misappropriation of trade secrets and fraud. The trial court held the defendants jointly and severally liable on both counts. This court affirmed in part and reversed in part. It held that the defendants were liable for misappropriation of trade secrets, because the product was lent for the express purpose of testing the product, and the defendants were under an implied duty to preserve the product in its original condition and not to use it for purposes other than testing; thus, the defendants' use of the product to produce copies was an unauthorized use sufficient to render them liable. The court reversed the finding of fraud as to the person who made the copies and his corporation, because they did not make affirmative misrepresentations to the manufacturer. Mineral Deposits Ltd. v. Zigan, 773 P.2d 606, 608.

Conn.1988. Com. (b) quot. and cit. in disc. An insurance company sued its former sales employee and his subsequent employer for the theft of trade secrets. The trial court found for the defendants. This court affirmed, holding that a customer list was not a trade secret where the list was not kept substantially confidential and where the former salesman had retained the monthly production reports and had established personal relationships with his customers. Robert S. Weiss & Assoc. v. Wiederlight, 208 Conn. 525, 546 A.2d 216, 223, 224.

Conn.App.2021. Cit. in sup.; com. (b) quot. in sup. Solar-development company that had unsuccessfully bid on several renewable-energy procurements by the Department of Energy and Environmental Protection filed a freedom of information request seeking disclosure of responses to the Department's requests for proposals made by successful bidders. After the Department denied company's request, the Freedom of Information Commission affirmed. Affirming, this court held, among other things, that the Commission correctly found that some of the information at issue contained "highly market sensitive" information, which derived independent economic value from its secrecy, such that it was exempt from disclosure as a trade secret within the meaning of Restatement of Torts § 757. Allco Renewable Energy Limited v. Freedom of Information Commission, 257 A.3d 324, 333.

Conn.App.1999. Com. (b) quot. in disc. Public utility challenged a decision of the trial court that required utility to turn over to competitor a study involving the cost of service to a particular customer. Utility argued that the study constituted a trade secret protected by statute. Affirming, this court held that the study and the information contained within it did not amount to a protectable trade secret, since utility took no real steps to keep it confidential or to prevent its widespread dissemination. Dept. of Public Utilities v. FOIC, 55 Conn.App. 527, 739 A.2d 328, 330.

Fla.App.2020. Com. (b) quot. in case

quot. in sup. Vegetation-clearance company sued, among others, competitor, alleging claims of conspiracy and unfair trade practice, and seeking production of bid documents that defendant had made to an energy company to secure a vegetation-clearing contract. The trial court granted plaintiff's motion to compel. This court granted defendant's petition for certiorari and remanded, holding that the trial court erred when it determined as a matter of law that defendant's bid documents contained no trade secrets. The court explained that defendant adequately pleaded that the bid documents included information that could be reverse-engineered to reveal its proprietary bid-development processes, which constituted trade secrets as defined by Restatement of Torts § 757, Comment *b*. Lewis Tree Service, Inc. v. Asplundh Tree Expert, LLC, 311 So.3d 206, 212.

Fla.App.2013. Com. (b) quot. in case quot. in ftn. After plaintiff sued defendant who allegedly injured her in a car accident, defendant sought production of various documents from surgical center that treated plaintiff following the accident. The trial court denied surgical center's motion for a protective order and ordered it to comply with defendant's discovery request. Granting surgical center's petition for a writ of certiorari and quashing the order, this court held, among other things, that the trial court erred by failing to determine whether the requested documents constituted trade secrets and, if so, by failing to require any protective measures to prevent dissemination of the information. The court noted that, while defendant had indicated in his response to the petition that he was willing to stipulate that the requested documents were trade secrets, it was doubtful that all of the requested documents constituted trade secrets, because they included contracts, salary information, and cost information as it pertained to plaintiff's procedure only. Gulfcoast Surgery Center, Inc. v. Fisher, 107 So.3d 493, 496.

Fla.App.2011. Com. (b) quot. in sup., cit. in case cit. in disc. Borrowers who consented to a foreclosure judgment in favor of assignee of mortgage, note, and guaranty, but who contested subsequent deficiency action, moved to compel disclosure of purchase documents between assignee and original lender, which assignee claimed contained proprietary acquisition pricing information. The trial court ordered production of unredacted copies of the documents and declined to conduct a preliminary in camera review; assignee petitioned for a writ of certiorari to quash the compelled disclosure. Granting assignee's petition, this court held that the trial court departed from the essential requirements of law by ordering disclosure without conducting an in camera review to determine whether the information was a trade secret, and without such a review, this court could not determine whether the acquisition pricing information was merely the price for a single transaction, which would not be protected as a trade secret, or a formula resulting in a price, which might be a protected trade secret. Summitbridge Nat. Investments LLC v. 1221 Palm Harbor, L.L.C., 67 So.3d 448, 450.

Fla.App.2000. Com. (c) quot. in case quot. in disc. Defense contractor that designed, manufactured, and sold "rate dampers" for laser-guided bomb systems sued competing corporation that was founded by its former employees, alleging misappropriation of trade secrets relating to the rate dampers it produced. After the trial court entered judgment awarding plaintiff damages and enjoined defendant from future misappropriation of plaintiff's trade secrets, it denied plaintiff's motion for contempt for violation of the injunction. This court affirmed, holding, inter alia, that the trial court properly denied plaintiff's motion for contempt, because the two designs were not similar and an expert testified that the two rate dampers functioned in substantially different ways and were designed in accordance with different specifications, performance requirements, and parts. Real-Time Lab., Inc. v. Predator Systems, 757 So.2d 634, 637.

Fla.App.1996. Com. (b) cit. in disc. Employer petitioned court for a writ of certiorari to quash an order directing one of its employees to answer questions at a deposition involving two companies involved in misappropriation-of-trade-secret litigation. At issue was whether one of the companies misappropriated a certain bacterial process belonging to the other company, or whether the process was known to others in the field. Denying the petition, the court held that, even though the companies might each have discovered the process independently, it could still be a trade secret, and that employee's knowledge could be relevant to a determination of

Cit.—cited; com.—comment; fol.—followed; sup.—support.
A complete list of abbreviations precedes page 1.

what was generally known and readily ascertainable to competitors. Bestechnologies v. Trident Envir. System, 681 So.2d 1175, 1175, 1176.

Fla.App.1989. Com. (b) quot. in disc. A manufacturer of thermal-therapy machines sought a temporary injunction to prevent a competitor from manufacturing, marketing, distributing, or selling a similar machine, pursuant to a confidential disclosure agreement entered into by the two parties prior to failed business negotiations in which the plaintiff disclosed allegedly confidential information to the defendant regarding planned improvements to the plaintiff's product. The trial court granted a temporary injunction. Affirming, this court concluded that the plaintiff's planned improvements were confidential information under the confidential disclosure agreement. The court stated that, since the plaintiff presented evidence that it disclosed confidential information to the defendant, which information it disclosed to no one else, even though the improvements may or may not have been common law trade secrets, the information divulged under the agreement was information that the plaintiff intended to keep secret and that gave the defendant an unintended competitive advantage. Concept, Inc. v. Thermotemp, Inc., 553 So.2d 1325, 1327, review denied 574 So.2d 140 (1990).

Hawaii, 2002. Cit. in case cit. in disc., com. (b) quot. in case quot. in ftn. Husband, an inventor of electronic products, appealed from family court's postdecree orders, which recalculated the amount of the marital estate and denied prejudgment interest. This court affirmed, holding, inter alia, that, in a dissolution action, husband's trade secrets were subject to equitable distribution pursuant to the state statute. The court noted that trade secrets carried the hallmarks of property, because they were assignable, could form the res of a trust, and pass to a trustee in bankruptcy. Therefore, the husband's trade-secret inventions, which existed premaritally, constituted premarital property. Teller v. Teller, 99 Hawai'i 101, 53 P.3d 240, 247.

Idaho, 2019. Cit. in sup.; com. (b) quot. in case quot. in sup. In insurance agent's declaratory-judgment action against insurer that terminated his contract, insurer filed counterclaims against agent, alleging, among other things, that agent misappropriated its trade secrets. The trial court granted summary judgment for agent on insurer's counterclaims. Affirming, this court held that, while insurer asserted that agent had admitted that he used insurer's customer list, the list at issue did not constitute a trade secret under Restatement of Torts § 757. The court reasoned, in part, that the list was almost wholly generated from alternative and independent sources, it contained generally known or public information such as contact information for certain individuals, and insurer took few efforts to maintain its secrecy. Trumble v. Farm Bureau Mutual Insurance Company of Idaho, 456 P.3d 201, 217, 218.

Idaho, 2015. Com. (b) quot. in case quot. in sup. Provider of spa and salon services sued former employee and competitor formed by employee, alleging, among other things, that defendants violated the Idaho Trade Secrets Act by using plaintiff's client list and other client-related information. The trial court granted summary judgment for defendants. Reversing and remanding, this court held that there were genuine factual disputes regarding the nature of the information at issue and whether it qualified as confidential information and a trade secret under the first Restatement of Torts § 757. The court pointed out that there were disputes as to whether plaintiff's owner and founder authorized the use and release of plaintiff's client list, whether plaintiff's business practices compromised the confidentiality of the client list, and whether employee actually took and used any of plaintiff's confidential information in the creation and promotion of competitor. La Bella Vita, LLC v. Shuler, 353 P.3d 420, 428.

Idaho, 2010. Com. (b) quot. in case quot. in sup. Auto-body supply company brought suit for violations of the Idaho Trade Secrets Act against competitor, paint supplier, and plaintiff's former employees who left to work for competitor, arguing that defendants, acting jointly and severally, acquired, disclosed, or used plaintiff's customer information using improper means. This court affirmed the trial court's dismissal of that claim except as to one former employee/store manager, holding that plaintiff failed to raise a genuine issue of material fact that any of the employees other than the store manager took customer lists, lists showing customer-buying preferences, and custom paint formulas; to the extent that customers left plaintiff and began using competitor, the evidence indicated that this was due to the relationships that employees had developed with the customers and not trade secrets taken from plaintiff. Wesco Autobody Supply, Inc. v. Ernest, 149 Idaho 881, 243 P.3d 1069, 1086.

Idaho, 1999. Cit. in headnote, cit. generally in case quot. in disc., com. (b) cit. and quot. in disc. Manufacturer of dehydrated-potato products sued former research engineer employee and a competitor that hired former employee, alleging misappropriation of trade secrets related to production of a hash-brown product. Trial court entered an injunction and awarded plaintiff $3.26 million. This court affirmed, holding, inter alia, that plaintiff's "Golden Grill" process was a trade secret under the Idaho Trade Secrets Act. The fact that plaintiff spent almost six years developing the Golden Grill product was sufficient evidence that the process was not generally known or readily ascertainable. Basic American, Inc. v. Shatila, 133 Idaho 726, 992 P.2d 175, 184.

Ill.App.2020. Cit. in sup. Provider of assembly services, which was hired to assemble and repair certain subassemblies for manufacturer of excavators and wheel loaders, sued manufacturer, alleging, among other things, that it misappropriated provider's assembly process when it decided to start using its own employees to build the subassemblies. The trial court granted summary judgment for manufacturer. Affirming, this court held that provider's assembly process did not qualify as a trade secret as a matter of law under the six-factor test set forth in Restatement of Torts § 757. The court reasoned that provider's description of its "trade secret" as a process that focused on efficiency, cost, quality, safety, and transportation contained generic terms that many companies would use to describe their assembly processes. National Tractor Parts Inc. v. Caterpillar Logistics Inc., 171 N.E.3d 1, 14, 15.

Ill.App.2016. Com. (a) quot. in sup. Manufacturer of a cable assembly and panel mount brought claims for misappropriation of trade secrets against competitor and former employees who left to work for competitor. The trial court entered judgment on a jury verdict for defendants, but denied defendants' post-trial motion for attorney's fees. Reversing in part and remanding, this court held that competitor had made an exceptionally strong case that it should be awarded attorney's fees, pointing to evidence that plaintiff failed to identify the person or entity that it had a confidential relationship with, and that plaintiff admitted that it could not prove how competitor misappropriated its allegedly secret information. The court noted that, under Restatement of Torts § 757, it was the employment of improper means to procure a trade secret, rather than mere copying or use, that was the basis of liability; thus, the specific circumstances under which defendants acquired or used plaintiff's allegedly secret information were crucial considerations in assessing whether a misappropriation took place. Conxall Corp. v. Iconn Systems, LLC, 61 N.E.3d 1081, 1098.

Ill.App.2007. Adopted in case cit. in sup. Former employee of chemical company sued former employer, seeking a declaration of his rights under an employment contract, and employer counterclaimed, alleging breach of the contract's noncompetition and nondisclosure provisions. Denying employer's motion for a preliminary injunction prohibiting employee from competing with employer or disclosing employer's trade secrets, this court held, inter alia, that it was unlikely that it would find that employer's customer lists were trade secrets, that employee disclosed or misappropriated employer's customer data, or that employer had traded on or used employer's chemical formulas or blends in any commercial way. McGough v. Nalco Co., 496 F.Supp.2d 729, 739.

Ill.App.2007. Cit. in sup., com. (b) cit. in case cit. in sup. Employee sued former employee for, among other things, allegedly acquiring and using on behalf of employer's competitor a spreadsheet containing employer's trade secrets. The trial court denied employer's motion for a preliminary injunction based on violations of the Illinois Trade Secrets Act. Affirming, this court held, inter alia, that, other than the efforts taken by employer to guard the secrecy of the information and possibly the time expended to create and maintain the spreadsheet, the remaining relevant Restatement First factors supported the trial court's finding that the information at issue did not constitute a trade secret, particularly in light of employee's unrebutted testimony that he could reproduce the spreadsheet in two to three days without information from employer.

Stenstrom Petroleum Services Group, Inc. v. Mesch, 375 Ill.App.3d 1077, 314 Ill.Dec. 594, 874 N.E.2d 959, 971, 972, 974, 975, 977.

Ill.App.2005. Com. (b) cit. in case quot. in disc. Manufacturer of computer-network-protection equipment and its exclusive sales representative moved for a preliminary injunction barring representative's former sales staff from using alleged trade secrets, claiming misappropriation by staff. The trial court denied plaintiffs' motion. Reversing in part, affirming in part, and remanding, this court held, inter alia, that representative's price books were misappropriated trade secrets, but that although customer lists developed by representative were secret and had value because they took significant "digging" to compile, they, along with bids and sales quotations, could not be deemed trade secrets because representative did not take reasonable steps to alert employees that the information was confidential. Liebert Corp. v. Mazur, 357 Ill.App.3d 265, 277, 293 Ill.Dec. 28, 41, 827 N.E.2d 909, 922.

Ill.App.1991. Com. (b) cit. and quot. in case cit. in disc., cit. generally in disc., and cit. in conc. and diss. op. A corporation that designed and sold custom calendars sued to enjoin a former employee from soliciting former customers and to require him to turn various documents allegedly containing trade secrets over to the trial court for examination. The trial court granted the plaintiff's request for a preliminary injunction. Reversing, this court held that the defendant did not misappropriate any trade secrets, since the information the defendant brought with him from the plaintiff to use on his new job was either given to him freely by the plaintiff or developed by the defendant from his working a client. A concurring and dissenting opinion argued that information or customers' names need not have been kept secret from the defendant for them to be trade secrets as to him and that the trial court was within its discretion in requiring the defendant to deliver all documents containing the foregoing information to the court clerk. Colson Co. v. Wittel, 210 Ill.App.3d 1030, 155 Ill.Dec. 471, 474, 475, 477, 569 N.E.2d 1082, 1085, 1086, 1088, appeal denied 141 Ill.2d 537, 162 Ill.Dec. 484, 580 N.E.2d 110 (1991).

Ill.App.1989. Com. (b) cit. in case quot. in sup. A former employee appealed the grant of a preliminary injunction enjoining him from using trade secrets and confidential information obtained during his employment with plaintiff, a record storage and retrieval service for health care facilities. The appellate court reversed, holding that the plaintiff had failed to prove that its pricing formula, although unique in the industry, was the result of information or a process that was not generally known to others. The employee was entitled to use the general skills and knowledge acquired during his employment to form a competing company. Service Centers of Chicago v. Minogue, 180 Ill.App.3d 447, 129 Ill.Dec. 367, 535 N.E.2d 1132, 1135.

Ill.App.1988. Com. (b) cit. in case cit. in disc. A former employee of a telecommunications corporation, who had access to the corporation's electronic circuitry blueprints and schematics, collaborated with two others to form a new telecommunications corporation, which subsequently produced an automatic wake-up system for hotels that was substantially similar to that previously produced by their former employer. The former employer sued the former employees and their corporation for the misappropriation and use of its trade secrets, seeking injunctive relief, damages, and an accounting. The trial court entered an injunction prohibiting the defendants from manufacturing or selling their product, and the defendants filed an interlocutory appeal. Affirming, this court held, inter alia, that from the evidence presented, the trial court properly determined that the schematics and circuitry used by the defendants were trade secrets. Televation Telecommunication Systems, Inc. v. Saindon, 169 Ill.App.3d 8, 119 Ill.Dec. 500, 522 N.E.2d 1359, 1363.

Ind.2004. Cit. in ftn. to diss. op. Former employer's successor sued former employee and his new employer, alleging that former employee used stolen trade secrets to lure plaintiff's customers to new employer. The trial court held that former employee was liable for misappropriating and converting plaintiff's trade secrets, but that new employer was not. The court of appeals affirmed in part and reversed in part. Affirming the trial court's judgment, this court held that new employer could not be held liable absent proof of scienter required by the Uniform Trade Secrets Act. The dissent argued that the Uniform Act's requirement of scienter did not conflict with the imposition of vicarious liability on a wrongdoer's employer, since the risk of liability would serve as an incentive for employers to discourage employees from using misappropriated trade secrets. Infinity Products, Inc. v. Quandt, 810 N.E.2d 1028, 1035.

Ind.1993. Cit. and quot. in sup., subsec. (b) quot. in part in disc. An oil company sought injunctive relief against a competitor allegedly using the company's trade secrets in order to obtain oil leases. Trial court granted plaintiff company a preliminary injunction but intermediate court of appeals reversed. This court affirmed the trial court's judgment, holding that information regarding the location of potential oil fields that the oil company generated only after seven months of investigation and after spending more than $150,000 on microwave radar surveys was not readily ascertainable by other means and was, therefore, entitled to protection as a trade secret. Amoco Production Co. v. Laird, 622 N.E.2d 912, 916, 918.

Iowa, 2008. Com. (b) quot. in case quot. in sup. Manufacturer of cement mixers sued former employees, competitor, competitor's officers, and customer, alleging misappropriation of trade secrets, inter alia. The trial court granted summary judgment for defendants. Reversing and remanding as to former employees and competitor and its officers, this court held that genuine issues of material fact existed as to whether former employees took advantage of their positions with plaintiff to obtain proprietary information that was then used for competitor's benefit, and as to whether competitor and its officers used their positions as potential buyers of plaintiff's business to obtain plaintiff's proprietary information for their own benefit. Cemen Tech, Inc. v. Three D Industries, L.L.C., 753 N.W.2d 1, 8.

Iowa, 1988. Com. (b) quot. in disc. and quot. in case quot. in disc. A publishing company sued a former employee for interference with contractual relations, breach of fiduciary duty and oral employment contract, and misappropriation of trade secrets, inter alia, after the employee opened a competing publishing company and published books by authors who previously had used the employer's company. The trial court entered judgment for the defendant on the ground that he had caused no interference with the plaintiff's contractual relations with the authors who went over to the defendant's publishing company and that the list of authors the plaintiff claimed had been misappropriated was not a trade secret. Affirming, this court held that the relationship between the authors and the plaintiff had deteriorated before any offer had been made by the defendant and that the list of authors was not a trade secret because it was openly disclosed to the public. The court also concluded that the plaintiff's claim that the defendant had breached his duty of loyalty and the oral employment contract was barred by the statute of limitations because the statute began to run when the plaintiff discovered that the defendant was working for his own publishing company while still employed by the plaintiff's company. Kendall/Hunt Pub. Co. v. Rowe, 424 N.W.2d 235, 246.

Me.2001. Cit. in disc., com. (b) quot. in disc. Engineer sued former employer to recover unpaid commissions. Employer counterclaimed for breach of contract and misappropriation of trade secrets. Trial court ruled that employee breached employment contract, but did not use or disclose employer's trade secrets. This court affirmed, holding, inter alia, that information that former employee used to design a dryer for employer's competitor was not a trade secret, as employer's design was not unique or inherently superior to other designs, and trial court did not err in analyzing the value of employer's information in terms of its utility as opposed to its actual economic value. Bernier v. Merrill Air Engineers, 770 A.2d 97, 107.

Md.2004. Com. (b) quot. in disc. Employer sought injunctive relief to prevent former employee from accepting employment with its primary competitor, alleging that former employee had misappropriated trade secrets that would provide competitor with unfair competitive advantage. Trial court granted preliminary injunction for employer. Vacating and remanding, this court noted the long history of Maryland's regulation of trade-secret protection, and although it agreed with the trial court that former employee had misappropriated employer's trade secrets, it held that the trial court based its grant of an injunction on a theory, the inevitable-disclosure doctrine, that did not apply in Maryland. LeJeune v. Coin Acceptors, Inc., 381 Md. 288, 849 A.2d 451, 460.

Md.Spec.App.1999. Cit. in disc., com. (b) quot. in cases quot. in disc. Corporation

Cit.—cited; com.—comment; fol.—followed; sup.—support.
A complete list of abbreviations precedes page 1.

sued former president for violations of the Maryland Uniform Trade Secrets Act, alleging that defendant misappropriated technology he developed for plaintiff while in plaintiff's employ. The trial court entered judgment for plaintiff. Affirming, this court held, in part, that the development of a process for separating adherent foreign matter from solid materials constituted a trade secret, as did the knowledge of such a process. That defendant resigned his position as a corporate officer one day before absconding with the information at issue was irrelevant to a consideration of his liability. Bond v. PolyCycle, Inc., 127 Md.App. 365, 732 A.2d 970, 973, 974, 976.

Md.Spec.App.1991. Cit. in disc.; com. (b) quot. in case quot. in disc., quot. in ftn. in law review. A vinyl-looseleaf-binder manufacturer sued its former employee, the employee's business and business partner, inter alia, for misappropriation of trade secrets. In the performance of his job, the defendant used confidential information regarding pricing, costs, profits, production rates, and marketing strategies. While still in the plaintiff's employ, the defendants formed a corporation that manufactured vinyl looseleaf binders. The trial court found that the defendants did not misappropriate trade secrets because the pricing and marketing information were not trade secrets under the state uniform trade secrets act. This court affirmed on the same grounds. The court stated that although all of the Restatement's factors were no longer required to find a trade secret under the act, those factors still provided helpful guidance to determine whether the information concerned constituted trade secrets within the definition of the act. Optic Graphics v. Agee, 87 Md.App. 770, 591 A.2d 578, 584, 585.

Md.Spec.App.1989. Com. (b) cit. in case quot. in disc. (Erron. cit. as § 757b.) A professional dental association sued two dentists, former members of the association, alleging wrongful use of patient information and unfair competition. The trial court found in favor of the defendants. This court affirmed, holding that the plaintiff's patient list was not a trade secret. The court said that, while the patients' names and addresses were not generally known outside of the practice and the list could not have been easily acquired by others, the plaintiff did not expend an extraordinary amount of money or effort to generate the patient list; it was developed as an incident of the practice. Additionally, the plaintiff took no measures to guard the secrecy of the patient list, or to restrict its accessibility. Allan M. Dworkin D.D.S., P.A. v. Blumenthal, 77 Md.App. 774, 551 A.2d 947, 950.

Mass.1998. Com. (b) cit. in case cit. in ftn. A company sued a corporation that provided executive-employee search services for injunctive relief and damages, alleging unfair and deceptive trade practices, deceit, and invasion of privacy. The defendant company's agents had misrepresented themselves to plaintiff's offices nationwide by using various aliases, and they obtained names, addresses, phone numbers, and positions of plaintiff's managerial and sales employees. The trial court granted defendant's motion to dismiss. This court affirmed in part, vacated in part, and remanded, holding, inter alia, that fact issues existed as to whether the information acquired by defendant was proprietary business information entitled to protection. The court stated that if a factfinder were to determine that the employee information was proprietary business information entitled to protection, but that plaintiff had not yet suffered damages, plaintiff could seek injunctive relief to restrict use of the employee information, if it could show that it may lose money incident to the use of the information. Plaintiff could attempt to show loss of its human-resource investment in recruiting, training, and retaining its valued employees, especially those women and minorities who may have been underrepresented in professional and executive positions. Warner-Lambert Co. v. Execuquest Corp., 427 Mass. 46, 691 N.E.2d 545, 547.

Mass.App.2000. Com. (b) quot. in case quot. in disc. Purported inventor sued research firm and individual defendants, seeking to be named as inventor or coinventor on patents issued to research firm and to recover damages for tortious interference with contractual relations, among other claims. Trial court granted defendants partial summary judgment. This court vacated in part, reversed in part, and remanded, holding, inter alia, that trial court had jurisdiction, since plaintiff's claim that individual defendants wrongfully induced firm to breach its agreement not to disclose his trade secrets did not require as an essential element a determi-

For earlier citations, see the Appendices, Supplements, or Pocket Parts, if any, that correspond to the subject matter under examination.

nation of a substantial question of federal patent law. Stark v. Advanced Magnetics, Inc., 50 Mass.App.Ct. 226, 736 N.E.2d 434, 440.

Mass.App.1991. Cit. in case quot. in disc., quot. in ftn. Alleging breach of contract, misappropriation of trade secrets, and breach of fiduciary duty to the estate, the administratrix of the deceased's estate sued the deceased's former employer for continuing after his death to use ice-cream formulas developed by the deceased before he came to work for the manufacturer. After the jury returned verdicts in favor of the estate, the trial court judge entered a judgment n.o.v. for the ice cream manufacturer. Affirming, this court held that the manufacturer's use of the disputed formulas was consensual and of right since the deceased had never attempted to keep the formulas secret from the manufacturer or tried to impose restrictions or conditions on their use. The court stated that the evidence that the formulas were only known by a small group of authorized personnel showed that the secret was guarded from competitors, not the manufacturer. Connors v. Howard Johnson Co., 30 Mass.App.Ct. 603, 571 N.E.2d 427, 429.

Miss.1993. Com. (a) cit. in disc., com. (b) cit. in case quot. in disc. A chemical company sued a competitor that was formed by its former employees, alleging misappropriation of trade secrets and willful interference with its business. The trial court dismissed these claims and entered judgment for defendant on its counterclaims. This court affirmed, holding, inter alia, that no trade secrets were involved because the formulas alleged to be trade secrets were generally known throughout the industry. The former employees had failed to sign a noncompetition agreement, and the knowledge they took with them was not acquired illegally, but through their employment and as a result of their own talents. Furthermore, plaintiff had obtained the trade secrets by wrongful means and could not prevent defendant from competing in light of the "unclean hands" doctrine. ACI Chemicals, Inc. v. Metaplex, Inc., 615 So.2d 1192, 1195.

Miss.1987. Com. (b) cit. in disc. A research company, alleging that a former employee had wrongfully misappropriated certain proprietary rice strains, sued to enjoin him from exploiting and profiting from certain rice farming operations. The chancery court granted the injunction, but after a hearing on the merits, it dissolved the restraining order and injunction. Affirming, this court held that the evidence supported the chancery court's finding that the employee did not steal the rice; it had been abandoned by the employer. Since the former employee had rightful possession of the rice, he was free to do whatever he wanted with it as long as he did not unfairly compete with his former employer, and the court declined to disturb the lower court's resolution of such fact questions. Rice Researchers, Inc. v. Hiter, 512 So.2d 1259, 1268.

Mo.App.2009. Cit. in sup., quot. in case quot. in sup., quot. and applied in cases cit. in ftn. Former employee sued former employers, seeking a declaration that defendants were not entitled to enforce the parties' noncompete and confidentiality agreement against him. After a bench trial, the trial court entered judgment in favor of plaintiff. Affirming as modified, this court held, inter alia, that the agreement was not enforceable against plaintiff to protect defendants' customer lists, rate sheets, or pricing processes. The court reasoned, in part, that the information contained in the rate sheets was not a process or device for continuous use in the business; rather, it consisted of frequently changing rates and fuel surcharges that were soon outdated and would not give a future employer a competitive advantage. Brown v. Rollet Bros. Trucking Co., Inc., 291 S.W.3d 766, 778, 779.

Mo.App.2005. Cit. in ftn. Various insurance companies brought action to enjoin state department of insurance from releasing to legal-aid society certain statistical insurance information provided to department by insurers doing business in state. The trial court granted insurers' injunction, holding that the information was a trade secret protected from disclosure under the Sunshine Act by, inter alia, the Uniform Trade Secrets Act. This court affirmed, holding, inter alia, that sufficient evidence supported a finding that the requested information had independent economic value to insurers or their competitors, the only trade-secret factor disputed by society, since insurers' expert explained how competitors could use company-specific premium data by zip code to their economic advantage. American Family Mut. Ins. Co. v. Missouri Dept. of Ins., 169 S.W.3d 905, 910.

Cit.—cited; com.—comment; fol.—followed; sup.—support.
A complete list of abbreviations precedes page 1.

Mo.App.1999. Com. (b) cit. in headnote, cit. in case quot. in sup., cit. generally in sup. A shoe insole manufacturer sued a competitor for misappropriation of trade secrets, tortious interference with a business expectancy, and conspiracy. Trial court granted defendant a directed verdict. This court reversed and remanded, holding, inter alia, that plaintiff's price book, which represented years of business experience, was a trade secret, because the information in it was not known outside of the business, was not independently known by employees, and would be valuable to competitors. Furthermore, employees knew that the price book was confidential and that access to it was limited. Lyn-Flex West, Inc. v. Dieckhaus, 24 S.W.3d 693, 698, 699.

Mo.App.1995. Com. (b) quot. in case quot. in disc. Company specializing in the repair of aircraft electrical components sought injunction to enforce noncompetition covenant purporting to prevent former shareholder who founded competing company from using information contained in first company's data sheets. The trial court entered judgment enjoining competition for a period of five years and this court affirmed, modifying the injunction to three years. It held that whether the data sheets, which contained information generally available to people in the business and might have constituted a process for the continuous use in the operation of the business, constituted protectable trade secrets was a close question that did not warrant resolution here, since first company had a protectable interest in customer contacts from which former shareholder was now attempting to benefit. The court revised the injunction after deciding that five years was longer than reasonably needed to protect first company from competition posed by former shareholder's newly formed company. AEE-EMF, Inc. v. Passmore, 906 S.W.2d 714, 721-722.

Mo.App.1993. Quot. in case quot. in sup. Gearbox manufacturer sued competitor and former employees working for competitor to enjoin them from revealing its trade secrets and using its trademark without authorization and requested other relief. The trial court granted plaintiff injunctive relief. Affirming in part, reversing in part, and remanding with directions, this court held, inter alia, that the finding that plaintiff's milling process qualified as a trade secret was supported by evidence that it was neither well known nor easily duplicated, that plaintiff took pains to ensure its secrecy, that its development required six months of concentrated effort by a large, highly trained staff, that it was continuing to be improved and refined, and that it was unique. Superior Gearbox Co. v. Edwards, 869 S.W.2d 239, 250.

Mo.App.1988. Cit. in case cit. in disc., com. (b) quot. in disc. An industrial-paint manufacturer sought to enjoin a former employee from working for a competitor. The trial court found for the plaintiff, holding that the parties' noncompete agreement's three-year, 350-mile restrictions were not more restrictive than reasonably necessary; however, the court limited the restrictions to two years and 125 miles. Affirming, this court held that the trial court did not exceed its equitable authority by modifying the restrictions of the covenant not to compete; that the durational and geographic limitations were not unreasonable; and that the evidence clearly supported the finding that the plaintiff had a protectible interest in trade secrets to support enforcement of the covenant. Mid-States Paint & Chemical Co. v. Herr, 746 S.W.2d 613, 617, 618.

N.J.1995. Com. (b) quot. and cit. in case quot. in disc. Public advocacy group, intervening in a products liability case against an acne drug manufacturer, sought to unseal records and documents filed in the underlying litigation in order to shed light on hazards posed by the drug. The trial court determined that 40 of 221 documents could be unsealed and, on remand, after dividing the documents into separate categories, decided to unseal 5 out of 175. The intermediate appellate court affirmed and advocacy group sought certification to clarify the standard for deciding when the denial of public access was justified. Reversing and remanding, this court held that a party attempting to overcome the rebuttable presumption of public access had to establish by a preponderance of the evidence that the need for secrecy outweighed the public's right to know, with different levels of protection accorded trade secrets, proprietary information and confidential information. Hammock by Hammock v. Hoffmann-LaRoche, Inc., 142 N.J. 356, 662 A.2d 546, 560.

N.J.1988. Com. (b) cit. in disc. An employer sued a former employee to enforce a holdover clause requiring the employee to

For earlier citations, see the Appendices, Supplements, or Pocket Parts, if any, that correspond to the subject matter under examination.

assign the right to a postemployment invention that did not involve a trade secret or proprietary information. The intermediate appellate court reversed the trial court's judgment in favor of the plaintiff. Affirming, this court held that the employee invention holdover agreement was not enforceable because the hardship on the employee outweighed the employer's need for protection, and there was no indication that the employee conceived the invention as a result of his employment with the company. Ingersoll-Rand Co. v. Ciavatta, 110 N.J. 609, 542 A.2d 879, 893.

N.J.Super.App.Div.2011. Com. (b) cit. and quot. in case cit. and quot. in sup. Newspaper brought an action under the Open Public Records Act against state-owned entertainment facility, after defendant refused to produce, in response to a request by one of plaintiff's reporters, unredacted copies of its contracts with event promoters for performances held in the facility. The trial court ordered defendant to release the unredacted records. Affirming, this court held, among other things, that the redacted financial terms contained in the contracts were neither "trade secrets" nor "proprietary commercial or financial information" that were exempt from disclosure under the Act. The court pointed out that the terms had circulated beyond defendant's staff and were generally known throughout the industry, and that the deals represented in the contracts appeared to be replicated nationwide in similar venues. Newark Morning Ledger Co. v. New Jersey Sports & Exposition Authority, 423 N.J.Super. 140, 31 A.3d 623, 640.

N.J.Super.App.Div.2010. Com. (b) cit. in case quot. in sup. Labor unions sued New Jersey Department of the Treasury, among others, under the Open Public Records Act (OPRA) and the common-law right of access, seeking to inspect all agreements relating to investments made by the Division of Investment in private equity funds with money from state-employee pension funds. Affirming the trial court's dismissal of plaintiffs' complaint, this court held, inter alia, that the investment agreements were trade secrets, as well as proprietary commercial financial information, not subject to disclosure; among other things, only the general and limited partners in Division's investment partnerships and others on a need-to-know basis had access to the investment agreements, each agreement contained a provision for sanctions for those who breached confidentiality, and the agreements were not filed with a public agency or made available to the general public. Communications Workers of America v. Rousseau, 417 N.J.Super. 341, 361, 9 A.3d 1064, 1076.

N.J.Super.2008. Com. (b) quot. in case quot. in sup. Labor unions sued New Jersey Department of the Treasury, among others, under the Open Public Records Act (OPRA) and the common-law right of access, seeking to inspect all agreements relating to investments made by the Division of Investment in private equity funds with money from state-employee pension funds. This court dismissed plaintiffs' complaint, holding, inter alia, that the documents were exempt as trade secrets from disclosure under OPRA; the agreements were not publicly disclosed, the firms' employees were subject to confidentiality agreements, the agreements were maintained in a locked filing cabinet, each agreement outlined a particular fund's organizational structures and investment strategies, the parties expended significant resources in crafting the agreements, and the information in the agreements was not easily acquired or duplicated by others. Communications Workers of America v. McCormac, 417 N.J.Super. 412, 438, 9 A.3d 1106, 1123.

N.J.Super.2002. Com. (b) quot. in case cit. in disc. and cit. generally in case cit. in ftn. Inventor sued company and its employee for misappropriation of trade secrets, among other claims, alleging that company based its "Crayola Paints" program on plaintiff's concepts without paying for his ideas and his proposed product line. Trial court granted company summary judgment. This court affirmed, holding that plaintiff's "mural in a can" marketing concept and product idea lacked novelty and failed to meet definition of a trade secret. Johnson v. Benjamin Moore & Co., 347 N.J.Super. 71, 95-97, 788 A.2d 906, 922, 923, certification granted, cause remanded 172 N.J. 176, 796 A.2d 893 (2002).

N.J.Super.2000. Cit. in sup., com. (b) cit. and quot. in case quot. in sup. Manufacturer of chemical products sued former employee for, inter alia, misappropriation of trade secrets. The trial court dismissed the complaint, reasoning, in part, that a product capable of being reverse engineered was

Cit.—cited; com.—comment; fol.—followed; sup.—support.
A complete list of abbreviations precedes page 1.

not protectable as a trade secret. Reversing on this point, this court held, among other things, that, under certain circumstances, a formula that was reverse engineered could be considered a trade secret; that defendant, having discovered a formula similar to but different from that of plaintiff, had not actually engaged in the process of reverse engineering; and that material factual issues existed as to whether plaintiff's formula was a trade secret. Rycoline Products, Inc. v. Walsh, 334 N.J.Super. 62, 756 A.2d 1047, 1053.

N.J.Super.1994. Com. (b) cit. generally in disc. and quot. in ftn. In a suit brought by a gambling casino against former employees who had allegedly obtained employment through fraud and misrepresentation, appeal was granted from the trial court's order refusing to quash a subpoena duces tecum issued by plaintiff against a nonparty that claimed trade-secret protection. Remanding, this court held that the trial judge should have reviewed the requested materials and taken any necessary testimony in camera, outside the presence of plaintiff's attorneys or representatives, and then reached a conclusion whether the subpoenaed information was protected from routine discovery procedure. Trump's Castle Assocs. v. Tallone, 275 N.J.Super. 159, 161-163, 645 A.2d 1207, 1208, 1209.

N.M.2008. Cit. in disc., com. (b) quot. in disc. Insureds sued insurer for bad faith. The trial court granted plaintiffs' motion to compel discovery of certain documents in defendant's possession. Following defendant's refusal to turn over the documents without a protective order on the ground that they contained trade secrets, the trial court entered a default judgment on liability; the court of appeals vacated and remanded. Holding that defendant had met its initial burden of asserting a trade secret, and that the trial court had abused its discretion in denying defendant's request for a hearing on the documents' trade-secret status, this court affirmed the court of appeals' vacation of the default judgment, and it remanded for the trial court to continue the case on its merits; while defendant's request for a protective order was rendered moot by subsequent events, plaintiffs, on remand, could move for sanctions, which would require a hearing on the trade-secret status of the documents at the time defendant refused to turn them over. Pincheira v. Allstate Ins. Co., 2008-NMSC-049, 144 N.M. 601, 190 P.3d 322, 327.

N.M.App.2007. Cit. in sup., cit. in case cit. in sup., cit. in diss. op.; com. (b) cit. in disc., cit. and quot. in sup., and quot. in diss. op. Insureds sued insurer and its agent, alleging that defendants routinely provided retirees like plaintiffs with false or misleading information concerning the benefits of uninsured motorist coverage. The trial court entered a default judgment against defendants after they violated an order requiring them to produce certain documents allegedly containing trade secrets. This court reversed and remanded to the trial court with instructions to reevaluate defendant's assertion of trade-secret privilege as to the documents in light of, among other things, the six factors listed in Restatement First of Torts § 757, Comment *b*. The dissent noted that the privilege did not necessarily attach to all information recognized as a trade secret. Pincheira v. Allstate Insurance Co., 142 N.M. 283, 164 P.3d 982, 986, 990, 994, 996, 1000, 1001.

N.Y.2018. Com. (b) quot. in diss. op. Manufacturer of plastic indicative security seals filed a complaint in federal court against competitor and three former employees who left manufacturer to work for competitor, alleging misappropriation of trade secrets, unfair competition, and unjust enrichment. The district court entered judgment on a jury verdict awarding plaintiff damages for defendants' unfair competition as measured by the development costs that defendants avoided due to their unlawful activity. Answering a question certified by the court of appeals, this court held that avoided costs were not awardable as compensatory damages in an action based on a theory of unfair competition; rather, damages had to be measured by the losses that the plaintiff actually incurred. The dissent cited the definition of "trade secret" set forth in Restatement of Torts § 757 in arguing that the majority's narrow interpretation of damages failed to recognize the unique nature of trade secrets, and that a plaintiff's loss in the value of a trade secret could be measured in several ways. E.J. Brooks Company v. Cambridge Security Seals, 105 N.E.3d 301, 316.

N.Y.2016. Com. (b) quot. in case quot. in sup. State joint commission on public ethics initiated a preliminary investigation of organization that acted as a not-for-profit partner of the mayor's office, alleging that

For earlier citations, see the Appendices, Supplements, or Pocket Parts, if any, that correspond to the subject matter under examination.

it failed to register and report as a lobbyist for the calendar year, despite having done so in prior years. This court granted in part commission's motion to compel organization to comply with a subpoena duces tecum and denied in part organization's motion for a protective order limiting production of certain allegedly privileged documents, holding that organization had not met its burden of establishing that the documents were privileged as trade secrets under Restatement of Torts § 757. The court reasoned, in part, that organization had not made any showing of how the information contained in the documents gave it a competitive advantage. New York State Joint Com'n on Public Ethics v. Campaign for One New York, Inc., 37 N.Y.S.3d 851, 861.

N.Y.1993. Com. (b) cit. and quot. in sup. Investment management firm sought a permanent injunction based on trade-secret misappropriation to bar defendant former employee from using a mathematical model for determining investment strategy that defendant had developed. The trial court entered judgment for defendant, and the intermediate appellate court affirmed as modified. Affirming, this court held, inter alia, that plaintiff's computerized mathematical stock selection model, which defendant had incorporated into his investment-strategy model, was not a trade secret subject to misappropriation, since a financial analyst could, based on public disclosures made by plaintiff, reproduce the calculations without access to the internal computer commands constituting plaintiff's software. Ashland Management Inc. v. Janien, 82 N.Y.2d 395, 604 N.Y.S.2d 912, 624 N.E.2d 1007, 1012, 1013.

N.Y.Sup.Ct.App.Div.2016. Com. (b) quot. in case quot. in sup. Owner of a communications network filed a petition to annul the state public service commission's determination that certain network-related documents that owner had filed with the state did not contain trade secrets and thus were not exempt from the state Freedom of Information Law. The trial court granted the petition in part, finding that all but three of the documents were exempt from disclosure as trade secrets, regardless of whether a likelihood of substantial competitive injury was shown. Affirming, this court held that it was unnecessary to require an entity that had established the existence of a bona fide trade secret to make a separate showing that disclosure of the trade secret would cause substantial injury to its competitive position. The court noted that, under the first Restatement of Torts § 757, an entity seeking trade-secret protection had to show that the information in question was a formula, pattern, device, or compilation of information that was used in its business and that gave it an opportunity to obtain an advantage over competitors who did not know or use the information. Verizon New York, Inc. v. New York State Public Service Com'n, 23 N.Y.S.3d 446, 451.

N.Y.Sup.Ct.App.Div.2016. Com. (b) cit. in sup. Manufacturer of a component used in a medical device filed a claim for misappropriation of trade secrets against medical-device manufacturer, alleging that defendant misappropriated plaintiff's process of producing the component, which was a trade secret, and improperly used that process to create its own component. The trial court denied defendant's motion for summary judgment. This court affirmed, holding that there was a genuine issue of material fact as to whether the alleged trade-secret process was provided to defendant under a duty of confidence. Citing Restatement of Torts § 757, Comment *b*, the court explained that plaintiff raised a triable issue of fact by providing evidence that plaintiff's president expressed concern over the confidentiality of the trade-secret process and that defendant made assurances that the process was protected and would not be stolen. Zylon Corp. v. Medtronic, Inc., 136 A.D.3d 462, 463, 26 N.Y.S.3d 279, 280.

N.Y.Sup.Ct.App.Div.2015. Com. (b) quot. in case quot. in sup. Inventor of a web application and inventor's companies sued former investment partner, alleging that defendant stole and illegally used plaintiffs' confidential ideas, technology, and business plans to develop a competing website. This court denied defendant's motion to dismiss plaintiffs' claim for trade-secret misappropriation, holding that plaintiffs sufficiently alleged that they possessed a trade secret within the meaning of the definition set forth in the first Restatement of Torts § 757. The court pointed to plaintiffs' allegations that defendant provided plaintiffs' confidential and proprietary technology and business plans to developers of the competing website despite being aware that the information was to be kept secret, that the

Cit.—cited; com.—comment; fol.—followed; sup.—support.
A complete list of abbreviations precedes page 1.

technology was valuable to plaintiffs and was not easily acquired or duplicated by others, and that plaintiffs took steps to maintain the secrecy of the information. Schroeder v. Pinterest Inc., 17 N.Y.S.3d 678, 690.

N.Y.Sup.Ct.App.Div.2007. Com. (b) quot. in case quot. in sup. Real estate broker who left brokerage to work for a former customer of brokerage sued brokerage, and brokerage counterclaimed for, among other things, misappropriation of trade secrets. The trial court denied summary judgment for plaintiff on defendant's counterclaims, ruling that issues of fact remained as to whether plaintiff misappropriated trade secrets belonging to defendant. This court reversed that portion of the decision and, as so modified, affirmed, holding that defendant failed to adequately rebut plaintiff's allegations that none of the information identified by defendant, including customer information or the terms of any proposals proffered by defendant to brokerage's former customer, qualified as trade secrets. Moser v. Devine Real Estate, Inc. (Florida), 42 A.D.3d 731, 736, 839 N.Y.S.2d 843, 849.

N.Y.Sup.Ct.App.Div.2006. Com. (b) quot. in case quot. in sup. Passengers who were injured in a car crash caused by a defective tire sued manufacturer and distributor of tire. The trial court denied in part plaintiffs' motion to compel disclosure of certain allegedly protected trade secrets. Modifying the order, and otherwise affirming, this court held, inter alia, that the tire's formula and composition were indispensable to plaintiffs' claims and thus were discoverable. The court noted that the tire was over 11 years old, and there was nothing to suggest that defendant still used the same formula; moreover, the tire's ingredients were not in fact secret, because the same information was available from other sources that regularly published the components of various tires as identified through a reverse-engineering process. Mann ex rel. Akst v. Cooper Tire Co., 33 A.D.3d 24, 816 N.Y.S.2d 45, 52, 53.

N.Y.Sup.Ct.App.Div.2003. Com. (b) quot. in case quot. in sup. Hotel-amenities supplier sued competitor, seeking to enjoin disclosure of confidential information, after competitor hired its former senior vice president for sales and marketing. Trial court granted supplier preliminary injunction. Reversing, this court held that no evidence existed that former vice president's new position was a threat to supplier's trade secrets so as to support issuance of preliminary injunction. Marietta Corp. v. Fairhurst, 301 A.D.2d 734, 738, 754 N.Y.S.2d 62, 66.

N.Y.Sup.Ct.App.Div.2000. Com. (b) quot. in case quot. in sup. In litigation based on allegations of unfair competition, plaintiff challenged trial court order dismissing the complaint as to three defendants. Reversing, this court held that material factual issues existed as to whether plaintiff's list of suppliers in China was sufficiently unknown in the trade as to constitute a trade secret. Howard Berger Co., Inc. v. Ye, 272 A.D.2d 445, 708 N.Y.S.2d 310, 310.

N.Y.Sup.Ct.App.Div.1999. Cit. in headnote, com. (b) quot. in case quot. in sup. Provider of building maintenance services sued two former employees, alleging that defendants engaged in unfair competition by using plaintiff's trade secrets to form a corporate competitor. Trial court granted plaintiff's motion for partial summary judgment. This court affirmed, holding that there was sufficient evidence that defendants exploited confidential information to obtain contracts with plaintiff's customers, and that they used plaintiff's proprietary secrets to build a competing business. Laro Maintenance Corp. v. Culkin, 267 A.D.2d 431, 700 N.Y.S.2d 490, 492.

N.Y.Sup.Ct.App.Div.1998. Cit. in headnote, com. (b) quot. in sup. After members of a real estate partnership unsuccessfully tried to repurchase from the mortgagee bank a building on whose mortgage the partners had defaulted, the partners sued an investment firm and the corporation that ultimately bought the property with the firm's assistance, alleging unfair competition, among other claims. Plaintiffs alleged that the information pertaining to the building's operation constituted trade secrets improperly disclosed by the investment firm to the purchasing corporation for the express purpose of enabling the purchasing corporation to make an attractive offer to the bank that would be comparable to plaintiffs' offer. The trial court dismissed plaintiff's complaint. This court affirmed as modified, holding, inter alia, that the data relating to the building's operations and to negotiations with tenants and unions was not of a genuinely secret nature. Similarly, the reports produced as a result of the audits may have been considered confiden-

For earlier citations, see the Appendices, Supplements, or Pocket Parts, if any, that correspond to the subject matter under examination.

tial, but they also failed to qualify as trade secrets. Wiener v. Lazard Freres & Co., 241 A.D.2d 114, 672 N.Y.S.2d 8, 10, 15.

N.Y.Sup.Ct.App.Div.1994. Com. (b) cit. in case cit. in disc. Reinsurance intermediary who developed reinsurance product sought permanent injunction against former director after he was heard boasting at insurance trade association conference that, unbound by any pledge of confidentiality, he would take away about $1 million in plaintiff's brokerage commissions. Reversing the trial court's denial of plaintiff's motion for renewal of preliminary injunction and granting renewal, this court held that it was undisputed that considerable effort was expended in developing the reinsurance scheme; whether product was true innovation or just marketing strategy, the court said that record was replete with evidence of plaintiff's efforts to maintain product's confidentiality and noted that defendant's boast provided substantial proof of scheme's value to industry competitors. U.S. Reinsurance Corp. v. Humphreys, 205 A.D.2d 187, 618 N.Y.S.2d 270, 273.

N.Y.Sup.Ct.App.Div.1993. Com. (b) cit. in sup. The former president and chief executive officer of a business sued the business and moved for a preliminary injunction to bar the business from enforcing a restrictive covenant against him. Affirming a partial grant of injunction, this court held that enforcement of the covenant was warranted to the extent of prohibiting the plaintiff from providing the business's competitors with confidential customer information acquired as a result of the employment. This information, said the court, would give the plaintiff an unfair opportunity and advantage over competitors who did not possess the information. Ward v. Arcade Bldg. Maintenance, Inc., 191 A.D.2d 368, 595 N.Y.S.2d 411, 412.

N.Y.Sup.Ct.App.Div.1991. Com. (b) cit. in disc. Alleging misappropriation of trade secrets, diversion of corporate opportunity, tortious interference with economic advantage, and unfair competition, an employer sued its former employees and their current employer seeking damages and a preliminary injunction. The trial court denied the employer's motion for a preliminary injunction and dismissed the claims for failure to state a cause of action and lack of in personam jurisdiction over the current employer. Affirming, this court held, inter alia, that the employer failed to state a cause of action for misappropriation of trade secrets. The court stated that the employer did not sufficiently assert that it had established precautionary measures to preserve its allegedly exclusive knowledge of the manufacturing process at issue. Precision Concepts, Inc. v. Bonsanti, 172 A.D.2d 737, 569 N.Y.S.2d 124, 126.

N.Y.Sup.Ct.App.Div.1987. Com. (b) cit. in disc. A defense contractor sued a former employee, inter alia, to recover damages arising from the breach of an employment agreement not to solicit business. The trial court entered judgment for the plaintiff. Affirming, this court held that the plaintiff was entitled to the damages awarded by the trial court, reasoning that the defendant utilized the plaintiff's confidential information, which was entitled to trade secret protection, to wrongfully solicit business. The court said that the defendant would have been liable for damages even in the absence of the contract restriction because a former employee was not entitled to solicit customers by the use of trade secrets or confidential information. Support Systems Assoc. v. Tavolacci, 135 A.D.2d 704, 522 N.Y.S.2d 604, 606.

N.Y.Sup.Ct.2020. Com. (b) quot. in case quot. in sup. Former employer that provided investment services in the secondary market sued former employee who made cold calls on behalf of employer to identify potential buyers and sellers, alleging that employee breached the confidentiality and non-compete provisions in the parties' employment agreement following her resignation. This court denied employer's motion for a preliminary injunction seeking to prevent employee from, among other things, disrupting employer's business by using its lists containing personal contact information for potential buyers and sellers, holding that employer failed to establish that the lists constituted protectable trade secrets under Restatement of Torts § 757. The court pointed out that employer failed to respond to employee's claims that the lists were publicly available. Setter Capital, Inc. v. Chateauvert, 130 N.Y.S.3d 905, 908.

N.Y.Sup.Ct.2014. Cit. in sup., cit. in case quot. in sup.; com (b) cit. and quot. in sup. and in ftn. Telecommunications company sought judicial review of the decision of the state public service commission that certain documents submitted by company to commission during the course of a regulatory

Cit.—cited; com.—comment; fol.—followed; sup.—support.
A complete list of abbreviations precedes page 1.

proceeding were not exempt from disclosure as trade secrets or confidential commercial information pursuant to the Freedom of Information Law (FOIL). Granting company's petition in part and denying it in part, this court held that company's cost information was a trade secret exempt from disclosure, and that only three of company's methods-and-procedures documents had to be disclosed. The court reasoned that, once commission concluded that the cost information and part of the method-and-procedures information constituted trade-secret material, the inquiry should have ended; no proof of substantial competitive injury was required by FOIL, and the material should have been determined to be exempt from disclosure under the statute. The court noted that, although the term "trade secret" was not defined under FOIL, courts applying New York law generally followed Restatement of Torts § 757 in determining whether information was entitled to protection as a trade secret. Verizon New York Inc. v. New York State Public Service Com'n, 991 N.Y.S.2d 841, 853, 854, 856-858, 860, 861.

N.Y.Sup.Ct.2009. Cit. in ftn., com. (b) quot. in case quot. in ftn. Newspaper publisher and journalist brought a proceeding challenging the Office of the State Comptroller's (OSC's) denial of their request under the Freedom of Information Law for certain records pertaining to the New York state public-employee payroll. Granting the petition, this court held, inter alia, that, although the metadata, record layouts, and documentation related to 14 databases to which petitioners sought access were proprietary or trade-secret information belonging to the vendor of the database-management software that OSC used to host the payroll application, OSC failed to show that merely providing petitioners with the requested data from specified payroll tables in an electronic spreadsheet format would constitute a breach of the vendor's proprietary rights or cause it to suffer a substantial competitive injury, especially since OSC had already provided petitioners with the data dictionary, consisting of a listing of the data elements comprising the 14 tables they sought. Hearst Corp. v. State, Office of State Comptroller, 24 Misc.3d 611, 630, 882 N.Y.S.2d 862, 877.

N.Y.Sup.Ct.2007. Com. (b) quot. in case quot. in sup. After two independent contractors hired by corporation to speak at half-day seminars whose object was to encourage realtors to attend a $425 all-day workshop resigned and opened up a similar business that targeted the mortgage industry, corporation sued the contractors for, in part, improper use of trade secrets. On defendants' motion for summary judgment, this court held that plaintiff's business model for attracting and selling to customers plainly did not constitute a trade secret, since the model was used by others, and plaintiff took no steps to protect the secrecy of the model, which was presented repeatedly during the free half-day seminars; concluding that, in opposition to defendants' showing, plaintiff failed to raise an issue of fact, the court ordered accordingly. Sales Strategies Group, Inc. v. Fenton, 16 Misc.3d 171, 173, 838 N.Y.S.2d 856, 858.

N.Y.Sup.Ct.2006. Com. (b) cit. and quot. in disc. State Insurance Department denied borough president's administrative appeals of its decisions to withhold certain records, filed by automobile insurers pursuant to state's anti-redlining statute, that president requested under Freedom of Information Law. This court annulled the denials, holding that department failed to demonstrate that the records qualified for the "trade secret" exemption. The court reasoned that the records could not be used by competitors to obtain an unfair advantage because they lacked information regarding pricing, profits, losses, or actual marketing plans, and that department did not apply any unique or proprietary methods to analyze the data, which could be obtained by the public by other means. Markowitz v. Serio, 11 Misc.3d 439, 443-445, 812 N.Y.S.2d 841, 844-846, reversed 39 A.D.3d 247, 833 N.Y.S.2d 444 (1st Dept.2007).

N.Y.Sup.Ct.2005. Com. (b) quot. in case quot. in disc. Independent contractor real-estate agent sued real-estate firm, asserting several causes of action after she was denied access to the various client/investor lists she kept on firm's computer and by her hand in hard copy following the termination of their business relationship The court denied in part firm's motion for summary judgment. The court held, inter alia, that agent's computerized lists, besides being considered convertible property, could also be afforded trade-secret protection, since agent had expended considerable time, effort, and cost in compiling them, thus precluding summary judgment on her

For earlier citations, see the Appendices, Supplements, or Pocket Parts, if any, that correspond to the subject matter under examination.

claim for misappropriation of proprietary information. Shmueli v. Corcoran Group, 9 Misc.3d 589, 802 N.Y.S.2d 871, 878.

N.Y.Sup.Ct.1995. Com. (b) cit. in case quot. in disc. Client sued accounting firm, alleging that firm breached its obligation to provide proper accounting services. Plaintiff argued that defendant's own policy and procedure manuals were relevant to a determination as to whether defendant followed its own guidelines. Defendant asserted that its audit manuals were trade secrets and that the manuals reflected defendant's approach to auditing developed over years of its experience. Trial court granted plaintiff's motion compelling defendant to respond to plaintiff's notice of discovery and inspection. This court granted defendant's motion to reargue the decision, holding that defendant's manuals constituted a trade secret and thus were not subject to discovery. The information in the manual was not indispensable to plaintiff's case, because if defendant did not follow its own procedures, such noncompliance was not proof as to whether defendant followed proper and sound accounting practice in providing its services to plaintiff. AIN Leasing v. Peat, Marwick & Mitchell, 166 Misc.2d 902, 636 N.Y.S.2d 584, 585.

N.Y.City Civ.Ct.2018. Com. (b) quot. in case quot. in sup. Yoga studio sued former employee who accepted a position at a competing studio, alleging that employee violated the parties' non-compete agreement by, among other things, soliciting studio's potential clients using a client list that the parties previously shared while conducting an online marketing campaign for studio. This court granted summary judgment for employee, holding, among other things, that studio failed to submit any evidence to establish that its list of potential clients was a trade secret that was entitled to protection under Restatement of Torts § 757. The court pointed out that studio did not show that it invested substantial time, effort, or expense in developing the list before the parties became partners, or that the list was not readily ascertainable from sources outside studio. Henderson v. Patel, 82 N.Y.S.3d 800, 804.

Ohio, 2016. Cit. in sup. Relator that ran a golf club brought a mandamus action against city agency that declined to comply with relator's request for records from public golf courses that city operated. The court of appeals denied in part plaintiff's request for a writ. This court affirmed, holding that the court of appeals correctly determined that defendant's customer list constituted trade secrets. The court cited Restatement of Torts § 757 for the definition of "trade secret" and concluded that defendant's customer list constituted a trade secret because it had economic value and was not available to the public or to defendant's contractual partners, a limited number of defendant's employees had access to the list, defendant took measures to protect the list, and defendant spent considerable effort and expense maintaining the list. Salemi v. Cleveland Metroparks, 49 N.E.3d 1296, 1302.

Ohio, 2013. Com. (b) cit. in case cit. in sup. Relator brought a public-records mandamus case against city and private, nonprofit corporation that operated and managed a public market for city, seeking unredacted copies of the lease agreements between corporation and merchants who subleased retail space at the market. After a trial, the magistrate denied the writ of mandamus, and the court of appeals rejected relator's objections. Affirming, this court held that the redacted terms and rental rates for market tenants' subleases were trade secrets and thus were exempt from disclosure under the public-records law. The court reasoned that the information derived independent economic value from not being generally known or readily ascertainable by others who might obtain economic advantage from knowing the information, and corporation took reasonable measures to keep the lease terms a secret under the standard precautions for the industry. State v. Corp. for Findlay Market, 135 Ohio St.3d 416, 421, 2013-Ohio-1532, 988 N.E.2d 546, 551.

Ohio, 2008. Com. (b) cit. in case quot. in disc. Actuarial firm sued former employee who organized a competing business while still employed by firm and then used firm's confidential information to successfully solicit 15 of its clients for his own business after resigning from firm. The trial court entered judgment in favor of firm. Affirming, this court held, inter alia, that firm's client list constituted a trade secret, and the fact that employee memorized the client list before leaving firm rather than taking any documents containing the confidential information from firm did not change the list's status as a trade secret or remove

Cit.—cited; com.—comment; fol.—followed; sup.—support.
A complete list of abbreviations precedes page 1.

it from the protection of Ohio's Uniform Trade Secrets Act. Al Minor & Assoc., Inc. v. Martin, 117 Ohio St.3d 58, 881 N.E.2d 850, 852.

Ohio, 2000. Cit. in disc., com. (b) quot. in case quot. in disc. Attorney petitioned for writ of mandate to compel state university to disclose documents relating to university's acquisition of private medical practice. University refused disclosure, arguing, among other things, that the information sought constituted trade secrets. Granting the petition in part and denying it in part, the court held, inter alia, that the fact that one of the requested documents related to a single event and was not used continuously in university's business did not preclude it from being a trade secret; however, university failed to show that the document in question retained independent economic value from not being readily ascertainable by proper means by university's competitors. State ex rel. Besser v. Ohio State Univ., 89 Ohio St.3d 396, 732 N.E.2d 373, 378.

Ohio, 1997. Com. (b) quot. in disc. A newspaper brought suit in mandamus under the Public Records Act, seeking records given by an insurer to the state department of insurance and pertaining to the proposed acquisition of the insurer by another insurer. This court granted the relators a limited writ of mandamus, holding that the documents were not confidential work papers and must be disclosed. The court also determined that some documents, or portions thereof, constituted trade secrets and had to be redacted from the record. However, the court determined that documents concerning the negotiations between the two insurers regarding how to settle the issues relating to the language in the principal agreement were not trade secrets. They did not disclose any information about the insurer's business or its business plans. Noting that the documents were negotiation documents for a sale that ultimately did not occur, the court stated that documents pertaining to draft contracts, bids, and letters of negotiation are not trade secrets. State ex rel. Plain Dealer v. Dept. of Ins., 80 Ohio St.3d 513, 687 N.E.2d 661, 673.

Ohio App.1993. Com. (b) quot. in part in sup. Designer/manufacturer of plastic injection mold that modified customer's model suction bowl, developed it to make a mold, and then produced suction bowls for customer, sued customer, alleging trade-secret misappropriation from customer's termination of parties' contract and subsequent self-manufacture of suction bowls. Affirming the trial court's entry of summary judgment for customer, this court held that no confidential relationship existed between the parties, since their employees had worked closely together in developing the revised suction-bowl specifications and plaintiff had permitted visitors to tour its facility without requiring them to execute written confidentiality agreements. R & R Plastics, Inc. v. F.E. Myers Co., 92 Ohio App.3d 789, 799-800, 637 N.E.2d 332, 339.

Ohio App.1990. Cit. in disc., com. (b) quot. in disc. A bank disclosed an inventor's system for categorizing check and credit card transactions, which the inventor had disclosed to it in confidence, to a company which subsequently used all aspects of the system. The inventor sued the bank and the user company for misappropriation of trade secrets, unjust enrichment, breach of implied contract, and breach of fiduciary duty. The trial court granted the defendants' motion for summary judgment, concluding that the plaintiff's system lacked sufficient novelty to merit protection. Reversing and remanding, this court held, inter alia, that jury questions existed as to whether the inventor's system qualified as a trade secret, since bank officers allegedly told the inventor that his system was novel in the banking industry. The court stated that although it was not necessary to establish the novelty required in the law of patents, at least some novelty was required to merit trade-secret protection for the inventor's system. Murray v. Bank One, Columbus, N.A., 64 Ohio App.3d 784, 582 N.E.2d 1124, 1126-1127.

Okl.2016. Com. (a) cit. in sup. and quot. in case quot. in sup. Developers of a bolus containing technology to monitor and track cattle brought a claim for conversion of personal and intellectual property against manufacturers they had hired to make boluses to their specifications, alleging that, after the parties' business relationship ended, defendants made and sold boluses using plaintiffs' confidential, proprietary information and tangible property. The trial court granted partial summary judgment for defendants. Reversing in part and remanding, this court held that defendants' alleged use of intangibles that were not information and of tangibles was not subject to the parties' nondisclosure agreement and was potentially subject to a claim for conversion. The court cited Restatement of Torts §§ 757 and 759 in explaining that Oklahoma had recognized the tort of misappropriation of confidential business information, under which one who received information that did not meet the definition of a "trade secret" and who was in a confidential relationship or obtained the information through improper means was potentially liable. American Biomedical Group, Inc. v. Techtrol, Inc., 374 P.3d 820, 825.

Okl.1986. Com. (b) cit. in disc. A corporation in the business of coating steel reinforcing bars with epoxy resin sued a company that allegedly misappropriated confidential business information about the coating process used by the plaintiff. The trial court entered judgment on a jury verdict for the defendant. Affirming, this court rejected the plaintiff's argument that it could recover for the defendant's disclosure of confidential information not rising to the level of a trade secret. The court stated that the jury's finding that the defendant was not guilty of fraud negated the necessary element of an improper means by which the information was procured and the fact that the coating process could not be distinguished as either a trade secret or confidential information discredited the plaintiff's theory. ABC Coating Co., Inc. v. J. Harris & Sons, 747 P.2d 266, 269.

Okl.App.2010. Com. (b) adopted in case cit. in sup., cit. and quot. in cases cit. in ftn., cit. in case cit. in sup., com. (c) quot. in ftn. Manufacturer that produced perforated pipe for use in the oil and gas industry sued two former employees, competitor, and competitor's employee, alleging breach of a confidentiality agreement and misappropriation of trade secrets. The trial court granted summary judgment for defendants. Reversing and remanding, this court held that disputed issues of fact remained as to whether plaintiff's methods, systems, and processes to simultaneously perforate multiple pipe joints constituted a trade secret, in light of evidence that plaintiff sought to maintain their secrecy, that they could not be duplicated by a casual observer, that the research and development required to produce them were expensive and time consuming, and that that portion of plaintiff's business was the most lucrative. Further, fact issues remained as to whether competitor's technology was a misappropriation of plaintiff's alleged trade secret, in light of evidence that competitor's methods, systems, and processes were essentially the same as plaintiff's. MTG Guarnieri Mfg., Inc. v. Clouatre, 239 P.3d 202, 209, 211.

Pa.Super.2011. Com. (b) quot. in sup. and quot. in case quot. in sup. Former employee sought, inter alia, an injunction to prevent former employer from enforcing a non-compete covenant, alleging that he possessed no confidential information about employer, and that his new position was with a non-competitor. The trial court found for plaintiff and issued the injunction. Affirming, this court held that plaintiff had demonstrated a likelihood that he would obtain a favorable ruling on the merits by showing that defendant had no legitimate interest to be protected by enforcement of the covenant, while plaintiff, who was in his late fifties and had received only one job offer after a long search, would suffer irreparable harm if it were enforced. The court rejected defendant's argument that the covenant was necessary to protect its trade secrets, reasoning that, because plaintiff was not privy to defendant's research and development, and any confidential information about pricing that he did possess was stale due to a lapse between bids and sale, plaintiff would not reveal any trade secrets. Shepherd v. Pittsburgh Glass Works, LLC, 25 A.3d 1233, 1244-1245.

Pa.Super.2010. Com. (b) quot. in case quot. in ftn. Employer sued former employee, alleging trade-secret misappropriation, breach of contract, and breach of fiduciary duty. After defendant refused to comply for a period of five years with any order of the trial court compelling discovery, arguing that plaintiff's claims were a pretext to obtain the alleged trade secrets of defendant and her own company, the trial court, inter alia, entered a default judgment against defendant as a discovery sanction. Affirming as to this issue, this court held that the trial court did not abuse its discretion or commit an error of law in concluding that the requested discovery was important because it was directly related to plaintiff's claims. The court noted that whether the discovery of trade secrets was allowed was determined according to the discretion of the trial court. Rohm and Haas Co. v. Lin, 992 A.2d 132, 143.

Pa.Super.2006. Com. (b) quot. and adopted in cases quot. in disc. Administra-

Cit.—cited; com.—comment; fol.—followed; sup.—support.
A complete list of abbreviations precedes page 1.

tors of two decedents' estates brought products-liability action against tire manufacturer, alleging that decedents' fatal automobile accident was caused by tire failure in one decedent's vehicle. The trial court denied defendant's motion for a protective order and ordered defendant to produce documents regarding the rubber compound formulas used to make the tires. Reversing and remanding, this court held, inter alia, that plaintiffs failed to demonstrate that they were entitled to the formulas. The court reasoned, in part, that it was undisputed that the formulas constituted valuable trade secrets, and that the formulas were not relevant or necessary to the litigation because they could not, in themselves, indicate whether a manufactured tire was defective. Crum v. Bridgestone/Firestone North American Tire, LLC, 907 A.2d 578, 585.

Pa.Super.2005. Cit. in disc., cit. in case cit. in disc., subsecs. (a) and (b) quot. in disc., com. (b) quot. in case quot. in disc. (Erron. cit. as Restatement Second of Torts.) Air-freshener manufacturer sued competitor and others for, inter alia, misappropriation of trade secrets, alleging that a trucker employed by both companies revealed confidential information from manufacturer's bills of lading to competitor. The trial court entered judgment for plaintiff. This court reversed in part, holding, inter alia, that the information displayed on plaintiff's bills of lading did not constitute a trade secret, since, among other things, the customers listed could easily be obtained from other sources, and no specific product-description or pricing information was shown. Pestco, Inc. v. Associated Products, Inc., 880 A.2d 700, 705-706, 708, 709, 711.

Pa.Super.2005. Com. (b) quot. in case quot. in disc. Healthcare system sued doctor on its management team for breach of contract after doctor resigned and started working for hospital in neighboring county, in violation of restrictive covenant in doctor's employment contract. Trial court granted in part and denied in part plaintiff's petition for a permanent injunction, prohibiting defendant from using or disclosing any information pertaining to plaintiff's patients. Affirming, this court held, inter alia, that plaintiff could not claim a protectable business interest in its fees and budget, as plaintiff failed to show that such data were a compilation of information that, if shared, would give a competitor a business advantage. Wellspan Health v. Bayliss, 869 A.2d 990, 997.

Pa.Super.2003. Quot. in sup., cit. in case cit. in sup., com. (b) cit. in case cit. in sup. Buyer of a travel company sued former company employees, seeking to enjoin them from contacting or soliciting any of the individuals named in company's customer lists. Trial court granted permanent injunction. This court affirmed, holding, inter alia, that trial court did not abuse its discretion in determining that the customer lists constituted trade secrets. Buyer presented testimony that the extensive compilations were both valuable and strictly maintained. Also, buyer had no reason to believe, in view of one defendant's representations and offer to buy the lists, that defendant had retained copies of the lists after his resignation and that the lists were no longer confidential. O.D. Anderson, Inc. v. Cricks, 815 A.2d 1063, 1070.

Pa.Super.2002. Com. (b) adopted in case quot. in sup. Cancer patient and his wife sued doctor and health-maintenance organization (HMO) for medical malpractice, and trial court denied HMO's motion for confidentiality order regarding discovery documents relating to physician hiring and compensation. Reversing and remanding, superior court held that, where evidence indicated that information was valuable to HMO, that HMO took measures to keep information secret, and that information could create competitive disadvantage to HMO if disclosed to competitors, information constituted trade secrets entitled to confidentiality. Dibble v. Penn State Geisinger Clinic, Inc., 806 A.2d 866, 871.

Pa.Super.1997. Com. (b) quot. in case quot. in sup. A gourmet fudge manufacturer sued a former employee and his corporation for misappropriation of trade secrets. Trial court granted plaintiff a permanent injunction. This court affirmed, holding that a trade secret injunction that permanently enjoins the defendants from engaging in the manufacture of a product is a proper means to protect trade secrets where the defendants' manufacture of that product is inextricably connected to their knowledge of the plaintiff's trade secrets. Plaintiff's president's testimony was sufficient to establish that the fudge recipe was a trade secret, because the president expended a large sum of money and a great deal of effort in developing the recipe; the president took steps to keep the recipe a

For earlier citations, see the Appendices, Supplements, or Pocket Parts, if any, that correspond to the subject matter under examination.

secret within the company; the recipe was not known outside of the company until defendant employee left the company; and, the president testified that the recipe had a multimillion-dollar value. Chris. M's Hand Poured Fudge v. Hennon, 699 A.2d 1272, 1274, 1275.

Pa.Super.1990. Cit. in conc. op. The owners of a company that created computer embroidery designs sued a former employee for theft of trade secrets, unfair competition, and unjust enrichment. The trial court granted a preliminary injunction preventing the defendant from using the plaintiffs' computer patterns, finding that the computer discs constituted trade secrets, that the plaintiffs had the exclusive right to use the designs, and that the trade secrets were disclosed while the defendant was an employee. This court affirmed, holding that these issues were beyond the scope of appellate review since the defendant's arguments on appeal related solely to the merits of the underlying action. A preliminary injunction was deemed appropriate since substantial legal questions were presented that needed to be resolved in order to determine the parties' rights. A concurring opinion stated that a "closer scrutiny" approach of engaging in a legal analysis of whether the discs constituted a trade secret was unnecessary, that the preliminary injunction was appropriately issued, and that the issue of whether the computer discs were trade secrets was a substantial legal question left to be determined. Chmura v. Deegan, 398 Pa.Super. 532, 581 A.2d 592, 594.

Pa.Super.1989. Cit. and quot. in disc., subsecs. (a) and (b) and com. (b) quot. in disc., com. (c) cit. in disc. A corporation that manufactured dental instruments sued to enjoin the defendant from acquiring a competitor of the plaintiff's, alleging that the injunction was necessary to prevent the disclosure by the defendant of allegedly confidential information obtained by the defendant about the plaintiff's business during ultimately unsuccessful negotiations between the parties regarding the sale of the plaintiff's business to the defendant. The trial court granted an injunction against the acquisition for a three-year period. This court affirmed, concluding that, because the defendant received trade secrets and other confidential information from the plaintiff through misrepresentations while in a confidential relationship with the plaintiff, an injunction was the appropriate remedy. Den-Tal-Ez, Inc. v. Siemens Capital Corp., 389 Pa.Super. 219, 566 A.2d 1214, 1224, 1228, 1229.

Pa.Super.1988. Com. (b) cit. and quot. in sup. An employer brought an action to enjoin a former employee from disclosing its supplier's price list, claiming that the list was a trade secret. The trial court issued a preliminary injunction, and the former employee appealed. Reversing, this court determined that the price list was not a trade secret because the information sought to be kept secret could be obtained by others through legitimate channels. Tyson Metal Products, Inc. v. McCann, 376 Pa.Super. 461, 546 A.2d 119, 121.

Pa.Cmwlth.2014. Adopted in case cit. in sup. (erron. cit. as Restatement Second). State department of public welfare filed a petition for review after the state office of open records ordered it to disclose, in response to a Right-to-Know Law request, certain rates related to the administration of its Medicare program that were set by contracts with managed-care organizations. Affirming in part, this court held, among other things, that department was required to disclose capitation rates, or the amounts paid in the Medicaid program per member, per month, because, among other things, the rates did not constitute trade secrets. The court reasoned that, other than confidentiality provisions in its contracts, department made no special effort to maintain the secrecy of the rates, and that department was in no danger of losing market share as a result of disclosure of the rates, because it was the commonwealth agency charged with administering the Medicaid program in the state and did not have any competitors. Com., Dept. of Public Welfare v. Eiseman, 85 A.3d 1117, 1126.

Tenn.App.2004. Quot. in case quot. in sup. Corporation sued former employees/officers for breach of fiduciary duty, unfair competition, and intentional inducement to breach a contract, inter alia. The trial court entered judgment for plaintiff. This court reversed in part, holding, inter alia, that the trial court erred in awarding judgment to plaintiff as to its breach-of-fiduciary-duty claim that defendants unlawfully solicited plaintiff's customers while officers of plaintiff, and that defendants unlawfully used or relied on confidential business information in soliciting plaintiff's clients after their resignation or termination. Plaintiff's customer information, specifically, client names, prices charged for services rendered, customer-contract-renewal dates, and identity of client representatives, did not constitute confidential business information. B & L Corp. v. Thomas and Thorngren, Inc., 162 S.W.3d 189, 211.

Tenn.App.1998. Quot. in case quot. in sup. Corporation sued former officer and his new company, alleging that defendant breached his fiduciary duty to plaintiff by forming his own company and by obtaining a contract with plaintiff's customer to perform a portion of the services formerly provided by plaintiff. The trial court entered a judgment awarding plaintiff damages. Reversing and remanding, this court held, inter alia, that plaintiff's customer rates did not constitute confidential information, and thus defendant's use of this information to obtain the customer's business did not result in a breach of fiduciary duty. Venture Express, Inc. v. Zilly, 973 S.W.2d 602, 606.

Tex.2009. Com. (b) cit. in case cit. in sup. Resident who lived near the site of a train collision that resulted in the release of toxic chlorine gas sued railroad for negligence. After the trial court denied railroad's motion to quash resident's notice of deposition requesting railroad's hazardous material rate structures, the court of appeals denied railroad's petition for a writ of mandamus. This court conditionally granted railroad's petition, holding, inter alia, that the rate structures were protectable trade secrets; railroad established that the manner and method it employed to calculate and arrive at shipping rates was not generally known or readily available to its competitors, its customers, other businesses, or even throughout the company, and it would be harmed by the competitive advantage rivals would gain if they found the information. In re Union Pacific R. Co., 294 S.W.3d 589, 592.

Tex.2006. Quot. in conc. op. Employer sued former at-will employee who left his position to work for a competitor, alleging breach of a covenant not to compete contained in an employment agreement signed by employee. The trial court granted summary judgment for employee, and the court of appeals affirmed. Reversing in part and remanding, this court held that employee became bound by his promise not to compete when employer later performed its corresponding promise to provide special training in its business methods and confidential information. A concurrence questioned the necessity of requiring an employer to provide consideration, in addition to employment, to make a confidentiality agreement entered at the commencement of or during employment enforceable post-termination, observing that this court had long held that an employee's fiduciary duty precluded the employee from misusing or misappropriating an employer's confidential information. Alex Sheshunoff Management Services, L.P. v. Johnson, 209 S.W.3d 644, 665.

Tex.2003. Com. (b) quot. in sup. Nonparticipating royalty-interest owners attempted discovery of the mineral-estate owner's geological seismic data to prove that the mineral-estate owner breached an implied duty to develop its land. Trial court rejected mineral-estate owner's claims that the data were trade secrets and ordered production of the data under a protective order. Appeals court denied mineral-estate owner's requested mandamus relief. This court conditionally granted mandamus relief and ordered trial court to vacate its order compelling the production of the seismic data. The court held that geological seismic data and its interpretations were trade secrets protected by the Texas Rules of Evidence, and that nonparticipating royalty-interest owners failed to establish claim against mineral-estate owner justifying discovery of the trade-secret data. In re Bass, 113 S.W.3d 735, 739.

Tex.1996. Cit. in headnote, quot. in case cit. in disc. In trade-secret-misappropriation litigation concerning an employee who brought to his new employer copies of computer programs taken from his former employer, the United States Court of Appeals for the Second Circuit certified to this court the question whether the discovery rule exception to § 16.003(a) of the Texas Civil Practice and Remedies Code applied, and, if not, whether application of the two-year statute of limitations violated the "open courts" provision of the Texas Constitution. In response, this court held that the exception did not apply in the context of intellectual-property trade-secret misappropriation, as the injury in such cases was not inherently undiscoverable within the two-year period, and that application of the two-year limitations period did not violate the "open courts" provision

For earlier citations, see the Appendices, Supplements, or Pocket Parts, if any, that correspond to the subject matter under examination.

of the state constitution. Computer Associates Intern. v. Altai, 918 S.W.2d 453, 453, 455.

Tex.1992. Com. (b) quot. in conc. op. Parents of a child who was injured when a bolt-action rifle discharged during loading sought a writ of mandamus in their products liability action to order the trial court to compel defendant manufacturer to produce documents containing alternative design information. Holding that the trial court abused its discretion by denying discovery, this court conditionally granted the writ. The concurring opinion argued that defendant did not meet its burden of establishing a right to protection based on the trade secret privilege. Chapa v. Garcia, 848 S.W.2d 667, 670.

Tex.App.2019. Cit. in case cit. in sup. (general cite). Trucking company that developed kits to convert truck engines from diesel to natural gas sued maintenance provider that serviced and repaired its trucks, which it later hired to install the kits on its trucks, alleging that defendant misappropriated its trade secrets when another business assumed operation of plaintiff's trucks and defendant continued to service the trucks for the other business. The trial court conducted a bench trial and ruled in favor of defendant. Affirming, this court pointed out that defendant stopped performing work related to the kits and only performed maintenance work for the other business, and held that the evidence was insufficient to establish that the identity of the other business was a trade secret under the six-factor test set forth in Restatement of Torts § 757. The court pointed out that the other business's identity was readily ascertainable by other means and was not substantially a secret, and that plaintiff did not make any efforts to keep the other business's identity a secret. EJ Madison, LLC v. Pro-Tech Diesel, Inc., 594 S.W.3d 632, 644.

Tex.App.2019. Com. (b) quot. in ftn. Photographer brought a lawsuit against public university, alleging that defendant violated state constitution provisions against takings without just compensation, because it violated plaintiff's copyright over his photographs by using them, without his permission, to promote its business school. The trial court denied defendant's motion to dismiss. This court reversed, vacated, and granted defendant's motion to dismiss, holding that, unlike government misappropriation of trade secrets, government violation of intellectual property rights did not constitute an unconstitutional taking. The court relied on Restatement of Torts § 757, Comment *b*, in defining the term "trade secret." University of Houston System v. Jim Olive Photography, 580 S.W.3d 360, 374.

Tex.App.2018. Quot. in case quot. in disc.; coms. (b) and (j) quot. in case quot. in disc. Distributor brought a lawsuit against manufacturer, manufacturer's subsidiary, and competitor, alleging, inter alia, that manufacturer misappropriated plaintiff's trade secrets, which had been given in confidence during negotiations for an exclusive distribution agreement, when manufacturer later established subsidiary as a distributor in the United States and entered into a distribution agreement with competitor. The trial court denied plaintiff's motion for temporary injunctive relief against defendants selling equipment in the United States. This court affirmed, holding that, although plaintiff established that there was a confidential relationship between it and manufacturer, the trial court reasonably could have concluded that plaintiff's information were not trade secrets. Citing Restatement of Torts § 757, the court explained that plaintiff established the existence of the confidential relationship when it demonstrated that it had shown a presentation containing confidential information to manufacturer and explicitly informed manufacturer that the presentation was confidential. Kana Energy Services, Inc. v. Jiangsu Jinshi Machinery Group Co. Ltd., 565 S.W.3d 347, 352-355.

Tex.App.2014. Com. (b) cit. in case quot. in sup. (general cite). Online broker filed a petition requesting presuit discovery from software developer and former employee of broker who left to work for developer, alleging that it appeared likely that employee and others had, in designing risk-analysis software for developer, misappropriated broker's confidential and proprietary assets in violation of the nondisclosure provisions in their employment contracts with broker. The trial court granted broker's petition and issued an order allowing the requested depositions and document production. This court directed the trial court to vacate its order and conditionally granted developer's petition for writ of mandamus, holding, inter alia, that developer established that all but one category of the information

Cit.—cited; com.—comment; fol.—followed; sup.—support.
A complete list of abbreviations precedes page 1.

sought by broker concerning developer's risk-analysis software constituted privileged trade-secret information. The court pointed to evidence that only two of developer's employees had access to the software's computer code, the software could not be duplicated by others without access to the underlying programming code, and the software was developer's only asset and was extremely valuable to developer. In re PrairieSmarts LLC, 421 S.W.3d 296, 307.

Tex.App.2013. Com. (b) cit. in case quot. in sup. Lessee of port authority property brought suit for declaratory and injunctive relief under the Texas Public Information Act (PIA), challenging state attorney general's ruling that certain lease information was not excepted from disclosure to a requestor under the PIA. The district court denied lessee its requested relief. Affirming, this court rejected lessee's argument that the lease information was "expressly confidential under other law," and therefore exempt from the PIA's mandatory disclosure requirement, because it was a common-law trade secret. The court concluded that lessee failed to conclusively establish that the lease information was a trade secret, reasoning that, while lessee did not generally make the information known outside its business, it failed to take reasonable precautions to protect its alleged trade secret by preventing port from disclosing the information, and failed to establish that the information was of sufficient value to lessee and its competitors to constitute a trade secret. Boeing Co. v. Abbott, 412 S.W.3d 1, 10.

Tex.App.2013. Subsecs. (a) and (b) quot. in case quot. in sup. Holders of a right of first refusal with respect to oil and gas prospects identified by development company sued former officer of company and related entities and individuals, alleging misappropriation of trade secrets and other claims, after defendants, acting without plaintiffs' knowledge, obtained a lease on a property identified in company's seismic map of a gas prospect. The trial court entered judgment on a jury verdict for plaintiffs. The trial court entered judgment on a jury verdict in favor of plaintiffs. Affirming, this court held that there was sufficient evidence to support the jury's finding that defendants' knowledge of the gas beneath the property was obtained through the unauthorized use of the map. The court pointed to evidence that defendants did not conduct any independent seismic research and that any well placement would be highly speculative without such research, but that defendants nevertheless bid over $1 million to lease the property, drilled wells on it, and drained the gas reservoir within six months. Lamont v. Vaquillas Energy Lopeno Ltd., LLP, 421 S.W.3d 198, 212.

Tex.App.2013. Cit. in ftn. Inventor and owners of a process for mining potash (potassium-containing ore) in a specific area that had anomalously high temperatures brought claims for misappropriation of trade secrets, inter alia, against inventor's former business partner and partner's company's subsidiary, alleging that defendants used plaintiffs' proprietary information in developing their own mining project. The trial court entered judgment on a jury verdict for plaintiffs. Affirming, this court held that there was sufficient evidence to support the jury's award of damages, which were based on considerations of, among other things, the amount of the present value of past and projected future revenues attributable to defendant's use of plaintiffs' trade secret. In making its decision, the court noted that the factors originally articulated in Restatement First of Torts § 757 were the foundation for both Georgia and Texas law on trade secrets. Southwestern Energy Production Co. v. Berry-Helfand, 411 S.W.3d 581, 608.

Tex.App.2013. Com. (b) quot. in case quot. in sup. Operator of county landfill brought an action against county and against state attorney general, seeking declaratory and injunctive relief under the Texas Public Information Act to prevent the disclosure, pursuant to an open-records request filed by a member of the public, of volume and pricing information contained in "waste tickets" generated when customers disposed of waste at the landfill, alleging that that information constituted a trade secret. After a bench trial, the trial court ordered county to disclose the information. This court reversed and rendered judgment that county was prohibited from disclosing the information, holding that a company's confidential pricing and rate information could qualify as a trade secret, and, here, the factors for determining whether information was a trade secret weighed strongly in favor of operator. Waste Management of Texas, Inc. v. Abbott, 406 S.W.3d 626, 631.

For earlier citations, see the Appendices, Supplements, or Pocket Parts, if any, that correspond to the subject matter under examination.

Tex.App.2013. Com. (b) quot. in case quot. in sup. In competitor's antitrust action against waste-disposal company, the trial court ordered company to produce various internal business records in their native, electronic format with all metadata. This court denied company's petition for mandamus relief, concluding, inter alia, that company failed to introduce any evidence that its compliance with the discovery order would require it to disclose trade secrets; merely claiming that trade secrets were at issue was not sufficient. Absent a showing by company that the disputed discovery contained trade secrets, competitor did not have to prove that the trade secrets were necessary for fair adjudication. In re Waste Management of Texas, Inc., 392 S.W.3d 861, 870.

Tex.App.2012. Cit. in sup., quot. in case cit. in sup., cit. in case cit. in disc. Natural-gas processor sued foreign limited-liability company, alleging theft of trade secrets. This court affirmed the trial court's denial of defendant's special appearance, holding that defendant had contacts with Texas out of which plaintiff's claim arose. The court concluded that defendant's use of plaintiff's trade secrets that allegedly occurred in Texas—i.e., defendant's marketing efforts and sales of products incorporating plaintiff's technology—was sufficient for liability, and thus defendant's Texas contacts were substantially connected to the operative facts of the litigation for purposes of establishing specific jurisdiction over defendant. Twister B.V. v. Newton Research Partners, LP, 364 S.W.3d 428, 438, 439.

Tex.App.2011. Com. (b) cit. in case cit. in sup. Former assistant to a real estate agent sued agent and his wife, alleging defamation and tortious interference with contract; defendants counterclaimed for theft of trade secrets. After the jury found for plaintiff on all three claims, the trial court, inter alia, denied defendants' motion for judgment n.o.v. as to the theft counterclaim. While reversing and remanding for a new trial on all of the claims, this court held that defendants did not conclusively prove that plaintiff knowingly stole trade secrets, since the jury could reasonably have found that plaintiff retained copies of only four nonconfidential and unprotected pages from defendants' policy and procedures manual, containing website passwords as to which all of defendants' employees had access. Downing v. Burns, 348 S.W.3d 415, 422.

Tex.App.2009. Com. (b) cit. in case cit. in sup. Licensor of technology for manufacturing polyethylene plastic brought action for misappropriation of trade secrets and breach of contract against licensee, after licensee sublicensed the technology to other companies without authorization. The trial court granted plaintiff's request for a temporary injunction. Affirming, this court held, among other things, that plaintiff, in demonstrated that its technology constituted a trade secret, presented some evidence tending to show that it acted with sufficient vigilance to maintain the secrecy of the technology; while defendant pointed to several agreements between plaintiff and other companies containing fixed-term secrecy clauses that had expired, plaintiff offered countervailing evidence to show that, under the unique circumstances of each agreement, the secrecy of the technology remained intact, despite the expiration of the secrecy clauses. INEOS Group Ltd. v. Chevron Phillips Chemical Co., LP, 312 S.W.3d 843, 849.

Tex.App.2008. Com. (b) cit. in sup. and cit. and quot. in cases cit. in sup. Development company sued energy company for breach of contract, alleging that defendant failed to reassign undeveloped acreage in accordance with obligations in certain gas leases. The trial court granted plaintiff's motion to compel production of documents stating defendant's reserve estimates and projected future revenues for wells covered by the leases. Conditionally granting defendant's petition for a writ of mandamus, this court held that defendant established that the data were trade secrets, and that plaintiff failed to show that disclosure of the information was necessary to prevent fraud or injustice. The court reasoned that the forecasts and conclusions of defendant and its consultants were not publicly available, defendant limited the information within its own organization and vigilantly guarded the data, and the information was highly valuable to the company. In re XTO Resources I, LP, 248 S.W.3d 898, 901-904.

Tex.App.2007. Adopted in case cit. in ftn. Manufacturer of fiberglass utility bodies and toppers for commercial vehicles sued competitor for, in part, tortious interference with prospective business relations, alleging that defendant's use of plaintiff's design drawings to create a stair-step topper for one of plaintiff's existing customers was independently tortious on the ground of trade-secret misappropriation. The trial court denied defendant's no-evidence motion for summary judgment on the tortious-interference claim. Affirming that portion of the decision, this court held, inter alia, that there was evidence that defendant misappropriated the design drawings because, by obtaining the drawings from plaintiff's customer, which was aware that the drawings were confidential, it discovered the drawings by improper means. Astoria Industries of Iowa, Inc. v. SNF, Inc., 223 S.W.3d 616, 636.

Tex.App.2005. Cit. in case cit. in disc., quot. in ftn. Manufacturer of replacement helicopter blades sued competitors, seeking injunction preventing defendants from using plaintiff's trade secrets. Trial court granted temporary injunction. This court affirmed, holding that plaintiff satisfied temporary injunction requirements for trade-secret-misappropriation claim. Defendants acquired trade-secret data through breach of confidential relationship. Plaintiff disclosed trade-secret data to defendants so that they could repair plaintiff's helicopters, but defendants had obligation to keep data confidential pursuant to confidentiality agreement. Work report containing data was not available through Attorney General publication centers, and drawings upon which report was based were not available through Freedom of Information Act request. IAC, Ltd. v. Bell Helicopter Textron, Inc., 160 S.W.3d 191, 199.

Tex.App.2004. Quot. in case quot. in disc. Employer brought suit for, in part, misappropriation of trade secrets against former employee who, after being laid off, accepted employment with competitor. Trial court granted summary judgment for employee. Affirming in part, this court held, inter alia, that, although customer information could be accorded trade-secret status, it would not do so automatically, and, instead, a substantial element of secrecy was required; here, employee's general knowledge of issues presented by customer's compensation system did not rise to level of trade secret. Trilogy Software, Inc. v. Callidus Software, Inc., 143 S.W.3d 452, 464, 466.

Tex.App.2003. Quot. in sup., adopted in case cit. in ftn., com. (b) quot. in case cit. in ftn. Company that designed converged architecture for delivering telecommunication services to residences sued developer of planned residential communities, alleging, among other things, misappropriation of trade secrets and breach in nondisclosure agreement,after developer invested in other company that intended to use company's secret information to market identical product. Trial court granted plaintiff a temporary injunction. Affirming, this court held, inter alia, that trial court did not abuse its discretion by granting temporary injunction where evidence established that plaintiff had probable right to relief on its claim for breach of nondisclosure agreement, which precluded defendant form using plaintiff's trade secrets to invest in company that intended to use plaintiff's secret information. Mabrey v. Sandstream, Inc., 124 S.W.3d 302, 310.

Tex.App.2002. Com. (b) quot. in case quot. in disc. (Erron. cit. as Restatement (Second) of Torts.) Decedent's mother sued tire manufacturer for negligence. After the trial court granted plaintiff's motion to inspect defendant's manufacturing plant, defendant moved for a writ of mandamus. Conditionally granting the writ, this court held that the trial court abused its discretion in ordering the inspection because plaintiff failed to show that she was entitled to discover defendant's trade secrets. In re Continental Tire North America, Inc., 74 S.W.3d 884, 886.

Tex.App.2000. Com. (b) quot. in case quot. in sup. Manufacturer of hair-care products sued drug and beauty company, among others, for, inter alia, tortious interference with exclusive distribution contracts existing between manufacturer and salons. The trial court granted defendant's motion for judgment n.o.v. Affirming, this court held, in part, that, even if defendant had been a willing participant in another party's breach of its exclusive distribution agreement with plaintiff, plaintiff had failed to establish that defendant had engaged in willful inducement, and that defendant's list of suppliers was protected from discovery as a trade secret. John Paul Mitchell v. Randalls Food Markets, 17 S.W.3d 721, 738.

Tex.App.1999. Com. (b) cit. in case cit. in disc. and quot. in case quot. in disc. Car insurers and trade associations sued the insurance commissioner, the attorney general, and a citizen to enjoin the disclosure of quarterly market reports that were submitted in connection with an assigned risk plan and were sought by the citizen under the Public Information Act. Trial

For earlier citations, see the Appendices, Supplements, or Pocket Parts, if any, that correspond to the subject matter under examination.

court entered injunctions prohibiting the department from releasing information to the citizen, holding that the market-report data constituted trade secrets. This court affirmed in part and reversed in part, holding, inter alia, that although the market-report information was not confidential information under the statute, the trial court did not abuse its discretion in granting a temporary injunction on the ground that the market report information, disclosing insurance sales by ZIP code, amounted to trade secrets. Birnbaum v. Alliance of American Insurers, 994 S.W.2d 766, 783.

Tex.App.1997. Cit. in headnote, com. (j) quot. in case quot. in disc. Manufacturer of premarinated beef fajitas sued competitor for misappropriation of trade secret, alleging that it disclosed its five-element process for creating the fajitas to defendant in confidence, and that defendant then used the process without plaintiff's authorization. The trial court entered judgment on a jury verdict for plaintiff. Reversing and remanding, this court held that plaintiff disclosed the process to defendant in confidence, and that defendant used the process in a manner unauthorized by plaintiff; however, the evidence was factually insufficient to support the jury's finding that the process constituted a trade secret, as the process was commonly known, having been published and widely distributed in the industry before defendant began using it. H.E. Butt Groc. Co. v. Moody's Qual. Meats, 951 S.W.2d 33, 33, 36.

Tex.App.1996. Cit. and quot. in disc., quot. in case quot. in disc. Company sued a former employee for misappropriation of trade secrets and sought to enjoin former employee from selling a competing product. Employee counterclaimed for malicious prosecution. Trial court entered judgment on jury verdict finding that the former employee did not convert any of employer's trade secrets. This court reversed and rendered judgment that the former employee take nothing by his counterclaim. The court held, inter alia, that employer had probable cause to file suit, because it had a legitimate interest in protecting confidential information relating to the design and manufacture of its derringer. American Derringer Corp. v. Bond, 924 S.W.2d 773, 776-778.

Tex.App.1996. Com. (b) quot. in case quot. in disc. Corporation that bought tool used for soil sampling in the oil and gas business brought action for misappropriation of trade secrets against competitor after competitor began using a similar tool. Defendant once worked for the company from which plaintiff bought its tool, but was no longer in company's employ at the time of the purchase. The trial court granted defendant's motion for partial summary judgment. Reversing as to costs but otherwise affirming, this court held, in part, that plaintiff could not recover for misappropriation of trade secrets in the absence of a confidential relationship between the parties. GeoChem Tech. Corp. v. Verseckes, 929 S.W.2d 85, 91.

Tex.App.1996. Cit. generally in case cit. in diss. op., com. (b) quot. in case quot. in diss. op. Defendant appealed from his conviction for commercial bribery and theft of trade secrets. Affirming in part, reversing in part, and remanding, this court held, inter alia, that the definition of trade secret in the jury charge tracked the definition set forth in the Texas Penal Code and correctly stated the law. The dissent argued that the trial court erred in failing to include an instruction to the jury that a trade secret must be a secret. McGowan v. State, 938 S.W.2d 732, 742.

Tex.App.1994. Quot. and cit. in sup., com. (b) quot. in disc., quot. in part in sup., and cit. in ftn., com. (m) quot. in part in sup. A business that provided heat-exchanger cleaning services for the oil and gas industry sued three competitors, asserting various claims, including one for misappropriation of trade secrets. Reversing the trial court's entry of judgment on jury verdict for plaintiff, rendering in part, and remanding in part, this court held, inter alia, that a deemed finding to supply the essential element of secrecy in the misappropriation claim could not be made to support judgment for plaintiff, since all defendants had objected to the trial court's failure to instruct jury that the allegedly misappropriated confidential information must be secret. Stewart & Stevenson v. Serv-Tech, Inc., 879 S.W.2d 89, 95, 96, 104.

Tex.App.1991. Com. (b) quot. in case quot. in disc. A supplier of industrial cleaners sued a corporate client and its wholly owned subsidiary for misappropriation of trade secrets, inter alia, alleging that the defendants benefited from the use and disclosure of the plaintiff's soap formula and confidential financial and customer data provided to them during discussions

Cit.—cited; com.—comment; fol.—followed; sup.—support.
A complete list of abbreviations precedes page 1.

concerning the defendants' possible acquisition of the plaintiff. The trial court entered judgment on a jury verdict awarding the plaintiff damages. Reversing and remanding, this court held that the evidence was insufficient to support the jury's finding of misappropriation. The court observed that the plaintiff did not prove actual use or disclosure of its trade secrets by the defendants to the plaintiff's competitive disadvantage. Atlantic Richfield v. Misty Products, 820 S.W.2d 414, 422.

Tex.App.1991. Cit. generally in case cit. in disc., com. (b) quot. in ftn. Former employees of a company were convicted by a jury of theft of trade secrets. The intermediate appellate court affirmed. Affirming, this court held, inter alia, that the combination of employment agreements, strict plant security, restricted computer access, the nonauthorization of disclosure of the subject programs, and the general nondisclosure of those programs by the company and its employees served to support trade-secret status of the computer programs that were the subject of the defendant's indictments. The court stated that these corporate actions and policies qualified as sufficient measures to protect trade-secret status under the statutory criteria. Schalk v. State, 823 S.W.2d 633, 636, certiorari denied 503 U.S. 1006, 112 S.Ct. 1763, 118 L.Ed.2d 425 (1992).

Tex.App.1990. Com. (a) quot. in disc., com. (b) cit. in disc. A health-care-services coordinator sued two of his former employees for breach of confidentiality and unfair competition in their use of trade secrets acquired during their tenure of employment. The trial court entered a judgment awarding the plaintiff damages and a three-year injunction enjoining, inter alia, the defendants from using any of the plaintiff's confidential health care forms and procedures. This court affirmed the judgment concerning this aspect of the injunction. Acknowledging that the trial court incorrectly stated the law in instructing the jury over the defendants' objection that a trade secret "may be only an idea," the court nonetheless rejected the defendants' point of error, stating that at no time did the defendants specify the grounds on which they were objecting to this part of the instruction, nor was any ground apparent in the record. Gonzales v. Zamora, 791 S.W.2d 258, 263, 264.

Tex.App.1988. Cit. in case quot. in disc., com. (b) quot. in disc. and cit. in case cit. in disc. A vibrator company sued two former employees who had resigned and formed a competitor company for damages and injunctive relief, alleging appropriation of trade secrets and confidential information in violation of their fiduciary duty. The trial court entered judgment on a jury verdict for the first former employee and against the second, and enjoined the competitor company from selling certain vibrators. This court affirmed in part, holding that the evidence at trial was factually sufficient to show that the plaintiff's customer cards, blueprints, and drawings were trade secrets, and their appropriation by the second former employee was a breach of fiduciary duty. The court modified the trial court's ruling as to the injunction, holding that the competitor company could manufacture, but not sell or lease, the specified vibrators. American Precision Vibrator Co. v. National Air Vibrator Co., 764 S.W.2d 274, 276.

Tex.App.1988. Quot. in case quot. in disc. An employer sued his former employee and the companies the former employee formed, seeking to enforce a covenant not to compete. The trial court granted a temporary injunction. Affirming, this court held that, although the employer was entitled to a temporary injunction, the injunction granted was overbroad in that it prohibited sales of any nature, not just those involving competitive items. Bertotti v. C.E. Shepherd Co., Inc., 752 S.W.2d 648, 652.

Tex.App.1987. Quot. in disc. A corporation engaged in selling and leasing diagnostic imaging equipment sought a temporary injunction against a former employee to prevent the employee from competing with the corporation. The trial court denied the corporation's application. Affirming, this court held that the information that the plaintiff sought to protect was not a trade secret because it was contained in the contracts distributed to the plaintiff's customers and could have been discovered by anyone. The court noted that information about the plaintiff's customers, prices, and services could not be accorded the court's protection because it was publicly available and generally known in the industry. Numed, Inc. v. McNutt, 724 S.W.2d 432, 435.

Tex.Crim.App.1998. Subsec. (b) quot. in ftn. Company owner who procured drawings used to manufacture original equipment manufacturers' replacement parts

For earlier citations, see the Appendices, Supplements, or Pocket Parts, if any, that correspond to the subject matter under examination.

was convicted in trial court of theft of trade secrets and appealed. Manufacturer's employee who sold him some of the drawings also appealed his conviction for trade secrets theft. In each case, the court of appeals affirmed in part and reversed in part. Affirming, this court held, inter alia, that evidence of employee nondisclosure agreements, plant security, and restricted access by third parties to the drawings supported a finding that manufacturers maintained substantial secrecy of the drawings at issue and sustained defendants' convictions for theft of trade secrets. The court said that trade-secret law had its origins in the civil law arena, noting that Texas law utilized the trade-secrets definition of Restatement of Torts § 757(b). Weightman v. State, 975 S.W.2d 621, 624.

Utah, 2016. Com. (b) quot. in sup., quot. in case cit. and quot. in sup. and cit. in ftn. Developer of a power-plant project brought, inter alia, an action against utility company that had submitted and selected its own bid to build a power plant, alleging that defendant misappropriated plaintiff's trade secrets regarding its vision for the project, despite having signed a confidentiality and nondisclosure agreement prior to entering into negotiations to purchase plaintiff's project assets. The trial court granted defendant's motion for summary judgment; the court of appeals reversed and remanded. On remand, the trial court entered judgment on a jury verdict for plaintiff. This court affirmed, holding that there was sufficient evidence to support a reasonable jury finding that a trade secret existed. The court relied on the factors set forth in Restatement of Torts § 757, Comment *b*, in determining that there was sufficient evidence to find that certain components of plaintiff's vision were not generally known or readily ascertainable. USA Power, LLC v. PacifiCorp, 372 P.3d 629, 651, 652.

Utah, 2010. Cit. in sup., com. (b) quot. in sup. Electric-power-plant developer sued utility company, alleging that it provided defendant with information about developing a power plant that constituted a trade secret, and that defendant misappropriated that trade secret when it chose to develop its own power plant rather than purchase the one proposed by plaintiff. The trial court granted summary judgment for defendant. Reversing and remanding, this court held that a compilation of information within the public domain could constitute a trade secret, and plaintiff raised a genuine issue of material fact as to misappropriation of its alleged trade secrets by defendant. The court additionally held that the six factors of Restatement of Torts § 757, Comment *b*, could be useful to trial courts in determining whether a compilation of items or ideas already in the public domain constituted a trade secret. USA Power, LLC v. PacifiCorp, 2010 UT 31, 235 P.3d 749, 760.

Utah App.2012. Com. (b) quot. in case quot. in sup. Concrete contractor sued, among others, competitor and former employee who left to work for competitor, alleging, inter alia, that defendants misappropriated plaintiff's trade secret labor and equipment rates and bid information. The trial court granted summary judgment for defendants. Affirming in part, this court held that plaintiff's labor and equipment pricing information was not entitled to trade-secret protection as a matter of law; among other things, plaintiff failed to set forth sufficient facts creating a genuine issue of material fact that the pricing information was not generally known and not readily ascertainable by proper means. CDC Restoration & Const., LC v. Tradesmen Contractors, LLC, 2012 UT App 60, 274 P.3d 317, 324.

Va.2016. Com. (f) quot. in ftn. Sublicensor of nuclear technology brought a claim for breach of the Virginia Uniform Trade Secrets Act against sub-licensees, alleging that defendants disclosed plaintiff's trade secrets to third parties without authorization. The trial court entered judgment on a jury verdict in favor of plaintiff. This court reversed and entered final judgment dismissing plaintiff's claims, holding that the trial court erred in failing to set aside the verdict on plaintiff's claim for misappropriation of trade secrets, because the sub-license gave defendants a perpetual, worldwide license to practice and use plaintiff's technology for all purposes, without restriction, and there could be no misappropriation where acquisition, disclosure, and use of a trade secret was expressly authorized by contract. The court reasoned, in part, that, under Restatement of Torts §§ 757 and 759, a valid contractual acquisition of a trade secret could not be characterized as an acquisition by "improper means." Babcock & Wilcox Company v. Areva NP, Inc., 788 S.E. 237, 260.

Va.1990. Com. (b) quot. in disc. A family-

Cit.—cited; com.—comment; fol.—followed; sup.—support.
A complete list of abbreviations precedes page 1.

owned manufacturing company obtained a patent for packaging material. After a bitter family dispute, the company sued its founder's son, who had been terminated, to prevent him from using the processes, techniques, and other secrets learned while employed at the company. The trial court entered an injunction against the former employee holding that the manufacturing process was a trade secret and that the employee's conduct constituted a misappropriation. Affirming, this court held, inter alia, that the manufacturing process satisfied the statutory definition of the term trade secret. The court stated that the company had used reasonable security measures to maintain the confidentiality of the material, that the material had a value and was generally unknown in the company's sales area, that the company had invested time, money, and effort in the research and development of the material, that the company had a competitive advantage, and that the material was a unique product. Dionne v. Southeast Foam Converting, 240 Va. 297, 397 S.E.2d 110, 113.

Wash.1999. Cit. generally in disc. Employer sued former employees for trade-secrets misappropriation, alleging that the employees solicited its clients using confidential information. Trial court held that the employees had misappropriated the trade secrets. Appellate court affirmed in part and reversed in part. This court affirmed, holding, inter alia, that information which had been determined to be a trade secret did not lose its protected status because it had been committed to memory rather than taken in written form. Ed Nowogroski Ins., Inc. v. Rucker, 137 Wash.2d 427, 971 P.2d 936, 944.

W.Va.1992. Cit. in case cit. in sup., com. (b) quot. generally in sup. and quot. in case cit. in sup. Worker injured by machine sought a writ of prohibition to prevent enforcement of a protective order issued in an underlying products-liability suit worker brought against the machine's manufacturer; the protective order limited plaintiff's access to defendant's technical files containing trade secrets. This court denied the writ, holding, inter alia, that the trial judge in the underlying action did not abuse her power in issuing the order, since both parties agreed that an order was necessary to the proceedings. The court also noted that the manufacturer's design drawings were not publicly known to anyone outside the company and to only a limited number within the company and that the manufacturer spent much time and money acquiring and protecting the disputed information. State ex rel. Johnson v. Tsapis, 187 W.Va. 337, 419 S.E.2d 1, 3.

Wis.2017. Cit. in ftn. to diss. op.; com. (b) cit. in diss. op. and quot. in case quot. in diss. op. Manufacturer of customized plastic parts, whose former employee left to form competitor with business partner, sued partner, among others, alleging that partner misappropriated plaintiff's trade secrets when employee formulated confidential bids on a project for both plaintiff and competitor while he was still working for plaintiff. The trial court granted summary judgment for partner. The court of appeals affirmed. Affirming, this court held that, even if plaintiff's bid was a trade secret, there was no evidence that employee disclosed the amount of the bid to partner. A dissent argued that the question of whether a trade secret existed under Wisconsin law and the Restatement of Torts § 757 was a question of fact to be determined by a trier of fact. Another dissent noted that, under § 757, a single or ephemeral event in the conduct of the business, such as the amount of a secret bid for a contract, could not constitute a trade secret. North Highland Inc. v. Jefferson Machine & Tool Inc., 898 N.W.2d 741, 755, 756, 769.

Wis.2006. Cit. generally in ftn. to diss. op., com. (b) cit. in case cit. in ftn. Former employer sued former employee and employee's new employer for, in part, misappropriation of trade secrets, alleging that, after resigning, employee used plaintiff's confidential information, including customer lists and pricing information, to solicit and acquire customers. The trial court granted summary judgment for defendants and the court of appeals affirmed. This court reversed in part and remanded, holding that, while the confidential information did not meet the definition of a trade secret provided in Wisconsin's trade-secret statute derived from the Uniform Trade Secrets Act (UTSA), plaintiff's related common-law claims were not precluded by the statute. The dissent argued that plaintiff could not maintain common-law claims for misappropriation of confidential information that did not rise to the level of a trade secret in a UTSA state such as Wisconsin. Burbank Grease Services, LLC v. Sokolowski, 294 Wis.2d 274, 717 N.W.2d 781, 791, 802.

For earlier citations, see the Appendices, Supplements, or Pocket Parts, if any, that correspond to the subject matter under examination.

Wis.1989. Com. (b) cit. in disc. and quot. in case quot. in disc. A manufacturer sought injunctive relief against former executive officers and a competitor on theories of misappropriation of a product formula and customer list trade secrets. The intermediate appellate court said that the trial court relied on evidence not admitted to establish the possibility of reverse engineering in denying injunctive relief, and affirmed the trial court's ruling that the formula was a trade secret, but held that the customer data was not. Reversing in part, this court held that the possibility of reverse engineering alone was not enough to deny a temporary injunction. Affirming in part, the court held that damages represented an adequate remedy for misappropriated customer data. The court said that the Restatement trade secret test, relied on by both courts below, was superseded by the Wisconsin Uniform Trade Secrets Act. Minuteman, Inc. v. Alexander, 147 Wis.2d 842, 434 N.W.2d 773, 776, 777.

Wis.App.2005. Cit. in disc., cit. in case cit. in disc., com. (b) cit. in ftn. After former employee of grease-collection company started working for a competing business and solicited former customers, former employer brought suit against former employee and competing business for, in part, misappropriation of trade secrets, alleging that employee used plaintiff's confidential customer information to his advantage. Trial court granted summary judgment for defendants. Affirming, this court held, inter alia, that plaintiff's customer list did not constitute a trade secret because all of the information contained therein was readily ascertainable from the customers themselves or by other proper means, and therefore was not protectable as confidential or unique. Burbank Grease Services, LLC v. Sokolowski, 278 Wis.2d 698, 693 N.W.2d 89, 94, 97.

Wis.App.1987. Com. (b) cit. in sup. and in ftn. After a purchaser of scrap paper containing a securities underwriter's customer information sold the information to a competitor of the underwriter, the underwriter sought to restrain any further disclosures. The trial court granted the plaintiff's motion for summary judgment, holding that the plaintiff was entitled to common law trade-secrets protection and that the defendant did not acquire title to the information as a good-faith purchaser. This court affirmed, holding that the information on the paper met all the criteria for trade-secret status and that it retained that status despite the accidental disclosure. The defendant did not acquire title to the information, said the court, and it would be inequitable to allow him to continue his use of it. B.C. Ziegler and Co. v. Ehren, 141 Wis.2d 19, 414 N.W.2d 48, 51.

Wyo.2014. Cit. in disc., cit. in case quot. in disc., com. (b) quot. in ftn. Nonprofit organizations submitted a request under the Wyoming Public Records Act (WPRA) to the state oil and gas conservation commission, seeking disclosure of the chemicals in several companies' hydraulic fracturing products. The commission denied the request, finding that the requested information was exempt from public disclosure as a trade secret under the WPRA, and the trial court affirmed. This court reversed and specified that, on remand, the trial court should apply the narrower definition of trade secret developed in federal case law under the Freedom of Information Act, rather than the broader definitions set forth in Restatement Third of Unfair Competition § 39 or Restatement of Torts § 757. The court noted that those sections of the Restatement focused on unfair competition and misappropriation, unlike the WPRA or FOIA, which sought to guarantee the public's right to access documents revealing the operations of the government. Powder River Basin Resource Council v. Wyoming Oil and Gas Conservation, 2014 WY 37, 320 P.3d 222, 233.

Wyo.2006. Cit. and quot. in disc., cit. in diss. op. After internet-based market-analysis company brought action for misappropriation of trade secrets in federal district court against former employees who formed competing company, the issue of whether such a cause of action existed in Wyoming was certified to this court for resolution. The court held, inter alia, that the tort was part of the common law adopted by the Wyoming legislature. The court observed that the Restatement of Torts § 757 version of the common-law tort had been supplanted by the law of unfair competition and trade regulation as set forth in the Restatement Third of Unfair Competition §§ 39-45, which the court adopted. The dissent argued that judicial adoption of the Restatement as the governing law was a usurpation of the legislature's authority and responsibility. Briefing.com v. Jones, 2006 WY 16, 126 P.3d 928, 931, 934, 936.

Cit.—cited; com.—comment; fol.—followed; sup.—support.
A complete list of abbreviations precedes page 1.

§ 758. Innocent Discovery of Secret—Effect of Subsequent Notice or Change of Position

C.A.3, 2000. Cit. in ftn., subsec. (b) and com. (a) cit. in ftn. British corporation sued Taiwanese corporation and Pennsylvania corporation with its principal place in business in New Jersey, alleging that defendants misappropriated trade secrets. Applying New Jersey law, New Jersey federal district court entered preliminary injunction for plaintiff. This court reversed, holding that Taiwanese law governed, because Taiwan had the greater interest in whether plaintiff had a protectible interest in information licensed to a Taiwanese licensee and whether defendant Taiwanese corporation acted unlawfully in acquiring it. New Jersey's interest in protecting trade-secret holders who exported their intellectual property to Taiwan was greatly outweighed by Taiwan's interest in setting standards for the protection of intellectual property in Taiwan. BP Chemicals Ltd. v. Formosa Chemical & Fibre Corp., 229 F.3d 254, 265.

C.A.7, 1991. Subsec. (b) cit. in disc. A manufacturer of newspaper printing presses sued a competitor and the competitor's president for misappropriation of trade secrets and RICO violations. The district court entered summary judgment for the defendants. Reversing and remanding, this court held that factual issues existed as to whether the plaintiff took reasonable precautions to keep its piece part drawings secret and whether the defendants obtained the drawings by improper means. Rockwell Graphic Systems, Inc. v. DEV Industries, Inc., 925 F.2d 174, 178.

E.D.Va.2001. Cit. in case quot. but dist., quot. in ftn. Employer, whose former employee allegedly disclosed trade secrets in his position with new employer, sued new employer for violation of the Virginia Uniform Trade Secrets Act (VUTSA). This court denied new employer's motion for partial summary judgment on the pleadings, holding that, under VUTSA, new employer could be liable for employee's trade-secret violation under theory of respondeat superior. Newport News Industrial v. Dynamic Testing, Inc., 130 F.Supp.2d 745, 753.

Ala.1992. Subsec. (b) quot. and cit. in sup., cit. generally in preface to statute quot. in sup., cit. in ftn., cit. in com. to statute quot. in sup. and in ftn. (Erron. cit. as § 758B.) The federal district court certified questions to this court to determine whether plaintiff, a defendant in a pending action, violated state legislation or common law in disclosing trade secret that she did not know was misappropriated by a third party at the time she obtained it. This court held that plaintiff violated state law when she disclosed the trade secret because she knew before disclosure that it was misappropriated. It concluded that the legislature intended for the statute to impose liability for knowledge of misappropriation at the time of disclosure regardless of the fact that plaintiff did not know the secret was misappropriated at the time she obtained it. IMED Corp. v. Systems Engineering Assoc., 602 So.2d 344, 346-349.

Ariz.App.1999. Com. (a) cit. in sup. Automobile-leasing company filed a motion for a permanent injunction against former senior-level manager, alleging that defendant misappropriated trade secrets. Reversing the trial court's denial of the motion and remanding, this court held, inter alia, that plaintiff's internal financial information and its customer-service worksheet were trade secrets entitled to protection according to the nondisclosure provision in the employment agreement. The court said that this case did not present a situation in which defendant innocently discovered a secret or in good faith paid value for it; there was no question that defendant had notice of the confidentiality of the information and used improper means to appropriate it. Enterprise Leasing Co. of Phoenix v. Ehmke, 197 Ariz. 144, 3 P.3d 1064, 1071.

Cal.App.1990. Cit. in disc. A vice president of a company that developed television game shows sold an idea for a program to a studio that then produced and aired the show. When he sold the idea, the vice president misrepresented to the studio that he, rather than his company, owned the rights to the program. The development company then sued the studio, alleging that the studio knew or should have known that the vice president did not own rights to the show. The trial court awarded the defendant summary judgment. Reversing, this court held that a triable issue of fact existed as to whether the studio had actual or constructive knowledge of the vice president's misrepresentations concerning the show. The court noted that the studio's potential liability for a continuing misappropriation would turn on such factors as whether it paid value in good faith to acquire the concept. Ralph Andrews Productions v. Paramount, 222 Cal.App.3d 676, 271 Cal.Rptr. 797, 802.

§ 759. Procuring Information by Improper Means

C.A.1, 1992. Cit. in disc. (Erron. cit. as Torts (Second).) A company, seeking to develop a new multimedia lighting system, entered into a business relationship with a reflector supplier. Later, as problems arose between the parties, the supplier ceased supplying reflectors, and the lighting company became insolvent and sued the supplier in district court. The jury returned a verdict for the lighting company on the breach of contract, fraud, and breach of good faith counts, and for the supplier on the remaining counts, including misappropriation of information. However, due to inconsistencies between the general verdict and the answers to special interrogatories, the district court granted the supplier's motion for a new trial. Pursuant to a new trial, which considered only the three counts on which the jury found for the lighting company, judgment was entered against the lighting company. Affirming, this court held that the grant of a new trial was proper, and the findings of the second trial were justified by the record. Cool Light Co., Inc. v. GTE Products Corp., 973 F.2d 31, 33.

D.Ariz.2015. Cit. in case quot. in disc. Financial advisor and his insurance agency brought claims for, among other things, unfair competition against competitor and former agency employees who left to work for competitor, alleging that defendants committed computer fraud, trespass, conversion, and other illegal acts in an effort to gain an unfair competitive advantage over plaintiff. This court granted, with leave to amend, defendants' motion to dismiss plaintiffs' claim for unfair competition, holding that Arizona did not appear to recognize a common-law claim for unfair competition as alleged in plaintiffs' complaint. The court noted that, while the first Restatement of Torts §§ 757 and 759 enumerated several theories of liability for unfair competition, including disclosure or use of another's trade secret and improper acquisition of information to advance a rival business interest, the Arizona Supreme Court had held that the universal test for unfair competition was whether the public was likely to be confused. Joshua David Mellberg LLC v. Will, 96 F.Supp.3d 953, 961.

D.D.C.2014. Cit. in case cit. in sup. Trade association that represented biopharmaceutical researchers and biotechnology companies brought an action to set aside a rule issued by the Federal Trade Commission (FTC), alleging that the rule violated the Administrative Procedure Act by placing the burden on the pharmaceutical industry to report transfers of exclusive patent rights. Granting defendant's motion for summary judgment, this court held that the rule was within the scope of defendant's jurisdiction and not arbitrary or capricious. The court pointed out that while, in the past, defendant had redacted certain information from the documents it released to the public during the comment period, there were other ways to seek the information, such as under common law, citing Restatement of Torts § 759. Pharmaceutical Research and Manufacturers of America v. Federal Trade Commission, 44 F.Supp.3d 95, 132.

N.D.Ga.1995. Com. (c) quot. in case quot. in disc. Company engaged in development and licensing of computerized hospital health-care systems sued competitor, among others, alleging, inter alia, misappropriation of trade secrets. Competitor counterclaimed, arguing misappropriation of confidential business information. Both parties moved for summary judgment. The court denied competitor's motion, holding that its failure to comply with discovery procedures precluded entry of summary judgment in its favor. However, it granted company's motion, holding that the information competitor sought to protect was neither confidential nor obtained by company by improper means, such as theft or fraud, as it was contained in a memo competitor had sent to company when the two were negotiating an ultimately unsuccessful merger. TDS Healthcare Systems v. Humana Hosp. Illinois, Inc., 880 F.Supp. 1572, 1584, 1584-1585.

N.D.Ga.1989. Quot. in disc. After an anchor manufacturer that was started up by a competitor's former president sued the competitor for alleged antitrust violations and unfair restraint of trade, the defendant counterclaimed for breach of fiduciary duty, misappropriation of confidential business information, and common law fraud and deceit, inter alia. This court denied both parties' motions for summary judgment, stating, as to the defendant's counterclaim, that there was a material issue of fact as to

Cit.—cited; com.—comment; fol.—followed; sup.—support.
A complete list of abbreviations precedes page 1.

whether the plaintiff's founder breached a fiduciary duty by making significant business arrangements to organize his competing business and solicited the defendant's sales agents while still employed by the defendant. The court added that it was for the jury to decide whether the founder obtained confidential business information by improper means. U.S. Anchor Mfg., Inc. v. Rule Industries, Inc., 717 F.Supp. 1565, 1576.

D.N.J.2009. Quot. in sup. (erron. cit. as § 789). Debt-collection agency sued former employee and former client, alleging that employee falsely informed client, among other things, that agency's employees were stealing confidential client information from agency, and that client conveyed the false allegations and certain confidential documents provided by employee to two of agency's other clients. Granting summary judgment for client, this court held, inter alia, that agency failed to show in support of its claim for breach of contract that employee's letter to client, which reiterated her allegations against agency in writing, included confidential business information protected by agency's contract with client. The court pointed out that the allegations were not the sort of confidential business practices protected by the common-law tort for disclosure of business secrets. Professional Recovery Services, Inc. v. General Elec. Capital Corp., 642 F.Supp.2d 391, 409.

W.D.N.C.1989. Com. (b) cit. in case quot. in disc. An employee sued his employer for misappropriation of a trade secret, inter alia, alleging that his invention constituted a trade secret when his employer disclosed and began use of it in connection with its business. The court denied the defendant's motion for summary judgment, rejecting the argument that the court could not grant state law protection to an invention that was patented under federal law. The court stated that it had jurisdiction over a claim of unfair competition when it was joined with a substantial and related claim under the patent laws and that a trade secret may be, but need not be, a device or process that was patentable. Additionally, the court noted that the plaintiff's invention fit the definition of a trade secret, since it was a device used in one's business which gave him an opportunity to obtain a competitive advantage. Moore v. American Barmag Corp., 710 F.Supp. 1050, 1059, affirmed 902 F.2d 44 (Fed.Cir.1990).

E.D.Pa.2022. Quot. in case quot. in sup. Tenured professor at university sued colleague and university, alleging that colleague misappropriated his trade-secret research data and used it to jointly file patent applications with university and to obtain private equity financing. This court denied in part colleague and university's motion to dismiss, holding that professor stated a claim for conversion under Restatement of Torts § 759 by alleging that colleague obtained his research data by misrepresenting to a student who was working for him that colleague had professor's permission to use the data, and that university knew of colleague's misdeed but nonetheless worked with colleague to file patents and monetize professor's research data, all while misrepresenting its involvement with colleague and their use of his data to him. Houser v. Feldman, 600 F.Supp.3d 550, 568.

E.D.Pa.2018. Quot. in case quot. in sup. Employer sued former employee, competitor, and competitor's CEO, who was also employee's romantic partner, alleging that employee passed employer's trade secrets to CEO and competitor in breach of her fiduciary duty to employer. This court denied in part CEO and competitor's motion to dismiss, holding that employer sufficiently stated a claim for procuring information by improper means against CEO and competitor under Restatement of Torts § 759 by alleging that CEO and competitor improperly procured trade secrets and other confidential information from employee and used that information to gain a competitive advantage over employer; however, the court dismissed the claim as to employee, noting that employee procured employer's information while she still worked for employer and was authorized to do so. Teva Pharmaceuticals USA, Inc. v. Sandhu, 291 F.Supp.3d 659, 681.

E.D.Pa.2010. Cit. in sup., coms. (b) and (c) quot. in sup. Salon owner sued competitor in connection with a takeover in which defendant seized plaintiff's business and began using plaintiff's name, license, equipment and furniture, employees, and customer lists. Granting in part plaintiff's motion for a preliminary injunction, this court held, among other things, that plaintiff had established a likelihood of success on the merits with respect to its claim for conversion of the customer lists; defendant was likely aware that plaintiff considered the lists to be confidential business information, and thus converted the lists when it induced plaintiff's employees to reveal them in breach of their duty to plaintiff. Pierre & Carlo, Inc. v. Premier Salons, Inc., 713 F.Supp.2d 471, 481, 482.

E.D.Pa.1997. Cit. in disc. Pennsylvania corporation brought RICO action against British medical schools and their agents, alleging that defendants misappropriated plaintiff's proprietary interest in medical scanner equipment and technology. Defendants moved to dismiss, arguing, among other things, that the court lacked personal jurisdiction over them. Denying the motion, the court held, in part, that in personam jurisdiction was proper under the "tort-out/harm-in" provision of the Pennsylvania Long Arm Statute, since defendants' alleged misappropriation of plaintiff's trade secrets in England caused harm to plaintiff in Pennsylvania, and that defendants had sufficient minimum contacts with Pennsylvania such that exercising jurisdiction over them would not offend traditional notions of fair play and substantial justice. Supra Medical Corp. v. McGonigle, 955 F.Supp. 374, 381.

M.D.Pa.2017. Quot. in sup.; com. (b) cit. in case quot. in sup. and cit. in ftn. Employer sued former employee who started a competing business while she was still working for employer, alleging, among other things, that employee was liable for procuring employer's information by improper means. This court granted employer partial summary judgment, holding that it was clear from the evidence that employee took employer's confidential business information, including data files, and used them at her competing business in violation of Restatement of Torts § 759, which had been adopted by Pennsylvania courts. The court noted that, under § 759, the information that was procured by improper means did not need to rise to the level of a trade secret, and only had to be confidential business information. Mifflinburg Telegraph, Inc. v. Criswell, 277 F.Supp.3d 750, 799.

Ariz.2014. Cit. in disc. Public-relations company brought unfair-competition and other claims against its former president and her competing company, alleging that defendants learned confidential and trade-secret information about plaintiff and intended to steal and exploit that information and plaintiff's customers to gain a competitive advantage. The trial court granted defendants' motion to dismiss, finding that the Arizona Uniform Trade Secrets Act (AUTSA) preempted plaintiff's common-law tort claims arising from the alleged misuse of confidential information even as to information not asserted to rise to the level of a trade secret. The court of appeals reversed in part. Agreeing with the result reached by the court of appeals, this court reversed the trial court's dismissal of plaintiff's unfair-competition claim and remanded that claim to that court, holding that the AUTSA did not displace common-law claims based on alleged misappropriation of confidential information that was not a trade secret. In making its decision, the court noted that it did not decide whether Arizona recognized a common-law claim for unfair competition under Restatement of Torts §§ 757 and 759. Orca Communications Unlimited, LLC v. Noder, 236 Ariz. 180, 184, 337 P.3d 545, 549.

Ind.2004. Cit. in ftn. to diss. op. Former employer's successor sued former employee and his new employer, alleging that former employee used stolen trade secrets to lure plaintiff's customers to new employer. The trial court held that former employee was liable for misappropriating and converting plaintiff's trade secrets, but that new employer was not. The court of appeals affirmed in part and reversed in part. Affirming the trial court's judgment, this court held that new employer could not be held liable absent proof of scienter required by the Uniform Trade Secrets Act. The dissent argued that the Uniform Act's requirement of scienter did not conflict with the imposition of vicarious liability on a wrongdoer's employer, since the risk of liability would serve as an incentive for employers to discourage employees from using misappropriated trade secrets. Infinity Products, Inc. v. Quandt, 810 N.E.2d 1028, 1035.

Okl.2016. Com. (c) quot. in case quot. in sup. Developers of a bolus containing technology to monitor and track cattle brought a claim for conversion of personal and intellectual property against manufacturers they had hired to make boluses to their specifications, alleging that, after the parties' business relationship ended, defendants made and sold boluses using plaintiffs' confidential, proprietary information and tangible property. The trial court granted partial summary judgment for defendants. Reversing in part and remanding, this court held that defendants' alleged use of intangibles that were not information and of tangibles was not subject to the parties' nondisclosure agreement and was potentially subject to a claim for conversion. The court cited Restatement of Torts §§ 757 and 759 in explaining that Oklahoma had recognized the tort of misappropriation of confidential business information, under which one who received information that did not meet the definition of a "trade secret" and who was in a confidential relationship or obtained the information through improper means was potentially liable. American Biomedical Group, Inc. v. Techtrol, Inc., 374 P.3d 820, 825.

Okl.1986. Quot. in disc., com. (b) cit. and quot. in disc., com. (c) quot. in disc. A corporation in the business of coating steel reinforcing bars with epoxy resin sued a company that allegedly misappropriated confidential business information about the coating process used by the plaintiff. The trial court entered judgment on a jury verdict for the defendant. Affirming, this court rejected the plaintiff's argument that it could recover for the defendant's disclosure of confidential information not rising to the level of a trade secret. The court stated that the jury's finding that the defendant was not guilty of fraud negated the necessary element of an improper means by which the information was procured, and the fact that the coating process could not be distinguished as either a trade secret or confidential information discredited the plaintiff's theory. ABC Coating Co., Inc. v. J. Harris & Sons, 747 P.2d 266, 270, 271.

Pa.Super.2005. Cit. and quot. in disc., com. (b) cit. in case quot. in disc. (erron. cit. as Restatement Second of Torts). Air-freshener manufacturer sued competitor and others, alleging that a trucker employed by both companies revealed confidential information from manufacturer's bills of lading to competitor. The trial court entered judgment for plaintiff. This court affirmed in part and reversed in part, holding, inter alia, that, while plaintiff could not recover for misappropriation of trade secrets, plaintiff could recover on an alternative claim for procuring information by improper means. The court concluded that, although the information on the bills of lading did not rise to the level of a trade secret, it was nonetheless confidential business information, and, because it was improperly revealed to rival, the requirements for this alternative claim were met. Pestco, Inc. v. Associated Products, Inc., 880 A.2d 700, 708, 709.

Pa.Super.1989. Cit. and quot. in disc., cit. in case cit. in disc., coms. cit. generally in disc. A corporation that manufactured dental instruments sued to enjoin the defendant from acquiring a competitor of the plaintiff's, alleging that the injunction was necessary to prevent the disclosure by the defendant of allegedly confidential information obtained by the defendant about the plaintiff's business during ultimately unsuccessful negotiations between the parties regarding the sale of the plaintiff's business to the defendant. The trial court granted an injunction against the acquisition for a three-year period. This court affirmed, concluding that, because the defendant received trade secrets and other confidential information from the plaintiff through misrepresentations while in a confidential relationship with the plaintiff, an injunction was the appropriate remedy. Den-Tal-Ez, Inc. v. Siemens Capital Corp., 389 Pa.Super. 219, 566 A.2d 1214, 1229, 1231.

Va.2016. Com. (c) cit. in ftn. Sub-licensor of nuclear technology brought a claim for breach of the Virginia Uniform Trade Secrets Act against sub-licensees, alleging that defendants disclosed plaintiff's trade secrets to third parties without authorization. The trial court entered judgment on a jury verdict in favor of plaintiff. This court reversed and entered final judgment dismissing plaintiff's claims, holding that the trial court erred in failing to set aside the verdict on plaintiff's claim for misappropriation of trade secrets, because the sub-license gave defendants a perpetual, worldwide license to practice and use plaintiff's technology for all purposes, without restriction, and there could be no misappropriation where acquisition, disclosure, and use of a trade secret was expressly authorized by contract. The court reasoned, in part, that, under Restatement of Torts §§ 757 and 759, a valid contractual acquisition of a trade secret could not be characterized as an acquisition by "improper means." Babcock & Wilcox Company v. Areva NP, Inc., 788 S.E. 237, 260.

§ 760. Misrepresentation in Marketing Goods of Which Another Is the Commercial Source—Liability to the Other

D.N.M.2010. Quot. in sup Buyer of end-

For earlier citations, see the Appendices, Supplements, or Pocket Parts, if any, that correspond to the subject matter under examination.

odontic equipment sued sellers for breach of contract and unfair trade practices; sellers brought various counterclaims sounding in contract and tort. Granting in part and denying in part buyer's motion for summary judgment on sellers' counterclaims, this court held, in determining that New Mexico law applied, that sellers' counterclaims of unfair competition, violation of the New Mexico Unfair Practices Act, and unlawful misappropriation fell into the category of torts. The court noted that the causes of action in the Restatement Third of Unfair Competition appeared to have grown out of the Restatement of Torts, implying that they should be categorized as torts. Guidance Endodontics, LLC v. Dentsply Intern., Inc., 708 F.Supp.2d 1209, 1225.

§ 761. False Advertising—Liability to Competitor

C.A.2, 1987. Quot. in case cit. in disc. A corporation with financial interests in the recordings of a deceased musician sued a competitor corporation under the Lanham Act and for tortious interference with economic advantage, alleging that the defendant marketed eight albums by fraudulently representing that the albums featured performances by the deceased musician. The trial court entered judgment n.o.v. for the defendant. Reversing in part and remanding, this court said that the plaintiff's Lanham Act claim did not require the plaintiff to prove that there was actual consumer confusion as a result of the defendant's marketing of the albums. The court also stated that the plaintiff's allegation that the defendant's recordings tended to create confusion among consumers sufficiently stated a claim of false advertising under the circumstances of this case, and the jury's finding of actual confusion caused by the defendant's misrepresentations was consistent with this claim. PPX Enterprises v. Audio Fidelity Enterprises, 818 F.2d 266, 272.

C.A.3, 1993. Cit. in case quot. in disc. In two cases, consumers of goods or services in interstate commerce sued vendors under the Lanham Act, alleging that, to their detriment, they purchased the goods or services in reliance on defendants' false advertising claims. Consolidating the two cases on appeal, this court affirmed the district courts' dismissals of plaintiffs' claims, holding that consumers did not have standing to bring suit for false advertising under the Lanham Act. The court stated that consumers fell outside the range of "reasonable interests" contemplated as protected by the false advertising prong of § 43(a) of the Lanham Act, which was primarily intended to protect commercial interests. Serbin v. Ziebart Intern. Corp., Inc., 11 F.3d 1163, 1167.

N.D.Ill.1987. Cit. but not fol. A manufacturer of electronic analgesic devices sued a competitor for breach of contract and unfair competition when negotiations for a joint marketing venture failed. The plaintiff sought a declaration that its product did not infringe any of the defendant's intellectual property rights. This court denied the defendant's motions to strike parts of the complaint, to dismiss, and to disqualify the plaintiff's attorney, holding that the allegations in the complaint sufficiently stated a claim for which relief could be granted. The court noted that on the facts alleged the plaintiff's only common law unfair-trade claim would be for false advertising, and that although the uniform deceptive trade practice and consumer fraud acts did not preempt a tort claim for false advertising, these statutes were so broad that such a claim would probably be superfluous. Pain Prevention Lab, Inc. v. Electronic Waveform Labs, Inc., 657 F.Supp. 1486, 1493.

D.N.M.2010. Quot. in sup. Buyer of endodontic equipment sued sellers for breach of contract and unfair trade practices; sellers brought various counterclaims sounding in contract and tort. Granting in part and denying in part buyer's motion for summary judgment on sellers' counterclaims, this court held, in determining that New Mexico law applied, that sellers' counterclaims of unfair competition, violation of the New Mexico Unfair Practices Act, and unlawful misappropriation fell into the category of torts. The court noted that the causes of action in the Restatement Third of Unfair Competition appeared to have grown out of the Restatement of Torts, implying that they should be categorized as torts. Guidance Endodontics, LLC v. Dentsply Intern., Inc., 708 F.Supp.2d 1209, 1225.

TORTS 2d

DIVISION NINE. INTERFERENCE WITH ADVANTAGEOUS ECONOMIC RELATIONS

Introductory Note

D.Hawaii Bkrtcy.Ct.2021. Intro. Note cit. in ftn. Trustee for Chapter 7 debtors filed an adversary proceeding against assignee of debtors' mortgage, alleging wrongful foreclosure as well as unfair and deceptive trade practices and unfair methods of competition in violation of a state statute. This court denied in part assignee's motion to strike trustee's jury demand, holding that trustee's request for declaratory and injunctive relief in connection with his wrongful-foreclosure claim did not deprive him of the right to a jury trial on his statutory claim. The court cited the Restatement Second of Torts in noting that unfair-competition and trade-regulation actions evolved from tort law, and that trustee's statutory claim was analogous to one that would traditionally be brought in a court of law. In re Simon, 634 B.R. 1057, 1062.

Wyo.2006. Intro. Note. quot. in disc. After internet-based market-analysis company brought action for misappropriation of trade secrets in federal district court against former employees who formed competing company, the issue of whether such a cause of action existed in Wyoming was certified to this court for resolution. The court held, inter alia, that the tort was part of the common law adopted by the Wyoming legislature. The court observed that earlier versions of the common-law tort had been supplanted by the law of unfair competition and trade regulation; the law of unfair competition and trade regulation had developed into an independent body of law that was no longer dependent on traditional principles of tort law. Briefing.com v. Jones, 2006 WY 16, 126 P.3d 928, 932.

CHAPTER 35. CONFUSION OF SOURCE [OMITTED. SEE INTRODUCTORY NOTE TO DIVISION 9.]

§ 712. General Principle [This section has been omitted from the Official Draft. See Introductory Note to Division 9.]

Or.App.2021. Com. (d) quot. in sup. (quoting T.D. No. 8, 1963). State initiated an action under the Unlawful Trade Practices Act against producers and sellers of energy drinks, alleging that defendants engaged in unlawful practices in advertising the drinks. After a bench trial, the trial court entered a verdict and judgment in favor of defendants. This court affirmed in part, holding that the trial court did not err in concluding that "materiality" was a requirement in proof of an unlawful trade practice under the statute. The court noted that Oregon courts had largely adopted the list of deceptive trade practices from the Uniform Deceptive Trade Practices Act, which in turn was derived from, among other sources, sections of the Restatement Second of Torts dealing with the likelihood-of-confusion test and false advertising of good, services, or businesses. State ex rel. Rosenblum v. Living Essentials, LLC, 497 P.3d 730, 741.

§ 715. Definition of Trade-Mark [This section has been omitted from the Official Draft. See Introductory Note to Division 9.]

E.D.Wis.1987. Cit. in disc. §§ 715-717 (T.D. No. 8, 1963), which have been omitted in the Official Draft. A brewing company marketed low-alcohol beer under the mark "LA" and threatened suit against other breweries who sought to use "LA" or "L.A." in the names of their low-alcohol beers. Two of the breweries who sought to use "LA" in

For earlier citations, see the Appendices, Supplements, or Pocket Parts, if any, that correspond to the subject matter under examination.

their brand names sued the senior user, requesting a declaratory judgment that "LA" was a generic mark and that their use of it did not constitute infringement or unfair competition. This court entered judgment for the plaintiffs, and held, inter alia, that the "LA" mark was merely descriptive, not distinctive, and that there was little likelihood of consumer confusion between the low-alcohol-beer products of the different companies, therefore the plaintiffs would not be liable to the defendant for unfair competition by their use of the "LA" mark. G. Heileman Brewing Co. v. Anheuser-Busch Inc., 676 F.Supp. 1436, 1470, affirmed 873 F.2d 985 (7th Cir.1989).

Wis.2008. Adopted in case cit. in sup. (citing § 715 of T.D. No. 8, 1963. § 715 has since been revised; see Official Text). Buyers of business with a tradename that included seller's family name sued seller for, among other things, tradename infringement, after seller formed a competing company with a tradename that also included seller's family name. The trial court entered judgment on a jury verdict in favor of buyers. The court of appeals affirmed the jury's finding that seller had infringed on business's tradename. Affirming that portion of the decision, this court held, inter alia, that the trial court's jury instructions on tradename infringement were not erroneous; Wisconsin courts had adopted an approach in which tradenames that had acquired trademark status were entitled to protection against infringement in the same manner and to the same extent as trademarks and, while ordinarily a party had a right to do business under his or her own name, that right could be voluntarily limited by contract. D.L. Anderson's Lakeside Leisure Co., Inc. v. Anderson, 2008 WI 126, 314 Wis.2d 560, 757 N.W.2d 803, 814.

Wis.App.1996. Cit. in ftn. (T.D. No. 8, 1963. Restatement, Second, Torts § 715, which was omitted from the official draft, corresponds to § 9 of the Restatement Third of Unfair Competition.) Company in the business of providing reprographic copying services to architects, engineers, publishers, and others sued competitor for trademark infringement. Following a bench trial, the trial court dismissed the complaint on the ground that there was insufficient likelihood of confusion between the parties' marks. Affirming, this court held, inter alia, that company's mark, which could also be considered a service mark, was a weak descriptive designation combining a geographical name with a shortened version of the term "reprographics"; that company's mark did not become strong or distinctive through secondary meaning; and that the minimal similarity of the two marks, as well as the sophistication of the parties' typical customers, supported the lower court's finding that there was no likelihood of confusion. Madison Reprographics v. Cook's Reprographics, 203 Wis.2d 226, 552 N.W.2d 440, 444.

§ 716. Definition of Trade Name [This section has been omitted from the Official Draft. See Introductory Note to Division 9.]

E.D.Wis.1987. Cit. in disc. §§ 715-717 (T.D. No. 8, 1963), which have been omitted from the Official Draft. A brewing company marketed low-alcohol beer under the mark "LA" and threatened suit against other breweries who sought to use "LA" or "L.A." in the names of their low-alcohol beers. Two of the breweries who sought to use "LA" in their brand names sued the senior user, requesting a declaratory judgment that "LA" was a generic mark and that their use of it did not constitute infringement or unfair competition. This court entered judgment for the plaintiffs, and held, inter alia, that the "LA" mark was merely descriptive, not distinctive, and that there was little likelihood of consumer confusion between the low-alcohol-beer products of the different companies, therefore the plaintiffs would not be liable to the defendant for unfair competition by their use of the "LA" mark. G. Heileman Brewing Co. v. Anheuser-Busch Inc., 676 F.Supp. 1436, 1470, affirmed 873 F.2d 985 (7th Cir. 1989).

Tex.App.2011. Com. (a) quot. in sup., com. (b) cit. in sup. (citing § 716 of T.D. No. 8, 1963. § 716 has since been revised; see Official Text). Radio show host sued festival promoter, alleging, among other things, that festival's name, which was the same as radio show's name, was a protectable trade name belonging to plaintiff. The trial court entered judgment on a jury verdict in favor of plaintiff. Reversing in part and remanding, this court held, among other things, that there was insufficient evidence that the name acquired a secondary meaning or special significance to support the jury's finding that the name was plaintiff's trade name; while plaintiff's use of the name at issue—to host a one or two-hour show once a week for 23 months, and then a daily three-hour show for three months—might qualify as evidence of length of use, it did not qualify as extensive use so as to establish secondary meaning. Funes v. Villatoro, 352 S.W.3d 200, 209, 212.

Wis.2008. Adopted in case cit. in sup. (citing § 716 of T.D. No. 8, 1963. § 716 has since been revised; see Official Text). Buyers of business with a tradename that included seller's family name sued seller for, among other things, tradename infringement, after seller formed a competing company with a tradename that also included seller's family name. The trial court entered judgment on a jury verdict in favor of buyers. The court of appeals affirmed the jury's finding that seller had infringed on business's tradename. Affirming that portion of the decision, this court held, inter alia, that the trial court's jury instructions on tradename infringement were not erroneous; Wisconsin courts had adopted an approach in which tradenames that had acquired trademark status were entitled to protection against infringement in the same manner and to the same extent as trademarks and, while ordinarily a party had a right to do business under his or her own name, that right could be voluntarily limited by contract. D.L. Anderson's Lakeside Leisure Co., Inc. v. Anderson, 2008 WI 126, 314 Wis.2d 560, 757 N.W.2d 803, 814.

Wis.App.1996. Cit. in ftn. (T.D. No. 8, 1963. Restatement, Second, Torts § 716, which was omitted from the official draft, corresponds to § 12 of the Restatement Third of Unfair Competition.) Company in the business of providing reprographic copying services to architects, engineers, publishers, and others sued competitor for trademark infringement. Following a bench trial, the trial court dismissed the complaint on the ground that there was insufficient likelihood of confusion between the parties' marks. Affirming, this court held, inter alia, that company's mark, which could also be considered a service mark, was a weak descriptive designation combining a geographical name with a shortened version of the term "reprographics"; that company's mark did not become strong or distinctive through secondary meaning; and that the minimal similarity of the two marks, as well as the sophistication of the parties' typical customers, supported the lower court's finding that there was no likelihood of confusion. Madison Reprographics v. Cook's Reprographics, 203 Wis.2d 226, 552 N.W.2d 440, 444.

§ 717. General Statement of Conditions of Infringement [This section has been omitted from the Official Draft. See Introductory Note to Division 9.]

E.D.Wis.1987. Cit. in disc. §§ 715-717, quot. in disc. (T.D. No. 8, 1963). §§ 715-717 have been omitted from the Official Draft. (Erron. cit. as § 17 on p. 1471.) A brewing company marketed low-alcohol beer under the mark "LA" and threatened suit against other breweries who sought to use "LA" or "L.A." in the names of their low-alcohol beers. Two of the breweries who sought to use "LA" in their brand names sued the senior user, requesting a declaratory judgment that "LA" was a generic mark and that their use of it was not infringement or unfair competition. This court entered judgment for the plaintiffs, and held, inter alia, that the "LA" mark was merely descriptive, not distinctive, and that there was little likelihood of consumer confusion between the low-alcohol-beer products of the different companies, therefore the plaintiffs would not be liable to the defendant for unfair competition by their use of the "LA" mark. G. Heileman Brewing Co. v. Anheuser-Busch Inc., 676 F.Supp. 1436, 1470, 1471, affirmed 873 F.2d 985 (7th Cir. 1989).

Wis.2008. Adopted in case cit. in sup. (citing § 717 of T.D. No. 8, 1963. § 717 has since been revised; see Official Text). Buyers of business with a tradename that included seller's family name sued seller for, among other things, tradename infringement, after seller formed a competing company with a tradename that also included seller's family name. The trial court entered judgment on a jury verdict in favor of buyers. The court of appeals affirmed the jury's finding that seller had infringed on business's tradename. Affirming that portion of the decision, this court held, inter alia, that the trial court's jury instructions on tradename infringement were not erroneous; Wisconsin courts had adopted an approach in which tradenames that had acquired trademark status were entitled to protection against infringement in the same manner and to the same extent as trademarks and, while ordinarily a party had a right to do business under his or her own name, that right could be voluntarily limited by contract. D.L. Anderson's Lakeside Leisure Co., Inc. v. Anderson, 2008 WI 126, 314 Wis.2d 560, 757 N.W.2d 803, 814.

Wis.App.1996. Cit. in ftn. (T.D. No. 8, 1963. Restatement, Second, Torts § 717, which was omitted from the official draft, corresponds to § 20 of the Restatement Third of Unfair Competition.) Company in the business of providing reprographic copying services to architects, engineers, publishers, and others sued competitor for trademark infringement. Following a bench trial, the trial court dismissed the complaint on the ground that there was insufficient likelihood of confusion between the parties' marks. Affirming, this court held, inter alia, that company's mark, which could also be considered a service mark, was a weak descriptive designation combining a geographical name with a shortened version of the term "reprographics"; that company's mark did not become strong or distinctive through secondary meaning; and that the minimal similarity of the two marks, as well as the sophistication of the parties' typical customers, supported the lower court's finding that there was no likelihood of confusion. Madison Reprographics v. Cook's Reprographics, 203 Wis.2d 226, 552 N.W.2d 440, 444.

§ 729. Factors in Determining Infringement-Resemblance of Marks [This section has been omitted from the Official Draft. See Introductory Note to Division 9.]

Or.App.2021. Com. (a) quot. in sup. (quoting T.D. No. 8, 1963). State initiated an action under the Unlawful Trade Practices Act against producers and sellers of energy drinks, alleging that defendants engaged in unlawful practices in advertising the drinks. After a bench trial, the trial court entered a verdict and judgment in favor of defendants. This court affirmed in part, holding that the trial court did not err in concluding that "materiality" was a requirement in proof of an unlawful trade practice under the statute. The court noted that Oregon courts had largely adopted the list of deceptive trade practices from the Uniform Deceptive Trade Practices Act, which in turn was derived from, among other sources, sections of the Restatement Second of Torts dealing with the likelihood-of-confusion test and false advertising of good, services, or businesses. State ex rel. Rosenblum v. Living Essentials, LLC, 497 P.3d 730, 741.

CHAPTER 37. INTERFERENCE WITH CONTRACT OR PROSPECTIVE CONTRACTUAL RELATION

§ 762. Privilege of Selecting Persons for Business Relations [This section has been omitted from the Official Draft. See Introductory Note to Division 9.]

N.J.Super.1994. Cit. in ftn. §§ 762-765 (citing Tentative Draft; these sections were omitted from the Restatement Second). Contractor severed business relations with mechanical subcontractor after subcontractor refused to comply with its request that subcontractor immediately stop dealing with contractor's competitor. Subcontractor sued contractor for tortious interference with contractual obligations and intentional interference with prospective economic advantages. The trial court dismissed; this court affirmed in part, holding that defendant's requests of plaintiff steered clear of a criminal law violation. Reversing in part, the court held that the filing of the proposed amended complaint, which should have been permitted, stated at least one cause of action under New Jersey antitrust law and that plaintiff could use an antitrust violation to satisfy the first Restatement's exception to nonliability for refusals to enter into business relations that had an illegal effect on competition. Van Natta Mech. Corp. v. Di Staulo, 277 N.J.Super. 175, 183, 649 A.2d 399, 404.

§ 763. Refusal in Public Utility Business [This section has been omitted from the Official Draft. See Introductory Note to Division 9.]

N.D.Ohio, 2022. Cit. in case cit. in sup. Former employee brought, among other things, a claim for tortious interference with business relationships against former employer, alleging that defendant retali-

Cit.—cited; com.—comment; fol.—followed; sup.—support.
A complete list of abbreviations precedes page 1.

ated against plaintiff by reassigning plaintiff's customers and business contacts developed prior to the parties' employment relationship. This court denied in part defendant's partial motion for judgment on the pleadings, holding that plaintiff's allegations regarding defendant's conduct supported a claim for tortious interference with business relationships. Citing Restatement Second of Torts § 763, the court explained that defendant failed to identify a legal interest it protected by reassigning plaintiff's customers and business contacts. Kenyon v. Union Home Mortgage Corp., 581 F.Supp.3d 951, 960.

N.J.Super.1994. Cit. in ftn. §§ 762-765 (citing Tentative Draft; these sections were omitted from the Restatement Second). Contractor severed business relations with mechanical subcontractor after subcontractor refused to comply with its request that subcontractor immediately stop dealing with contractor's competitor. Subcontractor sued contractor for tortious interference with contractual obligations and intentional interference with prospective economic advantages. The trial court dismissed; this court affirmed in part, holding that defendant's requests of plaintiff steered clear of a criminal law violation. Reversing in part, the court held that the filing of the proposed amended complaint, which should have been permitted, stated at least one cause of action under New Jersey antitrust laws and that plaintiff could use an antitrust violation to satisfy the first Restatement's exception to nonliability for refusals to enter into business relations that had an illegal effect on competition. Van Natta Mech. Corp. v. Di Staulo, 277 N.J.Super. 175, 183, 649 A.2d 399, 404.

§ 764. Refusal for Purpose of Monopoly [This section has been omitted from the Official Draft. See Introductory Note to Division 9.]

N.J.Super.1994. Cit. in ftn. §§ 762-765 (citing Tentative Draft; these sections were omitted from the Restatement Second). Contractor severed business relations with mechanical subcontractor after subcontractor refused to comply with its request that subcontractor immediately stop dealing with contractor's competitor. Subcontractor sued contractor for tortious interference with contractual obligations and intentional interference with prospective economic advantages. The trial court dismissed; this court affirmed in part, holding that defendant's requests of plaintiff steered clear of a criminal law violation. Reversing in part, the court held that the filing of the proposed amended complaint, which should have been permitted, stated at least one cause of action under New Jersey antitrust law and that plaintiff could use an antitrust violation to satisfy the first Restatement's exception to nonliability for refusals to enter into business relations that had an illegal effect on competition. Van Natta Mech. Corp. v. Di Staulo, 277 N.J.Super. 175, 183, 649 A.2d 399, 404.

§ 765. Concerted Refusal to Deal [This section has been omitted from the Official Draft. See Introductory Note to Division 9.]

N.J.Super.1994. Cit. in ftn. §§ 762-765 (citing Tentative Draft; these sections were omitted from the Restatement Second). Contractor severed business relations with mechanical subcontractor after subcontractor refused to comply with its request that subcontractor immediately stop dealing with contractor's competitor. Subcontractor sued contractor for tortious interference with contractual obligations and intentional interference with prospective economic advantages. The trial court dismissed; this court affirmed in part, holding that defendant's requests of plaintiff steered clear of a criminal law violation. Reversing in part, the court held that the filing of the proposed amended complaint, which should have been permitted, stated at least one cause of action under New Jersey antitrust laws and that plaintiff could use an antitrust violation to satisfy the first Restatement's exception to nonliability for refusals to enter into business relations that had an illegal effect on competition. Van Natta Mech. Corp. v. Di Staulo, 277 N.J.Super. 175, 183, 649 A.2d 399, 404.

RESTATEMENT THIRD

UNFAIR COMPETITION

Generally

C.A.5, 2007. Cit. in ftn. (general cite). Assignee of rights to computer program brought trade-secret-misappropriation claim against developers of competing program that was based in large part on assignee's program. On remand, the district court granted summary judgment for defendants. Affirming, this court, inter alia, upheld the magistrate judge's definition of "use" with respect to the third element of trade-secret misappropriation. The court reasoned, in part, that, under Texas law, which followed the Restatement Third of Unfair Competition, defendants "used" plaintiff's program by continuing to rely on it, either directly or on those portions incorporated into the competing program, to accelerate the development and marketability of the competing program. General Universal Systems, Inc. v. HAL, Inc., 500 F.3d 444, 451.

C.A.6, 2022. Cit. generally in case cit. in disc. Dietary-supplement developer sued customer, alleging that defendant misappropriated plaintiff's trade secrets regarding broccoli-seed extracts by hiring plaintiff's former employee, who provided plaintiff's confidential research and development information to defendant, and used it to create competing broccoli supplement products. The district court entered judgment on a jury verdict for plaintiff. This court affirmed, holding that substantial evidence supported a jury finding that defendant misappropriated plaintiff's trade secrets. The court observed that Kentucky frequently looked to the Restatement Third of Unfair Competition for analyzing trade-secrets issues. Caudill Seed & Warehouse Co., Inc. v. Jarrow Formulas, Inc., 53 F.4th 368, 380.

C.A.Fed.2011. Cit. generally in case cit. in disc. In an action by domestic manufacturer of cast steel railway wheels, the International Trade Commission found that importation of foreign competitor's wheels violated the Tariff Act. Affirming, this court held that a single federal standard, rather than the law of a particular state, determined what constituted a misappropriation of trade secrets sufficient to establish an "unfair method of competition" under the Tariff Act. The court noted that trade-secret law varied little from state to state and was generally governed by widely recognized authorities such as the Restatement Third of Unfair Competition. TianRui Group Co. Ltd. v. International Trade Com'n, 661 F.3d 1322, 1328.

D.Ariz.2021. Cit. generally in case cit. in disc. Female models, business women, and social-media personalities sued operator of strip club, alleging, inter alia, that defendant violated plaintiffs' right to publicity by using photographs of their likeness to advertise the strip club without plaintiffs' consent. After removal, this court denied in part defendant's motion for summary judgment, holding that state statutes protecting the right of publicity for soldiers did not preclude plaintiffs' common-law right-of-publicity claims. The court observed that state caselaw recognized the right of publicity set forth by the Restatement Third of Unfair Competition as a cause of action, because Arizona courts applied the Restatement so long as there was no law to the contrary. Longoria v. Kodiak Concepts LLC, 527 F.Supp.3d 1085, 1097.

N.D.Ill.2006. Cit. generally in disc. and in case cit. in disc. Developer of curing agent for epoxy resin sued distributor of competitor's equivalent product for, among other things, misappropriation of trade

Cit.—cited; com.—comment; fol.—followed; sup.—support.
A complete list of abbreviations precedes page 1.

secrets. This court denied defendant's motion to dismiss the claim, holding that it was possible that plaintiff could show that defendant misappropriated plaintiff's trade secrets under a broad reading of the word "use." The court pointed to plaintiff's allegations that distributor knew or should have known that competitor had manufactured its product by misappropriating developer's technology and had used its prior relationship with developer as its former distributor in order to price competitor's product cheaper than developer's and to solicit developer's customers. Cognis Corp. v. CHEMCENTRAL Corp., 430 F.Supp.2d 806, 812.

D.N.J.2011. Cit. generally in disc. and in ftn. In an action by former college football athlete against computer software developer for allegedly misappropriating his likeness and identity in a video game, this court declined to expressly adopt the Restatement Third of Unfair Competition's test for weighing the First Amendment rights of an author/creator against an individual's right of publicity, noting that New Jersey had yet to formally adopt that Restatement. Hart v. Electronic Arts, Inc., 808 F.Supp.2d 757, 791.

D.N.M.2014. Cit. generally in case cit. in sup. In a case brought by cancer-treatment facility against hospital owner and others, this court held that plaintiff alleged sufficient facts to form the basis of an unfair-competition claim. In making its decision, the court held that, in the absence of controlling law by New Mexico's supreme court, it would be appropriate to assume that that court would adopt the elements of an unfair-competition claim set forth in the Restatement Third of Unfair Competition. New Mexico Oncology and Hematology Consultants, Ltd. v. Presbyterian Healthcare Services, 54 F.Supp.3d 1189, 1235, 1236.

W.D.Pa.2022. Cit. generally in disc. and in case quot. in disc. Importer of steel products filed a state-law unfair-competition claim against competitor in state court, alleging that competitor misrepresented to the Department of Commerce that it was capable of manufacturing certain types and quantities of steel slab, resulting in the Department's denial of importer's request for an exemption from a tariff on importing such slab to fulfill customer orders. After competitor removed the action, this court granted competitor's motion to dismiss, holding that importer's state-law claim was preempted by the statutory and administrative framework governing the imposition of the tariff and the process for adjudicating an exemption request. The court rejected importer's argument that Pennsylvania would adopt the Restatement Third of Unfair Competition, which brought regulatory violations under the umbrella of unfair competition. NLMK Pennsylvania, LLC v. United States Steel Corporation, 592 F.Supp.3d 432, 444.

D.R.I.2019. Cit. generally in ftn. Medical-device manufacturer brought a lawsuit against competitor, alleging, inter alia, that defendant misappropriated plaintiff's trade secrets and breached a confidential relationship. This court granted in part defendant's motion to exclude the opinions of plaintiff's expert witness, holding that the expert's opinions rested on an unsound factual basis. The court noted that, in plaintiff's claim that it was entitled to recover all earned revenue from defendant's sales attributable to the misappropriation, plaintiff also argued that, under Restatement Third of Unfair Competition, the burden of apportioning revenue was placed on defendant. Alifax Holding SpA v. Alcor Scientific Inc., 387 F.Supp.3d 170, 172.

N.J.Super.1994. T.D. Nos. 1-4 cit. generally in ftn. Contractor severed business relations with mechanical subcontractor after subcontractor refused to comply with its request that subcontractor stop dealing with contractor's competitor. Subcontractor sued contractor for tortious interference with contractual obligations and intentional interference with prospective economic advantages. The trial court dismissed; this court affirmed in part, holding that defendant's requests of plaintiff steered clear of a criminal law violation. Reversing in part, the court held that the filing of the proposed amended complaint, which should have been permitted, stated at least one cause of action under New Jersey antitrust laws and that plaintiff could use an antitrust violation to satisfy the first Restatement of Torts § 762(b) exception to nonliability for refusals to enter into business relations that had an illegal effect on competition; it noted that there was no equivalent of that section in the Restatement of Unfair Competition. Van Natta Mech. Corp. v. Di Staulo, 277 N.J.Super. 175, 183, 649 A.2d 399, 404.

For earlier citations, see the Appendices, Supplements, or Pocket Parts, if any, that correspond to the subject matter under examination.

CHAPTER 1. THE FREEDOM TO COMPETE

Wyo.1992. Cit. in ftn. §§ 1-8 (T.D. No. 1, 1988). (§ 1 constitutes all of Ch. 1.) Oil company sued petroleum company with a substantially similar name for trade-name infringement and unfair competition. The trial court granted defendant's motion for summary judgment. Reversing and remanding, this court held that the 25-year-long use by plaintiff of its trade name, as well as its establishment of a dominant place in the market, warranting protection of its reputation, created an issue of fact as to whether plaintiff had developed a secondary meaning in its trade name. The court also stated that the trial court erred in restricting its analysis to confusion among customers, because this devalued other policy considerations that resulted in trade-name protection, such as consumer protection, property rights, economic efficiency, and universal concepts of justice. Powder River Oil v. Powder River Petroleum, 830 P.2d 403, 407.

§ 1. General Principles

C.A.3, 2009. Cit. and quot. in disc. Manufacturer of surgical implants and related devices and its exclusive distributor sued former distributor that allegedly made unauthorized sales of manufacturer's products after its distributorship was terminated. The district court granted summary judgment for manufacturer and distributor on former distributor's counterclaim for unfair competition. Affirming that portion of the decision, this court held that former distributor failed to show that its commercial relations were harmed by an incident at a hospital in which distributor "loudly accused" former distributor of illegally selling manufacturer's products, and that letters manufacturer sent to customers informing them that it only would insure and warrant products sold by authorized dealers such as distributor were not actionable, because they did not mention former distributor by name and were not defamatory under Pennsylvania law. Acumed LLC v. Advanced Surgical Services, Inc., 561 F.3d 199, 227.

C.A.7, 1994. Cit. in disc. (citing § 1 of T.D. No. 1, 1988. § 1 has since been revised; see Official Text). An insurer that had promised to indemnify an ambulance service for liability resulting from the infliction of advertising injury alleged that it did not have a duty under Wisconsin law to defend the insured against a wide-ranging antitrust and tort suit brought by a competitor ambulance service. District court granted insurer a declaratory judgment, holding that there was no duty and that the term "unfair competition" should be narrowly limited to acts of trademark infringement. Reversing, this court held that since part of competitor's suit alleged conduct within the scope of the insurance policy and none of the exclusions was applicable, insurer violated its duty to defend. The allegations that insured disseminated false information about competitor and campaigned to get the public to call 911 and ask for insured constituted charges of either defamation, product disparagement, or unfair competition. Curtis-Universal v. Sheboygan E.M.S., Inc., 43 F.3d 1119, 1124.

C.A.8, 2017. Com. (a) quot. in sup. Reseller of envelopes sued supplier after it began selling envelopes directly to plaintiff's customers, alleging, among other things, that defendant committed unfair competition by plotting to steal plaintiff's customers. The district court granted summary judgment for defendant. Affirming, this court held that plaintiff failed to support its assertion of unfairness. The court pointed out that defendant had repeatedly refused to sign a non-compete agreement with plaintiff, and that, under Restatement Third of Unfair Competition § 1, neither new entrants nor existing competitors were subject to liability for harm resulting solely from the fact of their participation in the marketplace. Tension Envelope Corporation v. JBM Envelope Company, 876 F.3d 1112, 1122.

C.A.8, 2016. Subsec. (a) cit. and quot. in disc. Local-exchange carrier ("LEC"), which contracted with conference-calling services provider, brought an action against interexchange carrier ("IXC"); IXC filed a third-party complaint against provider, alleging that defendant engaged in unfair competition by causing LEC to breach its contract with IXC by charging IXC under its tariff for traffic that terminated at conference-call bridges. Following a bench trial, the district court entered judgment for provider. This court affirmed in part, holding that the district court did not err in rejecting IXC's unfair-competition claim. The court rejected IXC's argument that

Cit.—cited; com.—comment; fol.—followed; sup.—support.
A complete list of abbreviations precedes page 1.

provider's business model was actionable under Restatement Third of Unfair Competition § 1(a), after concluding that it did not find that South Dakota would recognize that tort under these circumstances, because direct competition, an essential component of South Dakota's unfair-competition claim, was lacking here, and provider did not use any unfair methods to gain an advantage over IXC. Qwest Communications Corporation v. Free Conferencing Corporation, 837 F.3d 889, 898.

C.A.D.C.2020. Cit. in disc. (erron. cit. as Restatement Third of Torts). Restaurant owner brought claims of unfair competition against the President of the United States and limited-liability company that operated a hotel business held in trust for the sole benefit of the President, alleging that limited-liability company unfairly drew away plaintiff's customers by exploiting the surname of the President on the hotel business's name. After removal to federal court, the district court granted defendants' motion to dismiss. This court affirmed, holding that the District of Columbia did not recognize unfair-competition claims based on a person using their political prestige to enhance the success of his or her businesses. The court observed that plaintiff was unable to cite any caselaw recognizing the basis for his claims and only pointed to passages from Restatement Second of Torts §§ 539 and 540 and Restatement Third of Unfair Competition § 1 in asserting that the common law was evolving to favor fairness and commercial morality in trade. K&D LLC v. Trump Old Post Office LLC, 951 F.3d 503, 510.

D.Ariz.2019. Com. (a) quot. in disc. Manufacturer of pool float brought, among other things, a claim for unfair competition against competitors and owner of competitors, alleging that defendants unfairly designed, manufactured, and marketed a competing pool float by representing on an online marketplace that defendants' product was plaintiff's. This court entered judgment for defendants, holding that the record did not support a finding that defendants attempted to engage in unfair competition. The court explained that plaintiff failed to provide evidence that the online marketplace presented defendants' product as plaintiff's, which was necessary to establish that defendants infringed upon plaintiff's freedom to engage in business and competition under Restatement Third of Unfair Competition § 1, Comment *a*. Great American Duck Races Incorporated v. Kangaroo Manufacturing Incorporated, 398 F.Supp.3d 494, 508.

D.Ariz.2015. Com. (g) quot. in case quot. in disc. Financial advisor and his insurance agency brought claims for, among other things, unfair competition against competitor and former agency employees who left to work for competitor, alleging that defendants committed computer fraud, trespass, conversion, and other illegal acts in an effort to gain an unfair competitive advantage over plaintiff. This court granted, with leave to amend, defendants' motion to dismiss plaintiffs' claim for unfair competition, holding that Arizona did not appear to recognize a common-law claim for unfair competition as alleged in plaintiffs' complaint. The court noted that, although Restatement Third of Unfair Competition § 1 specified that methods of unfair competition that could potentially give rise to liability included a residual category encompassing unfair business practices, the Arizona Supreme Court had held that the universal test for unfair competition was whether the public was likely to be confused. Joshua David Mellberg LLC v. Will, 96 F.Supp.3d 953, 961, 962.

D.Ariz.1997. Quot. in sup. Two rivals provided telecommunications services in the same metropolitan area through construction and operation of local fiber-optic cable systems that connect consumers with long-distance companies. One of these "competitive access providers" (CAPs) entered into an exclusive agreement with the city power company. That CAP sued the city for injunctive and monetary relief after the city placed a moratorium on any use of the power company's facilities for fiber-optic construction until other CAPs were allowed equal access. The rival CAP intervened in the suit, alleging that the contracting CAP violated federal and state antitrust laws and engaged in tortious interference and unfair competition. This court denied both CAPs' motions for summary judgment, holding, inter alia, that, pursuant to the Restatement analysis, the rival CAP stated a viable unfair-competition claim. The court followed the Restatement's broad approach of finding that "unfair competition" reaches beyond the field of trademarks or trade secrets. Brooks Fiber Communications v. GST Tucson Lightwave, 992 F.Supp. 1124, 1131.

For earlier citations, see the Appendices, Supplements, or Pocket Parts, if any, that correspond to the subject matter under examination.

D.Del.Bkrtcy.Ct.2018. Cit. in disc. Chapter 11 debtor filed an adversary complaint against former chief operations officer and her new employer, alleging that defendants used plaintiff's trade secrets and misappropriated information to steal plaintiff's customers and employees as part of a premeditated course of action that included having chief operations officer leave her employment with plaintiff to join new employer. This court granted in part and denied in part defendants' motion for summary judgment, holding, inter alia, that plaintiff alleged the improper use of its customer lists by chief operations officer but not by new employer. The court noted that Missouri looked to Restatement Third of Unfair Competition § 1 in examining unfair-competition claims. In re Patriot National Inc., 592 B.R. 560, 583.

S.D.Iowa, 2017. Cit. and quot. in disc.; com. (g) cit. and quot. in disc. Local exchange carrier brought an action against long-distance carriers, alleging that defendants failed to pay billed switched-access charges for interstate services arising from conference-calling service arrangement; long-distance carriers counterclaimed, asserting that the arrangements, including revenue sharing, were per se illegal and amounted to traffic pumping. This court granted in part plaintiff's motion to dismiss defendants' unfair-competition counterclaim, holding that defendants failed to state a claim for unfair competition, and denied plaintiff's motion to dismiss with respect to the fraudulent-concealment and tortious-interference counterclaims. The court discussed plaintiff's reliance on the definition of "unfair competition" articulated in Restatement Third of Unfair Competition § 1 and noted that Iowa law was not modeled on this section. Aventure Communications Technology, LLC v. Sprint Communications Company L.P., 224 F.Supp.3d 706, 771-773.

S.D.Iowa, 2015. Cit. but not fol., subsecs. (a) and (b) quot. in disc., com. (g) quot. in disc. and cit. in case cit. in disc. Telecommunications company brought an unfair-competition claim against local-exchange carriers in connection with defendants' revenue-sharing agreements with free-conferencing-service companies. This court granted in part defendants' motion to dismiss, holding that plaintiff failed to state a claim for unfair competition under Iowa law, because plaintiff failed to allege that defendants or the free-conferencing-service companies were plaintiff's competitors, or that defendants were responsible for product confusion. The court rejected plaintiff's request that it adopt the definition of unfair competition found in Restatement Third of Unfair Competition § 1, which defined the tort in broader terms than Iowa law, noting that the Iowa Supreme Court had set forth the elements of the tort without looking to the Restatement. Qwest Communications Co. v. Aventure Communications Technology, LLC, 86 F.Supp.3d 933, 1007-1008,1010.

D.Kan.2022. Cit. and quot. in sup.; com. (g) quot. in sup. Provider of nursing-education resources sued creator of nursing-education videos, alleging, inter alia, that defendant engaged in unfair competition by using plaintiff's study materials to create study videos and sell related material without plaintiff's permission. This court granted in part and denied in part plaintiff's motion for summary judgment, holding that plaintiff's common-law unfair-competition claim was not preempted by federal copyright law and state statutes regarding trade-secrets misappropriation. The court cited Restatement Third of Unfair Competition § 1 in defining "unfair competition," and explained that, in this case, plaintiff's claim was distinct from federal copyright law, because it asserted an additional element that defendant breached the parties' confidential relationship by violating plaintiff's terms and conditions in using its materials to create study aids; furthermore, plaintiff's claim was not based on misappropriation of trade secrets. Assessment Technologies Institute, LLC v. Parkes, 588 F.Supp.3d 1178, 1222, 1223.

D.Kan.2014. Cit. in case quot. in sup.; subsecs. (a)(1)-(a)(3) quot. in case quot. in sup.; com. (g) quot. in sup. and quot. in case quot. in sup. In a dispute between two solar-panel companies that arose from the parties' competing discussions with city about leasing and installing their products on city's buildings, defendant filed counterclaims, alleging that plaintiffs made false representations to city about their products in an effort to dissuade city from doing business with defendant. This court denied plaintiffs' motion to dismiss defendant's counterclaims, holding that defendant sufficiently alleged that plaintiffs engaged in unfair competition in violation of Missouri

Cit.—cited; com.—comment; fol.—followed; sup.—support.
A complete list of abbreviations precedes page 1.

law by, among other things, engaging in "deceptive marketing," as defined by Restatement Third of Unfair Competition §§ 1 and 2. Energy Consumption Auditing Services, LLC v. Brightergy, LLC, 49 F.Supp.3d 890, 898-901.

D.Kan.2001. Cit. in sup., cit. in case cit. in sup., quot. in ftn., subsec. (a) quot. in sup. Aircraft navigational instrument provider sued competitor for Lanham Act violations and unfair competition, among other claims, alleging that defendant improperly obtained plaintiff's trade secrets, altered documents to misrepresent Federal Aviation Administration's position on plaintiff's products, and provided altered documents to plaintiff's customers. This court overruled defendant's motion to dismiss plaintiff's unfair-competition claim, predicting that Kansas Supreme Court would apply the general principles outlined in Restatement Third of Unfair Competition and allow an unfair-competition claim based on misuse of trade secrets and other confidential business information. Airport Systems Intern., Inc. v. Airsys ATM, Inc., 144 F.Supp.2d 1268, 1269, 1270, 1272.

W.D.Ky.2001. Subsec. (a) cit. in disc. Promoters of cable channel devoted to motor vehicles sued broadcasters for, in part, unfair competition, after defendants, which had expressed an interest in plaintiffs' idea and met with plaintiffs to obtain additional information, refused to invest in plaintiffs' project and instead invested in a similar channel. Granting defendants' motion for summary judgment, this court held, inter alia, that plaintiffs' unfair-competition claims arising from the misappropriation and use of plaintiffs' trade-secret information by defendants were preempted by the Kentucky Uniform Trade Secrets Act. Auto Channel, Inc. v. Speedvision Network, LLC, 144 F.Supp.2d 784, 790.

D.Md.2020. Quot. in case quot. in sup. Developer of senior-living community sued former employees, alleging that defendants misappropriated plaintiff's trade secrets and engaged in unfair competition when they downloaded plaintiff's confidential heat maps, pricing sheets, and underwritings during their employment and used them to create a competing business. This court granted plaintiff's motion for preliminary injunction, holding that plaintiff established the likelihood of success on the merits of its claims, because it provided sufficient evidence that the misappropriated information constituted trade secrets and that defendants unfairly interfered with plaintiff's business by misusing them. The court explained that plaintiff supplied substantial evidence that defendants used plaintiff's proprietary and confidential information while in plaintiff's employ to substantially interfere with its ability to compete, as defined by Restatement Third of Unfair Competition § 1, including evidence of email exchanges between defendants incorporating plaintiff's confidential underwritings and evidence that they downloaded plaintiff's proprietary information onto personal drives. Brightview Group, LP v. Teeters, 441 F.Supp.3d 115, 135.

D.Md.2012. Cit. and quot. in sup., cit. in ftn.; com. (g) quot. in sup. (general cite). As part of a wider action, nonexclusive franchisee dealership for truck manufacturer brought various claims against competing dealership and its owner, alleging, among other things, that competing dealership and owner engaged in unfair competitive behavior by making disparaging remarks about franchisee to its customers. Denying competing dealership and owner's motion to dismiss franchisee's unfair-competition claim, this court rejected their argument that franchisee failed to allege that their actions were accompanied by the taint of fraud or deception, concluding that misleading or deceptive conduct was not a necessary element of every unfair-competition claim. Paccar Inc. v. Elliot Wilson Capitol Trucks LLC, 905 F.Supp.2d 675, 690-692.

D.Mass.2004. Com. (a) cit. in disc. Sales representative for manufacturer of party goods sued manufacturer for unfair competition, inter alia, alleging that defendant withheld plaintiff's rightfully earned commissions, thereby interfering with his business and usurping his client. This court granted defendant summary judgment, holding that defendant was not liable for unfair competition, since parties properly defined scope of contractual rights and obligations and defendant engaged in business practices that were specifically authorized by contract. The parties' contract stated that plaintiff would be defendant's exclusive representative within plaintiff's territory, but that defendant had authority to remove account when it became too large for an independent contractor. Aisenberg v. Hallmark Marketing Corp., 337 F.Supp.2d 257, 263.

D.Minn.2014. Cit. but not fol., cit. in

cases cit. in disc.; subsec. (b) quot. in disc. Long-distance carrier, which delivered long-distance calls to telephone numbers assigned to free-conferencing-service companies through a local-exchange carrier, sued companies, alleging, among other things, that defendants engaged in unfair competition by causing the local-exchange carrier to violate statutes and abuse its regulatory status. This court granted in part defendants' motion to dismiss, holding that plaintiffs failed to identify an underlying tort in support of its claim for unfair competition. This court declined to predict that the Minnesota Supreme Court would permit unfair-competition claims predicated on statutory violations, and accordingly rejected plaintiff's argument that, under Restatement Third of Unfair Competition § 1, such a claim could be based on a violation of a state statute. Qwest Communications Co., LLC v. Free Conferencing, 990 F.Supp.2d 953, 974-976.

E.D.Mo.2009. Cit. in sup. Owner of federally registered trademark used to identify the source of various metrology products brought federal and state trademark claims and a state unfair-competition claim against competitor, alleging that competitor's unapproved use of its mark could deceive buyers as to the source, affiliation, or connection of competitor's products. Denying competitor's motion to dismiss, this court, inter alia, rejected competitor's argument that a Missouri unfair-competition claim could only be based on the misuse of trade secrets. The court noted that under both statutory and common law, unfair competition was established by showing that one party was passing off its product as that of another so that the public was deceived regarding the source of the goods, and that numerous Missouri unfair-competition cases concerned the alleged unfair use of trade names as opposed to trade secrets. Hubbs Mach. & Mfg., Inc. v. Brunson Instrument Co., 635 F.Supp.2d 1016, 1018, 1019.

D.N.H.1996. Com. (g) cit. in headnote and quot. in sup. Manufacturer of ball bearings sued competitors, alleging, in part, a state-law claim of unfair competition. The court held that plaintiff's allegations concerning competitors' false advertising stated an actionable claim for unfair competition under the common law of New Hampshire, and denied defendants' cross-motion insofar as it posited otherwise. The court stated that liability for deceptive marketing practices existed independent of specific statutory authority and that state consumer protection statutes provided supplemental, rather than exclusive, remedies for unfair competition. Pacamor Bearings, Inc. v. Minebea Co., Ltd., 918 F.Supp. 491, 492, 501.

D.N.J.2009. Com. (g) quot. in ftn. Holder of patents for a neuropathic pain drug sued generic-drug manufacturer, alleging patent infringement; manufacturer asserted various counterclaims. This court denied holder's motion to dismiss manufacturer's antitrust and unfair-competition counterclaims, noting that, when an antitrust plaintiff sufficiently alleged federal antitrust violations in its pleadings, it was fair to say that the conduct stated a claim under the much broader common-law tort of unfair competition; therefore, manufacturer's state-law unfair-competition counterclaims survived to the same extent, and for the same reasons, as its federal antitrust counterclaims. In re Gabapentin Patent Litigation, 649 F.Supp.2d 340, 350.

D.N.J.1999. Com. (g) quot. in part in disc. Drug manufacturer brought action against competitors, asserting various business torts. Denying defendants' motions to dismiss, the court held, in part, that even though plaintiff was arguably a third-party beneficiary of a consent decree entered earlier by the Federal Trade Commission (FTC), plaintiff lacked standing to enforce it, since government did not explicitly authorize third-party enforcement, and such authorization was required in order to overcome the presumption that government was acting solely in the public interest; that, despite plaintiff's lack of standing with respect to the FTC decree, its allegations of antitrust violations survived the motion to dismiss; and that antitrust violations, if proven, could support a finding that defendants engaged in unfair competition. Biovail Corp. Intern. v. Hoechst Aktiengesellschaft, 49 F.Supp.2d 750, 777.

D.N.M.2014. Subsec. (a) cit. and quot. in sup., cit. in cases cit. and quot. in sup.,; com. (g) cit. and quot. in sup., cit. in case quot. in sup. Cancer-treatment facility filed, inter alia, an unfair-competition claim against corporation that owned hospitals and insurance companies, alleging, among other things, that defendant misrepresented plaintiff's provider status to patients and coerced patients to switch to physicians

Cit.—cited; com.—comment; fol.—followed; sup.—support.
A complete list of abbreviations precedes page 1.

at its hospitals. Denying in part defendant's motion for summary judgment, this court held that plaintiff alleged sufficient facts to form the basis of an unfair-competition claim. The court determined that there was no indication that the New Mexico Supreme Court would conclude that plaintiff's claim was preempted by the Unfair Practices Act, or that it should not follow Restatement Third of Unfair Competition § 1, given that the supreme court had previously followed other Restatement provisions in the absence of controlling New Mexico law. New Mexico Oncology and Hematology Consultants, Ltd. v. Presbyterian Healthcare Services, 54 F.Supp.3d 1189, 1233-1236.

D.N.M.2010. Cit. and quot. in sup., com. (a) cit. in sup., Rptr's Note quot. in ftn. Buyer of endodontic equipment sued sellers for breach of contract and unfair trade practices; sellers brought various counterclaims sounding in contract and tort. Granting in part and denying in part buyer's motion for summary judgment on sellers' counterclaims, this court held, in determining that New Mexico law applied, that sellers' counterclaims of unfair competition, violation of the New Mexico Unfair Practices Act, and unlawful misappropriation fell into the category of torts. The court noted that, with respect to sellers' claim for common-law unfair competition, the categories at issue in this case were false advertising, trademark infringement, and trademark dilution. Guidance Endodontics, LLC v. Dentsply Intern., Inc., 708 F.Supp.2d 1209, 1225, 1249.

E.D.Pa.2021. Cit. in cases cit. in sup. Former employer brought, among other things, an unfair-competition claim against former employee and competitor, alleging that defendants misappropriated plaintiff's confidential information by obtaining unauthorized access to plaintiff's proprietary information and causing plaintiff pecuniary harm. This court denied defendants' motion to dismiss, holding that plaintiff satisfactorily alleged a common-law claim for unfair competition. The court relied on Restatement Third of Unfair Competition § 1 in defining the elements of an unfair-competition claim, and explained that a cause of action for unfair competition was recognized where there was evidence of unlawful use of confidential information and tortious interference with contracts. M3 USA Corporation v. Hart, 516 F.Supp.3d 476, 504.

E.D.Pa.2018. Cit. in disc. and in ftn.; subsec. (a) and (b) quot. in disc. Law firm brought an action against competing firm, alleging that defendant conducted an advertising campaign in violation of the Lanham Act by mostly referencing cases that it had referred to other firms, and violated Pennsylvania's Unfair Competition Law by engaging in deceptive marketing and trade-secret misappropriation with an advertising company. This court granted summary judgment for defendant, holding, inter alia, that plaintiff failed to produce evidence that any of defendant's false advertising deceived and influenced customers or proximately caused injury to plaintiff. The court noted that Pennsylvania followed Restatement Third of Unfair Competition § 1 in providing that one business could be liable for harm to the commercial relations of another. Larry Pitt & Associates v. Lundy Law LLP, 294 F.Supp.3d 329, 343.

E.D.Pa.2018. Cit. in sup., cit. in ftn., cit. in case cit. in sup. Employer sued former employee, competitor, and competitor's CEO, who was also employee's romantic partner, alleging that employee passed employer's trade secrets to CEO and competitor in breach of her fiduciary duty to employer. This court denied in part competitor's motion to dismiss, holding that employer sufficiently stated a claim for unfair competition against competitor under Restatement Third of Unfair Competition § 1 by alleging that competitor's misappropriation of employer's trade secrets caused harm to employer's commercial relations. The court pointed to employer's allegations that competitor used employer's trade secrets to advance the market position of its competing product and to make purchase decisions and set production goals that increased its profits and visibility in the market. Teva Pharmaceuticals USA, Inc. v. Sandhu, 291 F.Supp.3d 659, 679, 680.

E.D.Pa.2017. Cit. in sup.; subsec. (a) and com. (g) quot. in sup. Seller of medical devices brought an unfair-competition claim against competitor, alleging, among other things, that competitor actively recruited seller's employees and converted seller's customers by tortiously interfering with seller's agreements with customers and exploiting seller's employees' access to seller's confidential information. This court denied in part competitor's motion to dismiss, holding that seller's allegations were sufficient to state a claim for unfair competition under Restatement Third of Unfair Competition § 1. The court noted that, as a general matter, if the means of competition were otherwise tortious with respect to the injured party, they would also ordinarily constitute an unfair method of competition. DePuy Synthes Sales, Inc. v. Globus Medical, Inc., 259 F.Supp.3d 225, 246.

E.D.Pa.2016. Quot. in ftn., cit. in case quot. in ftn. Individual taxicab drivers and advocacy organization for taxicab companies filed claims for, among other things, unfair competition and tortious interference with contractual relations against transportation-network company, alleging that defendant wrongfully recruited plaintiffs' taxicab drivers and used money it gained from its illegal operation in an attempt to drive plaintiffs from the marketplace. This court granted defendant's motion to dismiss the amended complaint, holding, inter alia, that plaintiffs' allegations that defendant's operation was in violation of state law or municipal regulations could not support a private cause of action for unfair competition or tortious interference. The court explained that the scope of a common-law claim of unfair competition was coextensive with the definition set forth under Restatement Third of Unfair Competition § 1. Philadelphia Taxi Association, Inc. v. Uber Technologies, Inc., 218 F.Supp.3d 389, 394.

E.D.Pa.2014. Quot. in sup., cit. in ftn., cit. in case cit. in ftn. Law firm filed, inter alia, an unfair-competition claim against competitor that purchased from marketing company the exclusive rights to advertise on the exterior of regional buses, alleging that defendant acquired and used confidential information about plaintiff from the daughter of defendant's partner,who worked at marketing company. Denying in part defendant's motion to dismiss, this court held that plaintiff adequately stated a claim for unfair competition. Citing Restatement Third of Unfair Competition § 1, the court considered plaintiff's allegation that daughter provided competitively sensitive information regarding plaintiff's advertising budget and practices, and determined that plaintiff could have been able to establish that this constituted an appropriation of plaintiff's intangible trade values and could harm its commercial relations. Larry Pitt & Associates v. Lundy Law, LLP, 57 F.Supp.3d 445, 455, 456.

E.D.Pa.2012. Cit. in sup., quot. in ftn. Distributor of chemical products brought a common-law unfair-competition claim, inter alia, against agent of manufacturer of fumed silica product, alleging that defendant, in collusion with manufacturer and another distributor, improperly misappropriated and misused plaintiff's confidential market reports and lists of actual and prospective clients and customers. Denying defendant's motion to dismiss this claim, this court held that plaintiff sufficiently stated a claim for unfair competition by asserting that defendant lulled it into the belief that the parties had an agreement for an exclusive distributorship, and that, once in plaintiff's confidence, defendant became privy to confidential and valuable information that was shared with manufacturer and the other distributor and then used to lure clients away from plaintiff. ITP, Inc. v. OCI Co., Ltd., 865 F.Supp.2d 672, 683.

E.D.Pa.2011. Cit. in ftn. (general cite). In a contract dispute over the development of a sonar system, seller of sonar-processing modules brought a counterclaim for, inter alia, unfair competition against subcontractor hired by manufacturer to work on the sonar system. This court dismissed that counterclaim, holding that, because seller did not allege that customers were actually misled by subcontractor's website into thinking that subcontractor and manufacturer were the sole creators and designers of the sonar system, seller failed to state a claim under Pennsylvania law for unfair competition through false advertising. The court found, in addition, that seller failed to state a cognizable claim even under the slightly expanded definition of unfair competition in the Restatement Third of Unfair Competition. KDH Electronic Systems, Inc. v. Curtis Technology Ltd., 826 F.Supp.2d 782, 807.

E.D.Pa.2011. Cit. in ftn., com. (g) quot. in ftn. Trash-compactor distributor sued supplier, with whom it had a nonexclusive distribution agreement, alleging that supplier engaged in unfair competition under both the Lanham Act and the common law when it falsely informed city that it could buy compactors without soliciting bids from distributors. Denying defendant's motion to dismiss as to unfair competition, this court held that plaintiff sufficiently pled a violation of the Lanham Act by alleging that defendant made false or misleading state-

Cit.—cited; com.—comment; fol.—followed; sup.—support.
A complete list of abbreviations precedes page 1.

ments as to its own product when it convinced city that city had to buy compactors directly from defendant. Noting that several Pennsylvania courts had applied Restatement Third of Unfair Competition § 1 in analyzing unfair-competition claims, this court nevertheless concluded that it could deny defendant's motion to dismiss the common-law claims without determining the scope of those claims, because the parties seemingly agreed that liability under the Lanham Act could serve as a basis for common-law liability, and defendant offered no additional arguments beyond those used in opposing the Lanham Act claim. TriState HVAC Equipment, LLP v. Big Belly Solar, Inc., 836 F.Supp.2d 274, 288.

E.D.Pa.2010. Cit. in sup., quot. in ftn., com. (g) quot. in sup. Editor of an academic journal brought defamation and other claims against professor who sought authorship credit for an article that was published in the journal; professor counterclaimed, alleging that editor deliberately misrepresented that professor would receive authorship credit if he made sufficient contributions to the article. This court denied in part editor's motion to dismiss professor's counterclaims, holding, as to one of those counterclaims, that, whether it was asserted under a theory of commercial disparagement or unfair competition, it was not barred by the statute of limitations. The court noted that the Pennsylvania common-law tort of unfair competition was coextensive with the definition set forth in Restatement Third of Unfair Competition § 1. Giordano v. Claudio, 714 F.Supp.2d 508, 521, 522.

E.D.Pa.2009. Subsec. (a) cit. and quot. in sup., com. (g) quot. in sup. and cit. in ftn. Manufacturer of ion-exchange resins brought a claim for common-law unfair competition, inter alia, against competitor, three of competitor's employees, and manufacturer's former employees who had been hired by competitor. This court denied defendants' motions for summary judgment as to the unfair-competition claim, holding that a genuine issue of material fact existed as to whether competitor's employees knowingly participated in a scheme with plaintiff's former employees to misappropriate plaintiff's proprietary business information for competitor's benefit; while this claim would be preempted under the state uniform trade-secret statute to the extent the information at issue was determined to be trade-secret information, the claim could otherwise rest on confidential information that did not qualify for such status. Bro-Tech Corp. v. Thermax, Inc., 651 F.Supp.2d 378, 417, 418.

E.D.Pa.2009. Quot. in disc., cit. in case quot. in disc. Magazine publisher sued book publisher for copyright infringement and common-law unfair competition, alleging, among other things, that the name of defendant's book, "Famous Monster Movie Art of Basil Gogos," suggested an affiliation with the name of plaintiff's magazine, "Famous Monsters of Filmland." This court granted summary judgment for defendant, holding, inter alia, that plaintiff had abandoned its "Famous Monsters of Filmland" mark. In making its decision, the court noted that, while Pennsylvania trial courts had recently begun to apply the definition of unfair competition set forth in Restatement Third of Unfair Competition § 1, in this case it was appropriate to analyze plaintiff's common-law claim for unfair competition as if it were a Lanham Act claim of unfair competition. Warren Pub. Co. v. Spurlock, 645 F.Supp.2d 402, 430, 431.

E.D.Pa.2008. Cit. and quot. in ftn., com. (g) quot. in ftn. Roofing-materials manufacturer sued attic-ventilation-products inventor and his corporations, alleging breach of contract, inter alia. This court denied without prejudice plaintiff's motion to dismiss defendants' unfair-competition counterclaim, with the hope that when the motion was reasserted Pennsylvania courts would have provided more guidance on the controlling law for the claim. The court noted that, while, according to the Third Circuit, a claim of unfair competition under Pennsylvania law required proof of "passing off," the Pennsylvania Court of Common Pleas, as well as the federal Eastern District of Pennsylvania, had in recent years applied the Restatement Third's definition of unfair competition when faced with a Pennsylvania state-law unfair-competition claim; to date, however, no Pennsylvania appellate court had applied the Restatement Third. Building Materials Corp. of America v. Rotter, 535 F.Supp.2d 518, 526.

E.D.Pa.2003. Cit. in sup., quot. in ftn., com. (g) cit. and quot. in sup. Manufacturer of radio frequency tags brought tortious-interference claim, inter alia, in federal antitrust and state-law action against

For earlier citations, see the Appendices, Supplements, or Pocket Parts, if any, that correspond to the subject matter under examination.

competitor for competitor's alleged interference in supply agreement between manufacturer and electronics supplier. Trial court entered judgment on jury verdict for manufacturer on tort claims. This court held, inter alia, that where competitor was otherwise liable for tortious interference, it was not entitled to judgment as a matter of law on unfair-competition claim. ID Security Systems Canada, Inc. v. Checkpoint Systems Inc., 249 F.Supp.2d 622, 688, 689.

E.D.Pa.1997. Cit. in headnote, quot. in sup., cit. in disc., com. (g) quot. in disc. Fuel oil dealers sued electric utility for, inter alia, tortious interference with contract and unfair competition, alleging that utility offered and made cash payments to developers and contractors whose customers already heated with fossil oil in an effort to persuade them to convert those residences to electric heating systems. Utility moved for summary judgment. Denying the motion, the court held, in part, that material factual issues existed as to whether utility offered the conversion grants as a means of extolling the virtues of electric heating systems through the use of promotional incentives, or whether the grants constituted an improper method of interference. Summary judgment was equally inappropriate on dealers' claim for unfair competition, since questions remained as to whether utility's actions violated federal antitrust statutes. Yeager's Fuel v. Penn. Power & Light, 953 F.Supp. 617, 629, 668.

M.D.Pa.2017. Com. (g) quot. in disc. Employer sued former employee who started a competing business while she was still working for employer, alleging, among other things, that employee engaged in unfair competition by misleading others to believe that she was the proprietor of employer's business and that her competing business was operated by employer. This court granted employer partial summary judgment, holding that employee made several attempts to pass off her work as that of employers' in violation of state law. The court noted that, under Restatement Third of Unfair Competition § 1, a primary purpose of the prohibition against unfair competition was to identify and redress business practices that hindered rather than promoted the efficient operation of the market. Mifflinburg Telegraph, Inc. v. Criswell, 277 F.Supp.3d 750, 803.

W.D.Pa.2015. Cit. in sup. (general cite). Manufacturer of protective packaging and reflective insulation brought claims for, among other things, unfair competition against distributor of specialty building products in connection with defendant's alleged improper use of plaintiff's trademarks. After a bench trial, this court held that defendant was liable to plaintiff on plaintiff's federal and state-law claims for unfair competition. In making its decision, the court noted that the Pennsylvania common-law tort of unfair competition was coextensive with the definition set forth in the Restatement Third of Unfair Competition. Covertech Fabricating, Inc. v. TVM Bldg. Products, Inc., 124 F.Supp.3d 489, 538.

E.D.Wis.2014. Cit. in sup. Manufacturer of a patch used to cover large incisions made during abdominal surgery sued competitor and plaintiff's former director who left to form competitor, seeking to assert claims for, among other things, misappropriation of trade secrets, tortious interference with contract, and unfair competition. This court denied defendants' motion for summary judgment on plaintiff's claims for misappropriation of trade secrets and tortious interference, and further denied the motion as to the unfair-competition claim, holding that, although the parties did not discuss what type of unfair-competition claim was issue here, they agreed that the fate of the unfair-competition claim depended on the outcome of the trade-secret misappropriation and tortious-interference claims. The court noted that Restatement Third of Unfair Competition § 1 listed at least three distinct acts that gave rise to liability for unfair competition under the common law. Starsurgical Inc. v. Aperta, LLC, 40 F.Supp.3d 1069, 1085.

Alaska, 2012. Stat. Note cit. in ftn. Buyer of used motor home sued seller, among others, for, inter alia, violation of Alaska's Unfair Trade Practices and Consumer Protection Act (UTPA), after he discovered that the motor home was a different model year than seller had represented. The trial court entered judgment on a jury verdict finding that defendant did not violate UTPA. Reversing as to the UTPA claim, this court held that judgment should have been entered in favor of plaintiff, because the elements of a case for misrepresentation under UTPA—a statute which mirrored the Federal Trade Commission Act's prohibition on unfair or deceptive acts or practices in trade—were that defen-

Cit.—cited; com.—comment; fol.—followed; sup.—support.
A complete list of abbreviations precedes page 1.

dant made a material misrepresentation, and that that misrepresentation caused plaintiff damage, and those elements were established by the jury in the special verdict; specifically, the jury found that defendant misrepresented the model year of the motor home, that defendant knew or should have known that the statement was false or misleading, and that the misrepresentation was a legal cause of harm to plaintiff. Borgen v. A & M Motors, Inc., 273 P.3d 575, 583.

Ariz.2014. Com. (g) quot. in disc. Public-relations company brought unfair-competition and other claims against its former president and her competing company, alleging that defendants learned confidential and trade-secret information about plaintiff and intended to steal and exploit that information and plaintiff's customers to gain a competitive advantage. The trial court granted defendants' motion to dismiss, finding that the Arizona Uniform Trade Secrets Act (AUTSA) preempted plaintiff's common-law tort claims arising from the alleged misuse of confidential information even as to information not asserted to rise to the level of a trade secret. The court of appeals reversed in part. Agreeing with the result reached by the court of appeals; this court reversed the trial court's dismissal of plaintiff's unfair-competition claim and remanded that claim to that court, holding that the AUTSA did not displace common-law claims based on alleged misappropriation of confidential information that was not a trade secret. In making its decision, the court noted that it did not decide whether Arizona recognized a common-law claim for unfair competition, and that a claim for unfair competition under the Restatement Third of Unfair Competition did not fully exhaust the scope of statutory or common-law liability for unfair methods of competition. Orca Communications Unlimited, LLC v. Noder, 236 Ariz. 180, 184, 337 P.3d 545, 549.

Hawaii, 1999. Com. (g) at 9-11 cit. in ftn. Unsuccessful bidders on school-bus transportation contracts brought, inter alia, unfair competition claim against competitors, alleging that defendants, acting in concert, controlled and operated shell corporations to circumvent state agency's bidding rules and specifications. The trial court entered judgment for defendants. Affirming in part, this court held, inter alia, that, although defendants' conduct constituted unfair competition, there was insufficient evidence to show a dangerous probability of success in the relevant county or state school-bus markets to sustain plaintiffs' attempt-to-monopolize claim. Robert's Hawaii School Bus v. Laupahoehoe, 91 Hawai'i 224, 982 P.2d 853, 884.

La.1995. Com. (g) cit. in sup. The Gulf Coast Bank sued the Gulf Coast Bank and Trust Company for trade-name infringement, alleging that defendant's corporate name was deceptively similar to plaintiff's in violation of Louisiana's Trademark Act. Trial court granted defendant summary judgment and intermediate appellate court affirmed. This court reversed and remanded, holding that where one relies on secondary meaning to establish the distinctiveness of its name, one need not prove fraud to enjoin another from using its trade name, but must show that there is a likelihood of consumer confusion created by defendant's use of the trade name. The court stated that the basis of unfair competition has evolved from one of free trade, concerned primarily with the prevention of fraudulent practices, to one of fair trade, with its primary function being to prevent consumer confusion. Gulf Coast Bank v. Gulf Coast Bank & Trust Co., 652 So.2d 1306, 1318.

Mass.1991. Com. (c) cit. in sup. (citing § 1 of T.D. No. 1, 1988. § 1 has since been revised; see Official Text). A manufacturer and its subsidiary sued a competitor and the competitor's founder, alleging, inter alia, that in hiring away the subsidiary's general manager and then engaging him in a secret effort to recruit several of the subsidiary's other key employees, defendants knowingly joined in the general manager's breach of his duty to the subsidiary. The trial court held for plaintiffs. Following transfer of the defendants' interlocutory appeal to the supreme judicial court on its own motion, this court remanded, rejecting, as an independent basis for liability, the trial court's conclusion that defendants intended to cripple the subsidiary to ease defendants' entry into the market. The court noted that defendants' motives for engaging in the competition were, by themselves, insufficient to establish a basis for liability. Augat, Inc. v. Aegis, Inc., 409 Mass. 165, 565 N.E.2d 415, 422.

Mo.App.2012. Cit. but dist. Mortgage business operated by former wife sued former husband and his competitor company,

For earlier citations, see the Appendices, Supplements, or Pocket Parts, if any, that correspond to the subject matter under examination.

alleging unfair competition based upon company's use of deceptive advertising practices to pass itself off as wife's business and to trade on that business's established reputation. The trial court entered judgment on a jury verdict for plaintiff. Affirming, this court rejected defendants' argument that, because plaintiff's action was brought for the use of certain phrases commonly used in its advertisements, the action fell under the trade name or identifying phrases theory of liability set forth in Restatement Third of Unfair Competition § 1, and thus plaintiffs had to prove a secondary meaning to the unfair phrases at issue. The court held that the allegations were based on Restatement § 4, not § 1, because plaintiff specifically claimed that defendants were using plaintiff's distinctive marketing in an effort to pass off plaintiff's services as its own, and plaintiff presented significant evidence at trial that showed that rather than simply incorporating the use of particular phrases, defendants also incorporated the content, syntax, and message used by plaintiff in its advertising. American Equity Mortg., Inc. v. Vinson, 371 S.W.3d 62, 64, 65.

Mo.App.2008. Com. (g) cit. and quot. in sup. Trade organization representing orthodontists sought injunctive relief against publisher of directories listing businesses and professionals by category, alleging that publisher's listings for general dentists under the heading of "orthodontists" were false and misleading. The trial court granted defendant's motion to dismiss. Affirming, this court held, inter alia, that plaintiff failed to state a claim for common-law unfair competition. The court reasoned that it was not misleading or deceptive for a general dentist who performed orthodontist services to be listed under the heading "Dentists—Orthodontists," because a general dentist in Missouri was not required to undertake any additional specialized training to perform orthodontic services. American Ass'n of Orthodontists v. Yellow Book USA, Inc., 277 S.W.3d 686, 692, 694.

N.Y.Sup.Ct.App.Div.2012. Subsec. (1)(a) cit. in sup. Vehicle repair shop that was not a member of a direct repair program offered by automobile insurer sued insurer, alleging that insurer violated a state statute that prohibited deceptive acts or practices by engaging in conduct that misled plaintiff's customers into believing that they had to have their vehicles repaired at shops that were members of defendant's program. The trial court denied in part defendant's motion for summary judgment. Affirming as modified, this court held, among other things, that the allegation that defendant's deceptive practices diverted plaintiff's customers to competing businesses, resulting in over $5 million in lost business sales, constituted an allegation of a direct injury sufficient to confer standing on plaintiff under the statute. North State Autobahn, Inc. v. Progressive Ins. Group Co., 953 N.Y.S.2d 96, 106.

N.Y.Sup.Ct.2006. Com. (a) cit. in disc. State Insurance Department denied borough president's administrative appeals of its decisions to withhold certain records, filed by automobile insurers pursuant to state's anti-redlining statute, that president requested under Freedom of Information Law. This court annulled the denials, holding that department failed to demonstrate that the records qualified for the "trade secret" exemption. The court reasoned that the records could not be used by competitors to obtain an unfair advantage because they lacked information regarding pricing, profits, losses, or actual marketing plans, and that department did not apply any unique or proprietary methods to analyze the data, which could be obtained by the public by other means. Markowitz v. Serio, 11 Misc.3d 439, 445, 812 N.Y.S.2d 841, 846, reversed 39 A.D.3d 247, 833 N.Y.S.2d 444 (1st Dept.2007).

Ohio App.2003. Cit. in ftn. §§ 1-5. Insurer sought declaratory judgment that it did not have duty to defend insured based on policy exclusion in underlying trade-dress and patent-infringement suit. Trial court granted insured partial summary judgment on duty-to-defend claim, and awarded attorney's fees incurred in instant and underlying actions. Affirming in part, this court held, inter alia, that policy exclusion for intentional conduct did not relieve insurer of duty to defend underlying action even though underlying complaint alleged intentional conduct, where complaint also alleged unintentional conduct, underlying plaintiff could have prevailed on Lanham Act or common-law claims without showing intentional conduct, and proof of intent was required only to justify request for enhanced attorney's fees. Westfield Cos. v. O.K.L. Can Line, 155 Ohio App.3d 747, 757, 804 N.E.2d 45, 53.

Vt.2002. Com. (g) quot. in sup. Owners of

Cit.—cited; com.—comment; fol.—followed; sup.—support.
A complete list of abbreviations precedes page 1.

advertisement-based newspaper sued former operators of paper for conversion and unfair competition, alleging misappropriation of business assets. The trial court entered judgment on jury verdict for owners. Modifying conversion award and affirming, this court held, inter alia, that evidence that former operators took business assets such as customer lists, bookkeeping records, and office equipment supported unfair-competition claim based on misappropriation. Maguire v. Gorruso, 174 Vt. 1, 800 A.2d 1085, 1091.

CHAPTER 2. DECEPTIVE MARKETING

D.Colo.2007. Cit. in disc. §§ 2-6, constituting most of Ch. 2. Company that collected and sold insurance referrals to clients through a website sued competitor and its employee for, among other things, submitting hundreds of false insurance-quote inquiries to plaintiff's website. Granting in part defendant's motion to dismiss, this court held, inter alia, that plaintiff failed to state a claim for unfair competition. The court explained that, under Colorado law, unfair competition did not provide a cause of action for any alleged improper conduct by a competitor that deceived a plaintiff or its clients, but rather reached only conduct that involved either using or copying a plaintiff's products or service and deceiving or confusing the public as to the source of the business in question. NetQuote, Inc. v. Byrd, 504 F.Supp.2d 1126, 1132.

Wyo.1992. Cit. in ftn. §§ 1-8 (T.D. No. 1, 1988). (§§ 2-8 constitute all of Ch. 2.) Oil company sued petroleum company with a substantially similar name for trade-name infringement and unfair competition. The trial court granted defendant's motion for summary judgment. Reversing and remanding, this court held that the 25-year-long use by plaintiff of its trade name, as well as its establishment of a dominant place in the market, warranting protection of its reputation, created an issue of fact as to whether plaintiff had developed a secondary meaning in its trade name. The court also stated that the trial court erred in restricting its analysis to confusion among customers, because this devalued other policy considerations that resulted in trade-name protection, such as consumer protection, property rights, economic efficiency, and universal concepts of justice. Powder River Oil v. Powder River Petroleum, 830 P.2d 403, 407.

Introductory Note

D.N.M.2010. Intro. Note quot. in sup. Buyer of endodontic equipment sued sellers for breach of contract and unfair trade practices; sellers brought various counterclaims sounding in contract and tort. Denying buyer's motion for summary judgment with respect to sellers' counterclaim for common-law unfair competition based on false advertising, this court rejected buyer's contention that the claim failed because defendants had no evidence of actual confusion and evidence of actual confusion was necessary when the claimant's theory was based on literal falsity. The court noted that the Restatement Third of Unfair Competition § 2 required only that the representations be "likely to deceive or mislead prospective purchasers." Guidance Endodontics, LLC v. Dentsply Intern., Inc., 708 F.Supp.2d 1209, 1225, 1249.

§ 2. Deceptive Marketing: General Principle

C.A.Fed.2009. Com. (d) quot. in sup. Trademark applicant sought to register its mark—MOSKOVSKAYA—for vodka. The Trademark Trial and Appeal Board (Board) affirmed the refusal of the U.S. Patent and Trademark Office (PTO) to register the mark, concluding that it was primarily geographically deceptively misdescriptive of the goods. Vacating, this court held that the appropriate inquiry for materiality purposes was whether a substantial portion of the relevant consumers was likely to be deceived, not whether any absolute number or particular segment of the relevant consumers (such as foreign-language speakers) was likely to be deceived, and remanded to the Board for a determination of whether there was a prima facie case of material deception under the correct legal test. In re Spirits Intern., N.V., 563 F.3d 1347, 1355.

M.D.Ala.2007. Com. (b) quot. in disc. After owner of federal trademark registration for vitamin product replaced the original formulation of the product with an "improved" version that contained a different amount of active ingredient, company that marketed and distributed a "generic" version of the product sued trademark owner for, among other things, false advertising and trademark cancellation under the Lanham Act. This court granted summary judgment for defendant. In making its decision, the court noted that § 43(a) of the Lanham Act conferred protection against a myriad of deceptive commercial practices, and applied to both misrepresentations of source and other deceptive representations made in connection with the marketing of goods and services. Midlothian Laboratories, L.L.C. v. Pamlab, L.L.C., 509 F.Supp.2d 1065, 1076.

D.Ariz.2005. Quot. in part in disc. and in sup. Seller of cookware and dinnerware sued website operators for, inter alia, common-law trademark infringement and unfair competition, alleging that defendants posted on their website false and defamatory consumer complaints injurious to plaintiff's business and offered to alter their content to portray plaintiff in a good light if plaintiff paid a fee and monthly retainer. Denying in part defendants' motion to dismiss, this court held that although plaintiff did not allege that the appearance of plaintiff's mark on defendants' website was likely to cause confusion, the allegation that the website contained false and defamatory statements that injured plaintiff's business was sufficient to state a claim for common-law unfair competition. Hy Cite Corp. v. badbusinessbureau.com, L.L.C., 418 F.Supp.2d 1142, 1153.

D.Kan.2014. Cit. in case quot. in sup. In a dispute between two solar-panel companies that arose from the parties' competing discussions with city about leasing and installing their products on city's buildings, defendant filed counterclaims, alleging that plaintiffs made false representations to city about their products in an effort to dissuade city from doing business with defendant. This court denied plaintiffs' motion to dismiss defendant's counterclaims, holding that defendant sufficiently alleged that plaintiffs engaged in unfair competition in violation of Missouri law by, among other things, engaging in "deceptive marketing" as defined by Restatement Third of Unfair Competition §§ 1 and 2. Energy Consumption Auditing Services, LLC v. Brightergy, LLC, 49 F.Supp.3d 890, 898-899.

D.N.H.2014. Quot. in case quot. in disc. Purveyors of designer handbags brought, inter alia, a common-law unfair-competition claim against former owner of a flea market, alleging that defendant continued to provide his services to particular vendors whom he knew or had reason to know were selling counterfeit versions of plaintiff's products at the flea market. This court granted summary judgment for defendant on this claim, holding that, assuming that New Hampshire would recognize a viable unfair-competition claim, pursuant to the framework described in Restatement Third of Unfair Competition §§ 2 and 3, in a case where someone engaged in conduct that deceived the general buying public, plaintiff failed to identify any material representations made by defendant that likely deceived or misled a potential customer into believing that infringing products were genuine or authorized by plaintiff. Coach, Inc. v. Sapatis, 994 F.Supp.2d 192, 203.

D.N.H.1996. Quot. in sup. Manufacturer of ball bearings sued competitors, alleging, in part, a state-law claim of unfair competition. The court held that plaintiff's allegations concerning competitors' false advertising stated an actionable claim for unfair competition under the common law of New Hampshire, and denied defendants' cross-motion insofar as it posited otherwise. The court stated that liability for deceptive marketing practices existed independent of specific statutory authority and that state consumer protection statutes provided supplemental, rather than exclusive, remedies for unfair competition. Pacamor Bearings, Inc. v. Minebea Co., Ltd., 918 F.Supp. 491, 501.

D.N.M.2010. Cit. and quot. in sup., com. (b) cit. in sup., Rptr's Note quot. in ftn. Buyer of endodontic equipment sued sellers for breach of contract and unfair trade practices; sellers brought various counterclaims sounding in contract and tort. After concluding that sellers' common-law unfair-competition counterclaim sounded in tort and thus, pursuant to New Mexico's choice-of-law rule of lex loci delicti, was governed by New Mexico substantive law, this court denied buyer's motion for summary judgment with respect to sellers' unfair-competition counterclaim based on false advertising, rejecting buyer's contention that the claim failed because defendants had no evidence of actual confusion and evidence of actual confusion was necessary

Cit.—cited; com.—comment; fol.—followed; sup.—support.
A complete list of abbreviations precedes page 1.

when a claimant's theory was based on literal falsity. The court noted that the Restatement Third of Unfair Competition § 2 required only that the representations be "likely to deceive or mislead prospective purchasers." Guidance Endodontics, LLC v. Dentsply Intern., Inc., 708 F.Supp.2d 1209, 1225, 1249, 1252.

S.D.N.Y.2001. Cit. in ftn., com. (a) cit. generally in ftn. Cartoonist who had drawn a comic strip, including three characters, for a comic-book publisher sued publisher after it embarked on much more extensive and lucrative commercialization of those characters, including a motion picture. Plaintiff alleged that he owned the characters by virtue of state law, that he licensed them to defendant for limited purposes, and that he had a state-law claim for defendant's unlicensed uses. This court denied plaintiff's motion to remand the suit to state court for lack of subject-matter jurisdiction, holding, inter alia, that plaintiff's claim arose exclusively under the federal Copyright Act. DeCarlo v. Archie Comic Publications, Inc., 127 F.Supp.2d 497, 503, affirmed 11 Fed.Appx. 26 (2d Cir.2001).

E.D.Pa.2018. Cit. in sup. Law firm brought an action against competing firm, alleging that defendant conducted an advertising campaign in violation of the Lanham Act by mostly referencing cases that it had referred to other firms, and violated Pennsylvania's Unfair Competition Law by engaging in deceptive marketing and trade-secret misappropriation with an advertising company. This court granted summary judgment for defendant, holding, inter alia, that plaintiff failed to produce evidence that any of defendant's false advertising deceived and influenced customers or proximately caused injury to plaintiff. The court noted that a claim for deceptive marketing under Pennsylvania law, which followed Restatement Third of Unfair Competition § 2, was nearly identical to a Lanham Act claim. Larry Pitt & Associates v. Lundy Law LLP, 294 F.Supp.3d 329, 343.

E.D.Pa.2014. Cit. in sup. Law firm filed, inter alia, an unfair-competition claim against competitor, alleging, among other things, that defendant advertised for legal services it did not provide in order to refer those cases, for a fee, to firms with which defendant had a referral agreement. Denying in part defendant's motion to dismiss, this court held that plaintiff adequately stated a claim of unfair competition. In reaching its decision, the court pointed out that Restatement Third of Unfair Competition § 2's definition of "deceptive marketing" was nearly identical to that provided in the Lanham Act, and explained that it had previously denied defendant's motion to dismiss plaintiff's claim under the Lanham Act after determining that plaintiff adequately pleaded that claim. Larry Pitt & Associates v. Lundy Law, LLP, 57 F.Supp.3d 445, 456.

Mo.App.2012. Cit. in disc. Mortgage business operated by former wife sued former husband and his competitor company, alleging unfair competition based upon company's use of deceptive advertising practices to pass itself off as wife's business and to trade on that business's established reputation. The trial court entered judgment on a jury verdict for plaintiff. Affirming, this court rejected defendants' argument that, because plaintiff's action was brought for the use of certain phrases commonly used in its advertisements, the action fell under the trade name or identifying phrases theory of liability set forth in Restatement Third of Unfair Competition § 1, and thus plaintiffs had to prove a secondary meaning to the unfair phrases at issue. The court held that the allegations were based on Restatement § 4, not § 1, because plaintiff specifically claimed that defendants were using plaintiff's distinctive marketing in an effort to pass off plaintiff's services as its own, and plaintiff presented significant evidence at trial that showed that rather than simply incorporating the use of particular phrases, defendants also incorporated the content, syntax, and message used by plaintiff in its advertising. American Equity Mortg., Inc. v. Vinson, 371 S.W.3d 62, 64.

Neb.1996. Quot. in disc. Automobile dealership sued its liability insurer for breaching the parties' insurance contract by refusing to defend and indemnify it in the Iowa attorney general's lawsuit against it for unfair advertising practices. Affirming the trial court's dismissal of dealership's action, this court held, inter alia, that insurer was not contractually obligated to defend dealership, since the Iowa lawsuit was not one for unfair competition as the term was used in the insurance contract's advertising offense liability endorsement. The court said that unfair competition involved the "palming off" of one's goods as

For earlier citations, see the Appendices, Supplements, or Pocket Parts, if any, that correspond to the subject matter under examination.

the goods of another and did not refer to the conduct prohibited by the Iowa consumer protection statutes that dealership was alleged to have violated. John Markel Ford v. Auto-Owners Ins. Co., 249 Neb. 286, 293, 543 N.W.2d 173, 178.

N.Y.Sup.Ct.App.Div.2012. Cit. in sup. Vehicle repair shop that was not a member of a direct repair program offered by automobile insurer sued insurer, alleging that insurer violated a state statute that prohibited deceptive acts or practices by engaging in conduct that misled plaintiff's customers into believing that they had to have their vehicles repaired at shops that were members of defendant's program. The trial court denied in part defendant's motion for summary judgment. Affirming as modified, this court held, among other things, that plaintiff was not required to identify specific consumers who suffered pecuniary harm as a result of the allegedly deceptive conduct in order to show that the alleged conduct had a broad impact on consumers in violation of the statute. The court noted that the threshold requirement of consumer-oriented conduct could be satisfied where the allegedly deceptive acts were standardized such that they potentially affected similarly situated customers. North State Autobahn, Inc. v. Progressive Ins. Group Co., 953 N.Y.S.2d 96, 103, 106.

Ohio App.2003. Cit. in ftn. §§ 1-5. Insurer sought declaratory judgment that it did not have duty to defend insured based on policy exclusion in underlying trade-dress and patent-infringement suit. Trial court granted insured partial summary judgment on duty-to-defend claim, and awarded attorney's fees incurred in instant and underlying actions. Affirming in part, this court held, inter alia, that policy exclusion for intentional conduct did not relieve insurer of duty to defend underlying action even though underlying complaint alleged intentional conduct, where complaint also alleged unintentional conduct, underlying plaintiff could have prevailed on Lanham Act or common-law claims without showing intentional conduct, and proof of intent was required only to justify request for enhanced attorney's fees. Westfield Cos. v. O.K.L. Can Line, 155 Ohio App.3d 747, 757, 804 N.E.2d 45, 53.

§ 3. Commercial Detriment of Another

C.A.2, 2010. Com. (f) cit. in conc. and diss. op. Chain of clothing stores brought Lanham Act unfair-competition claim, inter alia, against supplier, alleging that defendant sold counterfeit jeans to plaintiff's competitors and, in the course of pursuing such sales, told other potential customers that plaintiff was a satisfied customer. The district court granted defendant's motion to dismiss. This court vacated and remanded, holding that plaintiff stated a claim for unfair competition even though it did not own the misused trademark at issue; while it might be difficult to prove, plaintiff sufficiently alleged that it lost sales of genuine brand-name jeans to defendant when customers purchased what they believed were also genuine jeans from defendant or from retailers who purchased from defendant, and that customers would believe that plaintiff was selling brand-name jeans at an inflated price. The concurring and dissenting opinion argued that plaintiff did not have standing to assert such a claim, pointing to, among other things, trademark owner's greater proximity than plaintiff to the injurious conduct alleged, and the potential for duplicative damages. Famous Horse Inc. v. 5th Ave. Photo Inc., 624 F.3d 106, 119.

C.A.2, 1995. Com. (d) cit. in sup. Author of book supporting the theory that the assassination of President John F. Kennedy resulted from a conspiracy sued second author and second author's publisher alleging, inter alia, violations of the Lanham Act. Plaintiff argued that advertisements for defendant author's book that included a photograph of plaintiff below the line "GUILTY OF MISLEADING THE AMERICAN PUBLIC," then the statement "ONE MAN. ONE GUN. ONE INESCAPABLE CONCLUSION" in connection with defendant author's thesis constituted false or misleading descriptions of fact. Affirming the district court's grant of summary judgment for defendants, this court held that both assertions were declarations of opinion, not fact, and, furthermore, that the ads, while summarizing arguments contained in plaintiff's book, did not disparage his work. Groden v. Random House, Inc., 61 F.3d 1045, 1051.

C.A.3, 1998. Com. (f) quot. in sup. Retail sellers of motor oil and other engine lubricants brought false-advertising claims under the Lanham Act against manufacturers of competing products. Affirming the district court's dismissal of the complaint,

Cit.—cited; com.—comment; fol.—followed; sup.—support.
A complete list of abbreviations precedes page 1.

this court held that plaintiffs lacked prudential standing under the Lanham Act. Plaintiffs' loss of sales did not impact their ability to compete or detract from their reputation or good will; plaintiffs were less directly injured than the manufacturers whose products they sold, and they were remote from defendants' allegedly harmful conduct; any damages were, if not speculative, then avoidable; and recognizing the right of every potentially injured party in the distribution chain to bring a private damages action would subject defendants to multiple liability for the same conduct and would result in administratively complex damages proceedings. Conte Bros. Automotive v. Quaker State-Slick 50, 165 F.3d 221, 233.

C.A.3, 1993. Com. (f) quot. in disc. (citing § 3 of T.D. No. 1, 1988, which is now § 3 of the Official Text). In two cases, consumers of goods or services in interstate commerce sued vendors under the Lanham Act, alleging that, to their detriment, they purchased the goods or services in reliance on defendants' false advertising claims. Consolidating the two cases on appeal, this court affirmed the district courts' dismissals of plaintiffs' claims, holding that consumers did not have standing to bring suit for false advertising under the Lanham Act. The court stated that consumers fell outside the range of "reasonable interests" contemplated as protected by the false-advertising prong of § 43(a) of the Lanham Act, which was primarily intended to protect commercial interests. Serbin v. Ziebart Intern. Corp., Inc., 11 F.3d 1163, 1177.

C.A.5, 2002. Com. (f) cit. in case cit. in spec. conc. op. Surgeon brought proposed class action and individual action against health-maintenance organizations (HMOs) under Lanham Act, alleging that HMOs' false advertising to consumers increased their market power over price of medical services, forcing him to accept reduced fees. Affirming district court's dismissal, court of appeals held that surgeon lacked constitutional standing to bring claims, as he could not prove that HMOs' conduct caused his reduction in income. Specially concurring judge asserted that surgeon lacked prudential Lanham Act standing, because link between his asserted commercial harm and allegedly false advertising was too attenuated, and his injury was not type of competitive harm protected by Act. Ford v. NYLCare Health Plans of the Gulf Coast, Inc., 301 F.3d 329, 337.

C.A.5, 2001. Com. (f) quot. in ftn. Household products manufacturer, plagued by rumors of links to Satanism, appealed from a dismissal of its lawsuit against a competitor and other defendants for defamation, fraud, and violations of the Lanham Act, RICO, and Texas state law. Affirming in part, this court held, inter alia, that plaintiff did not have prudential standing to bring a Lanham Act claim based on competitor's alleged misrepresentations about its pyramid scheme to competitor's own distributors. The court, however, reversed and remanded for fact finding as to RICO and Lanham Act claims based on competitor's dissemination of the Satanism rumor. Procter & Gamble Co. v. Amway Corp., 242 F.3d 539, 563, cert. denied 534 U.S. 945, 122 S.Ct. 329, 151 L.Ed.2d 243 (2001).

C.A.5, 2000. Cit. in case cit. in disc. Pizza manufacturer sued competitor for false advertising under the Lanham Act, alleging that defendant's advertising slogan "Better Ingredients. Better Pizza." was a misrepresentation of fact. District court entered judgment on jury verdict for plaintiff. This court vacated, reversed, and remanded, holding, inter alia, that the slogan standing alone was not an objectifiable statement of fact upon which consumers would be justified in relying, and thus it did not constitute a false or misleading statement of fact actionable under the Lanham Act. While the slogan, when appearing in comparative advertising, was given objectifiable meaning and became misleading, plaintiff failed to show that the misleading facts conveyed by the slogan were material to the consumers to which it was directed. Pizza Hut, Inc. v. Papa John's Intern., Inc., 227 F.3d 489, 496, cert. denied 532 U.S. 920, 121 S.Ct. 1355, 149 L.Ed.2d 285 (2001).

C.A.11, 2015. Com. (d) quot. in sup. Operator of duty-free stores in international airports sued manufacturer of beauty products sold in duty-free retail outlets, alleging contributory false advertising in violation of the Lanham Act based on statements that plaintiff's competitors made about plaintiff to airports that were seeking tenants for their duty-free retail spaces. The district court granted defendant's motion to dismiss. Affirming, this court held that plaintiff failed to plead sufficient facts from which a court could find that defendant induced or knowingly or intentionally participated in any of the allegedly false

For earlier citations, see the Appendices, Supplements, or Pocket Parts, if any, that correspond to the subject matter under examination.

statements made by plaintiff's competitors. The court noted that the Lanham Act's false-advertising provision allowed a plaintiff to base its claim not only on statements that were literally false, but also on statements that were misleading when considered in their full context, and that, under Restatement Third of Unfair Competition § 3, a statement framed as an opinion would be treated as one of fact if it fairly implied a factual basis. Duty Free Americas, Inc. v. Estee Lauder Companies, Inc., 797 F.3d 1248, 1277.

C.A.11, 2007. Com. (f) quot. in sup. Fast-food-restaurant franchisee brought a false-advertising claim under the Lanham Act against franchisor's competitor for misrepresenting the fairness of competitor's promotional games, after it was disclosed that the games had been rigged by a criminal ring led by an employee of the marketing company hired by competitor to operate the games. The district court dismissed the complaint for lack of prudential standing. Affirming, this court adopted the *Conte Bros.* five-factor test, rather than the so-called categorical approach applied in the majority of circuits, as the standard for determining whether a party had prudential standing to bring a false-advertising claim under the Lanham Act, and held, after weighing the five factors, that, on balance, plaintiff lacked such standing. Phoenix of Broward, Inc. v. McDonald's Corp., 489 F.3d 1156, 1164.

D.Conn.2018. Com. (d) cit. in case quot. in sup. Sellers of small tents for viewing outdoor sporting events during inclement weather brought a claim for false advertising in violation of the Lanham Act against competitors in connection with a series of comments that defendants posted on plaintiffs' social-media accounts, in which defendants stated that plaintiffs' products were "illegal knockoffs" and "very poor quality." This court granted defendants' motion to dismiss plaintiffs' false-advertising claim, holding that the offending comments about plaintiffs' products did not violate the Lanham Act, because they constituted statements of opinion and puffery, rather than false or misleading representations of fact that could give rise to Lanham Act liability under Restatement Third of Unfair Competition § 3. Anthem Sports, LLC v. Under the Weather, LLC, 320 F.Supp.3d 399, 414.

M.D.Fla.2012. Com. (b) quot. in sup. Federal Trade Commission (FTC) sued marketers/sellers of mortgage loan modification services, alleging that defendants violated section 5 of the FTC Act and the Telemarketing Sales Rule by making misrepresentations to homeowners. After a bench trial, this court ruled for the FTC, holding that defendants violated the Act and Rule by deceptively overstating the likelihood that homeowners would obtain a loan modification; defendants convinced thousands of cash-strapped homeowners who were facing imminent foreclosure to front thousands of dollars in cash to an opaquely defined "New Start Work Out Program" that had no independent authority to modify loans and operated as a mere "expediter" or intermediary between homeowners and lenders, by creating a "net impression" that portrayed a product or "program" that was materially different from the services actually provided. F.T.C. v. Washington Data Resources, 856 F.Supp.2d 1247, 1272-1273.

S.D.Fla.2019. Com. (b) quot. in case quot. in sup. The Federal Trade Commission brought an action for a preliminary injunction against healthcare indemnity provider and subsidiaries, alleging, inter alia, that defendants falsely represented to customers that defendants' healthcare indemnities were "comprehensive," meaning that they covered a variety of medical procedures, and were qualified health-insurance plans under the Affordable Care Act. This court granted plaintiff's motion for a preliminary injunction, holding that plaintiff was likely to succeed on the merits, because defendants made material misrepresentations to its customers. The court relied on Restatement Third of Unfair Competition § 3, Comment *b*, in defining "material representation," and explained that defendants' representations were material, because their customers were likely to attach importance to and be misled by the misrepresentations. Federal Trade Commission v. Simple Health Plans LLC, 379 F.Supp.3d 1346, 1360.

D.N.H.2014. Quot. in case quot. in disc. Purveyors of designer handbags brought, inter alia, a common-law unfair-competition claim against former owner of a flea market, alleging that defendant continued to provide his services to particular vendors whom he knew or had reason to know were selling counterfeit versions of plaintiff's products at the flea market. This court granted summary judgment for defendant on this claim, holding that, assuming that New Hampshire would recognize a viable unfair-competition claim, pursuant to the framework described in Restatement Third of Unfair Competition §§ 2 and 3, in a case where someone engaged in conduct that deceived the general buying public, plaintiff failed to identify any material representations made by defendant that likely deceived or misled a potential customer into believing that infringing products were genuine or authorized by plaintiff. Coach, Inc. v. Sapatis, 994 F.Supp.2d 192, 204.

D.N.H.1996. Cit. in headnote and quot. in sup. Manufacturer of ball bearings sued competitors, alleging, in part, a state-law claim of unfair competition. Denying plaintiff's motion for partial summary judgment, this court held, inter alia, that genuine issues of material fact existed as to whether defendants' alleged false advertising contained material representations and whether the representations had caused or were likely to cause a diversion of trade from plaintiff or harm to plaintiff's reputation or good will. Pacamor Bearings, Inc. v. Minebea Co., Ltd., 918 F.Supp. 491, 492, 501.

D.N.J.1998. Rptr's Note to com. (f) quot. in case quot. in disc. (citing § 3 of T.D. No. 1, 1988, which is now § 3 of the Official Text). Retailers of engine-treatment products sued a group of manufacturers for false advertising and consumer fraud, alleging that defendants engaged in a systematic nationwide campaign to advertise and promote their treatment products in an intentionally misleading manner. This court dismissed plaintiffs' complaint, holding, inter alia, that plaintiffs had not alleged that they were in direct competition with defendants, or that they were acting as surrogates for a direct competitor of defendants. Accordingly, plaintiffs did not have standing to sue for false advertising under § 43(a) of the Lanham Act. Conte Bros. Auto. v. Quaker State-Slick 50, Inc., 992 F.Supp. 709, 712, affirmed 165 F.3d 221 (3d Cir.1998).

D.N.M.2010. Quot. in sup. Buyer of endodontic equipment sued sellers for breach of contract and unfair trade practices; sellers brought various counterclaims sounding in contract and tort. Denying buyer's motion for summary judgment with respect to sellers' unfair-competition counterclaim based on false advertising, this court rejected buyer's contention that the claim failed because defendants had no evidence of actual confusion and evidence of actual confusion was necessary when a claimant's theory was based on literal falsity. The court noted that the Restatement Third of Unfair Competition § 2 required only that the representations be "likely to deceive or mislead prospective purchasers." Guidance Endodontics, LLC v. Dentsply Intern., Inc., 708 F.Supp.2d 1209, 1249, 1252.

N.D.N.Y.2016. Com. (d) cit. and quot. in sup. Yogurt manufacturer brought a claim against competitor, seeking a determination that plaintiff's advertising campaign did not amount to false advertising under the Lanham Act; defendant counterclaimed for false advertising and moved for the entry of a preliminary injunction, seeking to preclude plaintiff from making certain claims in its campaign pending the resolution of the merits of their dispute. This court granted defendant's motion for a preliminary injunction, holding that defendant was likely to prevail on its false-advertising counterclaim. Citing Restatement Third of Unfair Competition § 3, Comment *d*, the court noted that, although plaintiff's statements in its advertising campaign may have been literally true, there was a strong likelihood that a factfinder would conclude that the statements, when taken in the context of the advertisement, conveyed a message about defendant's product that was false. Chobani, LLC v. Dannon Company, Inc., 157 F.Supp.3d 190, 202.

N.D.N.Y.2016. Com. (d) cit. and quot. in sup. Yogurt manufacturer brought a claim for unfair competition through false advertising under the Lanham Act against competitor. Granting plaintiff's motion for entry of a preliminary injunction precluding defendant from making certain claims in its yogurt advertising campaign pending the resolution of the merits of their dispute, this court held that plaintiff was likely to prevail on its false-advertising claim. Citing Restatement Third of Unfair Competition § 3, Comment *d*, the court noted that, although defendant's statements in its advertising campaign may have been literally true, there was a strong likelihood that a factfinder would conclude that the statements, when taken in the context of the advertisement, conveyed a message about plaintiff's product that was false. General

For earlier citations, see the Appendices, Supplements, or Pocket Parts, if any, that correspond to the subject matter under examination.

Mills, Inc. v. Chobani, LLC, 158 F.Supp.3d 106, 119.

S.D.N.Y.1997. Cit. in disc. The sponsors of a toy fair brought, in part, a claim of unfair competition against the sponsors of a competing toy show. Partially granting plaintiffs' motion for a preliminary injunction, the court held, inter alia, that defendants' registration procedures constituted unfair competition under New York statutory and common law. The court stated that defendants hoped to utilize the good will and reputation of plaintiffs' toy fair to their advantage by capitalizing on the confusion likely to be caused by instituting a registration procedure strikingly similar to that long used by plaintiffs. Toy Manufacturers v. Helmsley-Spear, 960 F.Supp. 673, 682.

Ohio App.2003. Cit. in ftn. §§ 1-5. Insurer sought declaratory judgment that it did not have duty to defend insured based on policy exclusion in underlying trade-dress and patent-infringement suit. Trial court granted insured partial summary judgment on duty-to-defend claim, and awarded attorney fees incurred in instant and underlying actions. Affirming in part, this court held, inter alia, that policy exclusion for intentional conduct did not relieve insurer of duty to defend underlying action even though underlying complaint alleged intentional conduct, where complaint also alleged unintentional conduct, underlying plaintiff could have prevailed on Lanham Act or common-law claims without showing intentional conduct, and proof of intent was required only to justify request for enhanced attorney's fees. Westfield Cos. v. O.K.L. Can Line, 155 Ohio App.3d 747, 757, 804 N.E.2d 45, 53.

§ 4. Misrepresentations Relating to Source: Passing Off

W.D.Ark.1995. Com. (b) cit. in ftn. Insurer sought declaration as to whether it was obligated to defend its insured, a knife manufacturer, against charges that it infringed another manufacturer's trademark. Insurer moved for summary judgment on the ground that suits for trademark infringement were excluded from the policy providing a duty to defend actions based on advertising injury. Denying the motion, the court held that trademark infringement, which arose solely from the unauthorized use of another's mark, was, along with infringement of copyright, title, or slogan, an advertising injury against which insurer had a duty to defend. Union Ins. v. The Knife Co., Inc., 897 F.Supp. 1213, 1215.

D.Colo.2007. Cit. in sup. §§ 4-5. Company that collected and sold insurance referrals to clients through a website sued competitor and its employee for, among other things, submitting hundreds of false insurance-quote inquiries to plaintiff's website. Granting in part defendant's motion to dismiss, this court held, inter alia, that plaintiff failed to state a claim for unfair competition. The court explained that, under Colorado law, unfair competition did not provide a cause of action for any alleged improper conduct by a competitor that deceived a plaintiff or its clients, but rather reached only conduct that involved either using or copying a plaintiff's products or service and deceiving or confusing the public as to the source of the business in question. NetQuote, Inc. v. Byrd, 504 F.Supp.2d 1126, 1132.

S.D.Ind.1999. Cit. in disc. Cigarette manufacturer sought injunction to prevent competing but affiliated companies from importing back into the United States cigarettes meant for foreign distribution. Plaintiff argued that defendants' sale of a product materially different from the domestic version constituted trademark infringement, among other things. Issuing the injunction, the court held, in part, that the fact that plaintiff and defendants were related corporations did not necessarily render the Lanham Act inapplicable; that plaintiff had made a strong argument for infringement and had established that it would be irreparably injured in the absence of injunctive relief; and that the balance of hardships weighed in plaintiff's favor. Philip Morris, Inc. v. Allen Distributors, Inc., 48 F.Supp.2d 844, 852.

Cal.App.2000. Illus. 1, 3, and 5 and Rptr's Notes quot. in disc. After trademark holder and its licensee obtained a federal-court judgment in their favor in their action for trademark infringement and unfair competition against insured, whose insurer subsequently became insolvent, they brought this action for a declaratory judgment that the California Insurance Guarantee Association (CIGA) was obligated to pay their claim against insured. The trial court entered a stipulated judgment for CIGA. Affirming, this court held, inter alia, that plaintiffs' unfair-competition claim for trade-dress infringement was encompassed

Cit.—cited; com.—comment; fol.—followed; sup.—support.
A complete list of abbreviations precedes page 1.

within the insurance policy's exclusion for injury arising out of trademark infringement, and thus was excluded from coverage. Aloha Pacific, Inc. v. CIGA, 79 Cal.App.4th 297, 93 Cal.Rptr.2d 148, 165.

Cal.App.1999. Com. (b) quot. in sup. Insurer sought declaration that it was not obligated to defend and indemnify insured against competitor's business-tort claims. The trial court entered judgment on a jury verdict for insured. Reversing, this court held, in part, that "passing off" claims based entirely on advertising conduct infringing competitor's trade dress or trademark were expressly excluded under the policy provision barring coverage for claims for unfair competition arising from trademark infringement. Industrial Indem. Co. v. Apple Computer, 79 Cal.App.4th 817, 95 Cal.Rptr.2d 528, 536.

Idaho, 2010. Quot. in sup. Auto-body supply company that purchased the Idaho stores of an auto supply business sued plaintiff's competitor, paint supplier, and business's former employees who left plaintiff to work for competitor, asserting that defendants, through their joint and several efforts, purposefully engaged in unfair competition specifically designed to reduce plaintiff's ability to compete against defendants in the automotive paint-supply industry and to drive plaintiff out of business. The trial court refused to dismiss any of the former employees or competitor as to the unfair-competition claim, but dismissed paint supplier and its principal. Affirming as to that claim, this court held that a genuine issue of material fact existed as to whether employees were making representations likely to deceive or mislead customers when they continued to wear auto supply business's clothing and use its cell numbers while working for competitor. Wesco Autobody Supply, Inc. v. Ernest, 149 Idaho 881, 243 P.3d 1069, 1084.

Mo.App.2012. Cit. and quot. in sup. Mortgage business operated by former wife sued former husband and his competitor company, alleging unfair competition based upon company's use of deceptive advertising practices to pass itself off as wife's business and to trade on that business's established reputation. The trial court entered judgment on a jury verdict for plaintiff. Affirming, this court rejected defendants' argument that, because plaintiff's action was brought for the use of certain phrases commonly used in its advertisements, the action fell under the trade name or identifying phrases theory of liability set forth in Restatement Third of Unfair Competition § 1, and thus plaintiffs had to prove a secondary meaning to the unfair phrases at issue. The court held that the allegations were based on Restatement § 4, not § 1, because plaintiff specifically claimed that defendants were using plaintiff's distinctive marketing in an effort to pass off plaintiff's services as its own, and plaintiff presented significant evidence at trial that showed that rather than simply incorporating the use of particular phrases, defendants also incorporated the content, syntax, and message used by plaintiff in its advertising. American Equity Mortg., Inc. v. Vinson, 371 S.W.3d 62, 64-66.

Ohio App.2003. Cit. in ftn. §§ 1-5. Insurer sought declaratory judgment that it did not have duty to defend insured based on policy exclusion in underlying trade-dress and patent-infringement suit. Trial court granted insured partial summary judgment on duty-to-defend claim, and awarded attorney's fees incurred in instant and underlying actions. Affirming in part, this court held, inter alia, that policy exclusion for intentional conduct did not relieve insurer of duty to defend underlying action even though underlying complaint alleged intentional conduct, where complaint also alleged unintentional conduct, underlying plaintiff could have prevailed on Lanham Act or common-law claims without showing intentional conduct, and proof of intent was required only to justify request for enhanced attorney's fees. Westfield Cos. v. O.K.L. Can Line, 155 Ohio App.3d 747, 757, 804 N.E.2d 45, 53.

§ 5. Misrepresentations Relating to Source: Reverse Passing Off

C.A.2, 1999. Quot. in disc. Architects sued other architects and a hospital for violations of the Copyright Act and the Lanham Act, alleging that defendants copied plaintiff's drawings for the renovation of the hospital and falsely designated themselves as the source of his design for the renovation. New York federal district court granted defendants summary judgment. This court affirmed, holding, inter alia, that plaintiff failed to state a viable claim for reverse passing off under the Lanham Act, because plaintiff failed to establish substantial similarity. Whatever similarity existed between plaintiff's drawings and defendants' realizations related

For earlier citations, see the Appendices, Supplements, or Pocket Parts, if any, that correspond to the subject matter under examination.

only to ideas and concepts, elements that were not protected by copyright law. Attia v. Society of the New York Hospital, 201 F.3d 50, 59, cert. denied 531 U.S. 843, 121 S.Ct. 109, 148 L.Ed.2d 67 (2000).

C.A.2, 1994. Cit. in sup., com. (c) cit. and quot. in sup. (citing § 5 of T.D. No. 1, 1988. § 5 has since been revised; see Official Text). A publisher of children's books and its distributor sued another publisher of children's books, alleging that defendant violated the Lanham Act by publishing books that entered into the stream of commerce with a false designation of origin because a recipient of the books would likely think that the books originated with defendant, when they in fact originated with plaintiff. District court held that plaintiffs showed likelihood of success on Lanham Act claim and granted preliminary injunction in plaintiffs' favor. This court vacated the preliminary injunction and remanded, holding that while plaintiffs showed a likelihood of success on their claim that defendant falsely designated the source of its books and that this false designation would cause consumer confusion, a remand was necessary to determine whether plaintiffs could show irreparable economic harm from the false designation. Waldman Pub. Corp. v. Landoll, Inc., 43 F.3d 775, 780, 785.

D.Colo.2007. Cit. in sup. §§ 4-5. Company that collected and sold insurance referrals to clients through a website sued competitor and its employee for, among other things, submitting hundreds of false insurance-quote inquiries to plaintiff's website. Granting in part defendant's motion to dismiss, this court held, inter alia, that plaintiff failed to state a claim for unfair competition. The court explained that, under Colorado law, unfair competition did not provide a cause of action for any alleged improper conduct by a competitor that deceived a plaintiff or its clients, but rather reached only conduct that involved either using or copying a plaintiff's products or service and deceiving or confusing the public as to the source of the business in question. NetQuote, Inc. v. Byrd, 504 F.Supp.2d 1126, 1132.

N.D.Iowa, 2003. Cit. in case cit. in disc., com. (c) cit. and quot. in case cit. and quot. in sup. Manufacturer of self-propelled crop sprayers sued competitor for, in part, reverse palming off in violation of the Lanham Act. Denying in part defendant's motion for partial summary judgment, the court held, inter alia, that plaintiff stated a cognizable claim of reverse palming off, and that genuine issues of material fact existed as to whether defendant copied plaintiff's designs, whether the sprayer components that defendant incorporated into its own product were identical or substantially similar to plaintiff's designs, and whether plaintiff was harmed by the false representation of origin of the designs. Walker Mfg., Inc. v. Hoffmann, Inc., 261 F.Supp.2d 1054, 1072, 1073.

N.D.Iowa, 1995. Cit. in case cit. in disc. (citing § 5 of T.D. No. 1, 1988. § 5 has since been revised; see Official Text). Owner of a trademark for semi-trailers sued semi-trailer manufacturers and dealers alleging unfair competition under the Lanham Act and requesting an injunction. Plaintiff alleged both that defendants used a photograph of his product, without making significant modifications to the product, in an advertisement in which they represented the product to be one of their own, obscuring plaintiff's trademarks, and also that his trailers were uniquely and distinctively associated with him. This court denied the defendant dealers' motion to dismiss for lack of subject-matter jurisdiction, holding that plaintiff stated a cognizable federal claim of "reverse palming off" under the Lanham Act over which the court had subject-matter jurisdiction. Woodke v. Dahm, 873 F.Supp. 179, 189, affirmed 70 F.3d 983 (8th Cir.1995).

S.D.N.Y.1999. Com. (c) quot. in case quot. in disc. Musician sued former bandmates, among others, for, in part, violation of Lanham Act, alleging that defendants falsely attributed authorship of two songs by excluding his name. Granting defendants' motion to dismiss, the court held, inter alia, that plaintiff's Lanham Act claim was duplicative of a Copyright Act claim and thus was preempted by federal copyright law, since no affirmative act of falsely claiming originality was alleged beyond that implicit in any false-copyright claim. Weber v. Geffen Records, Inc., 63 F.Supp.2d 458, 463.

S.D.N.Y.1996. Com. (c) cit. in case quot. in sup. Photographer whose images were used, without his consent and without payment to him, in bottled-water advertisements appearing in the Russian and Finnish editions of an American magazine sued advertiser and seller of bottled water for,

Cit.—cited; com.—comment; fol.—followed; sup.—support.
A complete list of abbreviations precedes page 1.

inter alia, violations of the Lanham Act. Defendants moved to dismiss. Granting the motion in part and denying it in part, the court held, among other things, that plaintiff, having alleged that his images appeared in the foreign magazines above an erroneous copyright notice claiming copyright protection in favor of seller, had stated a claim against both defendants under § 43(a) of the Lanham Act. Noble v. Great Brands of Europe, Inc., 949 F.Supp. 183, 187.

S.D.N.Y.1995. Com. (c) quot. in case quot. in ftn. (citing § 5 of T.D. No. 1, 1988. § 5 has since been revised; see Official Text). In 1981, a writer published a novel that told the story of a man trapped in a repeating day, forced to live the same day over and over. In 1993, film makers released their film "Groundhog Day," which also featured a man caught in a repeating day. Writer sued film makers under the Copyright Act, the Lanham Act, and common law principles, alleging that defendants copied the novel's plot, mood, characters, pace, setting, and sequence of events. This court granted defendants summary judgment, holding, inter alia, that even assuming the Lanham Act applied in this case, no reasonable jury could find that defendants falsely designated the origin of their film by placing their names on what was essentially plaintiff's product. In addition, plaintiff had not raised a reasonable fact issue regarding the likelihood of confusion. Arden v. Columbia Pictures Industries, Inc., 908 F.Supp. 1248, 1263.

Ohio App.2003. Cit. in ftn. §§ 1-5. Insurer sought declaratory judgment that it did not have duty to defend insured based on policy exclusion in underlying trade-dress and patent-infringement suit. Trial court granted insured partial summary judgment on duty-to-defend claim, and awarded attorney's fees incurred in instant and underlying actions. Affirming in part, this court held, inter alia, that policy exclusion for intentional conduct did not relieve insurer of duty to defend underlying action even though underlying complaint alleged intentional conduct, where complaint also alleged unintentional conduct, underlying plaintiff could have prevailed on Lanham Act or common-law claims without showing intentional conduct, and proof of intent was required only to justify request for enhanced attorney's fees. Westfield Cos. v. O.K.L. Can Line, 155 Ohio App.3d 747, 757, 804 N.E.2d 45, 53.

§ 6. Misrepresentations in Marketing the Goods or Services of Another

D.N.M.2010. Rptr's Note quot. in ftn. Buyer of endodontic equipment sued sellers for breach of contract and unfair trade practices; sellers brought various counterclaims sounding in contract and tort. Granting in part and denying in part buyer's motion for summary judgment on sellers' counterclaims, this court held, in determining that New Mexico law applied, that sellers' counterclaims of unfair competition, violation of the New Mexico Unfair Practices Act, and unlawful misappropriation fell into the category of torts. The court noted that the causes of action in the Restatement Third of Unfair Competition appeared to have grown out of the Restatement of Torts, implying that they should be categorized as torts. Guidance Endodontics, LLC v. Dentsply Intern., Inc., 708 F.Supp.2d 1209, 1225.

§ 7. Contributory Liability of Printers, Publishers, and Other Suppliers

Mo.App.2008. Subsec. (1) quot. in ftn. Trade organization representing orthodontists sought injunctive relief against publisher of directories listing businesses and professionals by category, alleging that publisher's listings for general dentists under the heading of "orthodontists" were false and misleading. The trial court granted defendant's motion to dismiss. Affirming, this court held, inter alia, that plaintiff failed to state a claim for common-law unfair competition. The court rejected plaintiff's argument that defendant was contributorily liable for accepting and organizing advertisements by general dentists that conflicted with public policy set forth in a state statute regulating licensed dentists, reasoning that the statute regulated only dentists, not publishers. American Ass'n of Orthodontists v. Yellow Book USA, Inc., 277 S.W.3d 686, 695.

Wyo.1992. Cit. in ftn. (citing § 7 of T.D. No. 2, 1990. § 7 has since been revised; see Official Text). Oil company sued petroleum company with a substantially similar name for trade-name infringement and unfair competition. The trial court granted defendant's motion for summary judgment. Reversing and remanding, this court held that the 25-year-long use by plaintiff of its trade name, as well as its establishment of a dominant place in the market, warranting protection of its reputation, created an issue of fact as to whether plaintiff had developed a secondary meaning in its trade name. The court also stated that the trial court erred in restricting its analysis to confusion among customers, because this devalued other policy considerations that resulted in trade-name protection, such as consumer protection, property rights, economic efficiency, and universal concepts of justice. Powder River Oil v. Powder River Petroleum, 830 P.2d 403, 407.

§ 8. Contributory Liability of Manufacturers and Distributors

D.Md.1996. Quot. and cit. in disc., cit. generally in disc. In action brought under the Lanham Act, charity sued publisher for contributory trademark infringement in connection with the use of charity's name and mark in a book designed to instruct readers on ways to make money from "business opportunity" frauds and scams. Publisher moved to dismiss on the ground that charity could not sustain a claim for contributory infringement absent proof of direct infringement. Denying the motion, the court held, in part, that dismissal was inappropriate because it could not say, as a matter of law, that charity would be unable to present evidence of direct infringement. N.F.B. v. Loompanics Enterprises, 936 F.Supp. 1232, 1245.

CHAPTER 3. THE LAW OF TRADEMARKS

Wyo.1992. Cit. in ftn. §§ 9-27, 28-37 (T.D. Nos. 2, 1990, and 3, 1991), constituting all of Ch. 3; Rptr's Memo. at xvii cit. in ftn. (T.D. No. 3, 1991). Oil company sued petroleum company with a substantially similar name for trade-name infringement and unfair competition. The trial court granted defendant's motion for summary judgment. Reversing and remanding, this court held that the 25-year-long use by plaintiff of its trade name, as well as its establishment of a dominant place in the market, warranting protection of its reputation, created an issue of fact as to whether plaintiff had developed a secondary meaning in its trade name. The court also stated that the trial court erred in restricting its analysis to confusion among customers, because this devalued other policy considerations that resulted in trade-name protection, such as consumer protection, property rights, economic efficiency, and universal concepts of justice. Powder River Oil v. Powder River Petroleum, 830 P.2d 403, 407.

Generally

C.A.2, 1990. Ch. 3 cit. generally in sup. (P.D. No. 3, 1989). The manufacturer of a line of "Grand Baroque" silverware sued a competitor for trade-dress infringement and sought a preliminary injunction. The district court denied the motion for a preliminary injunction. Affirming, this court held that the manufacturer's silverware design was a functional feature of "Baroque" style silverware, and trademark protection of this ornamental feature would significantly hinder competitors by limiting the range of adequate alternative designs. The court determined that the doctrine of functionality applied to features of a product that were purely ornamental but that were essential to effective competition. It stated that although the competitor's design was found by the district court judge to be "substantially similar," it was not identical or virtually identical, and the similarity involved design elements necessary to compete in the market for baroque silverware. Wallace Intern. Silversmiths v. Godinger Silver Art, 916 F.2d 76, 81, cert. denied 499 U.S. 976, 111 S.Ct. 1622, 113 L.Ed.2d 720 (1991).

TOPIC 1. SUBJECT MATTER OF TRADEMARK LAW

Ind.2006. Cit. in disc. §§ 9-12, constituting the definition sections of Ch. 3, Topic 1. In a dispute between two law firms that had been established by two unrelated families with the same last name, who operated the firms under nearly identical names, older law firm sued newer law firm for unfair competition. The trial court granted summary judgment for defendant and the court of appeals affirmed. Affirming, this court held, inter alia, that summary judgment was proper on plaintiff's claim of trade-name infringement because plaintiff failed to demonstrate that its name had secondary meaning. The court reasoned that, while "distinctive" personal names or surnames were protectable as trade names, such names were not "inherently distinctive" and thus were only protectable as trade names if the person claiming rights in the name proved that the name had come to be uniquely associated with the person's particular business through use, which was not shown here. Keaton and Keaton v. Keaton, 842 N.E.2d 816, 821.

§ 9. Definitions of Trademark and Service Mark

U.S.2015. Com. (b) cit. in sup. Owner of the "SEALTIGHT" mark related to metal fasteners for the aerospace industry brought a trademark-infringement action against owner of the "SEALTITE" mark regarding fasteners for use in the construction trade. The district court refused to apply issue preclusion to the decision of the Trademark Trial and Appeal Board (TTAB) that SEALTITE was confusingly similar to SEALTIGHT, and the jury returned a verdict for defendant, finding no likelihood of confusion. The court of appeals affirmed. Reversing and remanding, this court held that TTAB decisions had preclusive effect if the ordinary elements of issue preclusion were met. The court cited Restatement Third of Unfair Competition § 9, Comment *b*, in noting that trademark law had a long history, going back at least to Roman times, and that the principle underlying trademark protection was that distinctive marks—words, names, symbols, and the like—could help distinguish a particular artisan's goods from those of others. B & B Hardware, Inc. v. Hargis Industries, Inc., 135 S.Ct 1293, 1299.

C.A.5, 2018. Quot. in ftn. Owner of a popular animated television series in which the main character worked at a fictional restaurant brought claims for trademark infringement and unfair competition against business that sought to open a seafood restaurant under the same name as the fictional restaurant and filed an application to register the name as a trademark. The district court granted summary judgment for plaintiff. Affirming, this court held, among other things, that, while plaintiff never registered the name of the restaurant as a trademark, plaintiff established ownership of a common-law trademark in the name through its use of the name as a source identifier. The court cited the definition of a trademark set forth in Restatement Third of Unfair Competition § 9 in explaining that a trademark was any word, name, symbol, or device, or any combination thereof, that a party used or intended to use to identify and distinguish the party's goods from those manufactured or sold by others. Viacom International v. IJR Capital Investments, L.L.C., 891 F.3d 178, 185.

C.A.5, 2010. Com. (f) quot. in ftn. Self-storage business sued competitor and construction company that built facilities for both business and competitor, alleging, among other things, infringement of a star design that it claimed as a service mark. The district court granted summary judgment for defendants. Affirming in part, this court held that the design was not legally protectable as a mark, because it was not inherently distinctive, and plaintiff had not raised a genuine issue of fact regarding secondary meaning. The court noted that, although trademarks and service marks were separately defined, their definitions under the Lanham Act closely tracked each other, and the cases construing the two terms informed the court's analysis equally. Amazing Spaces, Inc. v. Metro Mini Storage, 608 F.3d 225, 236.

C.A.7, 2016. Cit. in sup. Food-distribution company and its owner brought a trademark-infringement action against similarly named competitor that was owned by company's former employee, that hired owner after company suspended its operations, and that subsequently fired owner. The district court granted defendant's motion to dismiss. This court reversed and remanded, holding that the complaint failed to unambiguously establish the elements of the affirmative defense of acquiescence, because it did not allege that plaintiffs had made representations that they would not assert a right or claim regarding the trademark. Citing Restatement Third of Unfair Competition §§ 9 and 29, the court explained that the purpose of trademark protection was to identify the source of a good or service to consumers; and if the owner of a mark had, through his words or conduct, conveyed his consent to the defendant's use of the mark, then the mark's original source-identifying power was weakened. Hyson USA, Inc. v. Hyson 2U, Ltd., 821 F.3d 935, 939.

For earlier citations, see the Appendices, Supplements, or Pocket Parts, if any, that correspond to the subject matter under examination.

C.A.8, 1996. Cit. in ftn. Canadian beer company sent a letter to an American beer company accusing the competitor of infringing its trademarks by using terms such as "ice," "ice brewed," and "ice beer." American company brought suit seeking a declaratory judgment that the Canadian company had no protected rights in the generic "ice" terms. Canadian company counterclaimed alleging Lanham Act violations. Jury found that the "ice" terms at issue were not trademarks owned by the Canadian company. This court affirmed, holding, inter alia, that the district court properly instructed the jury that arbitrary or suggestive marks are entitled to trademark protection from the date that they are first used in an arbitrary or suggestive way on the product as marketed. Here, the jury rejected Canadian company's "genericide" theory, the basis for its unfair-competition claim, thus making it clear that the jury did not believe that the ice terms had been trademarks at any time. Anheuser-Busch, Inc. v. John Labatt Ltd., 89 F.3d 1339, 1345, cert. denied 519 U.S. 1109, 117 S.Ct. 944, 136 L.Ed.2d 833 (1997).

C.A.8, 1996. Quot. in ftn. State chartered bank whose official name was First National Bank, but which claimed to be known as First Bank, sought permanent injunction to prevent federally chartered bank registered as First Bank System from providing services in First National's primary market area. First National alleged that it was entitled to trademark protection because "First Bank" distinctly identified it as the supplier of certain banking services in the minds of its customers. The district court declined to issue the injunction. Affirming, this court held that First National, which conceded that "First Bank" was a descriptive term, failed to show that the term had acquired a secondary meaning by which customers associated "First Bank" with First National prior to First Bank System's registration of its trademark in 1971. First Bank v. First Bank System, Inc., 84 F.3d 1040, 1044.

C.A.10, 2021. Com. (f) quot. in ftn. Putative owner of service marks, who created a virtual-assistant program and an associated internet search engine, sued bank, alleging that defendant violated the Lanham Act and infringed upon plaintiff's service marks used for his virtual assistant and the domain name for the search engine by creating an almost identically-named virtual assistant used on a mobile banking application. The district court granted defendant's motion for summary judgment. This court affirmed in part, vacated in part, and remanded, holding that there was a genuine dispute of material fact as to whether plaintiff engaged in actual use of his mark for the virtual assistant, but he did not have a protectable interest under the Act for the mark used for the domain name of the search engine. The court cited Restatement Third of Unfair Competition § 9, Comment *f*, in noting that, while the term "service mark" was used to identify services and "trademark" was used to identify goods, both terms were governed by identical standards, and "trademarks" was frequently used to refer to both trademarks and service marks. Underwood v. Bank of America Corporation, 996 F.3d 1038, 1045.

C.A.11, 1996. Com. (f) cit. in headnote and ftn. (Erron. cit. as Restatement (Second) of Unfair Competition.) A company produced commercial study guides for various courses at a university by hiring students attending a university to take lecture notes, which it in turn marketed to the student body as a whole. The university sued the company for copyright infringement. District court entered judgment on jury verdict for the publisher. This court affirmed, holding that the district court properly entered directed verdicts on plaintiff's Lanham Act claims, because of the absence of substantial evidence that the information plaintiff sought to protect was both distinctive and nonfunctional. Noting that plaintiff had cited trademark, service mark, and trade dress cases, but had not clearly declared under which category its claims fell, the court stated that the same substantive legal principles applied equally to all three categories of marks. University of Florida v. KPB, Inc., 89 F.3d 773, 774, 776.

C.A.Fed.1995. Com. (c) cit. in ftn. Patent holder sued infringer for interference with patent rights. This court held that a patentee may recover damages for an infringer's interference with the patentee's market in unpatented goods. Dissent argued that damages may legally be obtained only for injury to patent rights, because the patent power may not be used to enact a general law of unfair competition protecting a patentee's unpatented business. King Instrument Corp. v. Perego, 72 F.3d 855, 857.

Cit.—cited; com.—comment; fol.—followed; sup.—support.
A complete list of abbreviations precedes page 1.

D.N.M.2010. Rptr's Note quot. in ftn. Buyer of endodontic equipment sued sellers for breach of contract and unfair trade practices; sellers brought various counterclaims sounding in contract and tort. Granting in part and denying in part buyer's motion for summary judgment on sellers' counterclaims, this court held, in determining that New Mexico law applied, that sellers' counterclaims of unfair competition, violation of the New Mexico Unfair Practices Act, and unlawful misappropriation fell into the category of torts. The court noted that the causes of action in the Restatement Third of Unfair Competition appeared to have grown out of the Restatement of Torts, implying that they should be categorized as torts. Guidance Endodontics, LLC v. Dentsply Intern., Inc., 708 F.Supp.2d 1209, 1225.

E.D.Pa.2005. Quot. in disc. Supplier of after-market automotive parts sued competitor, alleging that competitor infringed on supplier's unregistered trademarks by offering parts for sale that were stamped with an abbreviation of supplier's registered trademark, and by using supplier's part numbers to identify products in its catalog. This court granted defendant's motion for summary judgment, holding, inter alia, that no reasonable factfinder could conclude that the abbreviation or part numbers were valid and protectable trademarks, because there was insufficient evidence that consumers associated the abbreviation with plaintiff's registered mark, or that the part numbers functioned as a source identifier for plaintiff's goods in the minds of consumers. R & B, Inc. v. Needa Parts Mfg., Inc., 418 F.Supp.2d 684, 697.

Fla.App.2011. Com. (f) cit. in disc. Business group sued tourism council and festival organizer, seeking to enjoin organizer from interfering with its planned festival celebrating the satirical 1982 "secession" of the Florida Keys from the United States; organizer counterclaimed, alleging that the name that plaintiff had chosen to promote its festival infringed on and diluted the festival he had coordinated since 1990 under his trademark or service mark "Conch Republic Independence Celebration." The trial court granted summary judgment for business group. This court reversed, holding that organizer's mark was not generic, but descriptive, because, among other things, it identified its purpose—celebrating the satirical secession. The court accordingly remanded for a determination as to whether the mark had secondary meaning and primacy. Anderson v. Upper Keys Business Group, Inc., 61 So.3d 1162, 1167.

Fla.App.2001. Com. (c) cit. in disc. Homeowners' association brought suit to enjoin infringement and dilution of its trade name/service mark by real estate company. The trial court denied relief. Reversing and remanding, this court held that plaintiff's "Tortoise Island" name was arbitrary and distinctive, and that defendant's use of the name was likely to cause confusion on the part of the public, inviting the suggestion that defendant was sponsored by, approved by, or affiliated in some way with plaintiff's subdivision. The court also held that defendant's use of the name diluted the name's distinctive quality. Tortoise Island Homeowners Ass'n, Inc. v. Tortoise Island Realty, Inc., 790 So.2d 525, 530, 534.

Ind.2006. Com. (d) cit. in sup. In a dispute between two law firms that had been established by two unrelated families with the same last name, who operated the firms under nearly identical names, older law firm sued newer law firm for unfair competition, alleging, inter alia, that defendant "passed off" its services as plaintiff's. The trial court granted summary judgment for defendant and the court of appeals affirmed. Affirming, this court held, inter alia, that summary judgment was proper on the "passing off" claim because plaintiff failed to present any evidence of intentional misrepresentation or deception by defendant or anyone associated with it. The court pointed out that plaintiff had conceded at a hearing that defendant and its partners never intentionally misrepresented themselves as being the same as, or associated with, plaintiff, and that they never passed off their services as those of plaintiff. Keaton and Keaton v. Keaton, 842 N.E.2d 816, 819.

Iowa, 1999. Cit. in disc. Bank operating under the name "Commercial Savings Bank" brought trademark-infringement action against financial institution calling itself "Commercial Federal Bank." The trial court entered judgment for defendant on the ground that plaintiff had failed to establish the existence of a common-law trademark in "commercial." Affirming, this court held that "commercial" was a descriptive term that had become distinctive through secondary use; however, plaintiff

For earlier citations, see the Appendices, Supplements, or Pocket Parts, if any, that correspond to the subject matter under examination.

could not show that defendant's use of the term was likely to cause consumer confusion. Commercial Sav. v. Hawkeye Federal Sav., 592 N.W.2d 321, 326.

La.1995. Cit. and quot. in ftn., coms. (c), (d) and (e) cit. in sup. The Gulf Coast Bank sued the Gulf Coast Bank and Trust Company for trade-name infringement, alleging that defendant's corporate name was deceptively similar to plaintiff's in violation of Louisiana's Trademark Act. Trial court granted defendant summary judgment and intermediate appellate court affirmed. This court reversed and remanded, holding that where one relies on secondary meaning to establish the distinctiveness of its name, one need not prove fraud to enjoin another from using its trade name, but must show that there is a likelihood of consumer confusion created by defendant's use of the trade name. The court stated that the basis of unfair competition has evolved from one of free trade, concerned primarily with the prevention of fraudulent practices, to one of fair trade, with its primary function being to prevent consumer confusion. Gulf Coast Bank v. Gulf Coast Bank & Trust Co., 652 So.2d 1306, 1310, 1315, 1318, 1319.

La.App.1998. Coms. (c) and (d) cit. in disc. Supplier of school uniforms sued retailer for, inter alia, trade-name infringement. The trial court dismissed the complaint. Affirming, this court held, in part, that plaintiff's mark was not distinctive, since it was a descriptive name that had not acquired secondary meaning. Inka's S'Coolwear, Inc. v. School Time, L.L.C., 725 So.2d 496, 500.

Mich.App.2014. Coms. (c), (d), and (g) cit. in ftn. Owner of the trademark "TRAVIS" in connection with the food-service industry brought a trademark-infringement action under Michigan law against owner of the "Travis Grill," a restaurant that operated in the same geographical area as plaintiff's restaurant and licensees. The trial court granted an injunction against defendant's further use of the mark. Affirming, this court held that plaintiff's mark had priority, defendant's mark confused consumers, and defendant used the confusing mark in the sale of services in Michigan. The court, citing Restatement Third of Unfair Competition § 9, Comments *c* and *d*, opined that business owners who invested significant amounts of money and effort to convince consumers to identify their marks with their products and services needed a remedy against competitors who sought to "free ride" on this accumulated goodwill by copying or pirating already established marks. Janet Travis, Inc. v. Preka Holdings, L.L.C., 856 N.W.2d 206, 211, 212.

Tex.App.2012. Com. (f) cit. in disc. After licensee of a trademark and a service mark, which claimed to have acquired all rights in those marks, sold its retail store to purchasers, purchasers, based on the belief that they had purchased all rights in the marks, opened other retail outlets using the marks; licensee sued purchasers, alleging trademark and service mark infringement. Following a bench trial, the trial court rendered judgment in favor of defendants. Affirming in part, this court held that the trial court did not abuse its discretion when it concluded that plaintiff's claims were barred by laches, because plaintiff unreasonably delayed in asserting a right or claim in the marks, the delay was not excused, and it resulted in undue prejudice to defendant. The court pointed to evidence that plaintiffs filed suit over five years after they gained knowledge of defendants' alleged infringing use, and, during that time, defendants built up their business and entered into costly transactions with third parties under the assumption that they could use the marks. Condom Sense, Inc. v. Alshalabi, 390 S.W.3d 734, 739.

Vt.2002. Coms. (e) and (f) quot. and cit. in ftn. Owners of advertisement-based newspaper sued former operators of paper for conversion and unfair competition, alleging misappropriation of business assets. The trial court entered judgment on jury verdict for owners. Modifying conversion award and affirming, this court held, inter alia, that evidence that former operators took business assets such as customer lists, bookkeeping records, and office equipment supported unfair-competition claim based on misappropriation. Maguire v. Gorruso, 174 Vt. 1, 800 A.2d 1085, 1088.

Wis.2021. Quot. in disc. Sellers of a business that provided management services for a lakefront resort sued buyers of the business after buyers terminated agreements to manage units that sellers owned in the resort; buyers counterclaimed for trademark and trade-name infringement after sellers used the logo and trade name for the business without authorization when renting out their own units after the agreements were terminated. The trial

Cit.—cited; com.—comment; fol.—followed; sup.—support.
A complete list of abbreviations precedes page 1.

court granted summary judgment to sellers, and the court of appeals affirmed. Reversing and remanding, this court held, as a matter of law, that buyers became the exclusive owners of the logo and trade name for the business when they purchased the business from sellers, because it was a well-settled principle that trademarks and their associated goodwill passed with the sale of a business. In making its decision, the court cited the definitions of a trademark and a trade name set forth in Restatement Third of Unfair Competition §§ 9 and 12. Ritter v. Farrow, 955 N.W.2d 122, 128.

Wis.App.2002. Cit. in sup. Liability insurer brought suit for a declaratory judgment that it had no obligation to defend or indemnify insured in an underlying lawsuit brought against insured by its competitor for, in part, unfair competition. Reversing the trial court's grant of summary judgment for insured and remanding, this court held, inter alia, that, although the complaint set forth a claim for unfair competition, the claim was based on the theft of trade secrets rather than trademark or trade-dress infringement, and thus insurer had no duty to indemnify insured under the "infringement of trademark" provision of the insurance policies. Fireman's Fund Ins. Co. of Wisconsin v. Bradley Corp., 256 Wis.2d 643, 649 N.W.2d 685, 693, reversed, 2003 WI 33, 261 Wis.2d 4, 660 N.W.2d 666 (2003).

Wis.App.1996. Cit. in headnote, cit. and cit. generally in ftn. Company in the business of providing reprographic copying services to architects, engineers, publishers, and others sued competitor for trademark infringement. Following a bench trial, the trial court dismissed the complaint on the ground that there was insufficient likelihood of confusion between the parties' marks. Affirming, this court held, inter alia, that company's mark, which could also be considered a service mark, was a weak descriptive designation combining a geographical name with a shortened version of the term "reprographics"; that company's mark did not become strong or distinctive through secondary meaning; and that the minimal similarity of the two marks, as well as the sophistication of the parties' typical customers, supported the lower court's finding that there was no likelihood of confusion. Madison Reprographics v. Cook's Reprographics, 203 Wis.2d 226, 552 N.W.2d 440, 441, 444, 445.

§ 11. Definition of Certification Mark

E.D.Ark.2005. Com. (a) cit. in disc., com. (b) quot. in disc. and cit. generally in disc. Automobile-parts seller sued for declaratory judgment that its statements that it had "MQVP parts available" did not infringe on service mark of MQPV, an aftermarket parts monitoring program. Defendant counterclaimed for false designation and trademark infringement. This court granted plaintiff summary judgment on the counterclaim, holding, inter alia, that, although defendant's mark was not descriptive and thus could be protected whether or not it had acquired secondary meaning, plaintiff did not engage in false advertising and its use of the mark was not infringing, since plaintiff's statements created no likelihood of confusion among defendant's customers or potential customers. Mid-State Aftermarket Body Parts, Inc. v. MQVP, Inc., 361 F.Supp.2d 896, 902, 906, reversed and remanded 466 F.3d 630 (8th Cir.2006).

§ 12. Definition of Trade Name

Cal.App.1999. Coms. (a) and (b) quot. in ftn. Insurer sought declaration that it was not obligated to defend and indemnify insured against competitor's business-tort claims. The trial court entered judgment on a jury verdict for insured. Reversing, this court held, in part, that "passing off" claims based entirely on advertising conduct infringing competitor's trade dress or trademark were expressly excluded under the policy provision barring coverage for claims for unfair competition arising from trademark infringement. Industrial Indem. Co. v. Apple Computer, 79 Cal.App.4th 817, 95 Cal.Rptr.2d 528, 535.

Fla.App.2001. Com. (a) cit. in disc. Homeowners' association brought suit to enjoin infringement and dilution of its trade name/service mark by real estate company. The trial court denied relief. Reversing and remanding, this court held that plaintiff's "Tortoise Island" name was arbitrary and distinctive, and that defendant's use of the name was likely to cause confusion on the part of the public, inviting the suggestion that defendant was sponsored by, approved by, or affiliated in some way with plaintiff's subdivision. The court also held that defendant's use of the name diluted the name's distinctive quality. Tortoise Island Homeowners Ass'n, Inc. v. Tortoise Island Realty, Inc., 790 So.2d 525, 530, 534.

For earlier citations, see the Appendices, Supplements, or Pocket Parts, if any, that correspond to the subject matter under examination.

Ind.2006. Quot. in disc. In a dispute between two law firms that had been established by two unrelated families with the same last name, who operated the firms under nearly identical names, older law firm sued newer law firm for unfair competition. The trial court granted summary judgment for defendant and the court of appeals affirmed. Affirming, this court held, inter alia, that summary judgment was proper on plaintiff's claim of trade-name infringement because plaintiff failed to demonstrate that its name had secondary meaning. The court further held that, even if the family name had acquired a unique association with plaintiff, there was no evidence that plaintiff had any name recognition in defendant's location over 100 miles away, and the three instances of name confusion alleged by plaintiff were insufficient as a matter of law to establish actionable trade-name infringement. Keaton and Keaton v. Keaton, 842 N.E.2d 816, 820.

Ind.App.2014. Quot. in case quot. in sup. County visitor bureau brought claims for trademark infringement, inter alia, against operator of a hotel resort in the county, arising from defendant's use of the designation "Visit Michigan City LaPorte," which the bureau had selected as the branding identifier for the area, and the domain name visitmichigancitylaporte.com. On remand, the trial court entered judgment for plaintiff, and permanently enjoined defendant from using either the phrase or the domain name. Reversing, this court held that the designation was not subject to protection as a trade name and that there was no infringement, because the designation was primarily geographically descriptive and it had not acquired secondary meaning before defendant began using it. The court cited Restatement Third of Unfair Competition § 12 in noting that a trade name was a work, name, symbol, device, or other designation, or a combination of such designations, that was distinctive of a person's business or enterprise and distinguished it from the businesses or enterprises of others. Serenity Springs, Inc. v. LaPorte County Convention and Visitors Bureau ex rel. Bd. of Managers, 13 N.E.3d 487, 491.

La.1995. Cit. and quot. in ftn., com. (b) cit. in sup. The Gulf Coast Bank sued the Gulf Coast Bank and Trust Company for trade-name infringement, alleging that defendant's corporate name was deceptively similar to plaintiff's in violation of Louisiana's Trademark Act. Trial court granted defendant summary judgment and intermediate appellate court affirmed. This court reversed and remanded, holding that where one relies on secondary meaning to establish the distinctiveness of its name, one need not prove fraud to enjoin another from using its trade name, but must show that there is a likelihood of consumer confusion created by defendant's use of the trade name. The court stated that the basis of unfair competition has evolved from one of free trade, concerned primarily with the prevention of fraudulent practices, to one of fair trade, with its primary function being to prevent consumer confusion. Gulf Coast Bank v. Gulf Coast Bank & Trust Co., 652 So.2d 1306, 1318, 1319.

La.App.2006. Quot. in disc. After brother, who was essentially fired from his family jewelry business, opened a competing business with a similar name, family jewelry business sued brother and competing business, seeking, in part, to enjoin defendants from using its registered trade names, which included the family name in conjunction with the words "jewelers," "jewelry," and "diamonds." The trial court rendered judgment in favor of defendant. Reversing in part, this court held, inter alia, that plaintiff's registered trade names had acquired secondary meaning and were entitled to trade-name protection, but that defendant had sufficiently distinguished competing business by including both his first name and his surname in its trade name. Ramsey's Mfg. Jewelers, Inc. v. Ramsey, 924 So.2d 1045, 1049, writ denied 930 So.2d 26 (La.2006).

La.App.1998. Com. (b) cit. in disc. Supplier of school uniforms sued retailer for, inter alia, trade-name infringement. The trial court dismissed the complaint. Affirming, this court held, in part, that plaintiff's mark was not distinctive, since it was a descriptive name that had not acquired secondary meaning. Inka's S'Coolwear, Inc. v. School Time, L.L.C., 725 So.2d 496, 500.

Neb.2000. Com. (b) quot. in sup., com. (c) and Rptr's Note cit. in disc. Business owner who had registered the trade name "Husker Authentics" sued university for damages and injunctive relief, alleging that defendant was wrongfully using the trade name. Affirming the trial court's dismissal of the claim, this court held, inter alia, that

Cit.—cited; com.—comment; fol.—followed; sup.—support.
A complete list of abbreviations precedes page 1.

defendant had a common law right in the trade name "Husker Authentics" through its use of the name prior to registration of the name by plaintiff, and the registration therefore was invalid and had to be canceled. White v. Board of Regents, 260 Neb. 26, 35, 38, 614 N.W.2d 330, 337, 339.

R.I.2002. Quot. in sup. Lumber company sought injunctive relief to prevent competitor from using similar fictitious name. The trial court granted plaintiff permanent injunctive relief. Affirming, this court held that plaintiff was entitled to permanent injunctive relief preventing competitor from using deceptively similar trade name where plaintiff's trade name, while not inherently distinctive, had acquired secondary meaning through 40 years of continuous use. National Lumber & Building Materials Co. v. Langevin, 798 A.2d 429, 433.

Wis.2021. Quot. in disc. Sellers of a business that provided management services for a lakefront resort sued buyers of the business after buyers terminated agreements to manage units that sellers owned in the resort; buyers counterclaimed for trademark and trade-name infringement after sellers used the logo and trade name for the business without authorization when renting out their own units after the agreements were terminated. The trial court granted summary judgment to sellers, and the court of appeals affirmed. Reversing and remanding, this court held, as a matter of law, that buyers became the exclusive owners of the logo and trade name for the business when they purchased the business from sellers, because it was a well-settled principle that trademarks and their associated goodwill passed with the sale of a business. In making its decision, the court cited the definitions of a trademark and a trade name set forth in Restatement Third of Unfair Competition §§ 9 and 12. Ritter v. Farrow, 955 N.W.2d 122, 129.

Wis.App.1996. Cit. in headnote, cit. generally in ftn., cit. in disc., com. (b) cit. in ftn. Company in the business of providing reprographic copying services to architects, engineers, publishers, and others sued competitor for trademark infringement. Following a bench trial, the trial court dismissed the complaint on the ground that there was insufficient likelihood of confusion between the parties' marks. Affirming, this court held, inter alia, that company's mark, which could also be considered a service mark, was a weak descriptive designation combining a geographical name with a shortened version of the term "reprographics"; that company's mark did not become strong or distinctive through secondary meaning; and that the minimal similarity of the two marks, as well as the sophistication of the parties' typical customers, supported the lower court's finding that there was no likelihood of confusion. Madison Reprographics v. Cook's Reprographics, 203 Wis.2d 226, 552 N.W.2d 440, 441, 444, 445.

§ 13. Distinctiveness; Secondary Meaning

U.S.1992. Cit. in disc., com. (e) quot. in ftn., com. (a) cit. in disc., cit. in conc. op. (citing § 13 of T.D. No. 2, 1990, which is now § 13 of the Official Text). Owner of restaurant chain sued owner of similar restaurant chain for trade-dress infringement. Plaintiff patented its store's Mexican motif before defendant's opening of similarly decorated and designed stores. The district court granted judgment for plaintiff. The court of appeals affirmed. This court also affirmed, holding that plaintiff need not prove that trade dress had secondary meaning to be protected. The court accepted without discussion findings that plaintiff's trade dress was inherently distinctive. It did not require plaintiff to prove that its trade dress was uniquely associated with a specific source because such burden would be contrary to intent of federal legislation. A concurring opinion said that courts had recently accepted that trade dress was capable of having inherently distinctive meaning without proof of secondary meaning. Two Pesos, Inc. v. Taco Cabana, Inc., 505 U.S. 763, 766, 112 S.Ct. 2753, 2756, 2758, 2767, 120 L.Ed.2d 615, rehearing denied 505 U.S. 1244, 113 S.Ct. 20, 120 L.Ed.2d 947 (1992).

C.A.2, 2005. Com. (d) cit. in disc. Vodka producer brought state and federal trademark-infringement claims against rum and beer producers, alleging that an "O" design that it added to its label for a new orange-flavored vodka would be confused with "O" designs added to the labels of defendants' new lines of products. The district court rejected plaintiff's claims in their entirety. This court affirmed, holding, inter alia, that, although the district court erred in holding that plaintiff's design was not protectable as a trademark, plaintiff had not established a likelihood of confusion with defendants' products. The court

For earlier citations, see the Appendices, Supplements, or Pocket Parts, if any, that correspond to the subject matter under examination.

concluded that plaintiff's "O" design was protectable separately from the other design elements on plaintiff's vodka label because it was inherently distinctive, based on its sufficient stylization and novelty. Star Industries, Inc. v. Bacardi & Co. Ltd., 412 F.3d 373, 382, cert. denied 547 U.S. 1019, 126 S.Ct. 1570, 164 L.Ed.2d 298 (2006).

C.A.2, 1996. Com. (a) cit. in disc., com. (e) cit. generally in headnote and cit. in sup. Manufacturer of historic reproductions of "Mission furniture" sued competitor for trade-dress infringement. Vacating the district court's grant of a preliminary injunction for plaintiff and remanding for trial, this court held that the trade dress of reproductions was not inherently distinctive and that plaintiff was not likely to succeed in proving secondary meaning, since it was doubtful that consumers identified the Mission furniture trade dress with plaintiff rather than with the maker of the popular originals. L. & J.G. Stickley, Inc. v. Canal Dover Furniture, 79 F.3d 258, 259, 262, 263.

C.A.2, 1995. Subsec. (a) cit. in headnote and quot. in sup. Manufacturer of children's sweaters decorated with squirrel- and leaf-shaped appliques brought an action for trade-dress infringement under the Lanham Act and copyright infringement against competitor that introduced a line of similar sweaters. Vacating in part and affirming in part the district court's entry of judgment for plaintiff and remanding, this court held, inter alia, that plaintiff's sweater designs failed to qualify for protection of trade dress inherent in product design; since plaintiff's objective in the designs was primarily aesthetic, the designs were not primarily intended as source identification. Knitwaves, Inc. v. Lollytogs Ltd. (Inc.), 71 F.3d 996, 998, 1008.

C.A.2, 1995. Cit. in headnote, cit. in case quot. in sup., com. (d) cit. and quot. in sup., com. (e) cit. in disc. Manufacturer of makeup compacts sued competitor for trade-dress infringement under the Lanham Act, alleging that competitor infringed by packaging its compacts in a manner identical to manufacturer's. The district court granted competitor's motion for summary judgment and this court affirmed, holding that manufacturer failed to prove that its compacts' trade dress was inherently distinctive or had acquired distinctiveness through secondary meaning. The court explained that in a business such as compact manufacturing, the possibilities for trade dress were limited and, therefore, it was unlikely that consumers would ever consider one producer's dress striking or distinctive. Such was the case here where, additionally, manufacturer's compacts carried no distinguishing mark to identify it as the source of the items. Mana Products, Inc. v. Columbia Cosmetics Mfg., Inc., 65 F.3d 1063, 1065, 1069, 1070.

C.A.2, 1994. Cit. in ftn. (citing § 13 of T.D. No. 2, 1990, which is now § 13 of the Official Text). A publisher of children's books and its distributor sued another publisher of children's books, alleging that defendant violated the Lanham Act by publishing books that entered into the stream of commerce with a false designation of origin because a recipient of the books would likely think that the books originated with defendant, when they in fact originated with plaintiff. District court held that plaintiffs showed likelihood of success on Lanham Act claim and granted preliminary injunction in plaintiffs' favor. This court vacated the preliminary injunction and remanded, holding that while plaintiffs showed a likelihood of success on their claim that defendant falsely designated the source of its books and that this false designation would cause consumer confusion, a remand was necessary to determine whether plaintiffs could show irreparable economic harm from the false designation. Waldman Pub. Corp. v. Landoll, Inc., 43 F.3d 775, 784.

C.A.2, 1993. Cit. in ftn. but dist. (citing § 13 of T.D. No. 2, 1990, which is now § 13 of the Official Text). The owner of a trademarked and copyrighted television series sued a book author and publisher for, among other claims, trademark and copyright infringement. The district court entered judgment for plaintiff, holding, in part, that defendant had violated the Lanham Act and engaged in unfair competition, since reasonably prudent purchasers, on seeing the name "Twin Peaks" as part of the book's title, would be led to believe that plaintiff was the source of the goods. Vacating in part and remanding, this court determined that the district court had failed to fully examine the factors relevant to likelihood of confusion. The court noted that the stipulated facts would have required the district court to find secondary meaning, since the series was a media phenomenon and the title "Twin Peaks" was sufficiently well known that consumers as-

Cit.—cited; com.—comment; fol.—followed; sup.—support.
A complete list of abbreviations precedes page 1.

sociated it with plaintiff's work. Noting that while the "Twin Peaks" mark was at least suggestive, the court stated that the Second Circuit had required the trademark proprietor of literary titles to demonstrate secondary meaning notwithstanding the suggestive nature of the title. Twin Peaks Productions v. Publications Intern., 996 F.2d 1366, 1378.

C.A.2, 1992. Com. (e) quot. in disc. (citing § 13 of T.D. No. 2, 1990, which is now § 13 of the Official Text). A game-puzzle manufacturer sought a preliminary injunction based on trade-dress and copyright infringement against a competitor who developed a similar set of flat-to-cube game puzzles and used similar packaging. New York federal district court granted plaintiff's motion for a preliminary injunction, determining that plaintiff's trade dress was protected by the doctrine of secondary meaning in the making. This court vacated the preliminary injunction, holding, inter alia, that the doctrine of secondary meaning in the making should not be recognized under the Lanham Act, since the doctrine, by affording protection before prospective purchasers were likely to associate the trade dress with a particular sponsor, constrained unnecessarily the freedom to copy and compete. The court emphasized the level of protection afforded under existing law to prevent piracy in the early stages of product development. Laureyssens v. Idea Group, Inc., 964 F.2d 131, 138.

C.A.2, 1991. Coms. (b) and (e) and Rptr's Note cit. in disc. (citing § 13 of T.D. No. 2, 1990, which is now § 13 of the Official Text). A publisher of a book and audiotapes on the development of charisma that used the trade name "New Choices Press" sought to enjoin a magazine publisher from using the name "New Choices for the Best Years" for its magazine on retirement living. The district court granted defendant's motion for summary judgment. Affirming, this court held that plaintiff failed to raise a genuine issue of fact as to the likelihood of confusion. The court concluded that plaintiff's trade name was weak because it was not widely known. Lang v. Retirement Living Pub. Co., Inc., 949 F.2d 576, 581.

C.A.3, 1994. Cit. in case cit. in sup. (citing § 13 of T.D. No. 2, 1990, which is now § 13 of the Official Text). Manufacturer of plastic garden planters shaped like Grecian urns brought a trade-dress-infringement action against competitor and moved for a preliminary injunction. Affirming the district court's denial of plaintiff's motion, this court held that, since plaintiff was unable to show that its product's configuration was either inherently distinctive or had acquired a secondary meaning, plaintiff failed to demonstrate a likelihood of success on the merits. The court rejected the application of traditional trade dress doctrine to a claim that product configuration had been infringed. Duraco Products v. Joy Plastic Enterprises, Ltd., 40 F.3d 1431, 1440.

C.A.5, 2015. Com. (d) quot. in sup. Jewelry designer who sold dog trinkets made out of beads brought an action against bakery shop that owned a trademark for Mardi Gras bead-dog designs, seeking the cancelation of defendant's mark, a declaratory judgment that designer's activities did not violate any trademark laws, and damages. The district court granted in part plaintiff's motion for summary judgment, entered a declaratory judgment of noninfringement, and dismissed defendant's counterclaims. This court affirmed, holding that defendant failed to raise a genuine issue of material fact that its mark was legally protectable. Citing Restatement Third of Unfair Competition § 13, Comment *d*, the court considered defendant's use of the design mark and the manner in which defendant's design mark was used, and determined that defendant's design was not inherently distinctive because it was substantially similar to the well-known and traditional bead dog of Mardi Gras. Nola Spice Designs, L.L.C. v. Haydel Enterprises, Inc., 783 F.3d 527, 541, 542.

C.A.5, 2010. Quot. in sup. and in ftn., subsec. (a) quot. in ftn., com. (a) quot. in sup., com. (d) quot. in sup. and in ftn. Self-storage business sued competitor and construction company that built facilities for business and competitor, alleging, among other things, infringement of a design consisting of a raised five-pointed star set within a circle that it claimed as a service mark. The district court granted summary judgment for defendants. This court affirmed the district court's conclusion that the design was not legally protectable as a mark, holding, among other things, that the design was not inherently distinctive; the record was replete with similar or identical five-pointed stars, both raised and set in circles, and used in similar manners, such that no reasonable jury could find that plaintiff's design was even a mere refinement of this commonly adopted and well-known form of ornamentation. Amazing Spaces, Inc. v. Metro Mini Storage, 608 F.3d 225, 237, 241, 243, 245, 246.

C.A.5, 1999. Cit. in disc. Plaintiff, as assignee of registered service mark "SUGAR-BUSTERS" and author of best-selling diet book entitled "SUGAR BUSTERS! Cut Sugar to Trim Fat," sued authors and publisher of cookbook entitled "SUGAR BUST For Life!," asserting, in part, a claim for unfair competition under the Lanham Act. Vacating the district court's grant of plaintiff's motion for a preliminary injunction, this court remanded for a determination of whether plaintiff's book title had obtained secondary meaning by the time defendants' book was published and, if so, whether defendants' book title was likely to confuse or mislead consumers. Sugar Busters LLC v. Brennan, 177 F.3d 258, 268.

C.A.5, 1998. Coms. (c) and (e) cit. in disc. Golf course operator sued competitor for trademark infringement, alleging that defendant infringed and diluted plaintiff's mark by copying one of its holes. The district court entered judgment for plaintiff. Affirming, this court held, in part, that the design of plaintiff's hole was nonfunctional, under a test for either utilitarian or aesthetic functionality; that the design was descriptive and had acquired secondary meaning, as evidenced by plaintiff's extensive advertising, unsolicited publicity of the hole's trade dress in golf publications, and defendant's intent to copy and use the trade dress prominently in its own advertising; that plaintiff did not abandon its rights in a nearby lighthouse that was built at the same time as the golf course for purposes of being seen from the course; that the evidence supported the lower court's finding of a likelihood of confusion; and that defendant's use of the mark to suggest affiliation, sponsorship, or endorsement was more than nominative. Pebble Beach Co. v. Tour 18 I Ltd., 155 F.3d 526, 541, 546.

C.A.5, 1997. Com. (e) cit. in disc. A manufacturer sued for injunctive relief to bar a competitor from manufacturing and marketing a stand mixer, alleging that defendant unlawfully replicated plaintiff's mixer's product configuration. Affirming the district court's entry of a preliminary injunction in favor of plaintiff, this court held, inter alia, that, assuming arguendo that the unique product configuration of plaintiff's mixer could not be deemed inherently distinctive, the district could did not err in concluding that it had acquired secondary meaning, for purposes of a preliminary injunction. The court stated that, although plaintiff's evidence of the product's long and distinguished pedigree and the facts that the mixer had not changed in over 17 years and that no other mixers on the market resembled it were not conclusive, plaintiff had demonstrated a substantial likelihood of success on the merits. Sunbeam Products, Inc. v. West Bend Co., 123 F.3d 246, 253, cert. denied 523 U.S. 1118, 118 S.Ct. 1795, 140 L.Ed.2d 936 (1998).

C.A.10, 2016. Com. (d) quot. in sup. Manufacturer of retail metalworking parts and accessories brought a trademark-infringement action against competitor, alleging that defendant infringed on plaintiff's protected packaging—which used a combination of red, yellow, black, and white coloration—by packing its products using similar colors and a flame motif. The district court granted summary judgment for defendant. Affirming, this court held that plaintiff's use of color, which was not associated with any particular shape, pattern, or design, was not adequately designed to be inherently distinctive, and plaintiff failed to produce sufficient evidence that its use of color had acquired secondary meaning, such that the relevant public understood those colors to identify plaintiff as the source, as required to state a claim under Restatement Third of Unfair Competition § 13. Forney Industries, Inc. v. Daco of Missouri, Inc., 835 F.3d 1238, 1250.

C.A.10, 2008. Com. (e) cit. in diss. op. Ski resort that had a registered incontestable service mark in a geographically descriptive term, "Vail," that it used in conjunction with a purely descriptive term, "Ski," sued marketing service that had a registered service mark in the alphanumeric telephone number "1-800-SKI-VAIL," alleging infringement under the Lanham Act. After a bench trial, the district court concluded that plaintiff failed to show a likelihood of confusion between the two marks. Affirming, this court held, inter alia, that defendant's mark traded on "Vail" as a geographic ski destination, rather than as a mark identifying plaintiff or its resort. The dissent argued that the court erred in concluding that "Vail" was a weak mark, noting that a geographically descriptive

Cit.—cited; com.—comment; fol.—followed; sup.—support.
A complete list of abbreviations precedes page 1.

term acquired secondary meaning when prospective purchasers came to associate the term with a particular source. Vail Associates, Inc. v. Vend-Tel-Co., Ltd., 516 F.3d 853, 883.

C.A.Fed.2018. Com. (a) cit. in disc. Shoe manufacturer filed a complaint with the International Trade Commission (ITC), alleging that various competitors had infringed upon plaintiff's trademark by copying particular design elements constituting plaintiff's trademark. The ITC's administrative law judge found that plaintiff's trademark was valid but did not have a secondary meaning. The ITC reversed, finding that the trademark's lack of secondary meaning rendered it invalid. This court reversed and remanded, holding, inter alia, that plaintiff's trademark registration was not several distinct sets of rights arising from two kinds of marks as the ITC asserted, but rather a single mark that gave rise to several sets of rights. Citing Restatement Third of Unfair Competition § 13, Comment *a*, the court explained that, by establishing that its trademark was registered under the Lanham Act, plaintiff created a rebuttable presumption that the mark was distinctive and had secondary meaning. Converse, Inc. v. International Trade Commission Skechers U.S.A., Inc., 909 F.3d 1110, 1117.

E.D.Ark.2005. Com. (c) cit. in disc. Automobile-parts seller sued for declaratory judgment that its statements that it had "MQVP parts available" did not infringe on service mark of MQPV, an aftermarket parts monitoring program. Defendant counterclaimed for false designation and trademark infringement. This court granted plaintiff summary judgment on the counterclaim, holding, inter alia, that, although defendant's mark was not descriptive and thus could be protected whether or not it had acquired secondary meaning, plaintiff did not engage in false advertising and its use of the mark was not infringing, since plaintiff's statements created no likelihood of confusion among defendant's customers or potential customers. Mid-State Aftermarket Body Parts, Inc. v. MQVP, Inc., 361 F.Supp.2d 896, 905, reversed and remanded 466 F.3d 630 (8th Cir.2006).

W.D.Ark.1996. Coms. (a) and (e) cit. in disc.; cit. in case quot. in disc. (citing § 13 of T.D. No. 2, 1990, which is now § 13 of the Official Text). A producer of single-barb plastic fittings to connect tubing and piping sued a competitor, seeking a declaration of invalidity of certain of competitor's trademarks and trade dress. This court entered judgment for plaintiff, holding that the barb design and the slogan were not valid trademarks and were not entitled to protection under any provision of the federal trademark laws. In rejecting plaintiff's trade-dress claim, the court determined that the product designs were functional, that the designs were not inherently distinctive, and that the designs did not acquire distinctiveness through secondary meaning. Customer testimony indicated that customers could not make small distinctions among barb designs, and there was no proof of actual confusion at the point of sale. Regarding the trademark claims, plaintiff's slogan "INSTRUMENT QUALITY" was a descriptive phrase and not inherently distinctive, and it had not acquired distinctiveness through secondary meaning. Ark Plas Products, Inc. v. Value Plastics, Inc., 913 F.Supp. 1246, 1252, 1254, 1256.

D.Idaho, 1995. Cit. in case quot. in disc., com. (a) cit. in case quot. in disc. (citing § 13 of T.D. No. 2, 1990, which is now § 13 of the Official Text). Environmental organization, Committee for Idaho's High Desert, which unknowingly forfeited its corporate status, sought injunction under the Lanham Act to prevent second organization from incorporating and doing business as Committee for Idaho's High Desert, Inc. As defendant's views on the disposition of public land and resources were completely antithetical to plaintiff's, plaintiff alleged that defendant chose to incorporate under plaintiff's name for the purpose of harming it and defeating its environmental agenda. Entering judgment for plaintiff and enjoining defendant from using the name, the court held that plaintiff was entitled to protection because even though "Idaho's High Desert" was arguably geographically descriptive, it ceased to be once it was placed after the words "Committee for." Furthermore, the name had become distinctive through secondary meaning thanks to plaintiff's extensive advertising and exclusive use of the mark over 15 years. Committee for Idaho's High Desert v. Yost, 881 F.Supp. 1457, 1473, affirmed in part, reversed in part 92 F.3d 814 (9th Cir.1996).

E.D.La.2018. Com. (e) quot. in disc. After limited-liability company brought a petition seeking a declaratory judgment that

For earlier citations, see the Appendices, Supplements, or Pocket Parts, if any, that correspond to the subject matter under examination.

the registration of a service mark for its food hall was proper, city and landlord sought an injunction against limited-liability company and others, alleging, inter alia, that defendants were impermissibly using a trademark that city had previously attempted to register. This court granted plaintiffs' motion for a preliminary injunction, holding that it was substantially likely that plaintiffs would be able to establish secondary meaning for their mark in city's geographic area and successfully sue on the merits for trademark infringement. The court cited Restatement Third of Unfair Competition § 13, Comment *e*, in explaining that defendants and prospective customers of plaintiffs understood that the mark was heavily associated with plaintiffs' businesses in city's geographic area. Helpful Hound, L.L.C. v. New Orleans Building Corporation, 331 F.Supp.3d 581, 594.

E.D.La.2011. Sec. and com. (a) cit. in case cit. in disc. Sellers of ice-shaving machines and flavoring concentrates brought, inter alia, an unfair competition/false advertising claim under the Lanham Act against competitor. This court granted partial summary judgment for defendant, holding that plaintiffs had no claim for unfair competition insofar as they relied on the legal assertion that defendant's use of the trademarking symbols TM and (r) with certain generic product names constituted a literally false statement of fact. The court found that defendant's use of the (r) symbol with its ice-flavor marks for which it had obtained registration through the U.S. Patent and Trademark Office did not constitute a literally false statement, and subsequent loss of registration for those marks did not retroactively turn the use of the (r) symbol into such a statement. The court further concluded that, by using a TM, defendant stated that it was claiming rights to the flavor name as a trademark, not that it had trademark rights in the name or that it could meet its burden of proof as to secondary meaning. Southern Snow Mfg. Co. v. Snow Wizard Holdings, Inc., 829 F.Supp.2d 437, 449.

D.Md.1995. Com. (e) quot. in case quot. in sup. (citing § 13 of T.D. No. 2, 1990, which is now § 13 of the Official Text). Voluntary association of realtors brought an action for unfair competition, inter alia, against photographic service that used association's database of real estate listings to provide association members with photographs of real estate, alleging that defendant used plaintiff's trademarks in a way that was likely to confuse the public. Denying both parties' motions for summary judgment on the issue of defendant's use of plaintiff's marks "the Association," "the Board," "MCBR," and "MCAR," the court found that there was a genuine issue of material fact as to whether a likelihood of confusion existed regarding defendant's use of the marks. The court said that the weakness of plaintiff's marks weighed against a likelihood of confusion, since the marks were not inherently distinctive and there was no proof that the marks had acquired a secondary meaning that would make them distinctive. Montgomery County Ass'n of Realtors, Inc. v. Realty Photo Master Corp., 878 F.Supp. 804, 812.

D.Mass.2000. Com. (e) cit. in disc. Bathroom-faucet manufacturer sued competitor for trade-dress infringement and trade-dress dilution. District court granted manufacturer injunction on issue of dilution. Appellate court vacated and remanded. On remand, this court granted competitor's motion for summary judgment, holding, inter alia, that plaintiff's claim for trade-dress protection failed, because the functional elements of the manufacturer's faucet design had not acquired a secondary meaning, i.e., the public did not associate the trade-dress with the plaintiff. I.P. Lund Trading v. Kohler Co., 118 F.Supp.2d 92, 110.

D.Mass.2000. Com. (e) quot. in disc. Candle manufacturer sued competitor for, inter alia, trade-dress infringement. Entering partial summary judgment for defendant, the court held, among other things, that plaintiff's product was not inherently distinctive, nor had it acquired secondary meaning such that it was uniquely associated with a particular source; therefore, the claim for trade-dress infringement failed. Yankee Candle Co., Inc. v. Bridgewater Candle Co., LLC, 99 F.Supp.2d 140, 152, 153.

E.D.Mich.1998. Subsec. (a) and com. (e) cit. in headnote and quot. in part in disc. Manufacturer of a lounge chair and ottoman sued a competitor under the Lanham Act, claiming that the distinctive shape and design of its furniture were protected trade dress that defendant infringed by copying and marketing replicas. Granting defendant's motion for summary judgment, the court held, inter alia, that the design of

Cit.—cited; com.—comment; fol.—followed; sup.—support.
A complete list of abbreviations precedes page 1.

plaintiff's lounge chair and ottoman was not protectable trade dress. The court said that plaintiff failed to establish that the trade dress was inherently distinctive or that it had acquired secondary meaning. Herman Miller, Inc. v. Palazzetti Imports, 998 F.Supp. 757, 758, 759, 761, affirmed in part, reversed in part 270 F.3d 298 (6th Cir. 2001).

D.Neb.2015. Com. (e) quot. in sup. Seller of welding rods brought a trademark-infringement claim against former employee of seller's predecessor in connection with defendant's use of plaintiff's "LaGrange" mark, which was based on the name of plaintiff's founder, to sell welding rods in competition with plaintiff. This court granted summary judgment for plaintiff on its trademark-infringement claim, holding that there was no genuine dispute of fact that plaintiff's mark had acquired secondary meaning before defendant began using it. The court reasoned, in part, that, under Restatement Third of Unfair Competition § 13, personal names, while presumably descriptive, were frequently adopted as trademarks and readily recognized as such by consumers, and thus required less evidence than generic or distinctive marks to show that the mark had acquired secondary meaning. JDR Industries, Inc. v. McDowell, 121 F.Supp.3d 872, 888.

D.N.J.2002. Cit. in disc. Manufacturer of prescription medication "Xalatan" for treatment of glaucoma brought suit for trademark infringement and dilution against competitor, seeking to enjoin defendant's use of the trademark "Travatan." Denying plaintiff's motion for a preliminary injunction, this court held, inter alia, that any claim by plaintiff to exclusive rights to the suffix "ATAN" was weak because of the number of other pharmaceutical products that used the suffix and because of the existence of similar marks in the glaucoma market. Pharmacia Corp. v. Alcon Laboratories, Inc., 201 F.Supp.2d 335, 376.

D.N.J.2001. Com. (e) cit. in treatise cit. in disc. Maker of refrigerated cookie-dough products brought suit for infringement of its "BREAK & BAKE" trademark against companies that used similar marks for their presectioned cookie-dough products. Denying plaintiff's motion for a preliminary injunction, the court held, inter alia, that plaintiff was not likely to succeed in demonstrating that the mark had achieved secondary meaning at the time that defendants allegedly began infringing it; thus, it was unlikely that plaintiff would prevail on the merits of its infringement claim. J & J Snack Foods Corp. v. Nestle USA, Inc., 149 F.Supp.2d 136, 152.

E.D.N.Y.2021. Subsec. (a) quot. in case quot. in sup. Supplier of specialty Chinese foods sued competitor, alleging, among other things, trade-dress infringement after competitor developed its own logos and packaging that was identical or substantially indistinguishable from plaintiff's trade dress. This court granted in part defendant's motion to dismiss, holding that, while plaintiff plausibly alleged that its trade dress was inherently distinctive, it failed to demonstrate that it had a valid trade dress mark that was entitled to protection. The court cited Restatement Third of Unfair Competition § 13 in explaining that an inherently distinctive trade dress was one that was likely to serve primarily as a designator of origin of the product, taking into account the nature of the designation and the context in which it was used. Shandong Shinho Food Industries Co., Ltd. v. May Flower International, Inc., 521 F.Supp.3d 222, 257.

S.D.N.Y.1999. Quot. in disc. Stock exchange sued casino for, inter alia, trademark dilution and tarnishment in connection with defendant's use of a parody of plaintiff's trade name in defendant's stock-exchange-themed resort. Entering summary judgment for defendant, the court held, in part, that plaintiff's mark, which consisted of its name and a picture of the façade of its building, was not distinctive for purposes of trademark dilution, and that plaintiff had failed to show that the positive connotations associated with its mark were likely to be replaced by negative associations as a result of defendant's use. New York Stock Exc. v. New York, New York Hotel, 69 F.Supp.2d 479, 489.

S.D.N.Y.1996. Subsec. (a) quot. in case quot. in disc. Manufacturer of office and industrial furniture sued competitor for infringement of the trade dress of plaintiff's metal-frame stacking chair. Denying plaintiff's motion for a preliminary injunction, the court held that, although plaintiff had a protectable trade dress in the overall look of its stacking chair, plaintiff's six-to-nine-month delay in bringing this action precluded preliminary injunctive relief. The court found that the overall look of plaintiff's chair was inherently distinctive and

For earlier citations, see the Appendices, Supplements, or Pocket Parts, if any, that correspond to the subject matter under examination.

that plaintiff showed a likelihood of confusion, but not such an overwhelming likelihood that a preliminary injunction was justified in light of its delay in bringing this action. Krueger Intern., Inc. v. Nightingale Inc., 915 F.Supp. 595, 604.

N.D.Ohio, 2019. Com. (d) quot. in sup. Candy producer brought a lawsuit against competitor, alleging that defendant infringed upon the trade dress of plaintiff's candy package. This court granted plaintiff's motion for preliminary injunction, holding, inter alia, that plaintiff demonstrated that its claim was likely to succeed on the merits, because plaintiff's package design had acquired secondary meaning. The court quoted Restatement Third of Unfair Competition § 13, Comment *d,* in noting that plaintiff's design, which featured a red bag with white brand lettering and a display window, was not inherently distinctive, because the design only used commonplace symbols that did not themselves differentiate plaintiff's product from its competitors' products. Spangler Candy Company v. Tootsie Roll Industries, LLC, 372 F.Supp.3d 588, 601.

S.D.Ohio, 1993. Cit. in sup. (citing § 13 of T.D. No. 2, 1990, which is now § 13 of the Official Text). Women's apparel retailer sued department store chain and clothing manufacturer, alleging infringement of its trademark, "EXPRESS." Denying defendants' motions for summary judgment, the court held, inter alia, that genuine issues of material fact existed concerning the likelihood of confusion. The court stated that, in view of plaintiff's evidence that its mark appeared to occupy a significant presence in the retail marketplace, a fact issue existed regarding the mark's strength. Express, Inc. v. Sears, Roebuck & Co., 840 F.Supp. 502, 507.

E.D.Pa.2016. Com. (e) quot. in sup. Owner of the trademark "Parks" used to sell sausages and other food products sued owner of the trademark "Ball Park" used to sell frankfurters, alleging that defendant infringed on plaintiff's trademark when it launched a new line of premium frankfurters under the name "Park's Finest." Granting summary judgment for defendant, this court held, among other things, that plaintiff's survey, which detected a consumer confusion rate of 32.7%, did not constitute evidence of secondary meaning. Although proof of actual consumer confusion caused by another's use of a designation was evidence of secondary meaning under Restatement Third of Unfair Competition § 13, whether a likelihood of confusion detected by a survey was probative of secondary meaning depended on the format of the survey, and plaintiff's survey, which presented participants with images of each party's products and asked them if they perceived any connection or affiliation between any of the images, generated a rate of confusion that was not necessarily correlated to secondary meaning. Parks, LLC v. Tyson Foods, Inc., 186 F.Supp.3d 405, 425.

W.D.Pa.1993. Com. (e) quot. in disc. (citing § 13 of T.D. No. 2, 1990, which is now § 13 of the Official Text). Delaware manufacturer of plastic urn-like planters sued its competitors in the planter market, alleging trade-dress infringement and false advertising under the Lanham Act. Plaintiff moved for a preliminary injunction, seeking to enjoin defendants from any further marketing and sales of its Grecian-style plastic planters. The court refused to grant a preliminary injunction, holding, inter alia, that the likelihood of success on the merits was slim because plaintiff's product was generic and, thus, was unentitled to protection. The court stated that, even if the product was descriptive, plaintiff failed to prove that the urn planter had secondary meaning because there was no evidence that consumers perceived that the product emanated from a single source, or that the public identified plaintiff's planter with plaintiff's name. Duraco Products v. Joy Plastic Enterprises, 822 F.Supp. 1202, 1209, affirmed 40 F.3d 1431 (3d Cir.1994).

N.D.Tex.2022. Com. (d) cit. in sup. Bar that owned a registered trademark for a logo—consisting of two crossed revolvers outlined in black with a red star on each handle—filed an infringement action against clothing store that used a similar mark; defendant counterclaimed, alleging that it was the first to use the mark in commerce. This court granted defendant's motion for a preliminary injunction to stop plaintiff from using the mark, holding, among other things, that defendant was substantially likely to prevail in showing that the mark was protectable. The court cited Restatement Third of Unfair Competition § 13 in reasoning that, while a star lacked inherent distinctiveness such that a viewer would immediately recognize it as an indicator of origin, defendant's mark

Cit.—cited; com.—comment; fol.—followed; sup.—support.
A complete list of abbreviations precedes page 1.

incorporating stars was distinctive even without a showing of secondary meaning. Savage Tavern, Inc. v. Signature Stag, LLC, 589 F.Supp.3d 624, 642.

S.D.Tex.2017. Com. (d) quot. in case quot. in sup. Companies that delivered, serviced, and removed on-site portable toilets, dumpster units, and restroom trailers brought an action against competitor, alleging trademark-infringement and trademark-dilution claims based on defendant's name, logo, and colors of its portable toilets. This court denied defendant's motion for summary judgment, finding that plaintiff's mark was protectable and there was a genuine issue of material fact as to whether there was confusion between the marks. The court quoted Restatement Third of Unfair Competition § 13, Comment *d*, to explain that unless the symbol or design was striking, unusual, or otherwise likely to differentiate the products of a particular producer, the designation was not inherently distinctive; and the court reasoned that, here, plaintiff's mark was registered with the U.S. Patent and Trademark Office and was inherently distinctive. Texas Outhouse Inc. v. Fresh Can, LLC, 266 F.Supp.3d 928, 934.

S.D.Tex.2009. Com. (c) cit. in sup. Self-storage-services provider that used a logo consisting of a raised, five-pointed star set within a circle brought trademark-infringement and other claims against competitor that used a similar logo. Granting summary judgment for defendant, this court held, as a matter of law, that plaintiff's logo was not entitled to trademark protection, despite the fact that plaintiff had spent $723,138.75 advertising and promoting the logo for over 10 years. The court noted that substantial spending on advertising did not itself cause a mark to acquire secondary meaning, and there was no basis to conclude that plaintiff's 10-year use or spending on advertising had caused the public to think of plaintiff when they saw the logo. Amazing Spaces, Inc. v. Metro Mini Storage, 665 F.Supp.2d 727, 740.

S.D.Tex.2005. Com. (e) cit. in case cit. in disc. Former husband sued former wife, who produced and sold western jewelry in competition with former husband following their divorce, for various claims, including trade-dress infringement. This court held, among other things, that former husband failed to establish a protectible trade dress. Noting that in a product-design trade-dress case, the product design had to be shown to have acquired secondary meaning through empirical evidence, the court concluded that, based on the evidence presented at trial and the nature of the product and market, former husband failed to show that the asserted trade dress had inherent distinctiveness or had acquired secondary meaning, as most of the features of the asserted trade dress were design elements used by many producers of western jewelry. Berg v. Symons, 393 F.Supp.2d 525, 550.

S.D.Tex.1999. Com. (c) quot. in case quot. in disc. Publishers filed a declaratory-judgment action against a supplier of expensive clothes and furnishings, seeking a determination of their right to use "POLO" as a magazine title. Supplier counterclaimed for trademark infringement and dilution under the Lanham Act, and for unfair competition and injury to business reputation under state law. After balancing the interests of all concerned, this court ordered full injunctive relief for supplier, holding, inter alia, that the strength-of-the-mark analysis weighed in supplier's favor, because supplier had established trademarks in the fashion industry that were both famous and distinctive when associated with various items of men's and women's apparel, fashion accessories, fragrances, and home furnishings. Westchester Media Co. v. PRL USA Holdings, Inc., 103 F.Supp.2d 935, 947, affirmed in part, vacated in part 214 F.3d 658 (5th Cir.2000).

W.D.Wis.2017. Com. (e) quot. in disc. Information-technology company that sold electronic healthcare-record systems to large healthcare organizations brought an action against healthcare-management software provider and parent companies that maintained a health-and-wellness website associated with their own electronic healthcare-record system, alleging infringement of trademark used for plaintiff's interoperability application that resulted in customer confusion and unfair competition. This court granted defendants' motion for summary judgment, holding that there was no evidence that defendants' use of the mark caused actual confusion or a likelihood of confusion, or that defendants intended to confuse prospective customers, and there was little evidence that plaintiff's mark was strong, inherently or through development of secondary meaning. The court cited Restatement Third of Unfair Competition § 13, Comment *e*, in noting that prospective-customer surveys showing the strength of a mark could be particularly persuasive evidence but plaintiff did not produce such evidence. Epic Systems Corporation v. YourCareUniverse, Inc., 244 F.Supp.3d 878, 898.

Alaska, 2001. Com. (e) cit. in ftn. Theater owner sued operator of trolley tour service named "Fourth Avenue Theater Trolley Tours" for infringement of its trade name "Fourth Avenue Theatre." The trial court entered judgment on a jury verdict for plaintiff. Affirming in part, this court held, inter alia, that defendants infringed plaintiff's trade name. The court said that "Fourth Avenue Theatre" had acquired a secondary meaning prior to its use by defendants, and that the jury's finding of a likelihood of confusion was supported by the evidence. Alderman v. Iditarod Properties, Inc., 32 P.3d 373, 387.

Fla.1993. Cit. in ftn. as §§ 13-15, com. (b) cit. in ftn., com. (c) cit. and quot. in ftn. (citing § 13 of T.D. No. 2, 1990, which is now § 13 of the Official Text). The First Southern Bank sued to enjoin another bank from using the name "Great Southern Bank," alleging infringement and dilution of its trademark name and unfair competition. The trial court granted plaintiff injunctive relief and certified the question whether plaintiff bank's name was descriptive or generic so as not to be entitled to protection in the absence of proof that it had acquired a secondary meaning. This court remanded, holding that plaintiff bank's name contained laudatory, generic, and merely geographically descriptive elements so as not to be entitled to protection under either common or statutory law, but determination was necessary whether a secondary meaning in the name had developed in order to decide the dilution claim. In applying the suggestiveness test, the court stated that no great imagination was required to identify the product as banking services when the mark contained the word "bank," that many others used the word "southern" in their mark, and that businesses in the South had the need and right to use the term descriptively. Great Southern v. First Southern, 625 So.2d 463, 467-469.

Fla.App.2001. Com. (c) quot. in case quot. in disc., com. (e) cit. in disc. Homeowners' association brought suit to enjoin infringement and dilution of its trade name/service mark by real estate company. The trial court denied relief. Reversing and remanding, this court held that plaintiff's "Tortoise Island" name was arbitrary and distinctive, and that defendant's use of the name was likely to cause confusion on the part of the public, inviting the suggestion that defendant was sponsored by, approved by, or affiliated in some way with plaintiff's subdivision. The court also held that defendant's use of the name diluted the name's distinctive quality. Tortoise Island Homeowners Ass'n, Inc. v. Tortoise Island Realty, Inc., 790 So.2d 525, 530, 531.

Ind.2006. Com. (a) cit. in disc. In a dispute between two law firms that had been established by two unrelated families with the same last name, who operated the firms under nearly identical names, older law firm sued newer law firm for unfair competition. The trial court granted summary judgment for defendant and the court of appeals affirmed. Affirming, this court held, inter alia, that summary judgment was proper on plaintiff's claim of trade-name infringement because plaintiff failed to demonstrate that its name had secondary meaning. The court reasoned that, while "distinctive" personal names or surnames were protectable as trade names, such names were not "inherently distinctive" and thus were only protectable as trade names if the person claiming rights in the name proved that the name had come to be uniquely associated with the person's particular business through use, which was not shown here. Keaton and Keaton v. Keaton, 842 N.E.2d 816, 821.

Iowa, 2008. Coms. (c) and (e) cit. and quot. in sup. National bank brought action for trademark infringement against local bank, seeking, among other things, an injunction preventing defendant from using the name "Community State Bank." The trial court ruled in favor of plaintiff. The court of appeals reversed. Vacating the court of appeals and affirming the trial court, this court held, inter alia, that plaintiff had a valid common-law trademark in the name. The court reasoned, in part, that, while the name was descriptive, it had acquired the secondary meaning necessary to render it protectible; plaintiff had used the name continuously and exclusively for 12 years, plaintiff had spent significant amounts on advertising and had a substantially larger percentage of the market share in defendant's area, and surveys indicated that consumers considered the name a

Cit.—cited; com.—comment; fol.—followed; sup.—support.
A complete list of abbreviations precedes page 1.

brand indicating a source or type. Community State Bank, Nat. Ass'n v. Community State Bank, 758 N.W.2d 520, 525.

Iowa, 1999. Subsec. (b), coms. (a) and (e) cit. in sup., com. (c) cit. in ftn. Bank operating under the name "Commercial Savings Bank" brought trademark infringement action against financial institution calling itself "Commercial Federal Bank." The trial court entered judgment for defendant on the ground that plaintiff had failed to establish the existence of a common-law trademark in "commercial." Affirming, this court held that "commercial" was a descriptive term that had become distinctive through secondary use; however, plaintiff could not show that defendant's use of the term was likely to cause consumer confusion. Commercial Sav. v. Hawkeye Federal Sav., 592 N.W.2d 321, 328, 329, 331.

La.1995. Cit. in headnote and disc.; coms. (a) and (e) cit. in disc.; cit. in disc. and headnote as §§ 13-15; cit. in disc. as §§ 13-14. The Gulf Coast Bank sued the Gulf Coast Bank and Trust Company for trade name infringement, alleging that defendant's corporate name was deceptively similar to plaintiff's in violation of Louisiana's Trademark Act. Trial court granted defendant summary judgment and intermediate appellate court affirmed. This court reversed and remanded, holding that one need not prove fraud to enjoin another from using its trade name, but must show that there is a likelihood of consumer confusion created by defendant's use of the trade name. On remand, the court stated that plaintiff must establish secondary meaning since the name "Gulf Coast Bank" was not inherently distinctive. The word "Bank" was required to be in every bank's name and thus appeared to be a generic term, and the term "Gulf Coast" was geographic, denoting the general geographic area in which this bank operated. Gulf Coast Bank v. Gulf Coast Bank & Trust Co., 652 So.2d 1306, 1307, 1313, 1314, 1318.

La.App.2006. Cit. in disc., com. (e) cit. in disc.; cit. in disc. §§ 13-14. After brother, who was essentially fired from his family jewelry business, opened a competing business with a similar name, family jewelry business sued brother and competing business, seeking, in part, to enjoin defendants from using its registered trade names, which included the family name in conjunction with the words "jewelers," "jewelry," and "diamonds." The trial court rendered judgment in favor of defendant. Reversing in part, this court held, inter alia, that plaintiff's registered trade names had acquired secondary meaning and were entitled to trade-name protection, but that defendant had sufficiently distinguished competing business by including both his first name and his surname in its trade name. Ramsey's Mfg. Jewelers, Inc. v. Ramsey, 924 So.2d 1045, 1051, writ denied 930 So.2d 26 (La.2006).

La.App.2004. Cit. in sup., cit. in sup. §§ 13-15 and 13-14, coms. (a) and (e) cit. in sup. Shoe store sought injunction against national shoe retailer to prevent national retailer from using word "shoetique," which store had registered as trade name. Trial court granted national retailer summary judgment. Reversing and remanding, this court held that genuine issue of material fact as to whether the descriptive term "shoetique" had taken on a secondary meaning and therefore acquired a protectable proprietary character precluded summary judgment. McCain v. Designer Shoes Warehouse, LLC, 864 So.2d 784, 787, 788.

R.I.2002. Quot. in sup. Lumber company sought injunctive relief to prevent competitor from using similar fictitious name. The trial court granted plaintiff permanent injunctive relief. Affirming, this court held that plaintiff was entitled to permanent injunctive relief preventing competitor from using deceptively similar trade name where plaintiff's trade name, while not inherently distinctive, had acquired secondary meaning through 40 years of continuous use. National Lumber & Building Materials Co. v. Langevin, 798 A.2d 429, 433.

Vt.2002. Com. (e) quot. in ftn. Owners of advertisement-based newspaper sued former operators of paper for conversion and unfair competition, alleging misappropriation of business assets. The trial court entered judgment on jury verdict for owners. Modifying conversion award and affirming, this court held, inter alia, that evidence that former operators took business assets such as customer lists, bookkeeping records, and office equipment supported unfair-competition claim based on misappropriation. Maguire v. Gorruso, 174 Vt. 1, 800 A.2d 1085, 1088.

Wis.App.1996. Cit. in headnotes, cit. generally in ftn., subsecs. (a) and (b) cit. in disc., coms. (a), (b), and (e) cit. in disc., com. (c) cit. in ftn. Company in the business of providing reprographic copying services to architects, engineers, publishers, and others sued competitor for trademark infringement. Following a bench trial, the trial court dismissed the complaint on the ground that there was insufficient likelihood of confusion between the parties' marks. Affirming, this court held, inter alia, that company's mark, which could also be considered a service mark, was a weak descriptive designation combining a geographical name with a shortened version of the term "reprographics"; that company's mark did not become strong or distinctive through secondary meaning; and that the minimal similarity of the two marks, as well as the sophistication of the parties' typical customers, supported the lower court's finding that there was no likelihood of confusion. Madison Reprographics v. Cook's Reprographics, 203 Wis.2d 226, 552 N.W.2d 440, 441, 442, 444, 445, 448.

§ 14. Descriptive, Geographic, and Personal Name Designations

C.A.7, 2004. Com. (e) cit. in disc. Plush-toy manufacturer that began selling a camel named "Niles" in 1999 sued a competitor that began selling a camel also named "Niles" in 2000, alleging trademark infringement, product disparagement, and false advertising. District court dismissed plaintiff's claims. This court reversed in part and remanded, holding, inter alia, that plaintiff had a valid trademark in the name "Niles" as applied to its camel. The court said that treating the personal-name rule as a prohibition against ever using a personal name as a trademark, in the absence of secondary meaning, would lead to absurd results. Peaceable Planet, Inc. v. Ty, Inc., 362 F.3d 986, 989.

C.A.10, 2008. Com. (d) quot. in sup. Ski resort that had a registered incontestable service mark in a geographically descriptive term, "Vail," that it used in conjunction with a purely descriptive term, "Ski," sued marketing service that had a registered service mark in the alphanumeric telephone number "1-800-SKI-VAIL," alleging infringement under the Lanham Act. After a bench trial, the district court concluded that plaintiff failed to show a likelihood of confusion between the two marks. Affirming, this court held, inter alia, that defendant's mark traded on "Vail" as a geographic ski destination, rather than as a mark identifying plaintiff or its resort, and noted the proposition that merchants had to be free to indicate their place of business or the origin of their goods or services without unnecessary risk of infringement. Vail Associates, Inc. v. Vend-Tel-Co., Ltd., 516 F.3d 853, 868.

C.A.Fed.2009. Com. (c) cit. in sup. Trademark applicant sought to register its mark—MOSKOVSKAYA—for vodka. The Trademark Trial and Appeal Board (Board) affirmed the refusal of the U.S. Patent and Trademark Office (PTO) to register the mark, concluding that it was primarily geographically deceptively misdescriptive of the goods. Vacating, this court held that the appropriate inquiry for materiality purposes was whether a substantial portion of the relevant consumers was likely to be deceived, not whether any absolute number or particular segment of the relevant consumers (such as foreign-language speakers) was likely to be deceived, and remanded to the Board for a determination of whether there was a prima facie case of material deception under the correct legal test. In re Spirits Intern., N.V., 563 F.3d 1347, 1355.

E.D.Ark.2005. Cit. in disc., com. (a) quot. in disc. Automobile-parts seller sued for declaratory judgment that its statements that it had "MQVP parts available" did not infringe on service mark of MQPV, an aftermarket parts monitoring program. Defendant counterclaimed for false designation and trademark infringement. This court granted plaintiff summary judgment on the counterclaim, holding, inter alia, that, although defendant's mark was not descriptive and thus could be protected whether or not it had acquired secondary meaning, plaintiff did not engage in false advertising and its use of the mark was not infringing, since plaintiff's statements created no likelihood of confusion among defendant's customers or potential customers. Mid-State Aftermarket Body Parts, Inc. v. MQVP, Inc., 361 F.Supp.2d 896, 905, reversed and remanded 466 F.3d 630 (8th Cir.2006).

W.D.Ark.1995. Com. (a) and Rptr's Note to com. (a) cit. in disc. Insurer sought declaration as to whether it was obligated to defend its insured, a knife manufacturer, against charges that it infringed another manufacturer's trademark. Insurer moved for summary judgment on the ground that suits for trademark infringement were excluded from the policy providing a duty

Cit.—cited; com.—comment; fol.—followed; sup.—support.
A complete list of abbreviations precedes page 1.

to defend actions based on advertising injury. Denying the motion, the court held that trademark infringement, which arose solely from the unauthorized use of another's mark, was, along with infringement of copyright, title, or slogan, an advertising injury against which insurer had a duty to defend. Union Ins. v. The Knife Co., Inc., 897 F.Supp. 1213, 1217.

C.D.Cal.1998. Com. (e) cit. in ftn. (citing § 14 of T.D. No. 2, 1990, which is now § 14 of the Official Text). (Erron. cit. as com. 3.) Executors of the estate of Diana, Princess of Wales, as well as trustees of her memorial fund, brought trademark-dilution action against company that began producing and marketing commemorative items exploiting decedent's name and likeness. Defendant moved to dismiss. Granting the motion in part and denying it in part, the court held, inter alia, that, because of decedent's renown, it might not be possible for her name to acquire secondary meaning, and that plaintiffs had stated a claim for trademark dilution where they alleged that their marks, "Diana, Princess of Wales" and "Diana, Princess of Wales Memorial Fund," were famous, that defendant was using the marks commercially, that defendant's use began after the marks became famous, and that defendant's use diluted the marks' quality. Cairns v. Franklin Mint Co., 24 F.Supp.2d 1013, 1035.

C.D.Cal.1998. Com. (e) quot. in disc. Commercial illustrator brought unfair-competition action against toy manufacturer, alleging that defendant misappropriated and misused plaintiff's "Pearl Beach" trade name in connection with the promotion and distribution of its line of dolls. Specifically, plaintiff argued that defendant's actions resulted in reverse confusion in the marketplace. Entering judgment as a matter of law for defendant, the court held, in part, that, although plaintiff's mark was strong, she failed to establish a proximity of the goods, similarity of the marks, or evidence of actual confusion among purchasers; thus, plaintiff did not prove the type of confusion she was required to set forth in order to prevail under her "reverse confusion" theory. Walter v. Mattel, Inc., 31 F.Supp.2d 751, 759, affirmed 210 F.3d 1108 (9th Cir.2000).

N.D.Cal.1997. Com. (a) quot. in case quot. in disc. (citing § 14 of T.D. No. 2, 1990, which is now § 14 of the Official Text). The creator of a unique form of martial arts named "Kuk Sool Won" brought a trademark-infringement and unfair-competition action against a competitor. This court, among other dispositions, held that fact issues existed as to whether the term "Kuk Sool Won" was generic. However, the term "Kuk Sool" had become generic through public use and was not protected under principals of trademark law. Therefore, plaintiff could not prevent other martial art instructors from using the term "Kuk Sool" to identify instruction of this type of martial art. Suh v. Yang, 987 F.Supp. 783, 791.

D.D.C.2001. Com. (d) quot. in sup. Chilean wine producer that used trademark "Santa Rita" sought a preliminary injunction barring Bureau of Alcohol, Tobacco and Firearms (ATF) from designating Santa Rita Hills area of California as "American viticultural area," and allowing vintners in area to use phrase "Santa Rita Hills" on their labels. The district court denied producer's motion, holding, inter alia, that producer had no geographic interest in area, and therefore could not contest ATF's designation of distinct geographic region. Sociedad Anonima Vina Santa Rita v. U.S. Dept. of Treasury, 193 F.Supp.2d 6, 21.

S.D.Fla.1998. Cit. in disc. "Popular Bank" of Florida brought suit seeking an injunction prohibiting "Banco Popular de Puerto Rico" and "Banco Popular N.A. (Florida)" from using the marks Banco Popular or Popular Express in four counties in Florida. This court granted plaintiffs the preliminary injunction as to the name "Banco Popular," because plaintiff had established the priority and validity of its mark and defendants' use of that mark in South Florida was likely to cause customer confusion. However, the court denied plaintiff's request to enjoin the use of the name "Popular Express," because plaintiff did not demonstrate a likelihood of success on the merits by showing that its rights to the mark were prior and superior to defendants' use of the mark and that the mark was likely to cause consumer confusion. The court determined that, taken as a whole, "Popular Bank of Florida" was a descriptive mark. Popular Bank of Fla. v. Banco Popular de Puerto Rico, 9 F.Supp.2d 1347, 1356.

N.D.Ga.2010. Cit. in ftn. Medical practice that provided services under the name "Atlanta Allergy & Asthma Clinic" sued competitor that provided services under the name "Allergy & Asthma of Atlanta," alleging, among other things, trademark infringement. Denying the parties' cross-motions for summary judgment, this court held that disputed questions of fact remained as to whether plaintiff had a valid and protectable mark. The court explained that, while it was undisputed that plaintiff's mark was geographically descriptive, a descriptive mark was entitled to protection only if it had acquired secondary meaning, and the evidence presented was not conclusive on the question of whether plaintiff's mark had acquired secondary meaning among the consuming public. Atlanta Allergy and Asthma Clinic, P.A v. Allergy & Asthma of Atlanta, LLC, 685 F.Supp.2d 1360, 1367.

D.Idaho, 1995. Com. (d) cit. in disc. (citing § 14 of T.D. No. 2, 1990, which is now § 14 of the Official Text). Environmental organization, Committee for Idaho's High Desert, which unknowingly forfeited its corporate status, sought injunction under the Lanham Act to prevent second organization from incorporating and doing business as Committee for Idaho's High Desert, Inc. As defendant's views on the disposition of public land and resources were completely antithetical to plaintiff's, plaintiff alleged that defendant chose to incorporate under plaintiff's name for the purpose of harming it and defeating its environmental agenda. Entering judgment for plaintiff and enjoining defendant from using the name, the court held that plaintiff was entitled to protection because even though "Idaho's High Desert" was arguably geographically descriptive, it ceased to be once it was placed after the words "Committee for." Furthermore, the name had become distinctive through secondary meaning thanks to plaintiff's extensive advertising and exclusive use of the mark over 15 years. Committee for Idaho's High Desert v. Yost, 881 F.Supp. 1457, 1473, affirmed in part, reversed in part 92 F.3d 814 (9th Cir.1996).

S.D.Tex.2014. Com. (d) quot. in case quot. in sup. Owner of a trademark for "Sarco Creek Ranch," which sold thoroughbred horses from a ranch located next to Sarco Creek, brought claims for trademark infringement and unfair competition against another ranch located approximately 10 miles north on Sarco Creek, which provided hunting services under the same name. This court denied plaintiff's motion for a preliminary injunction, holding that plaintiff was unable to show a likelihood of success on the merits in light of defendant's defense that the trademark was primarily geographically descriptive. The court noted that, under Restatement Third of Unfair Competition § 14, merchants were generally free to indicate their place of business or the origin of their goods without unnecessary risk of infringement, and that an exception for obscure or remote place names that prospective purchasers would typically fail to recognize as indicating a geographic source did not apply, because, although Sarco Creek was a relatively small stream, it was historically significant and well-known to the largely local and niche-market customers targeted by both parties. Sarco Creek Ranch v. Greeson, 36 F.Supp.3d 726, 731.

Alaska, 2001. Com. (e) quot. in ftn. Theater owner sued operator of trolley tour service named "Fourth Avenue Theater Trolley Tours" for infringement of its trade name "Fourth Avenue Theatre." The trial court entered judgment on a jury verdict for plaintiff. Affirming in part, this court held, inter alia, that defendants infringed plaintiff's trade name. The court said that "Fourth Avenue Theatre" had acquired a secondary meaning prior to its use by defendants, and that the jury's finding of a likelihood of confusion was supported by the evidence. Alderman v. Iditarod Properties, Inc., 32 P.3d 373, 385.

Fla.1993. Cit. in ftn. as §§ 13-15; com. (b) cit. in ftn. (citing § 14 of T.D. No. 2, 1990, which is now § 14 of the Official Text). The First Southern Bank sued to enjoin another bank from using the name "Great Southern Bank," alleging infringement and dilution of its trademark name and unfair competition. Trial court granted plaintiff injunctive relief and certified the question whether plaintiff bank's name was descriptive or generic so as not to be entitled to protection in the absence of proof that it had acquired a secondary meaning. This court remanded, holding that plaintiff bank's name contained laudatory, generic, and merely geographically descriptive elements so as not to be entitled to protection under either common or statutory law, but determination was necessary whether a secondary meaning in the name had developed in order to decide the dilution claim. In applying the suggestiveness test, the court stated that no great imagination was

Cit.—cited; com.—comment; fol.—followed; sup.—support.
A complete list of abbreviations precedes page 1.

required to identify the product as banking services when the mark contained the word "bank," that many others used the word "southern" in their mark, and that businesses in the South had the need and right to use the term descriptively. Great Southern v. First Southern, 625 So.2d 463, 468, 469.

Ind.2006. Com. (e) cit. in disc. In a dispute between two law firms that had been established by two unrelated families with the same last name, who operated the firms under nearly identical names, older law firm sued newer law firm for unfair competition. The trial court granted summary judgment for defendant and the court of appeals affirmed. Affirming, this court held, inter alia, that summary judgment was proper on plaintiff's claim of trade-name infringement because plaintiff failed to demonstrate that its name had secondary meaning. The court reasoned that, while "distinctive" personal names or surnames were protectable as trade names, such names were not "inherently distinctive" and thus were only protectable as trade names if the person claiming rights in the name proved that the name had come to be uniquely associated with the person's particular business through use, which was not shown here. Keaton and Keaton v. Keaton, 842 N.E.2d 816, 821.

Ind.App.2013. Cit. in sup. County visitor bureau, which announced at a public meeting that it had selected the phrase "Visit Michigan City LaPorte" as the branding identifier for the area, sued operator of a hotel resort in the county, which registered the Internet domain name "visitmichigancitylaporte.com" immediately after the meeting, alleging trademark infringement, cybersquatting, and unfair competition. After a bench trial, the trial court permanently enjoined defendant from using the phrase or the domain name and ordered defendant to transfer the domain-name registration to plaintiff. Reversing and remanding, this court held, among other things, that plaintiff did not prove that defendant committed trademark infringement or cybersquatting, because it failed to establish that it held a valid and protectable trademark in the phrase. The court reasoned that the phrase was primarily geographically descriptive, rather than distinctive, and that it therefore was not subject to protection as a trademark, because it had not acquired secondary meaning before defendant began using it. Serenity Springs v. LaPorte County Convention and Visitors Bureau, 986 N.E.2d 314, 323.

Iowa, 2008. Quot. in sup. National bank brought action for trademark infringement against local bank, seeking, among other things, an injunction preventing defendant from using the name "Community State Bank." The trial court ruled in favor of plaintiff. The court of appeals reversed. Vacating the court of appeals and affirming the trial court, this court held, inter alia, that plaintiff had a valid common-law trademark in the name. The court concluded that, while the name was descriptive, it had acquired the secondary meaning necessary to render it protectible; plaintiff had used the name continuously and exclusively for 12 years, plaintiff had spent significant amounts on advertising and had a substantially larger percentage of the market share in defendant's area, and surveys indicated that consumers considered the name a brand indicating a source or type. Community State Bank, Nat. Ass'n v. Community State Bank, 758 N.W.2d 520, 525.

Iowa, 1999. Quot. in disc., com. (a) cit. in disc. Bank operating under the name "Commercial Savings Bank" brought trademark-infringement action against financial institution calling itself "Commercial Federal Bank." The trial court entered judgment for defendant on the ground that plaintiff had failed to establish the existence of a common-law trademark in "commercial." Affirming, this court held that "commercial" was a descriptive term that had become distinctive through secondary use; however, plaintiff could not show that defendant's use of the term was likely to cause consumer confusion. Commercial Sav. v. Hawkeye Federal Sav., 592 N.W.2d 321, 328.

La.1995. Cit. in headnote and disc.; cit. in disc. and headnote as §§ 13-15. The Gulf Coast Bank sued the Gulf Coast Bank and Trust Company for trade-name infringement, alleging that defendant's corporate name was deceptively similar to plaintiff's in violation of Louisiana's Trademark Act. Trial court granted defendant summary judgment and intermediate appellate court affirmed. This court reversed and remanded, holding that one need not prove fraud to enjoin another from using its trade name, but must show that there is a likelihood of consumer confusion created by

For earlier citations, see the Appendices, Supplements, or Pocket Parts, if any, that correspond to the subject matter under examination.

defendant's use of the trade name. On remand, the court stated that plaintiff must establish secondary meaning since the name "Gulf Coast Bank" was not inherently distinctive. The word "Bank" was required to be in every bank's name and thus appeared to be a generic term, and the term "Gulf Coast" was geographic, denoting the general geographic area in which this bank operated. Gulf Coast Bank v. Gulf Coast Bank & Trust Co., 652 So.2d 1306, 1307, 1313, 1314.

La.App.2006. Cit. in disc. §§ 13-14. After brother, who was essentially fired from his family jewelry business, opened a competing business with a similar name, family jewelry business sued brother and competing business, seeking, in part, to enjoin defendants from using its registered trade names, which included the family name in conjunction with the words "jewelers," "jewelry," and "diamonds." The trial court rendered judgment in favor of defendant. Reversing in part, this court held, inter alia, that plaintiff's registered trade names had acquired secondary meaning and were entitled to trade-name protection, but that defendant had sufficiently distinguished competing business by including both his first name and his surname in its trade name. Ramsey's Mfg. Jewelers, Inc. v. Ramsey, 924 So.2d 1045, 1051, writ denied 930 So.2d 26 (La.2006).

La.App.2004. Cit. in sup., cit. in sup. §§ 13-15 and 13-14. Shoe store sought injunction against national shoe retailer to prevent national retailer from using word "shoetique," which store had registered as trade name. Trial court granted national retailer summary judgment. Reversing and remanding, this court held that genuine issue of material fact as to whether the descriptive term "shoetique" had taken on a secondary meaning and therefore acquired a protectable proprietary character precluded summary judgment. McCain v. Designer Shoes Warehouse, LLC, 864 So.2d 784, 787.

R.I.2002. Cit. in sup. Lumber company sought injunctive relief to prevent competitor from using similar fictitious name. The trial court granted plaintiff permanent injunctive relief. Affirming, this court held that plaintiff was entitled to permanent injunctive relief preventing competitor from using deceptively similar trade name where plaintiff's trade name, while not inherently distinctive, had acquired secondary meaning through 40 years of continuous use. National Lumber & Building Materials Co. v. Langevin, 798 A.2d 429, 433.

Wis.App.1996. Cit. in headnote, cit. in sup., cit. and cit. generally in ftn. Company in the business of providing reprographic copying services to architects, engineers, publishers, and others sued competitor for trademark infringement. Following a bench trial, the trial court dismissed the complaint on the ground that there was insufficient likelihood of confusion between the parties' marks. Affirming, this court held, inter alia, that company's mark, which could also be considered a service mark, was a weak descriptive designation combining a geographical name with a shortened version of the term "reprographics"; that company's mark did not become strong or distinctive through secondary meaning; and that the minimal similarity of the two marks, as well as the sophistication of the parties' typical customers, supported the lower court's finding that there was no likelihood of confusion. Madison Reprographics v. Cook's Reprographics, 203 Wis.2d 226, 552 N.W.2d 440, 442, 444, 445, 447.

§ 15. Generic Designations

U.S.2020. Cit. in sup. Provider of online travel reservations and related services under the brand "Booking.com," which was also the domain name of its website, filed federal trademark applications to register four marks containing the term "Booking.com." A Patent and Trademark Office examining attorney denied the applications and the Trademark Trial and Appeals Board affirmed, concluding that "Booking.com" was generic and unregistrable. The court of appeals reversed, finding that "Booking.com" was descriptive, rather than generic, and that the term had acquired secondary meaning. Affirming, this court held that a term styled "generic.com" was a generic name for a class of goods or services and ineligible for trademark protection under Restatement Third of Unfair Competition § 15 only if the term had that meaning to consumers, and, because consumers did not perceive the term "Booking.com" to signify online hotel-reservation services as a class, "Booking.com" was not generic and was potentially eligible for federal trademark registration. United States Patent and Trademark Office v. Booking.com B.V., 140 S.Ct. 2298, 2303.

Cit.—cited; com.—comment; fol.—followed; sup.—support.
A complete list of abbreviations precedes page 1.

C.A.2, 1999. Cit. in headnotes, cit. in sup., com. (b) cit. in sup., com. (d) cit. in disc. Motorcycle manufacturer brought trademark-infringement action against provider of motorcycle products and services, seeking to enjoin defendant from using the word "hog" in reference to its business and goods and to prohibit defendant from employing a bar-and-shield logo similar to the one used by plaintiff. The district court entered judgment for plaintiff. Affirming in part, reversing in part, and remanding, this court held that "hog" was a generic term that was used to describe large motorcycles before plaintiff adopted it, and that plaintiff could not therefore enjoin defendant's use of the word; that defendant's use of the bar-and-shield logo for promotion and advertising did not constitute permissible trademark parody use; and that defendant's use of the logo was not made acceptable by the addition of the phrase "unauthorized dealer." Harley-Davidson, Inc. v. Grottanelli, 164 F.3d 806, 807, 810, 812.

C.A.2, 1999. Com. (a) cit. in disc. and quot. in sup., com. (b) quot. in disc. Japanese brewer that marketed and sold its sake in the United States under the "Otokoyama" brand name brought trademark-infringement action against competitor that imported and sold sake under the designation "Mutsu Otokoyama." Vacating the district court's grant of plaintiff's motion for a preliminary injunction and remanding, this court held that, because the district court erred in refusing to allow defendant to introduce evidence of the meaning and usage of "otokoyama" in Japan to support its claim that the mark was generic and therefore ineligible for protection as a trademark, the district court's finding that plaintiff was likely to succeed on the merits could not be sustained. Otokoyama Co. Ltd. v. Wine of Japan Import, Inc., 175 F.3d 266, 270-272.

C.A.2, 1994. Com. (d) cit. in disc. (citing § 15 of T.D. No. 2, 1990. § 15 has since been revised; see Official Text). Importer of Swiss pocket knives designated "Swiss Army knives" sued distributor of knives manufactured in China that were also designated "Swiss Army," alleging false advertising and unfair competition. The district court enjoined defendant from representing that its knife was a Swiss Army knife. Vacating and remanding, this court held, inter alia, that, although the phrase "Swiss Army knife" was not geographically descriptive and use of that phrase by defendant did not constitute false advertising, defendant was not absolved of liability for other forms of misrepresentation or unfair competition, such as "passing off," so that, if defendant wished to market such a knife, it could do so only in a manner that would not mislead the public into believing that the knife was manufactured by the Swiss manufacturers that made knives actually used by the Swiss military. Forschner Group, Inc. v. Arrow Trading Co., Inc., 30 F.3d 348, 359.

D.Ariz.2014. Com. (c) quot. in case quot. in sup. Buyers of 763 domain names that combined the word "google" with other terms sued owner of GOOGLE trademarks, seeking cancellation of defendant's marks on the basis that the marks had become generic. This court granted summary judgment for defendant, holding that, although a majority of the public used the word "google" as a verb to refer to the act of searching on the Internet without regard to what search engine was used, the primary significance of the word "google" to a majority of the public who utilized Internet search engines was as a designation of defendant's search engine. The court reasoned, in part, that, under Restatement Third of Unfair Competition § 15, casual and nonpurchasing uses of trademarks were not evidence of generic usage, because the primary significance of a trademark was determined by the use and understanding of the trademark in the context of purchasing decisions. Elliot v. Google Inc., 45 F.Supp.3d 1156, 1162.

N.D.Cal.2008. Cit. in disc. Bottled-water manufacturer that owned the registered trademark "Bottled at the Source" sued competitor, alleging federal trademark infringement, inter alia; defendant counterclaimed for cancellation of the trademark. This court granted summary judgment for defendant on plaintiff's claims and on the counterclaim, holding, inter alia, that the mark was generic and therefore invalid; defendant submitted undisputed evidence sufficient to overcome the presumption of validity created by registration of the mark, including proof of dozens of competitors using the mark, the media using the mark as a reference to a type of bottled water or a manufacturing process, and plaintiff's own use of the mark in a generic manner. CG Roxane LLC v. Fiji Water Co. LLC, 569 F.Supp.2d 1019, 1026.

For earlier citations, see the Appendices, Supplements, or Pocket Parts, if any, that correspond to the subject matter under examination.

D.Mass.1999. Com. (a) quot. in ftn. A dentist who used the service mark "Boston Dental" sued the "Boston Dental Group" for Lanham Act violations and unfair competition, among other claims. This court enjoined defendant from using the term "Boston Dental," holding, inter alia, that plaintiff was likely to succeed at trial in showing that the public had made the connection between the mark, "Boston Dental," and the services that plaintiff offered. There was evidence that the mark achieved secondary meaning, in that many patients and one of plaintiff's employees had confused plaintiff's dental practice with that of defendant. Boustany, D.M.D. v. Boston Dental Group, Inc., 42 F.Supp.2d 100, 106.

Fla.1993. Cit. in ftn. as §§ 13-15; com. (a) quot. in ftn. (citing § 15 of T.D. No. 2, 1990. § 15 has since been revised; see Official Text). The First Southern Bank sued to enjoin another bank from using the name "Great Southern Bank," alleging infringement and dilution of its trademark name and unfair competition. Trial court granted plaintiff injunctive relief and certified the question whether plaintiff bank's name was descriptive or generic so as not to be entitled to protection in the absence of proof that it had acquired a secondary meaning. This court remanded, holding that plaintiff bank's name contained laudatory, generic, and merely geographically descriptive elements so as not to be entitled to protection under either common or statutory law, but determination was necessary whether a secondary meaning in the name had developed in order to decide the dilution claim. In applying the suggestiveness test, the court stated that no great imagination was required to identify the product as banking services when the mark contained the word "bank," that many others used the word "southern" in their mark, and that businesses in the South had the need and right to use the term descriptively. Great Southern v. First Southern, 625 So.2d 463, 469.

Iowa, 2008. Com. (a) cit. in disc. National bank brought action for trademark infringement against local bank, seeking, among other things, an injunction preventing defendant from using the name "Community State Bank." The trial court ruled in favor of plaintiff. The court of appeals reversed. Vacating the court of appeals and affirming the trial court, this court held, inter alia, that plaintiff had a valid common-law trademark in the name. The court concluded that, while the name was descriptive, it had acquired the secondary meaning necessary to render it protectible; plaintiff had used the name continuously and exclusively for 12 years, plaintiff had spent significant amounts on advertising and had a substantially larger percentage of the market share in defendant's area, and surveys indicated that consumers considered the name a brand indicating a source or type. Community State Bank, Nat. Ass'n v. Community State Bank, 758 N.W.2d 520, 525.

Iowa, 1999. Subsec. (1) and com. (a) cit. in ftn. Bank operating under the name "Commercial Savings Bank" brought trademark-infringement action against financial institution calling itself "Commercial Federal Bank." The trial court entered judgment for defendant on the ground that plaintiff had failed to establish the existence of a common-law trademark in "commercial." Affirming, this court held that "commercial" was a descriptive term that had become distinctive through secondary use; however, plaintiff could not show that defendant's use of the term was likely to cause consumer confusion. Commercial Sav. v. Hawkeye Federal Sav., 592 N.W.2d 321, 327.

La.1995. Cit. in headnote and disc.; cit. in disc. and headnote as §§ 13-15. The Gulf Coast Bank sued the Gulf Coast Bank and Trust Company for trade-name infringement, alleging that defendant's corporate name was deceptively similar to plaintiff's in violation of Louisiana's Trademark Act. Trial court granted defendant summary judgment and intermediate appellate court affirmed. This court reversed and remanded, holding that one need not prove fraud to enjoin another from using its trade name, but must show that there is a likelihood of consumer confusion created by defendant's use of the trade name. On remand, the court stated that plaintiff must establish secondary meaning since the name "Gulf Coast Bank" was not inherently distinctive. The word "Bank" was required to be in every bank's name and thus appeared to be a generic term, and the term "Gulf Coast" was geographic, denoting the general geographic area in which this bank operated. Gulf Coast Bank v. Gulf Coast Bank & Trust Co., 652 So.2d 1306, 1307, 1313.

La.App.2004. Cit. in sup., cit. in sup.

§§ 13-15 and 13-14. Shoe store sought injunction against national shoe retailer to prevent national retailer from using word "shoetique," which store had registered as trade name. Trial court granted national retailer summary judgment. Reversing and remanding, this court held that genuine issue of material fact as to whether the descriptive term "shoetique" had taken on a secondary meaning and therefore acquired a protectable proprietary character precluded summary judgment. McCain v. Designer Shoes Warehouse, LLC, 864 So.2d 784, 787.

Vt.2002. Com. (a) quot. in ftn. Owners of advertisement-based newspaper sued former operators of paper for conversion and unfair competition, alleging misappropriation of business assets. The trial court entered judgment on jury verdict for owners. Modifying conversion award and affirming, this court held, inter alia, that evidence that former operators took business assets such as customer lists, bookkeeping records, and office equipment supported unfair-competition claim based on misappropriation. Maguire v. Gorruso, 174 Vt. 1, 800 A.2d 1085, 1088.

Wis.App.1996. Cit. in headnote, cit. generally in ftn., cit. in disc. Company in the business of providing reprographic copying services to architects, engineers, publishers, and others sued competitor for trademark infringement. Following a bench trial, the trial court dismissed the complaint on the ground that there was insufficient likelihood of confusion between the parties' marks. Affirming, this court held, inter alia, that company's mark, which could also be considered a service mark, was a weak descriptive designation combining a geographical name with a shortened version of the term "reprographics"; that company's mark did not become strong or distinctive through secondary meaning; and that the minimal similarity of the two marks, as well as the sophistication of the parties' typical customers, supported the lower court's finding that there was no likelihood of confusion. Madison Reprographics v. Cook's Reprographics, 203 Wis.2d 226, 552 N.W.2d 440, 441, 444, 445.

§ 16. Configurations of Packaging and Products: Trade Dress and Product Designs

U.S.1992. Com. (a) cit. in ftn. cit. in conc. op., com. (b) cit. in conc. op. (citing § 16 of T.D. No. 2, 1990. § 16 has since been revised; see Official Text). Owner of restaurant chain sued owner of similar restaurant chain for trade-dress infringement. Plaintiff patented its store's Mexican motif before defendant's opening of similarly decorated and designed stores. The district court granted judgment for plaintiff. The court of appeals affirmed. This court also affirmed, holding that plaintiff need not prove that trade dress had secondary meaning to be protected. The court accepted without discussion findings that plaintiff's trade dress was inherently distinctive. It did not require plaintiff to prove that its trade dress was uniquely associated with a specific source because such burden would be contrary to intent of federal legislation. A concurring opinion said that courts had recently accepted that trade dress was capable of having inherently distinctive meaning without proof of secondary meaning. Two Pesos, Inc. v. Taco Cabana, Inc., 505 U.S. 763, 763, 784, 787, 112 S.Ct. 2753, 2755, 2766, 2767, 120 L.Ed.2d 615, rehearing denied 505 U.S. 1244, 113 S.Ct. 20, 120 L.Ed.2d 947 (1992).

C.A.2, 2001. Com. (b) quot. in sup. Copyright holder sued maker of twisted cable jewelry, alleging copyright infringement, trade dress infringement under the Lanham Act, and unfair competition. The district court entered judgment for plaintiff. Reversing as to the trade-dress and unfair-competition claims, this court held, inter alia, that plaintiff failed to identify the specific common elements of its trade dress in its product line, and therefore its product design was protectible trade dress. Yurman Design, Inc. v. PAJ, Inc., 262 F.3d 101, 115.

C.A.2, 1997. Cit. in headnote, com. (b) cit. in disc. Swiss manufacturer of Swiss Army knives sued Chinese competitor for, inter alia, unfair competition. On remand from this court, the district court determined that, although defendant was free to identify its product by use of the phrase "Swiss Army knife," it was required to distinguish its product from that of plaintiff, either by changing the color of its knife to one not used by plaintiff or by adding language to the knife indicating that it was the maker. Affirming, this court held, in part, that the lower court did not err in failing to enjoin defendant from using the color red for its knives, because the color red did not distinguish defendant's knives from the

For earlier citations, see the Appendices, Supplements, or Pocket Parts, if any, that correspond to the subject matter under examination.

knives of any other manufacturer, nor did defendant's use of the color red create a likelihood of confusion as to the source of the product. Forschner Group, Inc. v. Arrow Trading Co., Inc., 124 F.3d 402, 404, 409.

C.A.2, 1997. Com. (a) quot. in part in disc., com. (b) cit. in disc. Manufacturer of the Toilet Bank, a novelty coin bank shaped like a tank toilet, sued competitor for, inter alia, trade dress infringement under the Lanham Act, alleging that competitor copied manufacturer's packaging for use with its Currency Can. The district court issued a preliminary injunction prohibiting competitor from producing, selling, or distributing the Currency Can in the packaging at issue or in any other packaging similar to that of manufacturer. Affirming, this court held that manufacturer's trade dress was inherently distinctive and nonfunctional, and that a substantial likelihood of confusion between the two products existed; consequently, the lower court did not err in issuing the preliminary injunction based upon its determination that manufacturer was likely to succeed on the merits of its claim. Fun-Damental Too, Ltd. v. Gemmy Industries Corp., 111 F.3d 993, 999, 1001.

C.A.2, 1997. Com. (b) cit. in case quot. in disc. Manufacturer of commercial outdoor furniture, called "site furniture," sued competitor for trade dress infringement. The district court granted manufacturer a preliminary injunction; the Second Circuit vacated and remanded. The district court reinstated the injunction, and this court again vacated, saying that manufacturer failed to articulate with sufficient particularity what was inherently distinctive about its trade dress. The court also suggested that packaging may be more distinctive to consumers than design. Landscape Forms, Inc. v. Columbia Cascade Co., 113 F.3d 373, 379.

C.A.2, 1996. Com. (b) cit. in disc. Merchandiser of troll dolls sued competitor for, inter alia, trade-dress infringement under the Lanham Act. The district court held in defendant's favor on the trade-dress infringement claim. Affirming in part, this court held, inter alia, that plaintiff failed to demonstrate that the trade dress of its troll dolls was either inherently distinctive or had acquired secondary meaning; since plaintiff's dolls were similar to the many other troll dolls on the market, their configuration did not serve primarily as a designator of their origin, and thus the dolls lacked inherent distinctiveness. The court stated that product-configuration trade dresses were less likely than package-configuration dresses to serve a source-identification function, noting that consumers were more likely to be attracted to a product for its features, rather than for the source-identifying role the features might play. EFS Marketing, Inc. v. Russ Berrie & Co., Inc., 76 F.3d 487, 491.

C.A.2, 1996. Com. (a) quot. in disc. Manufacturer of historic reproductions of "Mission furniture" sued competitor for trade-dress infringement. Vacating the district court's grant of a preliminary injunction for plaintiff and remanding for trial, this court held that the trade dress of reproductions was not inherently distinctive and that plaintiff was not likely to succeed in proving secondary meaning, since it was doubtful that consumers identified the Mission furniture trade dress with plaintiff rather than with the maker of the popular originals. L. & J.G. Stickley, Inc. v. Canal Dover Furniture, 79 F.3d 258, 262.

C.A.2, 1995. Cit. in disc. and in sup., com. (a) cit. in disc., com. (b) quot. in disc. Manufacturer of children's sweaters decorated with squirrel- and leaf-shaped appliques brought an action for trade-dress infringement under the Lanham Act and copyright infringement against competitor that introduced a line of similar sweaters. Vacating in part and affirming in part the district court's entry of judgment for plaintiff and remanding, this court held, inter alia, that plaintiff's sweater designs failed to qualify for protection of trade dress inherent in product design; since plaintiff's objective in the designs was primarily aesthetic, the designs were not primarily intended as source identification. Knitwaves, Inc. v. Lollytogs Ltd. (Inc.), 71 F.3d 996, 1005, 1008.

C.A.2, 1992. Cit. in disc., com. (b) cit. and quot. in disc. and cit. in ftn., Rptr's Note cit. in disc. (citing § 16 of T.D. No. 2, 1990. § 16 has since been revised; see Official Text). A game-puzzle manufacturer sought a preliminary injunction based on trade-dress and copyright infringement against a competitor who developed a similar set of flat-to-cube game puzzles and used similar packaging. New York federal district court granted plaintiff's motion for a preliminary injunction, determining that plaintiff's trade dress was protected by the doctrine of secondary meaning in the making. This court vacated the preliminary injunction, holding, inter alia, that the doctrine of secondary meaning in the making should not be recognized under the Lanham Act, since the doctrine, by affording protection before prospective purchasers were likely to associate the trade dress with a particular sponsor, constrained unnecessarily the freedom to copy and compete. The court emphasized the level of protection afforded under existing law to prevent piracy in the early stages of product development. Laureyssens v. Idea Group, Inc., 964 F.2d 131, 136, 138.

C.A.3, 1994. Com. (b) cit. and quot. in disc. and quot. in ftn. (citing § 16 of T.D. No. 2, 1990. § 16 has since been revised; see Official Text). Manufacturer of plastic garden planters shaped like Grecian urns brought a trade-dress infringement action against competitor and moved for a preliminary injunction. Affirming the district court's denial of plaintiff's motion, this court held that, since plaintiff was unable to show that its product's configuration was either inherently distinctive or had acquired a secondary meaning, plaintiff failed to demonstrate a likelihood of success on the merits. The court rejected the application of traditional trade-dress doctrine to a claim that product configuration had been infringed. Duraco Products v. Joy Plastic Enterprises, Ltd., 40 F.3d 1431, 1441, 1446, 1448, 1450.

C.A.4, 1999. Com. (b) cit. in disc. Home-furniture manufacturer sued competitor for, in part, violation of federal trade-dress law. Reversing the district court's grant of summary judgment for defendant and remanding, this court held, inter alia, that a genuine issue of material fact existed as to whether plaintiff's neo-Roman-design bedroom-furniture suite was inherently distinctive. Ashley Furniture Industries, Inc. v. SanGiacomo N.A. Ltd., 187 F.3d 363, 375.

C.A.4, 1996. Com. (a) cit. in disc. A company that engaged in the mail-order sale of tools and equipment sued a competitor for, inter alia, infringing the trade dress of the company's catalog. Affirming the district court's entry of judgment on a jury verdict for plaintiff, this court held that plaintiff presented sufficient evidence that its trade dress was nonfunctional and had acquired a secondary meaning and that defendant's infringement created a likelihood of confusion. Tools USA v. Champ Frame Straightening, 87 F.3d 654, 657.

C.A.5, 2010. Quot. in sup. Self-storage business sued competitor and construction company that built facilities for business and competitor, alleging, among other things, infringement of a star design that it claimed as a service mark. The district court granted summary judgment for defendants. While affirming as to plaintiff's claim for service-mark infringement, this court reversed and remanded plaintiff's claims for trade-dress infringement and unfair competition, holding that plaintiff did not have to establish that the design was legally protectable in order to protect the overall appearance of its facilities as trade dress; plaintiff's claimed trade dress, unlike the star design, consisted of the entirety of the facilities' design, including the placement of the star design under the roof peaks. Amazing Spaces, Inc. v. Metro Mini Storage, 608 F.3d 225, 251.

C.A.5, 1997. Com. (b) cit. in ftn. A manufacturer sued for injunctive relief to bar a competitor from manufacturing and marketing a stand mixer, alleging that defendant unlawfully replicated plaintiff's mixer's product configuration. Affirming the district court's entry of a preliminary injunction in favor of plaintiff, this court held, inter alia, that, since plaintiff's mixer's product configuration had acquired a secondary meaning, it was not necessary to reach the controversial question of whether product configurations could ever be considered inherently distinctive. The court noted that, although product configurations technically were regarded as trade dress, critics distinguished product configurations and designs from product packaging, which was more closely associated with traditional trademark law. Sunbeam Products, Inc. v. West Bend Co., 123 F.3d 246, 253, cert. denied 523 U.S. 1118, 118 S.Ct. 1795, 140 L.Ed.2d 936 (1998).

C.A.8, 2000. Com. (d) cit. in disc. Sponsor of home shows sued competitor for, inter alia, violations of the Lanham Act, alleging that defendant was sponsoring shows with names deceptively similar to those used by plaintiff. The district court entered judgment for plaintiff. Affirming, this court held that the names at issue constituted descriptive marks that had acquired secondary meaning. Home Builders Ass'n v. L & L Exhibition Management, 226 F.3d 944, 950.

E.D.Mich.1998. Com. (a) cit. generally in headnote and quot. in part in disc. Manufacturer of a lounge chair and otto-

For earlier citations, see the Appendices, Supplements, or Pocket Parts, if any, that correspond to the subject matter under examination.

man sued a competitor under the Lanham Act, claiming that the distinctive shape and design of its furniture were protected trade dress that defendant infringed by copying and marketing replicas. Granting defendant's motion for summary judgment, the court held, inter alia, that the design of plaintiff's lounge chair and ottoman was not protectable trade dress. The court said that plaintiff failed to establish that the trade dress was inherently distinctive or that it had acquired secondary meaning. Herman Miller, Inc. v. Palazzetti Imports, 998 F.Supp. 757, 758, 760, affirmed in part, reversed in part 270 F.3d 298 (6th Cir. 2001).

E.D.N.Y.2014. Com. (a) quot. in case quot. in ftn. Distributors of religious products, including prayer cards and framed prints featuring artwork produced by an Italian company, sued, among others, competitor that distributed the same products and plaintiff's former employee who left to help create competitor, alleging that defendants' catalog infringed the protectable trade dress of plaintiffs' catalog. This court granted summary judgment for defendants on plaintiffs' federal trade-dress claim, holding that, while Restatement Third of Unfair Competition § 16 provided that catalogs, like packaging, could dress products by promoting and displaying them for sale to potential customers and could thereby constitute protectable trade dress, no reasonable jury could find that plaintiffs' catalogs were inherently distinctive, or distinctive through their acquisition of secondary meaning, such that protection was warranted. Gerffert Co., Inc. v. Dean, 41 F.Supp.3d 201, 211.

N.D.N.Y.1997. Com. (b) quot. in case quot. in disc. A designer and manufacturer of child carriers sued a competitor for trade-dress infringement and unfair competition, alleging that the competitor had copied plaintiff's product, causing cheaper, inferior, and confusingly similar child carriers to be manufactured abroad. The district court granted plaintiff's motion for a preliminary injunction, but the Second Circuit vacated. This court granted defendant summary judgment, holding, inter alia, that plaintiff failed to state a viable claim for trade-dress infringement. The court determined that plaintiff failed as a matter of law to overcome the presumption that its dress was weak. In light of the absence of exclusivity during a period of less than two years prior to defendant's entry into the market and the lack of any direct evidence to the contrary, there was no reasonable basis for finding that plaintiff's dress was a strong source indicator because of secondary meaning. Tough Traveler, Ltd. v. Outbound Products, 989 F.Supp. 203, 211, affirmed 165 F.3d 15 (2d Cir.1998).

S.D.N.Y.2016. Com. (a) quot. in sup.; com. (b) quot. in ftn. Fashion company that purportedly held a trademark in the right to affix a metal plate to the toe of men's sneakers brought trademark-infringement and other claims against competitor. This court granted summary judgment for defendant, holding, among other things, that plaintiff failed to establish that the toe plate had acquired secondary meaning. The court cited Restatement Third of Unfair Competition § 16 in noting that the toe plate served a primarily aesthetic function and therefore did not qualify as a protectable trademark or product packaging, but, rather, as a product design, and that product-design features were not inherently distinctive and thus were not subject to trademark protection in the absence of secondary meaning. LVL XIII Brands, Inc. v. Louis Vuitton Malletier S.A., 209 F.Supp.3d 612, 650, 652.

S.D.N.Y.2016. Com. (b) quot. in case quot. in sup. Manufacturer of small plastic closures that were used to fasten bags of pastries, bread, and fruit sued competitor, seeking a declaration that its products did not infringe defendant's trademark or trade-dress rights in similar closures. After a bench trial, this court concluded that plaintiff was entitled to judgment declaring that its closures did not infringe or dilute any trademark or trade-dress rights claimed by defendant, and ordered the cancellation of defendant's trademark registration on the grounds that the claimed design of the closures was functional and not a proper subject of registration. The court cited Restatement Third of Unfair Competition § 16 in noting that rigorous application of the nonfunctionality requirement for trademark and trade-dress registration, which protected competition even at the cost of potential consumer confusion, was critical in a product-configuration case such as this one, because a monopoly right in the design of a product itself was more likely to preclude competition. Schutte Bagclosures Inc. v.

Kwik Lok Corporation, 193 F.Supp.3d 245, 261.

S.D.N.Y.2003. Com. (a) cit. in disc., com. (b) quot. in case quot. in disc. Fashion designer brought suit for trade-dress infringement against clothing retailer that allegedly borrowed heavily from plaintiff's innovative line of pants to create its own style of pants. Granting defendant's motion for summary judgment, the court held, inter alia, that plaintiff's line of pants did not have a consistent overall look, and was therefore unprotectable as a singular trade dress. The court said that, although plaintiff raised a fact question as to whether its trade dress was nonfunctional, aesthetic and otherwise, defendant presented sufficient evidence to support a finding that there was no material factual issue in dispute on the elements of likelihood of confusion and distinctiveness. Maharishi Hardy Blechman Ltd. v. Abercrombie & Fitch Co., 292 F.Supp.2d 535, 541.

S.D.N.Y.1998. Com. (a) cit. generally in headnote and cit. in case cit. in disc. Distributor of inexpensive novelty items sued competitors under the Lanham Act for allegedly infringing on an uncopyrighted "family" trade dress that plaintiff used when packaging its products. Entering judgment for defendants, the court held, inter alia, that plaintiff's Lanham Act claim failed because plaintiff had not consistently defined the elements of, or pursued the use of, a theme trade dress. The court held further that, even if plaintiff had consistently applied a single, identifiable theme trade dress to its packages, it could not prevail because its trade dress was descriptive within the market in which it competed, and the trade dress had not acquired secondary meaning. Regal Jewelry v. Kingsbridge Intern., 999 F.Supp. 477, 478, 486.

S.D.N.Y.1997. Com. (b) quot. in case quot. in sup. A shoe manufacturer sued a competitor for violations of federal law and asserted state-law claims, alleging violations of its intellectual property rights in its shoes featuring a "waffle" shoe-sole design. After this court held that defendant had not infringed plaintiff's waffle-sole trademark, defendant moved for cancellation of plaintiff's trademark. The court granted defendant's motion, holding, inter alia, that plaintiff's waffle trademark was not entitled to trademark protection and should be canceled. The court stated that the waffle sole lacked inherent distinctiveness because it was a product design and was merely a decorative feature of the goods that did not indicate source; in addition, the trademark did not serve primarily as a designator of origin of the product and thus lacked secondary meaning, or acquired distinctiveness. Aerogroup Intern. v. Marlboro Footworks, 977 F.Supp. 264, 267.

W.D.N.Y.2002. Com. (a) quot. in disc. Manufacturer of sugar-shell candy products sued competitor for trade-dress infringement. Granting plaintiff's motion for preliminary injunction, the court held that plaintiff's trade dress was distinctive, a likelihood of confusion existed between the parties' products as to source, and the balance of hardships tipped decidedly in plaintiff's favor. Masterfoods USA v. Arcor USA, Inc., 230 F.Supp.2d 302, 306.

M.D.N.C.1998. Com. (b) quot. in sup. A bedroom furniture manufacturer sued a competitor for trade-dress violations, among other claims, alleging that its furniture designs were infringed. This court granted defendant summary judgment, holding, inter alia, that because plaintiff had failed to demonstrate that it had a protectable trade-dress interest in its furniture design—either through proof of inherent distinctiveness or secondary meaning—plaintiff's claim under Section 43(a) of the Lanham Act failed as a matter of law. The court stated that no reasonable jury could find that the design was inherently distinctive, because the use of a high-gloss finish, columns, arches, and entablatures on bedroom furniture could not be characterized as arbitrary or fanciful, since such features were common to the furniture industry. Ashley Furniture Industries v. Sangiacomo N.A. Ltd., 11 F.Supp.2d 773, 777, 779, reversed 187 F.3d 363 (4th Cir. 1999).

S.D.Tex.2017. Quot. in disc. Manufacturer of medical-identification jewelry brought an action against its competitor, seeking to prevent defendant from using marketing methods and advertising materials that allegedly infringed its trade dress and copyright. This court denied plaintiff's motion for preliminary injunction, holding, inter alia, that plaintiff was unlikely to succeed in proving the merits of trade-dress infringement, because it failed to show that the unregistered claimed trade dress was inherently distinctive, was nonfunctional, and had acquired secondary meaning. In defining "trade dress," the court cited Re-

For earlier citations, see the Appendices, Supplements, or Pocket Parts, if any, that correspond to the subject matter under examination.

statement Third of Unfair Competition § 16 in noting that the design of elements constituting the total image and overall appearance of a product were eligible for protection as a mark. AMID, Inc. v. Medic Alert Foundation United States, Inc., 241 F.Supp.3d 788, 801.

Cal.App.2001. Com. (a) quot. in disc. Insureds sued commercial general liability insurer for breach of contract, alleging that defendant was obligated to defend them under the policy's advertising-injury coverage after they were sued in federal court for trade-dress infringement. Reversing the trial court's grant of summary judgment for insurer and remanding, this court held that the allegations charging insureds with trade-dress infringement, when read together with extrinsic evidence derived from photocopies of the allegedly infringing product from their catalog provided to insurer at the time of insureds' tender of their defense, were sufficient to charge the commission of an advertising injury potentially covered under the policies, and thus sufficed to establish insurer's duty to defend. El-Com Hardware, Inc. v. Fireman's Fund Ins. Co., 92 Cal.App.4th 205, 214, 111 Cal.Rptr.2d 670, 676, 677.

Cal.App.2000. Com. (a) quot. in disc. After trademark holder and its licensee obtained a federal-court judgment in their favor in their action for trademark infringement and unfair competition against insured, whose insurer subsequently became insolvent, they brought this action for a declaratory judgment that the California Insurance Guarantee Association (CIGA) was obligated to pay their claim against insured. The trial court entered a stipulated judgment for CIGA. Affirming, this court held, inter alia, that plaintiffs' unfair-competition claim for trade-dress infringement was encompassed within the insurance policy's exclusion for injury arising out of trademark infringement, and thus was excluded from coverage. Aloha Pacific, Inc. v. CIGA, 79 Cal.App.4th 297, 93 Cal.Rptr.2d 148, 162-164.

Cal.App.2000. Com. (a) cit. in ftn. Insured sued its liability insurer on a policy that covered "advertising injury," seeking a declaration of its right to a defense in a competitor's trade-dress-infringement action. Trial court granted insured summary judgment on the ground that insurer had a duty to defend, but concluded after a trial that insurer had no duty to indemnify insured for the $195,000 it paid to settle the underlying suit. This court reversed the order granting summary judgment and affirmed the judgment finding no duty to indemnify. The court held, inter alia, that the term "advertising" as used in the policy did not include an effort to sell, through a competitive bidding process, a product that was specifically manufactured for a single customer to meet the needs of a specific project. Thus, no duty to defend arose, because infringement did not occur in the course of advertising. Peerless Lighting Corporation v. American Motorists Insurance Co., 82 Cal.App.4th 995, 98 Cal.Rptr.2d 753, 756.

Fla.2006. Cit. in bar rules quot. in appendix to op. The Florida Bar petitioned this court to consider proposed amendments to the Rules Regulating the Florida Bar. The court, after acknowledging its jurisdiction, adopted the proposed amendments, including standards for certification of board-certified intellectual-property lawyers. Under the newly adopted standards, the term "trademark" was defined to include trademarks, service marks, certification marks, and collective marks, and was further defined to include trade dress, as that term was used in the Restatement Third, Unfair Competition § 16, and domain names. In re Amendments to the Rules Regulating the Florida Bar—Subchapters 6-25 and 6-26, 933 So.2d 1123, 1131.

Vt.2002. Cit. in ftn. Owners of advertisement-based newspaper sued former operators of paper for conversion and unfair competition, alleging misappropriation of business assets. The trial court entered judgment on jury verdict for owners. Modifying conversion award and affirming, this court held, inter alia, that evidence that former operators took business assets such as customer lists, bookkeeping records, and office equipment supported unfair-competition claim based on misappropriation. Maguire v. Gorruso, 174 Vt. 1, 800 A.2d 1085, 1088.

§ 17. Functional Designs

U.S.1995. Com. (c) quot. in disc. Manufacturer of green-gold dry-cleaning press pads sued competitor under the Lanham Act and for unfair competition, challenging defendant's use of the same color for the same purpose. The district court entered judgment for plaintiff but the intermediate

Cit.—cited; com.—comment; fol.—followed; sup.—support.
A complete list of abbreviations precedes page 1.

appellate court set it aside on the ground that color could not be registered as a trademark. Reversing, this court held that as long as the color to be registered served no nontrademark function, trademark protection was appropriate. The court warned, however, that a seemingly aesthetic component would be considered functional if it were an essential product ingredient without which a differently designed product would bestow no meaningful benefit on its maker, ultimately impeding legitimate competition. Qualitex Co. v. Jacobson Products Co., Inc., 514 U.S. 159, 115 S.Ct. 1300, 1306, 131 L.Ed.2d 248.

C.A.2, 2012. Com. (c) quot. in case quot. in sup. Designer of women's high-heeled shoes with high-gloss red lacquer outsoles that contrasted sharply with the color of the rest of the shoes brought a trademark-infringement action against competitor that marketed and sold a monochrome red shoe with a red sole. The district court denied plaintiff's request for a preliminary injunction. Reversing in part and remanding, this court held that the trademark was valid and enforceable as modified to limit the registration to a red lacquered outsole that contrasted with the color of the adjoining upper. The court explained that the district court could not adopt a per se rule of aesthetic functionality for color marks in the fashion industry that would effectively deny trademark protection to any deployment of a single color in an item of apparel; rather, a highly fact-specific analysis was required to determine whether recognition of trademark rights in the use of the color would significantly hinder competition by putting competitors at a significant non-reputation-related disadvantage. Christian Louboutin S.A. v. Yves Saint Laurent America Holdings, Inc., 696 F.3d 206, 221.

C.A.2, 1997. Com. (c) cit. in headnote, cit. in disc. Manufacturer of commercial outdoor furniture, called "site furniture," sued competitor for trade dress infringement. The district court granted manufacturer a preliminary injunction; the Second Circuit vacated and remanded. The district court reinstated the injunction, and this court again vacated, holding that manufacturer had not shown that its trade dress was inherently distinctive. The court agreed that a design is functional when it confers a significant benefit that cannot be duplicated practically by an alternative design, but that issue was not reached because manufacturer had not shown that its line of furniture was protectable. Landscape Forms, Inc. v. Columbia Cascade Co., 113 F.3d 373, 374, 377.

C.A.2, 1995. Com. (c) quot. in case quot. in sup. Competitor sued manufacturer of latex exercise bands whose levels of resistance were color-coded, seeking a declaration that defendant did not have legally enforceable trade-dress protection in the color system. The district court granted summary judgment for plaintiff on the trade-dress issue on the ground that the color sequence employed by defendant was functional and therefore not protectable. Reversing and remanding, this court held, inter alia, that genuine issues of material fact precluding summary judgment existed on the issue of functionality as to whether the benefit conferred by defendant's color sequence of identifying the resistance level of each band could be achieved by alternative means. Fabrication Enterprises, Inc. v. Hygenic Corp., 64 F.3d 53, 61.

C.A.2, 1995. Com. (c) cit. and quot. in disc. Manufacturer of children's sweaters decorated with squirrel- and leaf-shaped appliques brought an action for trade-dress infringement under the Lanham Act and copyright infringement against competitor that introduced a line of similar sweaters. Vacating in part and affirming in part the district court's entry of judgment for plaintiff and remanding, this court held, inter alia, that plaintiff's sweater designs failed to qualify for protection of trade dress inherent in product design; since plaintiff's objective in the designs was primarily aesthetic, the designs were not primarily intended as source identification. Knitwaves, Inc. v. Lollytogs Ltd. (Inc.), 71 F.3d 996, 1005, 1006.

C.A.2, 1993. Cit. in case cit. in sup., cit. generally in ftn., com. (c) and illus. 6 quot. in part in sup. (citing § 17 of T.D. No. 2, 1990. § 17 has since been revised; see Official Text). The seller of high-quality china sued a competitor for violation of the Lanham Act and unfair competition and dilution of its trademark under New York law. Reversing the district court's dismissal of plaintiff's claims, this court held, inter alia, that the competitor had failed to show that it needed to copy plaintiff's china design in order to compete in the market for hotel china, even if hotels did not buy china often, since the competitor did not show that it was at a significant competitive dis-

For earlier citations, see the Appendices, Supplements, or Pocket Parts, if any, that correspond to the subject matter under examination.

advantage in making initial sales without plaintiff's "basket" patterns. The design of hotel china, said the court, was not per se functional for infringement claim analysis purposes. Villeroy & Boch Keramische Werke v. THC Systems, 999 F.2d 619, 621.

C.A.2, 1992. Com. (a) cit. in disc., com. (b) quot. in disc. (citing § 17 of T.D. No. 2, 1990. § 17 has since been revised; see Official Text). A game puzzle manufacturer sought a preliminary injunction based on trade-dress and copyright infringement against a competitor who developed a similar set of flat-to-cube game puzzles and used similar packaging. New York federal district court granted plaintiff's motion for a preliminary injunction, determining that plaintiff's trade dress was protected by the doctrine of secondary meaning in the making. This court vacated the preliminary injunction, holding, inter alia, that the doctrine of secondary meaning in the making should not be recognized under the Lanham Act, since the doctrine, by affording protection before prospective purchasers were likely to associate the trade dress with a particular sponsor, constrained unnecessarily the freedom to copy and compete. The court emphasized the level of protection afforded under existing law to prevent piracy in the early stages of product development. Laureyssens v. Idea Group, Inc., 964 F.2d 131, 136, 138.

C.A.2, 1990. Com. (c) cit. in sup. and adopted., illus. 6-8 quot. in ftn. (citing § 17 of Prelim. Draft No. 3, 1989. § 17 has since been revised; see Official Text). The manufacturer of a line of "Grand Baroque" silverware sued a competitor for trade-dress infringement and sought a preliminary injunction. The district court denied the motion for a preliminary injunction. Affirming, this court held that the manufacturer's silverware design was a functional feature of "Baroque" style silverware, and trademark protection of this ornamental feature would significantly hinder competitors by limiting the range of adequate alternative designs. The court determined that the doctrine of functionality applied to features of a product that were purely ornamental but that were essential to effective competition. It stated that although the competitor's design was found by the district court judge to be "substantially similar," it was not identical or virtually identical, and the similarity involved design elements necessary to compete in the market for baroque silverware. Wallace Intern. Silversmiths v. Godinger Silver Art, 916 F.2d 76, 81-82, cert. denied 499 U.S. 976, 111 S.Ct. 1622, 113 L.Ed.2d 720 (1991).

C.A.4, 1996. Quot. in ftn. A company that engaged in the mail order sale of tools and equipment sued a competitor for, inter alia, infringing the trade dress of the company's catalog. Affirming the district court's entry of judgment on a jury verdict for plaintiff, this court held that plaintiff presented sufficient evidence that its trade dress was nonfunctional and had acquired a secondary meaning and that defendant's infringement created a likelihood of confusion. The court noted that the availability to competitors of alternative designs was a key factor in determining that a trade dress was nonfunctional. Tools USA v. Champ Frame Straightening, 87 F.3d 654, 659.

C.A.5, 2008. Cit. in case cit. in disc. (general cite). Four universities sued apparel company and its principal, alleging that defendants infringed their trademarks in violation of the Lanham Act and state law by selling t-shirts with universities' color schemes and other identifying indicia. The district court granted summary judgment for plaintiffs. Affirming, this court, inter alia, held that the colors, content, and context of the offending t-shirts were likely to cause confusion as to their source, sponsorship, or affiliation. The court rejected defendant's argument that universities' use of the colors on the t-shirts was functional and thus did not qualify for protection under the Lanham Act, concluding that the use was aesthetic. The court stressed that the Fifth Circuit had consistently rejected the concept of aesthetic functionality. Board of Supervisors for Louisiana State University Agricultural and Mechanical College v. Smack Apparel Co., 550 F.3d 465, 487.

C.A.5, 1998. Com. (c) cit. and quot. in ftn. Golf course operator sued competitor for trademark infringement, alleging that defendant infringed and diluted plaintiff's mark by copying one of its holes. The district court entered judgment for plaintiff. Affirming, this court held, in part, that the design of plaintiff's hole was nonfunctional, under a test for either utilitarian or aesthetic functionality; that the design was descriptive and had acquired secondary meaning, as evidenced by plaintiff's extensive advertising, unsolicited publicity of the hole's trade dress in golf publications, and

Cit.—cited; com.—comment; fol.—followed; sup.—support.
A complete list of abbreviations precedes page 1.

defendant's intent to copy and use the trade dress prominently in its own advertising; that plaintiff did not abandon its rights in a nearby lighthouse that was built at the same time as the golf course for purposes of being seen from the course; that the evidence supported the lower court's finding of a likelihood of confusion; and that defendant's use of the mark to suggest affiliation, sponsorship, or endorsement was more than nominative. Pebble Beach Co. v. Tour 18 I Ltd., 155 F.3d 526, 540.

C.A.7, 1995. Com. (c) quot. in case quot. in disc. Manufacturer of outdoor furniture sued competitor for trade-dress infringement. Vacating the district court's grant of a preliminary injunction in favor of plaintiff, this court held that the district court failed to consider whether the design of plaintiff's furniture was "functional" and thus not protectable trade dress, and it remanded for consideration of that issue. Landscape Forms, Inc. v. Columbia Cascade Co., 70 F.3d 251, 253.

C.A.8, 1994. Coms. (a) and (b) quot. in part in diss. op. (citing § 17 of T.D. No. 2, 1990. § 17 has since been revised; see Official Text). Packager of potpourri fragrances sued competitor in state court for infringement of trade dress. The case was removed to federal district court after amendment of the complaint to allege infringement of registered federal trademarks. Reversing and vacating the district court's finding of infringement, this court held that packaging in pillow-shaped double cellophane bags, closed at the top by gathering the excess cellophane and closing it with a colored cord tied in a square knot bow with an oval label, did not identify the manufacturer's product and did not have a secondary meaning. The trade dress, said the court, was merely functional. The dissent argued that defendant had engaged in a studied and extensive imitation of plaintiff's trade dress. Aromatique, Inc. v. Gold Seal, Inc., 28 F.3d 863, 883.

C.A.9, 2006. Cit. in disc. Maker of key chains and license-plate covers that bore exact replicas of two automobile manufacturers' trademarks sued the manufacturers for a declaratory judgment that its activities did not constitute trademark infringement, trademark counterfeiting, or trademark dilution. The district court granted partial summary judgment for plaintiff. Reversing and remanding, this court held, inter alia, that because plaintiff failed to show that defendants' logos and marks were aesthetic functional elements of plaintiff's products, the marks were entitled to trademark protection. The court rejected plaintiff's argument that the trademarks were functional features of plaintiff's products on the basis that they constituted the actual benefit that the consumer wished to purchase, stating that plaintiff's approach distorted basic principles of trademark law and the doctrine of functionality in particular. Au-Tomotive Gold, Inc. v. Volkswagen of America, Inc., 457 F.3d 1062, 1068, cert. denied 549 U.S. 1282, 127 S.Ct. 1839, 167 L.Ed.2d 323 (2007).

C.A.10, 1995. Cit. in disc., coms. (a) and (b) cit. in disc. Manufacturer of a household fan with a spiral grill sued competitor for trade dress infringement, alleging that defendant intentionally copied its grill design. District court entered an injunction for plaintiff, holding that grill could be protected under Lanham Act against copying by competitors. This court reversed, holding that where a disputed product configuration is part of a claim in a utility patent, and the configuration is a described, significant inventive aspect of the invention, so that without it the invention could not fairly be said to be the same invention, patent law prevented its protection as trade dress, even if the configuration was nonfunctional. It stated that trade-dress protection can directly interfere with the public's ability to practice patented inventions after the patents had expired, and that it undermined the principle that ideas in the public domain should stay there. Vornado Air Circulation Systems v. Duracraft Corp., 58 F.3d 1498, 1507.

C.A.11, 1996. Quot. in ftn. A company produced commercial study guides for various courses at a university by hiring students attending a university to take lecture notes, which it in turn marketed to the student body as a whole. The university sued the company for copyright infringement. District court entered judgment on jury verdict for the publisher. This court affirmed, holding that the district court properly entered directed verdicts on plaintiff's Lanham Act claims, because of the absence of substantial evidence that the information plaintiff sought to protect was both distinctive and nonfunctional. The court found no authority to the effect that a "sum of the digits" test would allow it to disregard the absence of two of the three

For earlier citations, see the Appendices, Supplements, or Pocket Parts, if any, that correspond to the subject matter under examination.

elements required under the Lanham Act for an unfair-competition claim. University of Florida v. KPB, Inc., 89 F.3d 773, 776.

C.A.Fed.1993. Subsec. (c) cit. in case cit. in sup. Manufacturer of fashion athletic shoes sued another shoe manufacturer, alleging design-patent and trade-dress infringement. The district court, finding that defendant's models were "strikingly similar" to plaintiff's design, entered judgment for plaintiff. Affirming in part, this court held, inter alia, that findings that the shoe design was not clearly functional and, thus, that defendant could be liable for trade-dress infringement were supported by evidence that the shoes could be made without plaintiff's design, so that copying it was not necessary in order for defendant to compete effectively. L.A. Gear, Inc. v. Thom McAn Shoe Co., 988 F.2d 1117, 1130, cert. denied 510 U.S. 908, 114 S.Ct. 291, 126 L.Ed.2d 240 (1993).

W.D.Ark.1996. Com. (b) cit. and quot. in disc. and cit. in headnote. A producer of single-barb plastic fittings to connect tubing and piping sued a competitor, seeking a declaration of invalidity of certain of competitor's trademarks and trade dress. This court entered judgment for plaintiff, holding that the barb design and the slogan were not valid trademarks and were not entitled to protection under any provision of the federal trademark laws. In rejecting plaintiff's trade-dress claim, the court determined that the product designs were functional, that the designs were not inherently distinctive, and that the designs did not acquire distinctiveness through secondary meaning. The fact that plaintiff could have adopted minor variations in design did not mean that there were sufficient alternative designs to render the design nonfunctional. Ark Plas Products, Inc. v. Value Plastics, Inc., 913 F.Supp. 1246, 1246, 1251.

N.D.Fla.2002. Quot. in ftn. Beef-packing company sued importer-exporter of frozen meat products for, in part, false designation of origin, alleging that defendant presented plaintiff's beef livers that were prepared for the Russian market as though they were packaged and processed in compliance with Egyptian labeling guidelines, in order to sell the livers at a higher price on the Egyptian market. Entering judgment for plaintiff, the court held that, because defendant's conduct caused a likelihood of confusion, defendant was liable on plaintiff's claim. The court noted that plaintiff's logo was inherently distinctive and primarily nonfunctional in that it afforded no benefits other than its significance as an indication of source. IBP, Inc. v. Hady Enterprises, Inc., 267 F.Supp.2d 1148, 1166, affirmed 52 Fed.Appx. 487 (11th Cir.2002).

S.D.Fla.2002. Cit. in case quot. in sup. Manufacturer of artificial sweetener brought action for copyright, trademark, and trade-dress infringement against participants in scheme to distribute and sell manufacturer's institutionally packaged product in counterfeit retail packaging. Granting in part manufacturer's motion for summary judgment as to defendant distributors, district court held, inter alia, that plaintiff sufficiently established trade-dress infringement by showing that its trade dress had acquired secondary meaning, that its trade dress was nonfunctional, and that defendants' counterfeit trade dress was so nearly identical to genuine product as to create likelihood of confusion to public. Monsanto Co. v. Campuzano, 206 F.Supp.2d 1252, 1265.

S.D.Fla.2002. Cit. in case quot. in sup. Manufacturer of artificial sweetener brought action for copyright, trademark, and trade-dress infringement against participants in scheme to distribute and sell manufacturer's institutionally packaged product in counterfeit retail packaging. Granting in part manufacturer's motion for summary judgment as to defendant who developed scheme, district court held, inter alia, that plaintiff sufficiently established trade-dress infringement by showing that its trade dress had acquired secondary meaning, that its trade dress was nonfunctional, and that defendants' counterfeit trade dress was so nearly identical to genuine product as to create likelihood of confusion to public. Monsanto Co. v. Campuzano, 206 F.Supp.2d 1239, 1247.

D.Kan.1997. Com. (b) quot. in disc. A Missouri corporation sued an Oklahoma corporation for trade-dress infringement, commercial misrepresentation, and unfair competition, alleging that the defendant corporation and its president infringed the trade dress of two of plaintiff's chemical injection pumps in violation of the Lanham Act. This court entered judgment for defendants, holding, inter alia, that plaintiff failed to establish that there was a likelihood of confusion by purchasers at the

Cit.—cited; com.—comment; fol.—followed; sup.—support.
A complete list of abbreviations precedes page 1.

point of sale of plaintiff's and defendant's pumps. On plaintiff's trade-dress-infringement claims, the court concluded that judgment for defendants was appropriate because plaintiff failed to establish that: (1) its trade dress was inherently distinctive or distinctive by proof of secondary meaning; and (2) there was a likelihood of confusion between the parties' pumps. Western Chemical Pumps, Inc. v. Superior Mfg., 989 F.Supp. 1112, 1129.

E.D.Mich.2002. Cit. in sup., quot. in disc., cit. generally in case cit. in disc., com. (c) quot. in disc., illus. 8 quot. in sup. Manufacturer of sinks with S-shaped dividers sued competitor for, in part, trade-dress infringement. Denying defendant's motion for summary judgment on the trade-dress claim, the court held, inter alia, that although defendant showed that the S-shaped divider was aesthetically functional, because the design conferred a significant benefit that could not practically be duplicated by use of alternative designs, defendant failed to show that it had not attained a secondary meaning. Goscicki v. Custom Brass & Copper Specialities, Inc., 229 F.Supp.2d 743, 751, 752.

E.D.Mich.1997. Com. (b) cit. and quot. in disc. and cit. in headnote. A manufacturer and seller of spring-mounted wind-resistant sign stands had sold the stands since 1968 under the trademark WINDMASTER. The manufacturer sued the manufacturer of a similar stand that was sold under the WINDBUSTER trade name, alleging that the WINDBUSTER stands infringed upon the WINDMASTER trademark and trade dress rights and constituted unfair competition pursuant to the Lanham Act. This court granted defendant summary judgment, holding, inter alia, that the dual-spring design asserted by plaintiff as trade dress was functional as a matter of law and not entitled to trade dress protection under the Lanham Act. The expired utility patents were especially strong evidence of the usefulness of the dual-spring design; the alternative designs suggested by plaintiff were few and unequal to the WINDMASTER sign stand in performance; and plaintiff's advertising emphasized the functional advantages of the dual-spring design rather than its look. Marketing Displays, Inc. v. Traffix Devices, Inc., 971 F.Supp. 262, 273, 275, affirmed 11 Fed.Appx. 547 (6th Cir.2001).

D.Minn.2000. Com. (b) quot. in disc. Manufacturer that registered color "canary yellow" as trademark for its sticky notes sued competitors for, in part, trademark infringement. Denying in part defendants' motion for summary judgment, the court held, inter alia, that genuine issues of material fact existed as to whether the color canary yellow was a functional aspect of the sticky-note product, based on plaintiff's evidence that any number of colors performed the job as well as or better than canary yellow, and that protecting canary yellow via trademark law would foreclose defendants from nothing other than their ability to trade on the good reputation of plaintiff's brand. Minnesota Mining and Man. v. Beautone Specialties, 82 F.Supp.2d 997, 1001.

N.D.N.Y.1995. Com. (c) quot. in case quot. in disc. (citing § 17 of T.D. No. 2, 1990. § 17 has since been revised; see Official Text). Manufacturer of playground equipment brought Lanham Act action against competitor, seeking to enjoin it from producing a line of equipment it claimed was virtually identical to its own. The court granted the injunction, holding that plaintiff's trade dress, consisting of flat wooden panels cut in shapes of objects and animals attractive to children and painted in basic colors and using protective white caps to cover protrusions, was distinctive and that plaintiff had shown strong similarities between the two product lines, a strong likelihood of confusion and at least one customer's actual confusion. The court rejected defendant's contention that plaintiff's trade dress was functional, reasoning that defendant did not prove that the design was essential for purposes of cost or safety or that competition was impossible without copying plaintiff's overall look. Kompan A.S. v. Park Structures, Inc., 890 F.Supp. 1167, 1181.

N.D.N.Y.1995. Com. (c) cit. but dist. In an action under § 43(a) of the Lanham Act, manufacturer of Mission-style furniture sought to enjoin competitor from producing a seemingly identical line of chairs, benches, and sideboards. The court granted plaintiff's motion for a preliminary injunction, holding that it had shown it had a protectible mark that had acquired distinctiveness through secondary meaning and that, absent the requested relief, potential customers were likely to become confused, causing plaintiff to suffer irreparable harm. The court disagreed with defendant's contention that injunctive relief was inappropriate because plaintiff was attempting to protect an aesthetically functional feature, explaining that defendant failed to prove that it would be at a significant competitive disadvantage if it were prevented from using the specific arrangements of plaintiff's trade dress. L. & J.G. Stickley, Inc. v. Canal Dover Furn. Co., 892 F.Supp. 413, 426, vacated 79 F.3d 258 (2d Cir.1996).

S.D.N.Y.2011. Com. (c) quot. in case quot. in sup. High fashion footwear designer sought injunctive relief against competitor for, inter alia, trademark infringement and unfair competition under the Lanham Act, alleging that the outsoles of competitor's shoes were a confusingly similar shade of red as that protected by designer's trademark on red outsoles. This court denied plaintiff's motion for a preliminary injunction, holding that it did not establish a likelihood of success against defendant, because it was unlikely to be able to prove that its red outsole trademark was protectable. The court reasoned that color was not protectable where it was functional, and, in fashion markets, color was functional where it served not solely to identify sponsorship, but was used primarily to advance expressive, ornamental and aesthetic purposes, as in defendant's functional use of red in a collection of monochromatic and color-coordinating shoes and garments; consequently, a trademark on a color for an item in the fashion industry, without some limitation, was overly broad. Christian Louboutin S.A. v. Yves Saint Laurent America, Inc., 778 F.Supp.2d 445, 450.

S.D.N.Y.2010. Com. (a) quot. in sup. Manufacturer of a foot file that had an egg-like appearance sued competitor that marketed a similar foot file, alleging, among other things, unfair competition under the Lanham Act. Granting defendants' motion to dismiss plaintiff's federal unfair-competition claim, this court held that plaintiff failed to allege that the trade dress of its foot file was nonfunctional, an essential element of such a claim. While plaintiff alleged that the trade dress was "arbitrary and fanciful," that phrase was not interchangeable with nonfunctional but, instead, was a term of art that specifically related to a different element of an infringement claim, distinctiveness; distinctiveness and nonfunctionality were clearly separate issues in the sphere of trademark law, since product trade dress that was functional was ineligible for protection regardless of its inherent or acquired distinctiveness. Telebrands Corp. v. Del Laboratories, Inc., 719 F.Supp.2d 283, 297.

S.D.N.Y.2001. Com. (b) quot. in sup. Corkscrew manufacturer brought, in part, claims for trade-dress infringement and unfair competition against competitor. Granting defendant's motion to dismiss the trade-dress-infringement claim, this court held, inter alia, that plaintiff's corkscrew's "rabbit's head" design was nonfunctional and protectable, but that there was no significant likelihood that defendant's corkscrew, which did not resemble a rabbit and was a purely functional device to pull corks from bottles, would be confused with plaintiff's corkscrew by purchasers or users. Metrokane, Inc. v. The Wine Enthusiast, 160 F.Supp.2d 633, 639.

S.D.N.Y.1994. Subsec. (c) quot. in case quot. in sup., illus. 6-8 cit. and quot. in sup. Knitwear manufacturer sued clothing retailer, among others, claiming that defendant infringed on plaintiff's trade dress and copyright by selling an alleged knockoff of plaintiff's Aran fisherman's sweater. Denying defendant's motion for partial summary judgment, the court held, inter alia, that defendant failed to show that plaintiff's design was aesthetically functional as a matter of law, such that its protection would effectively exclude competitors from the market; in the face of evidence suggesting the viability of alternative designs, defendant did not show at this stage of litigation that it would be foreclosed from competing in the market for Aran fisherman's sweaters if it were unable to market the design at issue here. Banff, Ltd. v. Limited, Inc., 869 F.Supp. 1103, 1112-1114.

W.D.Pa.2007. Com. (c) quot. in sup. Medical-equipment manufacturer sued competitor and its chief operating officer for, inter alia, federal trademark infringement under the Lanham Act, alleging its right to exclusive use of the color blue with black markings on its endoscopic probes. Granting summary judgment for defendants on this claim, this court held that there was no genuine issue regarding the fact that the blue color and black markings on the probes were "functional" and, therefore, such product features could not serve as trademarks; when a design's "aesthetic value" lay in its ability to confer significant benefit that could not practically be dupli-

Cit.—cited; com.—comment; fol.—followed; sup.—support.
A complete list of abbreviations precedes page 1.

cated by the use of alternative designs, it was deemed "functional," and, here, it was shown that the color blue enhanced endoscopic identification. ERBE Electromedizin GmbH v. Canady Technology LLC, 529 F.Supp.2d 577, 601.

D.R.I.2005. Cit. generally in disc., illus. 8 quot. in disc. Kitchenware-company owner who designed heart-shaped measuring spoons brought suit for, in part, trade-dress infringement against competitor that copied plaintiff's spoon sets and produced its own version to sell at a lower price. Granting defendant's motion for summary judgment, the court held, inter alia, that plaintiff failed to show that her product design served the primary nonfunctional purpose of identifying her as the source of the product. Because there was evidence that the heart-shape design was functional in the sense that its appeal produced demand, the aesthetic-functionality doctrine denied trade-dress protection. Bonazoli v. R.S.V.P. Intern., Inc., 353 F.Supp.2d 218, 226, 227, 230.

TOPIC 2. ACQUISITION AND PRIORITY OF RIGHTS

§ 18. Acquisition of Rights

E.D.Mich.2016. Com. (d) quot. in sup. Inventors of a spring-loaded drawer-organizer device brought a claim for trademark infringement against licensee of the right to manufacture, market, and sell the device, after defendant obtained a federal trademark registration for the name of plaintiffs' invention and began selling a competing device under the same name in nearly identical packaging. This court granted partial summary judgment for plaintiffs, holding that plaintiffs had created and maintained a common-law trademark for the name of their device. The court reasoned, in part, that, although plaintiffs themselves never manufactured or sold the devices, they demonstrated sufficient use of the mark under Restatement Third of Unfair Competition § 18 to satisfy the "use in commerce" requirement by showing that they had solicited retailers and manufacturers to produce a mold for the device before meeting defendant. Hoenig Developments, Inc. v. Dial Industries, Inc., 213 F.Supp.3d 895, 903.

D.N.J.2006. Quot. in sup. Online furniture retailer sued competitor for, in part, unfair competition and trademark infringement; competitor counterclaimed, alleging that it had trademark rights in over 90 unique, proprietary, and arbitrary product names. Denying competitor's motion for summary judgment on its claims with respect to the product names, this court held, inter alia, that competitor failed to establish that its unregistered product names were valid and protectable marks. The court found the evidence unclear as to how competitor actually used its product names, since competitor did not show where they appeared, if and how they were communicated to prospective purchasers, or even to what kinds of items they referred. Buying For The Home, LLC v. Humble Abode, LLC, 459 F.Supp.2d 310, 327.

S.D.N.Y.2007. Quot. in sup., cit. in ftn., com. (b) quot. in sup. and cit. in ftn., com. (d) quot. in ftn. Swedish manufacturer of professional laundry equipment brought action for trademark infringement and unfair competition against its exclusive United States distributor. Granting plaintiff's motion for a preliminary injunction, this court held, inter alia, that it appeared likely that plaintiff would be able to establish prior use of its "Wavy W" mark and that defendant would not be able to prove abandonment. The court found that plaintiff was apparently the first party to affix the mark to its products or to use it in marketing or advertising, and that any failure by plaintiff to exercise control over the use of it was in connection with products manufactured by others. AB Electrolux v. Bermil Industries Corp., 481 F.Supp.2d 325, 330, 334.

M.D.Tenn.1998. Quot. in disc. Restaurant owner sued union whose representatives had been distributing flyers bearing a parody of the restaurant's trademarked logo and listing a series of health violations, alleging that the union's actions violated plaintiff's trademark rights under the Lanham Act. Granting defendant's motion to dismiss, the court held, inter alia, that defendant did not use plaintiff's logo in commerce, as required for the imposition of liability under the Lanham Act, since defendant's purpose in distributing the flyers bearing the logo was not to advertise itself or its services, but to pressure an

For earlier citations, see the Appendices, Supplements, or Pocket Parts, if any, that correspond to the subject matter under examination.

employer in a labor dispute. WHS Entertainment v. United Paperworkers Intern., 997 F.Supp. 946, 950.

Ark.1997. Cit. in disc. The owner of the "Howard Funeral Home" brought a trade-name infringement action against a competitor that did business as "Eddie Howard Funeral Home," seeking to enjoin defendant from using the name "Howard" in connection with its funeral business. The chancery court declined to issue the injunction. Reversing, this court held, inter alia, that plaintiff had acquired a protectable interest in its trade name, without purchasing rights to it, by using the name in connection with its business over the course of time so that the trade name acquired a secondary meaning. Tri-County Funeral v. Eddie Howard Funeral, 330 Ark. 789, 957 S.W.2d 694, 698.

Ind.App.2014. Cit. and quot. in conc. and diss. op., quot. in ftn. to conc. and diss. op., com. (d) quot. in ftn. to conc. and diss. op. County visitor bureau sued operator of a hotel resort in the county for unfair competition and other claims in connection with allegations that defendant purchased and used the domain name visitmichigancitylaporte.com immediately after plaintiff publicly announced its selection of the designation "Visit Michigan City LaPorte" as the branding identifier for the area. On remand, the trial court entered judgment for plaintiff, and permanently enjoined defendant from using either the phrase or the domain name. Reversing, this court held that, as the designation had not become identified with plaintiff before defendant began using it, it was error for the trial court to find that defendant's use of the phrase was unfair competition. The concurring and dissenting opinion argued that priority of use in the designation lay with plaintiff for purposes of its unfair-competition claim, since, according to Restatement Third of Unfair Competition § 18, defendant's use of the designation merely to frustrate plaintiff's marketing plans in preparing to use a similar mark was not a bona fide use in the ordinary course of business. Serenity Springs, Inc. v. LaPorte County Convention and Visitors Bureau ex rel. Bd. of Managers, 13 N.E.3d 487, 494, 495.

La.1995. Cit. in headnote and disc. The Gulf Coast Bank sued the Gulf Coast Bank and Trust Company for trade name infringement, alleging that defendant's corporate name was deceptively similar to plaintiff's in violation of Louisiana's Trademark Act. Trial court granted defendant summary judgment and intermediate appellate court affirmed. This court reversed and remanded, holding that one need not prove fraud to enjoin another from using its trade name, but must show that there is a likelihood of consumer confusion created by defendant's use of the trade name. On remand, the court stated that plaintiff must establish secondary meaning. It noted that plaintiff had used its name since 1970 and had registered its trade name with the Secretary of State in 1984. Gulf Coast Bank v. Gulf Coast Bank & Trust Co., 652 So.2d 1306, 1307, 1313.

La.App.2006. Cit. in disc. After brother, who was essentially fired from his family jewelry business, opened a competing business with a similar name, family jewelry business sued brother and competing business, seeking, in part, to enjoin defendants from using its registered trade names, which included the family name in conjunction with the words "jewelers," "jewelry," and "diamonds." The trial court rendered judgment in favor of defendant. Reversing in part, this court held, inter alia, that plaintiff's registered trade names had acquired secondary meaning and were entitled to trade-name protection, but that defendant had sufficiently distinguished competing business by including both his first name and his surname in its trade name. The court noted that plaintiff's actual prior use of the trade names, a threshold requirement, was not at issue. Ramsey's Mfg. Jewelers, Inc. v. Ramsey, 924 So.2d 1045, 1051, writ denied 930 So.2d 26 (La.2006).

La.App.2004. Cit. in sup. Shoe store sought injunction against national shoe retailer to prevent national retailer from using word "shoetique," which store had registered as trade name. Trial court granted national retailer summary judgment. Reversing and remanding, this court held that genuine issue of material fact as to whether the descriptive term "shoetique" had taken on a secondary meaning and therefore acquired a protectable proprietary character precluded summary judgment. McCain v. Designer Shoes Warehouse, LLC, 864 So.2d 784, 787.

Mo.App.1993. Quot. in disc., com. (d) quot. in part in disc. (citing § 18 of T.D. No. 2, 1990. § 18 has since been revised; see

Official Text). Gearbox manufacturer sued competitor and former employees working for competitor to enjoin them from revealing its trade secrets and using its trademark without authorization and requested other relief. The trial court granted plaintiff injunctive relief. Affirming in part, reversing in part, and remanding with directions, this court held, inter alia, that, since any use competitor made of the accused mark before selling or distributing any gearboxes was not sufficient to create protectable trademark rights, plaintiff engaged in protected use of its mark before competitor engaged in such use of it, considering additionally competitor's knowledge of plaintiff's logo, indicating that its subsequent decision to use the accused mark was made in bad faith. Superior Gearbox Co. v. Edwards, 869 S.W.2d 239, 252.

Neb.2019. Adopted and quot. in case quot. in disc. and cit. in ftn. Home-construction company brought a lawsuit against competitor, alleging, among other things, that defendant misused plaintiff's trade name and committed deceptive trade practices by using a name substantially similar to plaintiff's trade name. The trial court entered judgment for plaintiff. This court affirmed, holding that defendant infringed upon plaintiff's trade name. The court rejected defendant's assertion that it did not use the infringing name as a trade name because the name was defendant's true legal name, and explained that defendant "used" the name as a trade name, as defined by Restatement Third of Unfair Competition § 18, by displaying it on advertising, social media, and elsewhere. Denali Real Estate, LLC v. Denali Custom Builders, Inc., 926 N.W.2d 610, 624.

Neb.2000. Cit. in disc., cit. and quot. in sup. and adopted, com. (a) cit. in disc., com. (d) cit. in sup. Business owner who had registered the trade name "Husker Authentics" sued university for damages and injunctive relief, alleging that defendant was wrongfully using the trade name. Affirming the trial court's dismissal of the claim, this court held, inter alia, that defendant had a common law right in the trade name "Husker Authentics" through its use of the name prior to registration of the name by plaintiff, and the registration therefore was invalid and had to be canceled. White v. Board of Regents, 260 Neb. 26, 35, 36, 614 N.W.2d 330, 337, 338.

Neb.App.2007. Adopted in case cit. in sup., quot. in sup. Security-services corporation that had acquired the successor-in-interest of a closely held security-systems company brought deceptive-trade-practices and trade-name-infringement claims against the company's former shareholders and the new security business that shareholders had started under the company's name, "A/C Security." The trial court entered judgment for plaintiff. Affirming, this court held that plaintiff had a legally protectable common-law interest in the trade name "A/C Security," and that defendants had violated that interest. The court reasoned that company's successor sold the trade name to plaintiff, and that plaintiff made use of the trade name in its ordinary course of business by, for example, continuing to honor company's old contracts. ADT Sec. Services, Inc. v. A/C Sec. Systems, Inc., 15 Neb.App. 666, 684, 736 N.W.2d 737, 757.

§ 19. Priority of Rights

C.A.1, 1992. Subsec. (a) cit. in disc., com. (d) cit. and quot. in disc., illus. 3 cit. in disc. (citing § 19 of T.D. No. 2, 1990. § 19 has since been revised; see Official Text). A cowboy sued a syndicator of an old television program featuring a fictional cowboy bearing striking similarities to plaintiff, alleging that defendant had violated federal and state trademark and unfair competition laws. Reversing the district court's judgment in plaintiff's favor, this court held that, since the suit depended upon relitigating issues that had already been decided against him in a prior suit against the network that originally provided the program, his new claims were collaterally estopped. The court stated that even if plaintiff provided evidence of his own expansion into television, an area where the network had priority using the mark, such expansion would be irrelevant because there was no evidence that the network or its syndicator used the mark in bad faith, with an intent or expectation of causing confusion, forestalling expansion under the mark by plaintiff, or harming plaintiff's reputation or good will. DeCosta v. Viacom Intern., Inc., 981 F.2d 602, 611, 612, cert. denied 509 U.S. 923, 113 S.Ct. 3039, 125 L.Ed.2d 725 (1993).

C.A.Fed.2018. Com. (b) cit. in disc. Shoe manufacturer filed a complaint with the International Trade Commission (ITC), alleging that various competitors had infringed upon plaintiff's trademark by copying particular design elements constituting plaintiff's trademark. The ITC's administrative law judge found that plaintiff's trademark was valid but did not have a secondary meaning. The ITC reversed, finding that the trademark's lack of secondary meaning rendered it invalid. This court reversed and remanded, holding, inter alia, that plaintiff's trademark registration was not several distinct sets of rights arising from two kinds of marks as the ITC asserted, but rather a single mark that gave rise to several sets of rights. The court cited Restatement Third of Unfair Competition § 19, Comment *b*, in explaining that plaintiff's validly registered trademark gave rise to a presumption of secondary meaning from the date of its registration onwards. Converse, Inc. v. International Trade Commission Skechers U.S.A., Inc., 909 F.3d 1110, 1117.

D.Del.1994. Com. (d) quot. in part in sup. (citing § 19 of T.D. No. 2, 1990. § 19 has since been revised; see Official Text). A temporary-employee placement company based in New Jersey sued a Florida competitor that had a Delaware office for service-mark infringement, unfair competition, and other claims. Granting in part the competitor's motion for summary judgment, the court held, inter alia, that no reasonable trier of fact could have inferred that the competitor adopted or decided to go forward with its "ACCUSTAFF" service mark, knowing that the placement company was using the "ACCU" mark and intending to reap some benefit from goodwill built up in the "ACCU" mark, so as to disqualify the competitor from protection of its mark. The expanding senior user, said the court, had to give way to the junior user's rights, established in good faith, in a geographically remote area, as the facts indicated at most that the competitor had knowledge of the service mark used by the placement company. ACCU Personnel, Inc. v. AccuStaff, Inc., 846 F.Supp. 1191, 1210.

D.D.C.2006. Rptr's Note to com. (b) cit. in disc. Association of law firms sued a two-member law partnership, seeking a declaratory judgment that it was the rightful owner of the "GLOBALAW" service mark; partnership, which claimed to have used the mark since 1988, counterclaimed for, in part, trademark infringement. Granting summary judgment for association on the counterclaim, this court held, inter alia, that partnership failed to establish that the mark, even if potentially protectable as a descriptive term, had accrued secondary meaning linking the mark to partnership in the minds of the purchasing public. The court observed that the scope of a party's rights to a descriptive term was limited to those geographic areas where secondary meaning existed before the alleged infringement began. Globalaw Ltd. v. Carmon & Carmon Law Office, 452 F.Supp.2d 1, 40.

S.D.Fla.1998. Com. (b) cit. in headnote and disc., com. (e) cit. in disc. "Popular Bank" of Florida brought suit seeking an injunction prohibiting "Banco Popular de Puerto Rico" and "Banco Popular N.A. (Florida)" from using the marks Banco Popular or Popular Express in four counties in Florida. This court granted plaintiffs the preliminary injunction as to the name "Banco Popular," because plaintiff had established the priority and validity of its mark and defendants' use of that mark in South Florida was likely to cause customer confusion. However, the court denied plaintiff's request to enjoin the use of the name "Popular Express," because plaintiff did not demonstrate a likelihood of success on the merits by showing that its rights to the mark were prior and superior to defendants' use of the mark and that the mark was likely to cause consumer confusion. The court determined that plaintiff failed to establish common law rights based on either actual use or zone of natural expansion. Popular Bank of Fla. v. Banco Popular de Puerto Rico, 9 F.Supp.2d 1347, 1348, 1354, 1355.

S.D.Iowa, 1995. Com. (d) cit. in disc. An Iowa bank named "First Bank" sued "First Bank System, Inc.," a Minnesota bank holding company that purchased an Iowa bank, requesting a permanent injunction against defendant's use of the terms "First Bank" or "First Bank Iowa." This court denied plaintiff's request, concluding that plaintiff had not proved a factual basis for its injunctive-relief claim. Equitable considerations precluded plaintiff from using the name "First Bank" exclusively in the three counties in question, because plaintiff's board of directors and management deliberately attempted to adopt the name "First Bank" knowing defendant was attempting to enter its market area and would likely use its registered name or a variant of the name "First Bank Systems." It noted that adoption of a mark or name already in use by another person is not in good faith if the name is adopted for the purpose of forestall-

Cit.—cited; com.—comment; fol.—followed; sup.—support.
A complete list of abbreviations precedes page 1.

ing the expansion of the mark and name by the prior user. First Bank v. First Bank System, Inc., 909 F.Supp. 657, 662.

D.Kan.2000. Cit. in disc. Bank sued competitor for service-mark infringement, alleging that the name of defendant's financial institution was confusingly similar to the one used by plaintiff. On remand, defendant moved for summary judgment. Denying the motion, the court held, in part, that material factual issues existed as to whether plaintiff's mark, which was weakly descriptive, had acquired secondary meaning in the disputed territory and, if so, whether secondary meaning was acquired before defendant began using the mark in that area in the same way or in a way likely to create consumer confusion. First Sav. Bank, F.S.B. v. U.S. Bancorp, 117 F.Supp.2d 1061, 1070.

E.D.Mich.2003. Cit. in case quot. in sup. Bank sued competitor under state and federal law for infringement of its service mark. Granting plaintiff's motion for a preliminary injunction, the court held, inter alia, that plaintiff had acquired common-law rights in its service mark, "Midwest Guaranty Bank," prior to any actual use by defendant of its mark, "Guaranty Bank," in the relevant geographic area of southeast Michigan. Midwest Guaranty Bank v. Guaranty Bank, 270 F.Supp.2d 900, 908.

W.D.Pa.1999. Cit. in sup. Bank holding company and its subsidiary brought trademark-infringement action against competing financial institution, seeking to enjoin defendant from using the mark "Laurel" in connection with banking services defendant offered in the Pittsburgh area. Entering partial summary judgment for plaintiff, the court held that "Laurel," as used here, was an arbitrary mark; that, while defendant was the senior user, plaintiff, having penetrated the relevant market first, had superior rights to the mark in the regional area at issue; and that the evidence supported the finding that defendant's actions would cause a likelihood of confusion. Laurel Capital Group, Inc. v. BT Financial Corp., 45 F.Supp.2d 469, 482.

Alaska, 2001. Rptr's Note, com. (b) quot. in ftn. Theater owner sued operator of trolley tour service named "Fourth Avenue Theater Trolley Tours" for infringement of its trade name "Fourth Avenue Theatre." The trial court entered judgment on a jury verdict for plaintiff. Affirming in part, this court held, inter alia, that defendants infringed plaintiff's trade name. The court said that "Fourth Avenue Theatre" had acquired a secondary meaning prior to its use by defendants, and that the jury's finding of a likelihood of confusion was supported by the evidence. Alderman v. Iditarod Properties, Inc., 32 P.3d 373, 389.

Ind.App.2014. Cit. in conc. and diss. op. County visitor bureau sued operator of a hotel resort in the county for unfair competition and other claims in connection with allegations that defendant purchased and used the domain name visitmichigancitylaporte.com immediately after plaintiff publicly announced its selection of the designation "Visit Michigan City LaPorte" as the branding identifier for the area. On remand, the trial court entered judgment for plaintiff, and permanently enjoined defendant from using either the phrase or the domain name. Reversing, this court held that, as the designation had not become identified with plaintiff before defendant began using it, it was error for the trial court to find that defendant's use of the phrase was unfair competition. The concurring and dissenting opinion argued that priority of use in the designation lay with plaintiff for purposes of its unfair-competition claim, citing Restatement Third of Unfair Competition § 19 in noting that only a person who had applied a designation as a trademark first had priority in the use of the designation over another user. Serenity Springs, Inc. v. LaPorte County Convention and Visitors Bureau ex rel. Bd. of Managers, 13 N.E.3d 487, 493.

La.1995. Com. (b) cit. in ftn. The Gulf Coast Bank sued the Gulf Coast Bank and Trust Company for trade-name infringement, alleging that defendant's corporate name was deceptively similar to plaintiff's in violation of Louisiana's Trademark Act. Trial court granted defendant summary judgment and intermediate appellate court affirmed. This court reversed and remanded, holding that where one relies on secondary meaning to establish the distinctiveness of its name, one need not prove fraud to enjoin another from using its trade name, but must show that there is a likelihood of consumer confusion created by defendant's use of the trade name. Fact issues existed as to the degree of protection that could be afforded plaintiff outside of the Acadiana area. The court noted that a senior user could protect its trade name in areas in which its reputation had extended even though that may be outside its area of operation. Gulf Coast Bank v. Gulf Coast Bank & Trust Co., 652 So.2d 1306, 1322.

Neb.2000. Cit. and quot. in sup. and adopted. Business owner who had registered the trade name "Husker Authentics" sued university for damages and injunctive relief, alleging that defendant was wrongfully using the trade name. Affirming the trial court's dismissal of the claim, this court held, inter alia, that defendant had a common law right in the trade name "Husker Authentics" through its use of the name prior to registration of the name by plaintiff, and the registration therefore was invalid and had to be canceled. White v. Board of Regents, 260 Neb. 26, 35, 36, 37, 614 N.W.2d 330, 338.

Wis.App.1994. Cit. in sup., com. (b) cit. in sup. (citing § 19 of T.D. No. 2, 1990. § 19 has since been revised; see Official Text). (erron. cit. as T.D. No. 3, 1991.) Purchaser of store in Oshkosh sought judgment declaring its rights under trade name; store in Milwaukee with same trade name counterclaimed. Affirming the trial court's finding that Oshkosh store built up its own secondary meaning in the Oshkosh area independent of the Milwaukee store, and that this finding was limited to a 20-mile radius, this court held that a contractual agreement that the seller entered into with purchaser stating that seller would not engage in a competing business within a 20-mile radius from Oshkosh store was probative of seller's understanding of the scope of the secondary meaning owned by him, since seller could sell only what he owned. Since counterclaiming store had registered the trade name first, it was the prima facie owner of the trade name beyond Oshkosh. Leon's Frozen Custard, Inc. v. Leon Corp., 182 Wis.2d 236, 513 N.W.2d 636, 639.

TOPIC 3. INFRINGEMENT OF RIGHTS

§ 20. Standard of Infringement

C.A.1, 2004. Com. (b) quot. in sup. Beacon Mutual, an insurer that had a lighthouse logo, sued competing insurer that changed its name to One Beacon and adopted lighthouse logo, alleging violations of Lanham Act and state trademark laws. District court granted defendant summary judgment, holding that plaintiff did not show substantial likelihood of confusion. This court reversed and remanded, holding that actual confusion was commercially relevant if infringer's use of mark could inflict commercial injury through diversion of sales, damage to goodwill, or loss of control over reputation on trademark holder. It held that likelihood-of-confusion inquiry was not limited to actual or potential purchasers, but also included others whose confusion threatened trademark owner's commercial interest in its mark. Here, there was sufficient evidence of actual confusion relevant to plaintiff's commercial interests. Beacon Mut. Ins. Co. v. OneBeacon Ins. Group, 376 F.3d 8, 16, on remand 376 F.Supp.2d 251 (D.R.I.2005).

C.A.2, 1997. Com. (b) cit. in headnote, cit. in disc. Manufacturer of commercial outdoor furniture, called "site furniture," sued competitor for trade-dress infringement. The district court granted manufacturer a preliminary injunction; the Second Circuit vacated and remanded. The district court reinstated the injunction, and this court again vacated, holding that manufacturer failed to establish that its trade dress was inherently distinctive. The court noted that the test for likelihood of confusion concerned the general public as well as potential purchasers, but third parties were relevant only if their views were related to the manufacturer's goodwill. If the general public was unaware of the manufacturer's trade dress, its confusion was irrelevant. Landscape Forms, Inc. v. Columbia Cascade Co., 113 F.3d 373, 374, 383.

C.A.2, 1991. Cit. in disc., cit. in sup. §§ 20-23, subsec. (1)(c) and com. (f) cit. in disc., Rptr's Note quot. in disc. (citing § 20 of T.D. No. 2, 1990. § 20 has since been revised; see Official Text). A publisher of a book and audiotapes on the development of charisma that used the trade name "New Choices Press" sought to enjoin a magazine publisher from using the name "New Choices for the Best Years" for its magazine on retirement living. The district court granted defendant's motion for summary judgment. Affirming, this court held that plaintiff failed to raise a genuine issue of fact as to the likelihood of confusion. The

Cit.—cited; com.—comment; fol.—followed; sup.—support.
A complete list of abbreviations precedes page 1.

court concluded that plaintiff's trade name was weak because it was not widely known. Lang v. Retirement Living Pub. Co., Inc., 949 F.2d 576, 579, 580, 583.

C.A.4, 2010. Com. (b) quot. in sup. Paper-products manufacturer brought, inter alia, a Lanham Act claim for contributory trademark infringement against competitor, after defendant started selling to distributors an inferior paper toweling it specifically manufactured for use in plaintiff's touchless paper-towel dispensers bearing plaintiff's trademarks. The district court granted summary judgment for defendant. Vacating and remanding, this court held, inter alia, that the district court erred in limiting its likelihood-of-confusion inquiry to distributors who purchased defendant's toweling and their respective end-user customers; plaintiff offered sufficient evidence for a reasonable jury to find that there was a likelihood of confusion among restroom visitors as to the source of the paper toweling being dispensed from plaintiff's dispensers when such dispensers were "stuffed" with defendant's toweling, and that the likelihood of confusion among such restroom visitors would adversely affect plaintiff's reputation among its laborers, lenders, investors, or other groups with whom plaintiff interacted. Georgia Pacific Consumer Products, LP v. Von Drehle Corp., 618 F.3d 441, 453.

C.A.5, 1998. Com. (b) cit. in disc. and cit. in ftn. Golf course operator sued competitor for trademark infringement, alleging that defendant infringed and diluted plaintiff's mark by copying one of its holes. The district court entered judgment for plaintiff. Affirming, this court held, in part, that the design of plaintiff's hole was nonfunctional, under a test for either utilitarian or aesthetic functionality; that the design was descriptive and had acquired secondary meaning, as evidenced by plaintiff's extensive advertising, unsolicited publicity of the hole's trade dress in golf publications, and defendant's intent to copy and use the trade dress prominently in its own advertising; that plaintiff did not abandon its rights in a nearby lighthouse that was built at the same time as the golf course for purposes of being seen from the course; that the evidence supported the lower court's finding of a likelihood of confusion; and that defendant's use of the mark to suggest affiliation, sponsorship, or endorsement was more than nominative. Pebble Beach Co. v. Tour 18 I Ltd., 155 F.3d 526, 545, 546.

C.A.7, 1995. Com. (g) cit. in sup. A broom manufacturer brought a trademark infringement action against a competitor, alleging infringement of its trademarked contrasting color bands on the bristles of its brooms. District court enjoined competitor from selling the infringing line of brooms and awarded monetary relief, representing competitor's profits from the sale. This court reversed, holding, inter alia, that it was pure speculation to conclude that anyone, let alone a significant fraction of the broom-buying public, could have been misled into believing that plaintiff's broom and defendant's broom were one and the same brand. The two brooms were not packaged alike and did not have similar names; while the "undressed" brooms were similar, they were not identical; the appearance of the brooms in advertising was dissimilar; and the trademark was a thin one, since adding a colored stripe was hardly a distinctive way of marking a product. Libman Co. v. Vining Industries, Inc., 69 F.3d 1360, 1364.

C.A.9, 2012. Com. (b) cit. in ftn. Technology companies brought an action under the Lanham Act against business, alleging that business's use of a name similar to companies' names constituted trademark infringement. The district court granted summary judgment for defendant. Vacating and remanding, this court held that genuine issues of material fact existed regarding the likelihood of confusion between the marks at issue, and the district court erred by failing to consider plaintiffs' evidence of non-consumer confusion on the part of: potential consumers, non-consumers whose confusion could create an inference that consumers were likely to be confused, and non-consumers whose confusion could influence consumers. The court pointed to evidence of actual confusion on the part of several non-consumers—including plaintiff's prospective employees, plaintiff's auditors and patent attorneys, a vendor, an investor, various trade publications, and certain trade-show organizers and attendees. Rearden LLC v. Rearden Commerce, Inc., 683 F.3d 1190, 1217.

C.A.9, 1999. Cit. in disc. §§ 20-23. Entertainment industry information provider using "MovieBuff" as trademark sought to enjoin video rental chain from using "moviebuff.com" as its web site domain name. The district court entered judgment for defendant. Reversing and remanding,

For earlier citations, see the Appendices, Supplements, or Pocket Parts, if any, that correspond to the subject matter under examination.

this court held that plaintiff established itself as the senior user of the mark, and that, given the similarity of the marks, the relatedness of product offerings, and the overlap in marketing and advertising channels, likelihood of consumer confusion existed. That defendant did not intend to confuse consumers was irrelevant under the circumstances. Brookfield Communications v. West Coast, 174 F.3d 1036, 1054.

C.A.10, 2013. Com. (g) cit. and quot. in sup. Retailer of replacement contact lenses brought a claim for service-mark infringement under the Lanham Act against competitor, alleging, among other things, that competitor infringed retailer's 1800CONTACTS mark by purchasing keywords resembling the mark so that potential customers using a search engine would be directed to competitor's website. The district court granted summary judgment for defendant. Affirming in part, this court held, inter alia, that no likelihood of confusion existed, because traditional analysis and actual marketplace data revealed that the keywords used by defendant were highly unlikely to divert consumers. The court concluded that plaintiff's survey showing an average 7.4% confusion rate was entitled to no more than minimal weight and thus was correctly excluded by the trial court, noting that other factors, such as hard data concerning how often consumers were lured to defendant's website, overwhelmingly indicated the unlikelihood of confusion. 1-800 Contacts, Inc. v. Lens.com, Inc., 722 F.3d 1229, 1249.

C.A.10, 2008. Com. (g) quot. in ftn. to diss. op. Ski resort that had a registered incontestable service mark in a geographically descriptive term, "Vail," that it used in conjunction with a purely descriptive term, "Ski," sued marketing service that had a registered service mark in the alphanumeric telephone number "1-800-SKI-VAIL," alleging infringement under the Lanham Act. After a bench trial, the district court concluded that plaintiff failed to show a likelihood of confusion between the two marks. Affirming, this court held, inter alia, that defendant's mark traded on "Vail" as a geographic ski destination, rather than as a mark identifying plaintiff or its resort. The dissent argued that the marks were confusingly similar and that the totality of factors weighed in favor of a finding that defendant's mark was likely to cause consumer confusion. Vail Associates, Inc. v. Vend-Tel-Co., Ltd., 516 F.3d 853, 875.

C.A.10, 1999. Cit. in disc. §§ 20-23. Seller of camouflage-patterned outdoor clothing under "King of the Mountain" trademark brought trademark-infringement action against promoter of "Jeep KING OF THE MOUNTAIN DOWNHILL SERIES" ski races. Affirming the district court's grant of summary judgment for defendant, this court held, in part, that no likelihood of confusion existed as to sponsorship of ski races. King of the Mountain Sports, Inc. v. Chrysler Corp., 185 F.3d 1084, 1090.

C.D.Cal.2014. Com. (b) cit. in sup. Biopharmaceutical company brought a trademark-infringement claim, inter alia, against competitor, alleging that defendant's use of the LITHERA trademark infringed its KYTHERA mark, which it used in connection its development of a product that was designed to reduce human body fat. Denying defendant's motion to dismiss, this court held that plaintiff's allegations tended to show a likelihood of confusion and therefore plausibly supported plaintiff's claim despite the fact that plaintiff's product was not yet commercially available. The court cited Restatement Third of Unfair Competition § 20, Comment *b*, in noting that, while the focus of the court's inquiry was on whether actual consumers were confused, plaintiff was correct that confusion by non-consumers, such as potential consumers, could also be relevant to the likelihood-of-confusion inquiry. Kythera Biopharmaceuticals, Inc. v. Lithera, Inc., 998 F.Supp.2d 890, 901.

C.D.Cal.2004. Rptr's Note cit. generally in ftn. Clothing manufacturer that used a moose in its brand name and logos brought trademark-infringement suit against clothing retailer, alleging that retailer's use of the word "moose" and a pictorial depiction of a moose on its apparel and in its advertising campaigns caused customer confusion. Denying plaintiff's motion for preliminary injunction, the court held that plaintiff failed to adequately demonstrate a likelihood of customer confusion. Although confusion was actionable even where consumer did not make a purchase, plaintiff's evidence of one instance of actual confusion occurring during the time that defendant was using a moose on its clothing insufficiently established confusion in any substantial manner. Moose Creek, Inc. v. Abercrombie & Fitch Co., 331 F.Supp.2d 1214, 1230, affirmed 114 Fed.Appx. 921 (9th Cir.2004).

Cit.—cited; com.—comment; fol.—followed; sup.—support.
A complete list of abbreviations precedes page 1.

C.D.Cal.1999. Com. (g) quot. in disc. Magazine publisher sought to enjoin operators of Internet search engines from programming their sites in such a way as to return search results that allegedly infringed and diluted plaintiff's trademark. Declining to issue the injunction, the court held that defendants' use of the generic terms "playboy" and "playmate" did not constitute use of the terms in their trademark forms and that, even if it did, plaintiff had failed to establish a likelihood of confusion, blurring of the marks, or tarnishment. Playboy Enterprises v. Netscape Communications, 55 F.Supp.2d 1070, 1083, affirmed 202 F.3d 278 (9th Cir.1999).

C.D.Cal.1998. Com. (f) quot. in disc., Rptr's Note quot. in disc. and quot. in ftn. Commercial illustrator brought unfair-competition action against toy manufacturer, alleging that defendant misappropriated and misused plaintiff's "Pearl Beach" trade name in connection with the promotion and distribution of its line of dolls. Specifically, plaintiff argued that defendant's actions resulted in reverse confusion in the marketplace. Entering judgment as a matter of law for defendant, the court held, in part, that, although plaintiff's mark was strong, she failed to establish a proximity of the goods, similarity of the marks, or evidence of actual confusion among purchasers; thus, plaintiff did not prove the type of confusion she was required to set forth in order to prevail under her "reverse confusion" theory. Walter v. Mattel, Inc., 31 F.Supp.2d 751, 757, 758, 760, affirmed 210 F.3d 1108 (9th Cir.2000).

D.Colo.2001. Cit. in disc. §§ 20-23. Tirestore owner brought suit against manufacturer of tie-down straps and cargo-control products for infringement of its "Bigfoot" trademark. Granting plaintiff's motion for a preliminary injunction, the court held, inter alia, that plaintiff showed a likelihood of success on the merits based on evidence that defendant's use of the mark was likely to cause confusion in the marketplace concerning the source or quality of the products. Big O Tires, Inc. v. Bigfoot 4X4, Inc., 167 F.Supp.2d 1216, 1222.

D.Kan.1998. Quot. in part in disc. Manufacturer of medical surgical instruments sued company that reconditioned such instruments for, inter alia, patent and trademark infringement, unfair competition, and tortious interference with contract and business expectancy. Defendant moved for summary judgment. Granting the motion, the court held, in part, that defendant was not liable for patent infringement, that the act of repairing trademarked goods did not constitute use of the mark, and that defendant engaged in no wrongful means that would support a claim for tortious interference with contract or business expectancy. U.S. Surgical Corp. v. Orris, Inc., 5 F.Supp.2d 1201, 1208, affirmed 185 F.3d 885 (Fed. Cir.1999).

D.Me.1995. Quot. in sup. A company that developed and marketed promotional campaigns for radio stations sued a radio station, its executives, and its graphic design consultant for federal copyright, trademark, and trade-dress infringement and certain related state law claims. This court granted in part and denied in part defendants' motion for summary judgment, holding, inter alia, that, considering all of the eight pertinent factors together, no reasonable jury could find a likelihood of confusion based on the facts presented. The court applied the eight factors with an eye to the potential for confusion solely among radio station marketing decisionmakers, noting that radio stations were plaintiff's customers; therefore, radio station marketing and promotion decisionmakers were the obvious class whose confusion was relevant. Such sophisticated purchasers were less likely to be confused as to the source or origin of a product than ordinary consumers of inexpensive goods or services. CMM Cable Rep., Inc. v. Ocean Coast Properties, Inc., 888 F.Supp. 192, 200.

D.Md.2002. Rptr's Note cit. in case cit. in disc. Provider of marine lending services sued competitor for trademark infringement. Granting defendant's motion for summary judgment, the court held that, as a matter of law, defendant's use of its trademark was not likely to cause confusion among consumers of the parties' services. The court said that plaintiff's evidence of actual confusion on the part of banks, trade magazines, and internet service providers was entitled to little weight, since those entities were not consumers of the services provided by the parties to prospective purchasers of boats. Sterling Acceptance Corp. v. Tommark, Inc., 227 F.Supp.2d 454, 464, affirmed 91 Fed.Appx. 880 (4th Cir.2004).

D.N.M.2010. Rptr's Note quot. in ftn. Buyer of endodontic equipment sued sellers for breach of contract and unfair trade

For earlier citations, see the Appendices, Supplements, or Pocket Parts, if any, that correspond to the subject matter under examination.

practices; sellers brought various counterclaims sounding in contract and tort. Granting in part and denying in part buyer's motion for summary judgment on sellers' counterclaims, this court held, in determining that New Mexico law applied, that sellers' counterclaims of unfair competition, violation of the New Mexico Unfair Practices Act, and unlawful misappropriation of trade values fell into the category of torts. The court noted that the causes of action in the Restatement Third of Unfair Competition appeared to have grown out of the Restatement of Torts, implying that they should be categorized as torts. Guidance Endodontics, LLC v. Dentsply Intern., Inc., 708 F.Supp.2d 1209, 1225.

E.D.N.Y.2001. Rptr's Note quot. in case quot. in sup. (citing § 20 of T.D. No. 2, 1990. § 20 has since been revised; see Official Text). Manufacturer of sweetener called NatraTaste sued competitors that manufactured NutraSweet for trademark and trade-dress infringement, inter alia. This court granted competitors summary judgment, holding that there was no fact issue as to existence of significant likelihood that reasonably prudent buyers of NatraTaste would be confused into buying NutraSweet. The weakness of plaintiff's expert's survey as evidence of actual confusion was shown by fact that there was no evidence of actual confusion in marketplace; it could be inferred from the absence of such evidence that there was minimal likelihood of confusion. Cumberland Packing Corp. v. Monsanto Co., 140 F.Supp.2d 241, 250.

E.D.N.Y.1994. Rptr's Note at 179 quot. in case cit. in disc. (citing § 20 of T.D. No. 2, 1990. § 20 has since been revised; see Official Text). Karate instructor sued producers and distributor of "The Karate Kid" films for service-mark infringement. The court granted judgment as a matter of law in favor of defendants, holding that plaintiff's mark, "The Karate Kid," which fell into the category of descriptive marks, never acquired a secondary meaning and that there was no legally sufficient evidentiary basis for a reasonable jury to find that a likelihood of consumer confusion, reverse or otherwise, existed. The court said that, in an assessment of the likelihood of consumer confusion, the relevant confusion was that which affected the purchasing and selling of the goods or services in question, and there was no protection against confusion generally. DeClemente v. Columbia Pictures Industries, Inc., 860 F.Supp. 30, 47.

S.D.N.Y.2011. Rptr's Note quot. in case quot. in sup. Company that developed a line of teeth-whitening products using the "Go SMiLE" trademark sued dentist who co-founded company and later sold his interest in it, alleging that defendant's marketing of a competing teeth-whitening product line under the "Glo" mark infringed plaintiff's trademarks. This court denied plaintiff's motion for a preliminary injunction, holding that plaintiff failed to establish a likelihood of success in proving that consumers would confuse plaintiff's marks with those used by defendant. The court found that plaintiff's evidence of consumer confusion was very weak and of limited probative value, in that it did not reflect actual confusion on the part of prospective end-users, but was limited to remarks—many of them vague—attributed to employees of a retail store where plaintiff's products were sold; trademark infringement protected only against mistaken purchasing decisions and not against confusion generally. GoSMiLE, Inc. v. Dr. Jonathan Levine, D.M.D. P.C., 769 F.Supp.2d 630, 645.

S.D.N.Y.2007. Rptr's Note to com. (b) quot. in case quot. in sup. (citing § 20 of T.D. No. 2, 1990. § 20 has since been revised; see Official Text). Online magazine that was targeted towards women aged 35 and under sued publishers of now-defunct print magazine that was targeted towards men aged 40 and over for allegedly infringing on its unregistered trademark by publishing under the same title. Granting summary judgment for defendants on plaintiff's Lanham Act claims, this court held, inter alia, that there was no genuine issue of material fact as to the likelihood of customer confusion. Addressing the factor of actual confusion, the court pointed out that, while plaintiff received several e-mails intended for defendant from businesses and survey respondents, there was no evidence linking the confusion represented by the e-mails to any potential or actual effect on customers' purchasing decisions. SLY Magazine, LLC v. Weider Publications L.L.C., 529 F.Supp.2d 425, 440.

S.D.N.Y.1992. Com. (b) quot. in sup., Rptr's Note (b) quot. in ftn. in sup. (citing § 20 of T.D. No. 2, 1990. § 20 has since been revised; see Official Text). The cover of a stylish weekly magazine was designed as a

Cit.—cited; com.—comment; fol.—followed; sup.—support.
A complete list of abbreviations precedes page 1.

caricature of the famous traditional cover design of an annual almanac. The almanac's publisher and licensing agent sued the magazine's publisher for trademark infringement, false designation of origin, unfair competition, unjust enrichment, and trademark dilution. The court entered judgment for the magazine publisher, holding that the caricature or takeoff on the cover design was clearly recognizable as a joke and thus caused no significant likelihood of confusion concerning its source, since the magazine's title was clearly printed in bold letters. Furthermore, the unauthorized use of the trademark was not for the purpose of source identification. Its use was for the purpose of comedy or parody, and thus it was part of a communicative message that fell under the protection of the First Amendment. Yankee Pub. Inc. v. News America Pub. Inc., 809 F.Supp. 267, 273, 276.

D.R.I.2003. Quot. in case quot. in sup. Insurance company brought a trademark-infringement action against competitor. Granting defendant's motion for summary judgment, the court held, inter alia, that plaintiff failed to make out a claim for trademark infringement because there was no showing that the confusion plaintiff identified was connected in any way to its commercial interests. Beacon Mutual Ins. Co. v. OneBeacon Ins. Group, 290 F.Supp.2d 241, 247, reversed and remanded 376 F.3d 8 (1st Cir.2004).

M.D.Tenn.2000. Quot. in disc. Fast-food chain brought damages suit for unfair competition and trademark infringement against parties that had purchased promotional toys from chain's franchisees and offered them for sale on cable shopping network prior to their release date in marketing campaign. Granting defendants' motions for summary judgment and partial summary judgment, the court held, inter alia, that plaintiff failed to prove likelihood of confusion among consumers regarding whether defendants were affiliated with plaintiff; plaintiff also failed to counter defendants' "first sale" defense that, after the first sale to franchisees, plaintiff's intellectual property rights did not entitle it to exercise control over the toys. McDonald's Corp. v. Shop at Home, Inc., 82 F.Supp.2d 801, 808.

E.D.Va.2006. Com. (b) cit. in disc. User of trade name "Worsham Sprinkler Company" brought infringement action to permanently enjoin competitor and its majority shareholder from using the trade name "Wes Worsham Fire Protection, LLC." Entering judgment for defendants, this court held that plaintiff failed to carry its burden of establishing a likelihood of confusion. The court stated that the analytic factor of actual confusion did not support plaintiff's position, since, considered as a whole, taking into account the sophistication of the customer base and the suppliers, the few instances of actual confusion that might have inflicted commercial injury on plaintiff in the form of diversion of sales, damage to goodwill, or loss of control over reputation were de minimis. Worsham Sprinkler Co., Inc. v. Wes Worsham Fire Protection, LLC, 419 F.Supp.2d 861, 882.

Alaska, 2015. Com. (b) quot. in ftn. Developer of a gated subdivision brought claims for trademark and trade-name infringement against realtors who listed a neighboring property for sale, alleging that realtors misappropriated a photograph of the subdivision's sign and included it in the listing for the neighboring property, with the intent of creating the impression that the property was part of the subdivision. The trial court granted summary judgment for realtors. Affirming, this court held that developer's common-law trade-name infringement claim failed for lack of damages; even if the subdivision's name had acquired secondary meaning, developer failed to show that it suffered any actual damages from realtors' use of its photograph of the sign in their listing. The court cited Restatement Third of Unfair Competition § 20 in noting that modern cases treated trademark and trade-name claims similarly, and that the standard of infringement was the same. Alaskasland.Com, LLC v. Cross, 357 P.3d 805, 827.

Colo.App.2004. Cit. in disc. §§ 20-23. Buyer of seller's partnership interest in a company that developed television programs based on newspaper classified ads sued seller for breach of contract and tortious interference; seller counterclaimed for breach of the parties' license agreement. Trial court entered judgment on jury verdict for seller on the counterclaim. This court reversed in part, holding, inter alia, that buyer's use of "Employment TV" instead of the licensed mark "Employment Television" was not a misleading use of seller's trademark, and thus did not constitute a breach of the license agreement, since the two

For earlier citations, see the Appendices, Supplements, or Pocket Parts, if any, that correspond to the subject matter under examination.

marks were so similar as to preclude confusion by the public. Employment Television Enterprises, LLC v. Barocas, 100 P.3d 37, 49.

Fla.1993. Cit. in ftn. as §§ 20-23. (citing § 20 of T.D. No. 2, 1990. § 20 has since been revised; see Official Text). The First Southern Bank sued to enjoin another bank from using the name "Great Southern Bank," alleging infringement and dilution of its trademark name and unfair competition. The trial court granted plaintiff injunctive relief and certified the question whether plaintiff bank's name was descriptive or generic so as not to be entitled to protection in the absence of proof that it had acquired a secondary meaning. This court remanded, holding that plaintiff bank's name contained laudatory, generic, and merely geographically descriptive elements so as not to be entitled to protection under either common or statutory law, but determination was necessary whether a secondary meaning in the name had developed in order to decide the dilution claim. In applying the suggestiveness test, the court stated that no great imagination was required to identify the product as banking services when the mark contained the word "bank," that many others used the word "southern" in their mark, and that businesses in the South had the need and right to use the term descriptively. Great Southern v. First Southern, 625 So.2d 463, 470.

Ind.2006. Com. (c) cit. in disc. In a dispute between two law firms that had been established by two unrelated families with the same last name, who operated the firms under nearly identical names, older law firm sued newer law firm for unfair competition. The trial court granted summary judgment for defendant and the court of appeals affirmed. Affirming, this court held, inter alia, that summary judgment was proper on plaintiff's claim of tradename infringement because plaintiff failed to demonstrate that its name had secondary meaning. In making its decision, the court observed that trade-name infringement occurred regardless of a defendant's subjective intent when the use of a name was likely to cause confusion, but once infringement was established, the scope of relief could be more extensive if defendant had intent to deceive. Keaton and Keaton v. Keaton, 842 N.E.2d 816, 820.

Iowa, 2008. Cit. and quot. in sup. National bank brought action for trademark infringement against local bank, seeking, among other things, an injunction preventing defendant from using the name "Community State Bank." The trial court ruled in favor of plaintiff. The court of appeals reversed. Vacating the court of appeals and affirming the trial court, this court held that defendant infringed plaintiff's valid common-law trademark in the name, concluding, among other things, that defendant's use of the name would cause a likelihood of confusion among customers in defendant's area. The court reasoned that, while defendant did not intend to pass off its business and services as those of plaintiff, all of the remaining factors set forth in the Restatement weighed in favor of plaintiff; among other things, several incidents of actual confusion between the parties by customers had occurred. Community State Bank, Nat. Ass'n v. Community State Bank, 758 N.W.2d 520, 527, 528.

Iowa, 1999. Cit. in disc., quot. in ftn., coms. (b) and (h) quot. in disc., com. (d) cit. in disc. Bank operating under the name "Commercial Savings Bank" brought trademark-infringement action against financial institution calling itself "Commercial Federal Bank." The trial court entered judgment for defendant on the ground that plaintiff had failed to establish the existence of a common-law trademark in "commercial." Affirming, this court held that "commercial" was a descriptive term that had become distinctive through secondary use; however, plaintiff could not show that defendant's use of the term was likely to cause consumer confusion. Commercial Sav. v. Hawkeye Federal Sav., 592 N.W.2d 321, 330, 332.

Mich.App.2014. Cit. in ftn. Owner of the trademark "TRAVIS" in connection with the food-service industry brought a trademark-infringement action under Michigan law against owner of the "Travis Grill," a restaurant that operated in the same geographical area as plaintiff's restaurant and licensees. The trial court granted an injunction against defendant's further use of the mark. Affirming, this court held that plaintiff's mark had priority, defendant's mark confused consumers, and defendant used the confusing mark in the sale of services in Michigan. The court, citing Restatement Third of Unfair Competition § 20, opined that, through the strict requirements for stating a claim for trademark infringement under Michigan law, courts ensured that

Cit.—cited; com.—comment; fol.—followed; sup.—support.
A complete list of abbreviations precedes page 1.

only words, devices, and symbols that functioned as trademarks—that is, those that consumers actually identified with a certain business owner's products or services—received legal protection. Janet Travis, Inc. v. Preka Holdings, L.L.C., 856 N.W.2d 206, 212.

Wis.App.1996. Cit. in headnote, cit. generally in ftn., cit. in disc. Company in the business of providing reprographic copying services to architects, engineers, publishers, and others sued competitor for trademark infringement. Following a bench trial, the trial court dismissed the complaint on the ground that there was insufficient likelihood of confusion between the parties' marks. Affirming, this court held, inter alia, that company's mark, which could also be considered a service mark, was a weak descriptive designation combining a geographical name with a shortened version of the term "reprographics"; that company's mark did not become strong or distinctive through secondary meaning; and that the minimal similarity of the two marks, as well as the sophistication of the parties' typical customers, supported the lower court's finding that there was no likelihood of confusion. Madison Reprographics v. Cook's Reprographics, 203 Wis.2d 226, 552 N.W.2d 440, 441, 444, 445.

§ 21. Proof of Likelihood of Confusion: Market Factors

U.S.2004. Com. (a) cit. in disc. Makeup manufacturer sued competitor for declaratory relief as to use of the term "microcolor"; competitor counterclaimed for trademark infringement. District court granted manufacturer summary judgment on trademark infringement counterclaim, but court of appeals reversed. This court vacated and remanded, holding that a plaintiff claiming infringement of incontestable mark had to show likelihood of consumer confusion as part of prima facie case, while defendant had no independent burden to negate likelihood of any confusion in raising affirmative defense that a term was used descriptively, not as a mark, fairly, and in good faith. The court determined that, in this case, court of appeals erroneously required manufacturer/counterclaim defendant to shoulder burden on issue of confusion. KP Permanent Make-Up, Inc. v. Lasting Impression I, Inc., 543 U.S. 111, 117, 125 S.Ct. 542, 548, 160 L.Ed.2d 440, on remand 408 F.3d 596 (9th Cir.2005).

C.A.1, 1996. Com. (a) quot. in disc. In action brought under the Lanham Act, union that was lobbying to become nursing-home employees' collective-bargaining representative sued employer for trademark infringement after employer used union's mark on anti-union propaganda it distributed to employees. The district court granted employer's motion for summary judgment. Affirming on other grounds, this court held that union could not recover absent proof of a likelihood of confusion as to the source of the materials bearing its mark and that, when all the relevant factors were considered, including one employee's inquiry regarding the veracity of the documents at issue, there was no triable issue of fact as to likelihood of confusion. IAM v. Winship Green Nursing Center, 103 F.3d 196, 201.

C.A.2, 2004. Com. (a) quot. in sup. Owner of trademark "Brennan's," used in connection with well-known New Orleans restaurant, brought suit for trademark infringement against owner of New York restaurant called "Terrance Brennan's Seafood and Chop House." District court denied plaintiff's motion for preliminary injunction. Affirming, this court held that district court did not abuse its discretion in finding that plaintiff did not demonstrate a likelihood of confusion, and thus was not likely to prevail on merits of trademark-infringement claim, where court noted minimal evidence of actual consumer confusion, use of the first name "Terrance" in defendant's mark, sophistication of relevant consumer market, and substantial geographic distance between the two restaurants. Brennan's, Inc. v. Brennan's Restaurant, LLC, 360 F.3d 125, 128.

C.A.2, 2003. Com. (i) cit. in case quot. in disc. Holder of "VIRGIN" trademark brought suit for trademark infringement against operators of retail stores selling wireless telephones and services under the trade name "VIRGIN WIRELESS." The district court denied plaintiff's motion for a preliminary injunction. Reversing and remanding, this court held that, because plaintiff's mark was entitled to protection, and there was a significant likelihood of confusion, plaintiff demonstrated irreparable harm and likelihood of success on the merits, and thus was entitled to a preliminary injunction. The court said that the VIRGIN mark was a strong mark, since, in relation to the sale of consumer electronic equipment, it was inherently distinctive, in

For earlier citations, see the Appendices, Supplements, or Pocket Parts, if any, that correspond to the subject matter under examination.

that it was arbitrary and fanciful. Virgin Enterprises Ltd. v. Nawab, 335 F.3d 141, 147.

C.A.2, 2000. Com. (a) quot. in disc. Shipping company ("Federal Express") sued a wholesale distributor of commercial espresso machines ("Federal Espresso"), alleging trademark infringement and trademark dilution. District court denied plaintiff's motion for a preliminary injunction, holding that plaintiff failed to show irreparable harm in the absence of the injunction. This court affirmed, holding, inter alia, that plaintiff did not show likelihood of confusion and hence did not show that it was likely to succeed on the merits of its claims. Federal Express Corporation v. Federal Espresso, Inc., 201 F.3d 168, 174.

C.A.2, 1999. Cit. in headnote, com. (c) quot. in disc. Motorcycle manufacturer brought trademark-infringement action against provider of motorcycle products and services, seeking to enjoin defendant from using the word "hog" in reference to its business and goods and to prohibit defendant from employing a bar-and-shield logo similar to the one used by plaintiff. The district court entered judgment for plaintiff. Affirming in part, reversing in part, and remanding, this court held that "hog" was a generic term that was used to describe large motorcycles before plaintiff adopted it, and that plaintiff could not therefore enjoin defendant's use of the word; that defendant's use of the bar-and-shield logo for promotion and advertising did not constitute permissible trademark parody use; and that defendant's use of the logo was not made acceptable by the addition of the phrase "unauthorized dealer." Harley-Davidson, Inc. v. Grottanelli, 164 F.3d 806, 807, 813.

C.A.2, 1997. Com. (a) quot. in sup., com. (i) quot. in disc. and in sup. A cosmetics manufacturer sued a competitor for trademark infringement, alleging that defendant's "100% BODY CARE" mark infringed plaintiff's "100%" mark for its skin-care moisturizer. The district court granted plaintiff permanent injunctive relief. Reversing and remanding, this court held that, while plaintiff's mark was suggestive, rather than descriptive, and thus was entitled to protection, despite the absence of secondary meaning, plaintiff was not entitled to relief in the present case, since it failed to establish the likelihood of confusion. The court said that the district court's finding that plaintiff's mark was moderately strong was clearly erroneous; there was no evidence that consumers associated the mark with plaintiff, and the district court had found that plaintiff's use of the mark was not original. Estee Lauder Inc. v. The Gap, Inc., 108 F.3d 1503, 1509-1511.

C.A.2, 1991. Cit. in sup. §§ 20-23, coms. (c) and (j) cit. in disc., Rptr's Note quot. in disc. (citing § 21 of T.D. No. 2, 1990. § 21 has since been revised; see Official Text). A publisher of a book and audiotapes on the development of charisma that used the trade name "New Choices Press" sought to enjoin a magazine publisher from using the name "New Choices for the Best Years" for its magazine on retirement living. The district court granted defendant's motion for summary judgment. Affirming, this court held that plaintiff failed to raise a genuine issue of fact as to the likelihood of confusion. The court concluded that plaintiff's trade name was weak because it was not widely known. Lang v. Retirement Living Pub. Co., Inc., 949 F.2d 576, 580, 582.

C.A.3, 1995. Cit. in disc. (citing § 21 of T.D. No. 2, 1990. § 21 has since been revised; see Official Text). Manufacturer of a directional control valve, a device commonly used in control panels of offshore oil-drilling rigs to facilitate emergency shutdowns, sued competitor for trade-dress infringement alleging that competitor marketed a valve that copied plaintiff's product configuration. District court entered permanent injunction against competitor, precluding it from reselling its valve. This court reversed, holding that plaintiff failed to show existence of a likelihood that an appreciable number of consumers of the relevant type of valves would be confused as to source of the valve or its affiliation with plaintiff. Noting that the "likelihood of confusion" test was not developed for product-configuration cases, but for trademark-infringement and unfair-competition cases, the court stated that not all of the enumerated "likelihood of confusion" factors would function the same way as to trade dress inhering in a product configuration. Versa Products Co., Inc. v. Bifold Co. (Mfg.) Ltd., 50 F.3d 189, 202, certiorari denied 516 U.S. 808, 116 S.Ct. 54, 133 L.Ed.2d 19 (1995).

C.A.4, 2006. Subsec. (a)(i) cit. in disc. Health-maintenance organization sued

Cit.—cited; com.—comment; fol.—followed; sup.—support.
A complete list of abbreviations precedes page 1.

physicians group for trademark infringement and dilution after group began using mark with the same two words used in organization's mark, transposed. The district court granted summary judgment for defendant. Affirming, this court held, among other things, that the substantial difference in the public presentations of the two marks significantly reduced the likelihood of confusion notwithstanding their textual similarity. The court observed that the two marks at issue had very different appearances in the marketplace because plaintiff's mark was almost always paired with another trademark owned by organization, as well as other accouterments, while defendant's was always presented plainly and without any graphics, either by itself, or at most with the suffix "P.C." CareFirst of Maryland, Inc. v. First Care, P.C., 434 F.3d 263, 271.

C.A.4, 1997. Com. (i) quot. in case quot. in disc. A franchisor of truck-stop service facilities that had 14 registered federal service marks containing the term PETRO sued a petroleum-distribution company that opened a fueling facility under the name JAMES RIVER PETRO CARD. Plaintiff alleged federal and common law trademark infringement and federal and common law unfair competition, among other claims. The federal district court entered judgment for defendant, holding that there was no likelihood of confusion, because PETRO was merely descriptive and a fairly weak mark. This court affirmed, holding, inter alia, that the district court's conclusion was not clearly erroneous. The court cited the district court's findings that PETRO did not have secondary meaning in the card lock business, that the lack of customer confusion evidence confirmed the weakness of PETRO as a mark, and that many other companies commonly used PETRO to describe petroleum-related goods and services. Noting that the frequency with which a term is used in other trademark registrations was relevant to the distinctiveness inquiry, the court stated that plaintiff submitted evidence showing that over 2,700 businesses in the United States used PETRO as part of their name. Petro Stopping Centers v. James River Petroleum, 130 F.3d 88, 93.

C.A.5, 2020. Com. (*i*) quot. in ftn. Manufacturer of hard-seltzer beverages named "BRIZZY" sued competitor that sold hard-seltzer beverages named "VIZZY," seeking a preliminary injunction, and alleging that defendant infringed upon plaintiff's mark. The district court denied plaintiff's motion for a preliminary injunction. This court affirmed, holding, inter alia, that plaintiff could not obtain a preliminary injunction, because it failed to prove that it was likely to succeed on the merits of its claims. The court explained that, although plaintiff's trademark was of a greater quality than a generic mark under Restatement Third of Unfair Competition § 21, Comment *i*, the fact that the mark was suggestive was only one factor in determining its strength for the purpose of its standing in the marketplace, and noted that suggestive marks did not weigh towards a finding that the marks were likely to cause confusion among the parties' customers. Future Proof Brands, L.L.C. v. Molson Coors Beverage Company, 982 F.3d 280, 290.

C.A.5, 2018. Com. (c) quot. in case quot. in sup. Civic organization brought a federal trademark-infringement action under the Lanham Act against another civic organization that used a similar logo, seeking to enjoin defendant from using its name and logo in political advertisements. The district court granted summary judgment for plaintiff. This court affirmed as modified to restrain only defendant's use of its logo, holding that the district court correctly concluded that there was a strong likelihood of confusion because the parties' marks looked exactly alike. While, under Restatement Third of Unfair Competition § 21, the relevant inquiry was whether two marks were sufficiently similar that prospective purchasers were likely to believe that the two users were somehow associated, rather than whether the marks were identical in every respect, the court noted that the two marks at issue here appeared to be essentially identical. Alliance for Good Government v. Coalition for Better Government, 901 F.3d 498, 511.

C.A.5, 2000. Subsec. (e) cit. in disc., com. (j) cit. in disc. and quot. in case quot. in disc. Magazine publisher sued for a declaration that its use of the title "POLO" for its magazine on equestrian sports and lifestyles did not infringe fashion designer's "Polo" mark; designer counterclaimed for, in part, trademark infringement and sought injunctive relief. Affirming the district court's finding of trademark infringement but vacating its issuance of a permanent injunction against publisher

For earlier citations, see the Appendices, Supplements, or Pocket Parts, if any, that correspond to the subject matter under examination.

and remanding, this court held, inter alia, that a likelihood of confusion existed because publisher's use of the mark evidenced an intent to trade on designer's reputation, and the consuming public could believe that there was an association between designer and publisher's magazine since magazines were within designer's natural zone of expansion. Westchester Media v. PRL USA Holdings, Inc., 214 F.3d 658, 666, on remand 2001 WL 34109374 (S.D.Tex.2001).

C.A.5, 1998. Cit. in headnotes, subsecs. (a), (d), and (e), and coms. (i) and (j) cit. in disc., subsec. (a)(1) and coms. (c) and (j) quot. in disc. Assignee and registrant of all trademarks, copyrights, and publicity rights belonging to Elvis Presley estate sued owner of bar operating as "The Velvet Elvis" for, inter alia, trademark infringement and unfair competition. The district court entered judgment for defendant. Reversing and remanding, this court held that the district court erred in isolating its consideration of defendant's advertising practices from its consideration of whether the name "The Velvet Elvis" infringed plaintiff's trade and service marks and therefore created a likelihood of confusion; that the strength of plaintiff's mark, the similarity of the parties' marks, and the similarity of products and services weighed in favor of finding a likelihood of confusion; that defendant's actions suggested an intent to confuse customers as to the source of its mark; and that the evidence supported a finding that defendant's advertising practices caused actual confusion among customers. Elvis Presley Enterprises, Inc. v. Capece, 141 F.3d 188, 189, 190, 197, 201, 202.

C.A.7, 2020. Cit. in case cit. in sup. Wine maker and subsidiary sued former employee and competitor formed by former employee, alleging, inter alia, that defendants engaged in unfair competition when former employee, using his position as president while employed by plaintiffs, used plaintiffs' resources without their knowledge or consent to sell wine under competitor's brand at a cheaper price. The trial court entered judgment on a jury verdict for plaintiffs on their unfair-competition claim, entered a damages award of nothing, and granted plaintiffs' request for disgorgement as alternative relief. This court affirmed, holding that, under Restatement Third of Unfair Competition § 37, disgorgement was an appropriate remedy for plaintiffs' unfair-competition claim. The court explained that the district court did not err in relying on § 37 for guidance in determining if disgorgement was an appropriate remedy, because Michigan caselaw had previously cited §§ 21 and 33 in addressing novel issues of unfair competition. Continental Vineyard, LLC v. Vinifera Wine Co., LLC, 973 F.3d 747, 759.

C.A.7, 2005. Cit. in sup. Seller of goods produced by Indians brought suit for damages against non-Indian manufacturer of Indian-style jewelry, alleging violation of Indian Arts and Crafts Act's prohibition against selling a good in a manner that falsely suggested it was an Indian product. District court entered judgment on a jury verdict for defendant. Affirming, this court held that the district court's failure to base the jury instruction on a regulation providing that unqualified use of the name of an Indian tribe in connection with a product was a representation that the product was an Indian product was harmless error. Because the jury question really involved the meaning that an average consumer would ascribe to the context in which the jewelry was sold, asking whether defendant falsely suggested that it was selling Indian products and asking whether it failed to qualify its use of tribal names came to the same thing. Native American Arts, Inc. v. Waldron Corp., 399 F.3d 871, 876.

C.A.7, 2002. Com. (i) quot. in disc. Automobile manufacturers sought declaratory judgment that front-end grille on their new sport utility vehicle did not dilute or infringe upon defendant manufacturer's trademark for a similar grille. Defendant filed counterclaims and moved for preliminary injunction against plaintiffs' use of grille. Affirming district court's denial of defendant's motion, court of appeals held that, notwithstanding that defendant could likely show that its grille design had acquired secondary meaning due to consistent use for over 50 years, defendant failed to show likelihood of consumer confusion where there was little overlap between vehicles' target markets, consumers were likely to use high degree of care in making car purchases, and there was no evidence that plaintiffs intended to pass off their vehicles as defendant's. AM General Corp. v. DaimlerChrysler Corp., 311 F.3d 796, 828.

C.A.9, 1999. Cit. in disc. §§ 20-23. Entertainment industry information provider using "MovieBuff" as trademark sought to enjoin video rental chain from using "moviebuff.com" as its web site domain name. The district court entered judgment for defendant. Reversing and remanding, this court held that plaintiff established itself as the senior user of the mark, and that, given the similarity of the marks, the relatedness of product offerings, and the overlap in marketing and advertising channels, likelihood of consumer confusion existed. That defendant did not intend to confuse consumers was irrelevant under the circumstances. Brookfield Communications v. West Coast, 174 F.3d 1036, 1054.

C.A.9, 1997. Com. (a) quot. in disc. The owner of copyrights and trademarks to the works of a children's book author brought an action for copyright and trademark infringement against a publisher, seeking to enjoin the publication and distribution of a parody of the O.J. Simpson murder trial written in the style of the author's works. Affirming the district court's entry of a preliminary injunction, this court held, inter alia, that a balance of hardships favoring plaintiff and serious questions for litigation on the likelihood of confusion existed as to the federal trademark-infringement and unfair-competition claims, as required for preliminary injunctive relief. The court indicated eight factors to be considered in an analysis of likelihood of confusion, while noting that no mechanistic formula or list could set forth in advance the variety of elements that comprised the market context from which likelihood of confusion must be determined. Dr. Seuss Enterprises, L.P. v. Penguin Books, 109 F.3d 1394, 1404.

C.A.10, 2013. Com. (*i*) quot. in sup. In a dispute between competing sellers of sinus-irrigation products, new entrant into the market sued existing seller, seeking a declaration that its SINUSENSE mark did not infringe on existing seller's federally registered SINUCLEANSE mark and two similar marks; existing seller counterclaimed for trademark infringement and unfair competition under the Lanham Act. The district court granted summary judgment for new entrant on existing seller's counterclaims and dismissed new entrant's declaratory-judgment claim as moot. Affirming, this court held that existing seller failed to raise a genuine factual issue regarding the likelihood of confusion, given the weakness of its mark. The court pointed out that existing seller presented no data on whether the average consumer was aware of the brand, and had conceded that the average person on the street would not know what SINUCLEANSE was. Water Pik, Inc. v. Med-Systems, Inc., 726 F.3d 1136, 1151.

C.A.10, 2008. Subsec. (c) quot. in ftn. to diss. op., coms. (c) and (f) quot. in sup., coms. (g) and (i) quot. in diss. op. Ski resort that had a registered incontestable service mark in a geographically descriptive term, "Vail," that it used in conjunction with a purely descriptive term, "Ski," sued marketing service that had a registered service mark in the alphanumeric telephone number "1-800-SKI-VAIL," alleging infringement under the Lanham Act. After a bench trial, the district court concluded that plaintiff failed to show a likelihood of confusion between the two marks. Affirming, this court held, inter alia, that defendant's mark traded on "Vail" as a geographic ski destination, rather than as a mark identifying plaintiff or its resort. The dissent argued that the marks were confusingly similar and that the totality of factors weighed in favor of a finding that defendant's mark was likely to cause consumer confusion. Vail Associates, Inc. v. Vend-Tel-Co., Ltd., 516 F.3d 853, 874, 875, 881, 883.

C.A.10, 1999. Cit. in disc. §§ 20-23. Seller of camouflage-patterned outdoor clothing under "King of the Mountain" trademark brought trademark-infringement action against promoter of "Jeep KING OF THE MOUNTAIN DOWNHILL SERIES" ski races. Affirming the district court's grant of summary judgment for defendant, this court held, in part, that no likelihood of confusion existed as to sponsorship of ski races. King of the Mountain Sports, Inc. v. Chrysler Corp., 185 F.3d 1084, 1090.

C.A.11, 2015. Rptrs' Note cit. and quot. in sup. Religious order of the Catholic Church filed an infringement action against non-Catholic organization, alleging that defendant infringed on its registered service marks. On remand, the district court entered judgment for defendant. This court affirmed in part, holding that the district court did not err in determining that plaintiff's incontestable marks were presumptively strong and that defendant failed to defeat the presumption. Citing Restatement Third of Unfair Competition § 21, the court noted that it was bound by precedent that diverged from the majority of the courts to find that incontestability affected

For earlier citations, see the Appendices, Supplements, or Pocket Parts, if any, that correspond to the subject matter under examination.

the strength of a mark for purposes of confusion, even though it conceived error in the precedent. Sovereign Military Hospitaller Order of Saint John of Jerusalem of Rhodes and of Malta v. Florida Priory of the Knights Hospitallers of the Sovereign Order of Saint John of Jerusalem, Knights of Malta, The Ecumenical Order, 809 F.3d 1171, 1183, 1184.

C.A.Fed.2004. Com. (a) quot. in case quot. in sup. Holder of the "Bowflex" trademark, which it used to market its patented home-exercise machines of the same name, sued competitor that was using its "CrossBow" trademark to sell its exercise equipment, alleging trademark infringement. District court granted plaintiff a preliminary injunction, which barred defendant from using plaintiff's trademark to sell its equipment. This court affirmed, holding that district court did not abuse its discretion in finding likelihood of confusion. The degree of similarity of the marks, proximity of the products and services, strength of the mark, and similarity of marketing channels were factors that district court properly found to favor plaintiff. Nautilus Group, Inc. v. ICON Health and Fitness, Inc., 372 F.3d 1330, 1346.

C.D.Cal.2013. Com. (a) quot. in case quot. in sup. Comic-book publisher sued custom-car business, alleging, among other things, that defendant infringed upon plaintiff's trademarks by manufacturing and selling vehicles and car kits modeled after a fictional high-tech automobile used by one of plaintiff's comic-book characters. Granting plaintiff's motion for partial summary judgment on its trademark-infringement claim, this court held that plaintiff had valid trademark rights in the marks at issue, and that the relevant *Sleekcraft* factors supported a finding of a likelihood of confusion as a matter of law. In making its decision, the court noted that, although courts looked to the *Sleekcraft* factors for guidance in determining the likelihood of confusion, that list of factors was not exhaustive and other variables could come into play depending on the particular facts presented in the case. DC Comics v. Towle, 989 F.Supp.2d 948, 956.

C.D.Cal.2008. Com. (a) quot. in disc. Seller of electrical parts, supplies, and equipment sued small wholesale distributor of consumer electronic goods, alleging that its federally registered "REXELL" service mark was infringed by defendant's design trademark. Granting summary judgment for plaintiff, this court held that a reasonable trier of fact would be compelled to find that the likelihood of consumer confusion about the source of the products and services was high, based on an eight-factor test used in the Ninth Circuit; although the court cautioned that the factors were not exhaustive and should not be applied rigidly or mechanistically, it pointed out that plaintiff's mark was strong, defendant's mark was virtually identical, and the goods and services at issue were highly related and complementary. Rexel, Inc. v. Rexel Intern. Trading Corp., 540 F.Supp.2d 1154, 1164.

N.D.Cal.2008. Com. (i) cit. and quot. in disc. Bottled-water manufacturer that owned the registered trademark "Bottled at the Source" sued competitor, alleging federal trademark infringement, inter alia; defendant counterclaimed for cancellation of the trademark. This court granted summary judgment for defendant on plaintiff's claims and on the counterclaim, holding, inter alia, that the mark was generic and therefore invalid; defendant submitted undisputed evidence sufficient to overcome the presumption of validity created by registration of the mark, including proof of dozens of competitors using the mark, the media using the mark as a reference to a type of bottled water or a manufacturing process, and plaintiff's own use of the mark in a generic manner. CG Roxane LLC v. Fiji Water Co. LLC, 569 F.Supp.2d 1019, 1025.

D.Colo.2001. Cit. in disc. §§ 20-23. Tire-store owner brought suit against manufacturer of tie-down straps and cargo-control products for infringement of its "Bigfoot" trademark. Granting plaintiff's motion for a preliminary injunction, the court held, inter alia, that plaintiff showed a likelihood of success on the merits based on evidence that defendant's use of the mark was likely to cause confusion in the marketplace concerning the source or quality of the products. Big O Tires, Inc. v. Bigfoot 4X4, Inc., 167 F.Supp.2d 1216, 1222.

D.D.C.2022. Com. (j) cit. in case cit. in disc. Private industry groups sued nonprofit organization, alleging, inter alia, that defendant violated plaintiffs' trademark logos when it scanned plaintiffs' industry regulations into electronic documents that it published on its website in order to educate the public. On remand, this court granted in part plaintiffs' motion for sum-

Cit.—cited; com.—comment; fol.—followed; sup.—support.
A complete list of abbreviations precedes page 1.

mary judgment, holding that, while defendant's use of plaintiffs' logos did not constitute nominative fair use, defendant's use of plaintiffs' trademarks for describing their works constituted nominative fair use. The court noted that, prior to remand, it cited Restatement Third of Unfair Competition § 21, Comment *j*, in finding that defendant's use of plaintiffs' trademarks did not qualify as nominative fair use and was likely to cause confusion. American Society for Testing and Materials v. Public.Resource. Org, Inc., 597 F.Supp.3d 213, 223.

D.D.C.2003. Com. (m) quot. in sup. Pursuant to a petition filed by six Native Americans, the Trial Trademark and Appeal Board entered a decision that cancelled six federal trademark registrations involving the professional football team, the Washington Redskins. This court reversed in part, holding that board's finding that the marks at issue might disparage Native Americans was not supported by substantial evidence, and board failed to apply correct legal standard to its own findings of fact. The court determined that the ultimate question of whether trademarks at issue might disparage Native Americans was a question of fact. The issue of disparagement, like the issue of likelihood of confusion, required fact-based judgment that depended heavily on circumstances of each case. Pro-Football, Inc. v. Harjo, 284 F.Supp.2d 96, 117.

S.D.Fla.1998. Com. (i) cit. in ftn. "Popular Bank" of Florida brought suit seeking an injunction prohibiting "Banco Popular de Puerto Rico" and "Banco Popular N.A. (Florida)" from using the marks Banco Popular or Popular Express in four counties in Florida. This court granted plaintiffs the preliminary injunction as to the name "Banco Popular," because plaintiff had established the priority and validity of its mark and defendants' use of that mark in South Florida was likely to cause customer confusion. However, the court denied plaintiff's request to enjoin the use of the name "Popular Express," because plaintiff did not demonstrate a likelihood of success on the merits by showing that its rights to the mark were prior and superior to defendants' use of the mark and that the mark was likely to cause consumer confusion. The court determined that, taken as a whole, "Popular Bank of Florida" was a descriptive mark. Popular Bank of Fla. v. Banco Popular de Puerto Rico, 9 F.Supp.2d 1347, 1356.

D.Kan.1992. Rptr's Note quot. in case quot. in sup. (citing § 21 of T.D. No. 2, 1990. § 21 has since been revised; see Official Text). A provider of electronic banking services sued a telephone company for trademark infringement and unfair competition after defendant used the same term to describe its combination telephone and retail credit card as plaintiff used on its debit cards used for accessing automatic teller machines. Granting defendant's motion for summary judgment, this court held that there was no genuine issue of material fact as to the likelihood of confusion among consumers over the source of either card. In determining that reasonable jurors could only conclude that the two products were substantially different, the court noted that plaintiff's contention that it would soon be offering a credit card was irrelevant to the inquiry of likelihood of confusion. Universal Money Centers v. American Tel. & Tel., 797 F.Supp. 891, 895, affirmed 22 F.3d 1527 (10th Cir.1994), cert. denied 513 U.S. 1052, 115 S.Ct. 655, 130 L.Ed.2d 558 (1994).

E.D.La.2018. Com. (c) quot. in disc. After limited-liability company brought a petition seeking a declaratory judgment that the registration of a service mark for its food hall was proper, city and landlord sought an injunction against limited-liability company and others, alleging, inter alia, that defendants were impermissibly using a trademark that city had previously attempted to register. This court granted plaintiffs' motion for a preliminary injunction, holding that it was substantially likely that plaintiffs would be able to establish on the merits that their trademark was infringed because defendants' use of their mark would confuse prospective customers. The court cited Restatement Third of Unfair Competition § 21, Comment *c*, in explaining that the similarity between marks was a heavily weighted factor in deciding whether one mark infringed upon another by confusing prospective customers. Helpful Hound, L.L.C. v. New Orleans Building Corporation, 331 F.Supp.3d 581, 600.

D.Me.2010. Com. (i) quot. in sup. After inventor and his company brought patent-infringement action against competitor, competitor counterclaimed for, among other things, trademark infringement, alleging that counter-defendants' two-tone pink skin marker for mammography infringed on its federally registered trademark for pink identification markers placed on the skin

For earlier citations, see the Appendices, Supplements, or Pocket Parts, if any, that correspond to the subject matter under examination.

for use in medical imaging. Granting summary judgment for counter-defendants, this court held that there was no likelihood of confusion between the parties' trademarks. The court reasoned, in part, that, because counter-plaintiff's pink was at neither the descriptive (relatively weak) nor the arbitrary (relatively strong) end of the distinctiveness scale, a factfinder could not find it to be either a strong or a weak mark based on the record. DeSena v. Beekley Corp., 729 F.Supp.2d 375, 399.

S.D.N.Y.2012. Cit. in case quot. in sup. Clothing designer sued retailer, alleging that defendant infringed his ownership and use rights in the marks "Lower East Side," "LES NYC," and "LES." Granting summary judgment for defendant, this court held, inter alia, that any claims of trademark protection under the Lanham Act for plaintiff's LES mark were barred by his failure to raise them in his complaint and, in any event, the claims would be substantively deficient, because plaintiff failed to show that a likelihood of confusion existed between his LES mark and defendant's marks "Lower East Side" and the letters "L," "E," and "S" on its men's t-shirts. The court reasoned that, while the minimal stylization of plaintiff's LES mark might enable a finding that it was inherently distinctive, there was no evidence that consumers associated the mark with plaintiff or his clothing company; plaintiff provided no data with respect to his advertising efforts, and there was nothing even to support the claim that his LES mark was on the market before defendant introduced its t-shirt. Lopez v. Gap, Inc., 883 F.Supp.2d 400, 420.

S.D.N.Y.2007. Rptr's Note to com. (j) quot. in case quot. in sup. (citing § 21 of T.D. No. 2, 1990. § 21 has since been revised; see Official Text). Online magazine that was targeted towards women aged 35 and under sued publishers of now-defunct print magazine that was targeted towards men aged 40 and over for allegedly infringing on its unregistered trademark by publishing under the same title. Granting summary judgment for defendants on plaintiff's Lanham Act claims, this court held, inter alia, that there was no genuine issue of material fact as to the likelihood of customer confusion. Addressing the "bridge the gap" factor, the court found it unlikely that plaintiff would enter defendants' market, and plaintiff provided no evidence that prospective purchasers were assuming that plaintiff would publish a print magazine aimed at defendants' target audience. SLY Magazine, LLC v. Weider Publications L.L.C., 529 F.Supp.2d 425, 440.

S.D.N.Y.1998. Com. (a) quot. in disc. A capital-management corporation brought suit seeking a preliminary injunction enjoining a competitor from using the trademark "Lexington" in connection with defendant's activities as a retail broker in the financial services industry. Plaintiff alleged that defendant's use of its service mark constituted trademark infringement and unfair competition. This court granted plaintiff's motion for a preliminary injunction, holding, inter alia, that defendant's use of the "Lexington" mark in connection with the sale of securities and investment advisory services created a likelihood of confusion between plaintiff's and defendant's services. Plaintiff's mark was arbitrary and it had secondary meaning. Lexington Management v. Lexington Capital Partners, 10 F.Supp.2d 271, 278.

S.D.N.Y.1997. Com. (i) quot. in case quot. in disc. In trademark-infringement action, author and publisher of *The Book of Virtues* sued competing publisher for, inter alia, violations of § 43(a) of the Lanham Act after defendant began distributing an audiobook for young readers entitled *The Children's Book of Virtues*. Entering judgment for plaintiffs and permanently enjoining defendant from the manufacture, publication, distribution, and sale of its children's book, the court held that plaintiffs' title was a descriptive mark that had acquired secondary meaning, and that plaintiffs, having shown, among other things, a similarity between the marks, that their title had substantial source-identifying strength when defendant entered the market, and that defendant intentionally copied their mark in bad faith, had established a significant likelihood of confusion. Simon & Schuster, Inc. v. Dove Audio, Inc., 970 F.Supp. 279, 297.

S.D.N.Y.1996. Cit. in headnote, com. (i) quot. in disc., cit. in ftn. In trademark-infringement action, cosmetics manufacturer that created a skin-care product called "100% Time Release Moisturizer" sought to enjoin competitor from introducing a line of products under the name "100% Body Care." Manufacturer contended that "100%" was a protectable mark, the simultaneous use of which by competitor would produce consumer confusion. The

Cit.—cited; com.—comment; fol.—followed; sup.—support.
A complete list of abbreviations precedes page 1.

court agreed that "100%" had independent commercial value and issued a permanent injunction, holding that "100%," when used in conjunction with "Time Release Moisturizer," created a suggestive mark that was entitled to trademark protection, and that competitor's use of the term "100%" was likely to cause confusion where, among other things, manufacturer's mark was moderately strong or distinctive, and the two products were directed at similar classes of buyers. Estee Lauder, Inc. v. The Gap, Inc., 932 F.Supp. 595, 597, 610, 611, reversed 108 F.3d 1503 (2d Cir.1997).

S.D.N.Y.1992. Rptr's Note quot. in ftn. (citing § 21 of T.D. No. 2, 1990. § 21 has since been revised; see Official Text). Camera manufacturer sought an injunction against a competitor, alleging trademark infringement and false designation, inter alia. Granting plaintiff injunctive relief, the court held, inter alia, that the fact that both parties were in the same market, plaintiff's $70-$90 low-end cameras having bridged the gap with the $75-$125 top end of defendant's product line, a greater likelihood of confusion existed than if they operated in different markets. The court noted that it was not considering evidence of plaintiff's intention to introduce an even less expensive camera, since plaintiff did not present any evidence that would indicate that consumers were aware of its plan to launch this new camera. Nikon, Inc. v. Ikon Corp., 803 F.Supp. 910, 919.

S.D.Ohio, 1993. Rptr's Notes, com. (j) cit. in disc. (citing § 21 of T.D. No. 2, 1990. § 21 has since been revised; see Official Text). Women's apparel retailer sued department store chain and clothing manufacturer, alleging infringement of its trademark, "EXPRESS." Denying defendants' motions for summary judgment, the court held, inter alia, that genuine issues of material fact existed concerning the likelihood of confusion. The court found that defendants failed to show an absence of a genuine issue of material fact regarding the relatedness of the goods that were sold by the parties. Express, Inc. v. Sears, Roebuck & Co., 840 F.Supp. 502, 507.

E.D.Pa.2009. Com. (c) cit. in case cit. in sup. Seller of toy marbles that contained laser-etched three-dimensional figures under the name "Warbles" brought trademark-infringement and other claims against competitor that sold a trading-card game using marbles under the name "Warballs." Denying plaintiff's motion for a preliminary injunction, this court held, inter alia, that plaintiff failed to demonstrate a likelihood of success on the merits based on the likelihood of confusion. Analyzing the degree of similarity of the two marks under the "sound, sight, and meaning trilogy" and in their market context, the court concluded that, while the sounds of the trademarks were nearly identical, the difference in the trade dresses of the trademarked goods were substantial. Noasha LLC v. Nordic Group of Companies, Ltd., 630 F.Supp.2d 544, 553.

W.D.Pa.1999. Subsec. (a) cit. in treatise cit. in disc. Bank holding company and its subsidiary brought trademark-infringement action against competing financial institution, seeking to enjoin defendant from using the mark "Laurel" in connection with banking services defendant offered in the Pittsburgh area. Entering partial summary judgment for plaintiff, the court held that "Laurel," as used here, was an arbitrary mark; that, while defendant was the senior user, plaintiff, having penetrated the relevant market first, had superior rights to the mark in the regional area at issue; and that the evidence supported the finding that defendant's actions would cause a likelihood of confusion. Laurel Capital Group, Inc. v. BT Financial Corp., 45 F.Supp.2d 469, 495.

D.S.C.1995. Com. (h) quot. in sup. Manufacturer of fishing rod with a clear tip on an opaque rod base sued competitor for trademark infringement and unfair competition after competitor began marketing a fishing rod with the same color configuration. On remand from the intermediate appellate court, the court entered judgment for competitor, holding that manufacturer was not entitled to a presumption of a likelihood of confusion, since competitor copied manufacturer's design in good faith and with the goal of highlighting to buyers the functional qualities inherent in this type of fishing rod. Furthermore, manufacturer had failed to establish a likelihood of confusion because its mark was not especially strong, the rods had different appearances but for the color configuration, and consumers typically examined fishing rods quite thoroughly before buying. Alternatively, competitor could invoke the "fair use" defense, since it copied the color configuration for descriptive purposes only and did not intend to confuse

For earlier citations, see the Appendices, Supplements, or Pocket Parts, if any, that correspond to the subject matter under examination.

buyers as to the source of its product. Shakespeare Co. v. Silstar Corp. of America, Inc., 906 F.Supp. 997, 1012, affirmed 110 F.3d 234 (4th Cir.1997).

N.D.Tex.2022. Com. (*i*) quot. in case quot. in sup. Bar that owned a registered trademark for a logo—consisting of two crossed revolvers outlined in black with a red star on each handle—filed an infringement action against clothing store that used a similar mark; defendant counterclaimed, alleging that it was the first to use the mark in commerce. This court granted defendant's motion for a preliminary injunction to stop plaintiff from using the mark, holding, among other things, that defendant was substantially likely to prevail in showing that plaintiff's use of the mark created a likelihood of confusion. The court cited Restatement Third of Unfair Competition § 21 in noting that plaintiff had conceded that the mark was strong, and analysis of the mark also showed that it was strong, given its creative nature, coupled with the lack of evidence of its use by third parties. Savage Tavern, Inc. v. Signature Stag, LLC, 589 F.Supp.3d 624, 648.

N.D.Tex.2011. Com. (c) quot. in sup. Consumer lending company sued competitor for, inter alia, trademark dilution, alleging that competitor's use of the term "cash store," the trademarked name of company's stores, was likely to cause confusion and dilute company's mark. This court granted, in relevant part, plaintiff's motion for a preliminary injunction, holding that plaintiff demonstrated a substantial likelihood of success on its dilution-by-blurring claim under Texas law. After concluding that the "cash store" mark was distinctive, the court held that, even in the absence of consumer confusion, an unauthorized user's adoption of another's mark lessened that mark's capacity to identify the true owner's goods and services; moreover, factors such as the identical name used by both parties and the moderate degree of recognition of plaintiff's mark among loan consumers in plaintiff's areas of operation showed a likelihood of confusion that made dilution even more likely. Cottonwood Financial Ltd. v. Cash Store Services, Inc., 778 F.Supp.2d 726, 750.

S.D.Tex.2009. Com. (c) quot. in case quot. in sup. Real estate broker sued competitor, alleging that defendant's real-estate yard signs and other advertising materials had a design and color arrangement confusingly similar to plaintiff's trademarks. Granting summary judgment for plaintiff on its trademark-infringement and unfair-competition claims, this court held, inter alia, that, despite some differences, the signs were similar enough in their most significant features to cause confusion in the market for real-estate-brokerage services. The court noted that a real-estate yard sign was intended to catch the attention of people driving past, and that, to a consumer driving by, the red, white, and blue tri-bar design common to the parties' signs, not the differences in smaller, less-significant design elements, stood out. RE/MAX Intern., Inc. v. Trendsetter Realty, LLC, 655 F.Supp.2d 679, 700.

S.D.Tex.1999. Coms. (c) and (j) quot. in cases quot. in disc., com. (i) quot. in disc. Manufacturer/distributor of weight-training equipment brought trademark-infringement action against health club, alleging that the name of defendant's facility was confusingly similar to plaintiff's marks. Granting plaintiff's request for injunctive relief, the court held that plaintiff's mark was arbitrary and sufficiently strong in the fitness industry that defendant's use of a similar mark was likely to cause consumer confusion, as was the visual similarity of the marks and the similarity of the parties' products and services; that irreparable injury was likely to result absent of injunctive relief; and that protecting plaintiff's mark by use of an injunction served the public interest. Quantum Fitness Corp. v. Quantum LifeStyle Centers, 83 F.Supp.2d 810, 819, 823, 826.

S.D.Tex.1999. Subsec. (e) cit. in case quot. in disc., com. (c) quot. in case quot. in disc., com. (j) cit. in case quot. in disc. and quot. in case quot. in disc. Publishers filed a declaratory-judgment action against a supplier of expensive clothes and furnishings, seeking a determination of their right to use "POLO" as a magazine title. Supplier counterclaimed for trademark infringement and dilution under the Lanham Act, and for unfair competition and injury to business reputation under state law. After balancing the interests of all concerned, this court ordered full injunctive relief for supplier, holding, inter alia, that the new POLO magazine, which was meant to appeal to the same markets in which supplier had acquired a widespread identity, was likely to confuse consumers about supplier's

Cit.—cited; com.—comment; fol.—followed; sup.—support.
A complete list of abbreviations precedes page 1.

association with the magazine, and that the similarity of the marks also suggested an identification between the magazine and supplier's products. Westchester Media Co. v. PRL USA Holdings, Inc., 103 F.Supp.2d 935, 951, 953, affirmed in part, vacated in part 214 F.3d 658 (5th Cir.2000).

W.D.Wis.2017. Com. (*i*) quot. in sup. Information-technology company that sold electronic healthcare-record systems to large healthcare organizations brought an action against healthcare-management software provider and parent companies that maintained a health-and-wellness website associated with their own electronic healthcare-record system, alleging infringement of trademark used for plaintiff's interoperability application that resulted in customer confusion and unfair competition. This court granted defendants' motion for summary judgment, holding that there was no evidence that defendants' use of the mark caused actual confusion or a likelihood of confusion, or that defendants intended to confuse prospective customers, and there was little evidence that plaintiff's mark was strong, inherently or through development of secondary meaning. The court quoted Restatement Third of Unfair Competition § 21, Comment *i*, in explaining that the incontestable status of plaintiff's mark did not control the likelihood-of-confusion analysis when making a determination of inherent strength. Epic Systems Corporation v. YourCareUniverse, Inc., 244 F.Supp.3d 878, 898.

Colo.App.2004. Cit. in disc. §§ 20-23. Buyer of seller's partnership interest in a company that developed television programs based on newspaper classified ads sued seller for breach of contract and tortious interference; seller counterclaimed for breach of the parties' license agreement. Trial court entered judgment on jury verdict for seller on the counterclaim. This court reversed in part, holding, inter alia, that buyer's use of "Employment TV" instead of the licensed mark "Employment Television" was not a misleading use of seller's trademark, and thus did not constitute a breach of the license agreement, since the two marks were so similar as to preclude confusion by the public. Employment Television Enterprises, LLC v. Barocas, 100 P.3d 37, 49.

Fla.1993. Cit. generally in headnote, cit. in ftn. as §§ 20-23; com. (i) quot. in ftn. (citing § 21 of T.D. No. 2, 1990. § 21 has since been revised; see Official Text).; cit. in ftn. (citing § 21 of T.D. No. 3, 1991. § 21 has since been revised; see Official Text). The First Southern Bank sued to enjoin another bank from using the name "Great Southern Bank," alleging infringement and dilution of its trademark name and unfair competition. The trial court granted plaintiff injunctive relief and certified the question whether plaintiff bank's name was descriptive or generic so as not to be entitled to protection in the absence of proof that it had acquired a secondary meaning. This court remanded, holding that plaintiff bank's name contained laudatory, generic, and merely geographically descriptive elements so as not to be entitled to protection under either common or statutory law, but determination was necessary whether a secondary meaning in the name had developed in order to decide the dilution claim. In applying the suggestiveness test, the court stated that no great imagination was required to identify the product as banking services when the mark contained the word "bank," that many others used the word "southern" in their mark, and that businesses in the South had the need and right to use the term descriptively. It further determined that the name "First Southern Bank" was merely descriptive, and therefore lacked the "distinctive quality" that the Florida dilution statute was designed to protect. Great Southern v. First Southern, 625 So.2d 463, 465, 467, 470, 471.

Iowa, 1999. Cit. in disc., coms. (a) and (h) quot. in disc., com. (i) quot. and cit. in sup. Bank operating under the name "Commercial Savings Bank" brought trademark-infringement action against financial institution calling itself "Commercial Federal Bank." The trial court entered judgment for defendant on the ground that plaintiff had failed to establish the existence of a common-law trademark in "commercial." Affirming, this court held that "commercial" was a descriptive term that had become distinctive through secondary use; however, plaintiff could not show that defendant's use of the term was likely to cause consumer confusion. Commercial Sav. v. Hawkeye Federal Sav., 592 N.W.2d 321, 330-332.

Md.Spec.App.20004. Quot. in case quot. in disc. After building-supplies retailer sued storm-door manufacturer for breach of contract, manufacturer counterclaimed for trademark infringement. The trial court

For earlier citations, see the Appendices, Supplements, or Pocket Parts, if any, that correspond to the subject matter under examination.

entered judgment for manufacturer on the counterclaim. Affirming, this court held, inter alia, that manufacturer's "Guardian" trademark was distinctive, and was, therefore, entitled to substantial protection. Mid South Bldg. Supply of Maryland, Inc. v. Guardian Door and Window, Inc., 156 Md.App. 445, 847 A.2d 463, 474.

Mich.App.2014. Com. (a) cit. in sup. Owner of the trademark "TRAVIS" in connection with the food-service industry brought a trademark-infringement action under Michigan law against owner of the "Travis Grill," a restaurant that operated in the same geographical area as plaintiff's restaurant and licensees. The trial court granted an injunction against defendant's further use of the mark. Affirming, this court held that plaintiff's mark had priority, defendant's mark confused consumers, and defendant used the confusing mark in the sale of services in Michigan. The court, citing Restatement Third of Unfair Competition § 21, Comment *a*, noted that any factor that was likely to influence the impression conveyed to prospective purchasers by the use of a mark was relevant when assessing the likelihood of confusion, and pointed to evidence that plaintiff's mark was descriptive and had acquired secondary meaning, the length of the mark's use (since the 1940s) suggested that it was widely recognized, the name of defendant's restaurant was almost identical to the mark, and defendant's mark had actually confused customers. Janet Travis, Inc. v. Preka Holdings, L.L.C., 856 N.W.2d 206, 221.

N.Y.Sup.Ct.1997. Com. (i) quot. in disc. New York hotel that used "Wyndham" as a name and mark sought injunction to prevent Texas-based North and Central American hotel chain from also using "Wyndham." Issuing an injunction limited to New York County, the court held that, considering factors such as strength of the mark, similarity of the marks, proximity of the products, and actual confusion, it was likely that plaintiff would sustain irreparable damage if denied exclusive use of the mark for the duration of its lease. Wyndham Co. v. Wyndham Hotel Co., 176 Misc.2d 116, 670 N.Y.S.2d 995, 998.

N.D.1997. Cit. in disc., subsec. (e) and com. (m) cit. in disc. An audio and visual production services company (KAT Video) brought suit seeking to enjoin a radio station from using the name "Kat" and a tiger logo, in violation of North Dakota's tradename and trademark laws. Trial court granted the radio station summary judgment. This court reversed and remanded, holding that fact issues existed as to similarity of the marks, proximity of the products, evidence of actual confusion, and degree of care used by an ordinary purchaser. The court applied the six-step analysis of likelihood of confusion as adopted by the Eighth Circuit. KAT Video v. KKCT-FM Radio, 560 N.W.2d 203, 208.

Ohio, 2020. Com. (*i*) cit. in sup. Flower shop that operated under the trade name "Wooster Floral & Gifts" filed an action under Ohio's Deceptive Trade Practices Act against competitor that purchased the internet domain name "woosterfloral.com" and used it to redirect internet traffic to its own website. The trial court conducted a bench trial and entered judgment in favor of defendant, and the court of appeals affirmed. Affirming, this court held that there was nothing to suggest that defendant's use of the domain name created customer confusion about the source, sponsorship, approval, or certification of goods or services, as required to state a claim under the Act. The court pointed out that plaintiff's trade name was geographically descriptive of both parties' businesses, which were both floral shops located in Wooster, Ohio, and that, under Restatement Third of Unfair Competition § 21, geographically descriptive marks were generally considered weaker than marks that were inherently distinctive. Wooster Floral & Gifts, L.L.C. v. Green Thumb Floral & Garden Center, Inc., 172 N.E.3d 60, 62.

S.C.App.1998. Quot. in disc. Marketer of a novelty glow-in-the-dark condom sued a competitor for common law trademark infringement, common law trade-dress infringement, civil conspiracy, and unfair trade practices, arising from competitor's willful appropriation of marketer's marks and packaging. The trial court found defendant liable and awarded plaintiff damages. Reversing in part, this court held, inter alia, that South Carolina did not recognize a cause of action for common law trade-dress infringement independent of the Lanham Act or South Carolina's Unfair Trade Practices Act. Global Protection Corp. v. Halbersberg, 332 S.C. 149, 503 S.E.2d 483, 486.

Wis.App.1996. Cit. in headnote, cit. generally in ftn., com. (i) cit. in sup. Company

Cit.—cited; com.—comment; fol.—followed; sup.—support.
A complete list of abbreviations precedes page 1.

in the business of providing reprographic copying services to architects, engineers, publishers, and others sued competitor for trademark infringement. Following a bench trial, the trial court dismissed the complaint on the ground that there was insufficient likelihood of confusion between the parties' marks. Affirming, this court held, inter alia, that company's mark, which could also be considered a service mark, was a weak descriptive designation combining a geographical name with a shortened version of the term "reprographics"; that company's mark did not become strong or distinctive through secondary meaning; and that the minimal similarity of the two marks, as well as the sophistication of the parties' typical customers, supported the lower court's finding that there was no likelihood of confusion. Madison Reprographics v. Cook's Reprographics, 203 Wis.2d 226, 552 N.W.2d 440, 442, 444, 446.

Wyo.1992. Cit. in ftn. (citing § 21 of T.D. No. 3, 1991. § 21 has since been revised; see Official Text). Oil company sued petroleum company with a substantially similar name for trade-name infringement and unfair competition. The trial court granted defendant's motion for summary judgment. Reversing and remanding, this court held that the 25-year-long use by plaintiff of its trade name, as well as its establishment of a dominant place in the market, warranting protection of its reputation, created an issue of fact as to whether plaintiff had developed a secondary meaning in its trade name. The court also stated that the trial court erred in restricting its analysis to confusion among customers, because this devalued other policy considerations that resulted in trade name protection, such as consumer protection, property rights, economic efficiency, and universal concepts of justice. Powder River Oil v. Powder River Petroleum, 830 P.2d 403, 407.

§ 22. Proof of Likelihood of Confusion: Intent of the Actor

C.A.2, 1997. Com. (c) cit. in headnote, quot. in disc. Manufacturer of commercial outdoor furniture, called "site furniture," sued competitor for trade dress infringement. The district court granted manufacturer a preliminary injunction; the Second Circuit vacated and remanded. The district court reinstated the injunction, and this court again vacated, holding that manufacturer had not established that its trade dress was inherently distinctive. It stated that simulating a competitor's design was not bad faith unless there was reason to infer an intention to deceive, and no such intent was shown here; thus, the district court erred in concluding that manufacturer had demonstrated a likelihood of confusion. Landscape Forms, Inc. v. Columbia Cascade Co., 113 F.3d 373, 375, 383.

C.A.2, 1991. Cit. in sup. §§ 20-23 (citing § 22 of T.D. No. 2, 1990. § 22 has since been revised; see Official Text). A publisher of a book and audiotapes on the development of charisma that used the trade name "New Choices Press" sought to enjoin a magazine publisher from using the name "New Choices for the Best Years" for its magazine on retirement living. The district court granted defendant's motion for summary judgment. Affirming, this court held that plaintiff failed to raise a genuine issue of fact as to the likelihood of confusion. The court concluded that plaintiff's trade name was weak because it was not widely known. Lang v. Retirement Living Pub. Co., Inc., 949 F.2d 576, 580.

C.A.4, 1997. Cit. in headnote, subsec. (2) quot. in sup., com. (c) quot. in sup. Manufacturer that owned trademark for fishing rods with a translucent tip and a contrasting opaque shaft brought infringement action against competitor that began marketing a similar item. Competitor argued that the design was functional or descriptive, and thus manufacturer's mark should be canceled. The district court agreed, and ordered the Patent and Trademark Office to cancel the mark. This court concluded that the mark, which had become incontestable, could not be canceled, and reversed and remanded for a consideration of the remaining infringement issues. On remand, the district court entered judgment for competitor. Affirming, this court held that where competitor intentionally copied manufacturer's design not for the purpose of exploiting manufacturer's good will but, rather, in the good faith pursuit of the creation of a stronger fishing rod, manufacturer was not entitled to the presumption of a likelihood of confusion; alternatively, competitor had established a fair use defense. Shakespeare Co. v. Silstar Corp. of America, Inc., 110 F.3d 234, 235, 239, 241.

C.A.5, 2000. Com. (c) cit. in disc. Magazine publisher sued for a declaration that its use of the title "POLO" for its magazine on equestrian sports and lifestyles did not infringe fashion designer's "Polo" mark; de-

For earlier citations, see the Appendices, Supplements, or Pocket Parts, if any, that correspond to the subject matter under examination.

signer counterclaimed for, in part, trademark infringement and sought injunctive relief. Affirming the district court's finding of trademark infringement but vacating its issuance of a permanent injunction against publisher and remanding for reconsideration of a disclaimer procedure, this court held, inter alia, that a likelihood of confusion existed because publisher's use of the mark evidenced an intent to trade on designer's reputation, and the consuming public could believe that there was an association between designer and publisher's magazine since magazines were within designer's natural zone of expansion. Westchester Media v. PRL USA Holdings, Inc., 214 F.3d 658, 666, on remand 2001 WL 34109374 (S.D.Tex.2001).

C.A.5, 1998. Cit. in headnotes, coms. (b) and (c) cit. in disc. Assignee and registrant of all trademarks, copyrights, and publicity rights belonging to Elvis Presley estate sued owner of bar operating as "The Velvet Elvis" for, inter alia, trademark infringement and unfair competition. The district court entered judgment for defendant. Reversing and remanding, this court held that the district court erred in isolating its consideration of defendant's advertising practices from its consideration of whether the name "The Velvet Elvis" infringed plaintiff's trade and service marks and therefore created a likelihood of confusion; that the strength of plaintiff's mark, the similarity of the parties' marks, and the similarity of products and services weighed in favor of finding a likelihood of confusion; that defendant's actions suggested an intent to confuse customers as to the source of its mark; and that the evidence supported a finding that defendant's advertising practices caused actual confusion among customers. Elvis Presley Enterprises, Inc. v. Capece, 141 F.3d 188, 190, 203.

C.A.9, 1999. Cit. in disc. §§ 20-23. Entertainment industry information provider using "MovieBuff" as trademark sought to enjoin video rental chain from using "moviebuff.com" as its web site domain name. The district court entered judgment for defendant. Reversing and remanding, this court held that plaintiff established itself as the senior user of the mark, and that, given the similarity of the marks, the relatedness of product offerings, and the overlap in marketing and advertising channels, likelihood of consumer confusion existed. That defendant did not intend to confuse consumers was irrelevant under the circumstances. Brookfield Communications v. West Coast, 174 F.3d 1036, 1054.

C.A.10, 1999. Cit. in disc. §§ 20-23. Seller of camouflage-patterned outdoor clothing under "King of the Mountain" trademark brought trademark-infringement action against promoter of "Jeep KING OF THE MOUNTAIN DOWNHILL SERIES" ski races. Affirming the district court's grant of summary judgment for defendant, this court held, in part, that no likelihood of confusion existed as to sponsorship of ski races. King of the Mountain Sports, Inc. v. Chrysler Corp., 185 F.3d 1084, 1090.

D.Colo.2001. Cit. in disc. §§ 20-23. Tire-store owner brought suit against manufacturer of tie-down straps and cargo-control products for infringement of its "Bigfoot" trademark. Granting plaintiff's motion for a preliminary injunction, the court held, inter alia, that plaintiff showed a likelihood of success on the merits based on evidence that defendant's use of the mark was likely to cause confusion in the marketplace concerning the source or quality of the products. Big O Tires, Inc. v. Bigfoot 4X4, Inc., 167 F.Supp.2d 1216, 1222.

D.Kan.1997. Com. (c) quot. in disc. A Missouri corporation sued an Oklahoma corporation for trade-dress infringement, commercial misrepresentation, and unfair competition, alleging that the defendant corporation and its president infringed the trade dress of two of plaintiff's chemical injection pumps in violation of the Lanham Act. This court entered judgment for defendants, holding, inter alia, that plaintiff failed to establish that there was a likelihood of confusion by purchasers at the point of sale of plaintiff's and defendant's pumps. Several witnesses testified that consumers in the chemical injection pump market usually understood that different manufacturers made products with similar designs. The manner of marketing the pumps also suggested that there was little likelihood that direct purchasers were confused as to the origin of the pumps. Finally, defendant's intent in manufacturing the pumps suggested that there was little likelihood of confusion. Western Chemical Pumps, Inc. v. Superior Mfg., 989 F.Supp. 1112, 1124.

E.D.N.Y.2018. Com. (c) quot. in case quot. in sup. Owner of various trademarks

Cit.—cited; com.—comment; fol.—followed; sup.—support.
A complete list of abbreviations precedes page 1.

containing the word "BOLD" brought a lawsuit against competitors, alleging that defendants sold competing bathroom-fixture products using a text logo with the word "BOLD" that infringed on plaintiff's trademarks. This court adopted the recommendation of a magistrate judge and granted in part plaintiff's motion for default judgment on other grounds, holding, inter alia, that defendants' continued use of plaintiff's marks did not support an inference that they did so with the intent to confuse. The court quoted Restatement Third of Unfair Competition § 22, Comment *c*, and Restatement of Torts § 729, Comment *f*, in observing that defendants' continued use of the marks did not conclusively prove defendants' intent to create confusion, but provided evidence suggesting that defendants knew their infringing use could create confusion under the current market conditions. Kohler Co. v. Bold International FZCO, 422 F.Supp.3d 681, 728.

S.D.N.Y.2000. Com. (c) quot. in ftn. Gem-grading laboratory sued its trademark sublicensee and others, alleging trademark infringement and dilution, false designation of origin, unfair competition, and breach of contract. Sublicensee counterclaimed for fraud and intentional interference with business relations. This court entered judgment for plaintiff, holding, inter alia, that sublicensee's grading of stones under plaintiff's name and issuance of plaintiff's certificates outside the Los Angeles area infringed plaintiff's marks, and that sublicensee's bad faith alone was sufficient to warrant the inference that his actions were likely to cause confusion. E.G.L. Gem Lab Ltd. v. Gem Quality Institute, Inc., 90 F.Supp.2d 277, 293, affirmed 4 Fed.Appx. 81 (2d Cir.2001).

D.S.C.1995. Cit. in headnote, subsec. (2) quot. in sup., com. (c) quot. in sup. Manufacturer of fishing rod with a clear tip on an opaque rod base sued competitor for trademark infringement and unfair competition after competitor began marketing a fishing rod with the same color configuration. On remand from the intermediate appellate court, the court entered judgment for competitor, holding that manufacturer was not entitled to a presumption of a likelihood of confusion, since competitor copied manufacturer's design in good faith and with the goal of highlighting to buyers the functional qualities inherent in this type of fishing rod. Furthermore, manufacturer had failed to establish a likelihood of confusion because its mark was not especially strong, the rods had different appearances but for the color configuration, and consumers typically examined fishing rods quite thoroughly before buying. Alternatively, competitor could invoke the "fair use" defense, since it copied the color configuration for descriptive purposes only and did not intend to confuse buyers as to the source of its product. Shakespeare Co. v. Silstar Corp. of America, Inc., 906 F.Supp. 997, 999, 1010, 1011, affirmed 110 F.3d 234 (4th Cir.1997).

S.D.Tex.1999. Com. (b) cit. in disc., com. (c) quot. in case quot. in disc. Publishers filed a declaratory-judgment action against a supplier of expensive clothes and furnishings, seeking a determination of their right to use "POLO" as a magazine title. Supplier counterclaimed for trademark infringement and dilution under the Lanham Act, and for unfair competition and injury to business reputation under state law. After balancing the interests of all concerned, this court ordered full injunctive relief for supplier, holding, inter alia, that a real likelihood of confusion existed where evidence showed that the publishers intended to target suppliers' consumers and customers in its advertising, in its layouts, and in some aspects of the contents of its relaunched magazine. Westchester Media Co. v. PRL USA Holdings, Inc., 103 F.Supp.2d 935, 957, 965, affirmed in part, vacated in part 214 F.3d 658 (5th Cir.2000).

Colo.App.2004. Cit. in disc. §§ 20-23. Buyer of seller's partnership interest in a company that developed television programs based on newspaper classified ads sued seller for breach of contract and tortious interference; seller counterclaimed for breach of the parties' license agreement. Trial court entered judgment on jury verdict for seller on the counterclaim. This court reversed in part, holding, inter alia, that buyer's use of "Employment TV" instead of the licensed mark "Employment Television" was not a misleading use of seller's trademark, and thus did not constitute a breach of the license agreement, since the two marks were so similar as to preclude confusion by the public. Employment Television Enterprises, LLC v. Barocas, 100 P.3d 37, 49.

Fla.1993. Cit. in ftn. as §§ 20-23. (citing § 22 of T.D. No. 2, 1990. § 22 has since been revised; see Official Text). The First South-

For earlier citations, see the Appendices, Supplements, or Pocket Parts, if any, that correspond to the subject matter under examination.

ern Bank sued to enjoin another bank from using the name "Great Southern Bank," alleging infringement and dilution of its trademark name and unfair competition. The trial court granted plaintiff injunctive relief and certified the question whether plaintiff bank's name was descriptive or generic so as not to be entitled to protection in the absence of proof that it had acquired a secondary meaning. This court remanded, holding that plaintiff bank's name contained laudatory, generic, and merely geographically descriptive elements so as not to be entitled to protection under either common or statutory law, but determination was necessary whether a secondary meaning in the name had developed in order to decide the dilution claim. In applying the suggestiveness test, the court stated that no great imagination was required to identify the product as banking services when the mark contained the word "bank," that many others used the word "southern" in their mark, and that businesses in the South had the need and right to use the term descriptively. Great Southern v. First Southern, 625 So.2d 463, 470.

§ 23. Proof of Likelihood of Confusion: Evidence of Actual Confusion

C.A.1, 1996. Com. (c) quot. in sup. In action brought under the Lanham Act, union that was lobbying to become nursing-home employees' collective-bargaining representative sued employer for trademark infringement after employer used union's mark on anti-union propaganda it distributed to employees. The district court granted employer's motion for summary judgment. Affirming on other grounds, this court held that union could not recover absent proof of a likelihood of confusion as to the source of the materials bearing its mark and that, when all the relevant factors were considered, including one employee's inquiry regarding the veracity of the documents at issue, there was no triable issue of fact as to likelihood of confusion. IAM v. Winship Green Nursing Center, 103 F.3d 196, 205.

C.A.2, 1991. Cit. in sup. §§ 20-23 (citing § 23 of T.D. No. 2, 1990. § 23 has since been revised; see Official Text). A publisher of a book and audiotapes on the development of charisma that used the trade name "New Choices Press" sought to enjoin a magazine publisher from using the name "New Choices for the Best Years" for its magazine on retirement living. The district court granted defendant's motion for summary judgment. Affirming, this court held that plaintiff failed to raise a genuine issue of fact as to the likelihood of confusion. The court concluded that plaintiff's trade name was weak because it was not widely known. Lang v. Retirement Living Pub. Co., Inc., 949 F.2d 576, 580.

C.A.5, 1998. Cit. in headnote, subsec. (2) and com. (d) cit. in disc. Assignee and registrant of all trademarks, copyrights, and publicity rights belonging to Elvis Presley estate sued owner of bar operating as "The Velvet Elvis" for, inter alia, trademark infringement and unfair competition. The district court entered judgment for defendant. Reversing and remanding, this court held that the district court erred in isolating its consideration of defendant's advertising practices from its consideration of whether the name "The Velvet Elvis" infringed plaintiff's trade and service marks and therefore created a likelihood of confusion; that the strength of plaintiff's mark, the similarity of the parties' marks, and the similarity of products and services weighed in favor of finding a likelihood of confusion; that defendant's actions suggested an intent to confuse customers as to the source of its mark; and that the evidence supported a finding that defendant's advertising practices caused actual confusion among customers. Elvis Presley Enterprises, Inc. v. Capece, 141 F.3d 188, 190, 204.

C.A.9, 1999. Cit. in disc. §§ 20-23. Entertainment industry information provider using "MovieBuff" as trademark sought to enjoin video rental chain from using "moviebuff.com" as its web site domain name. The district court entered judgment for defendant. Reversing and remanding, this court held that plaintiff established itself as the senior user of the mark, and that, given the similarity of the marks, the relatedness of product offerings, and the overlap in marketing and advertising channels, likelihood of consumer confusion existed. That defendant did not intend to confuse consumers was irrelevant under the circumstances. Brookfield Communications v. West Coast, 174 F.3d 1036, 1054.

C.A.10, 1999. Cit. in disc. §§ 20-23. Seller of camouflage-patterned outdoor clothing under "King of the Mountain" trademark brought trademark-infringement action against promoter of "Jeep KING OF THE

Cit.—cited; com.—comment; fol.—followed; sup.—support.
A complete list of abbreviations precedes page 1.

MOUNTAIN DOWNHILL SERIES" ski races. Affirming the district court's grant of summary judgment for defendant, this court held, in part, that no likelihood of confusion existed as to sponsorship of ski races. King of the Mountain Sports, Inc. v. Chrysler Corp., 185 F.3d 1084, 1090.

C.D.Cal.2006. Com. (b) quot. in disc. Manufacturer of musical instruments sued competitors, seeking, inter alia, a declaratory judgment that the body shape of its guitars did not infringe on competitors' trade dress. This court granted plaintiff's motion for summary judgment as to the trade-dress claim, holding, among other things, that there was no likelihood of confusion between plaintiff's and defendant's guitars. As one factor in this conclusion, the court found that there was no evidence of actual confusion, because the guitar reviews submitted by defendants merely described the features of defendants' guitars, without showing any confusion, and defendants admitted that they had not received any communications from third parties regarding plaintiff's products. Switchmusic.com, Inc. v. U.S. Music Corp., 416 F.Supp.2d 812, 824, appeal transferred by 183 Fed.Appx. 955 (Fed.Cir.2006).

C.D.Cal.1998. Com. (c) quot. in disc. Commercial illustrator brought unfair-competition action against toy manufacturer, alleging that defendant misappropriated and misused plaintiff's "Pearl Beach" trade name in connection with the promotion and distribution of its line of dolls. Specifically, plaintiff argued that defendant's actions resulted in reverse confusion in the marketplace. Entering judgment as a matter of law for defendant, the court held, in part, that, although plaintiff's mark was strong, she failed to establish a proximity of the goods, similarity of the marks, or evidence of actual confusion among purchasers; thus, plaintiff did not prove the type of confusion she was required to set forth in order to prevail under her "reverse confusion" theory. Walter v. Mattel, Inc., 31 F.Supp.2d 751, 760, affirmed 210 F.3d 1108 (9th Cir.2000).

D.Colo.2001. Cit. in disc. §§ 20-23. Tirestore owner brought suit against manufacturer of tie-down straps and cargo-control products for infringement of its "Bigfoot" trademark. Granting plaintiff's motion for a preliminary injunction, the court held, inter alia, that plaintiff showed a likelihood of success on the merits based on evidence that defendant's use of the mark was likely to cause confusion in the marketplace concerning the source or quality of the products. Big O Tires, Inc. v. Bigfoot 4X4, Inc., 167 F.Supp.2d 1216, 1222.

S.D.N.Y.1994. Cit. generally in disc. International sneaker and sportswear manufacturer brought Lanham Act action against discount retailer, among others, alleging that retailer's "private label" sneaker infringed on manufacturer's trademarks and trade dress. The court entered judgment for retailer, holding that there was no infringement. The results of manufacturer's mall-intercept interviews, offered as proof of consumers' actual confusion, were properly excluded as they constituted nothing more than responses to interviews conducted in what the court called a staged, artificial situation. Reebok Intern. Ltd. v. K-Mart Corp., 849 F.Supp. 252, 274.

E.D.Pa.1999. Com. (b) quot. in sup. Religious and missionary association sued similarly named organization for unfair competition and trademark violations. This court entered judgment for plaintiff, enjoining defendant from using plaintiff's trade name and trademark. The court held that there was a significant likelihood of confusion, that two of plaintiff's members had experienced actual confusion, and that plaintiff and defendant conducted business in a like manner. Gideons International, Inc. v. Gideon 300 Ministries, Inc., 94 F.Supp.2d 566, 585.

Colo.App.2004. Cit. in disc. §§ 20-23. Buyer of seller's partnership interest in a company that developed television programs based on newspaper classified ads sued seller for breach of contract and tortious interference; seller counterclaimed for breach of the parties' license agreement. Trial court entered judgment on jury verdict for seller on the counterclaim. This court reversed in part, holding, inter alia, that buyer's use of "Employment TV" instead of the licensed mark "Employment Television" was not a misleading use of seller's trademark, and thus did not constitute a breach of the license agreement, since the two marks were so similar as to preclude confusion by the public. Employment Television Enterprises, LLC v. Barocas, 100 P.3d 37, 49.

Fla.1993. Cit. in ftn. as §§ 20-23. (citing § 23 of T.D. No. 2, 1990. § 23 has since been revised; see Official Text). The First South-

For earlier citations, see the Appendices, Supplements, or Pocket Parts, if any, that correspond to the subject matter under examination.

ern Bank sued to enjoin another bank from using the name "Great Southern Bank," alleging infringement and dilution of its trademark name and unfair competition. The trial court granted plaintiff injunctive relief and certified the question whether plaintiff bank's name was descriptive or generic so as not to be entitled to protection in the absence of proof that it had acquired a secondary meaning. This court remanded, holding that plaintiff bank's name contained laudatory, generic, and merely geographically descriptive elements so as not to be entitled to protection under either common or statutory law, but determination was necessary whether a secondary meaning in the name had developed in order to decide the dilution claim. In applying the suggestiveness test, the court stated that no great imagination was required to identify the product as banking services when the mark contained the word "bank," that many others used the word "southern" in their mark, and that businesses in the South had the need and right to use the term descriptively. Great Southern v. First Southern, 625 So.2d 463, 470.

§ 24. Use of Another's Trademark on Genuine Goods

C.A.4, 2004. Com. (c) cit. in disc. Defendant operator of counterfeit-clothing business was charged with trafficking, money laundering, and conspiracy, after a search warrant of defendant's residence produced evidence that defendant was placing brand-name logos on clothing without authorization and selling it to the public. The district court denied defendant's motions to quash the search warrant and dismiss the indictment. After court ruled that defendant failed to establish any affirmative defenses, he entered a conditional plea of guilty to trafficking and conspiracy to commit money laundering, and was sentenced to prison. Affirming, this court held, inter alia, that the district court properly declined to dismiss the trademark-infringement indictment because defendant encroached on trademark owners' right to control the quality of the goods manufactured and sold under their trademark. U.S. v. Farmer, 370 F.3d 435, 441.

C.A.6, 2005. Com. (b) cit. in disc. Company that provided gymnastics instruction to children through the use of school buses retrofitted with athletic equipment sued competitor for infringement of its TUMBLEBUS mark and trade dress. The district court granted plaintiff's motion for a preliminary injunction. Affirming in part, this court held, inter alia, that the first-sale defense did not apply in this case because defendant was not using the mark to resell a genuine good produced by plaintiff, but rather was using the mark to promote her own mobile-gymnastics service. Thus, defendant's use of the first-sale defense did not render it unlikely that plaintiff would prevail on the merits of its infringement claim. Tumblebus Inc. v. Cranmer, 399 F.3d 754, 766, cert. denied 546 U.S. 824, 126 S.Ct. 361, 163 L.Ed.2d 68 (2005).

C.A.9, 1995. Com. (b) quot. in ftn. in sup. Manufacturer of hair-care products brought an action for trademark infringement and unfair competition against retailer that purchased the products from authorized dealers and resold them without plaintiff's authorization. The district court preliminarily enjoined defendant from selling the products. Reversing and remanding, this court held that the "first sale" doctrine, which precluded a producer from controlling the distribution of a trademarked product beyond the first sale, shielded defendant from liability for the mere resale of plaintiff's products, and the district court erred in granting plaintiff's motion for preliminary injunction. Sebastian Intern. v. Longs Drug Stores, 53 F.3d 1073, 1075.

N.D.Ill.2020. Quot. in sup. Manufacturer of sunglasses sued retailers, alleging, inter alia, that defendants violated plaintiff's trademarks on its sunglasses by selling their own products on an online market using plaintiff's marks without its permission; defendants argued that plaintiff sold its goods to third parties knowing that the goods would eventually be sold on the online market. This court denied defendants' motion for summary judgment, holding that there were genuine issues of material fact regarding defendants' affirmative defense under the first-sale doctrine, because a reasonable jury could find that not all of the sunglasses bearing plaintiff's trademark sold on the online market were plaintiff's genuine goods and were sold there with plaintiff's consent. The court explained that, under Restatement Third of Unfair Competition § 24, defendants could not avail themselves of the first-sale doctrine if plaintiff did not authorize a first sale of its trademarked goods, because trademarked goods were not considered genuine until the trademark owner authorized the sale of the goods under the mark. Maui Jim, Inc. v. SmartBuy Guru Enterprises, 459 F.Supp.3d 1058, 1081.

E.D.N.Y.2007. Com. (c) quot. in case quot. in sup. Italian pasta manufacturer and its exclusive United States distributor sued their freight forwarder/customs broker for allegedly seizing their pasta and selling it in the United States, ostensibly for the purpose of recovering a debt owed by manufacturer to defendant's subsidiary. This court denied the parties' cross-motions for summary judgment as to plaintiffs' claim for trademark infringement, holding, inter alia, that questions of fact remained as to whether defendant sold infringing goods under the "first sale doctrine." The court noted that, if a trademark owner did not approve the original sale of goods, the goods were not genuine as a matter of law. Italverde Trading, Inc. v. Four Bills of Lading Numbered LRNNN 120950, LRNNN 122950, LRNN 123580, MSLNV 254064, 485 F.Supp.2d 187, 210.

S.D.N.Y.2000. Com. (c) quot. in case quot. in disc. Former Major League Baseball player sued company that sold sports-related merchandise using the player's name, likeness, and signature, alleging violations of the Lanham Act and trademark infringement, among other claims. This court denied in part defendant's motion to dismiss, holding, inter alia, that plaintiff stated a viable Lanham Act claim, because defendant had no right to sell plaintiff's products after its license was terminated. Defendant erroneously concentrated on the date the goods were manufactured rather than on whether their subsequent sale was authorized, and plaintiff had not authorized the initial sale or release into the stream of commerce. Ryan v. Volpone Stamp Company, Inc., 107 F.Supp.2d 369, 382.

S.D.N.Y.1997. Cit. in headnotes, com. (c) quot. in sup. A clothing designer sued a contractor, alleging, among other claims, trademark counterfeiting, trademark infringement, unfair competition and/or false designation of origin under the Lanham Act. This court denied plaintiff's motion for summary judgment, holding, inter alia, that the law did not support defendant's argument that plaintiff's garments were "genuine" and therefore could not be subject to trademark infringement. The court stated that the issue of whether the goods were genuine was merely duplicative of the central question: whether defendant's alleged sales of, and offers to sell, plaintiff's garments were authorized. The court determined that fact issues existed as to the scope of the contractor's authority to sell seconds and overruns, and as to whether a taped telephone conversation between plaintiff's private investigator and defendant's employee showed that the employee offered to sell garments in violation of any authority. Liz Claiborne, Inc. v. Mademoiselle Knitwear, Inc., 979 F.Supp. 224, 225, 230.

N.D.Ohio, 2008. Com. (c) cit. in sup. Holder of trademark for pet grooming tools sued company that obtained a large number of holder's allegedly defective tools, which bore the trademark and had been slated for destruction, and resold some of the tools on the Internet and at flea markets without plaintiff's permission. Granting partial summary judgment for plaintiff, this court rejected defendant's argument that plaintiff was not entitled to protection under the Lanham Act because the tools were not significantly different from tools sold with trademark holder's permission in retail stores and thus genuine. The court held that the tools at issue could not be considered genuine, because there was no dispute that plaintiff did not authorize or approve their initial sale. FURminator, Inc. v. Kirk Weaver Enterprises, Inc., 545 F.Supp.2d 685, 690.

E.D.Pa.1990. Com. (b) cit. in disc. (citing § 24 of T.D. No. 2, 1990. § 24 has since been revised; see Official Text). A corporation engaged in the business of providing engineering services to owners of computers manufactured and sold by a manufacturer of high-performance computer systems sued the manufacturer, alleging, inter alia, tortious interference with contracts and prospective contractual relations, unfair competition, and breach of contract. The manufacturer counterclaimed, alleging copyright infringement, violations of the Lanham Act, unfair competition, and breach of contract. Entering judgment for the manufacturer on its Lanham Act and unfair competition counterclaims, the court held, inter alia, that plaintiff violated the Lanham Act and engaged in unfair competition, because the evidence that plaintiff made and placed labels on copies of its software for one of the manufacturer's computer systems that were virtually identical

For earlier citations, see the Appendices, Supplements, or Pocket Parts, if any, that correspond to the subject matter under examination.

to labels that the manufacturer made and affixed to its software was sufficient to establish that plaintiff had made a false description and designation of origin with respect to its software. Allen-Myland v. International Business Machines Corp., 746 F.Supp. 520, 553, supplemented 770 F.Supp. 1014 (E.D.Pa.1991).

M.D.Tenn.2000. Cit. in disc., com. (b) quot. in disc., com. (c) quot. in case quot. but dist. Fast-food chain brought damages suit for unfair competition and trademark infringement against parties that had purchased promotional toys from chain's franchisees and offered them for sale on cable shopping network prior to their release date in marketing campaign. Granting defendants' motions for summary judgment and partial summary judgment, the court held, inter alia, that plaintiff failed to prove likelihood of confusion among consumers regarding whether defendants were affiliated with plaintiff; plaintiff also failed to counter defendants' "first sale" defense that, after the first sale to franchisees, plaintiff's intellectual property rights did not entitle it to exercise control over the toys. McDonald's Corp. v. Shop at Home, Inc., 82 F.Supp.2d 801, 809, 811, 812.

E.D.Wis.2008. Com. (b) quot. in sup. Manufacturer of dietary supplements brought trademark-infringement suit against chiropractor/nutrition counselor, after manufacturer terminated defendant's account for selling the products over the Internet, and defendant then bought the products from other customers and continued to sell them over the Internet. Granting in part defendant's motion for summary judgment, this court held that, while the "first sale doctrine" did not protect unauthorized resellers who used other entities' trademarks when such use gave a reasonable impression that the resellers were authorized resellers for a product, defendant's website did not create such an impression, because it did not include any pictures of plaintiff's products and, most importantly, it prominently displayed a disclaimer in the first paragraph of the page where a customer could buy the products. Standard Process, Inc. v. Banks, 554 F.Supp.2d 866, 869.

§ 25. Liability Without Proof of Confusion: Dilution and Tarnishment

Note: The Reporter's Note to § 25, comment a, contains a typographical error at p. 277, column 1, line 45, incorrectly spelling the name of the author of the article "Reexamining Trademark Dilution," published at 44 Vand.L.Rev. 531 (1991). The author's name is David S. Welkowitz.

U.S.2003. Statutory Note cit. in disc. Affiliated corporations that owned "Victoria's Secret" trademark and operated over 750 stores nationwide sued owners of retail store named "Victor's Little Secret" in a strip mall in Kentucky, alleging trademark infringement, unfair competition, dilution, and violation of Kentucky trademark and unfair-competition law. District court granted defendants summary judgment on infringement and unfair-competition claims, but it ruled for plaintiffs on dilution claim and enjoined defendants from using mark. Court of Appeals affirmed. This court reversed and remanded, holding, inter alia, that Federal Trademark Dilution Act (FTDA) required that actual dilution be established; mere fact that consumers mentally associated junior user's mark with famous mark was not sufficient to establish actionable dilution. It noted that at least 25 states had passed statutes protecting trademarks from dilution before FTDA was enacted in 1995. Moseley v. V. Secret Catalogue, Inc., 537 U.S. 418, 429, 123 S.Ct. 1115, 1123, 155 L.Ed.2d 1.

C.A.1, 1998. Com. (e) cit. and quot. in disc. Faucet manufacturer sued competitors, claiming, in part, that defendants' faucet diluted plaintiff's faucet's trade dress within the meaning of the Federal Trademark Dilution Act (FTDA). The district court issued plaintiff a preliminary injunction on the dilution claim. Vacating in part and remanding, this court held, inter alia, that plaintiff's faucet's design, itself unregistered and not inherently distinctive, was not so strong a mark or so well publicized and known as to satisfy the FTDA's rigorous standard for fame and distinctiveness, and thus plaintiff did not meet its burden of showing likelihood of success. I.P. Lund Trading ApS, Kroin Inc. v. Kohler Co., 163 F.3d 27, 47.

C.A.2, 1999. Cit. in headnote, com. (i) quot. in ftn. Motorcycle manufacturer brought trademark-infringement action against provider of motorcycle products and services, seeking to enjoin defendant from using the word "hog" in reference to its business and goods and to prohibit defendant from employing a bar-and-shield logo similar to the one used by plaintiff. The district court entered judgment for plaintiff. Affirming in part, reversing in part, and remanding, this court held that "hog" was a generic term that was used to describe large motorcycles before plaintiff adopted it, and that plaintiff could not therefore enjoin defendant's use of the word; that defendant's use of the bar-and-shield logo for promotion and advertising did not constitute permissible trademark parody use; and that defendant's use of the logo was not made acceptable by the addition of the phrase "unauthorized dealer." Harley-Davidson, Inc. v. Grottanelli, 164 F.3d 806, 807, 813.

C.A.2, 1999. Subsec. (1)(a) quot. in part in ftn., com. (c) cit. in disc., com. (f) quot. in disc. Manufacturer of packaged foods sought declaration that its use of a fish-shaped, cheese-flavored cracker did not dilute the distinctive quality of competitor's mark. The district court granted competitor's motion to enjoin further production of manufacturer's cracker. Affirming, this court held, in part, that competitor was the senior user, that competitor's mark was moderately distinctive, that the similarities of manufacturer's item lessened the distinctive quality of that of competitor in the eyes of consumers, and that competitor had presented a strong case for dilution. Nabisco, Inc. v. PF Brands, Inc., 191 F.3d 208, 216, 217, 219, 220.

C.A.3, 2000. Com. (e) quot. in sup. Publisher of a weekly publication entitled "The Sporting News" sued publisher of a weekly sports-betting publication called "Las Vegas Sporting News" for trademark dilution under the Federal Trademark Dilution Act (FTDA). Affirming the district court's grant of plaintiff's motion for a preliminary injunction, this court held, inter alia, that a mark could be famous in a niche market when the mark had a high degree of distinctiveness within the market and when the parties were operating in the same or related markets. The court concluded that plaintiff's mark was famous in its niche and therefore was entitled to protection under the FTDA against defendant's use of a similar mark in the same market. Times Mirror Magazines v. Las Vegas Sports News, 212 F.3d 157, 164, cert. denied 531 U.S. 1071, 121 S.Ct. 760, 148 L.Ed.2d 662 (2001).

C.A.4, 1999. Com. (b) cit. and quot. in sup., stat. note cit. in disc. A circus that owned the trademark slogan "The Greatest Show on Earth" sued the state of Utah for trademark dilution for using the slogan "The Greatest Snow on Earth" as a tourism advertisement. District court entered judgment for the state, finding that plaintiff had not proved dilution. This court affirmed, holding, inter alia, that to establish dilution of a famous mark under the Federal Trademark Dilution Act required proof that (1) a defendant had made use of a junior mark sufficiently similar to the famous mark to evoke, in a relevant universe of consumers, a mental association of the two that (2) caused (3) actual economic harm to the famous mark's economic value by lessening its former selling power as an advertising agent for its goods or services. Ringling Bros.-Barnum & Bailey Combined Shows, Incorporated v. Utah Division of Travel Development, 170 F.3d 449, 453-455, 457.

C.A.5, 2001. Com. (e) cit. in disc. Car-rental company sued competitor for trademark dilution, and competitor filed counterclaim. District court denied both parties relief. Affirming in part, this court held that one company's slogan was not sufficiently famous, even in the car rental market, to warrant protection from dilution. Advantage Rent-A-Car v. Enterprise Rent-A-Car, Inc., 238 F.3d 378, 380.

C.A.5, 1998. Cit. in ftn., subsec. (1)(a) and com. (e) cit. in ftn. Golf course operator sued competitor for trademark infringement, alleging that defendant infringed and diluted plaintiff's mark by copying one of its holes. The district court entered judgment for plaintiff. Affirming, this court held, in part, that the design of plaintiff's hole was nonfunctional, under a test for either utilitarian or aesthetic functionality; that the design was descriptive and had acquired secondary meaning, as evidenced by plaintiff's extensive advertising, unsolicited publicity of the hole's trade dress in golf publications, and defendant's intent to copy and use the trade dress prominently in its own advertising; that plaintiff did not abandon its rights in a nearby lighthouse that was built at the same time as the golf course for purposes of being seen from the course; that the evidence supported the lower court's finding of a likelihood of confusion; and that defendant's use of the mark to suggest affiliation, sponsorship, or endorsement was more than nominative. Pebble Beach Co. v. Tour 18 I Ltd., 155 F.3d 526, 547.

For earlier citations, see the Appendices, Supplements, or Pocket Parts, if any, that correspond to the subject matter under examination.

C.A.6, 2010. Cit. and quot. in case cit. and quot. in disc.; cit. in sup., subsec. (g) cit. in sup. (erron. cit. as Restatement Third of Trademarks); com. (c) and illus. 3 quot. in ftn., com. (g) quot. in ftn. and in diss. op. International lingerie company brought suit for injunctive relief under the Trademark Dilution Revision Act against small retail store that sold sex toys and other sexually oriented products, alleging that defendant's use of the name "Victor's Little Secret" or "Victor's Secret" tarnished its own "Victoria's Secret" mark. On remand, the district court concluded that, even though the two parties did not compete in the same market, defendant's mark—because it was sex-related—disparaged and tended to reduce the positive associations and "selling power" of plaintiff's mark. This court affirmed, concluding that the new Act, which was expressly intended to overrule the Supreme Court's interpretation of the old Act in this very same case, created a rebuttable presumption, or at least a very strong inference, that a new mark used to sell sex-related products was likely to tarnish a famous mark if there was a clear semantic association between the two, and that that presumption had not been rebutted in this case. The dissent, noting that plaintiff had only presented evidence of a single individual who thought poorly of "Victor's Little Secret," and that even that individual's conception of "Victoria's Secret" remained unchanged, argued that plaintiff had not met its burden to show that its mark was likely to be diluted by way of tarnishment, and that the majority had sanctioned an almost nonexistent evidentiary standard. V Secret Catalogue, Inc. v. Moseley, 605 F.3d 382, 386-388, 392.

C.A.6, 2001. Com. (b) cit. generally in case cit. in disc. Lingerie retailer that owned the "Victoria's Secret" mark sued owners of adult specialty store, alleging, in part, that defendants' use of the name "Victor's Little Secret" constituted trademark dilution. Affirming the district court's grant of summary judgment for plaintiff, this court held that plaintiff's trademark was diluted by tarnishing, that is, associating it with defendants' sex toys and lewd coffee mugs, and that it was diluted by blurring, that is, linking plaintiff's chain of stores with a single, unauthorized establishment. V Secret Catalogue, Inc. v. Moseley, 259 F.3d 464, 472, cert. granted 535 U.S. 985, 122 S.Ct. 1536, 152 L.Ed.2d 463 (2002), reversed 537 U.S. 418, 123 S.Ct. 1115, 155 L.Ed.2d 1 (2003).

C.A.7, 1999. Com. (e) quot. in disc. Producer of plastic baskets used for floral bouquets at funerals sued competitor for, in part, trade-dress dilution under the Federal Trademark Dilution Act (FTDA). Reversing in part the district court's grant of summary judgment for defendant and remanding, this court held, inter alia, that fame of trade dress in niche market, like that of wholesalers and retail florists in this case, was sufficient to meet statutory criterion of being "famous" for purpose of qualifying for protection under the FTDA. Syndicate Sales, Inc. v. Hampshire Paper Corp., 192 F.3d 633, 640.

C.A.8, 1999. Com. (f) cit. in disc. Company that produced "Lean Cuisine" low-fat frozen entrees sued a competitor that produced "Michelina's Lean 'N Tasty" low-fat frozen entrees, alleging trademark infringement or dilution. District court granted defendant summary judgment. This court affirmed, holding, inter alia, that plaintiff's trademark dilution claim failed, because plaintiff did not show that defendant's mark caused consumers to associate plaintiff's mark with something other than plaintiff's frozen entrees. Luigino's, Inc. v. Stouffer Corporation, 170 F.3d 827, 832.

C.D.Cal.1999. Com. (f) quot. in disc. Magazine publisher sought to enjoin operators of Internet search engines from programming their sites in such a way as to return search results that allegedly infringed and diluted plaintiff's trademark. Declining to issue the injunction, the court held that defendants' use of the generic terms "playboy" and "playmate" did not constitute use of the terms in their trademark forms and that, even if it did, plaintiff had failed to establish a likelihood of confusion, blurring of the marks, or tarnishment. Playboy Enterprises v. Netscape Communications, 55 F.Supp.2d 1070, 1088, affirmed 202 F.3d 278 (9th Cir.1999).

C.D.Cal.1998. Com. (i) quot. in disc. Holder of federally registered trademarks sued web-site designer for trademark infringement and trademark dilution in connection with defendant's use of the marks in various web pages. Entering summary judgment for defendant, the court held, in part, that while plaintiff held valid and protectable marks, it had failed to establish a likelihood of confusion, and that defendant's use of the marks in a noncommercial setting, as a means of expressing customer dissatisfaction, constituted free speech protected by the First Amendment. Bally Total Fitness Holding Corp. v. Faber, 29 F.Supp.2d 1161, 1167.

M.D.Fla.1994. Com. (e) cit. and quot. in sup., com. (g) quot. in sup. (citing § 25 of T.D. No. 2, 1990. § 25 has since been revised; see Official Text). Textile manufacturer that registered its "Sunbrella" trademark on acrylic fabrics adaptable to outdoor applications sued hotel corporation that subsequently applied to register the "Sunbrella" mark to be used with provision of hotel services in connection with vacation packages, alleging, among other claims, unfair competition and violation of state antidilution statute. The court denied plaintiff's motion for preliminary injunction, holding, inter alia, that, until it could determine whether the "class of purchasers" requirement should be applied in a dilution claim under the state statute, it could not conclude that plaintiff was likely to succeed on the merits of its dilution claim. The court determined that the marks were similar and that plaintiff's mark was highly distinctive and was entitled to protection from dilution. It also stated that despite the sexual overtones of defendant's advertisements, it could not conclude that there was a likelihood of injury to business reputation through tarnishment. Glen Raven Mills, Inc. v. Ramada Intern., Inc., 852 F.Supp. 1544, 1554-1558.

S.D.Fla.1999. Cit. in ftn. Vacation cruise-ship line sued company that offered six-hour gambling cruises for, inter alia, trademark dilution, alleging that defendant's registered slogan was overly similar to the one used by plaintiff. Entering judgment for defendant, the court held, in part, that plaintiff had failed to establish that its mark was sufficiently famous for purposes of federal trademark law, or sufficiently distinctive for purposes of the Florida Dilution Act. Carnival Corp. v. SeaEscape Casino Cruises, Inc., 74 F.Supp.2d 1261, 1271.

D.Hawaii, 1996. Cit. generally in disc. In trademark-infringement action, owner of supermarket business called "Star Markets" sued owner of convenience stores that operated under the name "Star Mart" for violations of the Trademark Dilution Act of 1995. Entering partial summary judgment for defendant, the court held that plaintiff could not recover under the terms of the Act because it had not proven that its mark was sufficiently famous to merit antidilution protection. The court rejected the argument that a finding of trademark infringement necessitated a finding of dilution, explaining that infringement by confusion and dilution could coexist as legal findings in cases where a large number of consumers were confused, and, among those not confused, defendant's use illegally caused dilution by blurring or tarnishment. Star Markets, Ltd. v. Texaco, Inc., 950 F.Supp. 1030, 1037.

C.D.Ill.2000. Com. (e) cit. in disc. Manufacturer of coffee makers sued company that supplied coffeemaking products and related items for, inter alia, breach of contract, trademark infringement, and unfair competition. Entering partial summary judgment for plaintiff, the court held, in part, that defendant had breached the parties' licensing agreement; that, with respect to plaintiff's claim for trademark dilution, material factual issues existed as to whether its mark had become sufficiently famous; and that a triable issue existed as to whether plaintiff's claims were barred by laches or acquiescence. Bunn-O-Matic Corp. v. Bunn Coffee Service, Inc., 88 F.Supp.2d 914, 925.

N.D.Ill.1997. Com. (e) quot. in disc. Manufacturer of truck and van tool boxes and storage equipment bearing the federally registered trademark "Weather Guard" sued manufacturer of car covers for, inter alia, trademark infringement, unfair competition and dilution in connection with defendant's use of the mark "WeatherGUARD." Following a bench trial, the court entered judgment for defendant, holding, in part, that the claims for trademark infringement and unfair competition failed because plaintiff was unable to prove that defendant's use of "WeatherGUARD" created a likelihood of consumer confusion as to the source of its products, and that plaintiff's "Weather Guard" mark was not sufficiently distinctive to support a claim for dilution. Knaack Mfg. Co. v. Rally Accessories, Inc., 955 F.Supp. 991, 1005.

N.D.Ill.1996. Cit. in disc. Corporation sued individual for, inter alia, trademark infringement and for violations of the Federal Trademark Dilution Act and the Illinois Anti-Dilution Act after defendant registered plaintiff's corporate name as an Internet domain name. Both parties filed

For earlier citations, see the Appendices, Supplements, or Pocket Parts, if any, that correspond to the subject matter under examination.

motions for summary judgment. Granting plaintiff's motion on the dilution claims but denying it on the trademark-infringement claim, and denying defendant's motion entirely, the court held that defendant's registration of plaintiff's name as a domain name violated both the federal and state dilution acts because it lessened the capacity of a famous mark to identify and distinguish goods and services; however, material factual issues existed as to whether defendant's actions were likely to result in consumer confusion. Intermatic Inc. v. Toeppen, 947 F.Supp. 1227, 1237.

D.Me.1995. Com. (b) cit. in disc. A nonalcoholic beverage manufacturer that owned the trademarks "Royal Mistic" and "Mistic" brought a trademark-infringement action against a museum and its licensees, seeking to prevent defendants from manufacturing and distributing beverages under the name "Mystic Seaport." This court enjoined defendants from using the current label on their line of beverages, because there was a substantial likelihood of confusion among an appreciable number of ordinarily prudent purchasers in the alcoholic-beverage market. The court noted that Maine's antidilution statute mirrored the Massachusetts statute upon which most antidilution statutes were apparently based. Best Flavors, Inc. v. Mystic River Brewing Co., 886 F.Supp. 908, 918.

D.N.J.2006. Com. (e) quot. in case quot. in sup. Cigar seller sued pay-for-priority Internet search engine, alleging that defendant improperly sold to third parties the right to use seller's service marks and variations of those marks as Internet keywords or other devices to generate advertising revenues for defendant, in the process forcing customers looking for seller's cigars to wade through other websites, including competitors'. This court denied defendant's motion for summary judgment as to plaintiff's claims under federal and state antidilution statutes, holding, inter alia, that seller's marks were famous within the cigar market for purposes of the dilution statutes. The court noted, among other things, that seller had earned over a billion dollars under the marks, which had received extensive unsolicited third-party recognition in news articles and awards, and were prominent among search terms used by Internet browsers when looking for cigars. 800-JR Cigar, Inc. v. GoTo.com, Inc., 437 F.Supp.2d 273, 294.

D.N.J.2002. Com. (f) quot. in disc. and quot. generally in disc. Manufacturer of prescription medication "Xalatan" for treatment of glaucoma brought suit for trademark infringement and dilution against competitor, seeking to enjoin defendant's use of the trademark "Travatan." Denying plaintiff's motion for a preliminary injunction, this court held, inter alia, that the ultimate consumers in prescription-drug cases were physicians, who as sophisticated users were not confused by the two trademarks, and thus plaintiff failed to prove that there was a likelihood of confusion between the marks. Pharmacia Corp. v. Alcon Laboratories, Inc., 201 F.Supp.2d 335, 374, 380.

D.N.M.2010. Quot. in sup., cit. in disc. Buyer of endodontic equipment sued sellers for breach of contract and unfair trade practices; sellers brought various counterclaims sounding in contract and tort. Granting buyer's motion for summary judgment with respect to sellers' unfair-competition counterclaim based on trademark dilution, this court held that sellers' claim failed because sellers provided no evidence of the fame of their "Thermafil" mark in New Mexico, presented no argument why their mark would be considered famous under New Mexico law, and conceded that the mark was not famous outside the endodontic marketplace. Guidance Endodontics, LLC v. Dentsply Intern., Inc., 708 F.Supp.2d 1209, 1250, 1253.

S.D.N.Y.2002. Com. (f) cit. in disc., com. (i) quot. in case cit. in disc., Rptr's Note cit. in ftn. Owner of "TOMMY HILFIGER" trademark used in connection with high-end products, including fragrances, brought suit for, in part, trademark infringement against manufacturer of pet perfume called "Timmy Holedigger." Granting defendant's motion for summary judgment, the court held, inter alia, that plaintiff failed to prove that defendant's parody of plaintiff's trademark created a likelihood of confusion as to the source of the goods in question. Tommy Hilfiger Licensing, Inc. v. Nature Labs, LLC, 221 F.Supp.2d 410, 414, 415, 422.

S.D.N.Y.2000. Com. (i) quot. in ftn. in sup. Owner of bodybuilding course sued comic-book publisher for, inter alia, trademark infringement in connection with defendant's use of plaintiff's character in one of its story lines. Entering summary judgment for defendant, the court held, in part, that defendant had parodied the

Cit.—cited; com.—comment; fol.—followed; sup.—support.
A complete list of abbreviations precedes page 1.

character for purposes of expression, and that plaintiff's interest in preventing possible confusion was outweighed by defendant's First Amendment rights. Charles Atlas, Ltd. v. DC Comics, Inc., 112 F.Supp.2d 330, 337.

S.D.N.Y.2000. Com. (c) cit. in case quot. in ftn. The writer of a popular series of children's books and her publishing company brought suit seeking a declaratory judgment that they had not infringed the copyrights and trademarks of an author of a children's book in the 1980s. Both authors' works were based on a set of fictional characters called "Muggles." The other author counterclaimed for dilution and defamation, among other claims. This court granted in part and denied in part plaintiffs' motion to dismiss defendant's counterclaims. The court held, inter alia, that defendant sufficiently alleged the necessary elements to state a dilution claim under both federal and state law with respect to the "Muggle" and "Muggles" marks, namely that those marks became distinctive and acquired secondary meaning in the late 1980s (and had remained distinctive), and that plaintiffs' subsequent use of the "Muggles" mark in plaintiff writer's books had diluted the value of defendant's property. Scholastic, Inc. v. Stouffer, 124 F.Supp.2d 836, 848.

S.D.N.Y.1999. Coms. (c) and (g) cit. in disc. Stock exchange sued casino for, inter alia, trademark dilution and tarnishment in connection with defendant's use of a parody of plaintiff's trade name in defendant's stock-exchange-themed resort. Entering summary judgment for defendant, the court held, in part, that plaintiff's mark, which consisted of its name and a picture of the façade of its building, was not distinctive for purposes of trademark dilution, and that plaintiff had failed to show that the positive connotations associated with its mark were likely to be replaced by negative associations as a result of defendant's use. New York Stock Exc. v. New York, New York Hotel, 69 F.Supp.2d 479, 491.

M.D.N.C.1999. Com. (e) quot. in disc. Telephone company sued telephone directory companies for trademark infringement, among other claims, alleging that defendants infringed upon plaintiff's "walking fingers" logo in areas where plaintiff provided local phone service. This court granted defendants summary judgment, holding, inter alia, that plaintiff's Lanham Act claim failed, because plaintiff developed and implemented the "walking fingers" logo and placed the symbol in the public domain as a generic identifier of the yellow pages, by both its words and its actions. BellSouth Corp. v. White Directory Publishers, 42 F.Supp.2d 598, 613.

N.D.Ohio, 1999. Com. (e) cit. generally in case quot. in disc. Glassware manufacturer sued competitors for, inter alia, violations of the Lanham Act's anti-dilution provisions. Denying defendants' motion for summary judgment on this count of the complaint, the court held, in part, that material factual issues existed as to whether plaintiff's trade dress, while not inherently distinctive, had acquired secondary meaning or was famous; if it was famous, whether it became so after defendants began using it; whether defendants had used it in commerce; and whether the distinctive quality of the trade dress was diluted as a result of defendants' use. Libbey Glass, Inc. v. Oneida Ltd., 61 F.Supp.2d 700, 717.

W.D.Pa.2003. Subsec. (2) quot. in part in ftn. Professional-wrestling promoter sued seller of T-shirts and other consumer merchandise that featured graphics of dogs caricatured as plaintiff's wrestling characters, alleging, in part, trademark dilution. Granting defendant's motion for summary judgment, the court held, inter alia, that defendant's parodies of plaintiff's characters did not dilute plaintiff's trademarks by tarnishment. The court said that there was no evidence that defendant's merchandise was either inferior or offensive. World Wrestling Federation Entertainment Inc. v. Big Dog Holdings, Inc., 280 F.Supp.2d 413, 443.

W.D.Tenn.2001. Statutory Note cit. in disc. Food company sued petroleum company for trademark infringement of cartoon tiger. District court granted defendant summary judgment; court of appeals reversed. Granting in part and denying in part defendant's motions for summary judgment, this court held that, as matters of first impression, plaintiff's dilution claims were not barred by retroactive application of Federal Trademark Dilution Act (FTDA), and plaintiff was required to show actual dilution to bring action under FTDA; evidence precluded summary judgment on plaintiff's dilution-by-blurring claim under state and federal law; evidence was insufficient to

For earlier citations, see the Appendices, Supplements, or Pocket Parts, if any, that correspond to the subject matter under examination.

support plaintiff's dilution-by-tarnishment claim under state and federal law; and evidence precluded summary judgment on plaintiff's dilution-by-tarnishment claim relating to defendant's use of mark to promote alcohol and tobacco products. Kellogg Co. v. Exxon Mobil Corp., 192 F.Supp.2d 790, 797.

N.D.Tex.2011. Com. (f) quot. in sup., cit. in case cit. in disc., and quot. in ftn. Consumer lending company sued competitor for, inter alia, trademark dilution, alleging that competitor's use of the term "cash store," the trademarked name of company's stores, was likely to cause confusion and dilute company's mark. This court granted, in relevant part, plaintiff's motion for a preliminary injunction, holding that plaintiff demonstrated a substantial likelihood of success on its dilution-by-blurring claim under Texas law. After concluding that the "cash store" mark was distinctive, the court held that, even in the absence of consumer confusion, an unauthorized user's adoption of another's mark lessened that mark's capacity to identify the true owner's goods and services; moreover, factors such as the identical name used by both parties and the moderate degree of recognition of plaintiff's mark among loan consumers in plaintiff's areas of operation showed a likelihood of confusion that made dilution even more likely. Cottonwood Financial Ltd. v. Cash Store Services, Inc., 778 F.Supp.2d 726, 748, 750, 751, 753, 755.

S.D.Tex.2001. Cit. in disc. Trademark owner of "ERNEST & JULIO GALLO" sued owners of the domain name ERNESTANDJULIOGALLO.COM for violation of the Texas Anti-Dilution Statute and Anti-Cybersquatting Consumer Protection Act. Granting plaintiff partial summary judgment, this court held, inter alia, that defendants' bad-faith registration of domain name diluted plaintiff's distinctive mark, and risk of irreparable harm to plaintiff warranted permanent injunction. E. & J. Gallo Winery v. Spider Webs Ltd., 129 F.Supp.2d 1033, 1037.

E.D.Va.1999. Com. (e) cit. in disc. Owner of recognized but unregistered trademark sued competitor that was using a substantial portion of the mark in one of its Internet domain names for violations of the Lanham Act and the Federal Trademark Dilution Act. Entering judgment in part for plaintiff, the court held that the mark, which was descriptive, had acquired secondary meaning, and that defendant's use created a likelihood of confusion; therefore, plaintiff had stated a claim for trademark infringement. However, because plaintiff could not establish that the mark was famous, either within or outside a specialized market, its claim for dilution failed. Washington Speakers Bureau v. Leading Authorities, 33 F.Supp.2d 488, 503, affirming 217 F.3d 843 (4th Cir.2000).

Fla.1993. Cit. in ftn., subsec. (1) quot. in part in sup., com. (e) quot. in sup. and in ftn. (citing § 25 of T.D. No. 2, 1990. § 25 has since been revised; see Official Text). The First Southern Bank sued to enjoin another bank from using the name "Great Southern Bank," alleging infringement and dilution of its trademark name and unfair competition. The trial court granted plaintiff injunctive relief and certified the question whether plaintiff bank's name was descriptive or generic so as not to be entitled to protection in the absence of proof that it had acquired a secondary meaning. This court remanded, holding that plaintiff bank's name contained laudatory, generic, and merely geographically descriptive elements so as not to be entitled to protection under either common or statutory law, but a determination was necessary as to whether a secondary meaning in the name had developed in order to decide the dilution claim. The court stated that, because it found as a matter of law that the name "First Southern Bank" was merely descriptive, and therefore lacked the "distinctive quality" that the Florida dilution statute was designed to protect, there was no possibility of a violation of the dilution statute unless a "distinctive quality" had arisen because the name had acquired a secondary meaning. It noted that resolution of the dilution issue was a mixed one of law and fact. Great Southern v. First Southern, 625 So.2d 463, 470.

Ga.2016. Subsec. (1) cit. in sup.; coms. (c) and (*i*) quot. in sup. Corporation and its affiliated nursing homes brought an action under Georgia's trademark antidilution statute against law group that focused on suing nursing homes, regarding defendant's month-long, state-wide advertising campaign targeting plaintiffs. The trial court entered a permanent injunction prohibiting defendant from running advertisements about plaintiffs that included trade names, service marks, or logos. This court reversed in part as to one advertisement, holding that the advertisement did not violate the

Cit.—cited; com.—comment; fol.—followed; sup.—support.
A complete list of abbreviations precedes page 1.

statute. The court cited Restatement Third of Unfair Competition § 25 in determining that defendant did not dilute plaintiffs' trademarks by tarnishment, because defendant used plaintiffs' mark in a descriptive manner to identify a nursing-home facility in an advertisement for defendant's legal services. McHugh Fuller Law Group, PLLC v. PruittHealth, Inc., 794 S.E.2d 150, 155, 156.

La.1995. Cit. in disc. The Gulf Coast Bank sued the Gulf Coast Bank and Trust Company for trade-name infringement, alleging that defendant's corporate name was deceptively similar to plaintiff's in violation of Louisiana's Trademark Act. Trial court granted defendant summary judgment and intermediate appellate court affirmed. This court reversed and remanded, holding that where one relies on secondary meaning to establish the distinctiveness of its name, one need not prove fraud to enjoin another from using its trade name, but must show that there is a likelihood of consumer confusion created by defendant's use of the trade name. The court stated that the legislature amended the trademark and trade name act to add the anti-dilution statute, opining that the legislature recognized that an antidilution cause of action is not recognized under the law of unfair competition absent specific statutory authority. Gulf Coast Bank v. Gulf Coast Bank & Trust Co., 652 So.2d 1306, 1312.

§ 26. Contributory Infringement by Printers, Publishers, and Other Suppliers

C.D.Cal.1997. Com. (a) cit. in sup. Operator of aerospace development and production facility sued registrar of Internet domain names for, inter alia, trademark infringement, contributory infringement, and unfair competition, alleging, among other things, that defendant violated federal trademark law by accepting registrations of domain names similar or identical to plaintiff's "SKUNK WORKS" service mark. Granting defendant's motion for summary judgment, the court held, in part, that there was no trademark infringement because, in accepting registrations of domain names using the words "skunk works," defendant did not use plaintiff's mark in connection with the sale, distribution, or advertisement of goods and services, and that defendant was not liable for contributory infringement absent a showing that it had unequivocal knowledge that the domain names it was registering were being used to infringe plaintiff's mark. Lockheed Martin Corp. v. Network Solutions, Inc., 985 F.Supp. 949, 964, affirmed 194 F.3d 980 (9th Cir.1999).

§ 27. Contributory Infringement by Manufacturers and Distributors

D.Md.1996. Cit. and cit. generally in disc. In action brought under the Lanham Act, charity sued publisher for contributory trademark infringement in connection with the use of charity's name and mark in a book designed to instruct readers on ways to make money from "business opportunity" frauds and scams. Publisher moved to dismiss on the ground that charity could not sustain a claim for contributory infringement absent proof of direct infringement. Denying the motion, the court held, in part, that dismissal was inappropriate because it could not say, as a matter of law, that charity would be unable to present evidence of direct infringement. N.F.B. v. Loompanics Enterprises, 936 F.Supp. 1232, 1245.

S.D.N.Y.2008. Cit. and quot. but not fol. Trademark owner sued Internet marketing website for contributory trademark infringement under federal and common law, alleging that defendant facilitated and allowed the sale on its website of counterfeit silver jewelry bearing plaintiff's brand. Entering judgment for defendant, this court held that defendant was not liable for contributory infringement. The court concluded, inter alia, that the U.S. Supreme Court's *Inwood* test, rather than the "reasonable-anticipation" test articulated in the Restatement Third of Unfair Competition § 27, which test was rejected by the Supreme Court in *Inwood*, governed this claim; under the *Inwood* test, plaintiff's allegations were insufficient to establish that defendant knew or had reason to know of the infringement at issue. Tiffany (NJ) v. eBay, Inc., 576 F.Supp.2d 463, 502.

For earlier citations, see the Appendices, Supplements, or Pocket Parts, if any, that correspond to the subject matter under examination.

TOPIC 4. DEFENSES AND LIMITATIONS ON RELIEF

§ 28. Descriptive Use (Fair Use)

U.S.2004. Cit. in disc. Makeup manufacturer sued competitor for declaratory relief as to use of the term "microcolor"; competitor counterclaimed for trademark infringement. District court granted manufacturer summary judgment on trademark infringement counterclaim, but court of appeals reversed. This court vacated and remanded, holding that a plaintiff claiming infringement of incontestable mark had to show likelihood of consumer confusion as part of prima facie case, while defendant had no independent burden to negate likelihood of any confusion in raising affirmative defense that a term is used descriptively, not as a mark, fairly, and in good faith. The court determined that, in this case, court of appeals erroneously required manufacturer/counterclaim defendant to shoulder burden on issue of confusion. KP Permanent Make-Up, Inc. v. Lasting Impression I, Inc., 543 U.S. 111, 124, 125 S.Ct. 542, 551, 160 L.Ed.2d 440, on remand 408 F.3d 596 (9th Cir.2005).

C.A.2, 2009. Com. (c) quot. in sup. Clothing manufacturer sued fashion designer, alleging that defendant's proposed use of his personal name, "Joseph Abboud," in connection with his new collection of high-end men's clothing breached the parties' sales agreement transferring to plaintiff certain assets, including defendant's names, trademarks, and trade names, and constituted trademark infringement in violation of the Lanham Act. The district court entered judgment for plaintiff and granted it injunctive relief. Vacating and remanding, this court held, inter alia, that, with respect to defendant's "fair use" defense to the trademark-infringement claim, whether defendant sought to "use" his name "otherwise than as a mark" required individualized consideration of defendant's proposed advertisements. The court noted the relevance of the physical nature of the use in terms of size, location, and other characteristics in comparison with other descriptive matter, as well as the presence or absence of precautionary measures such as labeling. JA Apparel Corp. v. Abboud, 568 F.3d 390, 401.

C.A.2, 2001. Quot. but dist. Holder of trademark "The Children's Place" sued creator of website for infringement, unfair competition, and dilution after defendant registered domain names similar to its mark. District court issued injunction barring defendant from using 81 domain names. Affirming in part, this court held, inter alia, that holder was entitled to injunction under the Lanham Act prohibiting defendant from use of similar Internet domain names that could cause a likelihood of confusion among consumers. Defendant was not protected by doctrine of fair use where defendant did not use mark descriptively and where trial court found that defendant acted in bad faith. TCPIP Holding Co., Inc. v. Haar Communications, Inc., 244 F.3d 88, 103, on remand 2004 WL 1620950 (S.D.N.Y.2004).

C.A.2, 2000. Com. (c) quot. in disc., com. (d) cit. in disc. Holders of rights in swing-era song sued advertising agency and manufacturer of sporting goods for violations of the Lanham Act, alleging that defendants' use of an evocative version of the song in a commercial for manufacturer's golf clubs was likely to confuse consumers into associating the song with the product. The district court entered summary judgment for defendants. Reversing and remanding, this court held, in part, that a trademark did not protect the actual musical composition but, instead, its title, and that material factual issues existed as to whether defendants used the mark in a descriptive sense and, if so, whether they acted in good faith. EMI Catalogue v. Hill, Holliday, Connors, Cosmopulos, 228 F.3d 56, 65-67.

C.A.2, 1999. Cit. in disc. Manufacturer of packaged foods sought declaration that its use of a fish-shaped, cheese-flavored cracker did not dilute the distinctive quality of competitor's mark. The district court granted competitor's motion to enjoin further production of manufacturer's cracker. Affirming, this court held, in part, that competitor was the senior user, that competitor's mark was moderately distinctive, that the similarities of manufacturer's item lessened the distinctive quality of that of competitor in the eyes of consumers, and that competitor had presented a strong case for dilution. Nabisco, Inc. v. PF Brands, Inc., 191 F.3d 208, 221.

C.A.2, 1997. Com. (c) quot. in part in sup. Manufacturer of lip gloss that was marketed under the registered trademark

Cit.—cited; com.—comment; fol.—followed; sup.—support.
A complete list of abbreviations precedes page 1.

"Sealed with a Kiss" brought Lanham Act action against competitor that used the phrase "Seal it with a Kiss" in the promotional displays for its lipsticks. The district court entered summary judgment for competitor, finding that "Seal it with a Kiss" was not used to identify its product but, rather, as an invitation to consumers to test the lipsticks' durability by applying it, then sealing or imprinting a complimentary postcard. Affirming, this court held that defendant's use of the phrase "Seal it with a Kiss" was descriptive in nature and, therefore, within the fair-use defense to Lanham Act liability. Cosmetically Sealed Indus. v. Chesebrough-Pond's, 125 F.3d 28, 30.

C.A.2, 1995. Cit. in disc., com. (a) quot. in disc., com. (d) cit. in disc. Manufacturer of air fresheners in the shape of a pine tree for use in automobiles brought a trademark-infringement action against the maker of a pine-tree-shaped air freshener designed to be plugged into electrical outlets. The district court granted plaintiff summary judgment on defendant's fair-use defense but granted defendant summary judgment on the ground that no likelihood of confusion existed. This court affirmed the grant of summary judgment for defendant and reversed the district court's fair-use determination, holding that, because defendant used the pine-tree shape for descriptive purposes and not as a mark, its use of the shape was fair use; defendant's adoption of the shape with knowledge of plaintiff's use and without consulting counsel was not evidence of bad faith that would negate the fair-use defense, since defendant was entitled to use the mark descriptively notwithstanding plaintiff's use of the shape as a mark. Car-Freshner Corp. v. S.C. Johnson & Son, Inc., 70 F.3d 267, 269, 270.

C.A.4, 1997. Com. (b) quot. in case quot. in disc. Manufacturer that owned trademark for fishing rods with a translucent tip and a contrasting opaque shaft brought infringement action against competitor that began marketing a similar item. Competitor argued that the design was functional or descriptive, and thus manufacturer's mark should be canceled. The district court agreed, and ordered the Patent and Trademark Office to cancel the mark. This court concluded that the mark, which had become incontestable, could not be canceled, and reversed and remanded for a consideration of the remaining infringement issues. On remand, the district court entered judgment for competitor. Affirming, this court held that where competitor intentionally copied manufacturer's design not for the purpose of exploiting manufacturer's good will but, rather, in the good faith pursuit of the creation of a stronger fishing rod, manufacturer was not entitled to the presumption of a likelihood of confusion; alternatively, competitor had established a fair use defense. Shakespeare Co. v. Silstar Corp. of America, Inc., 110 F.3d 234, 238.

C.A.5, 1999. Cit. in disc., coms. (b) and (c) cit. in disc. Plaintiff, as assignee of registered service mark "SUGAR-BUSTERS" and author of best-selling diet book entitled "SUGAR BUSTERS! Cut Sugar to Trim Fat," sued authors and publisher of cookbook entitled "SUGAR BUST For Life!," asserting, in part, a claim for unfair competition under the Lanham Act. Vacating the district court's grant of plaintiff's motion for a preliminary injunction, this court remanded for a determination of whether defendants' use of their book title was protected by the fair-use doctrine, which allowed a party to use a term in good faith to describe its goods or services when the term was used in its descriptive, rather than in its trademark, sense. Sugar Busters LLC v. Brennan, 177 F.3d 258, 271.

C.A.5, 1998. Coms. (a) and (c) cit. in ftn. Golf course operator sued competitor for trademark infringement, alleging that defendant infringed and diluted plaintiff's mark by copying one of its holes. The district court entered judgment for plaintiff. Affirming, this court held, in part, that the design of plaintiff's hole was nonfunctional, under a test for either utilitarian or aesthetic functionality; that the design was descriptive and had acquired secondary meaning, as evidenced by plaintiff's extensive advertising, unsolicited publicity of the hole's trade dress in golf publications, and defendant's intent to copy and use the trade dress prominently in its own advertising; that plaintiff did not abandon its rights in a nearby lighthouse that was built at the same time as the golf course for purposes of being seen from the course; that the evidence supported the lower court's finding of a likelihood of confusion; and that defendant's use of the mark to suggest affiliation, sponsorship, or endorsement was more than nominative. Pebble Beach Co. v. Tour 18 I Ltd., 155 F.3d 526, 545.

For earlier citations, see the Appendices, Supplements, or Pocket Parts, if any, that correspond to the subject matter under examination.

C.A.9, 2010. Com. (c) cit. and quot. in sup. Owner of incontestable trademark DELICIOUS for young women's footwear brought suit for trademark infringement against seller of intimate apparel and beauty products, after defendant, as part of its promotion for a new line of beauty products, sold or gave away a hot pink tank top with the word "Delicious" written across the chest. The district court granted summary judgment for defendant. Reversing and remanding, this court held that genuine issues of material fact existed as to whether defendant's use of the word "Delicious" was protected by the Lanham Act's fair-use defense. The court pointed to evidence from which a reasonable jury could conclude that defendant was using "Delicious" as a trademark, and noted little evidence that defendant took precautionary measures to avoid confusion with plaintiff's mark; in addition, a jury could reasonably decide that defendant did not use the word "only to describe its goods." Fortune Dynamic, Inc. v. Victoria's Secret Stores Brand Management, Inc., 618 F.3d 1025, 1040-1042.

C.A.9, 2003. Com. (a) quot. in disc. The corporate owner of "The Beach Boys" trademark sued one of the band's former members for infringement. District court granted corporation summary judgment and issued permanent injunction against defendant's use of the trademark. This court affirmed, holding, inter alia, that the classic fair-use defense did not apply, because defendant did not use the mark in its primary, descriptive meaning of "boys who frequent a stretch of sand beside the sea." Instead, defendant used the mark in its secondary, trademark sense, which denoted the music band that popularized California surfing culture. Brother Records, Inc. v. Jardine, 318 F.3d 900, 906, cert. denied 540 U.S. 824, 124 S.Ct. 155, 157 L.Ed.2d 45 (2003).

C.D.Cal.2014. Com. (c) quot. in case quot. in sup. Hair-product distributor brought an action for trademark infringement, unfair competition, and false advertising against competitor, alleging that competitor developed a line of hair-care products confusingly similar in name and packaging design to distributor's products. This court denied plaintiff's motion for summary adjudication of defendant's affirmative defense of fair use. Citing Restatement Third of Unfair Competition § 28, Comment *c*, the court held that, despite the lack of evidence showing that defendant took precautionary measures to minimize the risk that the trademarked term and colors would be understood in its trademark sense, a reasonable jury could find that defendant did not use the term and colors as a trademark, but rather, to describe the product. Moroccanoil, Inc. v. Marc Anthony Cosmetics, Inc., 57 F.Supp.3d 1203, 1227.

N.D.Ga.2013. Com. (c) quot. in sup., quot. in case quot. in sup., cit. in treatise cit. in sup. Nutrition center that owned trademarks for "Don't diet. Lose IT!" and "Don't diet. Live IT!" brought a trademark-infringement action against publisher, alleging that defendant infringed on plaintiff's marks by using the phrases as subchapters in its publications. This court granted defendant's motion to dismiss, holding that defendant was likely to satisfy the elements of the fair-use defense, because plaintiff's complaint suggested that defendant's alleged use of the marks constituted a non-infringing use. Citing Restatement Third of Unfair Competition § 28, Comment *c*, the court determined that defendant did not use the trademarked phrases as identifiers of the source of the publications, but rather, used the phrases in their descriptive sense to indicate that the subchapters were about losing weight and maintaining weight loss. Southeast Clinical Nutrition Centers, Inc. v. Mayo Foundation for Medical Educ. and Research, 135 F.Supp.3d 1267, 1276, 1277.

S.D.Iowa, 2000. Cit. in disc. Software company sued computer manufacturer for trademark infringement, unfair competition, and dilution, alleging that defendant's launching of its most recent computer operating system, "MAC OS-9," for its personal computer constituted willful and intentional infringement of plaintiff's trademark "OS-9," a mark that had been federally registered since 1989. This court granted defendant summary judgment, holding, inter alia, that defendant established its fair-use defense, because the "OS-9" portion of "Mac OS-9" was a descriptive term and was not used as a trademark, and defendant used "Mac OS-9" fairly and in good faith. Microware Systems Corp. v. Apple Computer, Inc., 126 F.Supp.2d 1207, 1219, affirmed 238 F.3d 989 (8th Cir.2001).

D.Minn.1994. Com. (b) cit. in sup. (citing § 28 of T.D. No. 3, 1991. § 28 has since been revised; see Official Text). Hair-care prod-

Cit.—cited; com.—comment; fol.—followed; sup.—support.
A complete list of abbreviations precedes page 1.

uct manufacturer sued a competitor for trademark infringement, unfair competition, and deceptive trade practice, alleging that defendant's use of the phrase "Style Freeze" in connection with its line of hair-care products created a likelihood of confusion with the family of "STYLE" trademarks that plaintiff used for hair, skin, and nail-care products. This court denied both parties' motions for summary judgment, holding, inter alia, that a genuine issue of material fact existed as to the issue of likelihood of confusion because factual issues existed as to whether plaintiff's "STYLE" marks were descriptive or suggestive. Regarding the element of actual confusion, a factual issue existed as to the adequacy of the questions of defendant's market survey, which indicated that there was no actual confusion between its "style freeze" product and plaintiff's line of "STYLE" products. Dowbrands, L.P. v. Helene Curtis, Inc., 863 F.Supp. 963, 971.

S.D.N.Y.2010. Com. (c) quot. in case quot. in sup. Clothing manufacturer that purchased trademarks from clothing designer, including trademarks based on designer's name, sued designer for, among other things, trademark infringement based on designer's proposed use of his personal name in promoting his new clothing line. On remand, this court granted plaintiff injunctive relief, concluding, among other things, that designer's proposed advertisements would constitute trademark infringement not otherwise insulated by the fair-use defense. The court reasoned that the size and font of the name, which was virtually identical to the trademark sold to manufacturer, removed it from the realm of descriptive, nontrademark use, and created confusion that could not withstand scrutiny under the fair-use test, particularly given the prominence of the name in the ads. JA Apparel Corp. v. Abboud, 682 F.Supp.2d 294, 311.

S.D.N.Y.2008. Com. (c) quot. in sup. and in case quot. in sup. Competitor sued owner of the registered trademark LOVE POTION, seeking a declaratory judgment that its description of two of its fragrance products as "love potion fragrance" and "belly button love potion fragrance" did not infringe owner's trademark. This court granted in part competitor's motion for summary judgment, declaring that competitor did not infringe the mark, because its use of "love potion" constituted fair use, i.e., the use of a protected mark to describe certain aspects of goods, but not as a mark to identify the goods. The court noted that competitor's manner of use indicated a descriptive use, rather than use as a mark, since there was no TM symbol next to "love potion" on its products, the term was placed off-center on all of its packaging and printed in a smaller font size than its own mark, and the term was used with other words to form a phrase describing the products. Dessert Beauty, Inc. v. Fox, 568 F.Supp.2d 416, 426.

S.D.N.Y.2000. Coms. (a) and (d) cit. in disc. Interior designer brought infringement and defamation action against former client, operator of Internet web-sites critical of designer, claiming misuse of mark as "metatag" to cause search engines to list web-sites in response to user queries based on mark. This court denied designer's request for preliminary injunction barring continuation of web-sites, holding, inter alia, that the fair-use doctrine protected the web-site operator's use of the designer's mark, because web-site operator used the mark to indicate truthfully the mark's connection with the business of designer, and that operator's prior knowledge of designer's trade name did not necessarily infer a lack of good faith on operator's part. Bihari v. Gross, 119 F.Supp.2d 309, 322-323.

D.Or.2016. Com. (b) quot. in sup. Shoe manufacturer filed a trademark-infringement action against competitor, seeking to prevent defendant from selling shoes that plaintiff alleged were confusingly similar to plaintiff's registered trademarks and trade dress, including plaintiff's "Supernova" mark. This court granted plaintiff's motion for a preliminary injunction prohibiting competitor from selling the challenged shoes, holding that plaintiff was likely to succeed in overcoming defendant's descriptive-fair-use defense. The court explained, citing Restatement Third of Unfair Competition § 28, Comment *b*, that, as the degree of likely confusion between the marks increased, the likelihood that the use was fair decreased; and defendant was using "Supernova" as a mark, not as a descriptor, because there was no reference to the shoe's cosmic color scheme or any information suggesting that Supernova was anything other than the name of the shoe. Adidas America, Inc. v. Skechers USA, Inc., 149 F.Supp.3d 1222, 1246.

D.S.C.1995. Cit. in headnote, Rptr's Note

to com. (a) cit. in ftn., com. (b) quot. in sup. Manufacturer of fishing rod with a clear tip on an opaque rod base sued competitor for trademark infringement and unfair competition after competitor began marketing a fishing rod with the same color configuration. On remand from the intermediate appellate court, the court entered judgment for competitor, holding that manufacturer was not entitled to a presumption of a likelihood of confusion, since competitor copied manufacturer's design in good faith and with the goal of highlighting to buyers the functional qualities inherent in this type of fishing rod. Furthermore, manufacturer had failed to establish a likelihood of confusion because its mark was not especially strong, the rods had different appearances but for the color configuration, and consumers typically examined fishing rods quite thoroughly before buying. Alternatively, competitor could invoke the "fair use" defense, since it copied the color configuration for descriptive purposes only and did not intend to confuse buyers as to the source of its product. Shakespeare Co. v. Silstar Corp. of America, Inc., 906 F.Supp. 997, 1000, 1014, 1015, affirmed 110 F.3d 234 (4th Cir.1997).

§ 29. Consent

C.A.7, 2016. Cit. in sup. Food-distribution company and its owner brought a trademark-infringement action against similarly named competitor that was owned by company's former employee, that hired owner after company suspended its operations, and that subsequently fired owner. The district court granted defendant's motion to dismiss. This court reversed and remanded, holding that the complaint failed to unambiguously establish the elements of the affirmative defense of acquiescence, because it did not allege that plaintiffs had made representations that they would not assert a right or claim regarding the trademark. Citing Restatement Third of Unfair Competition §§ 9 and 29, the court explained that the purpose of trademark protection was to identify the source of a good or service to consumers; and if the owner of a mark had, through his words or conduct, conveyed his consent to the defendant's use of the mark, then the mark's original source-identifying power was weakened. Hyson USA, Inc. v. Hyson 2U, Ltd., 821 F.3d 935, 940.

W.D.Ark.2018. Coms. (a) and (d) cit. in disc.; com. (c) cit. and quot. in disc. Former authorized reseller of developer's software, which continued to sub-resell the software on its website after the termination of the parties' authorized-reseller relationship, sued developer for tortious interference with a business expectancy based on certain statements that developer made to consumers and to the public about it and its website; developer counterclaimed, alleging trademark infringement and other claims. This court granted in part developer's motion for summary judgment on its counterclaims, holding that developer satisfied all of the elements of a claim for trademark infringement and was entitled to injunctive relief, but concluded that developer was estopped from recovering any monetary damages. In making its decision, the court noted that, under Restatement Third of Unfair Competition § 29, a trademark license did not have to take the form of a written contract, and could arise through a course of conduct that clearly indicated to a reasonable person in the implied licensee's position that the holder of the trademark consented to a particular type of use of that mark by the licensee. Visual Dynamics, LLC v. Chaos Software Ltd., 309 F.Supp.3d 609, 617, 626, 627.

E.D.Mo.2012. Cit. in sup. Licensor of trademarks that were used in the identification and marketing of certain financially distressed retail properties brought, along with licensor's affiliate, claims for false designation of origin and unfair competition under the Lanham Act against, among others, special servicer of defaulted loans on the properties, which had entered into a licensing agreement with plaintiffs in connection with the trademarks, alleging that, after affiliate was terminated as the properties' manager, defendant wrongfully continued to use plaintiffs' trade names and trademarks with the intent to confuse consumers as to the management of the properties. Granting summary judgment for defendant, this court held, among other things, that the licensing agreement authorized defendant to use plaintiffs' marks, and, furthermore, there was no evidence that defendant did not have a good-faith belief that it had authorization to use the marks. Ariel Preferred Retail Group, LLC v. CWCapital Asset Management, 883 F.Supp.2d 797, 832.

Tex.App.2012. Cit. in disc. After licensee of a trademark and a service mark, which claimed to have acquired all rights in those

Cit.—cited; com.—comment; fol.—followed; sup.—support.
A complete list of abbreviations precedes page 1.

marks, sold its retail store to purchasers, purchasers, based on the belief that they had purchased all rights in the marks, opened other retail outlets using the marks; licensee sued purchasers, alleging trademark and service mark infringement. Following a bench trial, the trial court rendered judgment in favor of defendants. Affirming in part, this court held that the trial court did not abuse its discretion when it concluded that, because plaintiff's conduct with respect to the name and associated marks had been inequitable and marked by a want of good faith, plaintiff's claims were barred by the doctrine of unclean hands. The court pointed to evidence that the license agreement from the original owner of the marks to plaintiff did not permit plaintiff to assign or sub-license the marks, and, therefore, the sale to defendant was based on something that plaintiff did not have a right to do in the first place. Condom Sense, Inc. v. Alshalabi, 390 S.W.3d 734, 763.

Wis.App.1994. Cit. in diss. op., coms. (a) and (d) cit. in diss. op., com. (b) cit. in diss. op. and in ftn. to diss. op. (citing § 29 of T.D. No. 3, 1991. § 29 has since been revised; see Official Text). Purchaser of store in Oshkosh sought judgment declaring its rights under trade name; store in Milwaukee with same trade name counterclaimed. Affirming the trial court's finding that Oshkosh store built up its own secondary meaning in the Oshkosh area independent of the Milwaukee store, and that this finding was limited to a 20-mile radius, this court held that a contractual agreement that the seller entered into with purchaser stating that seller would not engage in a competing business within a 20-mile radius from Oshkosh store was probative of seller's understanding of the scope of the secondary meaning owned by him, since seller could sell only what he owned. Since counterclaiming store had registered the trade name first, it was the prima facie owner of the trade name beyond Oshkosh. A dissent argued that plaintiff's right did not derive from a good-faith adoption of the trade name by the purchased business but through consent of the counterclaiming business. Leon's Frozen Custard, Inc. v. Leon Corp., 182 Wis.2d 236, 513 N.W.2d 636, 642.

§ 30. Abandonment

C.A.2, 1996. Com. (a) cit. in disc. Manufacturer of historic reproductions of "Mission furniture" sued competitor for trade-dress infringement. Vacating the district court's grant of a preliminary injunction for plaintiff and remanding for trial, this court held that the trade dress of reproductions was not inherently distinctive and that plaintiff was not likely to succeed in proving secondary meaning, since it was doubtful that consumers identified the Mission furniture trade dress with plaintiff rather than with the maker of the popular originals. L. & J.G. Stickley, Inc. v. Canal Dover Furniture, 79 F.3d 258, 264.

C.A.4, 2000. Com. (b) cit. in disc. Manufacturer of rescue vehicles sued competitor for trademark infringement in connection with defendant's use of a mark almost identical to the one used by plaintiff. Defendant counterclaimed, arguing that plaintiff had abandoned the mark. The district court entered judgment on a jury verdict for plaintiff. Vacating and remanding, this court held, in part, that, while the lower court erred in failing to instruct the jury that, for purposes of abandonment, intent to resume use of a mark meant an intent to resume use in the reasonably foreseeable future, it was not error to omit an instruction explaining that an intent not to resume use became more likely as the period of nonuse became longer. Emergency One, Inc. v. American FireEagle, Ltd., 228 F.3d 531, 540.

C.A.5, 1998. Com. (c) cit. in disc. Golf course operator sued competitor for trademark infringement, alleging that defendant infringed and diluted plaintiff's mark by copying one of its holes. The district court entered judgment for plaintiff. Affirming, this court held, in part, that the design of plaintiff's hole was nonfunctional, under a test for either utilitarian or aesthetic functionality; that the design was descriptive and had acquired secondary meaning, as evidenced by plaintiff's extensive advertising, unsolicited publicity of the hole's trade dress in golf publications, and defendant's intent to copy and use the trade dress prominently in its own advertising; that plaintiff did not abandon its rights in a nearby lighthouse that was built at the same time as the golf course for purposes of being seen from the course; that the evidence supported the lower court's finding of a likelihood of confusion; and that defendant's use of the mark to suggest affiliation, sponsorship, or endorsement was more than nominative. Pebble Beach Co. v. Tour 18 I Ltd., 155 F.3d 526, 543.

For earlier citations, see the Appendices, Supplements, or Pocket Parts, if any, that correspond to the subject matter under examination.

C.A.6, 2005. Com. (a) quot. in disc. Company that provided gymnastics instruction to children through the use of school buses retrofitted with athletic equipment sued competitor for infringement of its TUMBLEBUS mark and trade dress. The district court granted plaintiff's motion for a preliminary injunction. Affirming in part, this court held, inter alia, that there was insufficient evidence that competitor's defense that plaintiff abandoned its rights in the mark through naked licensing was so strong as to make it unlikely that plaintiff would succeed on the merits of its trademark-infringement claim. The court said that abandonment of the mark in other parts of the United States did not effectuate a forfeiture of plaintiff's rights in the greater Louisville area. Tumblebus Inc. v. Cranmer, 399 F.3d 754, 766, cert. denied 546 U.S. 824, 126 S.Ct. 361, 163 L.Ed.2d 68 (2005).

C.A.7, 2011. Cit. in sup. Licensor of a trademark for a shop that sold bridal and bridesmaid dresses sued former licensees, alleging that defendants violated the Lanham Act by continuing to use the trademark without payment or a current license. The district court granted summary judgment for defendants. Affirming, this court held that plaintiff had abandoned the trademark by engaging in naked licensing. The court rejected plaintiff's argument that the high quality of defendants' business permitted unsupervised licensing; a licensor was required to ensure the *consistent* quality, not *high* quality, of the licensee's goods and services, and, here, plaintiff did not retain any control, via either the license agreement or course of performance, over the appearance or operations of defendants' business or even over what inventory defendants had to carry or avoid. Eva's Bridal Ltd. v. Halanick Enterprises, Inc., 639 F.3d 788, 789.

C.A.11, 2002. Com. (a) quot. in ftn. Radio station brought a trademark-infringement action against competitor. Affirming the district court's entry of a preliminary injunction in favor of plaintiff, this court held, inter alia, that the preliminary injunction was not overbroad in prohibiting defendant from making "curative uses" designed to dispel confusion, since a court did not have to permit curative steps to an infringer treading on the protectable rights of a current user. Cumulus Media, Inc. v. Clear Channel Communications, Inc., 304 F.3d 1167, 1179.

S.D.Ind.2015. Cit. in case quot. in sup. In a trade-dress infringement dispute between firearms manufacturers, defendants brought a counterclaim for abandonment against plaintiffs, alleging that plaintiffs engaged in naked licensing in the parties' prior settlement, by approving the design for a certain firearm and covenanting not to sue defendants for the sale of firearms based on that design. This court denied defendants' motion for summary judgment on its counterclaim, holding that plaintiffs did not grant defendants a license to manufacture the design, but rather, stipulated that the design did not infringe their trade dress. The court noted that, under Restatement Third of Unfair Competition §§ 30 and 33, a licensor could be held to have abandoned its trade dress if it engaged in naked licensing by allowing a licensee to use the trade dress without exercising reasonable control over the nature and quality of the goods made by the licensee. Heckler & Koch, Inc. v. German Sport Guns GmbH, 71 F.Supp.3d 866, 922.

N.D.Iowa, 2001. Com. (a) cit. in case quot. in disc. Plaintiff healthcare companies that were affiliated to provide services and products in Iowa and Illinois under common-law and state-registered trademarks "Trinity" and "Trinity Health" sued defendant healthcare companies that had acquired by assignment rights in federally registered service mark for "Trinity Healthcare Services." Defendants counterclaimed for infringement of their federally registered trademark. Plaintiffs counterclaimed, alleging challenges to federal mark. This court denied in part defendants' motion to dismiss, holding, inter alia, that plaintiffs' improper-tacking claim stated a claim upon which relief could be granted, because there were facts that could be proved consistent with allegations of improper tacking that would constitute abandonment of predecessor mark. Iowa Health System v. Trinity Health Corp., 177 F.Supp.2d 897, 920.

S.D.N.Y.1999. Com. (a) quot. in disc. Manufacturer of Indian pickles brought claims for trademark and copyright infringement against its former United States distributor and others, seeking, in part, to cancel defendants' registrations for "Priya" trademark. Defendants counterclaimed for, in part, trademark infringement. On defendants' counterclaim, the court held that defendants failed to demonstrate their ownership of a federal trademark, noting

Cit.—cited; com.—comment; fol.—followed; sup.—support.
A complete list of abbreviations precedes page 1.

existence of a serious question of abandonment in two of three markets of any common law rights they might have had in trademark prior to the federal registrations. Ushodaya Enterprises, Ltd. v. V.R.S. Intern., Inc., 63 F.Supp.2d 329, 338.

S.D.N.Y.1997. Subsec. (2)(a), coms. (a) and (b) cit. in disc. In trademark infringement action, putative United States registrant of the mark "TOPICLEAR" sought to enjoin French owner from infringing or threatening to infringe the mark in the United States. French owner argued that alleged registrant never had United States rights to the mark because, among other things, an agreement executed by the parties in 1992 that purported to transfer all of French owner's right, title, and interest in the mark to a corporation formed by French owner and alleged registrant was not binding. Entering judgment in part for alleged registrant and in part for French owner, the court held, inter alia, that alleged registrant did not develop any rights in the mark simply because he was one of French owner's United States resellers of TOPICLEAR; that, prior to the 1992 agreement, French owner had a protectible mark that was not abandoned; that the 1992 agreement was an enforceable contract assigning French owner's right in the mark to corporation; and that cancellation of alleged registrant's United States registration of the mark was appropriate. Aini v. Sun Taiyang Co., Ltd., 964 F.Supp. 762, 775, affirmed 159 F.3d 1348 (2d Cir.1998).

N.D.Ohio, 2001. Com. (d) cit. and quot. in disc. and quot. in treatise quot. in disc. Mattress retailer sued its licensee for trademark and trade-name infringement. Licensee counterclaimed, seeking a declaratory judgment that it had not infringed the trademark and trade name, and that licensor had abandoned the trademark and trade name. This court granted licensor summary judgment, holding, inter alia, that there was no merit in licensee's abandonment defense. The court determined that licensee could not raise a "naked licensing" defense based on licensor's failure to adequately control the quality of licensee's operations. Although the court allowed licensee to raise its naked licensing claim based on licensor's alleged failure to control the quality of an Indiana third-party licensee's operation, there was no evidence that a naked license in Indiana would diminish the trademark and trade name as a source of origin in this localized market area. Westco Group, Inc. v. K.B. & Associates, Inc., 128 F.Supp.2d 1082, 1090.

E.D.Pa.2009. Cit. in ftn. (general cite). Magazine publisher sued book publisher for copyright infringement and common-law unfair competition, alleging, among other things, that the name of defendant's book, "Famous Monster Movie Art of Basil Gogos," suggested an affiliation with the name of plaintiff's magazine, "Famous Monsters of Filmland." This court granted summary judgment for defendant, holding, inter alia, that plaintiff had abandoned its "Famous Monsters of Filmland" mark. In making its decision, the court noted that, while Pennsylvania trial courts had recently begun to apply the definition of unfair competition set forth in Restatement Third of Unfair Competition § 1, in this case it was appropriate to analyze plaintiff's common-law claim for unfair competition as if it were a Lanham Act claim of unfair competition. Warren Pub. Co. v. Spurlock, 645 F.Supp.2d 402, 443.

W.D.Tex.2014. Com. (c) cit. in sup. Operator of a garage-door repair-and-installation service brought a trademark-infringement action against competitor; defendant counterclaimed, seeking, among other things, cancellation of plaintiff's trademark based on his alleged abandonment of the mark by failure to police third-party use. This court denied in part plaintiff's motion to dismiss, holding that, while defendant faced a stringent burden of proving its abandonment counterclaim, at this stage of the proceedings, defendant had plausibly alleged that plaintiff's disregard of potentially infringing activity resulted in his mark ceasing to function as an indicator of origin and losing trade significance. The court noted that Restatement Third of Unfair Competition § 30 provided that abandonment would only result where a trademark had lost all significance as an indication of source or sponsorship through widespread unauthorized use. Garcia v. Global Development Strategies Inc., 44 F.Supp.3d 666, 673.

Me.2002. Quot. in sup. Real estate company sued similarly named insurance company to enjoin use of its business name. Trial court entered judgment for defendant, holding that plaintiff had abandoned the name "Knowles" and that defendant did not misappropriate the Knowles name when it

For earlier citations, see the Appendices, Supplements, or Pocket Parts, if any, that correspond to the subject matter under examination.

registered to do business under that name. This court vacated and remanded, holding that there was no evidence that plaintiff intended to abandon the name. Although plaintiff's former owner transferred capital stock in original "Knowles Company" to one of his business associates, he continued to use the name and sought to reacquire exclusive right to it. When defendant entered into licensing agreement with owner for right to use the Knowles name, defendant acknowledged that owner controlled it. The Knowles Co. v. Northeast Harbor Insurers, 2002 ME 6, 788 A.2d 587, 589-590, on remand 2003 WL 23162892 (Me.Super. 2003).

Neb.App.2007. Quot. in sup. Security-services corporation that had acquired the successor-in-interest of a closely held security-systems company brought deceptive-trade-practices and trade-name-infringement claims against the company's former shareholders and the new security business that shareholders had started under the company's name, "A/C Security." The trial court entered judgment for plaintiff. Affirming, this court concluded that, because successor had not abandoned the trade name "A/C Security" through its rebranding process, and was actively using the name when plaintiff acquired successor under a purchase agreement that transferred the name and other intellectual property to plaintiff, the defense of abandonment failed. ADT Sec. Services, Inc. v. A/C Sec. Systems, Inc., 15 Neb.App. 666, 685-686, 736 N.W.2d 737, 758.

§ 31. Unreasonable Delay (Laches)

C.A.4, 1998. Com. (d) cit. in disc. Operator of golf resort sued competitor under Lanham Act, alleging that competitor infringed operator's "PINEHURST" service mark by using that name in connection with its own golf courses. The district court entered summary judgment for operator on its claims of validity of mark and infringement, but denied its request for injunctive relief. Affirming in part, reversing in part, and remanding, this court held that the "PINEHURST" mark had acquired secondary meaning as a result of operator's long-time use of the name; that the evidence supported a finding that competitor's use of the mark created a likelihood of confusion; and that, while the defenses of laches and acquiescence did not prevent the issuance of a permanent injunction, they could bar operator's claim for damages. Resorts of Pinehurst, Inc. v. Pinehurst Nat. Corp., 148 F.3d 417, 423.

C.A.9, 2018. Com. (c) quot. in sup. Owner of a trademark for use on a line of gluten-free cookies sued operator of a chain of grocery stores that purchased the cookies from owner, alleging that defendant infringed on plaintiff's trademark by using a similar mark as part of a food-scoring system displayed on certain foods that it sold in its stores. The district court granted summary judgment for defendant based on the affirmative defense of laches, finding that plaintiff unreasonably delayed filing suit against defendant in an effort to sell its brand to defendant, rather than in an effort to settle the dispute. Vacating in part and remanding, this court held that the district court impermissibly resolved a disputed question of material fact—whether plaintiff was trying to settle its claims with defendant—in favor of the moving party. The court noted that it relied on Restatement Third of Unfair Competition § 31 in a prior action to conclude that laches did not bar a claim where a plaintiff waited two years to file suit, because during that period the parties were actively seeking to resolve the matter out of court. Eat Right Foods Ltd. v. Whole Foods Market, Inc., 880 F.3d 1109, 1118.

C.A.9, 2004. Com. (c) quot. in disc. A large Mexican grocery chain that had long used the trademark "Gigante" in Mexico but not the United States sued small American grocery chain that used name "Gigante" in Southern California. District court held that plaintiff's four-year delay in bringing suit barred plaintiff from enjoining defendant from using the mark. This court vacated and remanded, holding, inter alia, that district court properly applied laches factors to this case because plaintiff had not been diligent in enforcing its mark. Although defendant operated its first "Gigante" store at a loss for three years, it opened second store a year after plaintiff first learned of alleged infringement. Grupo Gigante SA De CV v. Dallo & Co., Inc., 391 F.3d 1088, 1102.

C.A.9, 2002. Com. (a) cit. in disc. Manufacturer of nutritional supplements sued competitor for false advertising under the Lanham Act. Affirming the district court's grant of summary judgment for defendant, this court held, inter alia, that plaintiff's suit was barred by laches, since it was filed after the analogous limitations period for

Cit.—cited; com.—comment; fol.—followed; sup.—support.
A complete list of abbreviations precedes page 1.

fraud under California law had expired, and plaintiff's delay in filing suit was both unreasonable and prejudicial. Jarrow Formulas, Inc. v. Nutrition Now, Inc., 304 F.3d 829, 836, cert. denied 537 U.S. 1047, 123 S.Ct. 600, 154 L.Ed.2d 520 (2002).

C.A.11, 2021. Com. (e) quot. in case quot. in sup. Illinois-based advertising and marketing company filed claims for trademark infringement and unfair competition under the Lanham Act against Florida-based advertising and marketing company that operated under the same name as plaintiff. After a jury rendered a verdict for plaintiff, the district court granted defendant's post-trial motion for judgment as a matter of law, finding that plaintiff's claims were barred by laches. While affirming the district court's conclusion that the doctrine of laches barred plaintiff's claims for monetary damages, this court remanded for consideration of plaintiff's request for injunctive relief to protect the public's interest in avoiding confusion. The court cited Restatement Third of Unfair Competition § 31 in explaining that, because of the public interest in preventing the deception of consumers, delay by a trademark owner ordinarily would not disable it from obtaining an injunction where there was strong evidence of likely or actual confusion. Pinnacle Advertising and Marketing Group, Inc. v. Pinnacle Advertising and Marketing Group, LLC, 7 F.4th 989, 1011.

C.A.11, 1997. Com. (e) quot. in sup. Manufacturer of commercial refrigerator components brought trademark-infringement action against competitor that began selling parts that were virtually identical to those produced by manufacturer, seeking damages and injunctive relief. The district court entered summary judgment for defendant, concluding that the action was barred by laches. Vacating and remanding, this court held that, for purposes of determining the extent of plaintiff's delay in bringing suit, the lower court should have considered the progressive encroachment theory in order to evaluate the point at which plaintiff could have demonstrated likelihood of confusion in its primary market, and that, even if laches barred a claim for monetary damages, injunctive relief might still be appropriate if the public interest in preventing consumer deception outweighed the effect of plaintiff's delay. Kason Industries v. Component Hardware Group, 120 F.3d 1199, 1207.

C.A.Fed.1992. Cit. in disc. (citing § 30 of T.D. No. 3, 1991, which is now § 31 of the Official Text). Patentee sued construction company for patent infringement nine years after first becoming aware of defendant's infringement. The district court granted defendant summary judgment based in part on the defense of laches. Reversing and remanding, this court held that laches was not established by undue delay of plaintiff and prejudice to defendant, but remained an equitable judgment of the district court in light of all the circumstances, and that the issue of laches must be tried. The court stated that, in making its decision on whether plaintiff dealt unfairly with defendant by not promptly bringing suit, the district court must weigh all pertinent facts, such as length of delay, seriousness of prejudice, reasonableness of excuses, and defendant's conduct or culpability. A.C. Aukerman Co. v. R.L. Chaides Const. Co., 960 F.2d 1020, 1040.

N.D.Ala.2017. Com. (a) quot. in ftn.; com. (e) cit. in case quot. in sup. Supplier of window-tinting products doing business under a trade name brought an action under the Lanham Act and state law for, inter alia, trademark infringement and dilution against competitors with similar name and identical products that refused to stop using the trade-marked name. This court denied defendants' motions to dismiss, holding, inter alia, that plaintiff's claims were not time barred, despite being filed outside of the applicable limitations period, because whatever delay occurred was excusable and did not unduly prejudice defendants, given that they had notice of the alleged infringement. The court referred to Restatement Third of Unfair Competition § 31's analysis of the uncertain role of the statute of limitations for Lanham Act claims and explained that an analogous statute of limitations should be used only as a jumping-off point to determine whether the doctrine of laches was a valid defense to plaintiff's claims. Solar Reflections, LLC v. Solar Reflections Glass Tinting, LLC, 256 F.Supp.3d 1248, 1253, 1255, 1256.

N.D.Cal.1997. Cit. in disc. The creator of a unique form of martial arts named "Kuk Sool Won" brought a trademark-infringement and unfair-competition action against a competitor. Defendant argued that plaintiff's unfair competition claim was barred by the four-year statute of limitations. This court, among other dispositions, denied defendant's counter-motion for summary judgment based upon the running of the statute of limitations for unfair competition. The court held, inter alia, that plaintiff's claim for unfair competition would not be barred by the four-year statute of limitations, since the alleged wrongs (i.e., the wrongful use and dilution of plaintiff's service marks) were multiple, continuous acts, and some of those acts had occurred within the limitations period. The court stated that each allegedly infringing display of defendant's service name on products or advertisements could create a separate cause of action for unfair competition and trademark infringement. Suh v. Yang, 987 F.Supp. 783, 796.

N.D.Ga.2006. Com. (e) cit. in case quot. in sup. Nonprofit organization that provided free air transportation to and from hospitals for persons with medical and financial difficulties sued similar organization that had a similar name for trademark infringement and related claims. This court denied defendant's motion for summary judgment, holding that plaintiff's claims were not barred by the doctrine of estoppel by laches. Noting that numerous instances of actual confusion between plaintiff and defendant had been alleged, the court reasoned in part that, even if plaintiff had unreasonably delayed in asserting its trademark rights, it would be inappropriate to grant summary judgment for defendant on equitable laches grounds because it was in the public interest to prevent consumer confusion, and plaintiff sought only injunctive relief. Angel Flight of Georgia, Inc. v. Angel Flight Southeast, Inc., 424 F.Supp.2d 1366, 1371.

C.D.Ill.2000. Cit. in disc. Manufacturer of coffee makers sued company that supplied coffeemaking products and related items for, inter alia, breach of contract, trademark infringement, and unfair competition. Entering partial summary judgment for plaintiff, the court held, in part, that defendant had breached the parties' licensing agreement; that, with respect to plaintiff's claim for trademark dilution, material factual issues existed as to whether its mark had become sufficiently famous; and that a triable issue existed as to whether plaintiff's claims were barred by laches or acquiescence. Bunn-O-Matic Corp. v. Bunn Coffee Service, Inc., 88 F.Supp.2d 914, 927.

D.Minn.2000. Com. (a) quot. in part in sup. Manufacturer that registered color "canary yellow" as trademark for its sticky notes sued competitors for, in part, trademark infringement. Granting in part defendants' motion for summary judgment, the court held, inter alia, that because defendants, which, since 1986, had spent millions of dollars manufacturing and promoting their yellow sticky-note products, showed that plaintiff's delay in pursuing trademark protection was inexcusable and that they suffered undue prejudice because of the delay, plaintiff was barred by laches from receiving damages and profits for the period prior to the filing of this suit. Minnesota Mining and Man. v. Beautone Specialties, 82 F.Supp.2d 997, 1004.

S.D.N.Y.2002. Cit. in disc. Cuban cigar manufacturer sued American manufacturer of tobacco products, challenging defendant's use and registration of the "COHIBA" trademark. Granting plaintiff's motion for summary judgment to dismiss defendant's equitable defenses of estoppel by acquiescence and equitable estoppel, the court held, inter alia, that defendant failed to establish evidence of any acts, conduct, or omissions on plaintiff's part on which defendant could rely. Plaintiff's three-year silence prior to filing its cancellation petition did not constitute cause for equitable estoppel, since defendant had made little effort to promote its COHIBA-branded cigars during that time, and thus plaintiff did not as a matter of law have a duty to speak. Emmpresa Cubana Del Tabaco v. Culbro Corp., 213 F.Supp.2d 247, 277.

Cal.App.2007. Com. (a) cit. in case quot. in disc. Manufacturer of a kitchen device used to make tarts sued former distributor of the device and Taiwanese corporations that sourced copies of the device for distributor, alleging, in part, a claim for trade-dress infringement in violation of the Lanham Act. The trial court granted a directed verdict for defendants on the trade-dress-infringement claims. Affirming, this court held, inter alia, that plaintiff's claims were barred by the equitable defense of laches; plaintiff delayed for 10 years in asserting its claims and thus they were presumptively untimely, its delay was unreasonable as a matter of law, and defendants, who invested significant resources in developing and selling the device, were prejudiced by the delay. Magic Kitchen LLC v. Good Things Intern. Ltd., 153 Cal.App. 4th 1144, 1156, 63 Cal.Rptr.3d 713, 722.

Md.Spec.App.20004. Quot. in disc. After building-supplies retailer sued storm-door manufacturer for breach of contract, manufacturer counterclaimed for trademark infringement. The trial court entered judgment for manufacturer on the counterclaim. Affirming, this court held, inter alia, that manufacturer's trademark-infringement claim was not barred by laches. The court said that manufacturer timely challenged the infringement, and retailer continued to infringe on the mark even after the counterclaim had been filed. Mid South Bldg. Supply of Maryland, Inc. v. Guardian Door and Window, Inc., 156 Md.App. 445, 847 A.2d 463, 485.

N.H.2004. Com. (e) cit. and quot. in disc. Condominium owners' association sued unit owner and board member who formed corporation operating under development's registered trade name for purposes of renting her units and others in the complex. Trial court granted plaintiff's motion for permanent injunction against use of trade name, but denied its request for monetary damages and attorney's fees. Affirming, this court held, inter alia, that although plaintiff's delay in asserting its rights was unreasonable, the public interest in avoiding confusion and mistake required that the doctrine of laches not be rigidly applied, because the strong likelihood of confusion outweighed any inequities to defendants. Nordic Inn Condominium Owners' Ass'n v. Ventullo, 151 N.H. 571, 864 A.2d 1079, 1088, 1089.

Tex.App.2012. Com. (a) cit. in disc. After licensee of a trademark and a service mark, which claimed to have acquired all rights in those marks, sold its retail store to purchasers, purchasers, based on the belief that they had purchased all rights in the marks, opened other retail outlets using the marks; licensee sued purchasers, alleging trademark and service mark infringement. Following a bench trial, the trial court rendered judgment in favor of defendants. Affirming in part, this court held that the trial court did not abuse its discretion when it concluded that plaintiff's claims were barred by laches, because plaintiff unreasonably delayed in asserting a right or claim in the marks, the delay was not excused, and it resulted in undue prejudice to defendant. The court pointed to evidence that plaintiffs filed suit over five years after they gained knowledge of defendants' alleged infringing use, and, during that time, defendants built up their business and entered into costly transactions with third parties under the assumption that they could use the marks. Condom Sense, Inc. v. Alshalabi, 390 S.W.3d 734, 758, 759.

§ 32. Plaintiff's Misconduct (Unclean Hands)

C.A.Fed.2015. Com. (c) cit. in sup. Applicant brought an action to register a mark for his band name "THE SLANTS," alleging that the name was intended to reclaim and take ownership of Asian stereotypes. The examiner for the Patent and Trademark Office refused to register the trademark based on the Lanham Act's disparagement proscription; the U.S. Trademark Trial and Appeal Board affirmed. The court of appeals affirmed the Board's decision. On rehearing en banc, this court vacated and remanded, holding that the disparagement proscription amounted to viewpoint discrimination in violation of the First Amendment and thus was unconstitutional. The court rejected government's argument that the denial of plaintiff's registration did not eliminate any common-law rights that might exist in his mark, and, citing Restatement Third of Unfair Competition § 32, Comment *c*, pointed out that plaintiff's common-law right to the trademark could be unenforceable under the doctrine of unclean hands. In re Tam, 808 F.3d 1321, 1344.

C.A.Fed.2009. Com. (b) quot. in sup. Trademark applicant sought to register its mark—MOSKOVSKAYA—for vodka. The Trademark Trial and Appeal Board (Board) affirmed the refusal of the U.S. Patent and Trademark Office (PTO) to register the mark, concluding that it was primarily geographically deceptively misdescriptive of the goods. Vacating, this court held that the appropriate inquiry for materiality purposes was whether a substantial portion of the relevant consumers was likely to be deceived, not whether any absolute number or particular segment of the relevant consumers (such as foreign-language speakers) was likely to be deceived, and remanded to the Board for a determination of whether there was a prima facie case of material deception under the correct legal test. In re Spirits Intern., N.V., 563 F.3d 1347, 1355.

For earlier citations, see the Appendices, Supplements, or Pocket Parts, if any, that correspond to the subject matter under examination.

TOPIC 5. LICENSING AND ASSIGNMENT OF RIGHTS

§ 33. Licensing of Trademarks

C.A.1, 2018. Quot. in sup. In Chapter 11 proceedings, debtor rejected an agreement in which it had granted licensee, among other things, a trademark license and the exclusive rights to sell certain of debtor's goods. The bankruptcy court determined that the rejection left licensee with only a pre-petition damages claim in lieu of any obligation by debtor to further perform under the agreement. Affirming, this court held that licensee did not retain its rights under the agreement post-rejection. The court pointed out that the Bankruptcy Code allowed a debtor to free itself from executory burdens, and reasoned that allowing licensee to retain the use of debtor's trademarks would force debtor to choose between performing executory obligations arising from the continuance of the license or risking the permanent loss of its trademarks; the court explained that, under Restatement Third of Unfair Competition § 33, a trademark owner's failure to monitor and exercise control over the quality of goods sold to the public under its trademark could result in abandonment of the trademark. In re Tempnology, LLC, 879 F.3d 389, 403.

C.A.3, 2006. Com. (b) quot. in sup. Corporation that was formed by, and handled sales and distribution for, family seed-corn partnership brought trademark-infringement and other claims against partnership. The district court granted summary judgment for plaintiff as to ownership of the family name as a trademark. Reversing and remanding, this court held, among other things, that it could not conclude as a matter of law that partnership had abandoned its rights to the trademark merely because it had ceased all direct use of it after corporation was founded. The court reasoned that a reasonable fact-finder could conclude that partnership, via an implied license agreement, consented to corporation's use of the mark and exercised adequate quality control over products represented by mark, particularly in light of the high degree of interlocking family ownership and control over corporation and partnership. Doeblers' Pennsylvania Hybrids, Inc. v. Doebler, 442 F.3d 812, 824.

C.A.6, 2005. Com. (b) quot. in disc. Company that provided gymnastics instruction to children through the use of school buses retrofitted with athletic equipment sued competitor for infringement of its TUMBLEBUS mark and trade dress. The district court granted plaintiff's motion for a preliminary injunction. Affirming in part, this court held, inter alia, that there was insufficient evidence that competitor's defense that plaintiff abandoned its rights in the mark through naked licensing was so strong as to make it unlikely that plaintiff would succeed on the merits of its trademark-infringement claim. The court said that abandonment of the mark in other parts of the United States did not effectuate a forfeiture of plaintiff's rights in the greater Louisville area. Tumblebus Inc. v. Cranmer, 399 F.3d 754, 764, 766, cert. denied 546 U.S. 824, 126 S.Ct. 361, 163 L.Ed.2d 68 (2005).

C.A.7, 2020. Cit. in case cit. in sup. Wine maker and subsidiary sued former employee and competitor formed by former employee, alleging, inter alia, that defendants engaged in unfair competition when former employee, using his position as president while employed by plaintiffs, used plaintiffs' resources without their knowledge or consent to sell wine under competitor's brand at a cheaper price. The trial court entered judgment on a jury verdict for plaintiffs on their unfair-competition claim, entered a damages award of nothing, and granted plaintiffs' request for disgorgement as alternative relief. This court affirmed, holding that, under Restatement Third of Unfair Competition § 37, disgorgement was an appropriate remedy for plaintiffs' unfair-competition claim. The court explained that the district court did not err in relying on § 37 for guidance in determining if disgorgement was an appropriate remedy, because Michigan caselaw had previously cited §§ 21 and 33 in addressing novel issues of unfair competition. Continental Vineyard, LLC v. Vinifera Wine Co., LLC, 973 F.3d 747, 759.

C.A.7, 2011. Quot. in sup., coms. (a), (b), and (c) quot. in sup., Rptr's Note to com. (c) cit. in sup. Licensor of a trademark for a shop that sold bridal and bridesmaid dresses sued former licensees, alleging that defendants violated the Lanham Act by continuing to use the trademark without payment or a current license. The district court granted summary judgment for defendants. Affirming, this court held that plaintiff had abandoned the trademark by

Cit.—cited; com.—comment; fol.—followed; sup.—support.
A complete list of abbreviations precedes page 1.

engaging in naked licensing. The court rejected plaintiff's argument that the high quality of defendants' business permitted unsupervised licensing; a licensor was required to ensure the *consistent* quality, not *high* quality, of the licensee's goods and services, and, here, plaintiff did not retain any control, via either the license agreement or course of performance, over the appearance or operations of defendants' business or even over what inventory defendants had to carry or avoid. Eva's Bridal Ltd. v. Halanick Enterprises, Inc., 639 F.3d 788, 789-791.

C.A.7, 2011. Com. (c) quot. in case quot. in disc. Chapter 11 debtor sought permission to sell its subsidiary's assets, including an executory contract between subsidiary and trademark licensee. The district court, inter alia, ruled that bankruptcy court's order barring assignment of the contract was erroneous. Affirming, this court held that the contract was a services agreement that could be assigned without licensee's consent; after the trademark sublicense in the contract expired, all that was left was a contract for services. The court rejected licensee's argument that the service provisions of the contract were actually a continuation of the trademark sublicense, i.e., an "implied" sublicense; if licensee had wanted to prevent subsidiary from assigning the service contract to another firm without licensee's permission, all it had to do was get subsidiary to agree to designate the contract as a trademark sublicense, which was not assignable in the absence of a provision authorizing assignment. In re XMH Corp., 647 F.3d 690, 697.

C.A.7, 1997. Coms. (b) and (c) cit. in disc. German manufacturer of special paper product brought trademark-infringement action against its American distributor. The district court entered judgment for distributor and, citing the doctrine of acquiescence, issued a preliminary injunction preventing manufacturer from using the trademarks or asserting any ownership rights to them. Vacating and remanding, this court held that manufacturer did not abandon all trademark rights through "naked" licensing, since it neither lost control of the manufacture of the basic product nor had any evidence of inadequate quality control on the part of distributor, and that, even assuming that manufacturer acquiesced in distributor's use of the marks, an acquiescence defense did not divest manufacturer of its right to use the marks. TMT North America, Inc. v. Magic Touch GmbH, 124 F.3d 876, 885, 887.

C.A.8, 2018. Com. (d) cit. in disc. Licensor of "Sturgis" marks designed for an annual motorcycle rally commonly known as "Sturgis" brought an action against souvenir providers that sold merchandise related to the rally and stores that sold providers' merchandise, alleging that defendants used the marks in violation of the Lanham Act and related South Dakota statutes. A jury rendered a verdict for plaintiff, and the district court denied in part defendants' motion for judgment as a matter of law. Affirming in part, this court held that the district court did not err in declining to apply licensee estoppel against defendants. The court cited Restatement Third of Unfair Competition § 33, Comment *d*, in noting that licensee estoppel was an equitable doctrine, and rejected plaintiff's argument that defendants were estopped from challenging the validity of its marks because one defendant had previously licensed one of the marks, explaining that plaintiff did not allege that the other defendants were alter egos of the licensee-defendant, and that licensee-defendant only admitted to the validity of the mark that it had licensed. Sturgis Motorcycle Rally, Inc. v. Rushmore Photo & Gifts, Inc., 908 F.3d 313, 321.

C.A.D.C.2011. Quot. in case quot. in disc. After two heating and air conditioning businesses with nearly identical names sued each other over which company had the right to use two trademarks naming the companies, the trial court concluded that first business, which was the licensor of the marks, was the proper owner of the trademarks, and that second business, as licensee of the marks, was estopped from challenging first business's ownership. This court affirmed, holding that, regardless of how it would define the contours of the licensee-estoppel doctrine, the equities in this case weighed in favor of applying licensee estoppel against second business, which, while having benefited from its license of the disputed marks for over two decades, was now asking the court to declare that the licensed trademarks had been void since 1993. Thus, the court found no need to determine whether licensee estoppel was an automatic bar to all trademark licensee challenges of its licensor's ownership or whether the court was required to engage in a totality-of-the-circumstances analysis. John C. Flood of Virginia, Inc. v. John C. Flood, Inc., 642 F.3d 1105, 1110.

D.D.C.2016. Quot. in case quot. in sup.; com. (a) quot. in case quot. in sup.; com. (c) quot. in sup. In a trademark dispute, California-based manufacturer and seller of a style of ice-cream bars and popsicles known as "paletas" sued Mexico-based competitor, alleging, among other things, that defendant had abandoned any rights to its purported registered or unregistered marks in the United States by engaging in "naked licensing." After a bench trial, this court held that defendant had satisfied the minimal level of control necessary to avoid abandonment through naked licensing under Restatement Third of Unfair Competition § 33. The court pointed out that defendant's licensees were closely related to defendant's directors and owners and regarded their businesses as being part of a family tradition that stretched back generations, and that defendant had retained and exercised authority over its licensees, even if it had done so with less rigor than might be considered ideal or expected in a typical licensing arrangement. Paleteria La Michoacana, Inc. v. Productos Lacteos Tocumbo S.A. DE C.V., 188 F.Supp.3d 22, 92, 93.

D.D.C.2010. Quot. in case quot. in sup. Plumbing business brought trademark-infringement action against its sister company, which was the successor in interest of the original owner and licensor of the trademarks. Granting summary judgment for defendant, this court held that plaintiff, as licensee of the trademarks, was estopped from claiming ownership of the trademarks under the naked-licensing doctrine. The court reasoned that plaintiff, in seeking to employ the doctrine, not as a defense to defendant's infringement claims, but as an offensive claim to transfer ownership of the trademarks from defendant to it based solely on its allegations that defendant's lack of supervision caused the quality of its goods and services to suffer, was attempting to benefit from its own misfeasance. John C. Flood of Virginia, Inc. v. John C. Flood, Inc., 700 F.Supp.2d 90, 97.

C.D.Ill.2000. Cit. in ftn. Manufacturer of coffee makers sued company that supplied coffeemaking products and related items for, inter alia, breach of contract, trademark infringement, and unfair competition. Entering partial summary judgment for plaintiff, the court held, in part, that defendant had breached the parties' licensing agreement; that, with respect to plaintiff's claim for trademark dilution, material factual issues existed as to whether its mark had become sufficiently famous; and that a triable issue existed as to whether plaintiff's claims were barred by laches or acquiescence. Bunn-O-Matic Corp. v. Bunn Coffee Service, Inc., 88 F.Supp.2d 914, 927.

N.D.Ill.2015. Cit. and quot. in disc.; com. (c) cit. and quot. in sup. Owner of trademarked karaoke accompaniment tracks brought a claim for unauthorized use of trademarks in violation of the Lanham Act, inter alia, against licensees of its trademarks; defendants counterclaimed, seeking a declaratory judgment that the trademarks were invalid because they were fraudulently procured. This court denied both parties' motions for summary judgment, holding that, although the record did not support a finding that plaintiff, itself, used its trademark in commerce, factual questions existed as to whether plaintiff exercised sufficient control over its licensees to establish indirect use of its trademarks. In the course of its discussion, the court referred to the standards set forth in Restatement Third of Unfair Competition § 33 for analyzing what constituted a trademark owner's reasonable control of its licensee. Slep-Tone Entertainment Corporation v. Coyne, 141 F.Supp.3d 813, 824, 825.

N.D.Ill.2014. Rptr's Note to com. (b) quot. in case quot. in sup. Trademark owner of a karaoke system brought an action against owner of a bar and grill that provided karaoke shows, alleging that defendant hired karaoke operators that used a pirated version of plaintiff's tracks; defendant filed counterclaims for, inter alia, fraudulent procurement of the trademarks, alleging that, when it applied for the trademarks registration, plaintiff misrepresented that it used the trademarks to conduct karaoke shows. This court denied in part plaintiff's motion to dismiss defendant's counterclaims, holding that defendant sufficiently stated a counterclaim for fraudulent procurement. Citing Restatement Third of Unfair Competition § 33, the court acknowledged that the "use in commerce" requirement of the Lanham Act could be satisfied by the use of a trademark by a licensee, but determined that the language in plaintiff's application did not

Cit.—cited; com.—comment; fol.—followed; sup.—support.
A complete list of abbreviations precedes page 1.

disclose that the requirement was met in such a way. Slep-Tone Entertainment Corporation v. Kalamata, Inc., 75 F.Supp.3d 898, 904.

N.D.Ill.1998. Quot. in ftn., com. (b) quot. in disc. and ftn. A marketing and distributing company sued competitors for unfair competition under the Lanham Act, among other claims, alleging that defendants' use of its trademark "STEALTH" on various shoes infringed its trademark. This court granted defendants summary judgment, holding, inter alia, that defendants' use of STEALTH did not create a likelihood of confusion, because the parties' products were dissimilar and defendants' use of a prominent house mark on the shoe upper and its relegation of STEALTH to the sole militated against confusion. S Industries, Inc. v. Stone Age Equipment, Inc., 12 F.Supp.2d 796, 804, 813.

S.D.Ind.2015. Cit. in case quot. in sup. In a trade-dress infringement dispute between firearms manufacturers, defendants brought a counterclaim for abandonment against plaintiffs, alleging that plaintiffs engaged in naked licensing in the parties' prior settlement, by approving the design for a certain firearm and covenanting not to sue defendants for the sale of firearms based on that design. This court denied defendants' motion for summary judgment on its counterclaim, holding that plaintiffs did not grant defendants a license to manufacture the design, but rather, stipulated that the design did not infringe their trade dress. The court noted that, under Restatement Third of Unfair Competition §§ 30 and 33, a licensor could be held to have abandoned its trade dress if it engaged in naked licensing by allowing a licensee to use the trade dress without exercising reasonable control over the nature and quality of the goods made by the licensee. Heckler & Koch, Inc. v. German Sport Guns GmbH, 71 F.Supp.3d 866, 922.

D.Mass.2012. Quot. in case quot. in ftn. Coin collector who claimed to have invented a new method to grade the "eye appeal" of coins brought claims for, among other things, violations of the Lanham Act against coin-grading service and service's competitor, alleging that, after he communicated some marketing proposals about his grading system to defendants, defendants added the plus (+) designation used in his method to their own systems without his permission. In granting in part defendants' motion to dismiss, this court noted that, while plaintiff contended that service gave a "naked license" of the "+" mark to competitor, he failed to allege the existence of a written or implied license agreement, a required element of a naked licensing claim; therefore, the court declined to decide whether service breached any duty, resulting in deceptive conduct that would mislead consumers, to control the quality of grading services that bore the "+" mark. Blake v. Professional Coin Grading Service, 898 F.Supp.2d 365, 385.

S.D.N.Y.2018. Com. (d) cit. in sup. Former licensees of the right to use a camouflage pattern that was protected by a utility patent sued licensor, seeking a declaration that plaintiffs' use of a second camouflage pattern that was owned by the federal government did not breach the parties' license. This court granted summary judgment for plaintiffs, holding that a provision of the license that required plaintiffs, upon termination of the license, to immediately cease all sales of products using both patterns, did not protect a legitimate business interest of defendant and was therefore unenforceable on public-policy grounds. The court reasoned, in part, that plaintiffs were not estopped from asserting that defendant had no rights in the second camouflage pattern based on the fact that they agreed to the license, noting that, under Restatement Third of Unfair Competition § 33, the doctrine of licensee estoppel was equitable in nature and not subject to rigid application. Navajo Air, LLC v. Crye Precision, LLC, 318 F.Supp.3d 640, 651.

S.D.N.Y.2004. Com. (d) quot. in ftn. Creator of popular computer game brought suit against export agency to whom creator had assigned international transaction licensing rights, seeking to determine lawful owner of game's intellectual property rights. Denying in part defendant's cross-motion for a preliminary injunction, the court held that neither side demonstrated a likelihood of success on the merits as to whether plaintiff could raise a defense of equitable estoppel to defendant's claim that its trademark obtained "incontestable" status because it was used in commerce for five continuous years after registration. The court also noted, but did not discuss, the applicability of the equitable doctrine of "licensee estoppel." Blue Planet Software, Inc. v. Games International, LLC, 334 F.Supp.2d 425, 439.

For earlier citations, see the Appendices, Supplements, or Pocket Parts, if any, that correspond to the subject matter under examination.

S.D.N.Y.2000. Com. (d) cit. in ftn. Gem-grading laboratory sued its trademark sublicensee and others, alleging trademark infringement and dilution, false designation of origin, unfair competition, and breach of contract. Sublicensee counterclaimed for fraud and intentional interference with business relations. This court entered judgment for plaintiff, holding, inter alia, that sublicensee's acceptance and use of the marks precluded his claim of invalidity, and that the doctrine of licensee estoppel barred the same claim by other defendants. The court disagreed with defendants' assertion that a prior Supreme Court case rejecting the doctrine of licensee estoppel as applied to patents should also be applied to abrogate the doctrine in the trademark realm. E.G.L. Gem Lab Ltd. v. Gem Quality Institute, Inc., 90 F.Supp.2d 277, 292, affirmed 4 Fed.Appx. 81 (2d Cir.2001).

S.D.N.Y.Bkrtcy.Ct.2021. Com. (b) quot. in sup. Buyers and designees of substantially all of Chapter 11 debtors' assets in a § 363 sale under the Bankruptcy Code filed an adversary proceeding against manager of debtors and against three other entities controlled by manager, seeking a declaration that certain intellectual-property licenses that the entities entered into with each other in connection with an amendment to a license agreement were void as fraudulent transfers. This court granted in part defendants' motion to dismiss, holding that plaintiffs failed to show that anything was transferred or assigned. The court explained that, because the license included quality-control measures that were not eliminated by the amendment, the amended license agreement contained licenses rather than assignments under Restatement Third of Unfair Competition § 33. In re KG Winddown, LLC, 632 B.R. 448, 490.

N.D.Ohio, 2001. Quot. in disc. Mattress retailer sued its licensee for trademark and trade-name infringement. Licensee counterclaimed, seeking a declaratory judgment that it had not infringed the trademark and trade name, and that licensor had abandoned the trademark and trade name. This court granted licensor summary judgment, holding, inter alia, that there was no merit in licensee's abandonment defense. The court determined that licensee could not raise a "naked licensing" defense based on licensor's failure to adequately control the quality of licensee's operations. Although the court allowed licensee to raise its naked licensing claim based on licensor's alleged failure to control the quality of an Indiana third-party licensee's operation, there was no evidence that a naked license in Indiana would diminish the trademark and trade name as a source of origin in this localized market area. Westco Group, Inc. v. K.B. & Associates, Inc., 128 F.Supp.2d 1082, 1089.

S.D.Ohio, 1993. Com. (b) quot. in sup. Women's apparel retailer sued department store chain and clothing manufacturer, alleging infringement of its trademark, "EXPRESS." Denying defendants' motions for summary judgment, the court held, inter alia, that a genuine issue of material fact existed as to whether plaintiff abandoned its mark through uncontrolled or "naked" licensing. Express, Inc. v. Sears, Roebuck & Co., 840 F.Supp. 502, 510.

N.D.Okl.2011. Com. (c) quot. but dist. Purported assignees of a trademark for bite-size chicken sued establishments with similar names to the mark alleging, inter alia, trademark infringement under the Lanham Act. This court granted defendants' motion for partial summary judgment, holding that the mark was abandoned following three consecutive years of nonuse by the mark's original owner. The court rejected plaintiffs' argument that the mark had remained protected because original owner had granted a license to a certain restaurant, which had used the mark for decades under plaintiffs' and their predecessors' control. The court explained that to overcome a presumption of abandonment, plaintiffs had to show that they maintained reasonable control over the goods and services sold under the mark, and, although such supervision could be conducted by a third party, plaintiffs' argument that this condition was satisfied by regular state department of health inspections failed, because that department was clearly never appointed to carry out quality control testing of restaurant's product, and only inspected for health and food safety violations. Original Rex, L.L.C. v. Beautiful Brands Intern., LLC, 792 F.Supp.2d 1242, 1260-1261.

Ariz.App.2010. Com. (b) quot. in sup. After corporate taxpayer filed a combined state income tax return in which it did not include income from subsidiary that held and managed trademarks transferred to it by taxpayer and licensed the trademarks back to taxpayer under a nonexclusive agreement, state department of revenue found that subsidiary was operationally integrated with taxpayer and had to be taxed with taxpayer as a unitary business. The board of tax appeals and the tax court affirmed. While affirming, this court rejected the tax court's reasoning that trademarks were intrinsically tied to historical users as a matter of law and that the trademarks at issue therefore could not be separated from taxpayer as the original holder of the marks. The court noted that the law permitted trademark licensing under any circumstances where the licensor exercised quality control over goods and services that reached the customer under the licensed mark, and that the benefits of the licensee's use accrued to the trademark owner. R.R. Donnelley & Sons Co. v. Arizona Dept. of Revenue, 224 Ariz. 254, 229 P.3d 266, 273.

Colo.App.2004. Com. (b) cit. in sup. Buyer of seller's partnership interest in a company that developed television programs based on newspaper classified ads sued seller for breach of contract and tortious interference; seller counterclaimed for breach of the parties' license agreement. Trial court entered judgment on jury verdict for seller on the counterclaim. This court reversed in part, holding, inter alia, that buyer's use of "Employment TV" instead of the licensed mark "Employment Television" was not a misleading use of seller's trademark, and thus did not constitute a breach of the license agreement, since the two marks were so similar as to preclude confusion by the public. Employment Television Enterprises, LLC v. Barocas, 100 P.3d 37, 49.

Mich.App.2014. Com. (a) quot. in sup., coms. (b) and (c) cit. in ftn. Licensor of a trademark for a video-rental business brought a trademark-infringement action against successor of licensee, after it refused to pay a fee to plaintiff and sign a licensing agreement. The trial court granted summary judgment for defendant, finding that plaintiff's trademark-infringement arguments were precluded because plaintiff engaged in naked licensing by allowing the original licensees to use the trademark for over a decade with almost no restrictions, and thus abandoned the trademark before defendant used it. The court explained that, under Restatement Third of Unfair Competition § 33, trademark owners were permitted to license their trademarks and retain their trademark rights against infringers only if they were careful to ensure that their trademarks remained a source identifier to consumers. Movie Mania Metro, Inc. v. GZ DVD's Inc., 857 N.W.2d 677, 690, 691, 693.

Wash.App.2018. Com. (b) quot. in disc. California-based marijuana business brought a lawsuit against Washington-based competitor, alleging, inter alia, trademark infringement and violations of the Washington Consumer Protection Act. The trial court granted defendant's motion for summary judgment, finding that plaintiff failed to allege the lawful use of its mark in the ordinary course of trade in Washington and therefore had no trademark rights in the mark in Washington. This court reversed and remanded, holding, inter alia, that plaintiff alleged the lawful use of the mark in Washington when it licensed the mark to a marijuana business in Washington, and licensee used the mark under the terms of a quality-control agreement between it and plaintiff. The court cited Restatement Third of Unfair Competition § 33, Comment *b*, in explaining that the benefits of a licensee's use of a protected mark, including its lawful use, were imparted onto the licensor as long as the licensor exercised reasonable control over the nature and quality of the licensee's goods or services. Headspace International LLC v. Podworks Corp., 428 P.3d 1260, 1265.

Wis.App.1994. Cit. in ftn. to diss. op. (citing § 33 of T.D. No. 3, 1991. § 33 has since been revised; see Official Text). Purchaser of store in Oshkosh sought judgment declaring its rights under trade name; store in Milwaukee with same trade name counterclaimed. Affirming the trial court's finding that Oshkosh store built up its own secondary meaning in the Oshkosh area independent of the Milwaukee store, and that this finding was limited to a 20-mile radius, this court held that a contractual agreement that the seller entered into with purchaser stating that seller would not engage in a competing business within a 20-mile radius from Oshkosh store was probative of seller's understanding of the scope of the secondary meaning owned by him, since seller could sell only what he owned. Since counterclaiming store had registered the trade name first, it was the prima facie owner of the trade name beyond Oshkosh. A dissent argued that plaintiff's right did not derive from a good faith adoption of the trade name by the purchased business but through consent of the counterclaiming business. Leon's Frozen Custard, Inc. v. Leon Corp., 182 Wis.2d 236, 513 N.W.2d 636, 642.

§ 34. Assignment of Trademarks

C.A.2, 2013. Quot. in sup. State-chartered entity of the Russian Federation sued purported licensees of certain United States-registered trademarks related to a brand of vodka, alleging that defendants' asserted title to the marks was invalid and that defendants' use of the marks infringed the rights of the Russian Federation, which was the true owner of the marks. The district court granted defendants' motion to dismiss. Affirming, this court held that plaintiff lacked standing to sue under the Lanham Act, because it was neither an "assign" of the Russian Federation nor the Federation's legal representative under the terms of the Act. The court reasoned, in part, that the documents submitted by plaintiff in support of its claim left the Russian Federation with not only ownership, but simply too great an operational interest in the marks for the court to consider the Federation as having assigned the marks to plaintiff for purposes of the Act. Federal Treasury Enterprise Sojuzplodoimport v. SPI Spirits Ltd., 726 F.3d 62, 75.

C.A.4, 2021. Cit. in sup. After the Trademark Trial and Appeal Board approved applications for registrations of the "iPad" mark filed by seller of touch-screen tablets, competitor that sold cloud-storage services under the "ipad" mark appealed; applicant counterclaimed for trademark infringement. The district court granted summary judgment for applicant on all of the parties' claims and counterclaims. This court affirmed, holding, among other things, that competitor was not the senior user of the mark. The court reasoned that applicant became the senior user when it acquired a prior user's then-pending trademark application for the same mark under Restatement Third of Unfair Competition § 34, which recognized that an assignee succeeded to an assignor's priority of use in a mark. RXD Media, LLC v. IP Application Development LLC, 986 F.3d 361, 370.

C.A.9, 2016. Quot. in sup. Owner of exotic-dance club that used the mark "Crazy Horse III" brought an action against owner of registered mark "Crazy Horse," seeking a declaratory judgment that plaintiff's use of the mark "Crazy Horse III" did not infringe on defendant's mark, because plaintiff was the assignee of a trademark co-existence agreement that assignor had entered into with the former owner of defendant's mark. The district court granted plaintiff's motion for summary judgment. Affirming, this court held that there were no genuine issues of material fact as to the validity of the agreement between former owner of defendant's mark and assignor, or as to the validity of the assignment of rights from assignor to plaintiff. Citing Restatement Third of Unfair Competition § 34, the court explained that a trademark owner could transfer ownership of a designation to another through an assignment. Russell Road Food and Beverage, LLC v. Spencer, 829 F.3d 1152, 1156.

C.A.10, 2001. Com. (b) quot. in sup. Oklahoma tire distributor that allegedly owned the trademark "Vittoria," which designated a well-known brand of bicycle tires, sued California sole proprietorship that allegedly bought Vittoria-branded tires overseas and imported them into United States in violation of plaintiff's trademarks. District court granted plaintiff partial summary judgment. This court affirmed, holding, inter alia, that assignment agreement between plaintiff and Italian tire company constituted a valid transfer of rights to use Vittoria trademark in United States. The court stated that transfer of assets was not a sine qua non for transferring goodwill associated with a trademark. Plaintiff's actions before and after transfer of trademark were calculated to maintain continuity in use of mark and public's perceptions of products associated with it. Vittoria North America, L.L.C. v. Euro-Asia Imports Inc., 278 F.3d 1076, 1083.

W.D.Ky.2017. Com. (c) quot. in sup. Seller of agricultural equipment that was painted green and yellow sued competitor, alleging that defendant violated federal trademark and common law by producing and distributing competing equipment bearing green and yellow colors that were indistinguishable from plaintiff's colors. After a bench trial, this court held that defendant's use of green and yellow on its equipment infringed on and diluted plaintiff's trademarks in violation of the Lanham Act and state common law. The court re-

Cit.—cited; com.—comment; fol.—followed; sup.—support.
A complete list of abbreviations precedes page 1.

jected defendant's argument that it had acquired the assets, including trademarks and goodwill, of a bankrupt entity that previously used green and yellow on its agricultural products, and that the entity's use could be attributed to defendant, finding that defendant failed to carry its burden of proving continuity with the entity's use of green and yellow by a preponderance of the evidence under Restatement Third of Unfair Competition § 34. Deere & Company v. FIMCO Inc., 302 F.Supp.3d 837, 862.

S.D.N.Y.1997. Com. (d) cit. in ftn. In trademark-infringement action, putative United States registrant of the mark "TOPICLEAR" sought to enjoin French owner from infringing or threatening to infringe the mark in the United States. French owner argued that alleged registrant never had United States rights to the mark because, among other things, an agreement executed by the parties in 1992 that purported to transfer all of French owner's right, title, and interest in the mark to a corporation formed by French owner and alleged registrant was not binding. Entering judgment in part for alleged registrant and in part for French owner, the court held, inter alia, that alleged registrant did not develop any rights in the mark simply because he was one of French owner's United States resellers of TOPICLEAR; that, prior to the 1992 agreement, French owner had a protectible mark that was not abandoned; that the 1992 agreement was an enforceable contract assigning French owner's right in the mark to corporation; and that cancellation of alleged registrant's United States registration of the mark was appropriate. Aini v. Sun Taiyang Co., Ltd., 964 F.Supp. 762, 774, affirmed 159 F.3d 1348 (2d Cir.1998).

TOPIC 6. REMEDIES

Ind.2006. Cit. in disc. §§ 35-37, constituting all of Ch. 3, Topic 6. In a dispute between two law firms that had been established by two unrelated families with the same last name, who operated the firms under nearly identical names, older law firm sued newer law firm for unfair competition. The trial court granted summary judgment for defendant and the court of appeals affirmed. Affirming, this court held, inter alia, that summary judgment was proper on plaintiff's claim of trade-name infringement because plaintiff failed to demonstrate that its name had secondary meaning. In making its decision, the court observed that trade-name infringement occurred regardless of a defendant's subjective intent when the use of a name was likely to cause confusion, but once infringement was established, the scope of relief could be more extensive if defendant had intent to deceive. Keaton and Keaton v. Keaton, 842 N.E.2d 816, 820.

§ 35. Injunctions: Trademark Infringement and Deceptive Marketing

C.A.2, 1994. Com. (f) quot. in part in sup. (citing § 35 of T.D. No. 3, 1991. § 35 has since been revised; see Official Text). An American drug company sued a German drug company, alleging that the German company had used the American company's trademark in violation of their contract and of the Lanham Act. Affirming in part and vacating in part the district court's grant of a permanent injunction severely limiting the German company's use of the mark and remanding for trial on damages as reserved by the trial court pending resolution of this appeal, this court held that the injunction was too broad in attempting to restrain uses that were protected under German law. In addition, said the court, further findings were necessary concerning whether the German company's use had a substantial effect on United States commerce, whether the German company was a citizen of the United States, and whether there was a conflict between the German company's rights under German law and the American company's rights under American law. Sterling Drug, Inc. v. Bayer AG, 14 F.3d 733, 746.

C.A.3, 2004. Cit. in disc., subsec. (2) quot. in disc. Bank sought declaratory judgment that competitor bank could not prevent it from using trademark for certain regional branch locations. District court denied defendant's motion for a permanent injunction, molded jury's verdict of infringement in favor of plaintiff, and sua sponte issued an injunction restraining defendant's use of the trademark instead. After balancing the equities and considering such factors as bad faith, devastating effects on busi-

For earlier citations, see the Appendices, Supplements, or Pocket Parts, if any, that correspond to the subject matter under examination.

ness and customers, and the public interest, this court reversed in part and remanded, holding, inter alia, that the district court's refusal to enjoin plaintiff's infringement in defendant's marketplace was an abuse of discretion. Citizens Financial Group, Inc. v. Citizens National Bank of Evans City, 383 F.3d 110, 117, 125, 126, cert. denied 544 U.S. 1018, 125 S.Ct. 1975, 161 L.Ed.2d 857 (2005).

C.A.9, 2002. Com. (c) cit. in disc. Toy manufacturer brought suit for, in part, trademark dilution against music companies that produced, marketed, and sold song using plaintiff's "Barbie" trademark. Affirming the district court's grant of summary judgment for defendants, this court held, inter alia, that use of the mark in the song fell within the noncommercial-use exemption to the Federal Trademark Dilution Act, since the song lampooned the Barbie image and commented humorously on the cultural values it represented. Mattel, Inc. v. MCA Records, Inc., 296 F.3d 894, 904, cert. denied 537 U.S. 1171, 123 S.Ct. 993, 154 L.Ed.2d 912 (2003).

C.D.Cal.2007. Com. (h) quot. in sup. Clothing company that applied for a federal trademark and purchased a similar registered federal trademark brought trademark-infringement action against, among others, competitor that sold clothing under a similar registered state trademark. Denying plaintiff's request for a preliminary injunction to prevent defendant from using its trademark outside the state in which it was registered, this court, inter alia, declined to address whether plaintiff had demonstrated a likelihood of consumer confusion with defendant's trademark, holding that plaintiff failed to demonstrate that it owned a protectible interest in any trademark by showing that it was the senior user of either trademark in which it claimed an interest. Pollution Denim & Co. v. Pollution Clothing Co., 547 F.Supp.2d 1132, 1138.

E.D.La.2018. Com. (h) quot. in disc. After limited-liability company brought a petition seeking a declaratory judgment that the registration of a service mark for its food hall was proper, city and landlord sought an injunction against limited-liability company and others, alleging, inter alia, that defendants were impermissibly using a trademark that city had previously attempted to register. This court granted plaintiffs' motion for a preliminary injunction, holding, inter alia, that plaintiffs demonstrated that they would suffer irreparable harm beyond mere speculation. The court cited Restatement Third of Unfair Competition § 35, Comment *h*, in explaining that it would grant preliminary injunctions in a trademark-infringement action if there were strong evidence of the likelihood of confusion of marks. Helpful Hound, L.L.C. v. New Orleans Building Corporation, 331 F.Supp.3d 581, 603.

E.D.Mich.2014. Subsec. (1)(b) cit. in case quot. in sup. Holder of trademarks used to sell automotive cylinder heads brought a trademark-infringement action against aluminum-wheel manufacturer, which used a similar logo on its wheels. The jury returned a verdict finding that defendant had infringed plaintiff's trademarks but that the infringement was not intentional and that plaintiff had not suffered any damages as a result of the infringement. This court, which had reserved the question of equitable remedies at trial until after the jury returned its verdict, held that plaintiff was entitled to a permanent injunction tailored to restore to plaintiff rightful control over its marks and eliminate the likelihood of confusion, while permitting defendant to remain in business. The court cited Restatement Third of Unfair Competition § 35(1)(b) in noting that courts would ordinarily award injunctive relief once a party had been found liable for trademark infringement, even if the jury had found in favor of the plaintiff but awarded no damages. CFE Racing Products, Inc. v. BMF Wheels, Inc., 2 F.Supp.3d 1029, 1032.

D.Minn.1993. Com. (b) quot. in disc. (citing § 35 of T.D. No. 3, 1991. § 35 has since been revised; see Official Text). Dog-food manufacturer sued competitor for trademark infringement and unfair competition, seeking injunctive relief and monetary damages. Denying defendant's motion for summary judgment with respect to injunctive relief, the court held, inter alia, that genuine issues of material fact as to whether defendant had ceased all uses of the allegedly infringing mark and as to the likelihood of confusion resulting from use of the two marks rendered any determination of plaintiff's entitlement to an injunction premature. Minnesota Pet-Breeders v. Schell & Kampeter, 843 F.Supp. 506, 511, affirmed 41 F.3d 1242 (8th Cir.1994).

E.D.Pa.1997. Quot. in disc., subsec. (2)(c)

Cit.—cited; com.—comment; fol.—followed; sup.—support.
A complete list of abbreviations precedes page 1.

cit. in headnote and in disc., coms. (b) and (c) cit. in headnotes (erron. cit. as subsecs. (b) and (c)), com. (b) quot. in disc., com. (c) cit. in disc. and quot. in ftn. and in sup. A swimsuit manufacturer brought suit against an apparel manufacturer, alleging that defendant infringed plaintiff's "MIRACLESUIT" trademark with its "THE MIRACLE BRA" line of products. The court granted plaintiff injunctive relief, ordering defendant not to use "THE MIRACLE BRA" mark on its swim wear unless it used a disclaimer and paid plaintiff a reasonable royalty. The court stated that equity should be the key consideration in determining which remedies to award in a case where only a possibility of confusion had been shown. The court denied plaintiff's request for attorney's fees, stating that defendant had not acted willfully, fraudulently, or in bad faith. A & H Sportswear v. Victoria's Secret Stores, 967 F.Supp. 1457, 1458, 1459, 1468, 1469, 1472, 1473, remanded 166 F.3d 197 (3d Cir.1999).

D.S.D.2009. Com. (c) cit. in treatise cit. in sup. Bank sued competitor, seeking relief for alleged violations of the Lanham Act, common-law service-mark infringement, and common-law unfair competition, as well as for the alleged violation of a preliminary injunction previously issued in plaintiff's prior action against defendant. Modifying its prior injunction to expand the area within which defendant was prohibited from using certain service marks, this court noted that, in determining the proper scope of the modified injunction, a court had to consider, among other things, the manner in which the plaintiff was harmed, the possible means by which the harm could be avoided, the viability of the defenses raised, the burden that would be placed on the defendant, and the potential effect upon lawful competition between the parties. First Nat. Bank in Sioux Falls v. First Nat. Bank South Dakota, SPC, Inc., 655 F.Supp.2d 979, 1002.

Alaska, 2015. Cit. in ftn., com. (a) quot. in ftn. Developer of a gated subdivision brought claims for trademark and trade-name infringement against realtors who listed a neighboring property for sale, alleging that realtors misappropriated a photograph of the subdivision's sign and included it in the listing for the neighboring property, with the intent of creating the impression that the property was part of the subdivision. The trial court granted summary judgment for realtors. Affirming, this court held that developer's common-law trade-name infringement claim failed for lack of damages; even if the subdivision's name had acquired secondary meaning, developer failed to show that it suffered any actual damages from realtors' use of its photograph of the sign in their listing. The court additionally concluded that defendant's injunction claim was moot, because the photograph had been removed from the listing; under Restatement Third of Unfair Competition § 35, when there was no proof of passing off, and when the infringement neither damaged the plaintiff nor profited the infringer, damages would not be awarded, because an injunction would satisfy the equities of the case. Alaskasland.Com, LLC v. Cross, 357 P.3d 805, 827.

§ 36. Damages: Trademark Infringement and Deceptive Marketing

C.A.2, 1996. Subsec. (2) and com. (i) cit. in headnote and cit. in sup. Yacht-racing association sued clothing designer for infringement of its "STAR CLASS" trademark and solid five-pointed star insignia. The district court granted plaintiff a permanent injunction against defendant's use of the "STAR CLASS" mark but denied injunctive relief as to the insignia; it also denied plaintiff's request for an accounting of profits, actual damages, and attorney's fees. Affirming in part, this court held, inter alia, that, because plaintiff offered no evidence of actual confusion caused by defendant's infringing use of the mark and presented no evidence of pecuniary loss, a remedy for actual damages was not available. ISCYRA v. Tommy Hilfiger, U.S.A., Inc., 80 F.3d 749, 750, 753.

C.A.3, 1999. Com. (c) cit. in sup. Swimwear manufacturer that used the mark "MIRACLESUIT" brought trademark infringement action against apparel manufacturer, challenging defendant's use of the mark "THE MIRACLE BRA" on lingerie and swimwear. The district court found no infringement with regard to lingerie but held that defendant's use of "THE MIRACLE BRA" on swimwear created a "possibility of confusion" with plaintiff's swimsuit, ordering defendant to pay past and future royalty fees to plaintiff. Remanding, this court held that the district court's use of a "possibility of confusion," rather than the prevalent "likelihood of confusion,"

For earlier citations, see the Appendices, Supplements, or Pocket Parts, if any, that correspond to the subject matter under examination.

standard was error, and, in light of plaintiff's failure to offer evidence of lost profits or other pecuniary harm, saw no basis to award damages or impose royalty fees. A & H Sportswear v. Victoria's Secret Stores, 166 F.3d 197, 209.

C.A.9, 2012. Subsec. (1) cit. in sup. Owner and operator of a skydiving center sued operator of an Internet and telephone based advertising service that made skydiving arrangements for customers and issued certificates that could be redeemed at various drop zones around the country, alleging false advertising, trademark infringement, and cybersquatting. The jury awarded plaintiff actual damages against defendant in the form of harm to plaintiff's goodwill and reputation. After the district court doubled the award of actual damages, this court reversed and reinstated the original actual damages award, holding that the jury's calculation was based upon reasonable inferences and represented a fair assessment of the damages suffered by plaintiff. Skydive Arizona, Inc. v. Quattrocchi, 673 F.3d 1105, 1112.

C.A.9, 2010. Com. (c) cit. in ftn., com. (h) quot. in sup. and cit. in ftn. Manufacturer of men's clothing brought an action for cybersquatting in violation of the Lanham Act against former employee, after defendant, upon leaving plaintiff to work for a competitor, removed plaintiff's website, which had been registered in defendant's name, and refused to return it. The district court entered judgment on a jury verdict in favor of plaintiff. Affirming, this court held that, while defendant's wrong made it impossible to know with any precision what plaintiff's sales would have been had he not committed his wrong, the jury had sufficient tools for estimating plaintiff's actual damages, including financial statements bracketing the period of loss and testimony regarding how much plaintiff spent recreating its website. DSPT Intern., Inc. v. Nahum, 624 F.3d 1213, 1223, 1224.

D.Mass.1992. Cit. and quot. in sup., coms. (c) and (h) quot. in part in sup. (citing § 36 of T.D. No. 3, 1991. § 36 has since been revised; see Official Text). Owner of federally registered trademark sought money damages for alleged infringement. The court granted defendant summary judgment, holding that plaintiff was not entitled to money damages in addition to the injunction it had already obtained, since plaintiff had proved unwilling and incapable of showing actual harm that must precede an award of such damages where defendant's carelessness in no way approached the active fraud or willful deception involved in palming off of one's own goods as another's. It noted that the lack of direct competition between the goods further undermined plaintiff's claim for damages and cited as the final factor influencing its determination the lack of a sound numerical basis for awarding money damages. Aktiebolaget Electrolux v. Armatron Intern., Inc., 829 F.Supp. 458, 466, 467, affirmed 999 F.2d 1 (1st Cir.1993).

D.N.J.2009. Com. (h) quot. in sup. and in ftn., com. (i) quot. in sup. Marketer/seller of x-ray contrast media sued competitor for false advertising in violation of the Lanham Act, alleging that defendant falsely advertised the superiority of its product over plaintiff's product. After a bench trial, this court held that, while certain of defendant's advertisements constituted actionable commercial promotion or advertisements and were false, plaintiff failed to establish causation in connection with its proffered damages. The court concluded that defendant's false advertising was not a material or substantial factor in the decision to award certain group purchasing organization contracts to defendant; the evidence showed that plaintiff's loss of sales resulted from a variety of other factors wholly unrelated to defendant's advertising. Bracco Diagnostics, Inc. v. Amersham Health, Inc., 627 F.Supp.2d 384, 487, 489.

E.D.N.Y.2009. Com. (h) quot. in sup. Operator of travel tours and cruises sued competitor, alleging trademark infringement, trademark dilution, and unfair competition under federal and state law. This court, which earlier granted plaintiff's motion for a default judgment, here adopted the magistrate judge's report and recommendation with regard to damages for lost profits. The magistrate judge noted that proof of a general decline in sales or a disruption of anticipated business growth following a defendant's misconduct was sufficient in some cases to justify an inference of causation, and calculated plaintiff's lost profits based on declining revenue, using a preinfringement "base line" to predict the revenue plaintiff would have generated absent the infringement. Victoria Cruises, Inc. v. Changjiang Cruise Overseas Travel Co., 630 F.Supp.2d 255, 262.

S.D.N.Y.1995. Subsec. (3) and com. (h)

Cit.—cited; com.—comment; fol.—followed; sup.—support.
A complete list of abbreviations precedes page 1.

cit. in sup. (citing § 36 of T.D. No. 3, 1991. § 36 has since been revised; see Official Text). Upscale shoe manufacturer sued competitor under Lanham Act for damages incurred when defendant imitated and sold plaintiff's P-sole shoes. In order to sample consumer reaction to and confusion over the shoes, plaintiff's employee conducted a survey of seemingly well-to-do passersby near its store. Defendant moved to exclude the survey and responses on the ground that their prejudicial value substantially outweighed any probative value. Granting in part and denying in part the motion, the court held that the survey itself, which did not conform to accepted survey techniques and used highly questionable methodology, would be excluded but that the testimony of the respondents was admissible for the purpose of establishing actual confusion, a prerequisite to an award of damages. Arche, Inc. v. Azaleia, U.S.A., Inc., 882 F.Supp. 334, 337.

E.D.Pa.1997. Subsec. (3)(b) cit. in headnote and in disc., com. (*o*) cit. in ftn. A swimsuit manufacturer brought suit against an apparel manufacturer, alleging that defendant infringed plaintiff's "MIRACLESUIT" trademark with its "THE MIRACLE BRA" line of products. The court granted plaintiff injunctive relief, ordering defendant not to use "THE MIRACLE BRA" mark on its swim wear unless it used a disclaimer and paid plaintiff a reasonable royalty. The court stated that equity should be the key consideration in determining which remedies to award in a case where only a possibility of confusion had been shown. A & H Sportswear v. Victoria's Secret Stores, 967 F.Supp. 1457, 1458, 1468, 1481, remanded 166 F.3d 197 (3d Cir. 1999).

Alaska, 2015. Quot. in ftn., com. (i) quot. in ftn. Developer of a gated subdivision brought claims for trademark and trade-name infringement against realtors who listed a neighboring property for sale, alleging that realtors misappropriated a photograph of the subdivision's sign and included it in the listing for the neighboring property, with the intent of creating the impression that the property was part of the subdivision. The trial court granted summary judgment for realtors. Affirming, this court held that developer's common-law trade-name infringement claim failed for lack of damages; even if the subdivision's name had acquired secondary meaning, developer failed to show that it suffered any actual damages from realtors' use of its photograph of the sign in their listing. The court noted that, under Restatement Third of Unfair Competition § 36, the recovery of damages for trade-name infringement ordinarily required proof that some consumers were actually confused or deceived. Alaskasland.Com, LLC v. Cross, 357 P.3d 805, 827.

Neb.App.2007. Cit. in sup., coms. (b), (c), and (g) cit. in disc. Security-services corporation that had acquired the successor-in-interest of a closely held security-systems company brought a trade-name-infringement claim against the company's former shareholders and the new security business that shareholders had started under the company's name. The trial court awarded plaintiff monetary damages. Affirming, this court held, as a matter of first impression, that an award of monetary damages based on the infringer's profits was an appropriate remedy for infringement of a common-law trade name/service mark in order to prevent unjust enrichment and deter future infringement, and that here, in light of defendants' intent to cause confusion and deception, the trial court did not err in awarding damages of 25% of defendants' gross profits. ADT Sec. Services, Inc. v. A/C Sec. Systems, Inc., 15 Neb.App. 666, 695, 698, 736 N.W.2d 737, 764, 766.

S.C.App.1998. Subsec. (1) and com. (e) quot. in sup., subsec. (2) cit. in sup. Marketer of a novelty glow-in-the-dark condom sued a competitor for common law trademark infringement, common law trade-dress infringement, civil conspiracy, and unfair trade practices, arising from competitor's willful appropriation of marketer's marks and packaging. The trial court found defendant liable and awarded plaintiff damages. Affirming in part, this court held, inter alia, that plaintiff was entitled to recover research and development costs. The court stated that plaintiff invested considerable time and expense in developing unique packaging for its product; by producing a substantially identical product, defendant prevented plaintiff from realizing the full benefit of its investment. Global Protection Corp. v. Halbersberg, 332 S.C. 149, 503 S.E.2d 483, 488.

Tex.App.2004. Cit. in disc. Trademark holder, which had previously brought trademark-infringement claims against company, brought suit alleging breach of resulting settlement agreement. Trial court rendered judgment and permanent injunction for holder. Affirming, this court held, inter alia, that, although this was a contract case, the measure of the benefit of the trademark holder's bargain was the same as the trademark-infringement remedies available for the infringing conduct, and awarding company's profits as compensation for holder's lost profits to prevent unjust enrichment or to deter future infringement was proper. Qaddura v. Indo-European Foods, Inc., 141 S.W.3d 882, 889.

Wis.App.2007. Com. (i) cit. in disc. and quot. in sup. Water bottler sued rival that used bottler's logo on delivery trucks and drivers' uniforms for six weeks after it acquired bottler's distributor, despite plaintiff's demands that it cease using the mark. After a jury returned a verdict for plaintiff on its trademark-infringement claim, the trial court changed the verdict and dismissed the claim with prejudice. This court reversed and remanded for reinstatement of the jury's verdict, holding, inter alia, that credible evidence supported the jury's finding that defendant's use of the logo caused confusion; while confusion could have been inferred by the jury based on plaintiff's loss of business during the period in question, plaintiff also offered direct proof of actual confusion, entitled to substantial weight, in the form of testimony from witnesses who had bought defendant's water thinking that it was plaintiff's. Western Wisconsin Water, Inc. v. Quality Beverages of Wisconsin, Inc., 2007 WI App 188, 305 Wis.2d 217, 738 N.W.2d 114, 119, 120.

§ 37. Accounting of Defendant's Profits: Trademark Infringement and Deceptive Marketing

C.A.1, 2008. Com. (b) quot. in sup. Seller of software products brought trademark-infringement action against provider of consulting services, asserting a theory of reverse confusion based on allegations that defendant saturated the market with a mark substantially similar to plaintiff's trademarks, which led potential customers to believe that defendant had acquired plaintiff and resulted in lost sales to plaintiff. The trial court entered judgment on a jury verdict for plaintiff, but denied plaintiff's request for an accounting of defendant's profits. Affirming, this court held, inter alia, that an accounting was not warranted as a proxy for legal damages, i.e., as a rough measure of harm to the plaintiff, in this case; reverse confusion did not lend itself to any automatic assumption that there was equivalence between defendant's profits and plaintiff's diverted sales. Visible Systems Corp. v. Unisys Corp., 551 F.3d 65, 81.

C.A.1, 2002. Com. (e) cit. but not fol. Roofing-products manufacturer sued competitor for infringement of its "Heritage" trademark. The district court awarded defendant's profits to plaintiff, ordered defendant to pay plaintiff's attorneys' fees, and issued a permanent injunction. Affirming, this court held, inter alia, that an accounting of defendant's profits where the products directly competed was not conditioned on a showing of fraud, bad faith, or palming off, and concluded that the award of defendant's entire profits was correct. Tamko Roofing Products, Inc. v. Ideal Roofing Co., Ltd., 282 F.3d 23, 36.

C.A.2, 1996. Com. (e) cit. in sup. Yacht-racing association sued clothing designer for infringement of its "STAR CLASS" trademark and solid five-pointed star insignia. The district court granted plaintiff a permanent injunction against defendant's use of the "STAR CLASS" mark but denied injunctive relief as to the insignia; it also denied plaintiff's request for an accounting of profits and attorney's fees, finding that defendant did not act in bad faith or willfully infringe plaintiff's mark. This court vacated the district court's denial of an accounting of profits and attorney's fees and remanded the issue of defendant's bad faith for reconsideration, holding that the district court's factual findings on defendant's bad faith were erroneous and incomplete. ISCYRA v. Tommy Hilfiger, U.S.A., Inc., 80 F.3d 749, 753.

C.A.2, 1992. Cit. in sup., subsec. (1)(a) quot. in disc., subsec. (2), coms. (b), (e), and (f), and Rptr's Notes cit. in disc. (citing § 37 of T.D. No. 3, 1991. § 37 has since been revised; see Official Text). Metal-polish manufacturer sued former distributor for trade-dress infringement, inter alia. The district court entered judgment on a jury verdict awarding defendant's profits to plaintiff and denied defendant's motion for a judgment n.o.v. Vacating the award and reversing in part, this court held that plaintiff was not entitled to recover defendant's profits by way of an accounting absent proof that defendant engaged in

Cit.—cited; com.—comment; fol.—followed; sup.—support.
A complete list of abbreviations precedes page 1.

willful deception. George Basch Co., Inc. v. Blue Coral, Inc., 968 F.2d 1532, 1539, 1540, cert. denied 506 U.S. 991, 113 S.Ct. 510, 121 L.Ed.2d 445 (1992).

C.A.3, 2005. Cit. in disc. Company that held trademark for fishing lure sued a member of its board of directors for, in part, trademark infringement, after defendant developed and marketed a competing fishing lure. The district court entered judgment awarding plaintiff damages, finding defendant liable for false designation of origin under the Lanham Act. Affirming in part, this court held that a showing of willful infringement was not a prerequisite to an accounting of a trademark infringer's profits for a violation of the false-designation-of-origin provision. Banjo Buddies, Inc. v. Renosky, 399 F.3d 168, 174.

C.A.5, 2017. Cit. but not fol.; com. (a) quot. in disc. Manufacturer of medical-device system brought an action for unfair competition by misappropriation and fraud against distributor that, after receiving proprietary information about the system as a distributor and through a lawsuit, began developing and marketing its own competing product. Following a jury verdict for plaintiff, the district court granted defendant's motion for judgment as a matter of law. This court affirmed the take-nothing judgment, holding, inter alia, that plaintiff failed to present evidence sufficient for a jury to determine lost profits with reasonable certainty, because it did not show evidence of net profits or business expenses. The court explained that plaintiff's reliance on Restatement Third of Unfair Competition § 37 was misplaced because this section pertained to making an award based on an accounting of a defendant's profits for deceptive marketing and trademark infringement and not a plaintiff's lost-profit damages. Motion Medical Technologies, L.L.C. v. Thermotek, Incorporated, 875 F.3d 765, 780.

C.A.7, 2020. Quot. in sup., cit. in case cit. in sup. Wine maker and subsidiary sued former employee and competitor formed by former employee, alleging, inter alia, that defendants engaged in unfair competition when former employee, using his position as president while employed by plaintiffs, used plaintiffs' resources without their knowledge or consent to sell wine under competitor's brand at a cheaper price. The trial court entered judgment on a jury verdict for plaintiffs on their unfair-competition claim, entered a damages award of nothing, and granted plaintiffs' request for disgorgement as alternative relief. This court affirmed, holding that disgorgement was an appropriate remedy. The court explained that the district court did not err in relying on Restatement Third of Unfair Competition § 37 for guidance in determining if disgorgement was an appropriate remedy for plaintiffs' unfair-competition claim, because Michigan frequently relied on the Restatement for determining novel unfair-competition issues. Continental Vineyard, LLC v. Vinifera Wine Co., LLC, 973 F.3d 747, 753, 759.

C.A.10, 1998. Subsec. (1)(a) quot. in part in sup. Patentee sued competitor for trademark infringement. The district court concluded that defendant infringed plaintiff's mark, granted plaintiff's request for injunctive relief, and awarded attorney fees; however, having found no actual damages, the court rejected plaintiff's request for monetary relief. Affirming in part, reversing in part, and remanding, this court held that plaintiff did not abandon his mark, that plaintiff could recover profits from defendant's misuse of the mark if he could show that defendant acted willfully or in bad faith, that defendant's failure to honor a cease and desist commitment could serve as proof of bad faith, and that attorney fees were properly awarded. Bishop v. Equinox Intern. Corp., 154 F.3d 1220, 1223, appeal after remand 256 F.3d 1050 (10th Cir.2001).

C.A.11, 2019. Com. (b) cit. in sup. Owner of trademarks that it licensed to a cosmetics producer for use in the sale of cosmetics brought an action under the Lanham Act against competitor of producer, seeking an injunction to prevent future infringement, an accounting, disgorgement of profits, and declaratory relief, along with fees and costs. The district court denied plaintiff's request for a jury trial, noting that plaintiff had disclaimed any request for actual damages and was seeking only equitable remedies, and, after a bench trial, ruled that there was no likelihood of confusion and that defendant made out a fair-use defense to infringement. Affirming, this court held, among other things, that plaintiff was not entitled to a jury trial on its claim for an accounting and disgorgement of profits. The court cited Restatement Third of Unfair Competition § 37 and Restatement of Torts

For earlier citations, see the Appendices, Supplements, or Pocket Parts, if any, that correspond to the subject matter under examination.

§ 747 in explaining that the remedies sought by plaintiff in the form of an accounting and disgorgement of profits were historically equitable, rather than legal, in nature. Hard Candy, LLC v. Anastasia Beverly Hills, Inc., 921 F.3d 1343, 1356.

C.A.Fed.2016. Subsec. (1) quot. in sup.; cit. in sup. (citing § 37(1) of T.D. No. 3, 1991, which is now § 37(1) of the Official Text); com. (e) cit. in case quot. in sup. (citing com. (e) of § 37 of T.D. No. 3, 1991, which is now com. (e) of § 37 of the Official Text). Owner of a patent for magnetic-snap fasteners filed an action for patent and trademark infringement against handbag manufacturer that had contracted with plaintiff to buy its fasteners, alleging that some of defendant's products contained counterfeit fasteners. The jury returned a verdict for plaintiff and, after reducing the amount of damages awarded by the jury, the district court entered judgment for plaintiff. This court affirmed, holding that plaintiff could not recover defendant's profits for trademark infringement, because the jury found that defendant's trademark infringement was not willful. The court cited Restatement Third of Unfair Competition § 37(1), in determining that willfulness was a requirement for a trademark-infringement claim. Romag Fasteners, Inc. v. Fossil, Inc., 817 F.3d 782, 785, 786.

C.D.Cal.2009. Cit. in case quot. in sup. Provider of classroom, home study, and Internet-based traffic-school courses and state-licensed driver's education courses to the public sued competitors for unfair competition and false advertising under state and federal law. After a bench trial, this court found defendants jointly and severally liable for false advertising and issued a permanent injunction against defendants. The court declined to award plaintiffs monetary damages, however, holding that plaintiffs were barred from obtaining a disgorgement of defendants' profits under the equitable doctrine of unjust enrichment; plaintiffs had unclean hands because they had engaged in deceptive advertising similar to defendants, there was a lack of evidence of injury caused by defendants, and injunctive relief alone was sufficient to protect the public interest. TrafficSchool.com, Inc. v. Edriver, Inc., 633 F.Supp.2d 1063, 1087.

N.D.Cal.1993. Com. (h) quot. in treatise quot. in disc. and cit. generally in sup. (citing § 37 of T.D. No. 3, 1991. § 37 has since been revised; see Official Text). Holders of exclusive licenses to sell products exhibiting photographs of popular musicians brought suit for damages against unlicensed producers and distributors of poster books and calendars that contained photographs of the same musicians. Entering judgment on a jury verdict for plaintiffs and issuing a permanent injunction, the court held, inter alia, that no decrease in the damages award was justifiable on the basis of allocation of defendants' fixed costs based on the infringing products' share of gross revenues, considering that defendants' proffer in support of such a decrease was unsatisfactory. Winterland Concessions Co. v. Fenton, 835 F.Supp. 529, 532-533.

S.D.Fla.1996. Com. (h) quot. in sup. In copyright-infringement action, infringer sought to deduct its total cost of advertising and selling the infringing item from its opponent's award of profits. The magistrate judge recommended that infringer be allowed to deduct 10% of its total advertising and selling expenses from opponent's recovery. Affirming, adopting, and ratifying the magistrate's report and recommendation, this court held that infringer was entitled to deduct only that percentage of its advertising and selling costs that were directly attributable to the marketing of the infringing goods. Burger King Corp. v. Pilgrim's Pride Corp., 934 F.Supp. 425, 426.

D.Mass.1992. Cit. and quot. in sup. com. (a) quot. in part in sup., coms. (b), (e), and (f) cit. in sup. (citing § 37 of T.D. No. 3, 1991. § 37 has since been revised; see Official Text). Owner of federally registered trademark sought money damages for alleged infringement. The court granted defendant summary judgment, holding that plaintiff was not entitled to money damages in addition to the injunction it had already obtained, since plaintiff had proved unwilling and incapable of showing actual harm that must precede an award of such damages where defendant's carelessness in no way approached the active fraud or willful deception involved in palming off of one's own goods as another's. It noted that the lack of direct competition between the goods further undermined plaintiff's claim for damages and cited as the final factor influencing its determination the lack of a sound numerical basis for awarding money damages. Aktiebolaget Electrolux v. Armatron Intern., Inc., 829 F.Supp. 458, 466, 467, affirmed 999 F.2d 1 (1st Cir.1993).

D.Minn.2015. Coms. (e) and (f) cit. in sup. Carpet-cleaning franchisor that owned trademark for the name "ZEROREZ" filed, inter alia, a trademark-infringement claim against competitor, alleging that defendant's online advertisements for "zero rez carpet cleaning" were confusingly similar to plaintiff's mark and that defendant misrepresented to customers that it was affiliated with plaintiff. This court granted in part plaintiff's motion for summary judgment, holding that there was sufficient evidence to support plaintiff's claim that defendant used the mark in a manner likely to cause customer confusion, and supplemental briefing was required before it could determine the profit disgorgement that plaintiff was entitled to receive. The court cited Restatement Third of Unfair Competition § 37, Comments *e* and *f*, and determined that an accounting of profits was appropriate because there was evidence that defendant acted in bad faith. Zerorez Franchising System, Inc. v. Distinctive Cleaning, Inc., 103 F.Supp.3d 1032, 1048.

S.D.N.Y.2013. Com. (a) quot. in sup. Seller of fresh produce sued competing seller of preserved produce, alleging that defendant willfully violated the Lanham Act by falsely advertising that its products were fresh when they were actually preserved. After a jury found in favor of plaintiff, this court granted plaintiff's subsequent motion for a permanent injunction, holding, among other things, that there was no way to know precisely what harm might result from any future violations by defendant. The court pointed out that the jury had awarded plaintiff damages based on an accounting of defendant's profits after finding that plaintiff had $0 in lost sales, and that the reason the Lanham Act authorized an accounting of defendant's profits was precisely because of the difficulty of proving that a plaintiff had lost sales due to a defendant's false advertising. Fresh Del Monte Produce Inc. v. Del Monte Foods Co., 933 F.Supp.2d 655, 664.

S.D.N.Y.2009. Subsec. (g) cit. but not fol. Trademark owner sued retailer for allegedly violating a consent injunction under which defendant agreed not to purchase or sell any merchandise bearing plaintiff's trademark without written permission. This court, which earlier ruled that defendant was in civil contempt and subject to disgorgement of profits, here held that the amount defendant was required to disgorge could be reduced by the income tax paid on its profits. The court rejected plaintiff's argument that income tax on profits should not be deducted from an award since the amount paid by the contemnor could be recouped as a deductible business expense, noting that the Second Circuit had recently upheld deductions for taxes in the trademark context and in contempt proceedings. Fendi Adele S.R.L. v. Burlington Coat Factory Warehouse Corp., 642 F.Supp.2d 276, 282.

S.D.N.Y.2000. Com. (e) cit. in case cit. in sup. Novelty manufacturer sued competitor for infringement of floral designs, and competitor filed counterclaim for trademark infringement and dilution with respect to inflatable furniture. Denying in part manufacturer's motion to dismiss counterclaims, this court held, inter alia, that competitor stated a claim for fraudulent trademark registration under the Lanham Act, notwithstanding that competitor's mark was unregistered. GMA Accessories, Inc. v. Idea Nuova, Inc., 157 F.Supp.2d 234, 242.

S.D.N.Y.1997. Cit. in headnote, com. (e) quot. in sup. Circus that was known as "The Greatest Show on Earth" brought trademark-infringement action against owner of establishment that called itself "The Greatest Bar on Earth," seeking an injunction and an accounting of defendant's profits. Defendant moved for summary judgment. Granting the motion, the court held, in part, that an accounting was unavailable as a remedy absent proof that defendant willfully infringed plaintiff's mark, and that, in this case, defendant's good faith was evidenced by the fact that it conducted a trademark search and chose a mark reflecting its bar's characteristics. Ringling Bros.-Barnum & Bailey v. B.E. Windows, 969 F.Supp. 901, 902, 904.

E.D.Pa.1997. Subsec. (2)(b) cit. in headnote and in disc. A swimsuit manufacturer brought suit against an apparel manufacturer, alleging that defendant infringed plaintiff's "MIRACLESUIT" trademark with its "THE MIRACLE BRA" line of products. The court granted plaintiff injunctive relief, ordering defendant not to use "THE MIRACLE BRA" mark on its swim wear unless it used a disclaimer and paid plaintiff a reasonable royalty. The court stated that equity should be the key consideration in determining which remedies to award in a case where only a pos-

For earlier citations, see the Appendices, Supplements, or Pocket Parts, if any, that correspond to the subject matter under examination.

sibility of confusion had been shown. A & H Sportswear v. Victoria's Secret Stores, 967 F.Supp. 1457, 1458, 1468, remanded 166 F.3d 197 (3d Cir.1999).

Cal.App.2014. Cit. in sup., com. (g) cit. and quot. in sup. Attorney-joint-advertising group brought common-law claims for unfair competition and "passing off," as well as a state-statutory unfair-competition claim, against owners of the rights to telephone numbers that closely resembled plaintiff's number, alleging that, when callers mistakenly dialed defendants' numbers in an effort to contact plaintiff, defendants intentionally referred them to attorneys who were not affiliated with plaintiff. The trial court ordered the entry of a default against defendants as a sanction for discovery abuse after they refused to appear at their depositions, and issued a default judgment awarding plaintiff damages in the amount that the attorneys paid defendants for misdirecting callers. Affirming, this court held that the amount of damages awarded against defendants was not excessive. The court reasoned that the funds that a defendant received for carrying out unfair competition constituted a portion of the net profits from that tortious conduct. Los Defensores, Inc. v. Gomez, 223 Cal.App.4th 377, 401-403, 166 Cal.Rptr.3d 899, 919-921.

Neb.App.2007. Cit. in sup., com. (b) cit. in sup. Security-services corporation that had acquired the successor-in-interest of a closely held security-systems company brought a trade-name-infringement claim against the company's former shareholders and the new security business that shareholders had started under the company's name. The trial court awarded plaintiff monetary damages. Affirming, this court held, as a matter of first impression, that an award of monetary damages based on the infringer's profits was an appropriate remedy for infringement of a common-law trade name/service mark in order to prevent unjust enrichment and deter future infringement, and that here, in light of defendants' intent to cause confusion and deception, the trial court did not err in awarding damages of 25% of defendants' gross profits. ADT Sec. Services, Inc. v. A/C Sec. Systems, Inc., 15 Neb.App. 666, 696-698, 736 N.W.2d 737, 764-766.

Tex.App.2004. Com. (b) cit. in disc. Trademark holder, which had previously brought trademark-infringement claims against company, brought suit alleging breach of resulting settlement agreement. Trial court rendered judgment and permanent injunction for holder. Affirming, this court held, inter alia, that, although this was a contract case, the measure of the benefit of the trademark holder's bargain was the same as the trademark-infringement remedies available for the infringing conduct, and awarding company's profits as compensation for holder's lost profits to prevent unjust enrichment or to deter future infringement was proper. Qaddura v. Indo-European Foods, Inc., 141 S.W.3d 882, 889.

CHAPTER 4. APPROPRIATION OF TRADE VALUES

D.Colo.2007. Cit. in disc. §§ 38-45, constituting Topics 1 and 2 of Ch. 4. Company that collected and sold insurance referrals to clients through a website sued competitor and its employee for, among other things, submitting hundreds of false insurance-quote inquiries to plaintiff's website. Granting in part defendant's motion to dismiss, this court held, inter alia, that plaintiff failed to state a claim for unfair competition. The court explained that, under Colorado law, unfair competition did not provide a cause of action for any alleged improper conduct by a competitor that deceived a plaintiff or its clients, but rather reached only conduct that involved either using or copying a plaintiff's products or service and deceiving or confusing the public as to the source of the business in question. NetQuote, Inc. v. Byrd, 504 F.Supp.2d 1126, 1132.

Generally

Ohio App.2020. Ch. 4 cit. generally in sup. Seller of a house, who had been ordered to pay a judgment to buyers based on her fraudulent failure to disclose termite damage, sued providers of continuing education for realtors, alleging that defendants appropriated her name in violation of a state statute by discussing her case in their materials. The trial court granted summary judgment for defendants. This court affirmed, holding that the statute did not apply, because defendants' use of plaintiff's name was informative and newsworthy and was not intended to promote, advertise, or market a product or take advantage of her name's commercial value, if any. The court noted that the Supreme Court of Ohio had relied heavily on Restatement Second of Torts § 652C when it adopted the right of publicity, and that, while the right of publicity was originally treated as a branch of the right of privacy, the American Law Institute had transferred its discussion of the right of publicity to Chapter 4 of the Restatement Third of Unfair Competition, in recognition that the tort's primary focus was the value of a person's name, vis-à-vis the person's ability to market it for commercial purposes. Harvey v. Systems Effect, LLC, 154 N.E.3d 293, 307.

TOPIC 1. MISAPPROPRIATION

E.D.Pa.1997. Cit. in disc. §§ 38-45; § 38 constitutes all of Ch. 4, Topic 1. Pennsylvania corporation brought RICO action against British medical schools and their agents, alleging that defendants misappropriated plaintiff's proprietary interest in medical scanner equipment and technology. Defendants moved to dismiss, arguing, among other things, that the court lacked personal jurisdiction over them. Denying the motion, the court held, in part, that in personam jurisdiction was proper under the "tort-out/harm-in" provision of the Pennsylvania Long Arm Statute, since defendants' alleged misappropriation of plaintiff's trade secrets in England caused harm to plaintiff in Pennsylvania, and that defendants had sufficient minimum contacts with Pennsylvania such that exercising jurisdiction over them would not offend traditional notions of fair play and substantial justice. Supra Medical Corp. v. McGonigle, 955 F.Supp. 374, 381.

Generally

Fla.1993. Cit. generally in ftn. (T.D. No. 4, 1993). The First Southern Bank sued to enjoin another bank from using the name "Great Southern Bank," alleging infringement and dilution of its trademark name and unfair competition. The trial court granted plaintiff injunctive relief and certified the question whether plaintiff bank's name was descriptive or generic so as not to be entitled to protection in the absence of proof that it had acquired a secondary meaning. This court remanded, holding that plaintiff bank's name contained laudatory, generic, and merely geographically descriptive elements so as not to be entitled to protection under either common or statutory law, but a determination was necessary as to whether a secondary meaning in the name had developed in order to decide the dilution claim. The court stated that, because it found as a matter of law that the name "First Southern Bank" was merely descriptive, and therefore lacked the "distinctive quality" that the Florida dilution statute was designed to protect, there was no possibility of a violation of the dilution statute unless a "distinctive quality" had arisen because the name had acquired a secondary meaning. It noted that resolution of the dilution issue was a mixed one of law and fact. Great Southern v. First Southern, 625 So.2d 463, 471.

§ 38. Appropriation of Trade Values

C.A.1, 2001. Coms. (a)-(c) cit. in ftn., Rptr's Note cit. in ftn. After cookware corporation brought claims for trade-dress infringement, unfair competition, and patent infringement against marketer of kitchen products, marketer sued insurer for breach of duty to defend and indemnify marketer under policy coverage for advertising injury. New Hampshire federal district court entered judgment for marketer. This court reversed and remanded, holding that the policy term "advertising" referred to conventional advertising, separate from the product itself, and that marketer failed to establish causal connection between claim for misappropriation of tea-kettle design and "advertising injury" coverage clause in policy. Ekco Group, Inc. v. Travelers Indem. Co. of Illinois, 273 F.3d 409, 412.

C.A.2, 2011. Com. (c) cit. in case quot. in disc. Securities brokerage firms sued news aggregator, alleging copyright infringement based on defendant's extensive excerpting of reports containing plaintiffs' trading recommendations, and "hot news" misappropriation based on defendant's continual electronic publication of plaintiffs' recommendations. After a bench trial, the district court found in favor of plaintiffs. Reversing in part and remanding, this court held that plaintiffs' misappropriation claim was preempted by federal copyright law. In making its decision, the court declined to adopt a prior panel opinion's five-part test for identifying a nonpreempted "hot news" misappropriation claim, which relied in part on the Restatement Third of Unfair Competition. Barclays Capital Inc. v. Theflyonthewall.com, Inc., 650 F.3d 876, 898.

C.A.2, 1997. Com. (c) cit. in sup. and cit. and quot. in ftn. The National Basketball Association (NBA) sued for an injunction preventing the manufacturer of a handheld pager from transmitting scores or other data about NBA games in progress via the pagers or any equivalent means, absent authorization from the NBA. District court entered a permanent injunction in the NBA's favor. This court vacated the injunction and dismissed the NBA's claim for misappropriation, holding, inter alia, that only a narrow "hot news" misappropriation claim survived preemption for actions concerning material within the realm of copyright. The court found the extra elements—those in addition to the elements of copyright infringement—that allowed a "hot news" claim to survive preemption were: (i) the time-sensitive value of factual information, (ii) the free-riding by a defendant, and (iii) the threat to the very existence of the product or service provided by the plaintiff. National Basketball Ass'n v. Motorola, Inc., 105 F.3d 841, 852, 853.

C.A.6, 1996. Cit. in disc., coms. and Rptr's Notes cit. in disc. An insured manufacturer of writing instruments sued its commercial general liability insurer, alleging that insurer was obligated to indemnify and defend insured in a competitor's underlying action against it for trademark infringement, unfair competition, and dilution. Reversing the district court's grant of summary judgment for insured and remanding, this court held, inter alia, that although the offense of "misappropriation of advertising ideas or style of doing business," which was covered under the insurance policy's advertising provisions, was not necessarily limited to the common law tort of misappropriation, it did not extend to claims of trademark and trade-dress infringement, and thus insurer had no duty to defend insured against the claims asserted by its competitor. Advance Watch Co., Ltd. v. Kemper Nat. Ins. Co., 99 F.3d 795, 802.

C.D.Cal.2007. Com. (c) quot. in sup. Photo archivist sued operator of a celebrity-gossip website, asserting, in addition to a standard copyright-infringement claim, a claim for "hot-news" misappropriation of its copyrighted paparazzi-type, time-sensitive photographs. This court denied defendant's motion to dismiss, holding that the hot-news tort was cognizable under California law, and plaintiff stated the elements for the tort by alleging that it expended substantial costs to gather the photographs, the photographs were time sensitive, the parties were direct competitors, defendant earned revenue by free-riding on plaintiff's work, continuation of defendant's activities would have removed plaintiff's incentive to gather the photographs, and defendant's activities substantially harmed plaintiff. The court rejected defendant's argument that the tort had to be strictly construed; so long as the above-mentioned elements were present, no further narrowing was required. X17, Inc. v. Lavandeira, 563 F.Supp.2d 1102, 1108.

D.Mass.2004. Com. (b) quot. in sup. Sales representative for manufacturer of party goods sued manufacturer for unfair competition, inter alia, alleging that defendant withheld plaintiff's rightfully earned commissions, thereby interfering with his business and usurping his client. This court granted defendant summary judgment, holding that defendant was not liable for unfair competition, since parties properly defined scope of contractual rights and obligations and defendant engaged in business practices that were specifically authorized by contract. The parties' contract stated that plaintiff would be defendant's exclusive representative within plaintiff's territory, but that defendant had authority to remove account when it became too large for an independent contractor. Aisenberg v. Hallmark Marketing Corp., 337 F.Supp.2d 257, 263.

E.D.Mich.1997. Coms. (b) and (c) quot. generally in disc. In patent infringement case, patentee of pull-pull cable assembly moved to have its unfair competition claim against automobile manufacturer voluntarily dismissed without prejudice. Denying the motion and entering summary judgment for manufacturer, the court held, in part, that, to the extent patentee's claims were based upon a common law theory of misappropriation, they were preempted by federal patent law. Nagle Industries, Inc. v. Ford Motor Co., 173 F.R.D. 448, 452, 453, affirmed 194 F.3d 1339 (Fed. Cir. 1999).

Cit.—cited; com.—comment; fol.—followed; sup.—support.
A complete list of abbreviations precedes page 1.

W.D.Mich.2021. Com. (b) and Rptrs' Note to com. (c) quot. in sup. Trademark owner sued competitors, alleging that defendants infringed upon plaintiff's trademark for its store logo and misappropriated plaintiff's goodwill by using a substantially similar logo for their stores and websites. This court granted in part defendants' motion for judgment on the pleadings, holding, inter alia, that plaintiff was barred from asserting a claim for misappropriation outside the bounds of trademark law and unfair competition. Citing Restatement Third of Unfair Competition § 38, the court reasoned that the underlying rationale of trademark law did not recognize residual common-law misappropriation claims outside the context of trade secrets. Sadieboo, Inc. v. MJ Tools Corp., 526 F.Supp.3d 285, 292.

D.N.M.2010. Cit. in sup., subsec. (b) quot. in sup. and cit. in disc., subsec. (c) quot. in sup., com. (a) quot. in ftn. Buyer of endodontic equipment sued sellers for breach of contract and unfair trade practices; sellers brought various counterclaims sounding in contract and tort. After concluding that sellers' common-law unfair-competition counterclaim sounded in tort and thus, pursuant to New Mexico's choice-of-law rule of lex loci delicti, was governed by New Mexico substantive law, this court denied buyer's motion for summary judgment with respect to sellers' unfair-competition counterclaim based on unlawful misappropriation of trade values, holding that a genuine issue of material fact existed as to whether buyer, without consent, used sellers' name for purposes of trade when it allegedly told its customers that its products were repackaged products made by sellers. Guidance Endodontics, LLC v. Dentsply Intern., Inc., 708 F.Supp.2d 1209, 1225, 1258.

S.D.N.Y.2010. Com. (b) cit. in sup., com. (c) quot. in sup. Financial-services firms sued Internet subscription news service, alleging that it misappropriated time-sensitive equity research recommendations in violation of the state common law of unfair competition. After a bench trial, this court concluded that plaintiffs' claim for "hot news" misappropriation was not preempted by federal law and issued an injunction with a limited period of exclusivity for the dissemination of the recommendations. The court opined that, while the Restatement Third of Unfair Competition recommended that the residual tort of misappropriation, established by prior precedent and imported into the common law of many states, be formally abrogated, it seemed to eschew closing the door entirely in that it acknowledged that "hot news" scenarios like the one at issue constituted "unusual circumstances" that presented the most compelling case for protection against appropriation. Barclays Capital Inc. v. Theflyonthewall.com, 700 F.Supp.2d 310, 334, 345.

Fla.App.1999. Cit. generally in disc. Developer's majority shareholder sued a property owner and a competitor for, inter alia, misappropriation of an idea. Trial court granted defendants' motion to dismiss. This court affirmed, holding that plaintiff's idea to use a spring-training baseball complex as the "anchor" of a planned unit development was not that type of novel or original idea that entitled it to the special protection afforded by the misappropriation cause of action. The court did not reach the issue of whether to adopt the Restatement (Third) of Unfair Competition in this area. Alevizos v. John D. and Catherine T. MacArthur Foundation, 764 So.2d 8, 13.

Ill.App.2012. Com. (c) quot. in disc. National securities exchange located in Chicago, which was the exclusive licensee of two stock indexes brought suit with the providers of the indexes against national securities exchange located in New York and clearing agency for index options, after defendant exchange announced its intention to offer index options based on the indexes without first obtaining a license from providers. The trial court granted summary judgment for plaintiffs and issued an injunction in their favor. Affirming, this court held that defendant exchange's proposed use of the indexes would constitute misappropriation under Illinois common law. The court noted that, while some case law and commentaries had viewed the tort of misappropriation with disfavor, the court was bound by the Illinois Supreme Court's prior controlling decision in an action involving similar facts. Chicago Bd. Options Exchange, Inc. v. International Securities Exchange, L.L.C., 2012 IL App (1st) 102228, 973 N.E.2d 390, 407.

Vt.2002. Com. (b) quot. but dist. Owners of advertisement-based newspaper sued former operators of paper for conversion

For earlier citations, see the Appendices, Supplements, or Pocket Parts, if any, that correspond to the subject matter under examination.

and unfair competition, alleging misappropriation of business assets. The trial court entered judgment on jury verdict for owners. Modifying conversion award and affirming, this court held, inter alia, that evidence that former operators took business assets such as customer lists, bookkeeping records, and office equipment supported unfair-competition claim based on misappropriation. Maguire v. Gorruso, 174 Vt. 1, 800 A.2d 1085, 1091.

TOPIC 2. TRADE SECRETS

D.Kan.2001. Cit. in sup. §§ 39-45, constituting Ch. 4, Topic 2. Aircraft navigational instrument provider sued competitor for Lanham Act violations and unfair competition, among other claims, alleging that defendant improperly obtained plaintiff's trade secrets, altered documents to misrepresent Federal Aviation Administration's position on plaintiff's products, and provided altered documents to plaintiff's customers. This court overruled defendant's motion to dismiss plaintiff's unfair-competition claim, predicting that Kansas Supreme Court would apply the general principles outlined in Restatement Third of Unfair Competition and allow an unfair-competition claim based on misuse of trade secrets and other confidential business information. Airport Systems Intern., Inc. v. Airsys ATM, Inc., 144 F.Supp.2d 1268, 1270.

E.D.Pa.1997. Cit. in disc. §§ 38-45; §§ 39-45 constitute all of Ch. 4, Topic 2. Pennsylvania corporation brought RICO action against British medical schools and their agents, alleging that defendants misappropriated plaintiff's proprietary interest in medical scanner equipment and technology. Defendants moved to dismiss, arguing, among other things, that the court lacked personal jurisdiction over them. Denying the motion, the court held, in part, that in personam jurisdiction was proper under the "tort-out/harm-in" provision of the Pennsylvania Long Arm Statute, since defendants' alleged misappropriation of plaintiff's trade secrets in England caused harm to plaintiff in Pennsylvania, and that defendants had sufficient minimum contacts with Pennsylvania such that exercising jurisdiction over them would not offend traditional notions of fair play and substantial justice. Supra Medical Corp. v. McGonigle, 955 F.Supp. 374, 381.

W.D.Pa.2014. Cit. in case quot. in ftn. §§ 39-45, constituting all of Ch. 4, Topic 2 (general cite). Lessee of a computer from a rent-to-own franchise store brought a purported class action asserting, inter alia, a state-law claim for invasion of privacy based on intrusion upon seclusion against lessor store, franchisor, and other franchisee stores, alleging that defendants secretly installed software on leased computers that permitted them to remotely and surreptitiously monitor use of the computers. Dismissing this claim, this court held that the tort of invasion of privacy was not cognizable under Wyoming law. While the Wyoming Supreme Court had previously adopted the tort of misuse or misappropriation of trade secrets as it appeared in Restatement Third of Unfair Competition, the court declined plaintiff's invitation to undertake the same type of analysis in order to find that Wyoming would recognize a cause of action for invasion of privacy as it appeared in the Restatement Second of Torts. Byrd v. Aaron's, Inc., 14 F.Supp.3d 667, 693.

Tex.App.2007. Cit. in ftn. §§ 39-45, constituting all of Ch. 4, Topic 2. Manufacturer of fiberglass utility bodies and toppers for commercial vehicles sued competitor for, in part, tortious interference with prospective business relations, alleging that defendant's use of plaintiff's design drawings to create a stair-step topper for one of plaintiff's existing customers was independently tortious on the ground of trade-secret misappropriation. The trial court denied defendant's no-evidence motion for summary judgment on the tortious-interference claim. Affirming that portion of the decision, this court held, inter alia, that there was evidence that defendant misappropriated the design drawings because, by obtaining the drawings from plaintiff's customer, which was aware that the drawings were confidential, it discovered the drawings by improper means. Astoria Industries of Iowa, Inc. v. SNF, Inc., 223 S.W.3d 616, 636.

Tex.App.2005. Cit. in ftn. §§ 39-45, constituting all of Ch. 4, Topic 2. Manufacturer of replacement helicopter blades sued competitors, seeking injunction preventing defendants from using plaintiff's trade secrets. Trial court granted temporary injunction. This court affirmed, holding that plaintiff satisfied temporary injunction requirements for trade-secret-misappropriation claim. Defendants acquired trade-secret data through breach of confidential relationship. Plaintiff disclosed trade-secret data to defendants so that they could repair plaintiff's helicopters, but defendants had obligation to keep data confidential pursuant to confidentiality agreement. Work report containing data was not available through Attorney General publication centers, and drawings upon which report was based were not available through Freedom of Information Act request. IAC, Ltd. v. Bell Helicopter Textron, Inc., 160 S.W.3d 191, 199.

Tex.App.2003. Cit. in ftn. §§ 39-45, constituting all of Ch. 4, Topic 2. Company that designed converged architecture for delivering telecommunication services to residences sued developer of planned residential communities, alleging, among other things, misappropriation of trade secrets and breach of nondisclosure agreement, after developer invested in other company that intended to use company's secret information to market identical product. Trial court granted plaintiff a temporary injunction. Affirming, this court held, inter alia, that trial court did not abuse its discretion by granting temporary injunction where evidence established that plaintiff had probable right to relief on its claim for breach of nondisclosure agreement, which precluded defendant from using plaintiff's trade secrets to invest in company that intended to use plaintiff's secret information. Mabrey v. SandStream, Inc., 124 S.W.3d 302, 310.

Tex.App.1996. Cit. in ftn. §§ 39-45, which constitute all of Ch. 4, Topic 2. Company sued a former employee for misappropriation of trade secrets and sought to enjoin former employee from selling a competing product. Employee counterclaimed for malicious prosecution. Trial court entered judgment on jury verdict finding that the former employee did not convert any of employer's trade secrets. This court reversed and rendered judgment that the former employee take nothing by his counterclaim. The court held, inter alia, that employer had probable cause to file suit, because it had a legitimate interest in protecting confidential information relating to the design and manufacture of its derringer. American Derringer Corp. v. Bond, 924 S.W.2d 773, 776.

Wyo.2017. Cit. in case cit. in sup. §§ 39-45, which constitutes all of Ch. 4, Topic 2. Computer renters filed claims for invasion of privacy against rent-to-own franchise, alleging that defendant installed software on leased computers that allowed defendant to track the location of the computer, capture screen shots and key strokes, and activate the webcam. The trial court granted summary judgment for defendant. The court of appeals affirmed. This court reversed, holding that Wyoming recognized a common-law cause of action for intrusion upon seclusion as set forth in Restatement Second of Torts § 652B, with damages as defined by § 652H. The court agreed with plaintiffs that the Restatement version of the tort of intrusion upon seclusion was the approach best suited to Wyoming common law, noting its prior reliance on Restatement Third of Unfair Competition §§ 39-45 to formulate a tort of trademark infringement. Howard v. Aspen Way Enterprises, Inc., 406 P.3d 1271, 1278.

Wyo.2006. Cit. and quot. in sup. and adopted, cit. generally in diss. op. §§ 39-45, constituting all of Ch. 4, Topic 2. After internet-based market-analysis company brought action for misappropriation of trade secrets in federal district court against former employees who formed competing company, the issue of whether such a cause of action existed in Wyoming was certified to this court for resolution. Holding that the tort was part of the common law adopted by the Wyoming legislature, the court adopted the cause of action and its elements as set forth in the Restatement Third of Unfair Competition, as the modern and most appropriate version of the cause of action. The dissent noted that Wyoming was alone in adopting the Restatement, and argued that the Restatement so closely resembled a system of statutes that its adoption as the governing law was a usurpation of the legislature's authority and responsibility. Briefing.com v. Jones, 2006 WY 16, 126 P.3d 928, 930-933, 936.

§ 39. Definition of Trade Secret

C.A.1, 2020. Com. (d) quot. in sup.; com. (f) and Rptr's Notes cit. in sup. Tax-planning and consulting firm sued its former managing director and his two compet-

For earlier citations, see the Appendices, Supplements, or Pocket Parts, if any, that correspond to the subject matter under examination.

ing businesses, alleging that director misappropriated firm's trade secrets by downloading without authorization copies of two reports that firm had prepared for its clients and using information from the reports for the competing businesses. After a non-jury trial, the district court found that defendants were liable for misappropriation of trade secrets. This court reversed, holding that plaintiff failed to satisfy its burden to prove the existence of trade secrets in the reports. The court noted that, under Restatement Third of Unfair Competition § 39, a person claiming rights in a trade secret bore the burden of defining the information for which protection was sought with sufficient definiteness to permit a court to apply the criteria for protection and to determine the fact of an appropriation. TLS Management and Marketing Services, LLC v. Rodríguez-Toledo, 966 F.3d 46, 53.

C.A.5, 2022. Com. (d) cit. in case cit. in ftn. Former employer filed a claim for misappropriation of trade secrets against former employee and competitor that hired employee, alleging that employee and competitor misappropriated employer's trade-secret transactional documents and customer lists. The district court denied employer's motion for a preliminary injunction. Affirming, this court held that employer failed to establish a likelihood of success on the merits of its claim for misappropriation of trade secrets. The court cited Restatement Third of Unfair Competition § 39 in reasoning that employer failed to show that employee and competitor had access to trade secrets in the transactional documents before he started working for competitor or that any of the customer information was not publicly available or ascertainable through proper means. CAE Integrated, L.L.C. v. Moov Technologies, Incorporated, 44 F.4th 257, 262.

C.A.5, 2013. Quot. in ftn. Defendant was convicted after a jury trial in district court for perjury and conspiracy to steal trade secrets concerning the manufacture of a type of chlorinated polyethylene (CPE) developed by his former employer. Affirming, this court held that, while the district court erred in excluding the testimony of defendant's engineering expert, which suggested that portions of employer's manufacturing process were in the public domain and were not trade secrets, that error did not affect the verdict and thus was harmless, because the relevant inquiry in a conspiracy case was not whether the information at issue was actually a trade secret, but whether the defendant believed the information to be a trade secret, and there was overwhelming evidence that defendant and his co-conspirators stole trade secrets and that defendant believed that he was stealing trade secrets. The court noted that, even though independent discovery and analysis of publicly available products were not improper means of acquiring information, a trade-secret owner retained protection against an improper acquisition, disclosure, or use. U.S. v. Wen Chyu Liu, 716 F.3d 159, 170.

C.A.5, 2013. Rptr's Note to com. (d) quot. in case quot. in sup. (erron. cit. as cmt.). Developer of complex-services software for oil companies sued consulting firm, alleging that defendant misappropriated its trade secrets. The district court entered judgment on a jury verdict for plaintiff. Affirming, this court held that reasonable jurors could have found that defendant misappropriated plaintiff's trade secrets under Texas law. The court concluded that sufficient evidence existed to support the jury's finding that plaintiff's technology contained trade secrets, pointing out that plaintiff was the only company offering complex-services software from 2000 to 2005 (the years prior to defendant's alleged misappropriation), that it guarded the secrecy of its technology by placing its software behind a firewall and sharing it subject to confidentiality agreements, and that its technology had value. Wellogix, Inc. v. Accenture, L.L.P., 716 F.3d 867, 874.

C.A.5, 2010. Com. (d) quot. in case cit. in sup., Rptr's Note to com. (d) cit. and quot. in case cit. in sup. (general cite). Owner of copyrighted software sued former customer, after a group of defendant's employees obtained a copy of plaintiff's software from an unknown source and used it without authorization. The district court entered judgment on a jury verdict in favor of plaintiff. This court reversed as to plaintiff's claims for misappropriation of trade secrets and unfair competition and rendered a take-nothing judgment for plaintiff, holding that, while plaintiff demonstrated defendant's total revenue, it failed to deduct unrelated revenue and costs to demonstrate defendant's profits related to the infringement. The court rejected plaintiff's

Cit.—cited; com.—comment; fol.—followed; sup.—support.
A complete list of abbreviations precedes page 1.

argument that its exhibit showing total revenue satisfied its burden of proof with regard to defendant's "sales" and that defendant subsequently had the burden of demonstrating which portions of its revenue were not attributable to the state-law claims, concluding that the Texas Supreme Court would not adopt the burden-shifting procedures of Restatement Second of Torts § 45, Comment *f.* MGE UPS Systems, Inc. v. GE Consumer and Indus., Inc., 622 F.3d 361, 370.

C.A.5, 2007. Cit. in ftn. (general cite). Assignee of rights to computer program brought trade-secret-misappropriation claim against developers of competing program that was based in large part on assignee's program. On remand, the district court granted summary judgment for defendants. Affirming, this court, inter alia, upheld the magistrate judge's definition of "use" with respect to the third element of trade-secret misappropriation. The court reasoned, in part, that, under Texas law, which followed the Restatement Third of Unfair Competition, defendants "used" plaintiff's program by continuing to rely on it, either directly or on those portions incorporated into the competing program, to accelerate the development and marketability of the competing program. General Universal Systems, Inc. v. HAL, Inc., 500 F.3d 444, 451.

C.A.5, 2004. Com. (d) quot. in disc. and cit. in ftn. Developer and licensor of tracking software for shipping industry sued licensee who, without authorization, created similar tracking system that incorporated elements of licensor's software. The district court granted summary judgment for defendant on plaintiff's copyright-infringement claims, and subsequently dismissed plaintiff's conversion, misappropriation, and trade-secret claims. Reversing only as to the trade-secret claim, this court held, inter alia, that a genuine issue of material fact existed as to whether plaintiff took reasonable precautions to protect and secure its software as a trade secret. General Universal Systems, Inc. v. Lee, 379 F.3d 131, 151, on remand 2005 WL 1828565 (S.D.Tex. 2005).

C.A.5, 1997. Quot. in disc., com. (f) cit. in disc. Lessor of portable female fiberglass boat mold sued lessee for, inter alia, violations of the Louisiana Uniform Trade Secrets Act and the Louisiana Unfair Trade Practices Act after defendant made certain modifications and contracted to sell the modified molds to customers. The district court granted defendant's motion for summary judgment. Reversing and remanding, this court held, in part, that the ship mold was a trade secret, the secrecy of which plaintiff took reasonable steps to maintain, and that defendant misappropriated the mold, together with its inherent pattern, method, technique, and process. Reingold v. Swiftships, Inc., 126 F.3d 645, 650, 652.

C.A.6, 2022. Quot. in sup.; com. (d) quot. in sup. Dietary-supplement developer sued customer, alleging that defendant misappropriated plaintiff's trade secrets regarding broccoli-seed extracts by hiring plaintiff's former employee, who provided plaintiff's confidential information to defendant. The district court entered judgment on a jury verdict for plaintiff. This court affirmed, holding, inter alia, that substantial evidence supported a jury finding that plaintiff's research efforts into its broccoli-seed extracts constituted a protectable combination trade secret. Citing Restatement Third of Unfair Competition § 39, the court explained that plaintiff set forth evidence demonstrating that it assembled a unique combination of processes and information to create its dietary supplements; furthermore, imposing liability on defendant would not have an anticompetitive effect, because former employee sent plaintiff's documents to defendant and provided years of research to defendant on plaintiff's manufacturing processes. Caudill Seed & Warehouse Co., Inc. v. Jarrow Formulas, Inc., 53 F.4th 368, 379-382.

C.A.6, 2020. Com. (f) quot. in sup. Producer of software and associated hardware that interacted with heating, ventilation, and air conditioning (HVAC) units to perform quality-control tests sued manufacturer of HVAC units, alleging that it improperly used plaintiff's software to aid a third party in developing competing software. After a jury awarded plaintiff damages, the district court reduced the award and denied plaintiff's post-trial motion seeking, among other things, to enjoin defendant from using plaintiff's hardware. This court affirmed in part, holding that the district court did not err in concluding that plaintiff's assembled hardware items were not protectable derivative works or trade secrets as a matter of law. The court cited Restatement Third of Unfair Compe-

For earlier citations, see the Appendices, Supplements, or Pocket Parts, if any, that correspond to the subject matter under examination.

tition § 39 in reasoning that plaintiff's hardware was a marketed product that was sold and freely shared, and thus was not a trade secret. ECIMOS, LLC v. Carrier Corporation, 971 F.3d 616, 643.

C.A.7, 2021. Com. (f) cit. and quot. in sup. Manufacturer of a spinal-implant device filed claims for trade-secret misappropriation and breach of contract against distributor of manufacturer's device to hospitals and surgeons, alleging that distributor funneled information about the device to its parent company to develop a competing device. After an evidentiary hearing, the district court granted manufacturer's motion for a preliminary injunction. Affirming on interlocutory appeal, this court held, among other things, that the district court did not err in concluding that information about the device could remain a protected trade secret after manufacturer patented, displayed, and sold the device to hospitals and surgeons. The court cited Restatement Third of Unfair Competition § 39 in explaining that a company did not forfeit trade-secret protection by publicly displaying or selling a product unless the trade secret was readily ascertainable upon examination of the product. Life Spine, Inc v. Aegis Spine, Inc., 8 F.4th 531, 540, 541.

C.A.7, 2003. Com. (e) quot. in ftn. Toy-design company sued toy manufacturer and its representatives for misappropriation of a trade secret in a realistic toy railroad track under Illinois Trade Secrets Act. Jury awarded plaintiff a royalty for a license, but district court granted judgment as a matter of law for defendants, holding that plaintiff did not have a protectable trade secret. This court reversed, reinstated jury verdict, and remanded for trial on damages, holding that plaintiff presented sufficient evidence for jury reasonably to conclude that factors of Restatement of Torts § 757 weighed in plaintiff's favor. The court stated that it was irrelevant under Illinois law that plaintiff did not actually use the concept in its business. Learning Curve Toys, Inc. v. PlayWood Toys, Inc., 342 F.3d 714, 727.

C.A.9, 2020. Com. (f) quot. in case quot. in sup. Developer of securities-trading management software sued former licensee, alleging that defendant misappropriated plaintiff's trade secrets when, after gaining access to the source code of plaintiff's software through the parties' licensing agreement, it created competing software substantially based off of plaintiff's system. The district court granted defendant's motion for summary judgment. This court reversed, holding, inter alia, that there was a genuine issue of material fact as to whether plaintiff took reasonable measures to keep the information secret. The court explained that plaintiff set forth evidence demonstrating that it required defendant to enter into confidentiality agreements to maintain the secrecy of plaintiff's proprietary system, and, under Restatement Third of Unfair Competition § 39, Comment *f*, such confidential disclosures to licensees did not destroy the information's status as a trade secret. InteliClear, LLC v. ETC Global Holdings, Inc., 978 F.3d 653, 661.

C.A.9, 2016. Quot. in sup. United States brought charges against former employee of an executive search firm, who left firm to start a competing business, alleging that employee accessed firm's lists of potential candidates without authorization in violation of the Computer Fraud and Abuse Act and the Economic Espionage Act. The district court sentenced defendant after a jury convicted him on all counts. Affirming in part, this court held that there was sufficient evidence for the jury to conclude that the lists were trade secrets, that defendant knew the lists were trade secrets, and that defendant knew that stealing the lists would harm firm by helping his own competing business. The court rejected defendant's argument that the lists were not trade secrets because they were composed of public information and firm sometimes shared the lists with clients, explaining that, under Restatement Third of Unfair Competition § 39, a trade secret could consist of a compilation of data, public sources, or a combination of proprietary sources; and a confidential disclosure of trade-secret information did not destroy its status as a trade secret. United States v. Nosal, 844 F.3d 1024, 1042.

C.A.10, 2011. Cit. in disc. (general cite). Developer of audio teleconferencing equipment sued former employees and their new employer, alleging misappropriation of trade secrets pursuant to the Utah Uniform Trade Secrets Act. The trial court issued a permanent injunction against defendants, and entered judgment on a jury verdict for plaintiff. In affirming, this court rejected defendants' argument that, had the district court correctly applied Massachusetts law,

Cit.—cited; com.—comment; fol.—followed; sup.—support.
A complete list of abbreviations precedes page 1.

it would have been required to conclude that plaintiff's sound-enhancement algorithm did not constitute a valid trade secret because plaintiff had, prior to the alleged misappropriation, ceased using the algorithm and declared that it had no value; defendants had abandoned their position that Massachusetts law applied to the misappropriation claim, subsequently arguing that Utah law applied. ClearOne Communications, Inc. v. Bowers, 643 F.3d 735, 769.

C.A.11, 2003. Subsec. (f) quot. in case quot. in disc. Company that conceived of beverage-label marketing and production process sued cola company for, inter alia, misappropriation of trade secrets arising from defendant's disclosure of plaintiff's information to company that printed labels for defendant's product in Argentina, which in turn used information to develop similar label. District court granted defendant summary judgment. This court affirmed, holding, inter alia, that although plaintiff possessed a trade secret under Georgia law, defendant did not misappropriate plaintiff's trade secrets when it had Argentinean company develop label. Plaintiff satisfied elements of establishing trade secret, since production process was unique to plaintiff and unknown to competitors, the information possessed actual or potential economic value, and plaintiff's oral insistence on confidentiality and written nondisclosure agreement were reasonable efforts to maintain secrecy of process. Penalty Kick Management Ltd. v. Coca Cola Co., 318 F.3d 1284, 1291.

C.A.Fed.2018. Com. (a) cit. in disc. Developer and seller of ambient-light sensors that had confidentially shared information with competitor during negotiations regarding a potential merger filed, inter alia, a claim for misappropriation of trade secrets against competitor, alleging that competitor released new sensors with the technical design plaintiff had disclosed. The district court entered judgment in part on a jury verdict for plaintiff awarding, among other things, disgorgement of defendant's profits. This court vacated and remanded the judgment awarding disgorgement relief, holding that plaintiff did not have a Seventh Amendment right to a jury decision on its request for disgorgement of defendant's profits. The court reasoned that plaintiff did not show that disgorgement was available at law for its claim for trade-secret misappropriation, and noted, citing Restatement Third of Unfair Competition § 39, Comment *a*, that claims for trade-secret misappropriation were first recognized in American and English equity courts in the nineteenth century. Texas Advanced Optoelectronic Solutions, Inc. v. Renesas Electronics America, Inc., 888 F.3d 1322, 1341.

C.A.Fed.2004. Com. (f) quot. in disc. Designer of spectrometer device brought patent-infringement suit against competitor, also alleging that defendant misappropriated trade secrets and engaged in unfair competition by using designer's technology in its own product. District court granted defendant summary judgment. Affirming in part, this court held, inter alia, that plaintiff failed to demonstrate a disputed issue of material fact with respect to the long-path gas cell trade-secret claim. The court determined that defendant's activities did not constitute misappropriation because the patent on plaintiff's device, which contained public information not protectable as a trade secret, was issued before defendant began incorporating any aspects of plaintiff's device into its own product. On-Line Technologies, Inc. v. Bodenseewerk Perkin-Elmer GMBH, 386 F.3d 1133, 1141, on remand 428 F.Supp.2d 67 (D.Conn.2006).

Ct.Fed.Cl.2013. Com. (f) cit. in case quot. in disc. Patentee sued the United States, alleging that two robotic manipulators that were developed by defendant acting through the National Aeronautics and Space Administration (NASA) infringed on its patents. Plaintiff filed a motion seeking access to certain structure drawings and photographs of one of the manipulators, which NASA had previously identified as proprietary information that was subject to a protective order. This court denied plaintiff's motion in part, holding that defendant had met its burden of showing that its proprietary-information designations were proper with respect to certain documents that were created for this litigation, and that such protection had not been waived by public disclosure. The court reasoned, in part, that, while information contained in an issued patent was ordinarily regarded as public, information related to new inventions and technology under development—especially those that were not already the subject of pending patent applications—was particularly sensitive proprietary in-

For earlier citations, see the Appendices, Supplements, or Pocket Parts, if any, that correspond to the subject matter under examination.

formation, and the documents at issue contained greater or different technical details than other publicly disclosed information about the manipulators. Ross-Hime Designs, Inc. v. United States, 109 Fed.Cl. 725, 731.

Ct.Fed.Cl.2006. Cit. in brief cit. in sup. In a contract dispute between government and terminated military contractor, replacement contractor intervened to protect its proprietary information. This court ruled that its temporary umbrella protective order issued to safeguard information designated by intervenor as proprietary would remain in place during discovery, agreeing with intervenor that the term "trade secret," under applicable state trade-secret law, was not limited to productive processes. The court stressed that, under its rules of court, it had broad discretion to order, among other things, that a trade secret or other confidential research, development, or commercial information not be disclosed or be disclosed only in a designated way. Armour of America v. U.S., 73 Fed.Cl. 597, 602.

C.D.Cal.2010. Cit. and quot. in ftn., com. (d) cit. in sup. Taxpayers sought to obtain a tax refund from the federal government by characterizing their False Claims Act qui tam award in a Medicare fraud case as capital gains rather than ordinary income. Granting summary judgment for defendant, this court held, among other things, that knowledge of the ongoing fraud was not a "trade secret" such that it could be considered a capital asset for purposes of the Internal Revenue Code; as a factual matter, the information was not secret, and as a legal matter, there was no "reasonable" manner in which a person who held information about ongoing illegality could prevent that information from being disclosed to the public, and thus such information could not be the subject of trade-secret protection. Alderson v. U.S., 718 F.Supp.2d 1186, 1198, 1199.

E.D.Cal.2017. Com. (e) cit. in sup., quot. in case quot. in disc. Online car dealer that had contracted with a software-development company to design and build new software to replace its existing online auction system filed a trade-secret-misappropriation claim against company, alleging, inter alia, that defendant stole the proprietary software to enhance its own product line. This court denied summary judgment for defendant, holding that the fact-intensive determination of whether the source code constituted a trade secret was an issue of fact for trial. The court relied on Restatement Third of Unfair Competition § 39, Comment *e*, for authority that the economic value of an alleged trade secret need not be great, could be demonstrated through circumstantial evidence of an investment of resources in producing the information, and did not require a showing of use by the trade-secret owner. Copart, Inc. v. Sparta Consulting, Inc., 277 F.Supp.3d 1127, 1153, 1154.

N.D.Cal.2013. Cit. and quot. in sup. Former employee of an executive search and placement company was charged with, among other things, theft of trade secrets from company's database, which he allegedly used in starting his own competing company in violation of the terms of his noncompete agreement with company. Granting in part employee's motion for a subpoena duces tecum, this court held that company was required to produce documents supporting the government's contention that the information contained in the database was valuable as well as documents addressing the extent to which company kept the information secret. The court reasoned that the requested documents were material to whether the information afforded an actual or potential economic advantage over others such that it constituted a trade secret that was capable of being stolen. U.S. v. Nosal, 291 F.R.D. 403, 410, 412.

N.D.Cal.1995. Cit. in headnotes, quot. in disc., cit. in ftn., com. (b) cit. in case quot. in disc. and cit. in ftn., com. (d) quot. in disc. and cit. in sup., com. (e) cit. in disc., com. (f) quot. in sup., com. (g) cit. in disc. Nonprofit religious corporation sought preliminary injunction to prevent former Church of Scientology member from disseminating over the Internet copyrighted "course" materials for which corporation claimed an exclusive license. Corporation alleged that member's actions constituted copyright infringement and misappropriation of trade secrets. The court issued an injunction prohibiting member from posting copyrighted materials, but held that corporation failed to show a likelihood of success on the merits of its trade-secret claim where, among other things, it did not define with particularity those aspects of the course materials it considered secret, and the materials at issue had already ap-

Cit.—cited; com.—comment; fol.—followed; sup.—support.
A complete list of abbreviations precedes page 1.

peared on the Internet prior to member's posting. The court noted that as long as a religious organization took reasonable steps to protect the confidentiality of materials that gave it a competitive economic edge over others who did not possess them, the materials could not be denied trade-secret protection solely because of their religious nature. Religious Technology Center v. Netcom On-Line Com., 923 F.Supp. 1231, 1234, 1235, 1250-1253.

D.Conn.2003. Com. (f) quot. in sup. Technology company brought patent-infringement and trade-secret-misappropriation suit against manufacturers of a gas cell and two instruments, alleging that defendants misappropriated trade secrets during visits to plaintiff's laboratory and designed a product that infringed one of its patents. This court granted defendants summary judgment, concluding, inter alia, that plaintiff offered no evidence to rebut defendants' showing that no defendant used any of the alleged trade secrets related to the gas cell before patent was issued. After its disclosure in plaintiff's patent, the gas cell was no longer a secret under the state trade-secrets statute, because it ceased to derive independent economic value. On-Line Technologies, Inc. v. Perkin-Elmer Corp., 253 F.Supp.2d 313, 324.

D.D.C.2004. Quot. in ftn. Education association that developed and administered standardized test taken by medical-school applicants sued company that provided test-preparation courses, alleging copyright infringement, misappropriation of trade secrets, and fraud by compromising confidentiality and security of plaintiff's test. Defendant filed affirmative defenses, alleging that Federal Copyright Act preempted plaintiff's cause of action for misappropriation of trade secrets. This court granted plaintiff's motion to strike this affirmative defense, holding, inter alia, that the question of whether registration of test forms under secure test regulations was sufficient to establish secrecy required in a trade-secrets-misappropriation claim went to merits of plaintiff's claim, and did not address whether Copyright Act would preempt misappropriation claim. Association of American Medical Colleges v. Princeton Review, Inc., 332 F.Supp.2d 11, 23.

S.D.Fla.2001. Com. (d) quot. in sup. Produce company sued competitor for, among other claims, misappropriation of trade secrets regarding a new variety of pineapple. This court granted in part competitor's motion to dismiss, but it allowed plaintiff an opportunity to plead more specifically what aspect of the pineapple it sought to protect as a trade secret, such as genetic code or growth technique. The court determined that plaintiff had sufficiently alleged that the pineapple variety was a trade secret, and that fact issues existed as to whether certain information regarding the variety was a trade secret. Del Monte Fresh Produce Co. v. Dole Food Co., Inc., 136 F.Supp.2d 1271, 1292-1293.

N.D.Ga.2014. Com. (f) quot. in case quot. in ftn. (erron. cit. as § 39(f)). Retailer brought a misappropriation-of-trade-secrets action against another company, alleging that defendant misappropriated plaintiff's trade secrets that were shared with defendant in anticipation of a potential merger of the two companies, but which defendant used to develop its own competing products. Granting summary judgment for defendant on that claim, this court held that plaintiff failed to identify any specific information it claimed was a trade secret. The court further noted that plaintiff did not identify a "unique integration" of information that would have been considered a trade secret under Restatement Third of Unfair Competition § 39, Comment *f*, but identified only broad categories of data as its supposed trade secrets. Purchasing Power, LLC v. Bluestem Brands, Inc., 22 F.Supp.3d 1305, 1314.

N.D.Ga.2011. Com. (f) quot. in case quot. in sup. Home healthcare and hospice provider sued three of its former employees and a competitor, alleging that employees took trade-secret materials before resigning to join competitor and had used those materials while working for competitor. This court held, inter alia, that plaintiff established that its referral logs and workbook constituted trade secrets, because, while the names of doctors and healthcare centers included in those materials could have been developed by other means, "public" sources of this information would not indicate which doctors or healthcare centers referred patients to in-home care, what ailments the patients suffered from, who provided the referrals, and other information that was uniquely developed by plaintiff and not generally available or ascertainable from other sources. Amedisys Holding, LLC v. Interim Healthcare of Atlanta, Inc., 793 F.Supp.2d 1302, 1311.

N.D.Ga.2007. Subsec. (f) quot. in case cit. in sup. Sootblower manufacturer sued its former manager of service operations, alleging, inter alia, that manager misappropriated various trade secrets for the benefit of plaintiff's main competitor; plaintiff brought a separate action for trademark misappropriation against competitor. After consolidating the two actions, this court denied in part defendants' motions for summary judgment, concluding that a dispute of fact existed concerning whether the identity and particular combination of the components selected and used in plaintiff's permanently lubricated sootblower carriage constituted a trade secret. The court noted that, just because certain or all of the components of a certain product were generally known did not necessarily preclude protection for a combination, compilation, or integration of the individual elements. Diamond Power Intern., Inc. v. Davidson, 540 F.Supp.2d 1322, 1337.

N.D.Ga.2001. Subsec. (f) cit. and quot. in case quot. in disc. Management company sued beverage company for, in part, misappropriation of trade secrets, arising from defendant's use of a marketing and promotional concept similar to plaintiff's "Magic Windows," which permitted the decoding of a message on the reverse side of a label after the bottle was emptied. Granting defendant's motion for summary judgment, the court held, inter alia, that defendant's promotional concept and process for printing labels were not misappropriated from plaintiff within the meaning of the Georgia Trade Secrets Act because they were independently developed by a third party. Penalty Kick Management Ltd. v. Coca-Cola Co., 164 F.Supp.2d 1376, 1379, affirmed 318 F.3d 1284 (11th Cir.2003).

S.D.Ind.2001. Quot. in disc. Medical-device manufacturer sued competitor for patent infringement. Denying the parties' cross-motions for protective orders covering trade secrets and other commercially sensitive information, the court held, inter alia, that plaintiff's proposed order failed to include any requirement that the competitive value of the information must have arisen from the information's secrecy, or that the designating party must have exerted reasonable efforts to maintain that secrecy. Cook, Inc. v. Boston Scientific Corp., 206 F.R.D. 244, 248.

S.D.Ind.1998. Com. (f) cit. in disc. Manufacturer/seller of oxygen regulators sued competitor for misappropriation of trade secrets. Denying plaintiff's request for injunctive relief, the court held, in part, that plaintiff did not show a likelihood of succeeding on the merits of its claim, as the information sought to be protected was readily ascertainable through reverse engineering of plaintiff's products, which had been on the market for some time; plaintiff failed to take reasonable steps to protect the confidentiality of the allegedly protected information; and defendant, to whom plaintiff once voluntarily disclosed the information at issue, never consented to keep it confidential. Flotec, Inc. v. Southern Research, Inc., 16 F.Supp.2d 992, 1000.

S.D.Iowa, 2020. Com. (e) quot. in case quot. in sup.; com. (f) quot. in sup.; com. (g) cit. and quot. in sup. Seller of packaged deli products sued competitor and former employee who began working for competitor after leaving plaintiff, alleging, among other things, that defendants misappropriated plaintiff's trade secrets, including the terms of its program agreements with retail and wholesale customers. This court granted plaintiff's request for a preliminary injunction, holding that plaintiff had demonstrated a fair chance of prevailing on its claim for trade-secret misappropriation under Iowa law. The court reasoned, in part, that the terms of plaintiff's program agreements qualified as trade secrets within the meaning of Restatement Third of Unfair Competition § 39, because they had independent economic value, and plaintiff took reasonable precautions to maintain their secrecy. Smithfield Packaged Meats Sales Corp. v. Dietz & Watson, Inc., 452 F.Supp.3d 843, 855-857, 860, 861.

S.D.Iowa, 2015. Com. (d) quot. in case quot. in sup. Former employer brought a claim under the Iowa Uniform Trade Secrets Act (IUTSA) for misappropriation of trade secrets against, among others, competitor that hired plaintiff's former employee, alleging that employee forwarded plaintiff's customer emails, backorder lists, and confidential information, and downloaded plaintiff's customer database. This court denied defendant's motion to dismiss, holding that plaintiff sufficiently stated a claim for relief for misappropriation of trade secrets under IUTSA. In concluding that the information was a trade secret, the court relied on caselaw that quoted Restatement Third of Unfair Competition § 39, Comment *d*, for the scope of "trade

Cit.—cited; com.—comment; fol.—followed; sup.—support.
A complete list of abbreviations precedes page 1.

secret." Seneca Companies, Inc. v. Becker, 134 F.Supp.3d 1148, 1153.

S.D.Iowa.2010. Com. (d) quot. and adopted in case quot. in sup., com. (e) quot. in case quot. in sup. Tire manufacturer sued competitor and two former employees who left to work for competitor, alleging misappropriation of trade secrets and other claims. Granting summary judgment for defendants, this court held that plaintiff failed to demonstrate that defendants misappropriated its pricing and pricing strategies, product costs, product development, customer lists, or customer contracts; plaintiff produced no evidence that employees brought to competitor anything more than their own respective "general skills and knowledge" of the tire industry, which did not constitute a trade secret even if they acquired it while under plaintiff's employ, or that competitor "knowingly allowed, endorsed, encouraged, induced, and/or permitted the use" of the alleged trade secrets. Titan Intern., Inc. v. Bridgestone Firestone North America Tire, LLC, 752 F.Supp.2d 1032, 1038, 1039.

S.D.Iowa, 2008. Com. (d) quot. in case quot. in disc. Advertising company sued television broadcasters for trade-secret misappropriation, among other claims, after defendants discontinued use of plaintiff's services, yet allegedly continued using plaintiff's advertising methods. Granting defendants' motion for summary judgment, this court found that while plaintiff's claimed "method" of laying out advertisement mailers fit the list of "trade secrets" set forth in the Iowa Uniform Trade Secrets Act, plaintiff failed to show the required economic value in its alleged trade secret because it failed to demonstrate a direct, or even a fairly implied, link between the asserted trade secret and its engagement for additional campaigns. Sun Media Systems, Inc. v. KDSM, LLC, 564 F.Supp.2d 946, 966.

D.Mass.2007. Com. (d) cit. in ftn. (general cite). Software developer sued competitor for, in part, trade-secret violation, alleging that competitor wrongfully stole and incorporated developer's software into its own product. Allowing in part defendant's motion to dismiss, this court held, inter alia, that plaintiff's trade-secret-violation claim failed because plaintiff did not allege that the relevant trade secret was in continuous use, as required by Massachusetts law. The court noted that, despite plaintiff's argument that the vitality of the continuous-use requirement, which had been adopted from the first Restatement of Torts, had been questioned by a Massachusetts federal-district-court judge in light of the new definition in the Restatement Third of Unfair Competition, the requirement, whatever its wisdom, was part of Massachusetts law, and this court was powerless to remove it. Portfolioscope, Inc. v. I-Flex Solutions Ltd., 473 F.Supp.2d 252, 255.

D.N.J.2000. Com. (g) cit. in disc. Provider of "report card" for summarizing mutual fund performance sued securities brokerage firm, alleging trademark infringement, misappropriation of ideas, unfair competition, and breach of implied-in-fact contract. Following dismissal of claims relating to trademark, firm moved for dismissal of remaining claims. Granting the motion in part, this court held, inter alia, that plaintiff's "report card" idea was not sufficiently novel to warrant protection as a confidentially submitted idea; therefore, defendant's use of a similar form was appropriate. Duffy v. Charles Schwab & Co., Inc., 123 F.Supp.2d 802, 813.

S.D.N.Y.2009. Quot. in case quot. in sup. In a consolidated securities class action litigation involving a collapsed Italian conglomerate, lead plaintiffs moved to unseal certain discovery materials that certain defendants designated as confidential pursuant to a protective order. Granting plaintiffs' motion, this court held, inter alia, that defendants failed to show that the disclosure of any of the particular documents at issue would reveal business information that was sufficiently valuable and secret that it could cause competitive harm to them. The court noted that, although a business's information did not have to be a "true" trade secret in order to warrant protection from disclosure under federal discovery rules, trade-secret law was instructive in gauging whether information constituted sensitive business information that courts should shield from public scrutiny. In re Parmalat Securities Litigation, 258 F.R.D. 236, 245.

E.D.Tenn.1995. Com. (f) cit. in disc. Manufacturer of seamless-palm gloves sued its marketer for, inter alia, unfair competition by misappropriation of trade secrets, alleging that marketer wrongfully continued to produce the gloves using manufacturer's know-how after manufacturer became economically defunct. The court

For earlier citations, see the Appendices, Supplements, or Pocket Parts, if any, that correspond to the subject matter under examination.

entered judgment on a jury verdict for manufacturer, then granted marketer's motion for judgment as a matter of law. It held that the glove characteristics manufacturer claimed were protectable—certain sizing specifications, the thinness of the leather used and the thumb stretch—were physical features that were all readily observed and easily ascertained or duplicated and, therefore, were not trade secrets. TGC Corp. v. HTM Sports, B.V., 896 F.Supp. 751, 759.

E.D.Tex.2009. Com. (e) quot. in sup.; com. (f) quot. in disc. (erron. cit. as subsec. (f)). Defense-systems technology company sued rivals, claiming that defendants misappropriated its trade secrets concerning infrared imaging equipment. This court granted in part and denied in part plaintiff's motion to exclude defendants' expert's opinions, holding, inter alia, that while expert's testimony that certain of the alleged trade secrets were readily ascertainable through reverse engineering was relevant to the defense of plaintiff's misappropriation claim, expert could not offer testimony that, based on this, plaintiff did not actually own the trade secrets, since that would be an inadmissible legal opinion. Additionally, expert's testimony as to the sparseness of plaintiff's documentation on the alleged trade secret was relevant as an opinion of fact that went to the value of the trade secret, although expert was not permitted to conclude that this rendered the alleged secret not protectable. Raytheon Co. v. Indigo Systems Corp., 598 F.Supp.2d 817, 821, 822.

S.D.Tex.2015. Com. (d) cit. in case cit. in sup. Supplier of materials to the oil-and-gas industry filed a claim for misappropriation of trade secrets against competitor and former employee who left plaintiff to work for competitor in connection with allegations that employee stole confidential information from plaintiff and provided it to competitor. This court denied summary judgment for defendants, holding that questions of fact remained as to whether plaintiff's list of customer contacts and their personal email accounts was protectable as a trade secret under Texas law, noting that some Texas courts had held that even if customer information was readily available in the industry, liability would be upheld if the defendant gained the information in usable form while working for the plaintiff. The court cited Restatement Third of Unfair Competition § 39 in support of the proposition that the existence of a trade secret was a question of fact to be decided by the judge or the jury as fact-finder, and that, whether customer information was generally known or readily ascertainable was a question of fact. A.M. Castle & Co. v. Byrne, 123 F.Supp.3d 909, 915.

S.D.Tex.2015. Rptr's Note cit. in sup. Former employer brought a claim for misappropriation of trade secrets, inter alia, against former employee and his new employer, alleging that former employee misappropriated confidential customer lists, vendor lists, sales data, and other information from former employer and subsequently provided the information to former employee's new employer. Plaintiff moved to compel defendants to submit to a court-supervised forensic inspection of defendants' computers and other electronic equipment. The magistrate judge denied plaintiff's motion. Affirming, this court held that plaintiff was not entitled to the inspection of defendants' computers and other electronic equipment, because plaintiff failed to identify any specific confidential information of which defendants were in wrongful possession. The court referred to the Reporter's Note to Restatement Third of Unfair Competition § 39, in noting that the existence of a trade secret was a question of fact to be decided by the factfinder. A.M. Castle & Co. v. Byrne, 123 F.Supp.3d 895, 902.

S.D.Tex.2015. Cit. in sup. Designer of a smartphone application brought a claim for trade-secret misappropriation, inter alia, against former business partner, alleging that defendant sold the application to unnamed parties without authorization. Granting summary judgment for defendant on that claim, this court held that plaintiff failed to show that defendant improperly "used" the source code for the application by removing it from an online store without authorization. While defendant may have improperly used secret information, such as his password or the password-protected instance of the application that he removed from the developer account, he did not use information that was inherently valuable as a trade secret under Restatement Third of Unfair Competition § 39. Beardmore v. Jacobsen, 131 F.Supp.3d 656, 675.

S.D.Tex.2013. Rptr's Note to com. (d) cit. and quot. in case cit. and quot. in sup. Manufacturer of butterfly valves used in

Cit.—cited; com.—comment; fol.—followed; sup.—support.
A complete list of abbreviations precedes page 1.

the transportation industry brought a trade-secret-misappropriation claim, inter alia, against competitor, among others, alleging that defendant unlawfully obtained plaintiff's trade secrets when it hired plaintiff's former employee to develop a competing line of valves. Denying defendant's motion for partial summary judgment, this court held that genuine issues of material fact existed as to whether plaintiff's drawings and dimensions rose to the level of trade secrets, whether plaintiff took reasonable steps to protect them, whether the information had been publicly disclosed, whether plaintiff's former employee wrongfully used the trade secrets, and whether plaintiff was damaged. Ultraflo Corp. v. Pelican Tank Parts, Inc., 926 F.Supp.2d 935, 959.

S.D.Tex.2011. Rptr's Note to com. (d) cit. in sup. Software developer sued, among others, consulting firm, alleging, among other things, misappropriation of trade secrets and theft of trade secrets in violation of Texas statutory and common law. After a jury returned a verdict in favor of developer, this court denied firm's renewed motion for judgment as a matter of law, holding, among other things, that developer presented sufficient evidence to allow a jury to conclude that trade secrets existed. The court pointed to developer's evidence that the source code for its software was maintained behind a firewall to ensure its secrecy, and that, though the functions of developer's software were known to the industry, other software companies did not have identical functions in their software. Wellogix, Inc. v. Accenture, LLP, 823 F.Supp.2d 555, 562.

W.D.Tex.Bkrtcy.Ct.2012. Cit. in disc., com. (d) quot. in case quot. in sup., Rptr's Note (n) to com. (d) quot. in disc. Chapter 11 debtor/oil and gas production company brought an adversary proceeding for, inter alia, misappropriation of trade secrets against potential prepetition buyer of its assets, alleging that defendant impermissibly used plaintiff's confidential information and trade secrets to acquire oil and gas leases in a hydrocarbon-rich area of south Texas. This court entered judgment for debtor on this claim, holding that: debtor's subsurface, production, and operations data qualified as trade secrets under the six-factor test of Restatement of Torts § 757, Comment *b*; defendant obtained those trade secrets through improper means—requesting and receiving debtor's secrets from debtor's employees and a contractor retained by debtor; and defendant used debtor's trade secrets in a way that was competitively disadvantageous to debtor and benefited defendant. In re TXCO Resources, Inc., 475 B.R. 781, 804, 805.

W.D.Wash.2012. Quot. in sup., cit. in case cit. in sup., com. (d) quot. in sup. Football scouting company that compiled scouting reports on prospective football-league draftees and assigned each player a grade sued sports writer, alleging, inter alia, that defendant misappropriated its trade secrets when he published on a website eight articles discussing plaintiff's player grades for eighteen college players. Denying the parties' cross-motions for summary judgment on this claim, this court held that the fact that plaintiff awarded a grade to a player was information under the plain language of Washington's Uniform Trade Secrets Act, and whether the grade was protected under trade-secret law was a question for the trier of fact, because factual disputes existed as to whether plaintiff had made reasonable attempts to preserve the secrecy of the information, and whether the grades received economic value from not being generally known. National Football Scouting, Inc. v. Rang, 912 F.Supp.2d 985, 996.

Alaska, 2012. Com. (d) quot. in sup. and cit. in ftn. Village, along with manufacturer of a component for power-generation facilities, sued quasi-independent state agency, alleging, among other things, that agency erroneously awarded certain contracts for power generation in remote Alaskan villages to manufacturer's competitor and that agency's employees improperly disclosed manufacturer's trade secrets to competitor. The trial court granted agency's motion for summary judgment. While affirming, this court held that plaintiffs raised a fact issue as to the existence of a trade secret with regard to manufacturer's method of programming or wiring a certain type of controller. The court cited manufacturer's evidence regarding the value of its information to its business and to its competitors, the amount of effort and money expended in developing the information, how difficult it would be for others to properly acquire or duplicate the same information and methods, and manufacturer's efforts to keep its information secret. Powercorp Alaska, LLC v. Alaska Energy Authority, 290 P.3d 1173, 1188.

For earlier citations, see the Appendices, Supplements, or Pocket Parts, if any, that correspond to the subject matter under examination.

Ark.App.2016. Com. (f) cit. in sup. Lubricant producer brought a claim for misappropriation of trade secrets against custom lubricant blending company. The trial court granted defendant's motion for summary judgment on the ground that plaintiff's lubricant formulas did not meet the definition of "trade secret" under Arkansas law. This court reversed, holding that there were questions of material fact as to the existence of a trade secret. Citing the definition of "secrecy" set forth in Restatement Third of Unfair Competition § 39, the court noted that a formula or process was able to maintain its status as a trade secret even though, as here, it could be reverse-engineered if the process of reverse-engineering was too difficult or costly; and a formula did not automatically lose its trade-secret status simply because the product's ingredients were, as here, publicly available by way of patent, because it could be a combination of factors in addition to the ingredients that rendered the formula secret. Gibraltar Lubricating Services, Inc. v. Pinnacle Resources, Inc., 486 S.W.3d 224, 228.

Cal.App.2014. Com. (e) quot. in sup. Company that invented a process for creating self-authenticating documents through the use of barcodes sued manufacturer of multifunction printers, alleging trade-secret misappropriation. After a bench trial, the trial court entered judgment for plaintiff. Affirming, this court held that substantial evidence supported the trial court's finding that plaintiff showed that its alleged trade secrets had independent economic value, actual or potential, from not being generally known to the public or other persons who could obtain economic value from their disclosure or use. The court noted that, according to Restatement Third of Unfair Competition § 39, Comment *e*, the value of information claimed as a trade secret could be established by direct or circumstantial evidence, and pointed to evidence that plaintiff kept secret all but the most general idea for its technology, that plaintiff's president was not aware of any existing similar technology when he started his company, and that defendant obtained patents based on plaintiff's technology. Altavion, Inc. v. Konica Minolta Systems Laboratory Inc., 226 Cal.App.4th 26, 62, 171 Cal.Rptr.3d 714, 743.

Cal.App.2010. Com. (b) cit. in ftn. Software developer that obtained a judgment against competitor for misappropriating trade secrets sued purchaser of competitor's software, alleging that defendant, by using competitor's software, misappropriated plaintiff's trade secret source code incorporated into that software. The trial court granted summary judgment for defendant. Affirming, this court held that plaintiff failed to establish that defendant had knowledge of the trade secrets at issue. The court noted the undisputed fact that defendant never possessed or had access to the source code and only had executable, machine-readable code compiled by its supplier from source code, and concluded that a defendant did not, by executing machine-readable software, "use" the underlying source code or acquire the requisite knowledge of any trade secrets embodied in that code. Silvaco Data Systems v. Intel Corp., 184 Cal.App.4th 210, 226, 109 Cal.Rptr.3d 27, 42.

Cal.App.2007. Cit. and quot. in sup., coms. (e) and (f) quot. in sup. Company that developed and marketed software sued former employee, two business entities of which he was a principal, and others for, among other things, trade-secret misappropriation of its computer code. After a nonjury trial, the trial court entered judgment for defendants, finding that plaintiff failed to establish that the code constituted a trade secret. Affirming, this court held, inter alia, that, while the trial court found that the code would provide "some help" to another programmer, such evidence did not compel a finding that the code had independent economic value, i.e., that it was sufficiently valuable and secret to afford an actual or potential economic advantage over others. Yield Dynamics, Inc. v. Tea Systems Corp., 154 Cal.App.4th 547, 562, 564, 567, 66 Cal.Rptr.3d 1, 16-18, 20.

Cal.App.2006. Com. (f) cit. in disc. Pesticide manufacturers brought suit for injunctive relief against state's department of pesticide regulation, alleging, inter alia, violation of the Uniform Trade Secrets Act. The trial court granted in part summary adjudication for department. Holding that triable factual issues existed, this court reversed in part and remanded, concluding that department's consideration of plaintiffs' previously submitted data in evaluating other manufacturers' applications for pesticide registration was misappropriation under the Act if the data were trade secrets, department used the data without the

Cit.—cited; com.—comment; fol.—followed; sup.—support.
A complete list of abbreviations precedes page 1.

express or implied consent of the data owner, and department knew or had reason to know that it obtained the data under circumstances giving rise to a duty to limit its use of the data. Syngenta Crop Protection, Inc. v. Helliker, 138 Cal.App.4th 1135, 1172, 42 Cal.Rptr.3d 191, 218, vacating 136 Cal.App.4th 1464, 40 Cal.Rptr.3d 278.

Cal.App.2004. Com. (f) cit. in disc. Trade association of motion-picture, computer, and consumer-electronics industries, which licensed content-scrambling system designed to prevent unauthorized use of digital versatile disks on players or drives that did not contain association's decryption technology, sought injunction against website operators to prevent disclosure of alleged trade secret that unscrambled encryption technology. Trial court issued preliminary injunction. On remand, this court reversed, holding, inter alia, that plaintiff did not show likelihood that it would prevail on merits of misappropriation claim where evidence did not show that proprietary information contained in descrambling system was not generally known when defendants posted it, and there was no evidence as to when defendants posted information. DVD Copy Control Ass'n, Inc. v. Bunner, 116 Cal.App. 4th 241, 251, 252, 10 Cal.Rptr.3d 185, 192, 193.

Conn.2007. Cit. in ftn., com. (a) quot. in disc. Publicly traded corporation sued its former CFO for meeting with third parties without its knowledge to discuss a hostile takeover. The trial court ruled, in part, that defendant violated the Connecticut Uniform Trade Secrets Act (CUTSA). Reversing in part, this court held, inter alia, that, while defendant's negotiations arguably were informed by his insider's knowledge of plaintiff's business, there was no evidence that defendant used or disclosed plaintiff's strategic plan as a whole within the meaning of CUTSA. Pointing out that the purpose of CUTSA was to protect against the competitive use of misappropriated trade secrets, the court reasoned that an employee who planned to purchase a publicly traded corporation from its shareholders was not competing with the shareholders, but, rather, was seeking to offer them a fair return on their investment. Lydall, Inc. v. Ruschmeyer, 282 Conn. 209, 234, 235, 919 A.2d 421, 437, 438.

Conn.1999. Rptr's Note quot. in ftn. and cit. in case cit. in ftn. Cheese manufacturer sued its former accountant and the accountant's new cheesemaking company for breach of fiduciary duty, misappropriation of trade secrets, misrepresentation, and conversion, among other claims. Trial court granted plaintiff injunctive relief and awarded damages, holding that plaintiff's cheesemaking process was entitled to protection under the trade secrets act. This court affirmed, holding, inter alia, that the trial court properly found plaintiff's business operations—from the specific sources and costs of its supplies, through the production of its cheese, to the distribution of its product to three specific customers and the prices charged to them—to be a protectable trade secret. Furthermore, plaintiff's trade secret derived independent economic value from not being generally known to those, such as defendants, who could profit from the knowledge of it. Elm City Cheese Company, Inc. v. Federico, 251 Conn. 59, 752 A.2d 1037, 1044, 1054.

Conn.App.2021. Cit. in ftn.; com. (d) quot. in sup. and in ftn. Solar-development company that had unsuccessfully bid on several renewable-energy procurements by the Department of Energy and Environmental Protection filed a freedom of information request seeking disclosure of responses to the Department's requests for proposals made by successful bidders. After the Department denied company's request, the Freedom of Information Commission affirmed. Affirming, this court held, among other things, that the Commission correctly found that some of the information at issue contained "highly market sensitive" information, which derived independent economic value from its secrecy, such that it was exempt from disclosure as a trade secret within the meaning of Restatement Third of Unfair Competition § 39. Allco Renewable Energy Limited v. Freedom of Information Commission, 257 A.3d 324, 335, 336.

Fla.App.2020. Com. (f) quot. in sup. Fulfillment-services provider sued former customer and competitor, alleging that defendants misappropriated plaintiff's trade secrets regarding its web-based inventory management software when customer, after having used plaintiff's software, provided plaintiff's confidential and proprietary information to competitor to create competing software. The trial court granted partial injunctive relief to plaintiff, entering an order for temporary injunction to prevent defendants from disclosing, causing to disclose, or aiding and abetting in the disclosure of plaintiff's proprietary information. This court affirmed in part, holding, inter alia, that the trial court did not err in finding that plaintiff's software system constituted a trade secret that defendants misappropriated. The court quoted Restatement Third of Unfair Competition § 39, Comment *f*, in explaining that, although not all components of plaintiff's software were unique, such as its login screens and product-description screens, the system as a whole had a unique compilation and could perform unique tasks that justified its status as a protected trade secret. Mapei Corporation v. J.M. Field Marketing, Inc, 295 So.3d 1193, 1199.

Idaho, 1999. Quot. in ftn. Manufacturer of dehydrated potato products sued former research engineer employee and a competitor that hired former employee, alleging misappropriation of trade secrets related to production of a hash-brown product. Trial court entered an injunction and awarded plaintiff $3.26 million. This court affirmed, holding, inter alia, that plaintiff's "Golden Grill" process was a trade secret under the Idaho Trade Secrets Act. The fact that plaintiff spent almost six years developing the Golden Grill product was sufficient evidence that the process was not generally known or readily ascertainable. Basic American, Inc. v. Shatila, 133 Idaho 726, 992 P.2d 175, 184.

Iowa, 2008. Com. (d) cit. and quot. in sup., coms. (e) and (f) quot. in sup. Manufacturer of cement mixers sued former employees, competitor, competitor's officers, and customer, alleging misappropriation of trade secrets, inter alia. The trial court granted summary judgment for defendants. Reversing and remanding as to former employees and competitor and its officers, this court held that genuine issues of material fact existed as to whether former employees took advantage of their positions with plaintiff to obtain proprietary information that was then used for competitor's benefit, and as to whether competitor and its officers used their positions as potential buyers of plaintiff's business to obtain plaintiff's proprietary information for their own benefit. Cemen Tech, Inc. v. Three D Industries, L.L.C., 753 N.W.2d 1, 7, 9-10, 10.

Mo.App.1995. Cit. and quot. in disc, cit. and quot. generally in ftn. Company specializing in the repair of aircraft electrical components sought injunction to enforce noncompetition covenant purporting to prevent former shareholder who founded competing company from using information contained in first company's data sheets. The trial court entered judgment enjoining competition for a period of five years and this court affirmed, modifying the injunction to three years. It held that whether the data sheets, which contained information generally available to people in the business and might have constituted a process for continuous use in the operation of the business, constituted protectable trade secrets was a close question that did not warrant resolution here, since first company had a protectable interest in customer contacts from which former shareholder was now attempting to benefit. The court revised the injunction after deciding that five years was longer than reasonably needed to protect first company from competition posed by former shareholder's newly formed company. AEE-EMF, Inc. v. Passmore, 906 S.W.2d 714, 722.

N.J.Super.App.Div.2010. Quot. in sup. Labor unions sued New Jersey Department of the Treasury, among others, under the Open Public Records Act and the common-law right of access, seeking to inspect all agreements relating to investments made by the Division of Investment in private equity funds with money from state-employee pension funds. Affirming the trial court's dismissal of plaintiffs' complaint, this court held, inter alia, that the investment agreements were trade secrets, as well as proprietary commercial financial information, not subject to disclosure; among other things, only the general and limited partners in Division's investment partnerships and others on a need-to-know basis had access to the investment agreements, each agreement contained a provision for sanctions for those who breached confidentiality, and the agreements were not filed with a public agency or made available to the general public. Communications Workers of America v. Rousseau, 417 N.J.Super. 341, 361, 9 A.3d 1064, 1076.

N.J.Super.2008. Quot. in case quot. in sup. (citing § 39 of T.D. No. 4, 1993. § 39 has since been revised; see Official Text). Labor unions sued New Jersey Department of the Treasury, among others, under the Open Public Records Act (OPRA) and the common-law right of access, seeking to

Cit.—cited; com.—comment; fol.—followed; sup.—support.
A complete list of abbreviations precedes page 1.

inspect all agreements relating to investments made by the Division of Investment in private equity funds with money from state-employee pension funds. This court dismissed plaintiffs' complaint, holding, inter alia, that the documents were exempt as trade secrets from disclosure under OPRA; the agreements were not publicly disclosed, the firms' employees were subject to confidentiality agreements, the agreements were maintained in a locked filing cabinet, each agreement outlined a particular fund's organizational structures and investment strategies, the parties expended significant resources in crafting the agreements, and the information in the agreements was not easily acquired or duplicated by others. Communications Workers of America v. McCormac, 417 N.J.Super. 412, 438, 9 A.3d 1106, 1123.

N.J.Super.1995. Com. (d) cit. in case cit. in disc. (citing § 39 of T.D. No. 4, 1993. § 39 has since been revised; see Official Text). Toy company sued a competitor and sales representatives who left the first company for the competitor, arising from the competitor's efforts to divert the toy company's customers. This court entered judgment for plaintiff, holding, inter alia, that the post-employment restrictive covenant not to compete was valid and enforceable, as modified. The court stated that the knowledge plaintiff sought to protect through the agreement went beyond merely the identity of plaintiff's customers, as it sought to protect employee's knowledge of the customers' buying habits, plaintiff's mark-up structure, merchandising plans, sales projections and product strategies. It noted that a competitor's knowledge of a particular customer's pricing and packaging requirements actually gives the competitor the ability to design for that customer's needs and to obtain an advantage over competitors who do not have this information. Platinum Management v. Dahms, 285 N.J.Super. 274, 666 A.2d 1028, 1038.

N.J.Super.1994. Quot. in disc., com. (d) quot. in disc. (citing § 39 of T.D. No. 4, 1993. § 39 has since been revised; see Official Text). In a suit brought by a gambling casino against former employees who had allegedly obtained employment through fraud and misrepresentation, appeal was granted from the trial court's order refusing to quash a subpoena duces tecum issued by plaintiff against a nonparty that claimed trade secret protection. Remanding, this court held that the trial judge should have reviewed the requested materials and taken any necessary testimony in camera, outside the presence of plaintiff's attorneys or representatives, and then reached a conclusion whether the subpoenaed information was protected from routine discovery procedure. Trump's Castle Assocs. v. Tallone, 275 N.J.Super. 159, 161, 162, 645 A.2d 1207, 1208.

N.M.2008. Com. (e) cit. in sup. Insureds sued insurer for bad faith. The trial court granted plaintiffs' motion to compel discovery of certain documents in defendant's possession. Following defendant's refusal to turn over the documents without a protective order on the ground that they contained trade secrets, the trial court entered a default judgment on liability; the court of appeals vacated and remanded. This court affirmed the court of appeals' vacation of the default judgment, and it remanded for the trial court to continue the case on its merits. The court held that, while defendant's request for a protective order was rendered moot by subsequent events, plaintiffs, on remand, could move for sanctions, which would require a hearing on the trade-secret status of the documents at the time defendant refused to turn them over; any analysis of the information's value was to focus on whether the documents retained more than a trivial value when plaintiffs sought to compel production. Pincheira v. Allstate Ins. Co., 2008-NMSC-049, 144 N.M. 601, 190 P.3d 322, 334.

N.M.App.2007. Rptr's Note to com. (d) quot. in diss. op. Insureds sued insurer and its agent, alleging that defendants routinely provided retirees like plaintiffs with false or misleading information concerning the benefits of uninsured motorist coverage. The trial court entered a default judgment against defendants after they violated an order requiring them to produce certain documents allegedly containing trade secrets. This court reversed and remanded to the trial court with instructions to reevaluate defendant's assertion of trade-secret privilege as to the documents in light of, among other things, the six factors listed in Restatement First of Torts § 757, Comment *b*. The dissent noted that the privilege did not necessarily attach to all information recognized as a trade secret. Pincheira v. Allstate Insurance Co.,

For earlier citations, see the Appendices, Supplements, or Pocket Parts, if any, that correspond to the subject matter under examination.

2007-NMCA-094, 142 N.M. 283, 164 P.3d 982, 1000, affirmed on other grounds 2008-NMSC-049, 144 N.M. 601, 190 P.3d 322 (N.M.2008).

N.Y.Sup.Ct.App.Div.2006. Cit. in case cit. in disc. Passengers who were injured in a car crash caused by a defective tire sued manufacturer and distributor of tire. The trial court denied in part plaintiffs' motion to compel disclosure of certain allegedly protected trade secrets. Modifying the order, and otherwise affirming, this court held, inter alia, that the tire's formula and composition were indispensable to plaintiffs' claims and thus were discoverable. The court noted that the tire was over 11 years old, and there was nothing to suggest that defendant still used the same formula; moreover, the tire's ingredients were not in fact secret, because the same information was available from other sources that regularly published the components of various tires as identified through a reverse-engineering process. Mann ex rel. Akst v. Cooper Tire Co., 33 A.D.3d 24, 816 N.Y.S.2d 45, 52.

N.Y.Sup.Ct.App.Div.1998. Quot. in sup. After members of a real estate partnership unsuccessfully tried to repurchase from the mortgagee bank a building on whose mortgage the partners had defaulted, the partners sued an investment firm and the corporation that ultimately bought the property with the firm's assistance, alleging unfair competition, among other claims. Plaintiffs alleged that the information pertaining to the building's operation constituted trade secrets improperly disclosed by the investment firm to the purchasing corporation for the express purpose of enabling the purchasing corporation to make an attractive offer to the bank that would be comparable to plaintiffs' offer. The trial court dismissed plaintiff's complaint. This court affirmed as modified, holding, inter alia, that the data relating to the building's operations and to negotiations with tenants and unions were not of a genuinely secret nature. Similarly, the reports produced as a result of the audits may have been considered confidential, but they also failed to qualify as trade secrets. Wiener v. Lazard Freres & Co., 241 A.D.2d 114, 672 N.Y.S.2d 8, 15.

Or.App.2021. Com. (b) quot. in ftn. Heavy-machinery seller sued former employee and competitor, alleging that defendants violated the state Uniform Trade Secrets Act when former employee divulged the identities of plaintiff's customers upon obtaining employment with competitor. The trial court granted defendants' motion for summary judgment. This court affirmed, holding that the identities of plaintiff's customers did not constitute trade secrets, because the identities of customers in plaintiff's geographic region constituted readily ascertainable information. The court noted that it looked to the Restatement Third of Unfair Competition in analyzing whether customer identities constituted trade secrets, because, under § 39, Comment *b*, the principles of trade-secret law set forth in the Restatement were applicable to actions under the Uniform Trade Secrets Act. Peterson Machinery Co. v. May, 496 P.3d 672, 680.

Tenn.App.2001. Com. (f) cit. in disc. and quot. in case quot. in disc. Former employer brought action seeking injunctive relief against ex-employee and his company, alleging that employee had violated confidentiality agreement by developing bone-void filler to compete with product produced by employer. Trial court initially issued temporary restraining order, but, following hearing, it dissolved injunction. Affirming, this court held, inter alia, that the evidence did not preponderate against trial court's dissolution of the injunction. The court recognized that portions of information might be available in the public domain, yet the integration of the information into a process not commonly known could still be protectible; however, this was not the case here. Wright Medical Technology, Inc. v. Grisoni, 135 S.W.3d 561, 589, 591, 592.

Tex.2011. Com. (d) quot. in disc. Company sued its former employee and others for breach of contract, inter alia, alleging that employee solicited business from company's clients in violation of a covenant not to compete that employee had signed as a precondition to accepting stock options. The trial court granted defendants' motion for partial summary judgment, finding the covenant unenforceable; the court of appeals affirmed. Reversing and remanding, this court held that, under Texas's Covenants Not to Compete Act, the covenant was ancillary to or part of an otherwise enforceable agreement because the business interest being protected (goodwill) was reasonably related to the consideration given (stock options). Addressing the dissent's antipathy to non-compete agreements reasonably related to goodwill that were not specifically tied to trade secrets, confidential information, or special training, the court noted that trade secrets were not necessarily well-defined and easily proved, as suggested by the Restatement Third of Unfair Competition's statement that it was "not possible to state precise criteria for determining the existence of a trade secret." Marsh USA Inc. v. Cook, 354 S.W.3d 764, 779.

Tex.2011. Cit. in ftn. to conc. op. Newspaper publishers sued Department of Public Safety under the Texas Public Information Act, seeking a writ of mandamus to compel complete disclosure of travel vouchers from the governor's security detail. The trial court issued the writ. The court of appeals affirmed. This court reversed and remanded, holding that the information sought might be protected from disclosure under the Act as "expressly confidential under other law [than the Act]," namely, the common-law right to be free from physical harm. The court concluded that some of the information in the vouchers could create a substantial threat of physical harm because it revealed specific details about the number of officers assigned to protect the governor, their general location in relation to him, and their dates of travel. The concurrence argued that, even if "other law" could include judicial decisions and the common law, the Act required that the "other law" declare the *information itself* confidential. As an example, the concurrence pointed to the law of trade secrets, under which the nature of the information itself was at issue. Texas Dept. of Public Safety v. Cox Texas Newspapers, L.P., 343 S.W.3d 112, 126.

Tex.2003. Com. (d) cit. and quot. in sup. Nonparticipating royalty-interest owners attempted discovery of the mineral-estate owner's geological seismic data to prove that the mineral-estate owner breached an implied duty to develop its land. Trial court rejected mineral-estate owner's claims that the data were trade secrets and ordered production of the data under a protective order. Appeals court denied mineral-estate owner's requested mandamus relief. This court conditionally granted mandamus relief and ordered trial court to vacate its order compelling the production of the seismic data. The court held that geological seismic data and its interpretations were trade secrets protected by the Texas Rules of Evidence, and that nonparticipating royalty-interest owners failed to establish claim against mineral-estate owner justifying discovery of the trade-secret data. In re Bass, 113 S.W.3d 735, 739, 740.

Tex.App.2014. Rptr's Note to com. (d) cit. in case quot. in sup. (general cite). Online broker filed a petition requesting presuit discovery from software developer and former employee of broker who left to work for developer, alleging that it appeared likely that employee and others had, in designing risk-analysis software for developer, misappropriated broker's confidential and proprietary assets in violation of the nondisclosure provisions in their employment contracts with broker. The trial court granted broker's petition and issued an order allowing the requested depositions and document production. This court directed the trial court to vacate its order and conditionally granted developer's petition for writ of mandamus, holding, inter alia, that developer established that all but one category of the information sought by broker concerning developer's risk-analysis software constituted privileged trade-secret information. The court pointed to evidence that only two of developer's employees had access to the software's computer code, the software could not be duplicated by others without access to the underlying programming code, and the software was developer's only asset and was extremely valuable to developer. In re PrairieSmarts LLC, 421 S.W.3d 296, 307.

Tex.App.2013. Com. (f) quot. in sup. Inventor and owners of a process for mining potash (potassium-containing ore) in a specific area that had anomalously high temperatures brought claims for misappropriation of trade secrets, inter alia, against inventor's former business partner and partner's company's subsidiary, alleging that defendants used plaintiffs' proprietary information in developing their own mining project. The trial court entered judgment on a jury verdict for plaintiffs. Affirming, this court held, among other things, that the fact that some of the information plaintiffs claimed to be part of their trade secret was in the public domain or contained in defendants' files did not necessarily lessen the value of the trade secret. The court pointed to evidence demonstrating that, without plaintiffs' trade secret, there was little or no thought of economically mining potash in the area, and the jury

For earlier citations, see the Appendices, Supplements, or Pocket Parts, if any, that correspond to the subject matter under examination.

could reasonably have deduced that plaintiffs' trade secret made such mining feasible where it was not feasible before. Bishop v. Miller, 412 S.W.3d 758, 767, 778, 779.

Tex.App.2013. Rptr's Note to com. (d) cit. in sup. Lessee of port authority property brought suit for declaratory and injunctive relief under the Texas Public Information Act (PIA), challenging state attorney general's ruling that certain lease information was not excepted from disclosure to a requestor under the PIA. The district court denied lessee its requested relief. Affirming, this court rejected lessee's argument that the lease information was "expressly confidential under other law," and therefore exempt from the PIA's mandatory disclosure requirement, because it was a common-law trade secret. The court concluded that lessee failed to conclusively establish that the lease information was a trade secret, reasoning that, while lessee did not generally make the information known outside its business, it failed to take reasonable precautions to protect its alleged trade secret by preventing port from disclosing the information, and failed to establish that the information was of sufficient value to lessee and its competitors to constitute a trade secret. Boeing Co. v. Abbott, 412 S.W.3d 1, 10.

Tex.App.2013. Rptr's Note to com. (d) quot. in case quot. in sup. Operator of county landfill brought an action against county and against state attorney general, seeking declaratory and injunctive relief under the Texas Public Information Act to prevent the disclosure, pursuant to an open-records request filed by a member of the public, of volume and pricing information contained in "waste tickets" generated when customers disposed of waste at the landfill, alleging that that information constituted a trade secret. After a bench trial, the trial court ordered county to disclose the information. This court reversed and rendered judgment that county was prohibited from disclosing the information, holding that a company's confidential pricing and rate information could qualify as a trade secret, and, here, the factors for determining whether information was a trade secret weighed strongly in favor of operator. Waste Management of Texas, Inc. v. Abbott, 406 S.W.3d 626, 631.

Tex.App.2013. Coms. (e) and (f) cit. in sup., Rptr's Note to com. (d) cit. in disc. In competitor's antitrust action against waste-disposal company, the trial court ordered company to produce various internal business records in their native, electronic format with all metadata. This court denied company's petition for mandamus relief, concluding, inter alia, that company failed to introduce any evidence that its compliance with the discovery order would require it to disclose trade secrets; merely claiming that trade secrets were at issue was not sufficient. Absent a showing by company that the disputed discovery contained trade secrets, competitor did not have to prove that the trade secrets were necessary for fair adjudication. In re Waste Management of Texas, Inc., 392 S.W.3d 861, 870.

Tex.App.2012. Cit. in case cit. in disc. Natural-gas processor sued foreign limited-liability company, alleging theft of trade secrets. This court affirmed the trial court's denial of defendant's special appearance, holding that defendant had contacts with Texas out of which plaintiff's claim arose. The court concluded that defendant's use of plaintiff's trade secrets that allegedly occurred in Texas—i.e., defendant's marketing efforts and sales of products incorporating plaintiff's technology—was sufficient for liability, and thus defendant's Texas contacts were substantially connected to the operative facts of the litigation for purposes of establishing specific jurisdiction over defendant. Twister B.V. v. Newton Research Partners, LP, 364 S.W.3d 428, 439.

Tex.App.2011. Com. (d) cit. in case cit. in sup. Former assistant to a real estate agent sued agent and his wife, alleging defamation and tortious interference with contract; defendants counterclaimed for theft of trade secrets. After the jury found for plaintiff on all three claims, the trial court, inter alia, denied defendants' motion for judgment n.o.v. as to the theft counterclaim. While reversing and remanding for a new trial on all of the claims, this court held that defendants did not conclusively prove that plaintiff knowingly stole trade secrets, since the jury could reasonably have found that plaintiff retained copies of only four nonconfidential and unprotected pages from defendants' policy and procedures manual, containing website passwords as to which all of defendants' employees had access. Downing v. Burns, 348 S.W.3d 415, 422.

Tex.App.2009. Rptr's Note to com. (d) cit. in case cit. in sup. Licensor of technol-

Cit.—cited; com.—comment; fol.—followed; sup.—support.
A complete list of abbreviations precedes page 1.

ogy for manufacturing polyethylene plastic brought action for misappropriation of trade secrets and breach of contract against licensee, after licensee sublicensed the technology to other companies without authorization. The trial court granted plaintiff's request for a temporary injunction. Affirming, this court held, among other things, that plaintiff, in demonstrated that its technology constituted a trade secret, presented some evidence tending to show that it acted with sufficient vigilance to maintain the secrecy of the technology; while defendant pointed to several agreements between plaintiff and other companies containing fixed-term secrecy clauses that had expired, plaintiff offered countervailing evidence to show that, under the unique circumstances of each agreement, the secrecy of the technology remained intact, despite the expiration of the secrecy clauses. INEOS Group Ltd. v. Chevron Phillips Chemical Co., LP, 312 S.W.3d 843, 849.

Tex.App.2008. Com. (d) quot. in case cit. in sup. Corporation that acquired water-purification company's assets, including its trade secrets, sued company's former president and his new company through which he had begun manufacturing water-purification systems, claiming, in part, misappropriation of trade secrets. After the jury returned a verdict for plaintiff, the trial court granted a take-nothing judgment n.o.v. for defendants. Affirming, this court held that plaintiff's misappropriation claim failed because it did not show that the formula of the compound used in the absorption stage of its water-purification process was a trade secret—plaintiff presented no evidence that the formula was unknown outside its business or that it was valuable; the formula was not discrete but only an approximate ratio of two common substances; and plaintiff failed to prove that defendants actually used the formula. Global Water Group, Inc. v. Atchley, 244 S.W.3d 924, 929, vacating on denial of rehearing 244 S.W.3d 584.

Tex.App.2008. Rptr's Note to com. (d) quot. in case cit. in sup. Development company sued energy company for breach of contract, alleging that defendant failed to reassign undeveloped acreage in accordance with obligations in certain gas leases. The trial court granted plaintiff's motion to compel production of documents stating defendant's reserve estimates and projected future revenues for wells covered by the leases. Conditionally granting defendant's petition for a writ of mandamus, this court held that defendant established that the data were trade secrets, and that plaintiff failed to show that disclosure of the information was necessary to prevent fraud or injustice. The court reasoned that the forecasts and conclusions of defendant and its consultants were not publicly available, defendant limited the information within its own organization and vigilantly guarded the data, and the information was highly valuable to the company. In re XTO Resources I, LP, 248 S.W.3d 898, 901.

Tex.App.2007. Com. (d) quot. in disc. and quot. in case cit. in ftn. Manufacturer of fiberglass utility bodies and toppers for commercial vehicles sued competitor for, in part, tortious interference with prospective business relations, alleging that defendant's use of plaintiff's design drawings to create a stair-step topper for one of plaintiff's existing customers was independently tortious on the ground of trade-secret misappropriation. The trial court denied defendant's no-evidence motion for summary judgment on the tortious-interference claim. Affirming that portion of the decision, this court held, inter alia, that there was more than a scintilla of evidence that the design drawings were a trade secret. The court noted that that the six factors used by Texas courts to determine whether a trade secret existed were relevant, but not dispositive, because it was not possible to state precise criteria for determining the existence of a trade secret. Astoria Industries of Iowa, Inc. v. SNF, Inc., 223 S.W.3d 616, 635.

Tex.App.2003. Rptr's Note, com. (d) cit. in ftn. Company that designed converged architecture for delivering telecommunication services to residences sued developer of planned residential communities, alleging, among other things, misappropriation of trade secrets and breach of nondisclosure agreement, after developer invested in other company that intended to use company's secret information to market identical product. Trial court granted plaintiff a temporary injunction. Affirming, this court held, inter alia, that trial court did not abuse its discretion by granting temporary injunction where evidence established that plaintiff had probable right to relief on its claim for breach of nondisclosure agreement, which precluded defendant from us-

For earlier citations, see the Appendices, Supplements, or Pocket Parts, if any, that correspond to the subject matter under examination.

ing plaintiff's trade secrets to invest in company that intended to use plaintiff's secret information. Mabrey v. SandStream, Inc., 124 S.W.3d 302, 310.

Vt.2002. Cit. and quot. in ftn. Manufacturer brought suit for, in part, trade-secret misappropriation against competitor established by former employees. Affirming the trial court's entry of judgment for defendant, this court held, inter alia, that, because plaintiff failed to take steps to put employees on explicit or implicit notice that the information conveyed to them during their employment was to be kept confidential, defendants did not receive the information in confidence, did not breach their duty of confidence to plaintiff, and were not liable for misappropriation. Omega Optical, Inc. v. Chroma Technology Corp., 174 Vt. 10, 800 A.2d 1064, 1067.

Wis.2006. Cit. in ftn. to diss. op. Former employer sued former employee and employee's new employer for, in part, misappropriation of trade secrets, alleging that, after resigning, employee used plaintiff's confidential information, including customer lists and pricing information, to solicit and acquire customers. The trial court granted summary judgment for defendants and the court of appeals affirmed. This court reversed in part and remanded, holding that, while the confidential information did not meet the definition of a trade secret provided in Wisconsin's trade-secret statute derived from the Uniform Trade Secrets Act (UTSA), plaintiff's related common-law claims were not precluded by the statute. The dissent argued that plaintiff could not maintain common-law claims for misappropriation of confidential information that did not rise to the level of a trade secret in a UTSA state such as Wisconsin. Burbank Grease Services, LLC v. Sokolowski, 294 Wis.2d 274, 717 N.W.2d 781, 802.

Wyo.2014. Cit. and quot. but dist., com. (a) quot. in sup., com. (b) quot. in ftn. Nonprofit organizations submitted a request to the state oil-and-gas-conservation commission under the Wyoming Public Records Act (WPRA), seeking disclosure of the chemicals in several companies' hydraulic fracturing products. The commission denied the request, finding that the requested information was exempt from public disclosure as a trade secret under the WPRA, and the trial court affirmed. This court reversed and remanded for application of the narrower definition of trade secret developed in federal case law under the Freedom of Information Act, instead of the broader definition set forth in Restatement Third of Unfair Competition § 39. The court noted that that section of the Restatement focused on unfair competition and misappropriation, unlike the WPRA or FOIA, which sought to guarantee the public's right to access documents revealing the operations of the government. Powder River Basin Resource Council v. Wyoming Oil and Gas Conservation, 2014 WY 37, 320 P.3d 222, 228, 232-234.

Wyo.2006. Cit. and quot. in sup. and adopted, cit. generally, cit. generally in diss. op., com. (a) cit. generally and cit. in ftn. After internet-based market-analysis company brought action for misappropriation of trade secrets in federal district court against former employees who formed competing company, the issue of whether such a cause of action existed in Wyoming was certified to this court for resolution. Holding that the tort was part of the common law adopted by the Wyoming legislature, the court adopted the cause of action and its elements as set forth in the Restatement Third of Unfair Competition, as the modern and most appropriate version of the cause of action. The dissent noted that Wyoming was alone in adopting the Restatement, and argued that the Restatement so closely resembled a system of statutes that its adoption as the governing law was a usurpation of the legislature's authority and responsibility. Briefing.com v. Jones, 2006 WY 16, 126 P.3d 928, 930-932, 936, 937.

§ 40. Appropriation of Trade Secrets

U.S.2001. Com. (c) cit. in conc. op. Teachers' union representatives, whose cellular-phone conversation about status of negotiations with school board was intercepted and recorded by unknown person, sued radio commentator who played tape of intercepted conversation and head of local group opposed to union who obtained tape and disclosed it to media, alleging violations of federal and state wiretapping laws. District court denied summary judgment, but the court of appeals reversed, holding that statutes were invalid. This court affirmed, holding that statutes violated defendants' First Amendment rights, since tape concerned matter of public importance. Concurrence argued that speakers had little or no legitimate interest in maintaining pri-

Cit.—cited; com.—comment; fol.—followed; sup.—support.
A complete list of abbreviations precedes page 1.

vacy of particular conversation, which suggested violence and raised public safety concern. Bartnicki v. Vopper, 532 U.S. 514, 121 S.Ct. 1753, 1767, 149 L.Ed.2d 787.

C.A.1, 2001. Com. (c) quot. in disc. Manufacturers of cigarettes and smokeless tobacco sued commonwealth, alleging, in part, that Massachusetts statute requiring tobacco companies marketing their products in the commonwealth to disclose for each brand the identity of each added ingredient in order of weight, measure, or count effected an uncompensated taking in violation of the Fifth and Fourteenth Amendments. The district court permanently enjoined enforcement of the statute. Reversing, this court held, inter alia, that the statute was a valid exercise of the police power, and, in the absence of explicit guarantees of confidentiality from the commonwealth, did not effect a regulatory taking of trade secrets. The court said that the property interest in trade secrets, and its dimensions, could be changed prospectively to address health and safety concerns. Philip Morris, Inc. v. Reilly, 267 F.3d 45, 61, on rehearing en banc 312 F.3d 24 (2002).

C.A.3, 2021. Quot. in case, quot. in sup. Developer of pharmaceutical technology sued competitor and former employee, alleging that defendants misappropriated plaintiff's trade secrets to develop competing technology. The district court granted defendants' motion to dismiss. This court vacated and remanded, holding, inter alia, that plaintiff satisfactorily alleged a claim for statutory trade-secret misappropriation, because plaintiff alleged that competitor induced employee into leaving plaintiff's employ based on his knowledge of the technology and that competitor used the information to develop competing technology for a fraction of the resources invested by plaintiff. The court relied on a broader definition of "use" set forth in Restatement Third of Unfair Competition § 40, which went beyond defendants' proposed definition limiting use of confidential information to replicating or obviously incorporating plaintiff's technology in competing products. Oakwood Laboratories LLC v. Thanoo, 999 F.3d 892, 909.

C.A.3, 2004. Com. (a) cit. in disc. Writer of proposed screenplay sued producer of television series for misappropriation and quantum meruit, seeking compensation for his role in creation and development of defendant's series. District court granted defendant summary judgment. This court affirmed in part, concluding that New Jersey Supreme Court, if addressed with the issue, would hold that ideas lost their novelty if they were in the domain of public knowledge before use, and that such ideas could not be misappropriated. Despite plaintiff's creativity in combining stories and facts existing in public domain, this mode of originality was not protected under New Jersey misappropriation law. All of the locations plaintiff identified to defendant existed in public domain, and many stories and plot lines that plaintiff provided existed in public record. Baer v. Chase, 392 F.3d 609, 627, on remand 2005 WL 1106487 (D. N.J.2005).

C.A.5, 2016. Cit. in ftn.; com. (c) cit. in disc., cit. in case cit. in disc., quot. in case quot. in disc. Developer of software under a government subcontract filed an action in state court against competitor hired by the government to replace plaintiff's software, alleging, among other things, trade-secret misappropriation in violation of Texas law. After defendant removed the action, the district court entered judgment on a jury verdict for plaintiff. Affirming, this court held that plaintiff presented sufficient evidence that defendant used plaintiff's trade secrets in developing defendant's product, despite a lack of evidence of similarity between the parties' products. The court cited Restatement Third of Unfair Competition § 40 in noting that trade-secret cases involving software did not require application of the "access plus similarity" test when direct evidence was unavailable; rather, Texas law recognized that "use" could include reliance on trade secrets to facilitate research and development. GlobeRanger Corporation v. Software AG United States of America, Incorporated, 836 F.3d 477, 497, 498.

C.A.5, 2015. Cit. in sup., cit. in case cit. in ftn.; com. (c) quot. in sup., cit. in ftn. Computer-program developer brought an action against its former client and competitor that took client's business, alleging that defendants stole trade secrets regarding plaintiff's program. The district court granted defendants' motion for summary judgment. This court affirmed, holding that a reasonable jury could not find that defendants used plaintiff's trade secrets. The court rejected plaintiff's reliance on the access-plus-similarity test set forth in Restatement Third of Unfair Competition § 40 and explained that the fact that both products performed the same general function was not sufficient to show substantial similarity. Spear Marketing, Inc. v. BancorpSouth Bank, 791 F.3d 586, 601, 602.

C.A.5, 2013. Quot. in case quot. in sup. Developer of complex-services software for oil companies sued consulting firm, alleging that defendant misappropriated its trade secrets. The district court entered judgment on a jury verdict for plaintiff. Affirming, this court held that reasonable jurors could have found that defendant misappropriated plaintiff's trade secrets under Texas law. The court concluded that sufficient evidence existed to support the jury's finding that defendant used plaintiff's trade secrets, pointing out, among other things, that defendant joined with another software company to develop a complex-services component for a client's pilot project; that, around the time that defendant and the other company partnered, they were able to access plaintiff's dynamic templates source code, which had been uploaded to a confidential online portal; that defendant's document referenced the "creation of . . . complex service templates," and then "right below" stated: "Use [plaintiff's] content"; and that the same document provided that the templates "better deliver similar or better functionality than [plaintiff] or we may have a problem." Wellogix, Inc. v. Accenture, L.L.P., 716 F.3d 867, 877.

C.A.5, 2012. Com. (c) quot. in case quot. in sup. Inventor of a drilling-fluids cleaning machine sued drilling-services company and company's attorney for misappropriation of trade secrets, inter alia, after company pulled out of negotiations over the right to manufacture the machine and modified one of its own products to perform the same function. The district court entered judgment on a jury verdict for plaintiff. Affirming as to the misappropriation claim, this court held that there was sufficient evidence upon which to conclude that company "used" a trade secret of plaintiff's under Texas law and Restatement Third of Unfair Competition § 40—i.e., exploited plaintiff's idea for the machine in a way that was likely to result in injury to plaintiff or enrichment to defendants. The court pointed to evidence showing, among other things, that defendants contrived to give themselves an exclusive interest in plaintiff's machine, thereby keeping competitors from purchasing the machine, and then produced a product that directly competed for market share. Bohnsack v. Varco, L.P., 668 F.3d 262, 279, 280.

C.A.5, 2007. Quot. in sup., cit. in ftn. (general cite). Assignee of rights to computer program brought trade-secret-misappropriation claim against developers of competing program that was based in large part on assignee's program. On remand, the district court granted summary judgment for defendants. Affirming, this court, inter alia, upheld the magistrate judge's definition of "use" with respect to the third element of trade-secret misappropriation. The court reasoned, in part, that, under Texas law, which followed the Restatement Third of Unfair Competition, defendants "used" plaintiff's program by continuing to rely on it, either directly or on those portions incorporated into the competing program, to accelerate the development and marketability of the competing program. General Universal Systems, Inc. v. HAL, Inc., 500 F.3d 444, 450, 451.

C.A.5, 1998. Subsec. (b) cit. in disc., com. (c) quot. in disc. Employer sued former employee in state court for misappropriation of trade secret. The trial court entered judgment on a jury verdict finding employee liable, but concluding that he acted without malice, ill will, or evil motive. Employee then filed Chapter 7 bankruptcy protection and employer sought a determination that employee's debt was nondischargeable under 11 U.S.C. § 523(a)(4). The bankruptcy court entered summary judgment for employer, concluding that employee was precluded from relitigating the issue of intent. The district court affirmed. Reversing and remanding, this court held that proof of commission of an intentional tort was not evidence of actual intent to cause injury, as was required by 11 U.S.C. § 523(a)(6), because one could commit an intentional tort without acting maliciously or willfully, and that, in this case, the jury did not decide the issue of employee's intent. Matter of Miller, 156 F.3d 598, 603, 604.

C.A.6, 2022. Com. (c) cit. and quot. in sup. Dietary-supplement developer sued customer, alleging that defendant misappropriated plaintiff's trade secrets regarding broccoli-seed extracts by hiring plaintiff's former employee, who provided plaintiff's confidential research and development information to defendant, and used

Cit.—cited; com.—comment; fol.—followed; sup.—support.
A complete list of abbreviations precedes page 1.

it to create competing broccoli supplement products. The district court entered judgment on a jury verdict for plaintiff. This court affirmed, holding, inter alia, that substantial evidence supported a jury finding that defendant acquired and used substantially all of plaintiff's information constituting a protectable trade secret over its research and development on broccoli supplements. Citing Restatement Third of Unfair Competition § 40, Comment *c*, the court explained that defendant was not required to have created identical competing products using every aspect of plaintiff's trade-secret information to be held liable for trade-secret misappropriation. Caudill Seed & Warehouse Co., Inc. v. Jarrow Formulas, Inc., 53 F.4th 368, 384, 386.

C.A.7, 2011. Cit. in disc. S corporation and its shareholders challenged the issue of deficiency notices by the Commissioner of Internal Revenue following Commissioner's finding that settlement income that corporation received in an underlying trade secrets misappropriation suit should have been taxed as ordinary income, rather than long-term capital gain. The tax court agreed with Commissioner and ordered deficiency judgments. Affirming, this court rejected plaintiffs' argument that the settlement was payment for damage to corporation's trade secrets, which it alleged were capital assets, holding that, because corporation's litigation strategy had been to seek profits and other types of monetary recovery that could properly be taxed as ordinary income, and not to focus on the damage to or destruction of its capital asset, the settlement was not in lieu of a replacement of capital, and was properly identified as ordinary income. Freda v. C.I.R., 656 F.3d 570, 574.

C.A.7, 2004. Subsec. (b)(3) cit. in disc. American manufacturer of kitchen appliances sued Dutch competitor, seeking declaration that it had not misappropriated defendant's trade secrets. Dutch company counterclaimed for copyright violation. District court dismissed plaintiff's suit and the counterclaim on basis that third-party company was an indispensable party. This court reversed in part and remanded, holding, inter alia, that district court erred in dismissing Dutch company's counterclaim; there was no basis for finding that third party was indispensable party since counterclaim was a joint-tortfeasor case and Dutch company was not required to join third party as another alleged tortfeasor. Salton, Inc. v. Philips Domestic Appliances and Personal Care B.V., 391 F.3d 871, 878, certiorari dismissed 545 U.S. 1151, 125 S.Ct. 2992, 162 L.Ed.2d 908 (2005).

C.A.9, 2010. Com. (c) quot. in sup. Small technology startup company sued developer of source code for company's software product, seeking a declaration that developer was its employee when he wrote the source code, such that it owned the copyright to the software. After a bench trial, the district court found for plaintiff. Reversing as to plaintiff's claim for misappropriation of trade secrets and remanding, this court held, inter alia, that, while it was undisputed that the source code as a whole was a trade secret, defendant did not misappropriate it; besides filing for a copyright and threatening to withhold the source code from plaintiff, defendant did not make any other "use" of it, and defendant's possession of it for some period of time did not result in a loss of secrecy or a loss in value, which was reflected in the fact that the district court did not award plaintiff damages for lost value or unjust enrichment. JustMed, Inc. v. Byce, 600 F.3d 1118, 1130, 1131.

C.A.11, 2020. Com. (c) quot. in case quot. in sup. Company that maintained a database for use in selling life-insurance policies filed a claim for misappropriation of trade secrets against competitor, alleging that defendant made misrepresentations to gain access to the database and hired a "hacker" to "scrape" data from the database for use in its own software. After a bench trial, the trial court found in favor of defendant. This court vacated and remanded for a determination as to whether the block of data that defendant took from plaintiff was large enough to constitute appropriation of the database itself, and whether the means that defendant employed were improper. The court cited Restatement Third of Unfair Competition § 40 in explaining that the use of any substantial portion of a trade secret was sufficient to subject the actor to liability, and that actions could be improper for purposes of trade-secret misappropriation even if not independently unlawful. Compulife Software Inc. v. Newman, 959 F.3d 1288, 1313, 1314.

C.A.11, 2003. Quot. in sup., com. (a) quot. in ftn., com. (c) quot. in sup. Company that conceived of beverage-label marketing and production process sued cola company for,

For earlier citations, see the Appendices, Supplements, or Pocket Parts, if any, that correspond to the subject matter under examination.

inter alia, misappropriation of trade secrets arising from defendant's disclosure of plaintiff's information to company that printed labels for defendant's product in Argentina, which in turn used information to develop similar label. District court granted defendant summary judgment. This court affirmed, holding, inter alia, that although plaintiff possessed a trade secret under Georgia law, defendant did not misappropriate plaintiff's trade secrets when it had Argentinean company develop label. Plaintiff failed to prove that defendant disclosed information enabling Argentinean company to learn plaintiff's trade secret or that company's label was substantially derived from plaintiff's label and not the result of independent creation. Penalty Kick Management Ltd. v. Coca Cola Co., 318 F.3d 1284, 1292-1293, 1298.

C.A.Fed.2013. Cit. in disc. Military shipbuilder brought an action for misappropriation of trade secrets against the United States under the Federal Tort Claims Act (FTCA), alleging that defendant wrongfully disclosed plaintiff's proprietary technical drawings for a special-operations craft to its rival for use in designing and constructing a nearly identical craft. After the district court entered judgment for plaintiff, the Fifth Circuit Court of Appeals vacated and remanded for transfer to the Court of Federal Claims on the basis that plaintiff's claim was rooted in breach of contract. This court affirmed the district court's transfer of the case, holding that, while plaintiff's stated claim was a tort-based claim for liability based on the Virginia law of trade-secret misappropriation and, on its face, was within the district court's jurisdiction under the FTCA, the Fifth Circuit did not clearly err in holding that plaintiff's claim depended on an adjudication of the government's contract obligation not to disclose plaintiff's designs and thus was presumptively limited by the Tucker Act to the Court of Federal Claims. U.S. Marine, Inc. v. U.S., 722 F.3d 1360, 1365.

E.D.Cal.2011. Com. (c) cit. in case quot. in sup. Developer of front-end software for use in the health insurance industry sued developer of back-end software after defendant terminated the parties' agreement to develop an integrated solution, alleging, among other things, misappropriation of trade secrets. This court denied plaintiff's motion for a preliminary injunction seeking to prevent defendant from marketing a software product that allegedly incorporated plaintiff's trade secrets, holding that plaintiff failed to show a reasonable probability of success on the merits. The court reasoned that, while defendant made use of plaintiff's knowledge of how the front end of healthcare insurance worked generally and, to some extent, how plaintiff's data inputs and outputs worked, plaintiff failed to show how definite pieces of its knowledge, pieces that themselves qualified as trade secrets, recognizably showed up in, or were "embodied in" defendant's programming. Agency Solutions.Com, LLC v. TriZetto Group, Inc., 819 F.Supp.2d 1001, 1028.

N.D.Cal.2018. Com. (c) cit. and quot. in sup. Manufacturer of data centers brought a lawsuit against competitors, alleging that defendants willfully and maliciously misappropriated plaintiff's trade secrets regarding its modular data centers. This court denied defendants' motion for judgment as a matter of law, holding, inter alia, that the jury's conclusion that defendants had used plaintiff's trade secrets improperly was not unreasonable in the light of the evidence. The court cited Restatement Third of Unfair Competition § 40 in explaining that expert testimony was unnecessary for the jury to find that a trade secret was used, because finding that there was "use" of a trade secret did not require a complex technical explanation, merely a demonstration that defendants' creation was substantially derived from plaintiff's secrets. BladeRoom Group Limited v. Emerson Electric Co., 331 F.Supp.3d 977, 986, 989.

D.Conn.2003. Com. (c) quot. in sup. and cit. generally in ftn. Technology company brought patent-infringement and trade-secret-misappropriation suit against manufacturers of a gas cell and two instruments, alleging that defendants misappropriated trade secrets during visits to plaintiff's laboratory and designed a product that infringed one of its patents. This court granted defendants summary judgment, concluding, inter alia, that plaintiff offered no evidence to rebut defendants' showing that no defendant used any of the alleged trade secrets related to the gas cell before patent was issued. There was no authority that a dead-end flirtation with another's trade secret that resulted in no profit from, or disclosure or waste of, the secret could support finding of misappropriation.

Cit.—cited; com.—comment; fol.—followed; sup.—support.
A complete list of abbreviations precedes page 1.

On-Line Technologies, Inc. v. Perkin-Elmer Corp., 253 F.Supp.2d 313, 323-324, 332.

D.Del.2004. Com. (c) cit. in disc. Golf-ball manufacturer brought patent-infringement suit against competitor, and competitor counterclaimed for misappropriation of trade secrets relating to golf-ball technology. District court granted plaintiff's motion for partial summary judgment on the counterclaim. Denying defendant's motion for reconsideration, the court held that although proof of the use of another's trade secret in the course of research and development could be actionable, no reasonable fact finder could conclude from defendant's evidence that plaintiff's polyurethane golf balls were substantially derived from defendant's formulas, ingredients, and processes. Callaway Golf Co. v. Dunlop Slazenger Group Americas, Inc., 325 F.Supp.2d 457, 461.

N.D.Ga.2014. Com. (c) quot. in case quot. in sup. Company that marketed and sold high-end web-based camera systems sued competitor and several individuals employed by or associated with competitor, alleging that defendants engaged in corporate espionage to misappropriate plaintiff's trade secrets. This court granted summary judgment for defendant on plaintiff's misappropriation claim, holding that plaintiff failed to present evidence that defendants obtained plaintiff's trade secrets through improper means, or that defendants used a substantial portion of plaintiff's trade secrets to create a product that was substantially derived from those trade secrets. The court reasoned, in part, that, under Restatement Third of Unfair Competition § 40, if the contribution made by a trade secret was so slight that the defendant's product or process could be said to derive from other sources of information or from independent creation, the trade secret was not "used" for purposes of imposing liability for misappropriation of trade secrets. EarthCam, Inc. v. OxBlue Corp., 49 F.Supp.3d 1210, 1225.

N.D.Ga.2014. Com. (c) quot. in case quot. in sup. Retailer brought a misappropriation-of-trade-secrets action against another company, alleging that defendant misappropriated plaintiff's trade secrets that were shared with defendant in anticipation of a potential merger of the two companies, but which defendant used to develop its own competing products. Granting summary judgment for defendant on that claim, this court held that plaintiff failed to identify any specific information it claimed was a trade secret. The court further concluded that, even if the disclosed information had constituted a trade secret, plaintiff failed to show that any such information was "misappropriated." Citing Restatement Third of Unfair Competition § 40, Comment *c*, the court noted that if the contribution made by the trade secret was so slight that the defendant's product or process could be said to derive from other sources of information or from independent creation, the trade secret had not been "used" for purposes of imposing liability; and, here, plaintiff presented insufficient circumstantial evidence to show any misappropriation beyond a generalization about the similarity of the parties' products. Purchasing Power, LLC v. Bluestem Brands, Inc., 22 F.Supp.3d 1305, 1315.

N.D.Ga.2007. Com. (f) quot. in case quot. in sup. Sootblower manufacturer sued its former manager of service operations, alleging, inter alia, that manager misappropriated various trade secrets for the benefit of plaintiff's main competitor; plaintiff brought a separate action for trademark misappropriation against competitor. After consolidating the two actions, this court denied in part defendants' motions for summary judgment, concluding that a question of fact existed concerning whether competitor "used" or "disclosed" trade secrets for purposes of plaintiff's misappropriation claim under the Georgia Trade Secrets Act. The court noted that the evidence concerning competitor's CEO's sudden awareness of the components of plaintiff's sootblower's carriage could lead a factfinder to conclude that competitor later "used" that information because it likely would improve its own efforts to provide rebuild and repair services for plaintiff's systems. Diamond Power Intern., Inc. v. Davidson, 540 F.Supp.2d 1322, 1340.

N.D.Ill.2020. Cit. in cases cit. and quot. in sup.; com. (c) quot. in sup., cit. in case cit. in sup. Manufacturer of digital radios filed a claim for misappropriation of trade secrets against competitor under the Defend Trade Secrets Act, alleging that competitor hired three engineers from manufacturer's Malaysian office, who stole manufacturer's confidential documents and used them to develop and sell competing radios. This court denied in part competitor's motion to preclude manufacturer from

For earlier citations, see the Appendices, Supplements, or Pocket Parts, if any, that correspond to the subject matter under examination.

relying on extraterritorial damages, holding that manufacturer introduced sufficient evidence to support a finding that "use" of the alleged trade secrets occurred domestically, such that the Act could apply extraterritorially. The court pointed out that it was undisputed that competitor advertised, promoted, and marketed products embodying the allegedly stolen trade secrets domestically at numerous trade shows, and reasoned that such actions constituted "use" under Restatement Third of Unfair Competition § 40. Motorola Solutions, Inc. v. Hytera Communications Corp. Ltd., 436 F.Supp.3d 1150, 1164, 1165.

N.D.Ill.2006. Com. (c) quot. in sup. Developer of curing agent for epoxy resin sued distributor of competitor's equivalent product for, among other things, misappropriation of trade secrets. This court denied defendant's motion to dismiss the claim, holding that it was possible that plaintiff could show that defendant misappropriated plaintiff's trade secrets under a broad reading of the word "use." The court pointed to plaintiff's allegations that distributor knew or should have known that competitor had manufactured its product by misappropriating developer's technology and had used its prior relationship with developer as its former distributor in order to price competitor's product cheaper than developer's and to solicit developer's customers. Cognis Corp. v. CHEMCENTRAL Corp., 430 F.Supp.2d 806, 812.

N.D.Ind.2007. Com. (a) cit. in sup. Modular-home designer brought, in part, a tort claim for unfair competition against competitor, alleging that defendant misappropriated plaintiff's trade secrets, technical drawings, and confidential information to create a line of modular homes identical to one of plaintiff's models, and that, by way of its advertising, defendant improperly promoted the drawings as being its own work, in an effort to deprive plaintiff of customers. Denying in part defendant's motion for partial judgment on the pleadings, this court held that, based on the pleadings, the Indiana Uniform Trade Secrets Act (IUTSA) did not preempt plaintiff's unfair-competition claim. The court found that, at this stage, the claim, as alleged by plaintiff, did not simply restate the same operative facts underlying plaintiff's trade-secret-misappropriation claim, and did not necessarily conflict with IUTSA. Patriot Homes, Inc. v. Forest River Housing, Inc., 489 F.Supp.2d 865, 875.

N.D.Ind.Bkrtcy.Ct.2006. Subsec. (b) cit. in disc., com. (c) quot. in disc. Bank that refinanced automobile loan to debtor, who later transferred the vehicle title to nonparty without authorization in exchange for a promise that nonparty would complete the loan payments, brought adversary proceeding against debtor, seeking a determination that the debt was nondischargeable, inter alia, as a debt for willful and malicious injury. This court ruled that the debt was not excepted from discharge because debtor's actions in arranging for full satisfaction of the debt established a lack of willful intent to injure the bank's interests in the vehicle. The court observed that merely because a tort was classified as intentional did not indicate that any injury caused was willful; for example, the tort of misappropriation of trade secrets was wrongful regardless of whether injury to owner of the trade secrets was substantially certain to occur. In re Whiters, 337 B.R. 326, 341, 342.

S.D.Ind.Bkrtcy.Ct.2010. Com. (c) quot. in case quot. in sup. Off-duty police officer/private security guard brought adversary proceeding against Chapter 11 debtor, seeking a determination that debtor's indebtedness to her for personal injuries sustained in an altercation in a tavern in which she attempted to subdue and handcuff debtor were excepted from discharge as arising from conduct that was willful or malicious as a matter of law. This court granted summary judgment for guard, concluding that debtor's alleged indebtedness to guard was caused by a "willful injury." The court noted that merely because a tort was classified as intentional did not mean that any injury caused by the tortfeasor was willful, citing by way of example the torts of misappropriation of proprietary information and misuse of trade secrets, which were wrongful regardless of whether injury was substantially certain to occur. In re Roberts, 431 B.R. 914, 920.

D.Kan.2001. Cit. in sup. and in ftn. Aircraft navigational instrument provider sued competitor for Lanham Act violations and unfair competition, among other claims, alleging that defendant improperly obtained plaintiff's trade secrets, altered documents to misrepresent Federal Aviation Administration's position on plaintiff's products, and provided altered documents to plaintiff's customers. This court overruled defendant's motion to dismiss plain-

Cit.—cited; com.—comment; fol.—followed; sup.—support.
A complete list of abbreviations precedes page 1.

tiff's unfair-competition claim, predicting that Kansas Supreme Court would apply the general principles outlined in Restatement Third of Unfair Competition and allow an unfair-competition claim based on misuse of trade secrets and other confidential business information. Airport Systems Intern., Inc. v. Airsys ATM, Inc., 144 F.Supp.2d 1268, 1269, 1270.

E.D.La.Bkrtcy.Ct.2018. Com. (c) cit. in case quot. in disc. After her baby died following prolonged labor, mother brought a lawsuit against midwife who had subsequently filed for Chapter 7 bankruptcy, alleging that midwife's debt owed to mother should not be discharged, because midwife had acted willfully and maliciously in trying to deliver mother's baby given that midwife violated several state safety regulations regarding at-home deliveries. This court entered judgment for midwife, holding that, although midwife might have acted recklessly, she did not act willfully and maliciously, because she did not intend for the baby to suffer severe harm or die. The court analogized this action to caselaw citing Restatement Third of Unfair Competition § 40, Comment *c*, in explaining that midwife's acts that led to the baby's death, while done intentionally, were not done with the purpose of harming the baby. In re Dehler, 593 B.R. 301, 308.

D.N.J.2000. Com. (a) cit. in disc., com. (c) cit. in ftn. Provider of "report card" for summarizing mutual fund performance sued securities brokerage firm, alleging trademark infringement, misappropriation of ideas, unfair competition, and breach of implied-in-fact contract. Following dismissal of claims relating to trademark, firm moved for dismissal of remaining claims. Granting the motion in part, this court held, inter alia, that plaintiff's "report card" idea was not sufficiently novel to warrant protection as a confidentially submitted idea; therefore, defendant's use of a similar form was appropriate. Duffy v. Charles Schwab & Co., Inc., 123 F.Supp.2d 802, 808, 817.

D.N.J.1997. Subsec. (a) and com. (b) cit. in ftn., com. (c) cit. generally in headnote and cit. and quot. in disc., Rptr's Notes quot. in disc. A German drug manufacturer brought suit against several competitors, alleging that defendants misappropriated its trade secrets involved in the manufacture of a laboratory version of erythropoietin. Denying defendants' motion for summary judgment, the court held, inter alia, that genuine issues of material fact existed as to whether plaintiff's purported trade secrets were, in fact, secret; whether plaintiff took reasonable precautions to protect the secrecy of its alleged trade secrets; and whether one defendant used plaintiff's alleged trade secrets to plaintiff's detriment. The court refused to find that the defendant's use of plaintiff's purported trade secrets for evidentiary purposes during prior commercial litigation was privileged. Merckle GmbH v. Johnson & Johnson, 961 F.Supp. 721, 722, 730, 733, 734.

E.D.N.Y.2012. Com. (c) cit. and quot. in sup. After clients brought a putative class action for securities fraud against investment firm, they sought a ruling that an injunction issued in firm's parallel trade-secret-misappropriation case against three former employees did not prevent the employees from testifying in depositions in this case. Granting in part clients' motion, this court held that there was nothing in the injunction that prohibited deposition testimony in this case. The court reasoned that the express purpose of the injunction was to protect firm's trade-secret information from further disclosure or use, and, clearly, deposition testimony by former employees, under the protection of a confidentiality order, with sealed, attorney's-eyes-only transcripts, could not reasonably be expected to constitute or lead to further disclosure or use of defendant's confidential information; rather, it would allow the trier of fact to determine the truth or falsity of the allegations, a use that was fully consistent with protecting trade secrets. Goodman v. Genworth Financial Wealth Management, 881 F.Supp.2d 347, 354, 355.

N.D.N.Y.2018. Com. (c) quot. in case quot. in sup. In an action by manufacturer of drug testing kits against competitor, plaintiff filed a motion to amend or supplement the complaint to add claims for, among other things, misappropriation of trade secrets against its former employee, who left plaintiff to work for defendant. This court granted plaintiff's motion in part, holding that plaintiff stated a claim for misappropriation of trade secrets by pleading facts that plausibly alleged the existence of trade secrets and that it made an effort through a confidentiality agreement to keep the trade secrets confidential. The court pointed to plaintiff's allegations

For earlier citations, see the Appendices, Supplements, or Pocket Parts, if any, that correspond to the subject matter under examination.

that employee had access to proprietary and confidential information regarding plaintiff's contracts, pricing, product costs, internal sales strategies, legal and regulatory procedures, and competitive positions within plaintiff's industry during his employment with plaintiff, and noted that, under Restatement Third of Unfair Competition § 40, use of a trade secret could include any exploitation of the trade secret that was likely to result in injury to the owner or enrichment to the defendant. American Bio Medica Corporation v. Bailey, 341 F.Supp.3d 142, 158.

E.D.Tex.2019. Com. (c) quot. in case quot. in sup. Business and subsidiaries brought a lawsuit against former employees and competitors, alleging that defendants misused plaintiffs' trade secrets regarding products for spraying limestone, which defendants obtained during inquiries into an investment agreement with plaintiffs. This court adopted the recommendations of a magistrate judge and granted in part and denied in part defendants' motion for summary judgment, holding, inter alia, that plaintiffs failed to provide evidence that the allegedly misappropriated information, except for certain formulas, were trade secrets. Citing Restatement Third of Unfair Competition § 40, the court determined that, if "use" was a required element of plaintiffs' misappropriation claim under Texas law, plaintiffs' evidence that defendants referred to plaintiffs' formulas in their marketing and promotional materials created a genuine issue of material fact as to whether defendants "used" plaintiffs' formulas. StoneCoat of Texas, LLC v. ProCal Stone Design, LLC, 426 F.Supp.3d 311, 344.

N.D.Tex.2015. Com. (c) quot. in case quot. in sup. (general cite). Employer sued two former employees who left to work for a competitor, alleging, among other things, misappropriation of trade secrets. This court denied defendants' motion for summary judgment on plaintiff's misappropriation claim, holding that the evidence suggested that one defendant took potentially confidential information from plaintiff and had it in his possession after his termination, and, while plaintiff did not allege exactly how the information was used, the court was unwilling to find that no fact question existed as to whether the information was used. The court relied in part on language from Restatement Third of Unfair Competition § 40, which stated that, as a general matter, any exploitation of a trade secret that was likely to result in injury to the trade-secret owner or enrichment to the defendant was a "use" for purposes of a trade-secret misappropriation claim. Merritt Hawkins & Associates, LLC v. Gresham, 79 F.Supp.3d 625, 638.

N.D.Tex.2014. Com. (c) quot. in ftn. Developer of radio-frequency-identification technology that was installed for the U.S. Navy as part of a subcontract sued competitor, alleging that defendant improperly gained access to plaintiff's technology while working on a subsequent project for the Navy, and then used that access to reverse-engineer its own similar technology. This court denied defendant's motion for summary judgment on plaintiff's claim for misappropriation of trade secrets, holding, among other things, that questions of fact remained as to whether defendant unlawfully accessed and used plaintiff's technology. The court noted that, although the record at this stage did not clearly indicate which particular components of plaintiff's technology defendant acquired or used, Restatement Third of Unfair Competition § 40 provided that, as a general matter, any exploitation of a trade secret that was likely to result in injury to the trade-secret owner or enrichment to the defendant was a use for purposes of trade-secret liability. GlobeRanger Corp. v. Software AG, 27 F.Supp.3d 723, 739.

S.D.Tex.2015. Com. (c) quot. in case quot. in disc. Designer of a smartphone application brought a claim for trade-secret misappropriation, inter alia, against former business partner, alleging that defendant sold the application to unnamed parties without authorization. Granting summary judgment for defendant on that claim, this court held that plaintiff failed to show that defendant improperly "used" the source code for the application, which was publicly available to download for free for several weeks. In making its decision, the court noted that, under Restatement Third of Unfair Competition § 40"use" included any exploitation of a trade secret that was likely to result in injury to the trade-secret owner or enrichment to the user. Beardmore v. Jacobsen, 131 F.Supp.3d 656, 673.

S.D.Tex.2011. Quot. in case quot. in ftn. National tax consulting firm sued former employee who left firm to work for firm's competitor, alleging, among other things,

Cit.—cited; com.—comment; fol.—followed; sup.—support.
A complete list of abbreviations precedes page 1.

that employee took firm's confidential or proprietary customer lists and pricing information and disclosed it to competitor. Granting summary judgment for employee on firm's claim for misappropriation of trade secrets, this court held that, even if firm's pricing information was confidential or proprietary, the record showed no basis to infer that employee disclosed that information to competitor or that competitor used that information to firm's disadvantage; firm had not raised a fact issue that it was damaged by employee's disclosure of the information, a necessary element of a claim for misappropriation of trade secrets. Alliantgroup, L.P. v. Feingold, 803 F.Supp.2d 610, 625.

S.D.Tex.2011. Quot. in sup. Software developer that provided complex services solutions to oil and gas clients sued, among others, consulting firm with which it had partnered to make a joint presentation to a client, alleging misappropriation of trade secrets and other claims, after firm decided to partner with another software developer instead. Denying firm's motion for summary judgment, this court held, among other things, that there were genuine issues of material fact with respect to whether firm used developer's trade secrets. In making its decision, the court cited a Fifth Circuit opinion noting with approval that, under the Restatement Third of Unfair Competition, as a general matter, any exploitation of trade secrets that was likely to result in injury to the trade secret owner or enrichment to the defendant was "use" for purposes of a claim for misappropriation of trade secrets. Wellogix, Inc. v. Accenture, LLP, 788 F.Supp.2d 523, 540.

S.D.Tex.2010. Quot. in case quot. in ftn. Employer sued former employees for allegedly breaching noncompetition and nonsolicitation covenants contained in the parties' written employment agreements and using employer's trade secrets and proprietary information in setting up and operating a competing company. Denying summary judgment for employees on employer's claim for misappropriation of confidential, proprietary, and trade secret information, this court held that questions of fact remained as to whether employees took and used employer's pricing, business plan, financial, or other information determined by the court to be entitled to trade-secret protection. The court pointed to evidence that employees forwarded themselves e-mails containing employer's income/loss statements and reports, retained multiple boxes of documents containing employer's information, and only recently disclosed the existence of those materials. Rimkus Consulting Group, Inc. v. Cammarata, 688 F.Supp.2d 598, 666.

S.D.Tex.Bkrtcy.Ct.2014. Com. (c) quot. in case quot. in disc. (general cite). Claimant/manufacturer filed a proof of claim in Chapter 11 debtor's bankruptcy proceeding, alleging, inter alia, that debtor and its employees civilly conspired to misappropriate claimant's trade secrets. Debtor moved to estimate the claim, and filed an objection to the claim. This court found, among other things, that claimant failed to legally justify its request for multiple recovery of profits both affected and unaffected by the acquired trade secret as well as avoided costs, but was entitled to recover debtor's net profits earned using some of claimant's drawings. While the Fifth Circuit recently acknowledged the liberal construction of the term "use" of trade secrets contained in Restatement Third of Unfair Competition § 40, Comment *c*—which construed it as any exploitation of the trade secret that was likely to result in injury to the trade-secret owner or enrichment to the defendant—claimant in this case was not entitled to damages for debtor's sold, but unchanged parts and for claimant's drawings that debtor never exploited, because those trade secrets were useless to debtor. In re Mud King Products, Inc., 514 B.R. 496, 524.

W.D.Tex.Bkrtcy.Ct.2012. Com. (c) quot. in case quot. in sup. Chapter 11 debtor/oil and gas production company brought an adversary proceeding for, inter alia, misappropriation of trade secrets against potential prepetition buyer of its assets, alleging that defendant impermissibly used plaintiff's confidential information and trade secrets to acquire oil and gas leases in a hydrocarbon-rich area of south Texas. This court entered judgment for debtor on this claim, holding that: debtor's subsurface, production, and operations data qualified as trade secrets under the six-factor test of Restatement of Torts § 757, Comment *b*; defendant obtained those trade secrets through improper means—requesting and receiving debtor's secrets from debtor's employees and a contractor retained by debtor; and defendant used debtor's trade secrets in a way that was competitively disadvan-

For earlier citations, see the Appendices, Supplements, or Pocket Parts, if any, that correspond to the subject matter under examination.

tageous to debtor and benefited defendant. In re TXCO Resources, Inc., 475 B.R. 781, 820, 821.

E.D.Wis.2010. Com. (c) cit. and quot. in sup. Manufacturer of a safety vacuum release system (SVRS) for swimming pools sued motor manufacturer it asked to produce a pool pump motor for the SVRS, alleging misappropriation of trade secrets and other claims. Granting in part defendant's motion for partial summary judgment, this court held that plaintiff's claim for misappropriation of trade secrets was barred by the applicable Wisconsin statute of limitations, because plaintiff knew that defendant was "using" plaintiff's proprietary information more than three years before the parties' first tolling agreement; defendant had informed plaintiff that it had built a "prototype load sensor motor," which placed plaintiff on clear notice that it was employing plaintiff's proprietary information in manufacturing or producing a load sensor motor and relying on the information to assist and accelerate its research and development of a SVRS, a clear "use" of plaintiff's trade secrets. Fail-Safe LLC v. A.O. Smith Corp., 744 F.Supp.2d 831, 852, 853.

Cal.App.2010. Cit. in sup., com. (d) quot. in sup., Rptr's Note to com. (d) quot. in sup. Software developer that obtained a judgment against competitor for misappropriating trade secrets sued purchaser of competitor's software, alleging that defendant, by using competitor's software, misappropriated plaintiff's trade secret source code incorporated into that software. The trial court granted summary judgment for defendant. Affirming, this court held that plaintiff failed to establish that defendant had knowledge of the trade secrets at issue. The court noted the undisputed fact that defendant never possessed or had access to the source code and only had executable, machine-readable code compiled by its supplier from source code, and concluded that a defendant did not, by executing machine-readable software, "use" the underlying source code or acquire the requisite knowledge of any trade secrets embodied in that code. Silvaco Data Systems v. Intel Corp., 184 Cal.App.4th 210, 226, 109 Cal.Rptr.3d 27, 42.

Cal.App.2000. Coms. (c) and (d) cit. in disc. After former employees allegedly misappropriated former employer's trade secrets and used them in a new competing business, former employer and its parent corporation sued competitor's shareholders, officers, and directors for, in part, trade-secret misappropriation, seeking to hold defendants personally liable. Reversing the trial court's grant of summary judgment for defendants, this court held, inter alia, that genuine issues of material fact existed as to whether defendants knew, or had reason to know, of the alleged tortious acts when they invested in competitor, took control of it, and continued its operations. PMC, Inc. v. Kadisha, 78 Cal.App.4th 1368, 93 Cal.Rptr.2d 663, 673, 675.

Tex.2011. Cit. in ftn. to conc. op. Newspaper publishers sued Department of Public Safety under the Texas Public Information Act, seeking a writ of mandamus to compel complete disclosure of travel vouchers from the governor's security detail. The trial court issued the writ. The court of appeals affirmed. This court reversed and remanded, holding that the information sought might be protected from disclosure under the Act as "expressly confidential under other law [than the Act]," namely, the common-law right to be free from physical harm. The court concluded that some of the information in the vouchers could create a substantial threat of physical harm because it revealed specific details about the number of officers assigned to protect the governor, their general location in relation to him, and their dates of travel. The concurrence argued that, even if "other law" could include judicial decisions and the common law, the Act required that the "other law" declare the *information itself* confidential. As an example, the concurrence pointed to the law of trade secrets, under which the nature of the information itself was at issue. Texas Dept. of Public Safety v. Cox Texas Newspapers, L.P., 343 S.W.3d 112, 126.

Tex.App.2021. Com. (a) cit. in ftn. In an action by prospective seller of a hospital in Texas for unfair competition and other claims against California-based vice president of prospective buyer, who downloaded seller's sensitive information, this court, on interlocutory appeal, affirmed the trial court's grant of vice president's motion to dismiss for lack of personal jurisdiction. In making its decision, the court noted that seller did not specify the branch of unfair competition alleged, but that, under Restatement Third of Unfair Competition § 40, unfair competition could include torts

Cit.—cited; com.—comment; fol.—followed; sup.—support.
A complete list of abbreviations precedes page 1.

for misappropriation, infringement, unjust enrichment, and breach of confidence. Steward Health Care System LLC v. Saidara, 633 S.W.3d 120, 124.

Tex.App.2017. Com. (c) quot. in case quot. in sup. After the breakup of a limited partnership and the sale of its assets, general partner, among others, brought a lawsuit against limited partners and competitor that purchased partnership's assets at a foreclosure sale, alleging, inter alia, that limited partners' general manager used his position to acquire for competitor partnership's trade-secret cement-production data that had been invented by plaintiff. The trial court entered judgment for plaintiff. This court affirmed in part, holding that evidence supported the trial court's finding that defendants conspired to ensure that partnership's trade secrets were sold during the foreclosure sale of the partnership's assets to competitor. The court explained that, under Restatement Third of Unfair Competition § 40, Comment *c*, competitor's employment of plaintiff's manufacturing techniques that resulted in injury to partnership constituted "use" of the trade secret. Pike v. Texas EMC Management, LLC, 579 S.W.3d 390, 407.

Tex.App.2013. Cit. in ftn., cit. in cases cit. in ftn.; com. (c) quot. in sup. and cit. in case cit. in ftn. Inventor and owners of a process for mining potash (potassium-containing ore) in a specific area that had anomalously high temperatures brought claims for misappropriation of trade secrets, inter alia, against inventor's former business partner and partner's company's subsidiary, alleging that defendants used plaintiffs' proprietary information in developing their own mining project. The trial court entered judgment on a jury verdict for plaintiffs. Affirming, this court held, among other things, that, while plaintiffs acknowledged that defendants' operating plan did not copy plaintiffs' plan "in toto," defendants' plan was very similar and used major pieces of plaintiffs' plan. The court noted that use of any substantial portion of a trade secret was sufficient to subject the actor to liability, and that an actor was liable for using a trade secret with independently created improvement or modification if the result was substantially derived from the trade secret. Bishop v. Miller, 412 S.W.3d 758, 774.

Tex.App.2013. Com. (c) quot. in case quot. in sup. Petroleum engineer and geologist brought an action for, inter alia, misappropriation of a trade secret against oil-and-gas operator, alleging that defendant used plaintiffs' proprietary geological-and-engineering study, which identified several favorable prospects for the production of oil and gas from a specific lime formation, to plan their own drilling program at that specific location. The trial court entered judgment on a jury verdict for plaintiffs. Affirming in part, this court held that the evidence supported the jury's finding that plaintiffs' study was a trade secret. While the raw data used in the study was drawn from public or semi-public sources, the study involved a massive compilation and analysis requiring thousands of hours of work over a period of several years. Southwestern Energy Production Co. v. Berry-Helfand, 411 S.W.3d 581, 597.

Tex.App.2012. Cit. in disc., com. (c) quot. in sup. Natural-gas processor sued foreign limited-liability company, alleging theft of trade secrets. This court affirmed the trial court's denial of defendant's special appearance, holding that defendant had contacts with Texas out of which plaintiff's claim arose. The court concluded that defendant's use of plaintiff's trade secrets that allegedly occurred in Texas—i.e., defendant's marketing efforts and sales of products incorporating plaintiff's technology—was sufficient for liability, and thus defendant's Texas contacts were substantially connected to the operative facts of the litigation for purposes of establishing specific jurisdiction over defendant. Twister B.V. v. Newton Research Partners, LP, 364 S.W.3d 428, 438, 439.

Vt.2002. Cit. in sup., subsec. (b)(1) quot. in disc. Manufacturer brought suit for, in part, trade-secret misappropriation against competitor established by former employees. Affirming the trial court's entry of judgment for defendant, this court held, inter alia, that, because plaintiff failed to take steps to put employees on explicit or implicit notice that the information conveyed to them during their employment was to be kept confidential, defendants did not receive the information in confidence, did not breach their duty of confidence to plaintiff, and were not liable for misappropriation. Omega Optical, Inc. v. Chroma Technology Corp., 174 Vt. 10, 800 A.2d 1064, 1066, 1069.

Wash.1999. Com. (a) cit. in ftn. Employer sued former employees for trade-secret mis-

For earlier citations, see the Appendices, Supplements, or Pocket Parts, if any, that correspond to the subject matter under examination.

appropriation, alleging that the employees solicited its clients using confidential information. Trial court held that the employees had misappropriated the trade secrets. Appellate court affirmed in part and reversed in part. This court affirmed, holding, inter alia, that information which had been determined to be a trade secret did not lose its protected status because it had been committed to memory rather than taken in written form. Ed Nowogroski Ins., Inc. v. Rucker, 137 Wash.2d 427, 971 P.2d 936, 941.

§ **41. Duty of Confidence**

S.D.Ind.1998. Cit. in headnote, quot. in disc., subsec. (b) cit. in disc. Manufacturer/seller of oxygen regulators sued competitor for misappropriation of trade secrets. Denying plaintiff's request for injunctive relief, the court held, in part, that plaintiff did not show a likelihood of succeeding on the merits of its claim, as the information sought to be protected was readily ascertainable through reverse engineering of plaintiff's products, which had been on the market for some time; plaintiff failed to take reasonable steps to protect the confidentiality of the allegedly protected information; and defendant, to whom plaintiff once voluntarily disclosed the information at issue, never consented to keep it confidential. Flotec, Inc. v. Southern Research, Inc., 16 F.Supp.2d 992, 993, 1005-1006, 1006.

E.D.La.2018. Subsec. (b)(2) quot. in sup. Developer of a hydrate-remediation system used in the oil and gas industry sued competitor that worked with plaintiff to develop the system, alleging that defendant breached the parties' nondisclosure agreement by using plaintiff's confidential information for its own benefit. This court denied defendant's motion for summary judgment, holding that there were genuine disputes of fact as to whether the nondisclosure agreement covered confidential information that plaintiff disclosed to its contractors and clients without any restrictions as to use or distribution. The court noted that the agreement's exclusion of such information had a clear parallel in the law of trade secrets as set forth in Restatement Third of Unfair Competition § 41, which provided that voluntary disclosure of information destroyed its status as a trade secret, but that an owner of a trade secret would not lose the secret by disclosure to another if the owner created a duty in some manner and placed that duty upon the other not to disclose or use the secret. Wright's Well Control Services, LLC v. Oceaneering International, Inc., 292 F.Supp.3d 735, 747.

D.N.J.1998. Cit. and quot. in disc. A freight company acquired rights to computer programs through its affiliation with a Taiwan company. The Taiwan company was previously associated with a New Jersey cargo management company, and it had issued to the New Jersey company and its affiliates a license permitting the companies to make limited use of the software. When the Taiwan company became associated with the freight company, the limited license expired. The freight company sued the New Jersey company and its affiliates for copyright infringement, trade-secret misappropriation, and breach of contract, alleging wrongful use of the software after the license expired. This court denied the New Jersey company's motions for summary judgment, holding, inter alia, that plaintiff stated a viable trade-secret-misappropriation claim. In light of the relationships between the companies, as well as the nexus between these relationships and plaintiff's claim, a reasonable factfinder could hold the New Jersey defendant liable for the acts of its affiliates under general agency law. The nature of defendant's relationships with and control over the affiliates remained a fact issue for the jury. Expediters Intern. v. Direct Line Cargo Management, 995 F.Supp. 468, 481.

M.D.N.C.2002. Subsec. (d) quot. in disc. Supplier of aftermarket components and toner for remanufactured laser toner cartridges sued competitor, alleging that defendant tortiously interfered with a nondisclosure agreement signed by one of plaintiff's former employees hired away by defendant. Denying defendant's motion for summary judgment, this court held, inter alia, that plaintiff's interpretation of the agreement as being restricted to confidential information presented a genuine issue of material fact as to the scope of the nondisclosure agreement. Static Control Components, Inc. v. Darkprint Imaging, Inc., 200 F.Supp.2d 541, 549.

E.D.Wis.2010. Cit. and quot. in sup., cit. in ftn., subsec. (b)(1) cit. in sup. Manufacturer of a safety vacuum release system (SVRS) for swimming pools sued motor manufacturer it asked to produce a pool pump motor for the SVRS, alleging misap-

Cit.—cited; com.—comment; fol.—followed; sup.—support.
A complete list of abbreviations precedes page 1.

propriation of trade secrets and other claims. Granting defendant's motion for partial summary judgment on plaintiff's claim for misappropriation of trade secrets, this court held, among other things, that there was no evidence that a joint venture relationship existed between the parties such that defendant owed an implied duty of confidence to plaintiff; given that there was no agreement in place between the parties to engage in a joint venture, defendant had no reason to know that plaintiff's disclosure of information to defendant was intended to be in confidence. Fail-Safe LLC v. A.O. Smith Corp., 744 F.Supp.2d 831, 859, 860, 864.

Cal.2003. Com. (d) quot. in ftn. to conc. op. Trade association for motion-picture industry brought suit for injunctive relief against web-site operator's republication of source code for software designed to circumvent the encryption of movies stored on DVDs, alleging that defendant misappropriated trade secrets. The trial court issued a preliminary injunction. The court of appeal reversed. Reversing and remanding, this court held that the preliminary injunction did not violate defendant's free-speech rights under either the state or federal constitution. A concurring opinion argued that plaintiff did not establish a likelihood of prevailing on its trade-secret claim, noting that it was doubtful that the alleged trade secret, which was obtained through reverse engineering, was acquired by improper means. DVD Copy Control Association, Inc. v. Bunner, 31 Cal.4th 864, 901, 4 Cal.Rptr.3d 69, 101, 75 P.3d 1, 28, on remand 116 Cal.App.4th 241, 10 Cal.Rptr.3d 185 (2004).

Ind.App.2001. Subsec. (b) cit. in case cit. in disc. Auto-parts manufacturer sued former customer and others for misappropriation of trade secrets and interference with contractual relations. Trial court granted defendants summary judgment. This court affirmed, holding, inter alia, that trial court properly granted summary judgment on the misappropriation claims, because there was no protectible trade secret. Although plaintiff took some measures within its own company and with its own employees to protect the information contained in its shackle machines, it did very little to protect the information from outside sources; therefore, trial court could have found as a matter of law that plaintiff had not taken reasonable steps to maintain the secrecy of its proprietary information. Zemco Mfg., Inc. v. Navistar Intern. Transp. Corp., 759 N.E.2d 239, 247.

Iowa, 1999. Quot. in disc. Manufacturer of draft sensor devices sued competitor for tortious interference with contract, civil conspiracy, and misappropriation of trade secrets after two of plaintiff's employees resigned and went into business selling a similar item to defendant. The trial court entered judgment on a jury verdict for plaintiff on the claims for tortious interference and conspiracy. Affirming in part, reversing in part, and remanding, this court held that nondisclosure-confidentiality agreements and invention-assignment provisions executed by employees were reasonable and enforceable; that defendant was liable for tortious interference with these contracts; that plaintiff's recovery on its claim for civil conspiracy was duplicative of the damages awarded for tortious interference; and that defendant was not entitled to a pro tanto credit of a $60,000 settlement agreed to by plaintiff and employees, since the settlement involved claims for trademark and patent infringement and breach of contract. Revere Transducers, Inc. v. Deere & Co., 595 N.W.2d 751, 761.

Tex.2011. Cit. in ftn. to conc. op. Newspaper publishers sued Department of Public Safety under the Texas Public Information Act, seeking a writ of mandamus to compel complete disclosure of travel vouchers from the governor's security detail. The trial court issued the writ. The court of appeals affirmed. This court reversed and remanded, holding that the information sought might be protected from disclosure under the Act as "expressly confidential under other law [than the Act]," namely, the common-law right to be free from physical harm. The court concluded that some of the information in the vouchers could create a substantial threat of physical harm because it revealed specific details about the number of officers assigned to protect the governor, their general location in relation to him, and their dates of travel. The concurrence argued that, even if "other law" could include judicial decisions and the common law, the Act required that the "other law" declare the *information itself* confidential. As an example, the concurrence pointed to the law of trade secrets, under which the nature of the information itself was at issue. Texas Dept. of Public

For earlier citations, see the Appendices, Supplements, or Pocket Parts, if any, that correspond to the subject matter under examination.

Safety v. Cox Texas Newspapers, L.P., 343 S.W.3d 112, 126.

Tex.App.2018. Cit. in disc.; cit. in case cit. in ftn. (general cite). Distributor brought a lawsuit against manufacturer, manufacturer's subsidiary, and competitor, alleging, inter alia, that manufacturer misappropriated plaintiff's trade secrets, which had been given in confidence during negotiations for an exclusive distribution agreement, when manufacturer later established subsidiary as a distributor in the United States and entered into a distribution agreement with competitor. The trial court denied plaintiff's motion for temporary injunctive relief against defendants selling equipment in the United States. This court affirmed, holding that, although plaintiff established that there was a confidential relationship between it and manufacturer, the trial court reasonably could have concluded that plaintiff's information were not trade secrets. The court cited Restatement Third of Unfair Competition § 41 in defining "trade secrets" to not include customer lists if such information were publicly available; the court also noted that Restatement of Torts § 757 had been incorporated into Restatement Third of Unfair Competition § 41. Kana Energy Services, Inc. v. Jiangsu Jinshi Machinery Group Co. Ltd., 565 S.W.3d 347, 353.

Tex.App.2013. Com. (b) cit. in sup. Holders of a right of first refusal with respect to oil and gas prospects identified by development company sued former officer of company and related entities and individuals, alleging misappropriation of trade secrets and other claims, after defendants, acting without plaintiffs' knowledge, obtained a lease on a property identified in company's seismic map of a gas prospect. The trial court entered judgment on a jury verdict in favor of plaintiffs. Affirming, this court held that there was sufficient evidence to support the jury's finding that the map was, at all times, a trade secret, noting that plaintiffs acted to protect the map and that defendants' actions and secrecy confirmed their knowledge of the map's value. The court rejected defendants' argument that the map lost its status as a trade secret when plaintiffs showed the map to potential working-interest investors, noting that trade-secret status was not destroyed simply by showing a protected item to prospective buyers, customers, or licensees. Lamont v. Vaquillas Energy Lopeno Ltd., LLP, 421 S.W.3d 198, 212.

Vt.2002. Subsec. (b)(1) quot. in disc. Manufacturer brought suit for, in part, trade-secret misappropriation against competitor established by former employees. Affirming the trial court's entry of judgment for defendant, this court held, inter alia, that, because plaintiff failed to take steps to put employees on explicit or implicit notice that the information conveyed to them during their employment was to be kept confidential, defendants did not receive the information in confidence, did not breach their duty of confidence to plaintiff, and were not liable for misappropriation. Omega Optical, Inc. v. Chroma Technology Corp., 174 Vt. 10, 800 A.2d 1064, 1069.

Wis.2006. Cit. in ftn. to diss. op. Former employer sued former employee and his new employer for, in part, misappropriation of trade secrets and related common-law claims, alleging that, after resigning, employee used plaintiff's confidential information, including customer lists and pricing information, to solicit and acquire customers. The trial court granted summary judgment for defendants and the court of appeals affirmed. This court reversed in part and remanded, holding that, while the confidential information did not meet the definition of a trade secret provided in Wisconsin's trade-secret statute derived from the Uniform Trade Secrets Act (UTSA), plaintiff's common-law claims were not precluded by the statute. The dissent argued that plaintiff could not maintain common-law claims for misappropriation of confidential information that did not rise to the level of a trade secret in a UTSA state such as Wisconsin. Burbank Grease Services, LLC v. Sokolowski, 294 Wis.2d 274, 717 N.W.2d 781, 802.

§ 42. Breach of Confidence by Employees

C.A.3, 2021. Com. (g) quot. in ftn. Developer of pharmaceutical technology sued competitor and former employee, alleging that defendants misappropriated plaintiff's trade secrets to develop competing technology. The district court granted defendants' motion to dismiss. This court vacated and remanded, holding, inter alia, that plaintiff satisfactorily alleged a claim for statutory trade-secret misappropriation. The court noted that dismissal of plaintiff's trade-secrets claim was not necessarily fatal to its other claims, because, under Restatement Third of Unfair Competition § 42, Comment *g*, defendants could have

Cit.—cited; com.—comment; fol.—followed; sup.—support.
A complete list of abbreviations precedes page 1.

also incurred liability if their conduct violated confidentiality agreements that more broadly defined what constituted confidential information, but plaintiffs failed to challenge the dismissal of those claims on such grounds. Oakwood Laboratories LLC v. Thanoo, 999 F.3d 892, 904.

Ill.App.1995. Quot. in disc. Former employer sued former employee, seeking enforcement of a covenant not to compete. Reversing the trial court's dismissal of the complaint, this court held that the noncompetition covenant signed by defendant, who had been employed by plaintiff under an oral at-will employment agreement for a period of several years, was ancillary to the primary purpose of the ongoing employment relationship and thus was enforceable. Abel v. Fox, 274 Ill.App.3d 811, 211 Ill.Dec. 129, 135, 654 N.E.2d 591, 597.

Ind.App.2004. Cit. in case cit. in sup., cit. generally in sup., com. (e) quot. in sup. Motor repair shop sued its former employee and the competitor that hired former employee, alleging violation of the Indiana Uniform Trade Secret Act (IUTSA), statutory conversion, and breach of fiduciary duty. Trial court entered judgment for defendants. This court reversed, holding, inter alia, that former employee's compilation of servo motor repair data was owned by plaintiff and was entitled to trade-secret protection under IUTSA. The court stated that data compilation fell squarely within the scope of a servo motor repair technician's assigned duties, and that all information assembled in data compilation was obtained during former employee's working hours at plaintiff's shop, even though former employee compiled data in his home computer on his own time. Northern Elec. Co., Inc. v. Torma, 819 N.E.2d 417, 422, 423.

Iowa, 2008. Coms. (b) and (c) cit. in sup., com. (d) cit. in disc. and quot. in sup. Manufacturer of cement mixers sued former employees, competitor, competitor's officers, and customer, alleging misappropriation of trade secrets, inter alia. The trial court granted summary judgment for defendants. Reversing and remanding as to former employees and competitor and its officers, this court held that genuine issues of material fact existed as to whether former employees took advantage of their positions with plaintiff to obtain proprietary information that was then used for competitor's benefit, and as to whether competitor and its officers used their positions as potential buyers of plaintiff's business to obtain plaintiff's proprietary information for their own benefit. Cemen Tech, Inc. v. Three D Industries, L.L.C., 753 N.W.2d 1, 7, 8.

N.Y.Sup.Ct.App.Div.2001. Com. (e) cit. in disc. Former employee of an investment firm formed his own company, which sued other firms for misappropriation of trade secrets that former employee allegedly developed to be used in designing a new kind of complex financial transaction while he was employed by firm. Trial court granted defendants' motion to dismiss. This court affirmed, holding that the alleged trade secrets were created by former employee while acting within the scope of his assigned duties as an employee of a firm responsible for designing and promoting investment banking transactions, and any such trade secrets were therefore owned by the employers ab initio. Pullman Group, LLC. v. Prudential Ins. Co. of America, 288 A.D.2d 2, 733 N.Y.S.2d 1, 2.

Or.App.2021. Com. (f) quot. in sup and. in ftn. Heavy-machinery seller sued former employee and competitor, alleging that defendants misappropriated plaintiff's trade secrets when former employee divulged the identities of plaintiff's customers upon obtaining employment with competitor. The trial court granted defendants' motion for summary judgment. This court affirmed, holding that the identities of plaintiff's customers did not constitute trade secrets, because heavy-machinery dealers in plaintiff's geographic region knew who its customers were. Citing Restatement Third of Unfair Competition § 42, the court explained that solicitation of plaintiff's customers by plaintiff's competitors demonstrated that the identities of the customers constituted readily ascertainable information, and noted that, barring an express agreement between former employee and plaintiff to the contrary, former employee could solicit plaintiff's customers upon leaving plaintiff's employ. Peterson Machinery Co. v. May, 496 P.3d 672, 680-683.

Tenn.App.2001. Com. (b) cit. in case cit. in disc. Former employer brought action seeking injunctive relief against ex-employee and his company, alleging that employee had violated confidentiality agreement by developing bone-void filler to compete with product produced by employer. Trial court initially issued tempo-

For earlier citations, see the Appendices, Supplements, or Pocket Parts, if any, that correspond to the subject matter under examination.

rary restraining order, but, following hearing, it dissolved injunction. Affirming, this court held, inter alia, that, similar to common-law principles, the agreement between employee and employer prohibited employee from using or disclosing employer's confidential information, but did not apply to publicly available information; although some information employer sought to protect was of the type that could be deemed confidential, majority of it was not entitled to protection. Wright Medical Technology, Inc. v. Grisoni, 135 S.W.3d 561, 588.

Vt.2002. Cit. in sup., com. (b) cit. in sup., com. (c) quot. in sup. Manufacturer brought suit for, in part, trade-secret misappropriation against competitor established by former employees. Affirming the trial court's entry of judgment for defendant, this court held, inter alia, that, because plaintiff failed to take steps to put employees on explicit or implicit notice that the information conveyed to them during their employment was to be kept confidential, defendants did not receive the information in confidence, did not breach their duty of confidence to plaintiff, and were not liable for misappropriation. Omega Optical, Inc. v. Chroma Technology Corp., 174 Vt. 10, 800 A.2d 1064, 1066.

Wash.1999. Cit. generally in sup. and ftn., coms. (b) and (c) cit. in sup. and headnote, com. (f) quot. in sup. Employer sued former employees for trade-secret misappropriation, alleging that the employees solicited its clients using confidential information. Trial court held that the employees had misappropriated the trade secrets. Appellate court affirmed in part and reversed in part. This court affirmed, holding, inter alia, that information which had been determined to be a trade secret did not lose its protected status because it had been committed to memory rather than taken in written form. Ed Nowogroski Ins., Inc. v. Rucker, 137 Wash.2d 427, 971 P.2d 936, 942, 944, 945.

§ 43. Improper Acquisition of Trade Secrets

C.A.3, 2016. Quot. in sup.; com. (c) quot. in sup. Communications-equipment manufacturer brought, inter alia, a claim for unfair competition against its former contractor, alleging that defendant took action to directly compete with plaintiff by improperly gaining access to plaintiff's communications systems, soliciting plaintiff's former employees, and using information defendant learned when it was plaintiff's contractor. The district court granted defendant's motion for judgment as a matter of law. Vacating, this court held that plaintiff presented sufficient evidence to support a reasonable jury finding that there was unfair competition under a misappropriation theory. The court cited Restatement Third of Unfair Competition § 43 in providing a nonexhaustive list of conduct that constituted improper means of acquiring a trade secret, and concluded that, here, a jury could find that defendant's methods of gaining proprietary information constituted misappropriation. Avaya Inc., RP v. Telecom Labs, Inc., 838 F.3d 354, 387.

C.A.5, 2013. Quot. in ftn. Defendant was convicted after a jury trial in district court for perjury and conspiracy to steal trade secrets concerning the manufacture of a type of chlorinated polyethylene (CPE) developed by his former employer. Affirming, this court held that, while the district court erred in excluding the testimony of defendant's engineering expert, which suggested that portions of employer's manufacturing process were in the public domain and were not trade secrets, that error did not affect the verdict and thus was harmless, because the relevant inquiry in a conspiracy case was not whether the information at issue was actually a trade secret, but whether the defendant believed the information to be a trade secret, and there was overwhelming evidence that defendant and his co-conspirators stole trade secrets and that defendant believed that he was stealing trade secrets. The court noted that, even though independent discovery and analysis of publicly available products were not improper means of acquiring information, a trade-secret owner retained protection against an improper acquisition, disclosure, or use. U.S. v. Wen Chyu Liu, 716 F.3d 159, 170.

C.A.5, 2013. Cit. in case quot. in sup. Developer of complex-services software for oil companies sued consulting firm, alleging that defendant misappropriated its trade secrets. The district court entered judgment on a jury verdict for plaintiff. Affirming, this court held that reasonable jurors could have found that defendant misappropriated plaintiff's trade secrets under Texas law. The court concluded that sufficient evidence existed to support the

Cit.—cited; com.—comment; fol.—followed; sup.—support.
A complete list of abbreviations precedes page 1.

jury's finding that defendant improperly acquired plaintiff's trade secrets, pointing out that plaintiff entered into six confidential marketing agreements with defendant; that, through the marketing agreements, defendant had access to plaintiff's trade secrets; that defendant also had access to plaintiff's trade secrets uploaded to a confidential online portal; and that defendant's email referenced "harvesting IP" from plaintiff. Wellogix, Inc. v. Accenture, L.L.P., 716 F.3d 867, 876.

C.A.7, 2006. Com. (c) cit. in sup. Parent company of manufacturer brought suit under the state trade-secrets statute against competing business formed by engineer who had worked for manufacturer as an independent contractor. The district court granted summary judgment for defendant. Vacating and remanding, this court held, inter alia, that engineer did not acquire any rights in manufacturer's trade-secret data just because he used those data in the performance of his duties, and that fact issues as to whether engineer was aware that manufacturer treated at least some of the data it provided as trade secrets, and whether engineer disclosed or improperly used manufacturer's confidential information precluded summary judgment. Hicklin Engineering, L.C. v. Bartell, 439 F.3d 346, 349.

S.D.Ind.1998. Cit. in disc. Manufacturer/seller of oxygen regulators sued competitor for misappropriation of trade secrets. Denying plaintiff's request for injunctive relief, the court held, in part, that plaintiff did not show a likelihood of succeeding on the merits of its claim, as the information sought to be protected was readily ascertainable through reverse engineering of plaintiff's products, which had been on the market for some time; plaintiff failed to take reasonable steps to protect the confidentiality of the allegedly protected information; and defendant, to whom plaintiff once voluntarily disclosed the information at issue, never consented to keep it confidential. Flotec, Inc. v. Southern Research, Inc., 16 F.Supp.2d 992, 1000, 1001.

S.D.Iowa, 2020. Com. (d) quot. in case quot. in sup. Seller of packaged deli products sued competitor and former employee who began working for competitor after leaving plaintiff, alleging, among other things, that defendants misappropriated plaintiff's trade secrets, including the terms of its program agreements with retail and wholesale customers. This court granted plaintiff's request for a preliminary injunction, holding that plaintiff had demonstrated a fair chance of prevailing on its claim for trade-secret misappropriation under Iowa law. The court reasoned, in part, that the evidence suggested that defendants employed improper means of acquiring the program terms within the meaning of Restatement Third of Unfair Competition § 43, because employee appeared to have obtained the information in violation of the nondisclosure and confidentiality agreements he had signed with plaintiff. Smithfield Packaged Meats Sales Corp. v. Dietz & Watson, Inc., 452 F.Supp.3d 843, 858.

S.D.Iowa, 2009. Com. (d) quot. in case quot. in sup. Employer, a provider of lease equipment financing, sued former employee, alleging that defendant misappropriated plaintiff's trade secrets when he, together with his new corporation, used plaintiff's customer spreadsheet to book leases on behalf of a competitor. Entering judgment for plaintiff on the misappropriation claim, this court held that plaintiff's customer spreadsheet, which contained potential customers' names, addresses, Social Security numbers, and a credit evaluation performed by plaintiff's employees, and was prepared using a proprietary formula to determine how much credit a potential leasing customer could receive from plaintiff, could legally be considered a trade secret; plaintiff did not release this information to the public because it would give competitors an advantage knowing the precise terms on which plaintiff would be willing to extend credit to potential leasing customers. NCMIC Finance Corp. v. Artino, 638 F.Supp.2d 1042, 1077.

S.D.Tex.2010. Cit. in case quot. in sup. Developers of algorithms to maximize yields for natural gas and oil reservoirs brought, inter alia, a claim for misappropriation of trade secrets against various corporations and individuals, alleging that, after defendants falsely represented that they were interested in collaborating with plaintiffs to develop software using plaintiffs' algorithms, they instead incorporated into their own software the proprietary information that plaintiffs revealed. Denying defendants' motion to dismiss that claim, this court held that, since plaintiffs alleged that defendants obtained the algorithms by fraud, they sufficiently alleged that the trade secrets were discovered by improper means; additionally, plaintiffs sufficiently alleged that defendants "used" the trade secrets to derive a profit, and that they were damaged as a result. Terra Nova Sciences, LLC v. JOA Oil and Gas Houston, LLC, 738 F.Supp.2d 689, 696.

Conn.1999. Quot. in conc. and diss. op. Cheese manufacturer sued its former accountant and the accountant's new cheesemaking company for breach of fiduciary duty, misappropriation of trade secrets, misrepresentation, and conversion, among other claims. Trial court granted plaintiff injunctive relief and awarded damages, holding that plaintiff's cheesemaking process was entitled to protection under the trade secrets act. This court affirmed, holding, inter alia, that the trial court properly found plaintiff's business operations—from the specific sources and costs of its supplies, through the production of its cheese, to the distribution of its product to three specific customers and the prices charged to them—to be a protectable trade secret. Furthermore, plaintiff's trade secret derived independent economic value from not being generally known to those, such as defendants, who could profit from the knowledge of it. Concurring and dissenting opinion argued that plaintiff's production methods or lists of suppliers and customers were not trade secrets. Elm City Cheese Company, Inc. v. Federico, 251 Conn. 59, 752 A.2d 1037, 1060.

Iowa, 2008. Coms. (c) and (d) quot. in sup. Manufacturer of cement mixers sued former employees, competitor, competitor's officers, and customer, alleging misappropriation of trade secrets, inter alia. The trial court granted summary judgment for defendants. Reversing and remanding as to former employees and competitor and its officers, this court held that genuine issues of material fact existed as to whether former employees took advantage of their positions with plaintiff to obtain proprietary information that was then used for competitor's benefit, and as to whether competitor and its officers used their positions as potential buyers of plaintiff's business to obtain plaintiff's proprietary information for their own benefit. Cemen Tech, Inc. v. Three D Industries, L.L.C., 753 N.W.2d 1, 10, 11.

Tex.App.2013. Cit. and quot. in sup., com. (c) quot. in sup. Holders of a right of first refusal with respect to oil and gas prospects identified by development company sued former officer of company and related entities and individuals, alleging misappropriation of trade secrets and other claims, after defendants, acting without plaintiffs' knowledge, obtained a lease on a property identified in company's seismic map of a gas prospect. The trial court entered judgment on a jury verdict for plaintiffs. The trial court entered judgment on a jury verdict in favor of plaintiffs. Affirming, this court held that there was sufficient evidence to support the jury's finding that defendants' knowledge of the gas beneath the property was obtained through the unauthorized use of the map. The court pointed to evidence that defendants did not conduct any independent seismic research and that any well placement would be highly speculative without such research, but that defendants nevertheless bid over $1 million to lease the property, drilled wells on it, and drained the gas reservoir within six months. Lamont v. Vaquillas Energy Lopeno Ltd., LLP, 421 S.W.3d 198, 213, 215.

Tex.App.2013. Quot. in disc. Petroleum engineer and geologist brought an action for, inter alia, misappropriation of a trade secret against oil-and-gas operator, alleging that defendant used plaintiffs' proprietary geological-and-engineering study, which identified several favorable prospects for the production of oil and gas from a specific lime formation, to plan their own drilling program at that specific location. The trial court entered judgment on a jury verdict for plaintiffs. Affirming in part, this court held that, while it was unnecessary for the trial court to have instructed the jury that a defendant misappropriated a trade secret if he or she disclosed or used it after learning about it by improper means, the inclusion of that information, as well as the definition of "improper means," in the jury instruction was harmless. The court noted that there was no dispute that plaintiffs disclosed their proprietary information to defendant pursuant to a confidentiality agreement. Southwestern Energy Production Co. v. Berry-Helfand, 411 S.W.3d 581, 607, 608.

Tex.App.2007. Cit. in ftn. Manufacturer of fiberglass utility bodies and toppers for commercial vehicles sued competitor for, in part, tortious interference with prospective business relations, alleging that defen-

Cit.—cited; com.—comment; fol.—followed; sup.—support.
A complete list of abbreviations precedes page 1.

dant's use of plaintiff's design drawings to create a stair-step topper for one of plaintiff's existing customers was independently tortious on the ground of trade-secret misappropriation. The trial court denied defendant's no-evidence motion for summary judgment on the tortious-interference claim. Affirming that portion of the decision, this court held, inter alia, that there was evidence that defendant misappropriated the design drawings because, by obtaining the drawings from plaintiff's customer, which was aware that the drawings were confidential, it discovered the drawings by improper means. Astoria Industries of Iowa, Inc. v. SNF, Inc., 223 S.W.3d 616, 636, 637.

§ 44. Injunctions: Appropriation of Trade Secrets

C.A.3, 2007. Quot. in sup. Employer sued former employee who left employer to work for competitor, seeking, among other things, an injunction to enforce a one-year covenant not to compete. The district court granted in part defendant's motion to dismiss, without explicitly denying plaintiff's motion for an injunction. Vacating the dismissal, reinstating plaintiff's motion, and remanding, this court held, inter alia, that it had interlocutory jurisdiction because the district court had effectively denied plaintiff injunctive relief. The court noted that, while injunctive relief was potentially available for plaintiff's surviving claim alleging misappropriation of trade secrets, under Pennsylvania law, a broader injunction of the type sought by plaintiff was only available for such claims when it was virtually impossible for an employee to perform his duties for a new employer without in effect giving it the benefit of his confidential information. Victaulic Co. v. Tieman, 499 F.3d 227, 234.

C.A.7, 2011. Cit. in disc. S corporation and its shareholders challenged the issue of deficiency notices by the Commissioner of Internal Revenue following Commissioner's finding that settlement income that corporation received in an underlying trade secrets misappropriation suit should have been taxed as ordinary income, rather than long-term capital gain. The tax court agreed with Commissioner and ordered deficiency judgments. Affirming, this court rejected plaintiffs' argument that the settlement was payment for damage to corporation's trade secrets, which it alleged were capital assets, holding that, because corporation's litigation strategy had been to seek profits and other types of monetary recovery that could properly be taxed as ordinary income, and not to focus on the damage to or destruction of its capital asset, the settlement was not in lieu of a replacement of capital, and was properly identified as ordinary income. Freda v. C.I.R., 656 F.3d 570, 574.

C.A.11, 2021. Com. (f) cit. in sup. Seller of software for processing alcohol-sales invoices sued competitor, alleging misappropriation of trade secrets. The district court entered judgment on a jury verdict awarding plaintiff compensatory and punitive damages but denied plaintiff's request for a permanent injunction that would broadly prohibit defendant from using either company's software. This court affirmed in part, holding that the district court correctly refused plaintiff's requested injunction against defendant. The court explained that, under Restatement Third of Unfair Competition § 44, in the trade-secret context, an injunction had to be time-limited and could last only until the defendant could have acquired the trade-secret information by proper means. Financial Information Technologies, LLC v. iControl Systems, USA, LLC, 21 F.4th 1267, 1280.

Ct.Fed.Cl.2011. Cit. in ftn. Munitions-assembly-systems manufacturer sued the United States, alleging that the U.S. Air Force breached the parties' cooperative research and development agreement by releasing plaintiff's proprietary information to unauthorized recipients, including its competitors. After this court entered judgment for plaintiff on liability, it awarded plaintiff damages for the loss of its proprietary information as an income-producing asset, concluding that plaintiff showed that the damages it sought were foreseeable and caused by the Air Force's breach of the agreement. The court noted that, at least in the private sector, a party threatened by the breach of a confidentiality agreement could sometimes obtain an injunction preventing the disclosure, but that presumably was not the case with a contract with the government, as specific performance of such an agreement was not an available remedy. Spectrum Sciences and Software, Inc. v. U.S., 98 Fed.Cl. 8, 17.

D.Me.2004. Com. (d) cit. in ftn. Developer of automated trading program sued custom software company and its owner for misappropriating its trade secret and violating the parties' nondisclosure agreement. After

For earlier citations, see the Appendices, Supplements, or Pocket Parts, if any, that correspond to the subject matter under examination.

the jury returned a verdict against defendant owner, plaintiff moved for injunctive relief, seeking, in part, to permanently enjoin defendant from all programming of any automated trading systems. Granting in part plaintiff's motion, the court held, inter alia, that plaintiff was entitled to an injunction prohibiting defendant from using plaintiff's computer program or its concepts; however, an injunction barring defendant from all programming of automated trading systems was broader than the terms of the nondisclosure agreement and was not warranted. Pearl Investments, LLC v. Standard I/O, Inc., 297 F.Supp.2d 335, 338.

E.D.Mo.2000. Cit. in disc., subsec. (3) quot. in part in disc. Inventor of surgical cable device sued competitor for, inter alia, misappropriation of trade secrets. After the jury returned a verdict awarding plaintiff $700,000 in actual damages, plaintiff moved for injunctive relief, seeking to prevent defendant from making or selling its invention for a period of 28 months. Denying the motion, the court held that the damages award represented the amount the jury believed would fairly compensate plaintiff for the harm caused by defendant's actions, and therefore injunctive relief against defendant's future sales would be duplicative of the legal remedy already elected. Whiteside Biomechanics v. Sofamor Danek Group, 88 F.Supp.2d 1009, 1019, affirmed 13 Fed.Appx. 950 (Fed. Cir.2001).

E.D.Va.2015. Com. (b) cit. in sup.; com. (c) cit. and quot. in ftn. Government contractor brought a claim in state court for misappropriation of trade secrets, inter alia, against competitor; defendant removed the case to federal court, asserting federal-question jurisdiction. This court granted plaintiff's motion to remove the case back to state court, holding that federal-question jurisdiction did not exist here because the complaint asserted exclusively state-law claims that did not depend on federal law. The court rejected defendant's argument that federal-question jurisdiction was proper because one of plaintiff's requested remedies was disqualification of defendant as a bidder in a federal contract, and, referring to a state court's ability to order injunctive relief in misappropriation-of-trade-secret cases under Restatement Third of Unfair Competition § 44, the court noted that the remedy sought by plaintiff was not a matter solely within the province of a federal court. Aegis Defense Services, LLC v. Chenega-Patriot Group, LLC, 141 F.Supp.3d 479, 484-485.

E.D.Va.2012. Subsec. (2) cit. and quot. in sup., com. (d) quot. in disc. Manufacturer of para-aramid fibers used to make body armor and other products, sued competitor, alleging misappropriation of trade secrets in violation of the Virginia Uniform Trade Secrets Act. The jury returned a verdict for plaintiff and awarded it compensatory and punitive damages. This court granted plaintiff's subsequent motion for a permanent injunction, holding that it was appropriate for the injunction—which prohibited defendant's production of any para-aramid fiber for 20 years, its use of plaintiff's trade secrets, and its disclosure of the trade secrets within its organization or otherwise, and required defendant to return the stolen secrets to plaintiff—to apply extraterritorially and be worldwide in scope. The court noted that several authorities supported the proposition that geographical limitations on the scope of injunctive relief in trade-secret cases were ordinarily inappropriate. E.I. DuPont de Nemours and Co. v. Kolon Industries, Inc., 894 F.Supp.2d 691, 713-716.

Cal.App.2004. Com. (c) quot. in sup. Trade association of motion-picture, computer, and consumer-electronics industries, which licensed content-scrambling system designed to prevent unauthorized use of digital versatile disks on players or drives that did not contain association's decryption technology, sought injunction against website operators to prevent disclosure of alleged trade secret that unscrambled encryption technology. Trial court issued preliminary injunction. On remand, this court reversed, holding, inter alia, that evidence failed to show that plaintiff would suffer irreparable harm if injunction against disclosure of information was not issued where the information had already become public knowledge. DVD Copy Control Ass'n, Inc. v. Bunner, 116 Cal.App. 4th 241, 254, 10 Cal.Rptr.3d 185, 194.

Mass.2021. Cit. in sup. Law firm sued competing firm and former nonequity employees who left law firm to form competing firm, alleging that defendants stole plaintiff's proprietary materials, including its research library, electronic databases, and administrative materials. After a jury found defendants liable for conversion and other claims, the trial court issued a permanent injunction enjoining defendants from using plaintiff's research library and electronic databases only. This court reversed in part and remanded, holding that the trial court abused its discretion by excluding plaintiff's administrative files from the scope of the permanent injunction. The court cited Restatement Third of Unfair Competition § 44 in reasoning that, by allowing defendants to continue to use plaintiff's administrative files, the trial court improperly permitted them to continue to benefit from their theft. Governo Law Firm LLC v. Bergeron, 166 N.E.3d 416, 427.

Mass.App.2011. Subsec. (2) cit. in sup. Developer of an innovative method to produce a specialized encapsulant used in making solar cells sued competitor and former employee who left to work for competitor, alleging misappropriation of trade secrets and other claims. The trial court found in favor of plaintiff and permanently enjoined defendants from using plaintiff's trade-secret manufacturing process. Affirming, this court held that a permanent injunction against the use of a trade secret manufacturing process was not unreasonable merely because it was permanent. The court noted that plaintiff's method had not entered the public domain and that it was not susceptible of "reverse engineering." Specialized Technology Resources, Inc. v. JPS Elastomerics Corp., 80 Mass.App.Ct. 841, 848, 957 N.E.2d 1116, 1122.

Mass.App.1993. Subsec. (2) cit. in sup., com. (c) quot. in sup. (citing § 44 of T.D. No. 4, 1993. § 44 has since been revised; see Official Text). The operators of a billiard parlor sued for injunctive relief to prevent a competitor from opening, alleging unfair trade practices and theft of trade secrets. This court, affirming the trial court's grant of an injunction only preventing the competitor from revealing financial information including accounting procedures obtained from the plaintiffs, held, inter alia, that enjoining the competitor from owning and operating a billiard parlor would have been inappropriate, in light of the public interest in competition and the lack of evidence that plaintiffs would suffer harm from the opening of a competing establishment. Jillian's Billiard v. Beloff Billiards, 35 Mass.App.Ct. 372, 376, 619 N.E.2d 635, 638-639.

§ 45. Monetary Relief: Appropriation of Trade Secrets

C.A.2, 2017. Cit. in disc., cit. in cases cit. in disc. and in ftn.; com. (d) cit. in disc.; com. (f) and Rptr's Note to com. (f) quot. in disc. Employer sued competitor and three former employees who left to work for competitor, alleging misappropriation of trade secrets, unfair competition, and unjust enrichment in violation of New York law. The district court entered judgment on a jury verdict awarding employer damages. While affirming the judgment as to liability, this court certified to the New York Court of Appeals the question of whether, under New York law, a plaintiff asserting claims for misappropriation of trade secrets, unfair competition, and unjust enrichment could recover damages that were measured by the costs the defendant avoided due to its unlawful activity. The court noted that, although Restatement Third of Unfair Competition § 45 appeared to support the avoided-costs approach, it was unclear whether the Restatement accurately described New York law with respect to calculating damages in trade-secret and unfair-competition cases. E.J. Brooks Company v. Cambridge Security Seals, 858 F.3d 744, 749, 750.

C.A.2, 1998. Com. (f) quot. in disc. Computer-software company sued competitor for misappropriation of trade secrets. Following a bench trial, the district court entered judgment for plaintiff in the amount of $14 million. Affirming in part and vacating in part, this court held, inter alia, that the damages award was too great, and that, under the reasonable royalty rule, plaintiff was entitled to damages in the amount of $7.7 million. Vermont Microsystems, Inc. v. Autodesk, Inc., 138 F.3d 449, 450.

C.A.3, 2016. Quot. in ftn. Communications-equipment manufacturer brought, inter alia, a claim for unfair competition against its former contractor, alleging that defendant took action to directly compete with plaintiff by improperly gaining access to plaintiff's communications systems, soliciting plaintiff's former employees, and using information defendant learned when it was plaintiff's contractor. The district court granted defendant's motion for judgment as a matter of law. Vacating, this court held that plaintiff presented sufficient evidence to support a reasonable jury finding that there was unfair competition under a misappropriation theory. The court noted that New Jersey law, like Restatement Third of Unfair Competition

For earlier citations, see the Appendices, Supplements, or Pocket Parts, if any, that correspond to the subject matter under examination.

§ 45, allowed recovery under a disgorgement theory in cases of unfair competition, and that, here, plaintiff could show damages under either a lost-profit theory or a disgorgement theory. Avaya Inc., RP v. Telecom Labs, Inc., 838 F.3d 354, 387.

C.A.5, 2010. Com. (f) cit. and quot. but not fol. Owner of copyrighted software sued former customer, after a group of defendant's employees obtained a copy of plaintiff's software from an unknown source and used it without authorization. The district court entered judgment on a jury verdict in favor of plaintiff. This court reversed as to plaintiff's claims for misappropriation of trade secrets and unfair competition and rendered a take-nothing judgment for plaintiff, holding that, while plaintiff demonstrated defendant's total revenue, it failed to deduct unrelated revenue and costs to demonstrate defendant's profits related to the infringement. The court rejected plaintiff's argument that its exhibit showing total revenue satisfied its burden of proof with regard to defendant's "sales" and that defendant subsequently had the burden of demonstrating which portions of its revenue were not attributable to the state-law claims, concluding that the Texas Supreme Court would not adopt the burden-shifting procedures of Restatement Second of Torts § 45, Comment *f*. MGE UPS Systems, Inc. v. GE Consumer and Indus., Inc., 622 F.3d 361, 369, 370.

C.A.6, 2022. Coms. (b) and (c) quot. in sup.; com. (d) quot. in sup. and in diss. op.; illus. 2 quot. in diss. op. Dietary-supplement developer sued customer, alleging that defendant misappropriated plaintiff's trade secrets regarding broccoli-seed extracts by hiring plaintiff's former employee, who provided plaintiff's confidential research and development information to defendant, and used it to create competing broccoli supplement products. The district court entered judgment on a jury verdict for plaintiff. This court affirmed, holding, inter alia, that plaintiff was entitled to restitution damages and compensatory damages, including partial research and development costs. Citing Restatement Third of Unfair Competition § 45, the court explained that plaintiff's recovery included costs that defendant avoided by misappropriating plaintiff's research information. The dissent argued that § 45 did not entitle plaintiff to damages arising from research and development unless the trade secrets were destroyed by public disclosure, and here, the record did not indicate that defendant's misappropriation caused such destruction. Caudill Seed & Warehouse Co., Inc. v. Jarrow Formulas, Inc., 53 F.4th 368, 387, 390, 392, 396.

C.A.7, 2011. Cit. in disc. S corporation and its shareholders challenged the issue of deficiency notices by the Commissioner of Internal Revenue following Commissioner's finding that settlement income that corporation received in an underlying trade secrets misappropriation suit should have been taxed as ordinary income, rather than long-term capital gain. The tax court agreed with Commissioner and ordered deficiency judgments. Affirming, this court rejected plaintiffs' argument that the settlement was payment for damage to corporation's trade secrets, which it alleged were capital assets, holding that, because corporation's litigation strategy had been to seek profits and other types of monetary recovery that could properly be taxed as ordinary income, and not to focus on the damage to or destruction of its capital asset, the settlement was not in lieu of a replacement of capital, and was properly identified as ordinary income. Freda v. C.I.R., 656 F.3d 570, 574, 575.

C.A.10, 2014. Com. (g) quot. in sup. Computer-software company brought an action for trade-secret misappropriation against former director of the company, alleging that, after defendant had a falling out with his colleagues, he stole the computer source code on which company's products depended and shared it with a rival company that quickly produced a competing software product. The district court entered judgment on a jury verdict awarding plaintiff damages of $2.92 million on a theory of reasonable-royalty damages. Affirming, this court held, inter alia, that Utah's trade-secret statute, which governed defendant's case, expressly allowed a reasonable-royalty-measure of damages when the misappropriator used or disclosed the trade secret, even where, as here, he never used the secret for his own personal profit. The court further held that the amount of the award was not unreasonable as a matter of law, because the jury could reasonably have found that defendant assumed for himself a license that allowed him the right to share the trade secret with a rival, and to permit (if not compel) its commercial exploitation by that rival, leav-

Cit.—cited; com.—comment; fol.—followed; sup.—support.
A complete list of abbreviations precedes page 1.

ing the remaining financial value of the (former) secret seriously compromised. Storagecraft Technology Corp. v. Kirby, 744 F.3d 1183, 1185, 1186, 1189.

C.A.10, 2008. Com. (d) cit. in disc., com. (g) quot. in sup. Inventor sued manufacturer of medical devices, alleging that it misappropriated his trade secrets and breached a confidentiality agreement by incorporating his inventions into one of its medical devices after the parties failed to reach a license agreement regarding the inventions. The district court entered judgment on a jury verdict for plaintiff. Affirming, this court held, inter alia, that the district court did not err in allowing plaintiff to recoup unjust-enrichment damages against defendant; while the unjust-enrichment award put plaintiff in a much better position than if he had entered a licensing agreement with defendant, under Utah law, defendant, as the party that acted wrongfully, had to assume the risk it took by misappropriating rather than licensing plaintiff's trade secrets. The court also noted that unjust-enrichment awards could in these circumstances serve a legitimate deterrent function. Russo v. Ballard Medical Products, 550 F.3d 1004, 1021.

Ct.Fed.Cl.2011. Com. (d) quot. in ftn. Munitions-assembly-systems manufacturer sued the United States, alleging that the U.S. Air Force breached the parties' cooperative research and development agreement by releasing plaintiff's proprietary information to unauthorized recipients, including its competitors. After this court entered judgment for plaintiff on liability, it awarded plaintiff damages for the loss of its proprietary information as an income-producing asset, concluding that plaintiff showed that the damages it sought were foreseeable and caused by the Air Force's breach of the agreement. The court pointed out the distinction between recovering, on the one hand, the value of a lost income-generating asset, as here, and, on the other, expectation damages in the form of lost profits, and noted that the Restatement Third of Competition recognized a similar distinction with respect to the monetary relief appropriate for the tort of trade-secret appropriation. Spectrum Sciences and Software, Inc. v. U.S., 98 Fed.Cl. 8, 15.

N.D.Cal.2018. Com. (f) quot. in sup. Manufacturer of data centers brought a lawsuit against competitors, alleging that defendants willfully and maliciously misappropriated plaintiff's trade secrets regarding its modular data centers. This court denied defendants' motion for judgment as a matter of law, holding, inter alia, that the jury had reasonably concluded based on the evidence that defendants were unjustly enriched when they caused plaintiff to lose a contract by misappropriating plaintiff's trade secrets. The court cited Restatement Third of Unfair Competition § 45, Comment *f*, in explaining that the unjust-enrichment award was appropriate because the burden of proof was on defendants to establish the extent of defendants' earnings from the contract that were not attributable to plaintiff's trade secrets, and determined that the jury's finding that portions of defendants' earnings were due to the misappropriation was supported by substantial evidence. BladeRoom Group Limited v. Emerson Electric Co., 331 F.Supp.3d 977, 988.

D.Md.2011. Quot. in sup. Former employee sued former employer, alleging that employer retaliated for whistle-blowing activities; employer counterclaimed for, inter alia, misappropriation of trade secrets. Denying in part employee's motion for summary judgment, this court rejected employee's argument that because employer did not demonstrate actual business loss, it could not prove damages. The court explained that damages could include both the actual loss and the unjust enrichment caused by employee's own pecuniary gain from the appropriation, and, here, if employer proved that employee took and used trade secrets to create products that were incorporated into successful bids for government contracts, the amount of compensation received by employee under those contracts could serve as a basis for employer's unjust-enrichment recovery. Glynn v. Impact Science & Techology, Inc., 807 F.Supp.2d 391, 433.

S.D.N.Y.2019. Coms. (d) and (h) quot. in sup.; com. (f) quot. in case quot. in sup. In Chapter 11 proceedings for debtor that sold telecommunications equipment, former supplier of power supplies to debtor filed a proof of claim in connection with a lawsuit that it had previously filed against debtor for misappropriation of trade secrets. After the bankruptcy court issued a decision estimating supplier's claim against debtor, supplier appealed, alleging that the bankruptcy court erred in failing to assume debtor's liability for purposes of its estima-

For earlier citations, see the Appendices, Supplements, or Pocket Parts, if any, that correspond to the subject matter under examination.

tion, and in failing to award damages for unjust enrichment and lost profits. Affirming, this court cited Restatement Third of Unfair Competition § 45 in holding that the bankruptcy court did not err by inquiring into the value of supplier's trade secrets throughout the period of the alleged misappropriation, and into the extent to which supplier's trade secrets might have been independently discoverable or worked around by debtor during that period, or by basing its estimate on the reasonably royalty debtor would have paid to supplier in light of its cost savings attributable to the misappropriation, rather than based on its unjust enrichment and supplier's lost profits. In re Avaya Inc., 602 B.R. 445, 458, 463.

S.D.N.Y.2002. Com. (g) quot. in ftn. in sup. Computer-systems designer that had ceased operations sued competitor for, in part, trade-secret misappropriation. The court ruled that the appropriate measure of damages, where defendant did not profit from the alleged infringement, was a reasonable royalty. The royalty could result in a lump-sum payment based on a reasonable royalty as applied to expected sales or a running royalty based on actual sales. LinkCo, Inc. v. Fujitsu Ltd., 232 F.Supp.2d 182, 186.

D.R.I.2019. Cit. in ftn.; coms. (b) and (f) quot. in sup. Producer of automated clinical instruments used to analyze human blood samples sued competitor and former employee who left plaintiff to work for competitor, alleging misappropriation of trade secrets and other claims. After a jury found that defendants willfully misappropriated plaintiff's trade secrets in violation of Rhode Island law and awarded plaintiff damages for unjust enrichment, this court denied in part defendants' motions for judgment as a matter of law or for a new trial or remittitur, holding that the jury's award of damages—in the amount of one year of profits attributable to the unfair head start defendants gained by misappropriating plaintiff's trade secrets—was a rational appraisal of plaintiff's damages for defendants' unjust enrichment under Restatement Third of Unfair Competition § 45. Alifax Holding Spa v. Alcor Scientific Inc., 404 F.Supp.3d 552, 574.

W.D.Wash.2019. Com. (f) quot. in case quot. in disc. Software developer brought a lawsuit against university, alleging, inter alia, that defendant misappropriated plaintiff's trade secrets by transferring plaintiff's confidential and proprietary software information while using a competitor's data-management system. This court granted in part defendant's motion for summary judgment, holding that plaintiff failed to allege damages for its misappropriation claim. The court explained that, under Restatement Third of Unfair Competition § 45, Comment *f*, the traditional form of relief for misappropriation of trade secrets was disgorgement of a defendant's profits that were attributable to the use of the trade secrets, and determined that, here, plaintiff did not present any evidence of such profits resulting from defendant's purported use of the trade secrets. Inteum Company, LLC v. National University of Singapore, 371 F.Supp.3d 864, 884.

Alaska, 2015. Com. (g) quot. in ftn. Developer of a gated subdivision sued realtors who listed a neighboring property for sale, alleging that realtors misappropriated a photograph of the subdivision's sign and included it in the listing for the neighboring property, with the intent of creating the impression that the property was part of the subdivision. The trial court granted summary judgment for realtors. Affirming, this court held that, although the Copyright Act did not preempt a passing-off claim, such a claim required damages, which developer failed to prove with respect to the photograph of the subdivision's sign. The court rejected developer's argument that a "reasonable royalty" measure of damages was appropriate for a passing-off claim under Restatement Third of Unfair Competition § 45, noting that, while such a measure was often used in patent cases and in the context of trade secrets, its use in trademark was atypical. Alaskasland.Com, LLC v. Cross, 357 P.3d 805, 827.

Kan.2011. Com. (d) cit. in disc. Pipe-coating company sued former employees seeking damages, a restraining order, and an injunction against further use of purportedly misappropriated trade secrets, alleging that employees wrongfully took and used, among other things, a secret coating formula developed by company. The trial court found for plaintiff and required defendants to pay a limited-term royalty for any sales to plaintiff's customers based on use of the formula; the court of appeals affirmed in part, but found that the royalty injunction was not warranted. Affirming in part, reversing in part, and remanding, this

Cit.—cited; com.—comment; fol.—followed; sup.—support.
A complete list of abbreviations precedes page 1.

court held that, although defendants were liable for misappropriating the trade secret, evidence that plaintiff was lax in protecting the secret, that defendants' formula differed from plaintiff's, and that other companies used similar processes, could be exceptional circumstances that justified the imposition of royalties in lieu of other, more substantial damages. Progressive Products, Inc. v. Swartz, 292 Kan. 947, 258 P.3d 969, 979.

Mass.App.2011. Com. (f) quot. in sup. Developer of an innovative method to produce a specialized encapsulant used in making solar cells sued competitor and former employee who left to work for competitor, alleging misappropriation of trade secrets and other claims. The trial court found in favor of plaintiff. Affirming, this court held that the use of disgorgement of profits to compensate plaintiff for defendants' misuse of its trade secrets was appropriate. The court noted that, while the precise scope of plaintiff's monetary loss was difficult to quantify, the record supported the trial judge's implicit conclusion that plaintiff, which enjoyed a 25% global market share in a highly specialized product, suffered a loss of sales when it suddenly faced competition from another producer in its own backyard based on improper use of its trade-secret manufacturing process. Specialized Technology Resources, Inc. v. JPS Elastomerics Corp., 80 Mass.App.Ct. 841, 849, 957 N.E.2d 1116, 1123.

Mass.App.1993. Subsec. (1) cit. in disc., com. (b) quot. in part in disc. (citing § 45 of T.D. No. 4, 1993. § 45 has since been revised; see Official Text). The operators of a billiard parlor sued for injunctive relief to prevent a competitor from opening, alleging unfair trade practices and theft of trade secrets. This court, affirming the trial court's grant of an injunction only preventing the competitor from revealing financial information including accounting procedures obtained from the plaintiffs, held, inter alia, that, as the competing parlor had not yet opened, there was no basis for an award of damages, as these would have been highly speculative. The court noted also that the plaintiffs had not sought damages in their pleadings. Jillian's Billiard v. Beloff Billiards, 35 Mass.App.Ct. 372, 375, 619 N.E.2d 635, 638.

N.Y.2018. Cit. in disc. and in diss. op. (general cite); coms. (d) and (f) cit. in sup. Manufacturer of plastic indicative security seals filed a complaint in federal court against competitor and three former employees who left manufacturer to work for competitor, alleging misappropriation of trade secrets, unfair competition, and unjust enrichment. The district court entered judgment on a jury verdict awarding plaintiff damages for defendants' unfair competition as measured by the development costs that defendants avoided due to their unlawful activity. Answering a question certified by the court of appeals, this court held that avoided costs were not awardable as compensatory damages in an action based on a theory of unfair competition; rather, damages had to be measured by the losses that the plaintiff actually incurred. The court cited Restatement Third of Unfair Competition § 45 in support of its conclusion that the amount of avoided costs should not be used as a measure of damages in unfair-competition cases. E.J. Brooks Company v. Cambridge Security Seals, 105 N.E.3d 301, 306, 315, 326, 327.

Tex.App.2013. Com. (d) cit. in sup. and quot. in ftn., com. (g) cit. in sup. and in ftn., coms. (d)-(g) cit. in ftn. Inventor and owners of a process for mining potash (potassium-containing ore) in a specific area that had anomalously high temperatures brought claims for misappropriation of trade secrets, inter alia, against inventor's former business partner and partner's company's subsidiary, alleging that defendants used plaintiffs' proprietary information in developing their own mining project. The trial court entered judgment on a jury verdict for plaintiffs. Affirming, this court held, among other things, that there was sufficient evidence in the record to support the jury's finding that plaintiffs were entitled to $1,696,428.55 in damages for defendants' misappropriation of trade secrets, which was based on the jury's determination of what a reasonable royalty would have been had the parties negotiated for use of plaintiffs' trade secrets at the time the information was used. In making its decision, the court noted that there were several possible measures of damages in trade-secrets cases in addition to reasonable royalty, including the plaintiff's lost profits, the defendant's gain, and the defendant's savings from using the trade secrets. Bishop v. Miller, 412 S.W.3d 758, 776, 778.

Vt.2002. Subsec. (1) quot. in sup. Owners

of advertisement-based newspaper sued former operators of paper for conversion and unfair competition, alleging misappropriation of business assets. The trial court entered judgment on jury verdict for owners. Modifying conversion award and affirming, this court held, inter alia, that evidence that former operators took business assets such as customer lists, bookkeeping records, and office equipment supported unfair-competition claim based on misappropriation. Maguire v. Gorruso, 174 Vt. 1, 800 A.2d 1085, 1092.

Wash.App.2018. Com. (f) quot. in disc. Car dealership brought a lawsuit against competitor, alleging that defendant's employee had taken a customer list owned by plaintiff when he left plaintiff's employ and misused it to increase defendant's car sales. The trial court entered judgment for plaintiff. This court reversed and remanded, holding, inter alia, that the trial court erred by providing incorrect jury instructions for calculating plaintiff's damages resulting from defendant's willful and malicious misuse of plaintiff's customer list. The court cited Restatement Third of Unfair Competition § 45 in explaining that damages for willful and malicious misuse of a trade secret had to be calculated based off of defendant's sales attributable to the use of the customer lists, rather than all of defendant's sales following defendant obtaining the list. ADA Motors, Inc. v. Butler, 432 P.3d 445, 450.

Wash.App.2009. Com. (f) quot. in sup. and adopted. Design engineer contested drill manufacturer's application to terminate a 2001 injunction enjoining manufacturer from misappropriating engineer's design of a particular seafloor drilling technology. The trial court dissolved the injunction, and also ruled that engineer failed to prove that he suffered any damages from manufacturer's licensing to a third party of technology almost identical to his own design. Affirming, this court held that the undivided price of manufacturer's contract with the third party was the correct basis upon which to calculate the proper amount of restitutionary unjust-enrichment damages, and thus manufacturer's royalty payments to engineer based on revenues from the contract properly compensated him; the evidence did not require a separate damages award based on the license agreement, since the trial court could reasonably have concluded that the license of engineer's technology could not realistically have been separated from the overall contract price but, rather, served as an inducement to third party that did not have independent value. Petters v. Williamson & Associates, Inc., 151 Wash.App. 154, 210 P.3d 1048, 1054.

Wis.2002. Com. (e) quot. in sup. Seller of prosthetic components brought suit for trade-secret misappropriation against former manufacturer of its components. The trial court granted defendant's motion for a mistrial. The court of appeals reversed and remanded for a new trial. Affirming, this court held that evidence that defendant marketed defective products incorporating plaintiff's trade secret was relevant and admissible to show plaintiff's damages. World Wide Prosthetic Supply, Inc. v. Mikulsky, 251 Wis.2d 45, 640 N.W.2d 764, 769.

Wis.App.2001. Com. (e) cit. in disc. Seller of prosthetic components sued company that formerly manufactured the components for it, alleging that defendant's continued production of the components after their relationship ended constituted misappropriation of trade secrets, and that the misappropriation had caused it to lose profits. The trial court granted defendant's motion for mistrial on the ground that evidence that the components were defective had been erroneously admitted to prove damages. Reversing and remanding, this court held that evidence that the product defendant allegedly produced and distributed after misappropriating plaintiff's trade secrets was defective was admissible to prove that plaintiff suffered actual loss caused by the misappropriation. World Wide Prosthetic Supply, Inc. v. Mikulsky, 246 Wis.2d 461, 471, 631 N.W.2d 253, 258, affirmed 251 Wis.2d 45, 640 N.W.2d 764 (2002).

TOPIC 3. RIGHT OF PUBLICITY

C.A.3, 2013. Cit. in ftn. §§ 46-49, constituting all of Chapter 4, Topic 3. College athlete sued videogame producer, alleging that it violated his right of publicity, as recognized under New Jersey law, when it misappropriated his likeness and bio-

Cit.—cited; com.—comment; fol.—followed; sup.—support.
A complete list of abbreviations precedes page 1.

graphical information for use as a digital avatar in its series of college football video games. The district court granted defendant's motion for summary judgment, finding that the games were entitled to freedom-of-expression protection under the First Amendment. Reversing and remanding, this court applied the "transformative use" test for resolving conflicts between the right of publicity and the First Amendment, and held that the games at issue did not sufficiently transform plaintiff's identity such that they escaped the right-of-publicity claim. The court reasoned, in part, that, defendant's digital avatar of plaintiff closely matched plaintiff's appearance and biographical details, and was depicted as playing football at the same school where plaintiff once played; the inclusion of other creative and interactive elements in the games was not sufficient to transform the avatar into something that was primarily defendant's own expression, rather than plaintiff's likeness. Hart v. Electronic Arts, Inc., 717 F.3d 141, 151.

D.Ariz.2020. Cit. in sup. §§ 46-49, which constitutes all of Ch. 4, Topic 3. Models sued owner of a strip club, alleging that defendant posted advertisements using plaintiffs' images on the strip club's Facebook page to advertise the strip club without their permission. This court denied defendant's motion for summary judgment on plaintiffs' claim alleging that defendant was liable for violating plaintiffs' right of publicity by misappropriating their likenesses, holding that genuine issues of material fact remained as to whether defendant posted plaintiffs' images on its Facebook page. The court noted that, while in most jurisdictions the interest in personal privacy could not be assigned and did not survive death, Arizona courts had clarified that the right of publicity was in essence a property right under Restatement Third of Unfair Competition §§ 46-49. Pinder v. 4716 Incorporated, 494 F.Supp.3d 618, 631, 633.

§ 46. Appropriation of the Commercial Value of a Person's Identity: The Right of Publicity

C.A.3, 2013. Cit. and quot. but dist. College athlete sued videogame producer, alleging that it violated his right of publicity, as recognized under New Jersey law, when it misappropriated his likeness and biographical information for use as a digital avatar in its series of college football video games. The district court granted defendant's motion for summary judgment, finding that the games were entitled to freedom-of-expression protection under the First Amendment. Reversing and remanding, this court applied the "transformative use" test for resolving conflicts between the right of publicity and the First Amendment, and held that the games at issue did not sufficiently transform plaintiff's identity such that they escaped the right-of-publicity claim. The court reasoned, in part, that, defendant's digital avatar of plaintiff closely matched plaintiff's appearance and biographical details, and was depicted as playing football at the same school where plaintiff once played; the inclusion of other creative and interactive elements in the games was not sufficient to transform the avatar into something that was primarily defendant's own expression, rather than plaintiff's likeness. Hart v. Electronic Arts, Inc., 717 F.3d 141, 155-156.

C.A.6, 2003. Cit. and quot. in sup., com. (b) cit. and quot. in diss. op., com. (c) cit. and quot. in sup., com. (d) quot. in diss. op., statutory note cit. in diss. op. Professional golfer's licensing agent sued publisher of artwork that depicted golfer, alleging, in part, violation of golfer's right of publicity. District court granted defendant summary judgment. This court affirmed, concluding, inter alia, that, in deciding whether sale of prints violated plaintiff's right of publicity, the court would look to Ohio case law and Restatement Third of Unfair Competition. It stated that transformative-elements test adopted by California Supreme Court would assist in determining where proper balance was between First Amendment and plaintiff's intellectual property rights. Dissent argued that defendant's prints gained their commercial value by exploiting fame and celebrity status that plaintiff worked to achieve, and that it was hard to discern any transformative or creative contribution in the prints so as to entitle them to First Amendment protection. ETW Corp. v. Jireh Pub., Inc., 332 F.3d 915, 930, 942, 943, 952-954, 960.

C.A.6, 2003. Cit. in case cit. in ftn., quot. in ftn., com. (c) cit. in case cit. in disc. Civil-rights icon sued record producer, musicians, and others, alleging that defendants' use of her name as the title of their song constituted false advertising under Lanham Act, defamation, tortious interference with business relationship, and intrusion on her right of publicity. District court granted defendants summary judgment. This court reversed in part, holding, inter alia, that there was a fact issue on Lanham Act claim as to whether use of plaintiff's name as a title to the song and on album cover was artistically related to song's content or whether use of plaintiff's name was nothing more than a misleading advertisement for the sale of the song. Plaintiff's right-of-publicity claim also presented fact issue as to whether song title was "wholly unrelated" to song's content. Parks v. LaFace Records, 329 F.3d 437, 458, 460, cert. denied 540 U.S. 1074, 124 S.Ct. 925, 157 L.Ed.2d 744 (2003).

C.A.6, 2001. Com. (c) quot. in disc. Furniture company sued competitor under the Lanham Act, alleging that defendant produced imitations of a lounge chair and ottoman designed for plaintiff. The district court entered judgment on a jury verdict for plaintiff on several claims, dismissed two others, and entered a permanent injunction against defendant, allowing defendant to fairly identify the original designers of the reproduced furniture. Affirming in part, this court held, inter alia, that the district court did not abuse its discretion by creating a "fair use" exception in its permanent injunction issued pursuant to the jury verdict for plaintiff. Herman Miller, Inc. v. Palazzetti Imports and Exports, Inc., 270 F.3d 298, 320.

C.A.10, 1996. Cit. in disc., coms. (c) and (g) cit. in disc. A company brought suit to obtain a declaratory judgment that its parody trading cards featuring active major league baseball players did not infringe on the publicity rights of members of the Major League Baseball Players Association (MLBPA). District court held that the trading cards constituted expression protected by the First Amendment, and therefore read a parody exception into Oklahoma's statutory right of publicity. This court affirmed, holding that plaintiff's First Amendment right to free expression outweighed MLBPA's proprietary right of publicity. The justifications for the right of publicity were not nearly as compelling as those offered for other forms of intellectual property, and the cards were an important form of entertainment and social commentary. Cardtoons v. Major League Baseball Players, 95 F.3d 959, 967, 973, 975.

C.A.11, 2016. Quot. in sup. Nonprofit corporation that owned the name and likeness of a historically significant civil-rights activist filed, inter alia, a right-of-publicity claim against national retail corporation that sold products containing the activist's name, image, and likeness without first obtaining permission from plaintiff. The district court entered summary judgment for defendant. This court affirmed, holding that the products that defendant sold were protected by a qualified privilege because they communicated a matter of public importance. The court cited Restatement Third of Unfair Competition § 46, for the common-law right of publicity, and explained that this privacy right was not absolute and that a qualified privilege could be afforded as a defense in cases such as this, where the products contained information on a historical figure. Rosa and Raymond Parks Institute for Self Development v. Target Corp., 812 F.3d 824, 830.

C.A.Fed.2022. Quot. in sup. Applicant of trademark appealed the decision of the U.S. Trademark Trial and Appeal Board, alleging that the Board violated his First Amendment right to free speech by denying his request to trademark the phrase "TRUMP TOO SMALL" to criticize the former President of the United States. This court reversed the Board's decision, holding that certain Lanham Act provisions prohibiting registration of trademarks that consisted of or comprised the name of particular living individuals without their written consent violated First Amendment rights. The court explained that, while the government had interests in protecting state-law publicity rights, as set forth by Restatement Third of Unfair Competition § 46, the President's right of publicity was constrained against speech critical of him. In re Elster, 26 F.4th 1328, 1334.

M.D.Ala.2015. Cit. and quot. in sup. Corporation that owned the name and likeness of a woman who became an icon of the civil rights movement after she refused to surrender her seat to a white passenger on a racially segregated bus sued operator of retail stores, alleging that defendant violated plaintiff's right to publicity under Michigan law in connection with its unauthorized sale of seven books and a movie about the woman. This court granted summary judgment for defendant, holding that defendant's sale of the books and movie depicting the woman's life story without plaintiff's consent did not violate plaintiff's ownership rights in the woman's name or likeness, because they were biographical works. The court cited Restatement Third of Unfair Competition §§ 46 and 47 in explaining that Michigan courts did not extend the right-of-publicity tort to prohibit unlicensed works of biography. Rosa and Raymond Parks Institute for Self Development v. Target Corp., 90 F.Supp.3d 1256, 1262.

D.Ariz.2021. Cit. in sup., cit. in case cit. in sup.; coms. (b) and (g) quot. in sup. Female models, business women, and social-media personalities sued operator of strip club, alleging, inter alia, that defendant violated plaintiffs' right to publicity by using photographs of their likeness to advertise the strip club without plaintiffs' consent. After removal, this court denied in part defendant's motion for summary judgment, holding that state statutes protecting the right of publicity for soldiers did not preclude plaintiffs' common-law right-of-publicity claims. Citing Restatement Third of Unfair Competition § 46, the court explained that the one-year statute of limitations for personal-injury claims did not bar plaintiffs' claims, because they arose from defendant's purported violation of plaintiffs' property rights. Longoria v. Kodiak Concepts LLC, 527 F.Supp.3d 1085, 1097, 1098.

D.Ariz.2020. Com. (b) quot. in sup.; com. (d) quot. in case quot. in sup. Models sued owner of a strip club, alleging that defendant posted advertisements using plaintiffs' images on the strip club's Facebook page to advertise the strip club without their permission. This court denied defendant's motion for summary judgment on plaintiffs' claim alleging that defendant was liable for violating plaintiffs' right of publicity by misappropriating their likenesses, holding that genuine issues of material fact remained as to whether defendant posted plaintiffs' images on its Facebook page. The court cited Restatement Third of Unfair Competition § 46 in reasoning that the identity of even an unknown person could possess commercial value, and that the evaluation of the relative fame of a plaintiff was more properly relevant to the determination of appropriate relief. Pinder v. 4716 Incorporated, 494 F.Supp.3d 618, 631, 633, 634.

D.Ariz.2019. Com. (g) quot. in case quot. in sup. Grill manufacturer brought a right-of-publicity claim against competitor, alleging that defendant used the names and likenesses of the inventors of wood-pellet grills in advertising defendant's competing products, which violated an intellectual-property agreement between plaintiff and the inventors, and seeking a preliminary injunction against defendant's association and use of those names and likenesses. This court granted plaintiff's motion for a preliminary injunction, holding that plaintiff established a likelihood of success on the merits for its right-of-publicity claim under Restatement Third of Unfair Competition § 46. The court explained that plaintiff demonstrated that it had obtained the exclusive rights to the inventors' names and likenesses through the intellectual-property agreement, and that defendant violated those rights by issuing marketing statements with the images of the inventors, by referencing the story behind the inventors' creation of the grill, and by claiming that the competing products were "brought to you proudly" by the inventors. Traeger Pellet Grills, LLC v. Dansons US, LLC, 421 F.Supp.3d 876, 887.

D.Ariz.2006. Cit. in sup. Former players for basketball team sued licensor, apparel manufacturer, and others, alleging that defendants improperly licensed and made use of players' names, likenesses, and player numbers for use on a clothing line without players' consent. This court denied defendants' motion for summary judgment as to plaintiffs' claim for invasion of the right of publicity, holding, inter alia, that plaintiffs were permitted to assert such a claim under Arizona law, because the Restatement clearly recognized the right of publicity, both as a tort claim and as an unfair-competition claim, and, in the absence of Arizona law to the contrary, Arizona courts followed the Restatement. Lemon v. Harlem Globetrotters Intern., Inc., 437 F.Supp.2d 1089, 1100.

D.Ariz.2000. Cit. and quot. in sup., com. (e) quot. in sup. A professional golfer who made a "hole in one" for $1 million at a golf tournament sued video producer, alleging that defendant's use of plaintiff's name and golf shot in a promotional video constituted a violation of his right to publicity. This court denied defendant's motion to dismiss, holding, inter alia, that plaintiff had adequately stated a claim for violation of the right to publicity. Even though plaintiff appeared in only six seconds of the eight-minute videotape, the incidental-use doctrine did not apply, because inclusion of plaintiff's name and shot was integral to defendant's advertisement and clearly enhanced the marketability of its service. Pooley v. National Hole-In-One Association, 89 F.Supp.2d 1108, 1111, 1115.

C.D.Cal.2012. Com. (c) quot. in disc. and in sup. and quot. in case quot. in sup., com. (d) quot. in disc., coms. (h) and (i) quot. in sup. University that claimed to own a world-famous deceased physicist's right of publicity as a beneficiary under his will and thus exclusive control of the exploitation of his name and likeness sued automobile manufacturer, alleging unauthorized use of the physicist's image in a magazine advertisement. This court denied summary judgment for plaintiff, holding that plaintiff's claim was barred, because the New Jersey Supreme Court would likely find that the postmortem right of publicity under New Jersey common law endured for no more than 50 years after death, and more than 50 years had elapsed between the physicist's death in 1955 and the filing of this lawsuit in 2010. The court reasoned that a maximum duration of 50 years appropriately reflected the balance between meaningful enforcement of the right of publicity after a famous individual's death and the public's interest in free expression. Hebrew University of Jerusalem v. General Motors LLC, 903 F.Supp.2d 932, 936-939.

C.D.Cal.2012. Com. (h) quot. in sup. University that claimed to have inherited exclusive control of the name and likeness of a world-famous deceased physicist brought, inter alia, a cause of action for infringement of the right of publicity against automobile manufacturer, arguing that defendant's use of the physicist's image in a magazine advertisement implied and created the false impression that physicist's estate and/or plaintiff were associated with the advertisement. This court denied in part defendant's motion for summary judgment, holding, among other things, that, although plaintiff had presented sufficient evidence to create at least a genuine dispute of fact concerning whether physicist exploited his right of publicity during his lifetime, under New Jersey law, establishing a post mortem right of publicity did not require evidence of lifetime exploitation of that right. Hebrew University of Jerusalem v. General Motors LLC, 878 F.Supp.2d 1021, 1030.

C.D.Cal.2011. Com. (f) quot. in sup. Actress brought a putative class action against online provider of image copyright licenses, alleging that by displaying sample images of her on a website, provider violated her common law and statutory rights of publicity by exploiting her name, image, and likeness for financial gain without her consent. Granting summary judgment for defendant, this court held that plaintiff impliedly consented to the display of the sample images, whether or not the displaying parties were the photographers themselves or, like defendant, were distributors for the photographers. The court reasoned that plaintiff consented to have photographers at red carpet events take the pictures in question, knew that it was the custom and practice in the entertainment industry that red carpet photographs were widely used and disseminated, knew that photographers could employ third parties to assist them in distributing such photos, and had hitherto voiced no objections to such practices over a 40-year period. Jones v. Corbis Corp., 815 F.Supp.2d 1108, 1113.

N.D.Ga.2013. Quot. in sup. Retired professional wrestler brought, inter alia, a claim for violation of the right of publicity against entertainment corporation, alleging that defendant repeatedly used his name and likeness on its websites for its own commercial gain without his permission and without compensating him. Granting defendant's motion to dismiss, this court held that plaintiff failed to state a claim for violation of his right of publicity, because, under Georgia's "newsworthiness" exception to the right of publicity, the references to plaintiff's name on defendant's websites were matters of public interest and protected by the First Amendment. The court concluded that defendant's use on its websites of plaintiff's identity was not for a commercial transaction or a commercial use, because plaintiff's identity was not being used to sell a product in an advertisement, but, instead, was referred to as part of the historical events of professional wrestling. Somerson v. World Wrestling Entertainment, Inc., 956 F.Supp.2d 1360, 1369.

W.D.Ky.1995. Com. (a) quot. in disc., com. (d) quot. in ftn. in sup. Clothing designer who was photographed wearing one of her creations sued publisher of magazine that ran photo and T-shirt manufacturer that subsequently used the photo on its shirts for invasion of privacy. The court granted defendants' motion to dismiss

Cit.—cited; com.—comment; fol.—followed; sup.—support.
A complete list of abbreviations precedes page 1.

inasmuch as the complaint stated claims for intrusion upon seclusion, giving unreasonable publicity to plaintiff's private life, and placing her in a false light, but denied their motion to the extent that plaintiff alleged unauthorized appropriation of her likeness, holding that if she could prove a property interest in her likeness because of its commercial value and her intent to profit from it, she could recover. The court explained that while the cause of action was not limited to celebrities, the amount of damages would vary depending on the extent of the plaintiff's fame. Finally, the court denied plaintiff's request to add a claim for intentional infliction of emotional distress on the ground that defendants' behavior was not outrageous. Cheatham v. Paisano Publications, Inc., 891 F.Supp. 381, 385-386, 386.

E.D.Mich.2000. Quot. in disc. Heirs and personal representatives of musician depicted in television miniseries sued various entities and individuals involved with the production for, inter alia, misappropriation of likeness/violation of the right of publicity, defamation, and "false light" invasion of privacy. On motions to dismiss, the court held, in part, that the depiction of a life story, particularly where some of the events were fictionalized, did not give rise to a cause of action for violation of the right of publicity, and that defamation and "false light" claims brought by musician's de facto mother did not survive her death under the law of Mississippi, the state of mother's domicile. Ruffin-Steinback v. dePasse, 82 F.Supp.2d 723, 729, affirmed 267 F.3d 457 (6th Cir.2001).

E.D.Mich.1999. Quot. but dist. §§ 46-47. Public figure whose name was used as the title of a rap song sued the entertainers who wrote, performed, marketed, and distributed the song, asserting, in part, a claim for unfair competition under state law. Granting defendants' motion for summary judgment, the court stated that plaintiff's purported reliance on Restatement (Third) of Unfair Competition §§ 46-47 to support her state-law unfair-competition claim was misplaced because the Restatement did not apply to the use of a person's identity in entertainment, among other things. The court noted that, as a public figure, plaintiff simply was not entitled to control every conceivable presentation of her name and likeness. Parks v. LaFace Records, 76 F.Supp.2d 775, 784, affirmed in part, reversed in part and remanded 329 F.3d 437 (6th Cir.2003).

D.Minn.2017. Com. (g) quot. in sup. Personal representative of the estate of musical artist brought an action against sound engineer and related entities, seeking to enjoin further distribution of copyrighted material, and alleging that defendants' release of decedent's previously-unreleased recordings of performances violated, inter alia, decedent's common-law right of publicity. This court denied in part defendants' motion to dismiss, holding that, under Minnesota common law, a right of publicity was a property interest that was descendible and enforceable by a decedent's estate. The court quoted Restatement Third of Unfair Competition § 46, Comment *g*? noting that it was in accordance with the weight of authority of courts that had addressed the right of publicity, and determined that the right of publicity was a property right that survived death and was enforceable by a decedent's estate. Paisley Park Enterprises, Inc. v. Boxill, 299 F.Supp.3d 1074, 1082.

E.D.Mo.2006. Quot. in disc., com. (d) quot. in case quot. in disc., com. (c) quot. in disc. Professional baseball players' association intervened in a rights dispute between distributor of fantasy-sports products and baseball-team owners' interactive media/ Internet arm, asserting, along with the latter, counterclaims against distributor for violation of baseball players' right of publicity. Granting distributor's motions for summary judgment and dismissing the counterclaims, this court held, inter alia, that distributor did not violate players' claimed right of publicity, because the undisputed facts established that distributor did not use in fantasy baseball games players' names separately or in conjunction with their playing records as a symbol of their identity or with the intent to obtain a commercial advantage, and such use did not contravene the policy behind the right of publicity. C.B.C. Distribution and Marketing, Inc. v. Major League Baseball Advanced Media, L.P., 443 F.Supp.2d 1077, 1084, 1088-1090.

D.N.J.2011. Com. (b) quot. in disc. Former college football athlete sued computer software developer, alleging that defendant violated his right of publicity under New Jersey law by misappropriating and incorporating his identity and likeness for a commercial purpose in connection with

For earlier citations, see the Appendices, Supplements, or Pocket Parts, if any, that correspond to the subject matter under examination.

defendant's video games. Granting summary judgment for defendant, this court held that defendant's First Amendment right to free expression outweighed plaintiff's right of publicity. The court reasoned, in part, that defendant's use of plaintiff's image was part of an expressive act by defendant that might have drawn upon public familiarity with plaintiff's college football career, but did not explicitly state that he endorsed or contributed to the creation of the game; defendant's use of plaintiff's image was clearly related to the game and was not simply an advertisement for an unrelated product. Hart v. Electronic Arts, Inc., 808 F.Supp.2d 757, 772.

D.N.M.2010. Quot. in sup., com. (b) quot. in sup. Buyer of endodontic equipment sued sellers for breach of contract and unfair trade practices; sellers brought various counterclaims sounding in contract and tort. This court denied buyer's motion for summary judgment with respect to sellers' unfair-competition counterclaim based on unlawful misappropriation of trade values, holding that a genuine issue of material fact existed as to whether buyer, without consent, used sellers' name for purposes of trade when it allegedly told its customers that its products were repackaged products made by sellers. Guidance Endodontics, LLC v. Dentsply Intern., Inc., 708 F.Supp.2d 1209, 1258, 1259.

N.D.Ohio, 2004. Com. (f) quot. in disc. Television news anchor's participation in a wet t-shirt contest, during which she removed her clothing, was recorded without her notice or consent. Upon learning that her performance and image later appeared in videos and on various websites, some of which charged viewers for access, anchor sought a preliminary injunction against the production companies and website owners and operators to prohibit their continued use of her image. Granting the injunction, this court determined, inter alia, that the anchor's claims had a substantial likelihood of success on the merits. Defendants' unauthorized usage of anchor's image for commercial purposes, such as an advertisement for defendants' videos and other products or services, was not a form of expressive material protected by the First Amendment. Bosley v. Wildwett.com, 310 F.Supp.2d 914, 931.

E.D.Pa.2000. Cit. generally in disc. Due to a tracking device on a stolen car, a police raid of garages yielded 13 stolen cars and four arrests. One of the arrestees was found not guilty of charges stemming from the arrest, but a newspaper article named him as an arrestee and included a mug shot of him. After the tracking-device manufacturer distributed a brochure that included the newspaper article in which arrestee appeared, arrestee sued the manufacturer for defamation and invasion of privacy. This court denied in part defendants' motion to dismiss, holding, inter alia, that plaintiff stated a viable claim for invasion of privacy on the basis of appropriation, because plaintiff sufficiently alleged that defendant used plaintiff's name and likeness to advertise defendant's business product and for commercial purposes. The court noted that a federal court had incorrectly predicted that the Pennsylvania Supreme Court would clarify the law of appropriation and the right of publicity by adopting the Restatement (Third) of Unfair Competition. Fanelle v. LoJack Corporation, 79 F.Supp.2d 558, 563.

E.D.Pa.1997. Cit. in headnotes, cit. and quot. in disc. Well-known civil rights activist sued movie producers for, inter alia, "false light" invasion of privacy in connection with the manner in which he was portrayed in defendants' film. Plaintiff also alleged that defendants violated his right of publicity by using his photograph on the compact disc cover for the movie soundtrack. Defendants moved for summary judgment. Granting the motion, the court held that, despite some minor inaccuracies, a movie scene showing plaintiff and his associates legally purchasing guns did not place plaintiff in a false light; that a scene depicting a confrontation between plaintiff and another member of his organization did place plaintiff in a false light, but plaintiff failed to establish by clear and convincing evidence that defendants acted maliciously or with reckless disregard for the truth when they included that scene; and that use of plaintiff's photograph on the CD cover was not actionable because such use was not for trade or commercial purposes. Seale v. Gramercy Pictures, 964 F.Supp. 918, 919, 929-930, affirmed 156 F.3d 1225 (3d Cir.1998).

E.D.Pa.1996. Cit. in headnotes, cit. and quot. in sup. Civil rights leader whose name and likeness appeared, without his consent, in a film and book depicting the civil rights movement, as well as on the cover of the accompanying musical CD/

cassette soundtrack, sued movie producer, among others, for, inter alia, violations of his right of publicity and "false light" invasion of privacy. Defendants moved for summary judgment. Granting the motion in part and denying it in part, the court held that the use of plaintiff's name and likeness in connection with the film and book, the subject matter of which concerned plaintiff, was not actionable as a violation of his right of publicity because such use was not for purposes of trade but, rather, for the purpose of First Amendment expression; that material factual issues existed as to whether the use of plaintiff's name and likeness in connection with the CD/cassette was for purposes of trade or commercial purposes; and that material factual issues existed as to whether certain scenes in the film depicted plaintiff in a false light. Seale v. Gramercy Pictures, 949 F.Supp. 331, 331, 332, 336.

W.D.Pa.2003. Cit. generally in case cit. in disc., quot. in disc. Professional-wrestling promoter sued seller of T-shirts and other consumer merchandise that featured graphics of dogs caricatured as plaintiff's wrestling characters, claiming violations of common-law publicity rights on behalf of wrestlers. Granting defendant's motion for summary judgment, the court held, inter alia, that defendant's parodies of plaintiff's wrestling characters constituted expressive commentary that deserved First Amendment protection and outweighed the state-law interest in protecting plaintiff's rights of publicity. World Wrestling Federation Entertainment Inc. v. Big Dog Holdings, Inc., 280 F.Supp.2d 413, 444.

Ala.App.2004. Com. (b) cit. in sup. Client sued tattoo artist and his studio for invasion of privacy, after artist submitted, without plaintiff's permission, photographs of a tattoo on plaintiff's breast to a national tattoo magazine. The trial court granted defendants summary judgment. This court reversed and remanded, holding that plaintiff, who alleged injuries to her feelings and not to economic interests in her property right to her likeness, stated a viable claim for commercial-appropriation invasion of privacy, since in Alabama the commercial-appropriation invasion-of-privacy tort did not base its liability solely on commercial rather than psychological interests. To do so would substitute the commercial-appropriation invasion-of-privacy tort for the tort of violating the right to publicity. Minnifield v. Ashcraft, 903 So.2d 818, 825.

Ariz.App.2021. Com. (a) adopted in case cit. in sup. Actresses, models, and social-media influencers sued owner of a country-western-themed nightclub and dance bar, alleging that defendant edited photos of plaintiffs taken during unrelated professional photo shoots and used them in online advertisements without their consent. The trial court granted defendant's motion for judgment on the pleadings and dismissed plaintiffs' claims alleging violation of their right of publicity and false light invasion of privacy. This court reversed and remanded, holding, among other things, that Arizona courts expressly recognized a cause of action for common-law right of publicity consistent with Restatement Third of Unfair Competition § 46, and that an Arizona statute regulating the right of publicity for soldiers supplemented, but did not supplant, the common-law protection against non-consensual publicity and the complementary right of publicity. Canas v. Bay Entertainment, LLC, 498 P.3d 1082, 1085.

Ariz.App.2014. Cit. and quot. in sup., com. (a) cit. in sup., coms. (c), (d), and (g) quot. in sup., com. (h) cit. and quot. in sup. After daughter wrote online commentaries about her aging mother's daily challenges and a fond remembrance following her mother's death, daughter's sister, who was the personal representative of their mother's estate, objected to the writings and listed on the inventory of estate assets a claim against daughter for violation of mother's right of publicity. Daughter petitioned to compel closure of the estate, and the trial court disallowed sister's claim. Affirming, this court held that a right of publicity existed under Arizona law and it could be enforced by one's estate after death, but daughter's commentaries in this case did not, as a matter of law, give rise to such a claim, because they were expressive works that did not employ mother's name or likeness for purposes of trade. The court noted that the right of publicity at issue here was defined by Restatement Third of Unfair Competition § 46 as the right to the commercial value of a person's identity and, as a property right, was descendible, and therefore could be enforced by a decedent's estate. In re Estate of Reynolds, 235 Ariz. 80, 327 P.3d 213, 215-217.

Cal.App.2007. Coms. (b) and (c) cit. in disc., com. (d) quot. in sup. Professional model sued corporation that allegedly used his image on a coffee label without his

For earlier citations, see the Appendices, Supplements, or Pocket Parts, if any, that correspond to the subject matter under examination.

consent and without remuneration, asserting, in part, statutory and common-law appropriation claims. The trial court entered judgment on a jury verdict awarding plaintiff damages and profits. Reversing and remanding, this court held, inter alia, that the single-publication rule applied to the claims, and that, unless a reasonable person in plaintiff's position had no meaningful ability to discover the publication of his image, plaintiff was required to have filed a lawsuit within the limitations period of two years of when defendant either first published or republished the image. The court noted that, to recover profits under the statute, plaintiff had to show that the profits were attributable to the use of his identity or persona, rather than an iconic image of a coffee taster. Christoff v. Nestle USA, Inc., 152 Cal.App.4th 1439, 62 Cal.Rptr.3d 122, 129, 130, 143.

Cal.App.2001. Cit. in disc. Former major league baseball players sued Major League Baseball in two suits for, inter alia, violating their common law right of publicity, alleging that defendant appropriated their names and likenesses by using their names, voices, signatures, autographs, and likenesses without their consent and without compensation. Trial courts granted defendant summary judgment. After consolidating appeals, this court affirmed, holding, in part, that public interest favoring free dissemination of information as to baseball's history outweighed any proprietary interests at stake. Defendant's uses were entitled to receive full constitutional protection accorded to noncommercial speech, since uses involved statements of historical fact, descriptions of those facts, or video depictions of them. Gionfriddo v. Major League Baseball, 94 Cal.App.4th 400, 114 Cal.Rptr.2d 307, 313.

Cal.App.1996. Quot. in part in disc. Actors sued film distributor for violations of California's "right to publicity" statute after distributor released a film in which actors appeared, but did not pay them for their performances. Plaintiffs alleged that defendant was liable for having misappropriated their images and likenesses without their consent. The trial court granted defendant's motion for summary judgment and this court affirmed, holding that plaintiffs' action was preempted by federal copyright law. Fleet v. CBS, Inc., 50 Cal.App.4th 1911, 58 Cal.Rptr.2d 645, 649, limited by 92 Cal.Rptr.2d 713, 78 Cal.App. 4th 362 (2000).

Colo.2001. Coms. (a) and (b) cit. in disc. Newsletter publisher published an article identifying a woman by name and photograph and detailing his investigation of woman's theft of bearer bonds and her subsequent criminal conviction. Woman sued publisher, alleging that her privacy was invaded by appropriation of her name and likeness. Trial court granted defendant summary judgment, but appellate court reversed. This court held that the tort of invasion of privacy by appropriation of another's name or likeness was cognizable under Colorado law, and that plaintiff was not required to provide evidence of the value of her name or likeness. The court, however, reversed with directions to reinstate trial court's order because defendant's publication was privileged. Joe Dickerson & Associates, LLC v. Dittmar, 34 P.3d 995, 1000.

Ind.App.2014. Com. (g) quot. in ftn. Dentist brought claims for defamation per se, invasion of privacy, disclosure of private facts, and identity theft, inter alia, against former boyfriend, alleging that, after she ended the parties' relationship, he began sending letters informing her employers and colleagues that she had herpes. The trial court denied defendant's motion to transfer venue. Reversing, this court held that defendant was entitled to transfer venue, because plaintiff alleged injury to her reputation, privacy, and identity, and none of those things were transferable, intangible personal chattels that could serve as a basis for establishing preferred venue under the state's trial rules. In making its decision, the court noted that, under Restatement Third of Unfair Competition § 46, Comment *g*, the interest in the commercial value of a person's identity, or the right to publicity, was freely assignable to others. Belcher v. Kroczek, 13 N.E.3d 448, 452.

Ky.2001. Coms. (a) and (b) cit. in ftn. Deceased musician's estate sued musician's son, alleging that defendant violated musician's common-law and statutory right of publicity by using musician's voice and likeness in a music video. Trial court granted defendant summary judgment, and the appellate court affirmed. This court affirmed, holding, inter alia, that the statutory right of publicity did not apply to a work protected by the First Amendment where there was a genuine connection between the use of the musician's likeness and the content of the creative work. The court noted that many of the principles of the common-law right of publicity could be used in construing the statute. Montgomery v. Montgomery, 60 S.W.3d 524, 528.

Mo.2003. Cit. in sup., com. (d) cit. in sup. After professional hockey player learned of the existence of a comic book that contained a villainous character sharing his name, he brought suit for, in part, misappropriation of name against the comic book's creators, publishers, and marketers. The trial court granted defendants' motion for judgment n.o.v. Reversing in part and remanding, this court held, inter alia, that plaintiff, whose lawsuit was more precisely labeled a right-of-publicity action, presented sufficient evidence to prove that his name was used as a symbol of his identity, the evidence established that defendants used his name for a commercial advantage, and defendants' use of plaintiff's name was not protected under the First Amendment. Doe v. TCI Cablevision, 110 S.W.3d 363, 369, 370, cert. denied 540 U.S. 1106, 124 S.Ct. 1058, 157 L.Ed.2d 892 (2004).

N.Y.Sup.Ct.1995. Com. (i) quot. in sup. (citing § 46 of T.D. No. 4, 1993, which is now § 46 of the Official Text). Members of the 1969 World Champion New York Mets baseball team sued a corporation that was selling clothing items emblazoned with a group photograph of the team, alleging that the corporation violated their rights to publicity under New York Civil Rights Law. This court granted plaintiffs summary judgment and enjoined defendant from selling the clothing, holding, inter alia, that the Federal Copyright Act did not preempt plaintiffs' suit, because even if a copyright existed, the infringement of the right of publicity could occur. The court stated that right of publicity in a particular performance was distinguishable from a right to commercial exploitation of one's own identity. Shamsky v. Garan, Inc., 167 Misc.2d 149, 632 N.Y.S.2d 930, 935.

Ohio App.2020. Cit. in sup. Seller of a house, who had been ordered to pay a judgment to buyers based on her fraudulent failure to disclose termite damage, sued providers of continuing education for realtors, alleging that defendants appropriated her name in violation of a state statute by discussing her case in their materials. The trial court granted summary judgment for defendants. This court affirmed, holding that the statute did not apply, because defendants' use of plaintiff's name was informative and newsworthy and was not intended to promote, advertise, or market a product or take advantage of her name's commercial value, if any. The court noted that the Supreme Court of Ohio had relied heavily on Restatement Second of Torts § 652C when it adopted the right of publicity, and that, while the right of publicity was originally treated as a branch of the right of privacy, the American Law Institute had transferred its discussion of the right of publicity to Restatement Third of Unfair Competition § 46, in recognition that the tort's primary focus was the value of a person's name, vis-à-vis the person's ability to market it for commercial purposes. Harvey v. Systems Effect, LLC, 154 N.E.3d 293, 307, 308.

§ 47. Use for Purposes of Trade

C.A.3, 2013. Cit. and quot. but dist.; com. (c) cit. and quot. but dist., cit. in ftn. College athlete sued videogame producer, alleging that it violated his right of publicity, as recognized under New Jersey law, when it misappropriated his likeness and biographical information for use as a digital avatar in its series of college football video games. The district court granted defendant's motion for summary judgment, finding that the games were entitled to freedom-of-expression protection under the First Amendment. Reversing and remanding, this court applied the "transformative use" test for resolving conflicts between the right of publicity and the First Amendment, and held that the games at issue did not sufficiently transform plaintiff's identity such that they escaped the right-of-publicity claim. The court reasoned, in part, that, defendant's digital avatar of plaintiff closely matched plaintiff's appearance and biographical details, and was depicted as playing football at the same school where plaintiff once played; the inclusion of other creative and interactive elements in the games was not sufficient to transform the avatar into something that was primarily defendant's own expression, rather than plaintiff's likeness. The court opined that, contrary to the reading of certain other courts, the transformative-use test comported with the language of Restatement Third of Unfair Competition § 47, Comment c. Hart v. Electronic Arts, Inc., 717 F.3d 141, 156, 157, 161, 165.

C.A.5, 2000. Cit. in disc. Musicians sued record company and music producer for

For earlier citations, see the Appendices, Supplements, or Pocket Parts, if any, that correspond to the subject matter under examination.

misappropriation of their names and likenesses under Texas state law. Affirming the district court's entry of judgment on a jury verdict for plaintiffs, this court held, inter alia, that, because a person's name and likeness in themselves were not copyrightable, and because the state-law tort for misappropriation did not conflict with federal copyright law, plaintiffs' claims were not preempted by the Copyright Act. Brown v. Ames, 201 F.3d 654, 658, 660.

C.A.6, 2003. Com. (c) cit. and quot. in sup., com. (d) cit. in sup. Professional golfer's licensing agent sued publisher of artwork that depicted golfer, alleging, in part, violation of golfer's right of publicity. District court granted defendant summary judgment. This court affirmed, concluding that in deciding whether sale of prints violated plaintiff's right of publicity, the court would look to Ohio case law and Restatement Third of Unfair Competition. It stated that transformative-elements test adopted by California Supreme Court would assist in determining where proper balance was between First Amendment and plaintiff's intellectual property rights. Defendant's work had substantial informational and creative content that outweighed any adverse effect on plaintiff's market, his work did not violate golfer's right of publicity, and the work was entitled to First Amendment protection. ETW Corp. v. Jireh Pub., Inc., 332 F.3d 915, 930, 931, 937.

C.A.6, 2003. Quot. in case quot. in ftn., com. (c) quot. in sup. Civil-rights icon sued record producer, musicians, and others, alleging that defendants' use of her name as the title of their song constituted false advertising under Lanham Act, defamation, tortious interference with business relationship, and intrusion on her right of publicity. District court granted defendants summary judgment. This court reversed in part, holding, inter alia, that there was a fact issue on Lanham Act claim as to whether use of plaintiff's name as a title to the song and on album cover was artistically related to song's content or whether use of plaintiff's name was nothing more than a misleading advertisement for the sale of the song. Plaintiff's right-of-publicity claim also presented fact issue as to whether song title was "wholly unrelated" to song's content. Parks v. LaFace Records, 329 F.3d 437, 458, 461, cert. denied 540 U.S. 1074, 124 S.Ct. 925, 157 L.Ed.2d 744 (2003).

C.A.6, 2001. Quot. in disc., cit. generally in disc. Family members and business associates of former members of famous musical group sued producers and broadcaster of miniseries about the group, alleging, in part, violation of their rights of publicity. Affirming the district court's dismissal of the claim, this court held, inter alia, that the use of plaintiffs' fictionalized likenesses in a work protected by the First Amendment and the advertising incidental to that use did not give rise to a claim for relief under plaintiffs' rights of publicity. Ruffin-Steinback v. dePasse, 267 F.3d 457, 461, 462.

C.A.9, 2017. Quot. in sup. Former student athletes who appeared in photographs owned by the National Collegiate Athletic Association (NCAA) brought statutory and common-law claims for violation of their right to publicity and unfair competition against company that contracted with the NCAA to store, host, and license the photographs, alleging that defendant exploited their likenesses by selling non-exclusive licenses permitting consumers to download the photographs for non-commercial art use. The district court granted defendant's special motion to strike pursuant to California's anti-SLAPP statute, holding that the federal Copyright Act preempted plaintiffs' claims. Affirming, this court held, among other things, that, although a publicity-right claim could proceed when a likeness was used non-consensually on merchandise or in advertising, where, as here, a likeness was captured in a copyrighted artistic visual work and the work was being distributed for personal use, a publicity-right claim was little more than a thinly disguised copyright claim. The court reasoned that the right of publicity had to be construed in accordance with Restatement Third of Unfair Competition § 47, which limited liability to misappropriation for purposes of trade. Maloney v. T3Media, Inc., 853 F.3d 1004, 1018.

C.A.9, 2013. Com. (c) cit. in case cit. but not fol., com. (d) quot. in case quot. in disc. Former college football player brought a putative class action against developer of video games, alleging that defendant's use of class members' likenesses in its video games, which allowed users to control avatars representing college athletes as those avatars participated in simulated games, violated their rights of publicity under California law. The district court

Cit.—cited; com.—comment; fol.—followed; sup.—support.
A complete list of abbreviations precedes page 1.

denied defendant's motion to strike the complaint as a strategic lawsuit against public participation (SLAPP) under California's anti-SLAPP statute. Affirming, this court held, inter alia, that defendant's use of college athletes' likenesses in its video games did not qualify for First Amendment protection, and thus did not merit a defense under the anti-SLAPP statute, because it literally recreated plaintiff in the very setting in which he had achieved his renown, with no significant transformative or creative contribution. Furthermore, the court declined to extend the *Rogers* test governing false-enforcement claims under the Lanham Act—under which titles of artistic and literary works that used a celebrity's name were protected unless they explicitly misled consumers—to right-of-publicity claims. In re NCAA Student-Athlete Name & Likeness Licensing Litigation, 724 F.3d 1268, 1281.

C.A.Fed.2022. Coms. (b) and (c) quot. in sup. Applicant of trademark appealed the decision of the U.S. Trademark Trial and Appeal Board, alleging that the Board violated his First Amendment right to free speech by denying his request to trademark the phrase "TRUMP TOO SMALL" to criticize the former President of the United States. This court reversed the Board's decision, holding that certain Lanham Act provisions prohibiting registration of trademarks that consisted of or comprised the name of particular living individuals without their written consent violated First Amendment rights. Citing Restatement Third of Unfair Competition § 47, Comment *c*, the court explained that the use of the President's identity primarily for the purpose of communicating information or expressing ideas generally was not an actionable violation of his right to publicity. In re Elster, 26 F.4th 1328, 1337, 1338.

M.D.Ala.2015. Cit. in case quot. in sup., com. (c) quot. in case quot. in sup. Corporation that owned the name and likeness of a woman who became an icon of the civil rights movement when she refused to surrender her seat to a white passenger on a racially segregated bus sued operator of retail stores, alleging that defendant violated plaintiff's right to publicity under Michigan law in connection with its unauthorized sale of seven books and a movie about the woman. This court granted summary judgment for defendant, holding that defendant's sale of the books and movie depicting the woman's life story without plaintiff's consent did not violate plaintiff's ownership rights in the woman's name or likeness, because they were biographical works. The court cited Restatement Third of Unfair Competition §§ 46 and 47 in explaining that Michigan courts did not extend the right-of-publicity tort to prohibit unlicensed works of biography. Rosa and Raymond Parks Institute for Self Development v. Target Corp., 90 F.Supp.3d 1256, 1262, 1263.

D.Ariz.2021. Cit. in case cit. in sup. Female models, business women, and social-media personalities sued operator of strip club, alleging, inter alia, that defendant violated plaintiffs' right to publicity by using photographs of their likeness to advertise the strip club without plaintiffs' consent. After removal, this court denied in part defendant's motion for summary judgment, holding that state statutes protecting the right of publicity for soldiers did not preclude plaintiffs' common-law right-of-publicity claims. The court pointed out that Arizona caselaw recognized the right of publicity as a cause of action, citing an Arizona case that relied on Restatement Third of Unfair Competition § 47 in foreclosing right-of-publicity claims asserted by an estate on the grounds that expressive works were exempt from such liability. Longoria v. Kodiak Concepts LLC, 527 F.Supp.3d 1085, 1096, 1097.

D.Ariz.2000. Quot. in sup. A professional golfer who made a "hole in one" for $1 million at a golf tournament sued video producer, alleging that defendant's use of plaintiff's name and golf shot in a promotional video constituted a violation of his right to publicity. This court denied defendant's motion to dismiss, holding, inter alia, that plaintiff had adequately stated a claim for violation of the right to publicity. Even though plaintiff appeared in only six seconds of the eight-minute videotape, the incidental-use doctrine did not apply, because inclusion of plaintiff's name and shot was integral to defendant's advertisement and clearly enhanced the marketability of its service. Pooley v. National Hole-In-One Association, 89 F.Supp.2d 1108, 1112.

C.D.Cal.2012. Com. (c) quot. in sup. University that claimed to own a world-famous deceased physicist's right of publicity as a beneficiary under his will and thus exclusive control of the exploitation of his name and likeness sued automobile manu-

For earlier citations, see the Appendices, Supplements, or Pocket Parts, if any, that correspond to the subject matter under examination.

facturer, alleging unauthorized use of the physicist's image in a magazine advertisement. This court denied summary judgment for plaintiff, holding that plaintiff's claim was barred, because the New Jersey Supreme Court would likely find that the postmortem right of publicity under New Jersey common law endured for no more than 50 years after death, and more than 50 years had elapsed between the physicist's death in 1955 and the filing of this lawsuit in 2010. The court reasoned that a maximum duration of 50 years appropriately reflected the balance between meaningful enforcement of the right of publicity after a famous individual's death and the public's interest in free expression. Hebrew University of Jerusalem v. General Motors LLC, 903 F.Supp.2d 932, 940.

M.D.Fla.2002. Quot. in sup., com. (c) quot. in sup. Relatives of fishing crew killed in shipwreck brought action for unauthorized commercial misappropriation and invasion of privacy against producers and distributors of movie about shipwreck. Granting summary judgment for defendants, district court held, inter alia, that use of plaintiffs' and decedents' names and likenesses in motion picture and its related advertising did not constitute appropriation for commercial purpose under state law. Tyne v. Time Warner Entertainment Co., 204 F.Supp.2d 1338, 1341-1342.

S.D.Fla.2010. Quot. in sup. Author sued media companies, asserting, among other things, a claim under Florida statute for unauthorized publication of name or likeness in connection with a television program broadcast by defendants and an upload to a video-sharing website. Granting without prejudice defendants' motion to dismiss for failure to state a claim, this court held that, under the facts as alleged in plaintiff's complaint, plaintiff's name and likeness were not used for trade, commercial, or advertising purposes, because his name and likeness were not used to promote a product or service separate and apart from the television show/upload in which they were included. Fuentes v. Mega Media Holdings, Inc., 721 F.Supp.2d 1255, 1258-1259.

N.D.Ga.2013. Sec. and com. (c) cit. and quot. in sup. Retired professional wrestler brought, inter alia, a claim for violation of the right of publicity against entertainment corporation, alleging that defendant repeatedly used his name and likeness on its websites for its own commercial gain without his permission and without compensating him. Granting defendant's motion to dismiss, this court held that plaintiff failed to state a claim for violation of his right of publicity, because, under Georgia's "newsworthiness" exception to the right of publicity, the references to plaintiff's name on defendant's websites were matters of public interest and protected by the First Amendment. The court concluded that defendant's use on its websites of plaintiff's identity was not for a commercial transaction or a commercial use, because plaintiff's identity was not being used to sell a product in an advertisement, but, instead, was referred to as part of the historical events of professional wrestling. Somerson v. World Wrestling Entertainment, Inc., 956 F.Supp.2d 1360, 1369-1371.

E.D.Mich.2000. Quot. and cit. in disc., com. (c) quot. and cit. in disc. Heirs and personal representatives of musician depicted in television miniseries sued various entities and individuals involved with the production for, inter alia, misappropriation of likeness/violation of the right of publicity, defamation, and "false light" invasion of privacy. On motions to dismiss, the court held, in part, that the depiction of a life story, particularly where some of the events were fictionalized, did not give rise to a cause of action for violation of the right of publicity, and that defamation and "false light" claims brought by musician's de facto mother did not survive her death under the law of Mississippi, the state of mother's domicile. Ruffin-Steinback v. dePasse, 82 F.Supp.2d 723, 729-731, affirmed 267 F.3d 457 (6th Cir.2001).

E.D.Mich.1999. Quot. but dist. §§ 46-47. Public figure whose name was used as the title of a rap song sued the entertainers who wrote, performed, marketed, and distributed the song, asserting, in part, a claim for unfair competition under state law. Granting defendants' motion for summary judgment, the court stated that plaintiff's purported reliance on Restatement (Third) of Unfair Competition §§ 46-47 to support her state-law unfair-competition claim was misplaced because the Restatement did not apply to the use of a person's identity in entertainment, among other things. The court noted that, as a public figure, plaintiff simply was not entitled to control every conceivable presentation of her name and likeness. Parks v. LaFace

Cit.—cited; com.—comment; fol.—followed; sup.—support.
A complete list of abbreviations precedes page 1.

Records, 76 F.Supp.2d 775, 784, 785, affirmed in part, reversed in part and remanded 329 F.3d 437 (6th Cir.2003).

D.Minn.2014. Cit. and quot. in sup. Former professional football players filed a putative class action against professional football league, alleging that defendant's use of video footage of plaintiffs playing football violated their publicity rights, caused consumer confusion, and unjustly enriched defendant. Granting summary judgment for defendant, this court held that, while Minnesota recognized the common-law tort of misappropriation of the right of publicity, plaintiffs' publicity-rights claims arising under Minnesota law were barred by the defense of newsworthiness, because defendant's use of plaintiffs' identities in the challenged film productions was a matter of public interest and for the purpose of giving information to the public. The court reasoned that Minnesota courts were likely to apply a newsworthiness defense to a publicity-rights claim consistent with Restatement Third of Unfair Competition § 47. Dryer v. National Football League, 55 F.Supp.3d 1181, 1199.

E.D.Mo.2006. Com. (c) quot. in case quot. in sup. Professional baseball players' association intervened in a rights dispute between distributor of fantasy-sports products and baseball-team owners' interactive media/Internet arm, asserting, along with the latter, counterclaims against distributor for violation of baseball players' right of publicity. Granting distributor's motions for summary judgment and dismissing the counterclaims, this court held, inter alia, that distributor's use of players' names separately or in conjunction with their playing records in fantasy baseball games did not violate players' claimed right of publicity. The court further concluded that, even if players had a right of publicity in their names and playing records and distributor had violated this right, such right of publicity had to give way to distributor's First Amendment right to freedom of expression. C.B.C. Distribution and Marketing, Inc. v. Major League Baseball Advanced Media, L.P., 443 F.Supp.2d 1077, 1096.

D.N.J.2011. Coms. (a) and (c) quot. in case quot. in sup. Former college football athlete sued computer software developer, alleging that defendant violated his right of publicity under New Jersey law by misappropriating and incorporating his identity and likeness for a commercial purpose in connection with defendant's video games. Granting summary judgment for defendant, this court held that defendant's First Amendment right to free expression outweighed plaintiff's right of publicity. The court reasoned, in part, that defendant's use of plaintiff's image was part of an expressive act by defendant that might have drawn upon public familiarity with plaintiff's college football career, but did not explicitly state that he endorsed or contributed to the creation of the game; defendant's use of plaintiff's image was clearly related to the game and was not simply an advertisement for an unrelated product. Hart v. Electronic Arts, Inc., 808 F.Supp.2d 757, 793.

N.D.Ohio, 2004. Quot. but dist., com. (a) quot. in disc. (erron. cit. as § 46, com. (c)), com. (b) quot. in disc., com. (c) cit. in disc. (erron. cit. as § 46, com. (c)). Television news anchor's participation in a wet t-shirt contest, during which she removed her clothing, was recorded without her notice or consent. Upon learning that her performance and image later appeared in videos and on various websites, some of which charged viewers for access, anchor sought a preliminary injunction against the production companies and website owners and operators to prohibit their continued use of her image. Granting the injunction, this court determined, inter alia, that the anchor's claims had a substantial likelihood of success on the merits. Defendants' unauthorized usage of anchor's image for commercial purposes, such as an advertisement for defendants' videos and other products or services, was not a form of expressive material protected by the First Amendment. Bosley v. Wildwett.com, 310 F.Supp.2d 914, 922, 925.

S.D.Ohio, 2016. Com. (c) cit. in disc. Couple brought an action for, among other things, invasion of privacy against author, alleging that defendant published an erotic book that used plaintiffs' engagement photograph on the cover without plaintiffs' permission. This court denied defendant's motion for judgment on the pleadings, holding that plaintiffs stated a sufficient false-light invasion-of-privacy claim. The court rejected defendant's argument that his use of the photograph was justified under the incidental-use doctrine and Restatement Third of Unfair Competition § 47, Comment *c*, explaining that the doctrine only applied to persons with celebrity or other notorious

For earlier citations, see the Appendices, Supplements, or Pocket Parts, if any, that correspond to the subject matter under examination.

status, which plaintiffs did not have, and plaintiffs did not claim a right-of-publicity tort. Roe v. Amazon.com, 170 F.Supp.3d 1028, 1035.

N.D.Okl.1994. Cit. in ftn., com. (c) quot. generally in disc. (citing § 47 of T.D. No. 4, 1993. § 47 has since been revised; see Official Text). Declaratory-judgment action was brought to determine if manufacturer of trading cards displaying caricatured likenesses of active major league baseball players violated the players' association's rights under Oklahoma's right-of-publicity statute. Granting manufacturer's motion for summary judgment, the court applied copyright law to the right of publicity to recognize a parody exception to the Oklahoma statute; since manufacturer's product fell within this exception, despite the fact that it was a parody that was sold for commercial gain, the product did not violate the statute. Cardtoons v. Major League Baseball Players Ass'n, 868 F.Supp. 1266, 1271, 1273.

E.D.Pa.1997. Quot. in disc., com. (c) quot. in part in disc. Well-known civil rights activist sued movie producers for, inter alia, "false light" invasion of privacy in connection with the manner in which he was portrayed in defendants' film. Plaintiff also alleged that defendants violated his right of publicity by using his photograph on the compact disc cover for the movie soundtrack. Defendants moved for summary judgment. Granting the motion, the court held that, despite some minor inaccuracies, a movie scene showing plaintiff and his associates legally purchasing guns did not place plaintiff in a false light; that a scene depicting a confrontation between plaintiff and another member of his organization did place plaintiff in a false light, but plaintiff failed to establish by clear and convincing evidence that defendants acted maliciously or with reckless disregard for the truth when they included that scene; and that use of plaintiff's photograph on the CD cover was not actionable because such use was not for trade or commercial purposes. Seale v. Gramercy Pictures, 964 F.Supp. 918, 930, affirmed 156 F.3d 1225 (3d Cir.1998).

E.D.Pa.1996. Cit. in headnotes, cit. and quot. in sup., com. (a) cit. in sup., com. (c) cit. and quot. in sup. Civil rights leader whose name and likeness appeared, without his consent, in a film and book depicting the civil rights movement, as well as on the cover of the accompanying musical CD/cassette soundtrack, sued movie producer, among others, for, inter alia, violations of his right of publicity and "false light" invasion of privacy. Defendants moved for summary judgment. Granting the motion in part and denying it in part, the court held that the use of plaintiff's name and likeness in connection with the film and book, the subject matter of which concerned plaintiff, was not actionable as a violation of his right of publicity because such use was not for purposes of trade but, rather, for the purpose of First Amendment expression; that material factual issues existed as to whether the use of plaintiff's name and likeness in connection with the CD/cassette was for purposes of trade or commercial purposes; and that material factual issues existed as to whether certain scenes in the film depicted plaintiff in a false light. Seale v. Gramercy Pictures, 949 F.Supp. 331, 331, 332, 336.

W.D.Pa.2003. Quot. in ftn. Professional-wrestling promoter sued seller of T-shirts and other consumer merchandise that featured graphics of dogs caricatured as plaintiff's wrestling characters, claiming violations of common-law publicity rights on behalf of wrestlers. Granting defendant's motion for summary judgment, the court held, inter alia, that defendant's parodies of plaintiff's wrestling characters constituted expressive commentary that deserved First Amendment protection and outweighed the state-law interest in protecting plaintiff's rights of publicity. World Wrestling Federation Entertainment Inc. v. Big Dog Holdings, Inc., 280 F.Supp.2d 413, 444.

Ariz.App.2014. Cit. in disc., quot. in sup.; com. (c) quot. in sup. After daughter wrote online commentaries about her aging mother's daily challenges and a fond remembrance following her mother's death, daughter's sister, who was the personal representative of their mother's estate, objected to the writings and listed on the inventory of estate assets a claim against daughter for violation of mother's right of publicity. Daughter petitioned to compel closure of the estate, and the trial court disallowed sister's claim. Affirming, this court held that a right of publicity existed under Arizona law and it could be enforced by one's estate after death, but daughter's commentaries in this case did not, as a matter of law, give rise to such a claim, because they were expressive works that did not employ mother's name or likeness for purposes of trade. The court noted that Restatement Third of Unfair Competition § 47, Comment c, made clear that the mere sale of an expressive work that used one's likeness or name did not constitute use of the other's identity "for purposes of trade" as required to give rise to a claim for relief. In re Estate of Reynolds, 235 Ariz. 80, 327 P.3d 213, 217, 218.

Cal.App.2001. Cit. in disc. Former major league baseball players sued Major League Baseball in two suits for, inter alia, violating their common law right of publicity, alleging that defendant appropriated their names and likenesses by using their names, voices, signatures, autographs, and likenesses without their consent and without compensation. Trial courts granted defendant summary judgment. After consolidating appeals, this court affirmed, holding, in part, that public interest favoring free dissemination of information as to baseball's history outweighed any proprietary interests at stake. Defendant's uses were entitled to receive full constitutional protection accorded to noncommercial speech, since uses involved statements of historical fact, descriptions of those facts, or video depictions of them. Gionfriddo v. Major League Baseball, 94 Cal.App.4th 400, 114 Cal.Rptr.2d 307, 317.

Fla.2005. Quot. in sup., quot. in case quot. in sup., com. (c) quot. in sup. After an author wrote a book about fishing vessel's crewmembers who were killed in storm, a movie company produced a film depicting the lives and deaths of the crewmembers. The crewmembers' families sued the movie company in federal court for violation of Florida's commercial-misappropriation law and false-light invasion of privacy. The district court granted defendants summary judgment, and the court of appeals certified question. Answering the question, this court held that the term "commercial purpose" as used in the misappropriation statute did not apply to publications, including motion pictures, that did not directly promote a product or service. Tyne v. Time Warner Entertainment Co., 901 So.2d 802, 805, 807.

Ky.2001. Com. (b) cit. in ftn. Deceased musician's estate sued musician's son, alleging that defendant violated musician's common-law and statutory right of publicity by using musician's voice and likeness in a music video. Trial court granted defendant summary judgment, and the appellate court affirmed. This court affirmed, holding, inter alia, that the statutory right of publicity did not apply to a work protected by the First Amendment where there was a genuine connection between the use of the musician's likeness and the content of the creative work. The court noted that many of the principles of the common-law right of publicity could be used in construing the statute. Montgomery v. Montgomery, 60 S.W.3d 524, 528.

Mo.2003. Com. (c) cit. and quot. in sup. and cit. generally in disc. After professional hockey player learned of the existence of a comic book that contained a villainous character sharing his name, he brought suit for, in part, misappropriation of name against the comic book's creators, publishers, and marketers. The trial court granted defendants' motion for judgment n.o.v. Reversing in part and remanding, this court held, inter alia, that plaintiff, whose lawsuit was more precisely labeled a right-of-publicity action, presented sufficient evidence to prove that his name was used as a symbol of his identity, the evidence established that defendants used his name for a commercial advantage, and defendants' use of plaintiff's name was not protected under the First Amendment. Doe v. TCI Cablevision, 110 S.W.3d 363, 369, 371, 373, 374, cert. denied 540 U.S. 1106, 124 S.Ct. 1058, 157 L.Ed.2d 892 (2004).

Ohio App.2020. Cit. in case quot. in sup.; com. (c) quot. in case quot. in sup. Seller of a house, who had been ordered to pay a judgment to buyers based on her fraudulent failure to disclose termite damage, sued providers of continuing education for realtors, alleging that defendants appropriated her name in violation of a state statute by discussing her case in their materials. The trial court granted summary judgment for defendants. This court affirmed, holding that the statute did not apply, because defendants' use of plaintiff's name was informative and newsworthy and was not intended to promote, advertise, or market a product or take advantage of her name's commercial value, if any. The court cited Restatement Third of Unfair Competition § 47 in noting that the right of publicity as recognized by statute and common law was fundamentally constrained by the public and constitutional interest in freedom of expression, and that the use of a person's identity primarily for the purpose of communicating information or expressing ideas was not generally actionable as a violation of the person's right of publicity. Harvey v. Systems Effect, LLC, 154 N.E.3d 293, 308.

§ 48. Injunctions: Appropriation of the Commercial Value of a Person's Identity

C.A.6, 2001. Com. (c) quot. in disc. Furniture company sued competitor under the Lanham Act, alleging that defendant produced imitations of a lounge chair and ottoman designed for plaintiff. The district court entered judgment on a jury verdict for plaintiff on several claims, dismissed two others, and entered a permanent injunction against defendant, allowing defendant to fairly identify the original designers of the reproduced furniture. Affirming in part, this court held, inter alia, that the district court did not abuse its discretion by creating a "fair use" exception in its permanent injunction issued pursuant to the jury verdict for plaintiff. Herman Miller, Inc. v. Palazzetti Imports and Exports, Inc., 270 F.3d 298, 318, 327.

C.A.9, 2008. Com. (c) quot. in case quot. in disc. United States Department of Justice sued owner of movie theaters for allegedly violating Title III of the Americans with Disabilities Act by placing wheelchair seating in the front rows of its stadium-style multiplexes. The district court issued a nationwide injunction specifying compliance for the affected multiplexes, ruling that owner's existing facilities violated line-of-sight regulations implementing the Act. Reversing and remanding, this court held, inter alia, that the district court abused its discretion in neglecting comity concerns pertaining to the Fifth Circuit's less stringent interpretation of the regulations. The court cited by analogy a Sixth Circuit decision involving the right of publicity, which indicated that, while a court had jurisdiction to grant broad relief, an injunction protecting the right of publicity was ordinarily limited to conduct in jurisdictions that provided protection comparable to the forum state. U.S. v. AMC Entertainment, Inc., 549 F.3d 760, 773.

§ 49. Monetary Relief: Appropriation of the Commercial Value of a Person's Identity

D.Ariz.2021. Cit. in sup. Female models, business women, and social-media personalities sued operator of strip club, alleging, inter alia, that defendant violated plaintiffs' right to publicity by using photographs of their likeness to advertise the strip club without plaintiffs' consent. After removal, this court denied in part defendant's motion for summary judgment, holding that the undisputed facts demonstrated that defendant violated plaintiffs' interests in their likeness by publishing the advertisements using plaintiffs' photographs. The court observed that a factfinder was needed to determine plaintiffs' damages, and, under Restatement Third of Unfair Competition § 49, plaintiffs could look to a variety of theories in establishing their damages, including measuring the fair-market value of defendant's unauthorized use. Longoria v. Kodiak Concepts LLC, 527 F.Supp.3d 1085, 1099.

D.Ariz.2020. Com. (b) quot. in disc. Models sued owner of a strip club, alleging that defendant posted advertisements using plaintiffs' images on the strip club's Facebook page to advertise the strip club without their permission. This court denied defendant's motion for summary judgment on plaintiffs' claim alleging that defendant was liable for violating plaintiffs' right of publicity by misappropriating their likenesses, holding that genuine issues of material fact remained as to whether defendant posted plaintiffs' images on its Facebook page. The court cited Restatement Third of Unfair Competition § 49 in noting that, while in most jurisdictions the interest in personal privacy could not be assigned and did not survive death, Arizona courts had clarified that the right of publicity was in essence a property right. Pinder v. 4716 Incorporated, 494 F.Supp.3d 618, 631.

D.Ariz.2006. Com. (d) cit. and quot. in sup. Former players for basketball team sued licensor, apparel manufacturer, and others, alleging that defendants improperly licensed and made use of players' names, likenesses, and player numbers for use on a clothing line without players' consent. This court denied defendants' motion for summary judgment as to plaintiffs' claim for invasion of the right of publicity. Rejecting defendants' argument that plaintiffs presented no evidence of resulting injury, the court held, inter alia, that plaintiffs could show damages by establishing defendants' sales, because disgorgement of profits was available as a remedy under a right-of-publicity claim. In this regard, the court also held that plaintiffs, who had the burden of proving individual damages at trial, could rely on certain documents to identify sales on an individual basis, but not on a report that calculated aggregate damages. Lemon v. Harlem Globetrotters Intern., Inc., 437 F.Supp.2d 1089, 1103, 1106.

N.D.Ill.2015. Cit. in ftn. Former professional athlete filed a misappropriation-of-identity claim against supermarket conglomerate and supermarket chain owned by conglomerate, alleging that defendants used plaintiff's image in a magazine advertisement by featuring a picture of a jersey with plaintiff's name and the number he wore as a player. This court granted in part plaintiff's motion for summary judgment, finding that defendants violated the Illinois Right of Publicity Act, but denied plaintiff's motion to exclude defendants' expert testimony on damages, holding that plaintiff's damages could be ascertained by using various methods to calculate the fair-market value of the misappropriation, including defendants' expert's method. Citing Restatement Third of Unfair Competition § 49, Comment *d*, the court noted that, while the parties had agreed that damages were limited to the fair-market value of the misappropriation, some courts used disgorgement of profits as another measure of damages. Jordan v. Dominick's Finer Foods, 115 F.Supp.3d 950, 959.

N.D.Ohio, 2004. Com. (c) quot. in disc. (Erron. cit. as § 46, com. (b), illus. 2.) Television news anchor's participation in a wet t-shirt contest, during which she removed her clothing, was recorded without her notice or consent. Upon learning that her performance and image later appeared in videos and on various websites, some of which charged viewers for access, anchor sought a preliminary injunction against the production companies and website owners and operators to prohibit their continued use of her image. Granting the injunction, this court determined, inter alia, that the anchor's claims had a substantial likelihood of success on the merits. Defendants' unauthorized usage of anchor's image for commercial purposes, such as an advertisement for defendants' videos and other products or services, was not a form of expressive material protected by the First Amendment. Bosley v. Wildwett.com, 310 F.Supp.2d 914, 925.

Mo.2003. Com. (b) cit. in disc. After professional hockey player learned of the existence of a comic book that contained a villainous character sharing his name, he brought suit for, in part, misappropriation of name against the comic book's creators, publishers, and marketers. The trial court granted defendants' motion for judgment n.o.v. Reversing in part and remanding, this court held, inter alia, that plaintiff, whose lawsuit was more precisely labeled a right-of-publicity action, presented sufficient evidence to prove that his name was used as a symbol of his identity, the evidence established that defendants used his name for a commercial advantage, and defendants' use of plaintiff's name was not protected under the First Amendment. Doe v. TCI Cablevision, 110 S.W.3d 363, 368.

Mo.App.2006. Com. (b) quot. in case quot. in sup., com. (c) quot. in sup., com. (d) cit. and quot. in sup. Former professional hockey player sued creator of comic-book series and production company that issued the series, asserting a right-of-publicity claim involving the use of his name without his consent for a villainous character in the series. On remand, the trial court entered judgment on a jury verdict awarding plaintiff damages. Affirming, this court held, inter alia, that the trial court did not abuse its discretion in admitting plaintiff's experts' testimony regarding lost endorsement opportunities and plaintiff's entitlement to royalties from comic-series products because of the use of his name. In addition, the trial court's jury instruction correctly allowed plaintiff to recover for future damage to the commercial value of his name. Doe v. McFarlane, 207 S.W.3d 52, 67, 69, 70, 75, 76.

†

For earlier citations, see the Appendices, Supplements, or Pocket Parts, if any, that correspond to the subject matter under examination.